FRANCIS MESLET

ABANDONED WORLD

AN AI-GENERATED EXPLORATION

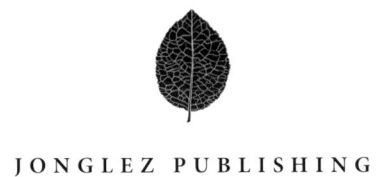

JONGLEZ PUBLISHING

Foreword

For the last fifteen years or so, I've been trying to capture the mysterious beauty of abandoned locations. By photographing the decay of places that were once living environments for humans, I wanted to bear witness to the fragility of our world and the futility of trying to hinder the passage of time. Taking stock of these places that had fallen into disuse took me back to the past, but inevitably also led me to question our future.

My work as an urban explorer came to an abrupt halt during the Covid pandemic of 2020. I had been planning a week-long photo trip for several months, and what was about to turn into a worldwide pandemic seemed no more than scaremongering at the time. So, on 19 February 2020, I set off for Italy as planned. Turin, Genoa, Bologna, Florence, Livorno ... some twenty places over five busy days, ultimately covering almost 3,000 km. It wasn't until I returned to France on 25 February that I began to realise the scale of the pandemic and how lucky I was to have escaped. Just a few days later, several fellow photographers ended up stuck at the border.

How could I pursue my passion without being able to travel? After two years of on-and-off confinement, I finally caught the virus in the summer of 2022 and was forced to remain quarantined at home yet again. It was at this point that, looking for a way to survive the isolation, I discovered how to generate images using artificial intelligence. I had seen a few articles on the websites I'd been monitoring. As I kept coming across the same information, I began to start testing all the apps available at the time to alleviate my boredom — but above all to satisfy my curiosity.

As an advertising creative and photographer, I've been involved in the world of images ever since graduating from the National School of Art and Design of Nancy (ENSAD Nancy) in 1986. Over the course of my studies and my professional career, I've been able to experiment with producing images in many different forms and techniques: drawing, painting, engraving, photography, computer graphics, 3D, video, animation ... always led by my curiosity and fascinated by the effect that images have on the viewer. As a result, producing images using AI was a natural extension of my work.

To avoid losing myself and to set a certain standard, I tried to use this new technology to expand on my photographic work on abandoned places. As an artistic director with some three decades of experience, I took enormous pleasure in framing, directing, guiding and wrestling with the generation of these images, which I wanted to be as realistic as possible while still retaining the general style of my photographic work. The hardest part was censoring myself and not succumbing to the siren song.

I think a picture is worth a thousand words. As long as the people who see my work in this book have been informed that it's generative imagery, I don't have to justify myself, nor do I have to ask anyone's permission.

I hope you'll enjoy taking this imaginary journey of discovery with me.

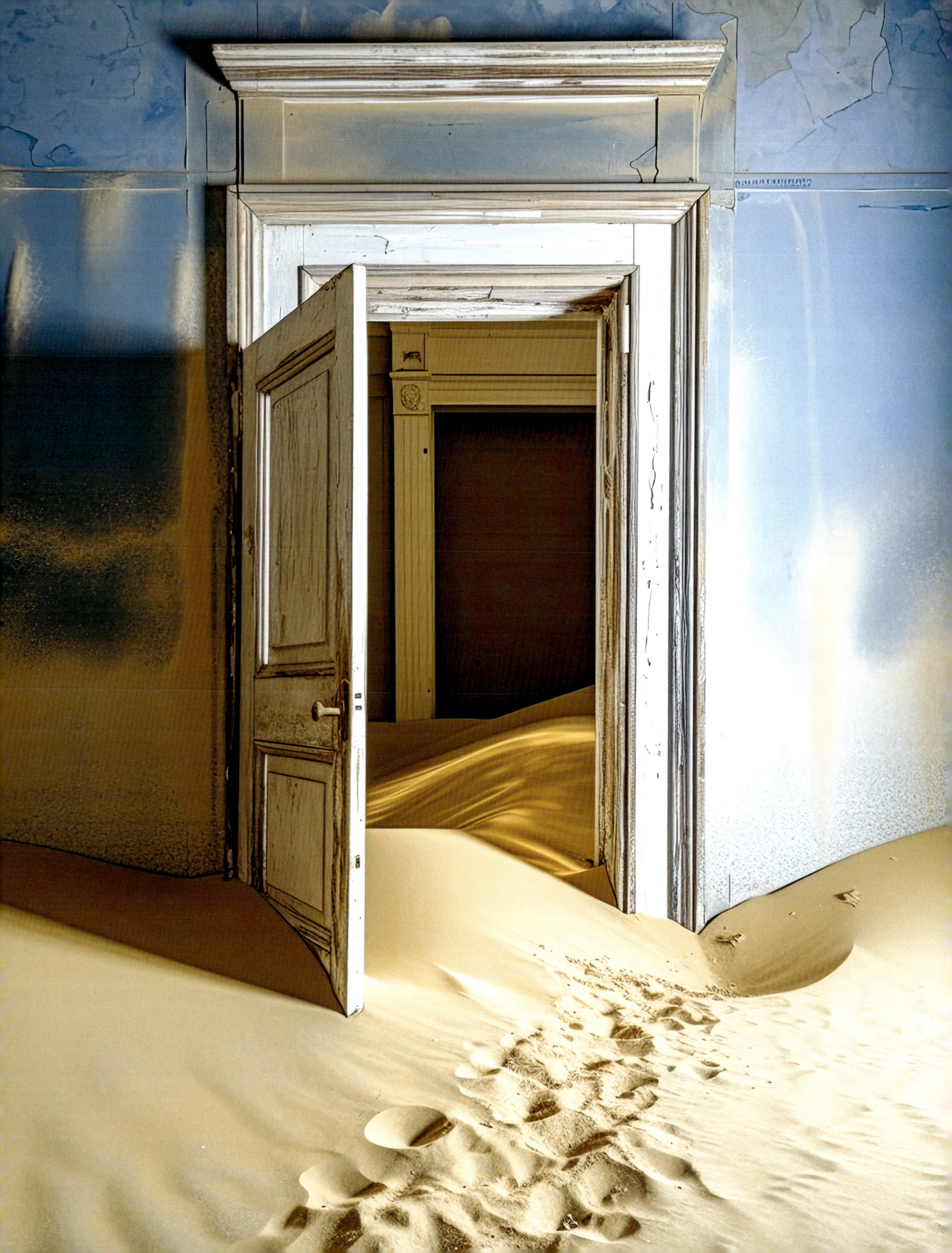

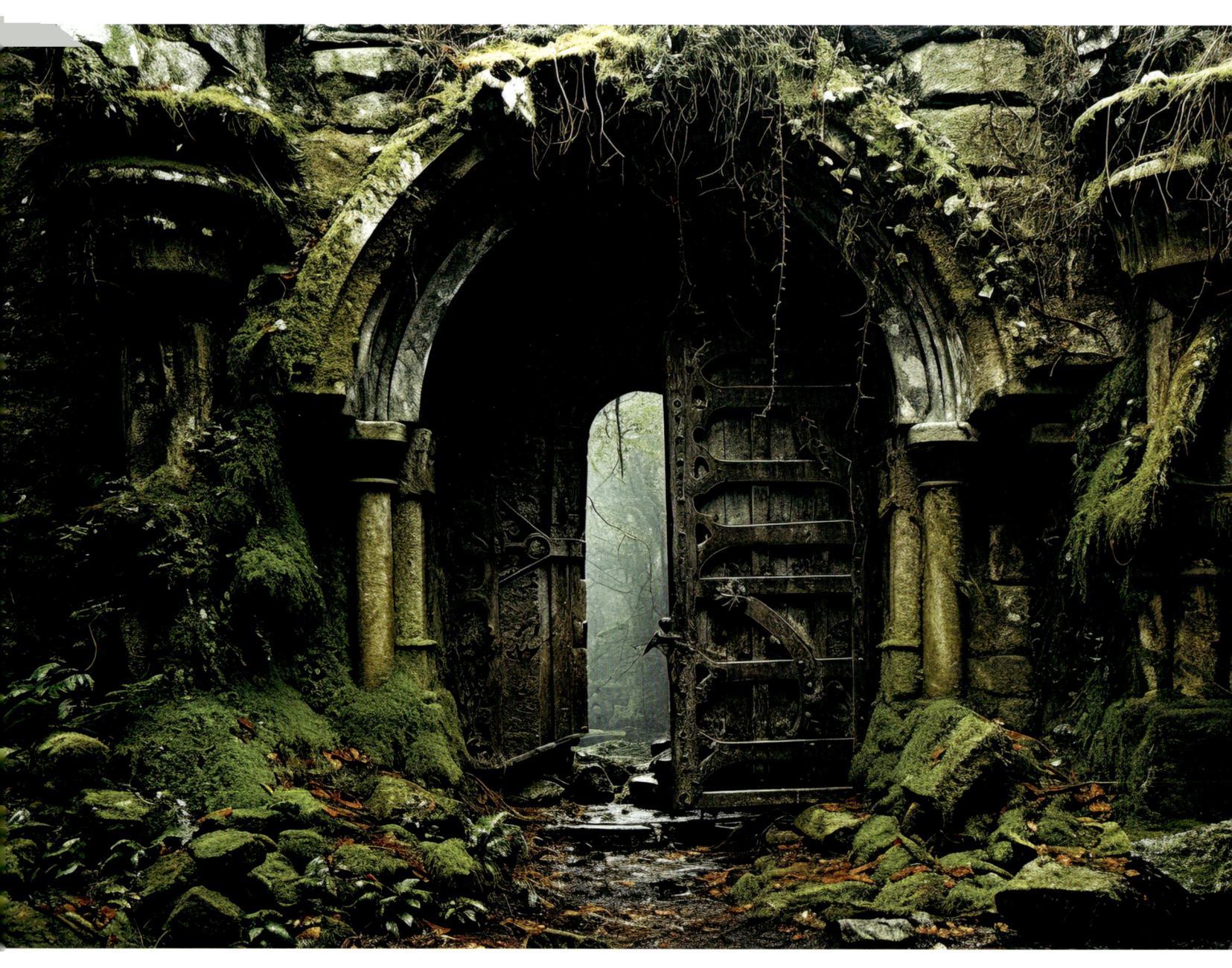

Introduction

The streets had become theatres where reality intermingled with artificial projections. Photographers, masters of the captured moment, had faded into the shadows of artificial intelligence, which now generated images of images. Every street corner was dotted with drones, feeding an infinite database of fictitious moments, projecting simulacra of emotions and life. Society had embraced the convenience of algorithms, abandoning the magic and authenticity of photography. Memories were no longer lived moments, but compositions generated by computers. Spontaneity had been sacrificed on the altar of algorithmic perfection, with every pixel subjected to meticulous analysis.

Reduced to ghosts in an all-digital world, photographers had seen their art supplanted by the implacable efficiency of the algorithm. Galleries had become sanctuaries of silence. In virtual exhibitions, haggard visitors wandered in continuous lines between images generated by binary codes, far from the thrill of a single capture. Emotions were filtered by algorithms, and faces were frozen in blissful smiles, all governed by the inexorable coldness of data streams.

And yet, there were still a few people who held out against this era of programmed images: artists who sought to capture the elusive, to transcribe the reality of this dehumanised digital world. These dissident photographers, armed with their old cameras, were trying to re-establish the lost connection with the human eye. In dark places impenetrable to algorithms, these clandestine artists whispered visual stories, fragile testimonies of humanity in the face of the growing domination of data.

Haunted by the vestiges of the past, a photographer was making his way through the rubble of a once bustling civilisation. As geopolitical turmoil plunged the world into unprecedented transformation, he had set himself the task of capturing the soul of abandoned places.

With his camera slung over his shoulder, he navigated through the debris of derelict monuments, silent testaments to the resilience of our heritage in the face of the ravages of time. Cafés, theatres and libraries, all deserted, had become sanctuaries for nature, which was reclaiming its rights. The sun's rays filtered through the broken windows, illuminating scenes worthy of the poetry of dereliction. These abandoned places were blank pages that the photographer strove to fill with the essence of their past. Each shot was an attempt to revive the forgotten splendour, to reveal the beauty in the decay. The cracked walls, the gutted floors, everything became a painting on which the lens inscribed its vision, a symbiosis of dilapidation and grace.

His work was much more than simple photographic documentation. It was an attempt to reconcile the present and the past, a meditation on the fragility of collective memory. He saw beauty in the abandonment, poetry in the deterioration. A guardian of history, a hunter of ephemeral moments, his images revealed the duality of time, the coexistence of decline and radiance. With his sharp eye, he reinvented himself as a poet of decrepitude, a composer of deserted places, capturing with his lens the soul of neglect, making each image a silent cry in the desert of contemporary indifference.

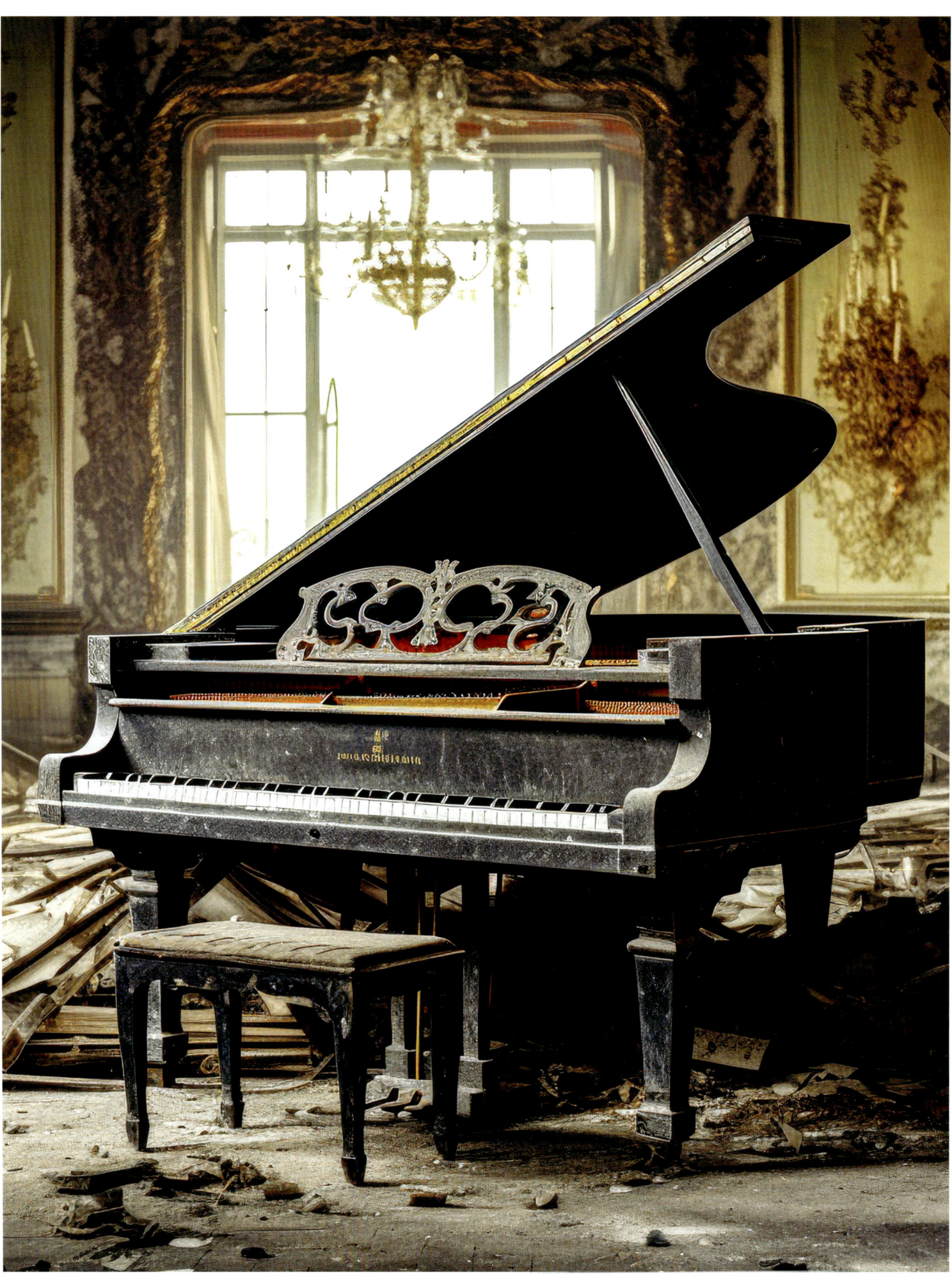

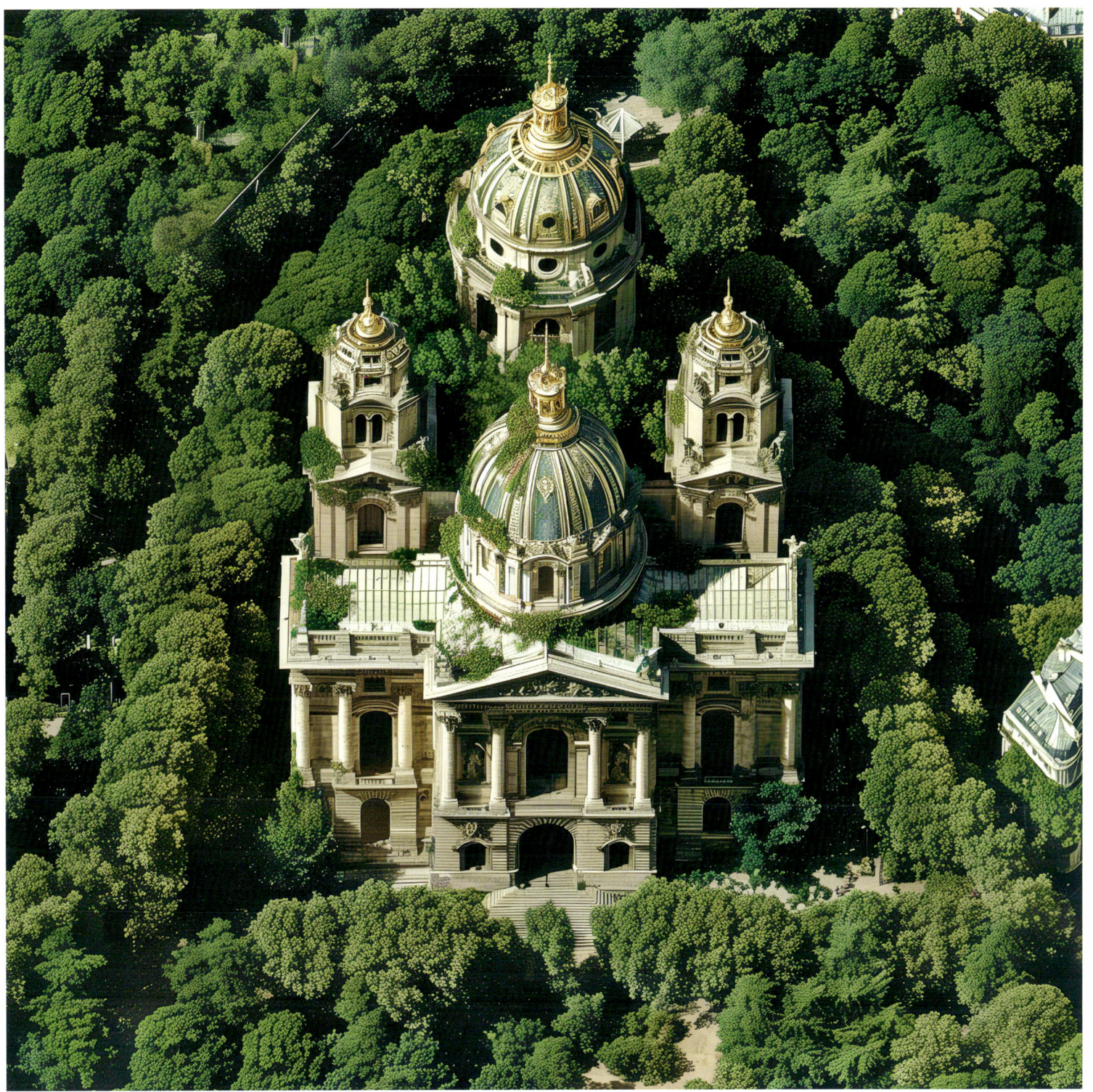

In the hush of libraries

The world has changed; the rise of digitalisation has turned everything upside down. Books, those precious paper gems, have been replaced by screens, bits and bytes. Information and culture are just a click away, so quick and easy that most people have forgotten that libraries even exist.

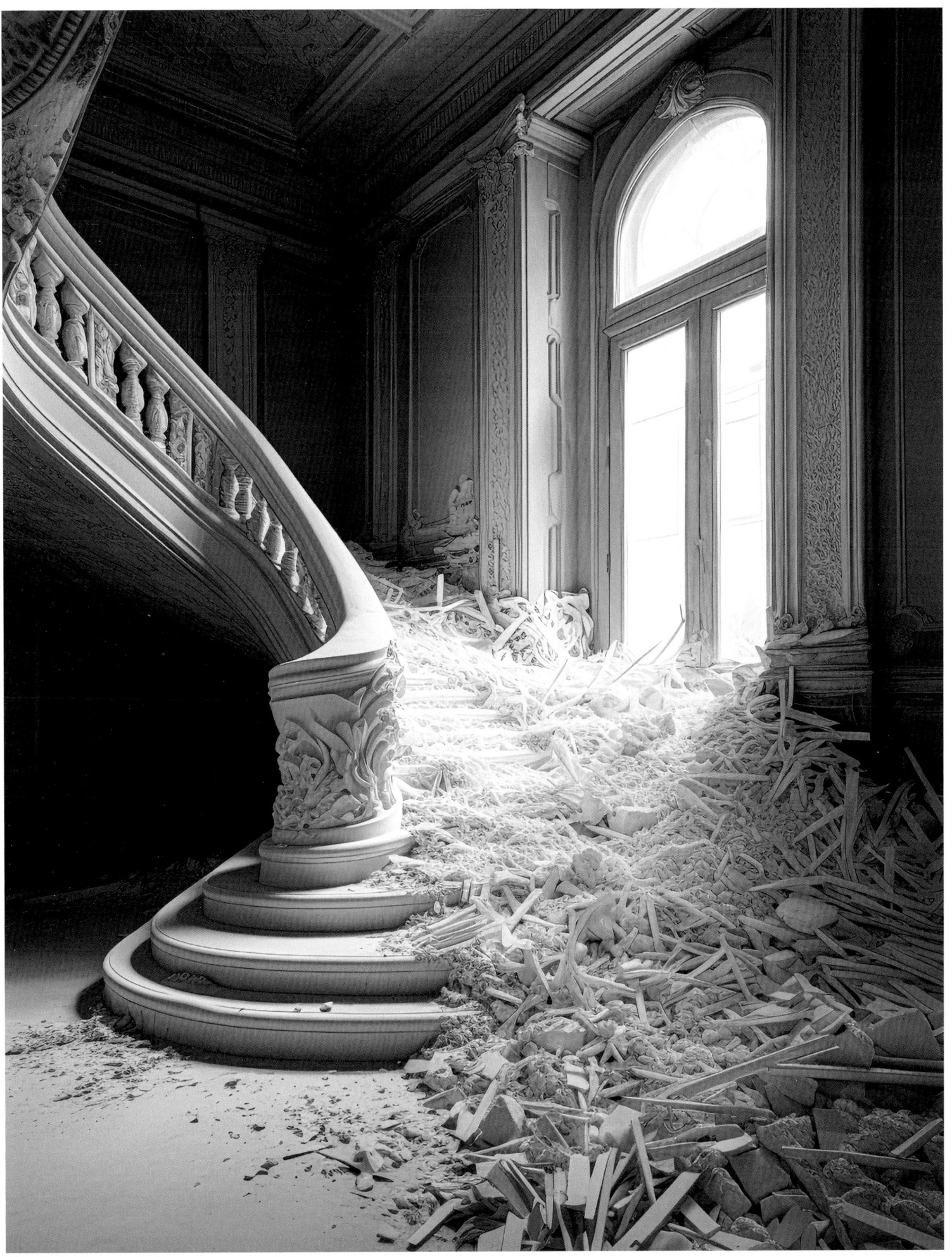

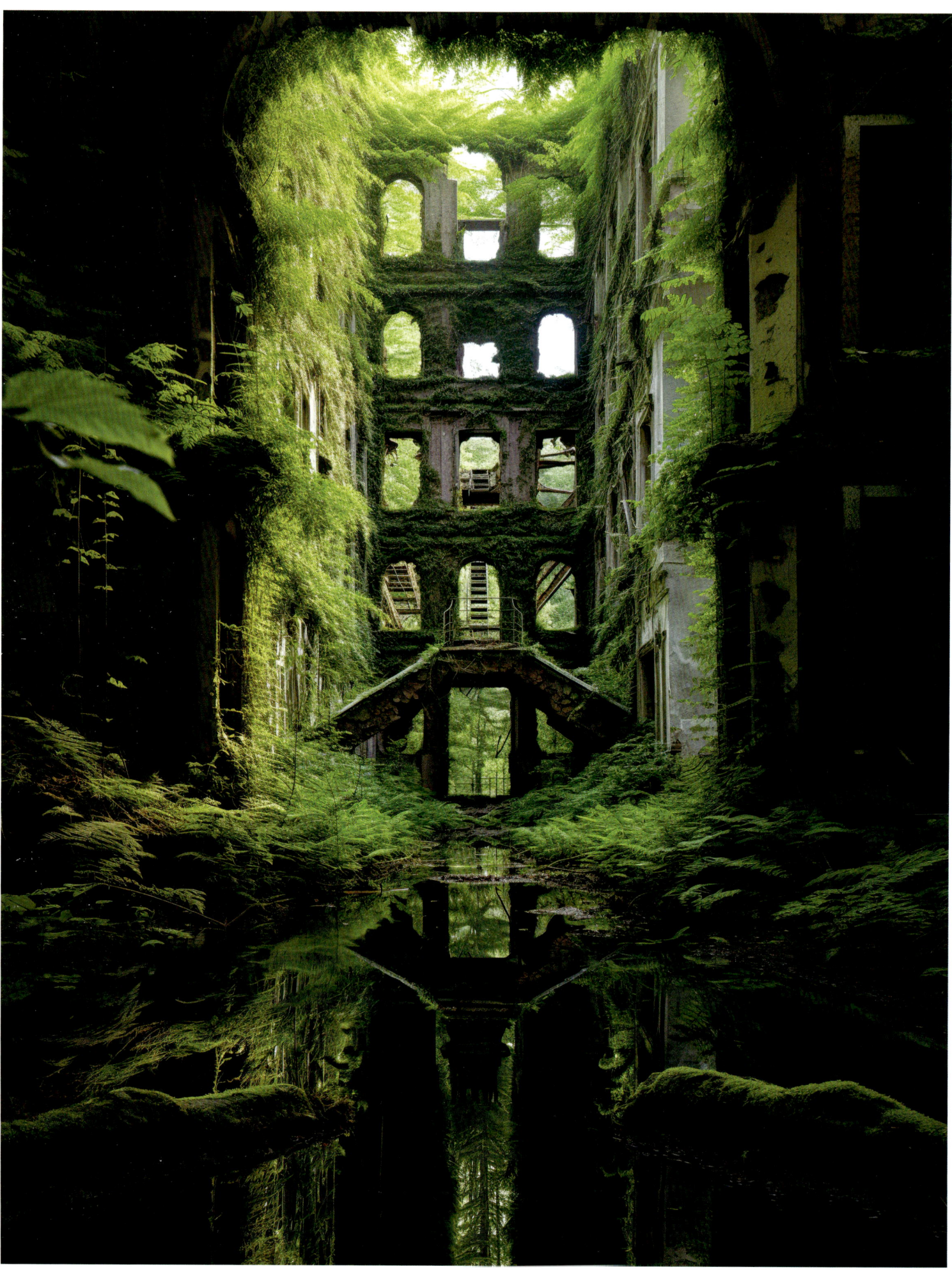

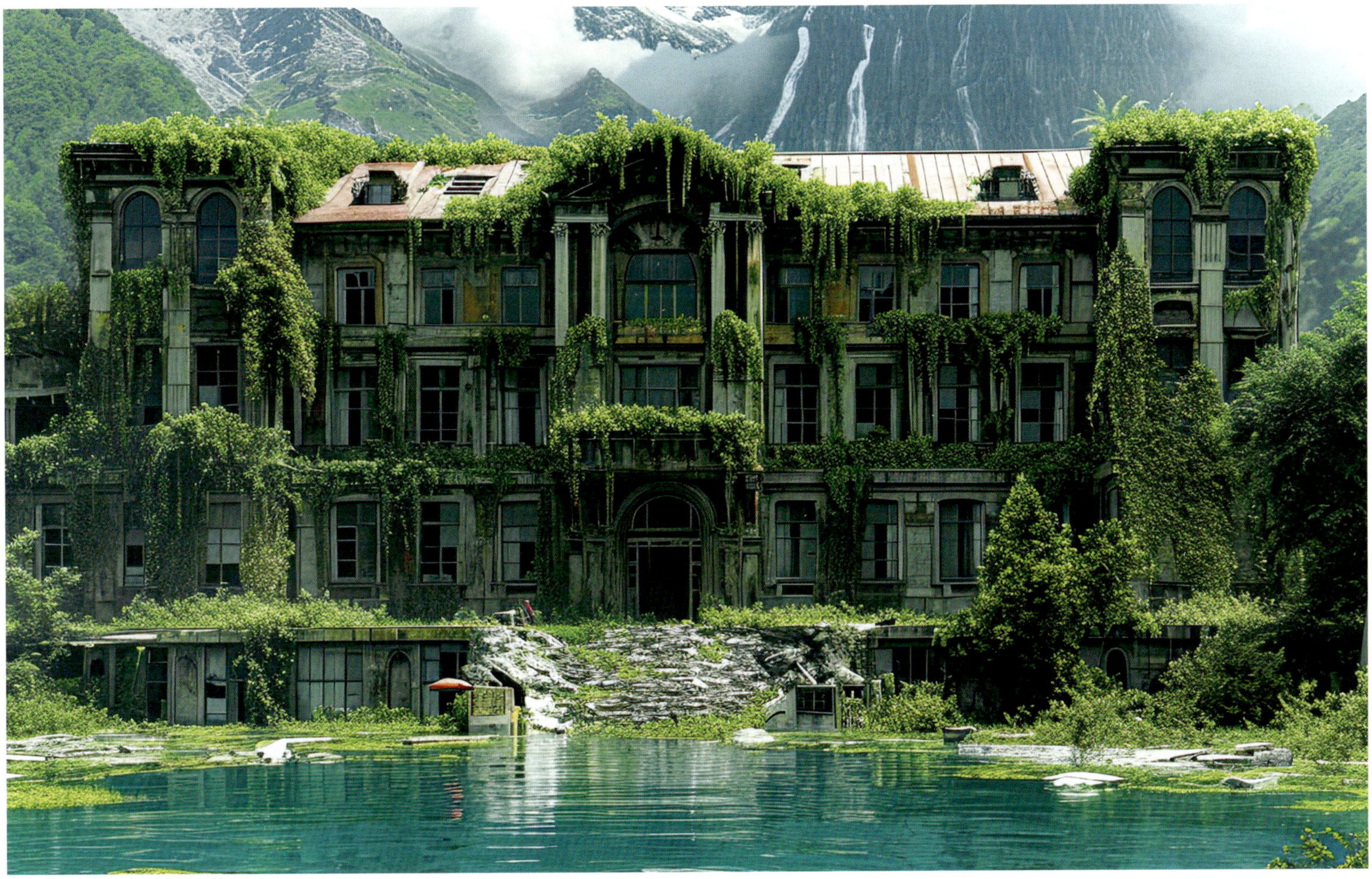

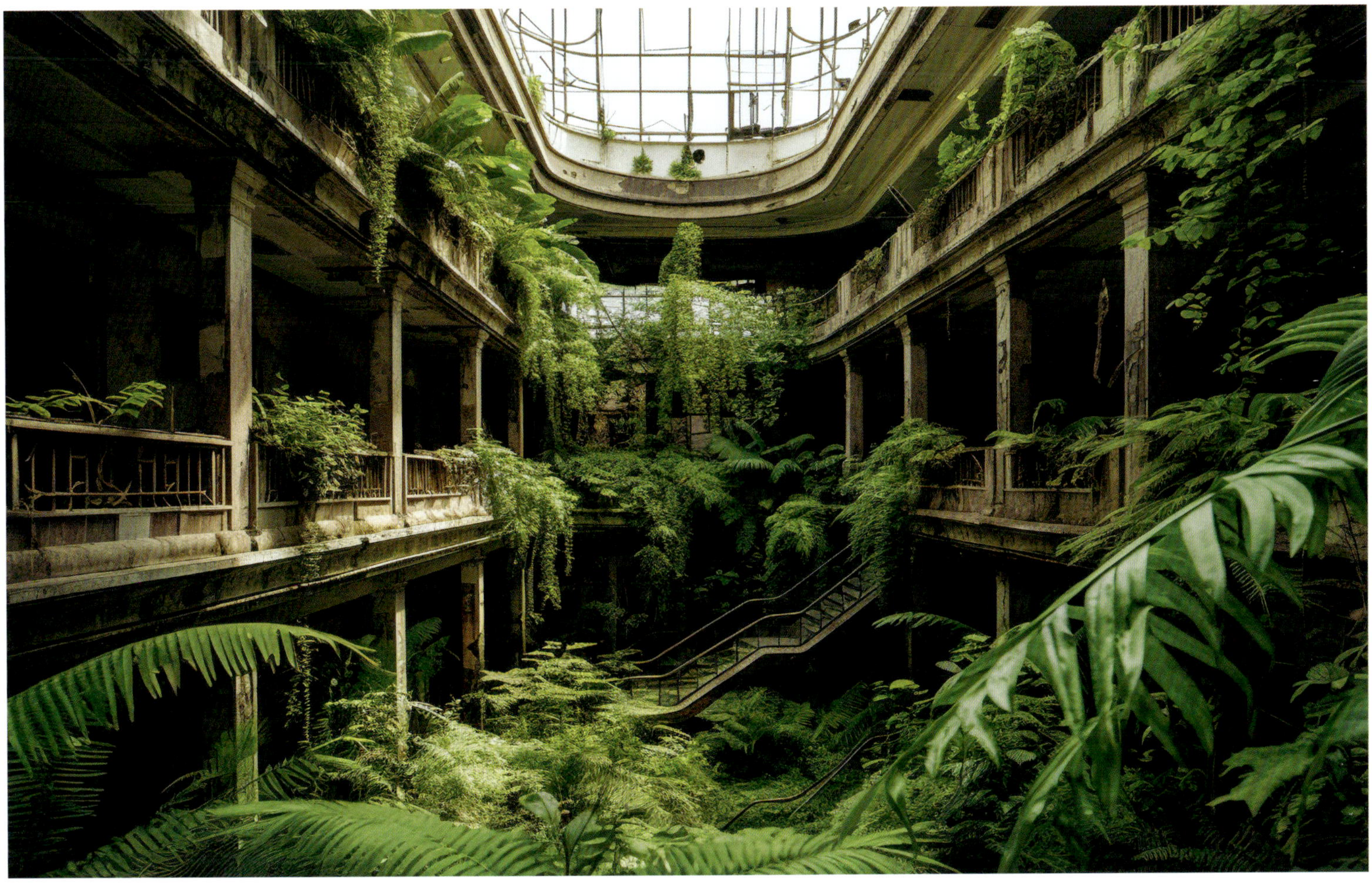

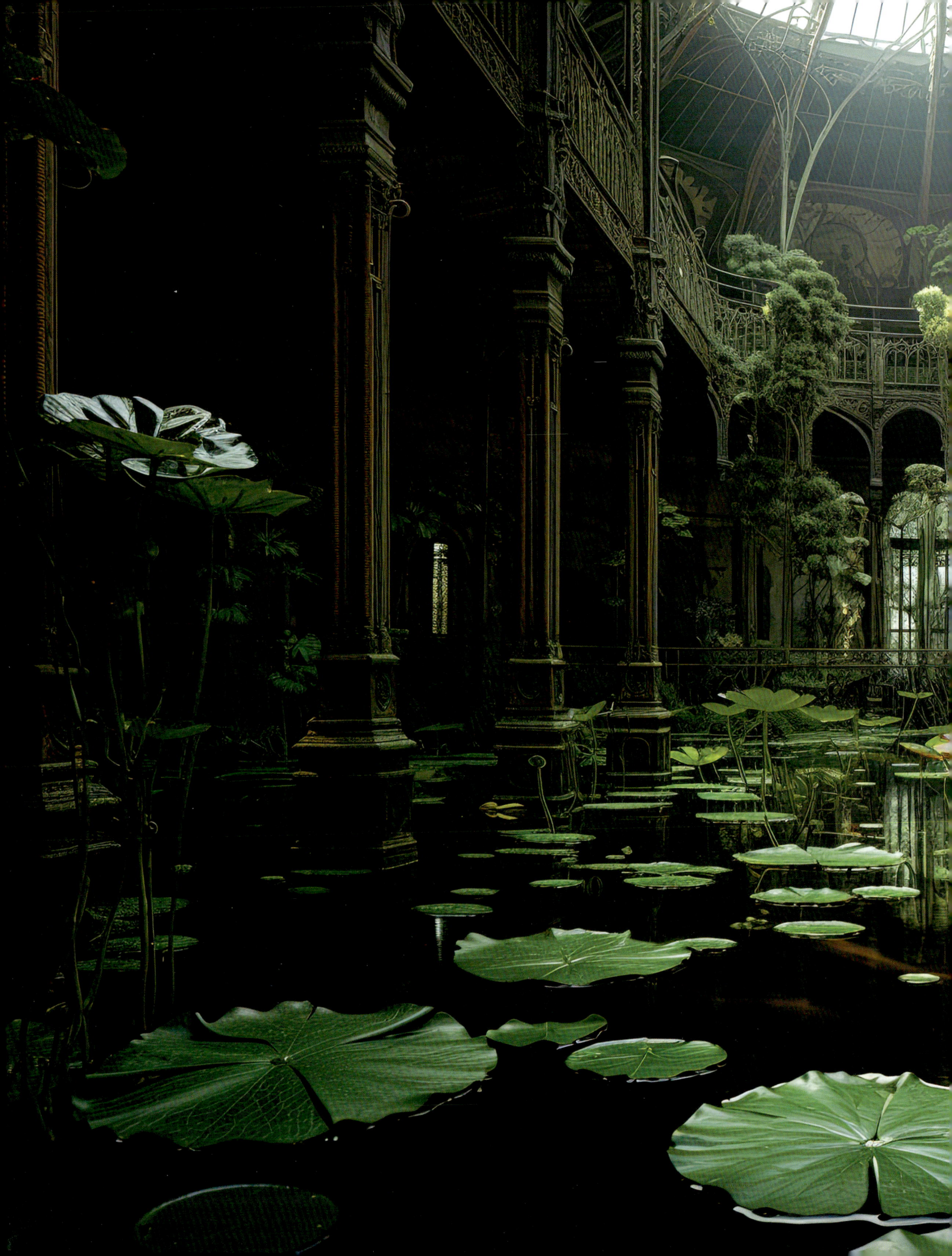

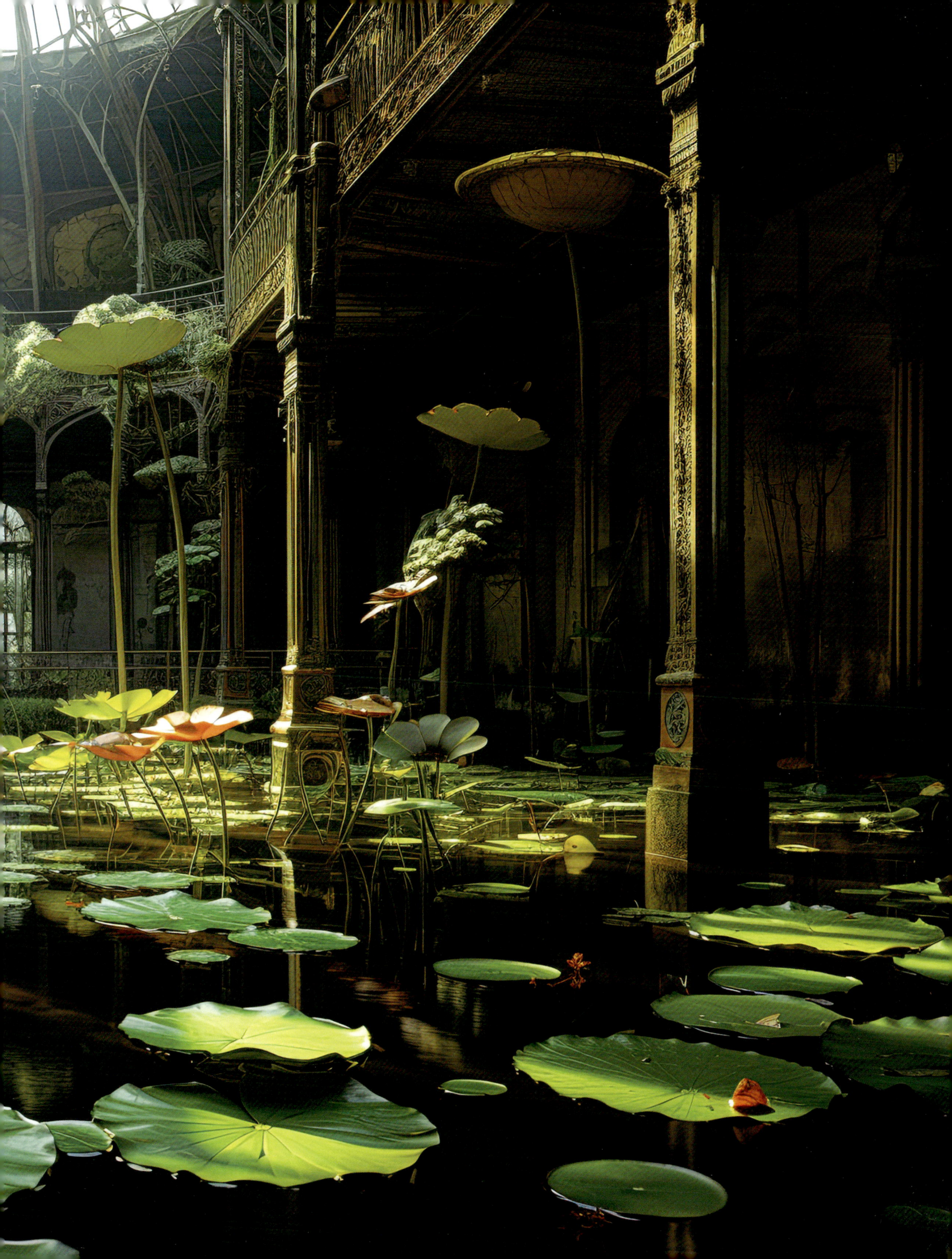

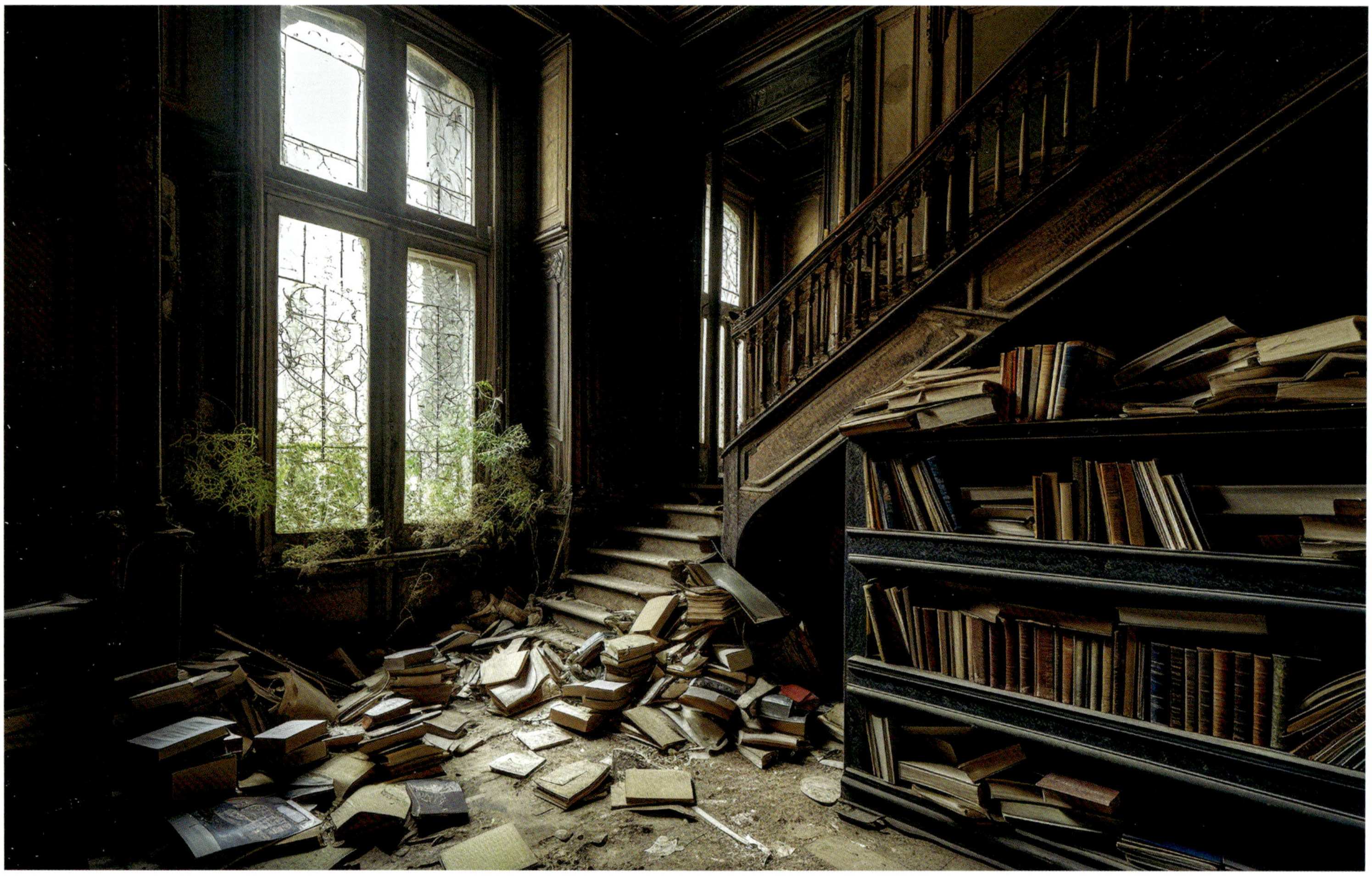

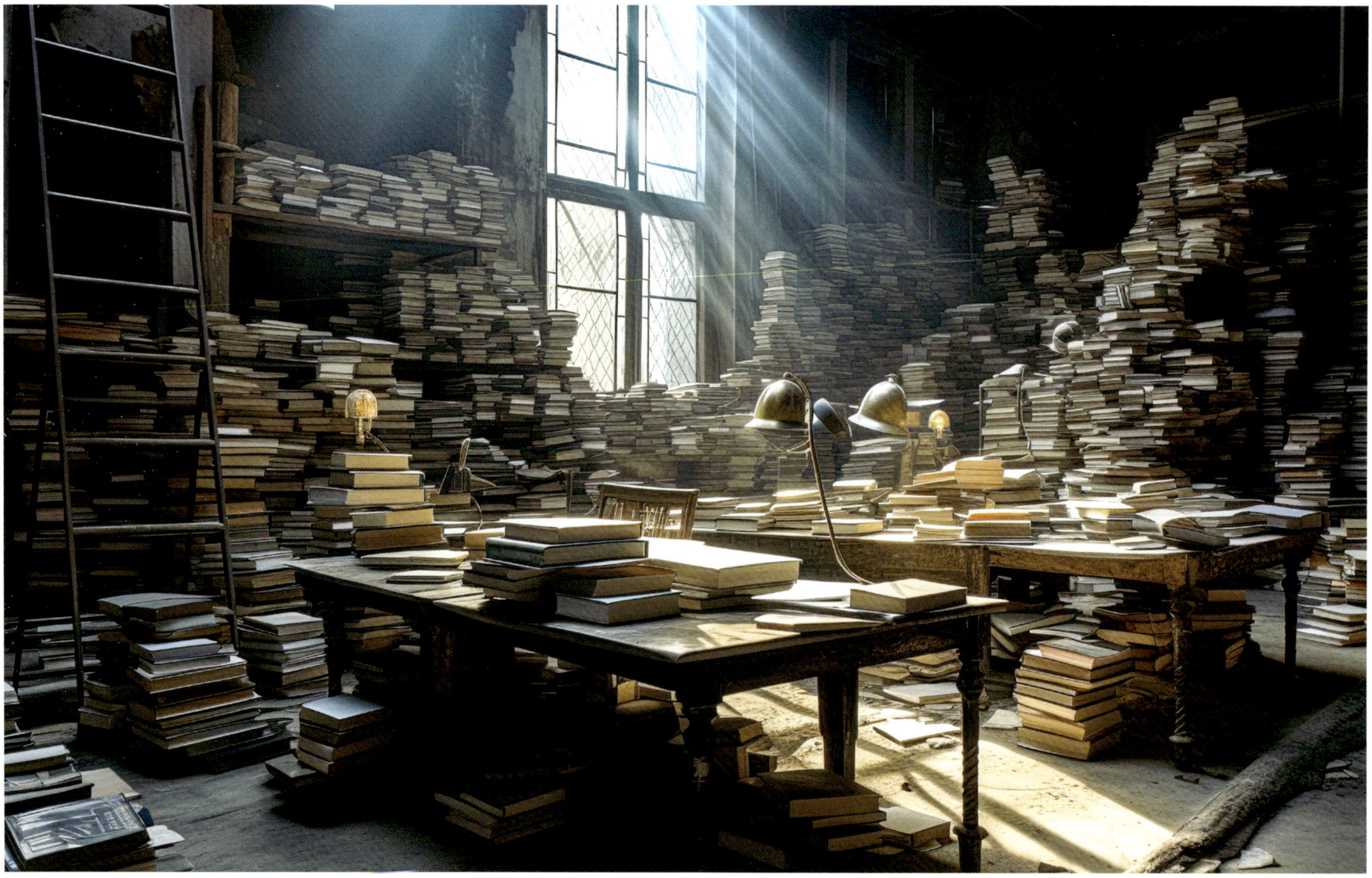

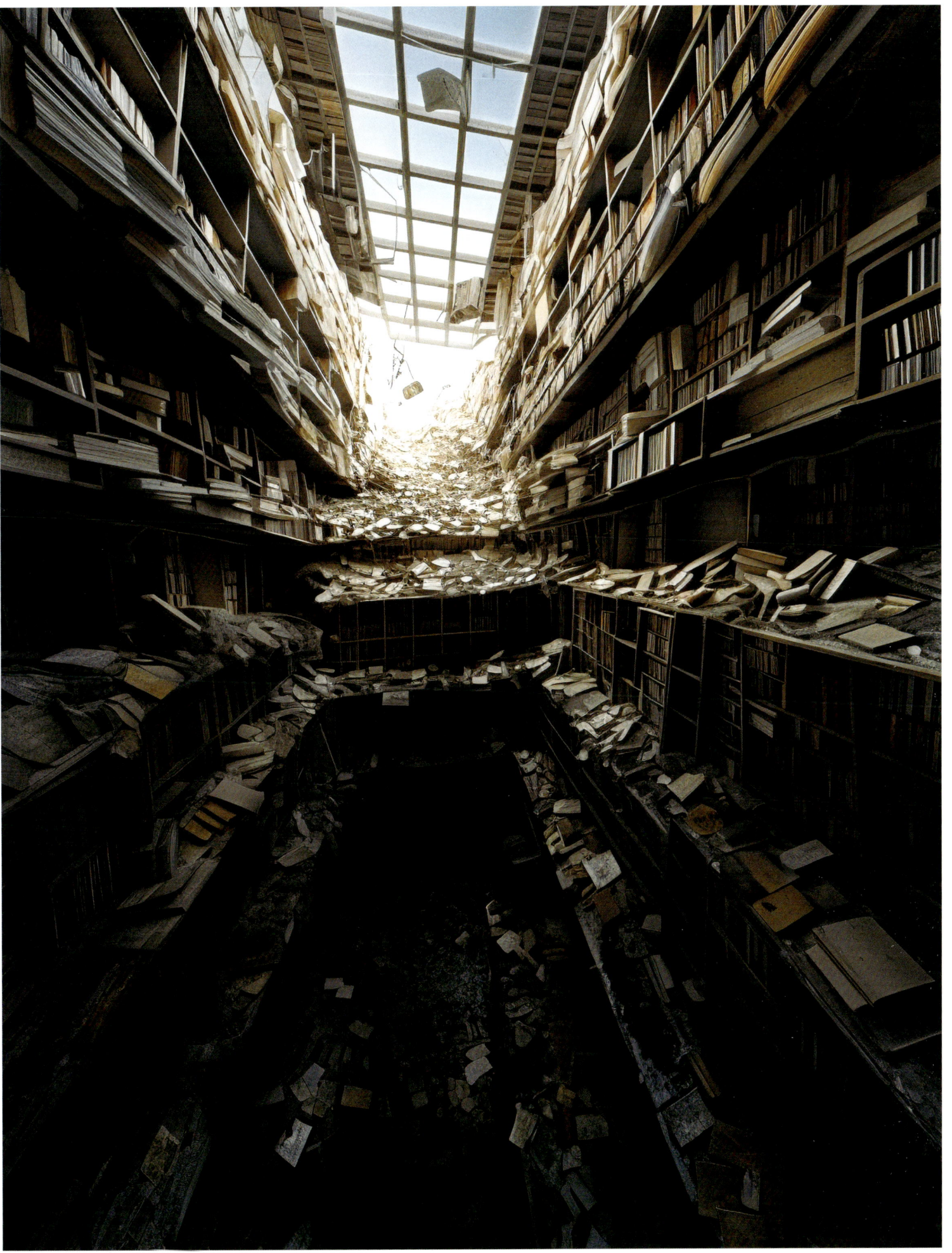

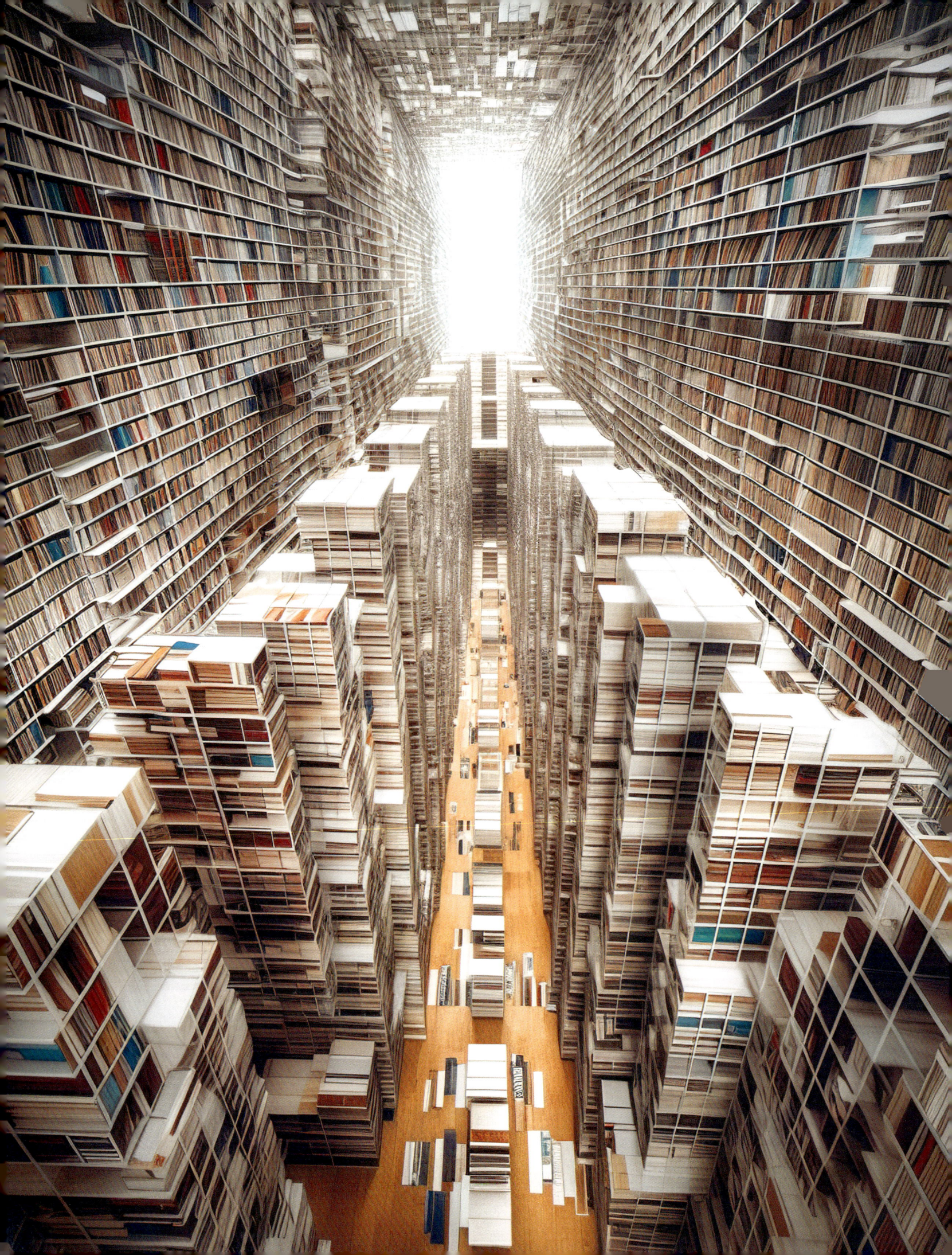

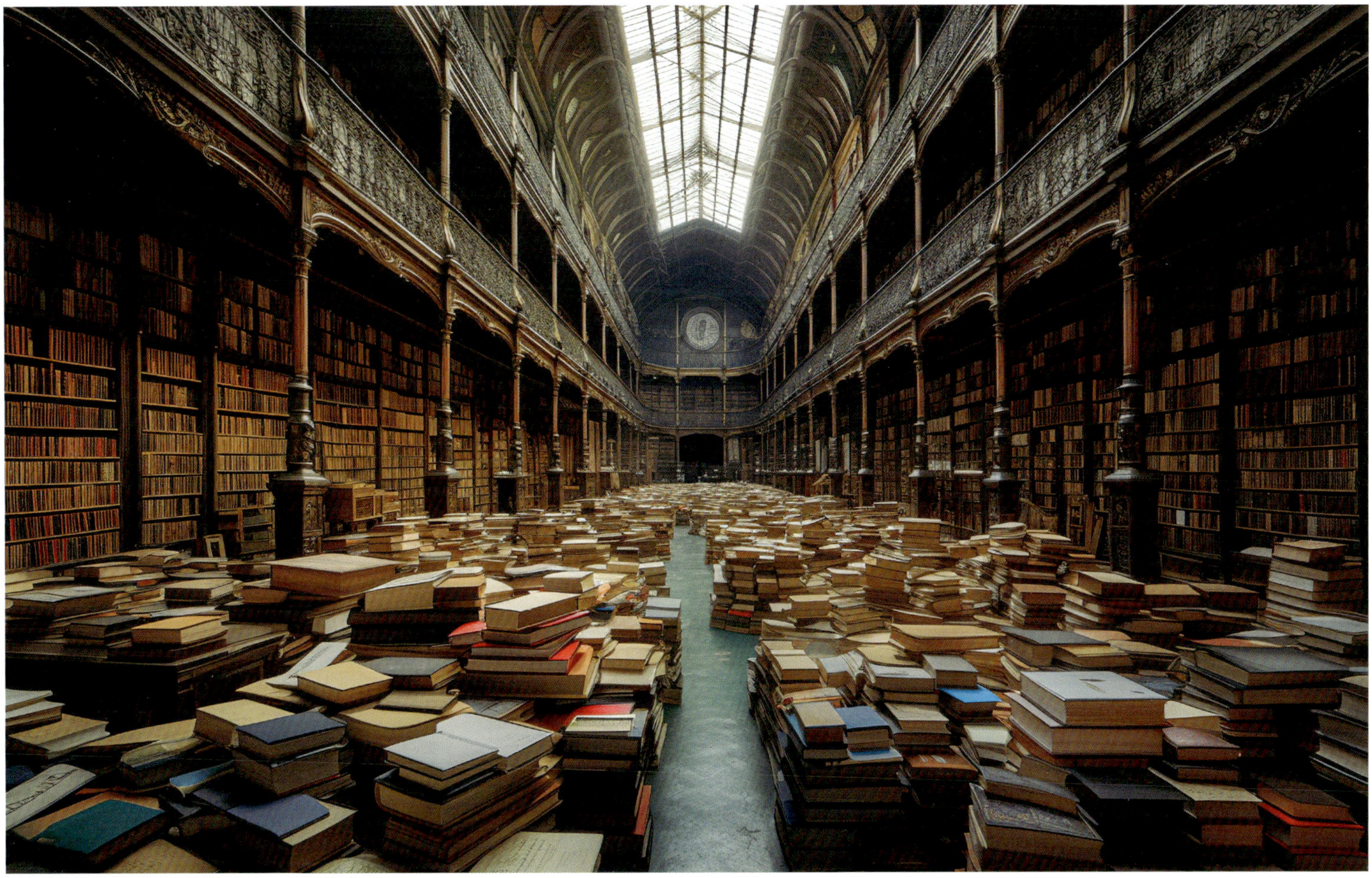

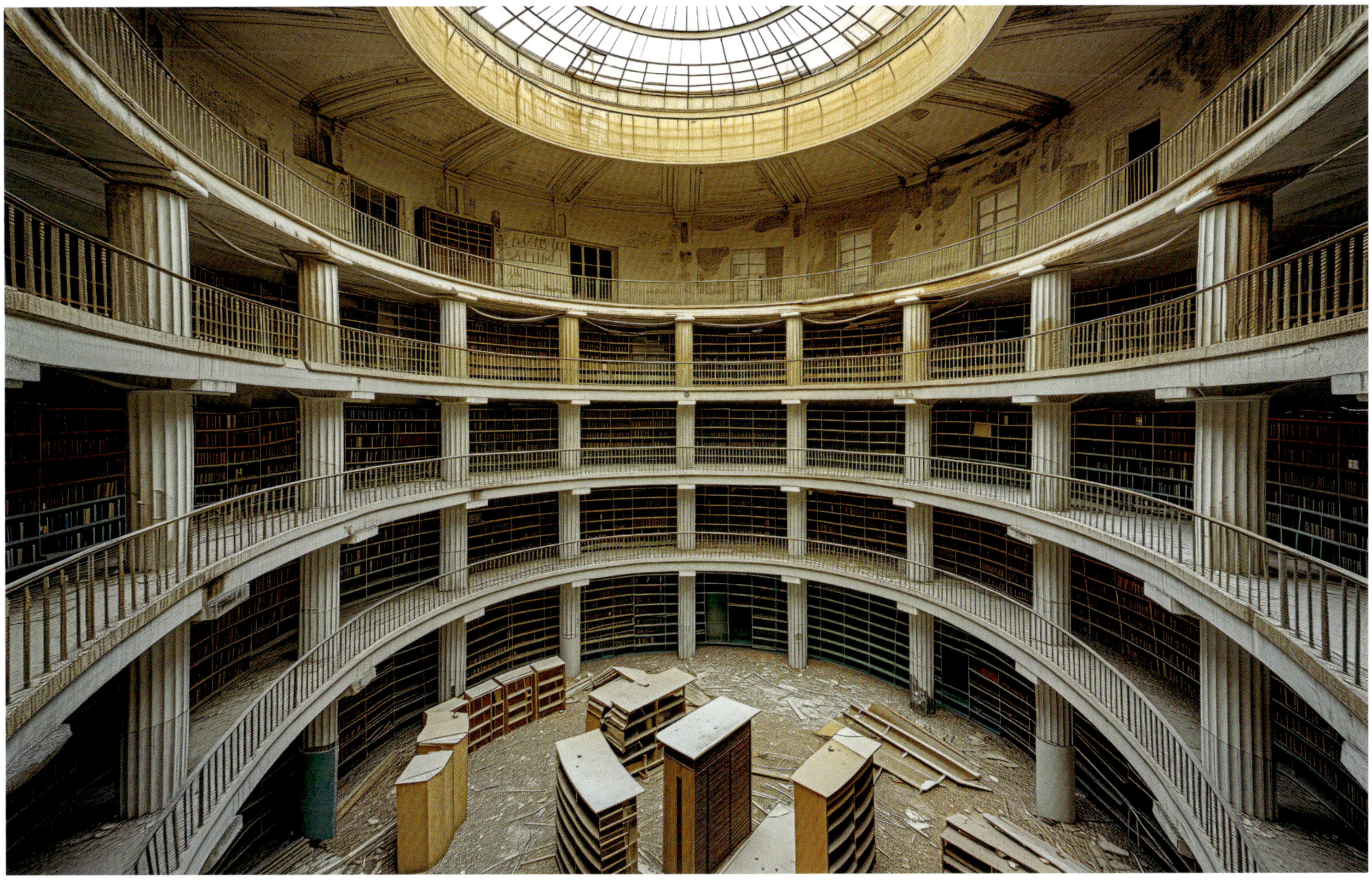

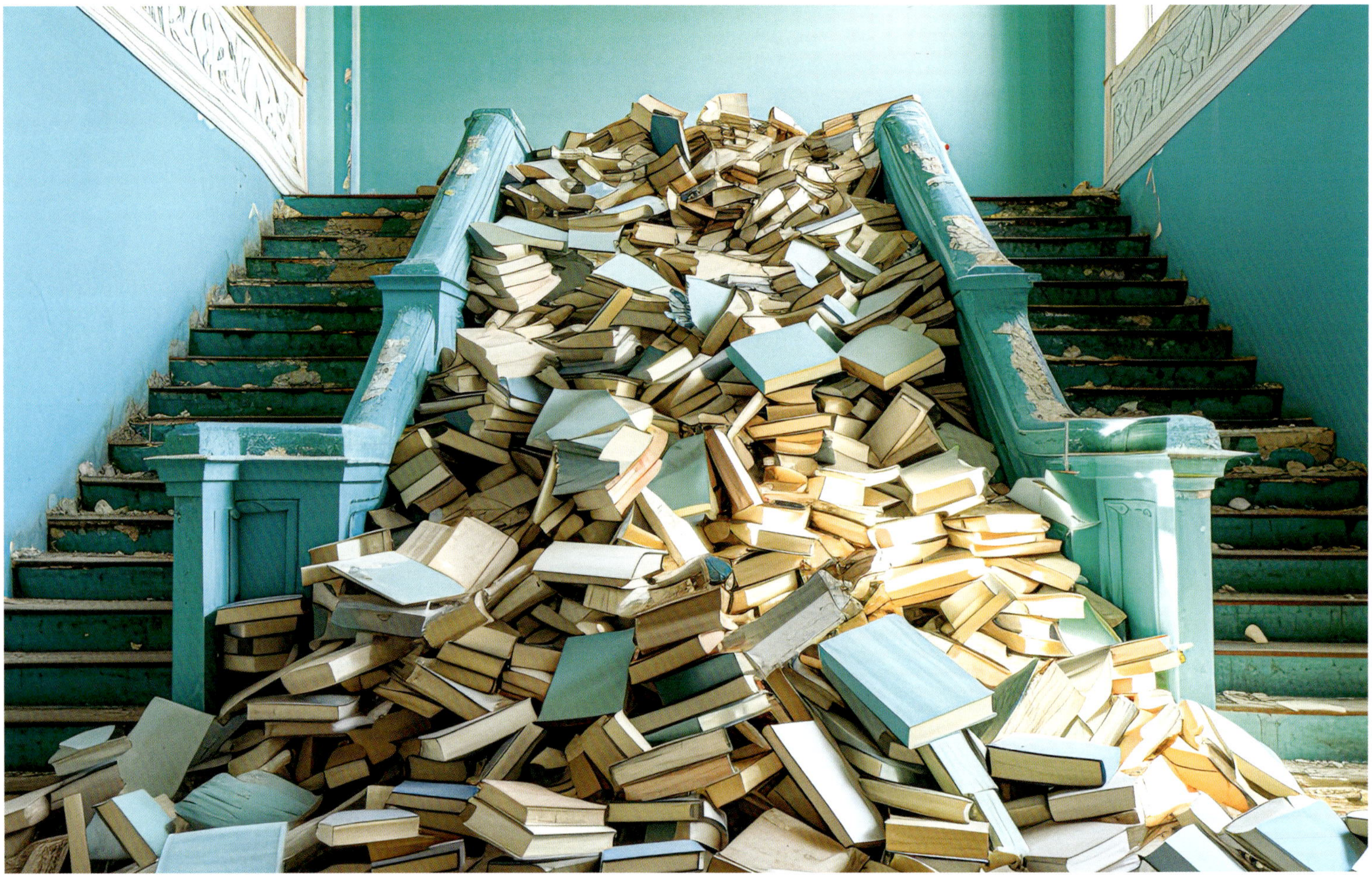

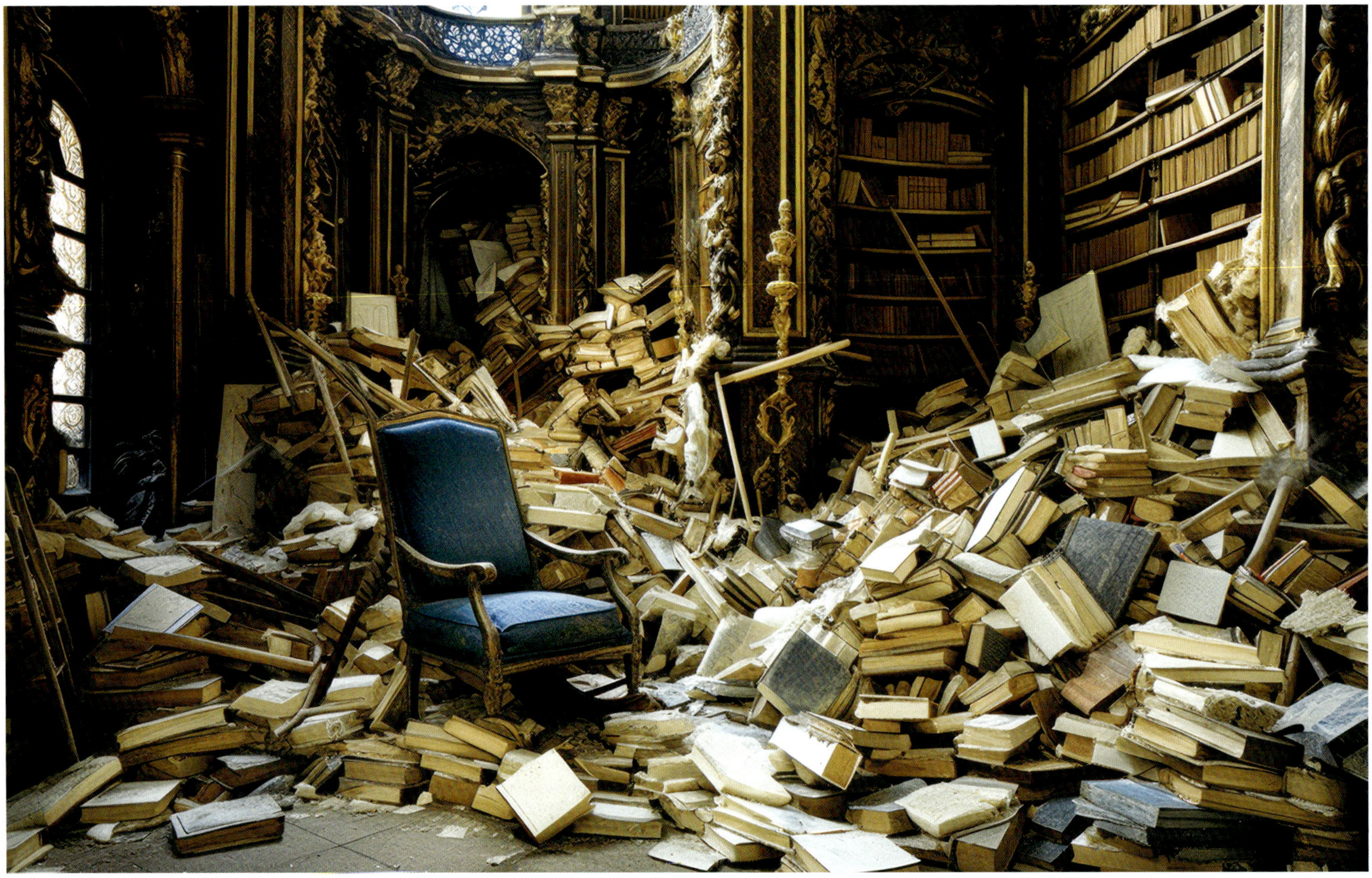

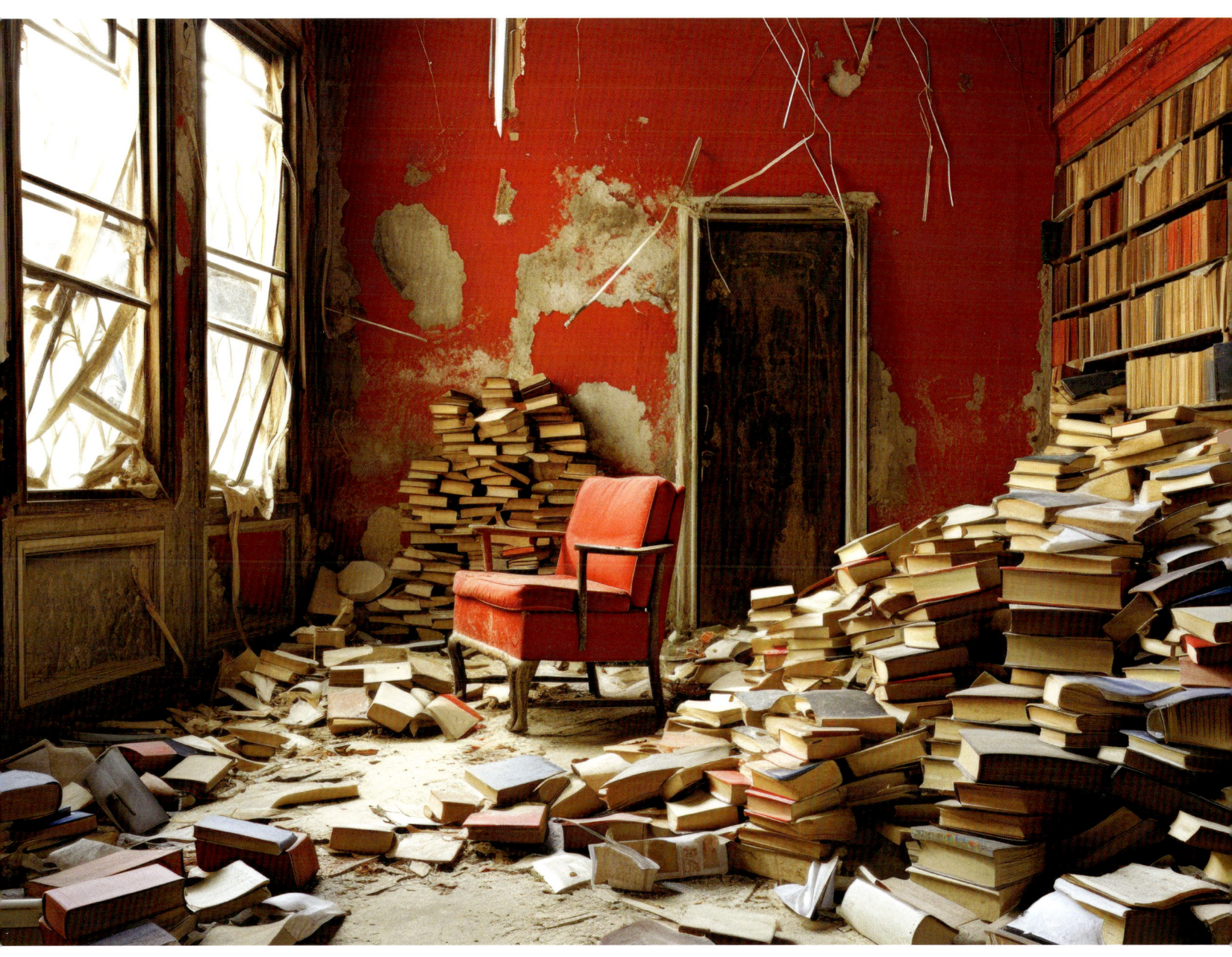

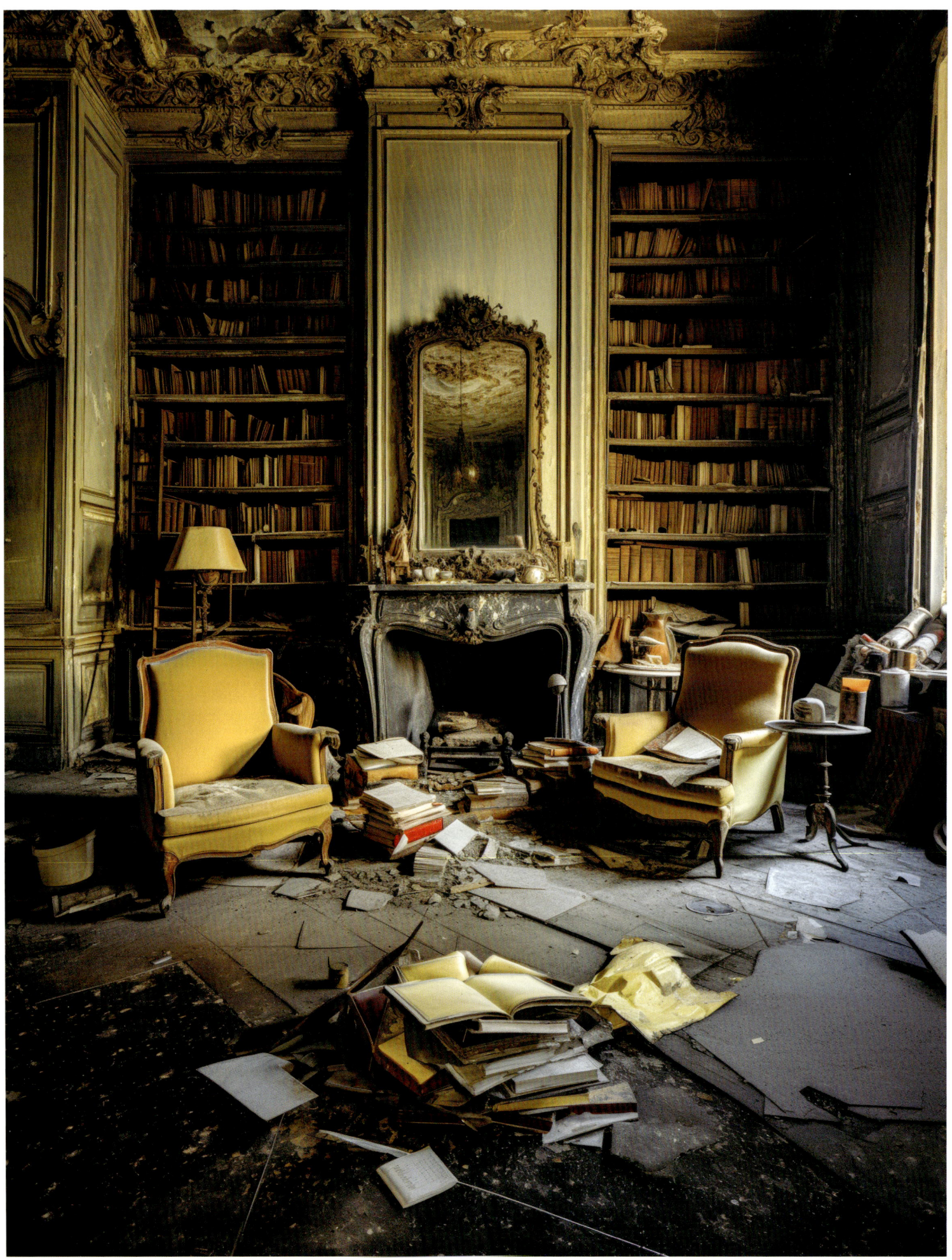

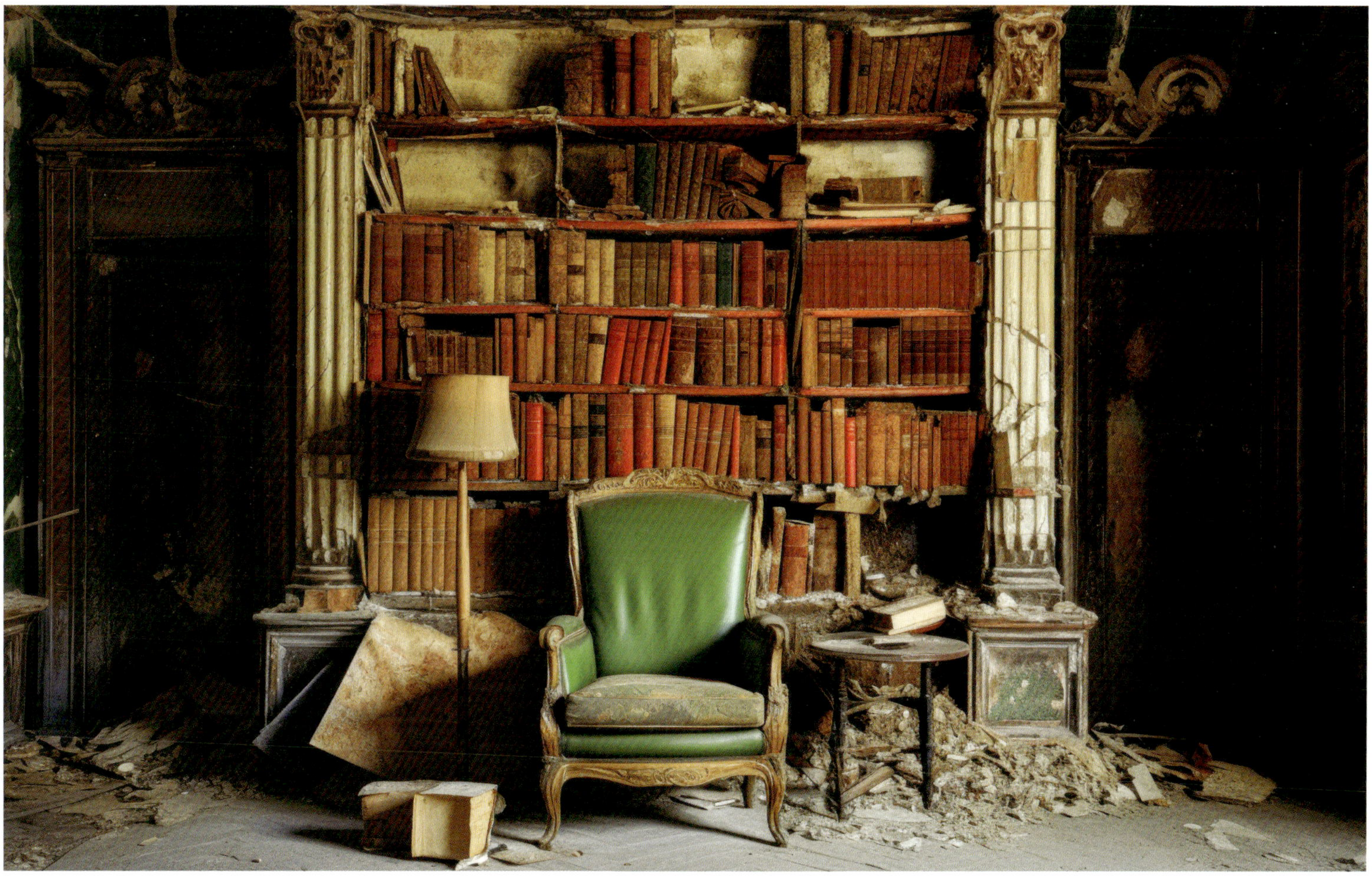

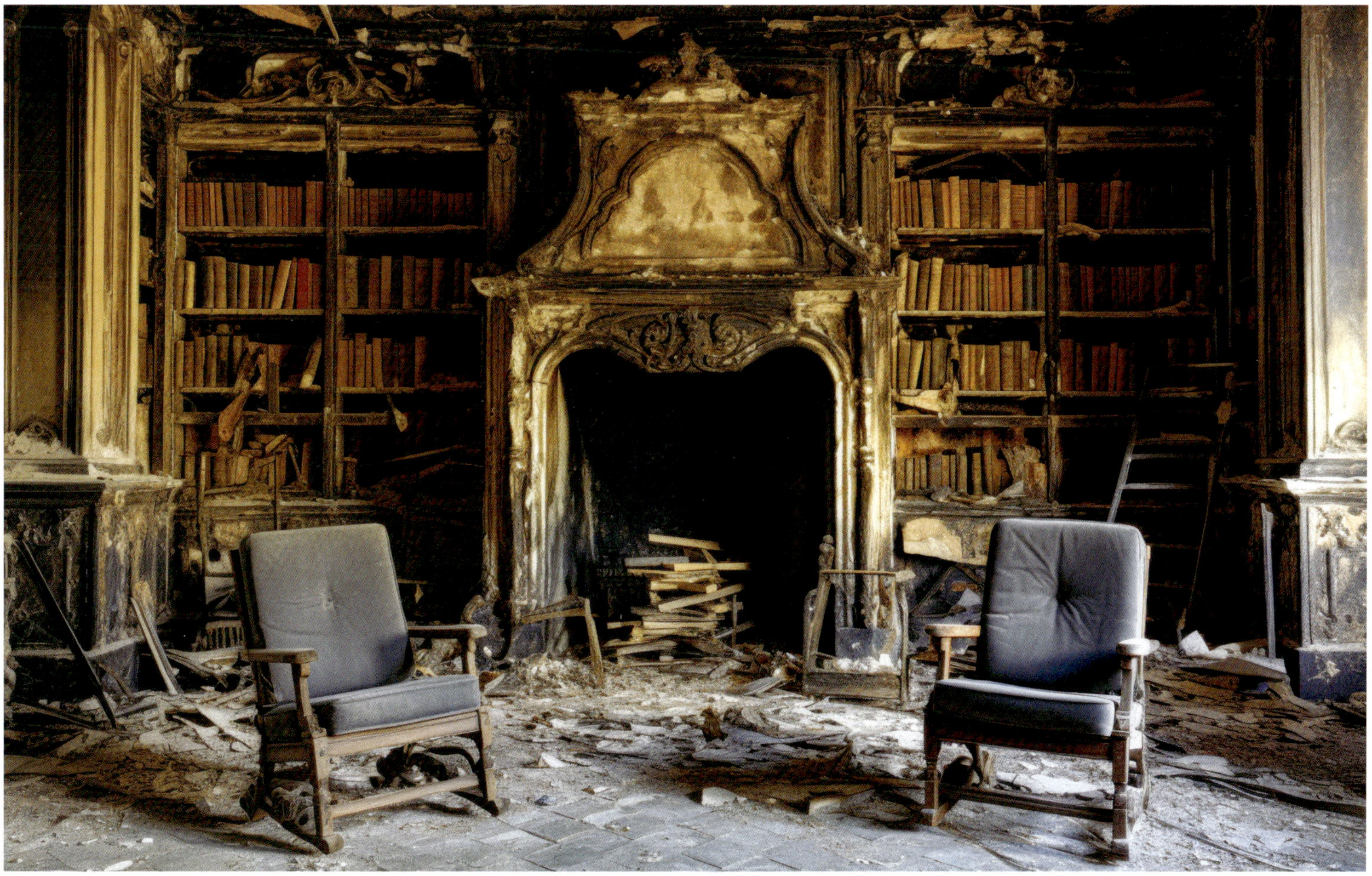

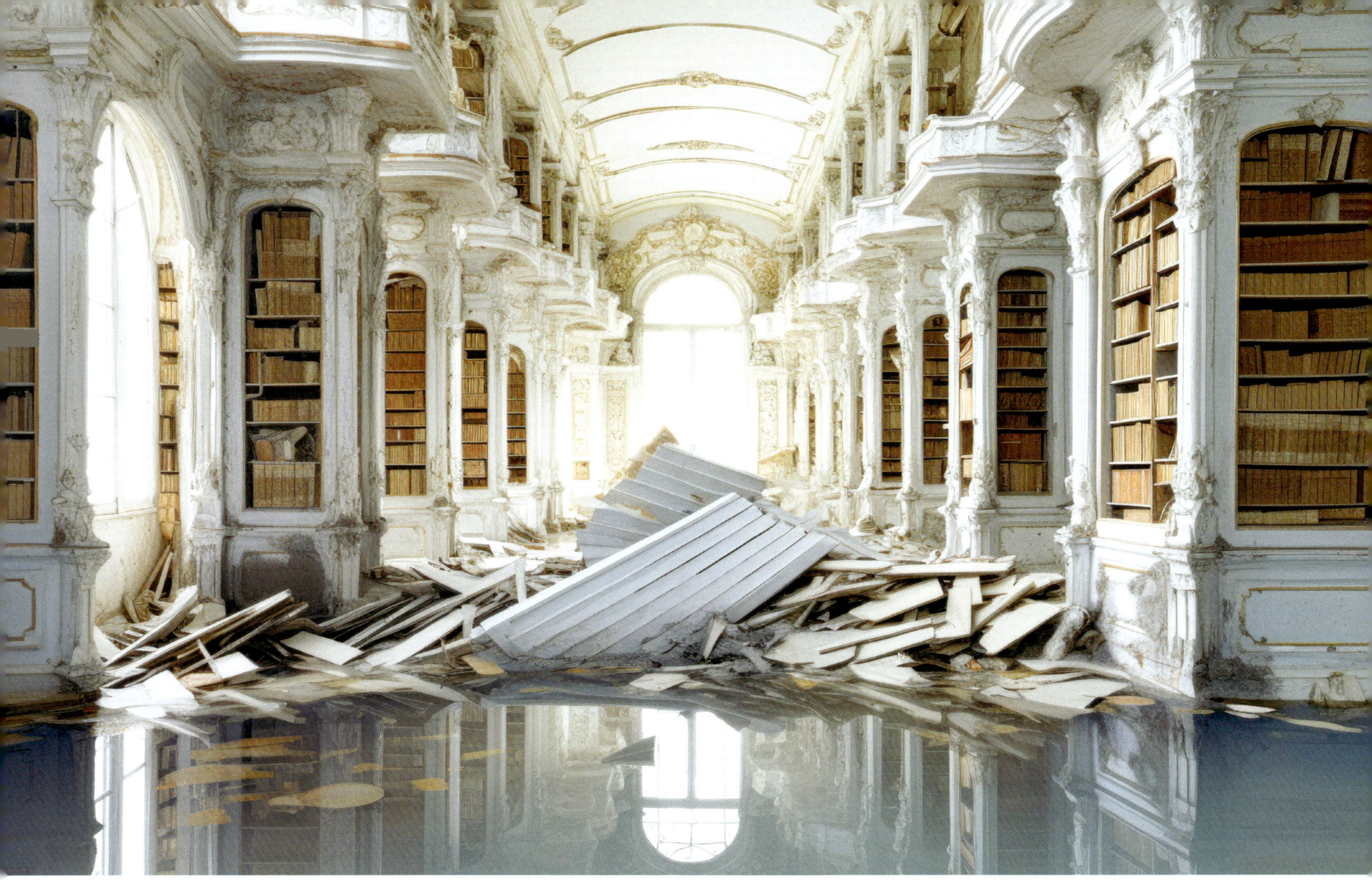

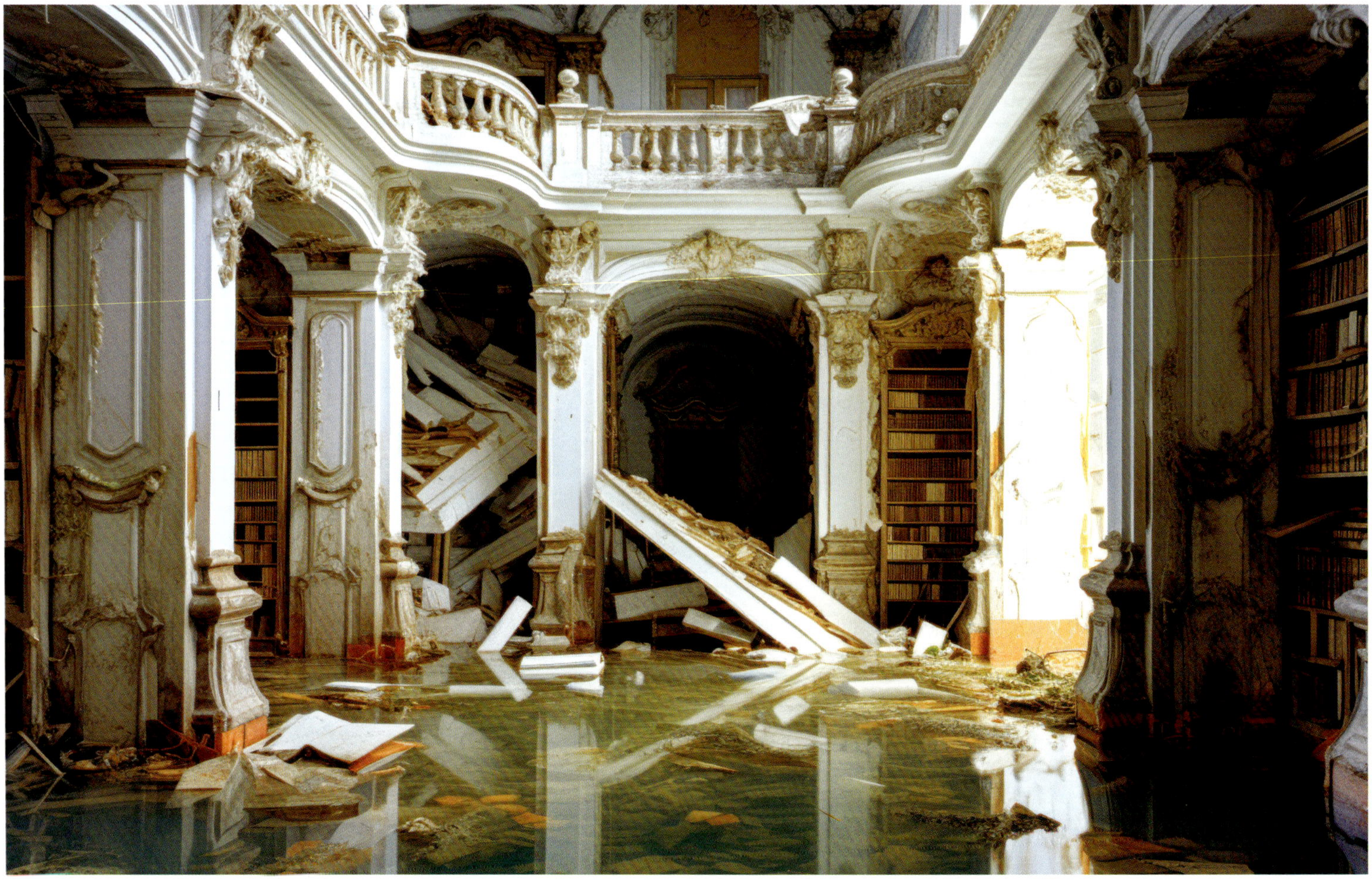

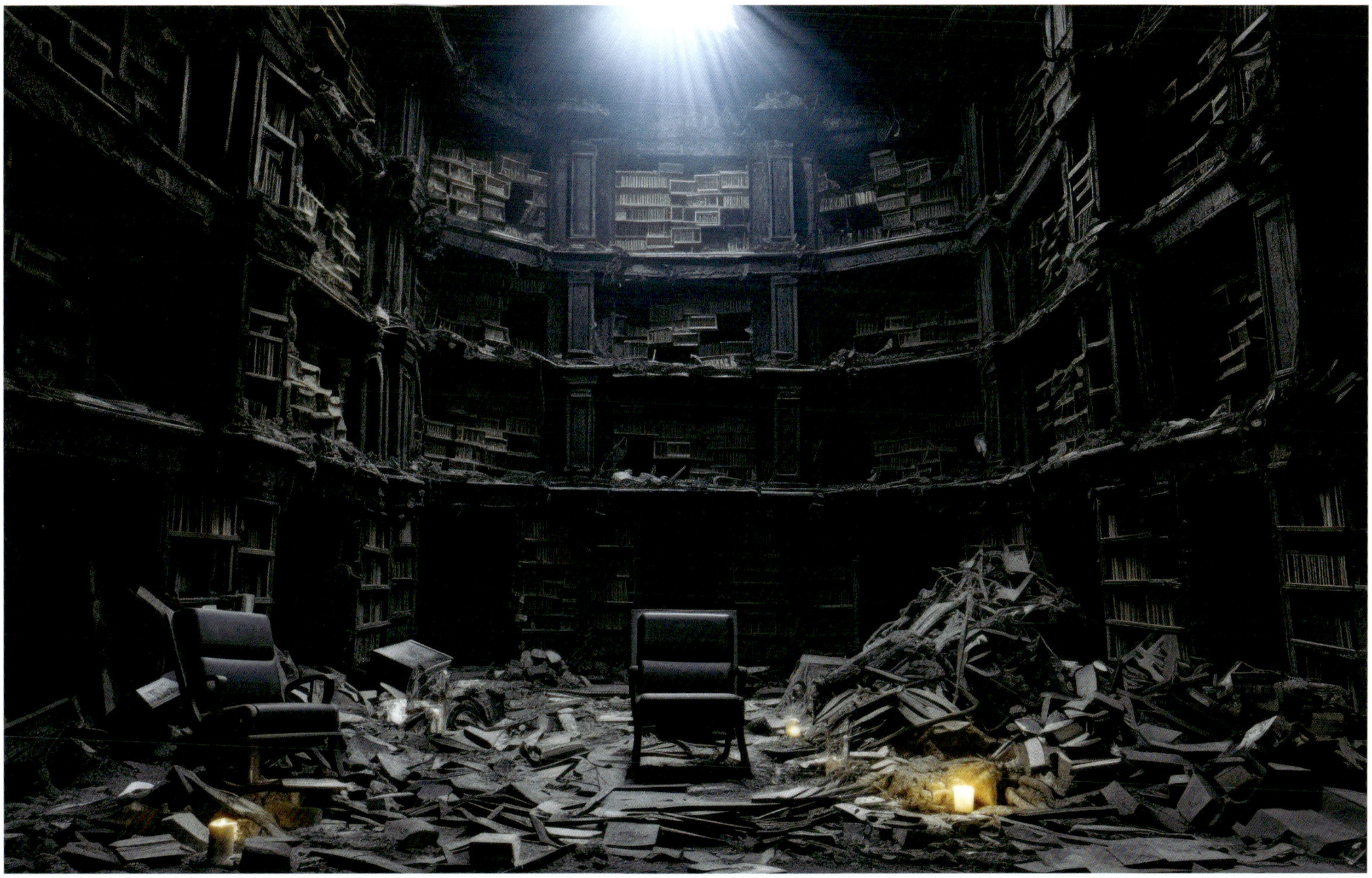

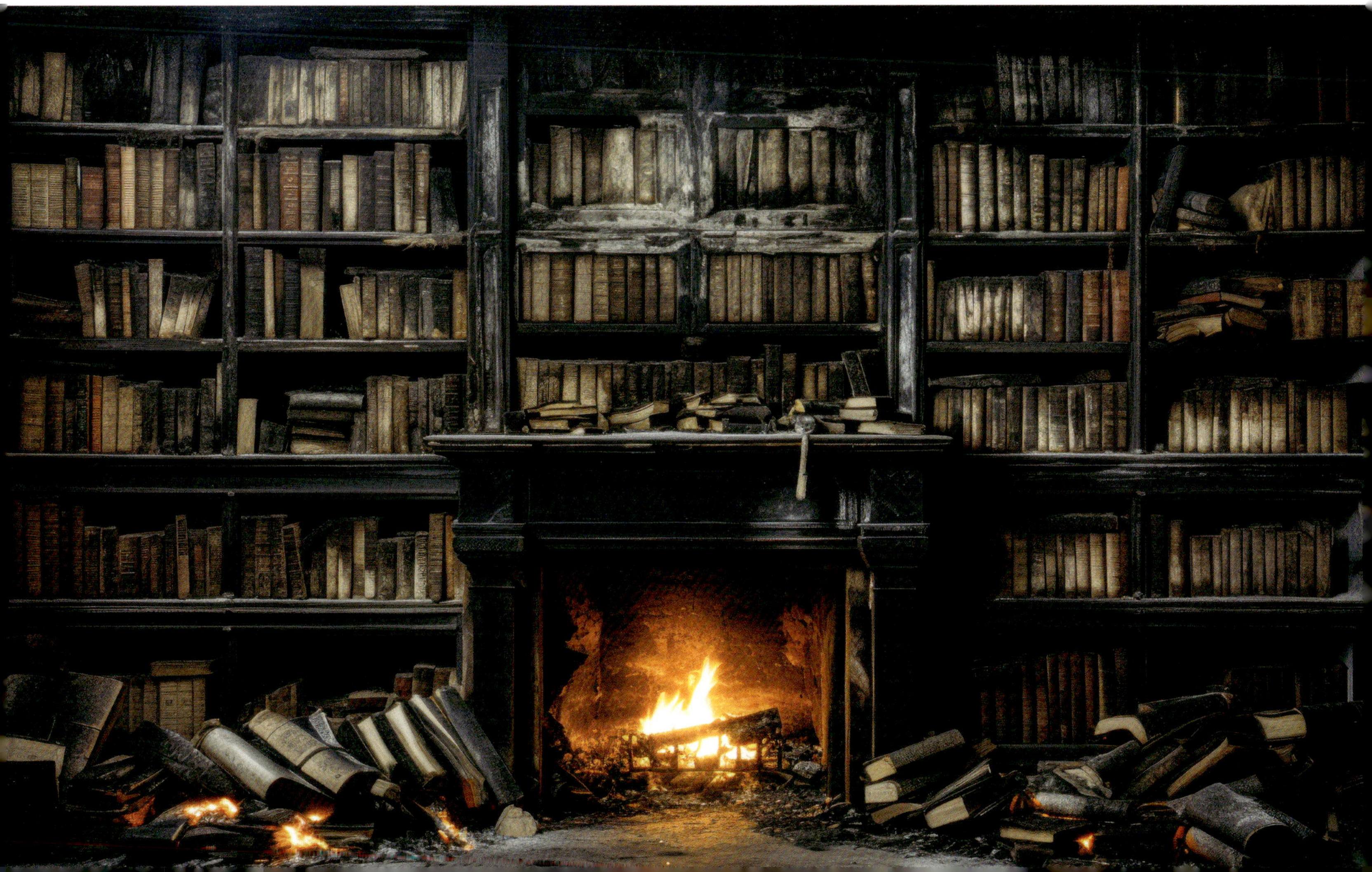

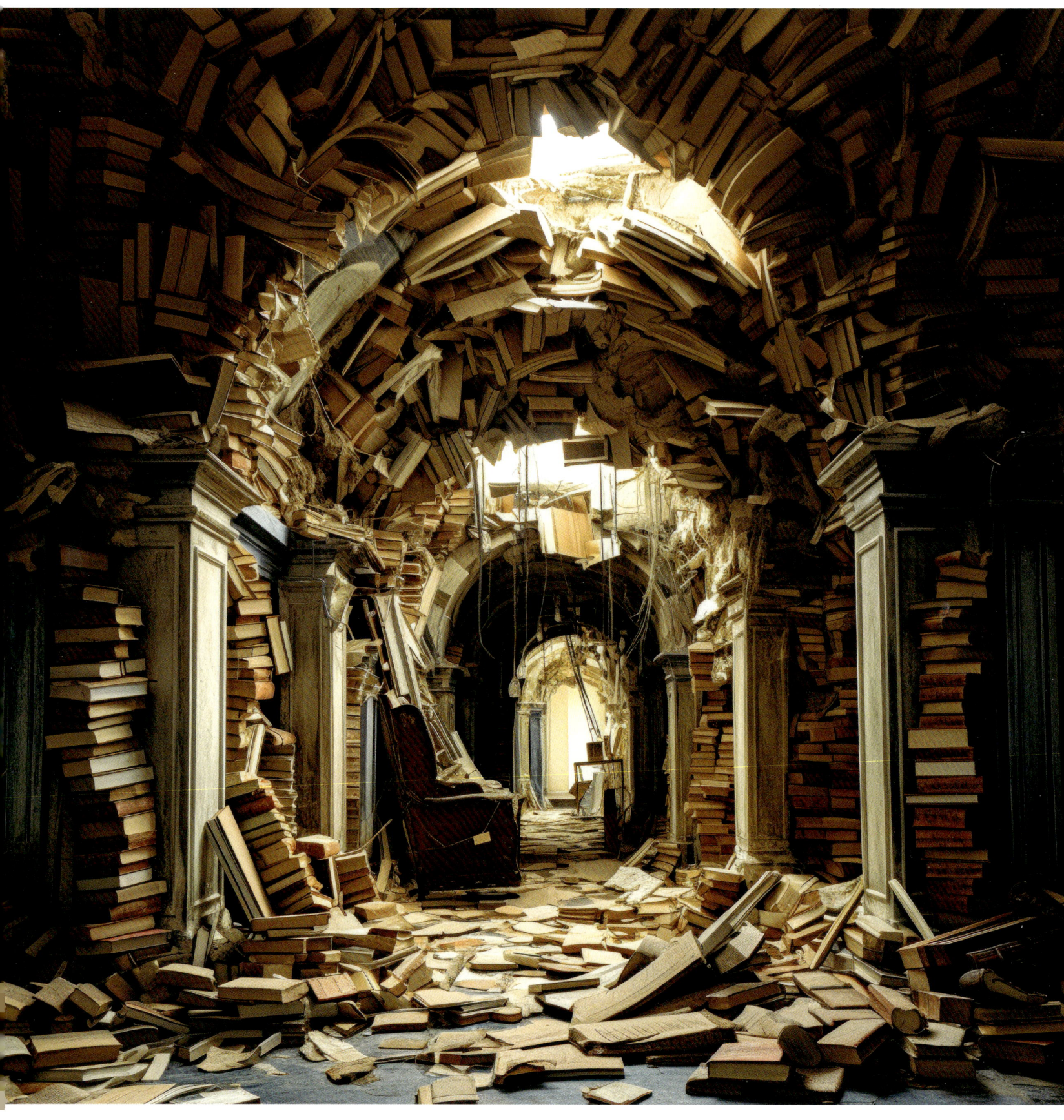

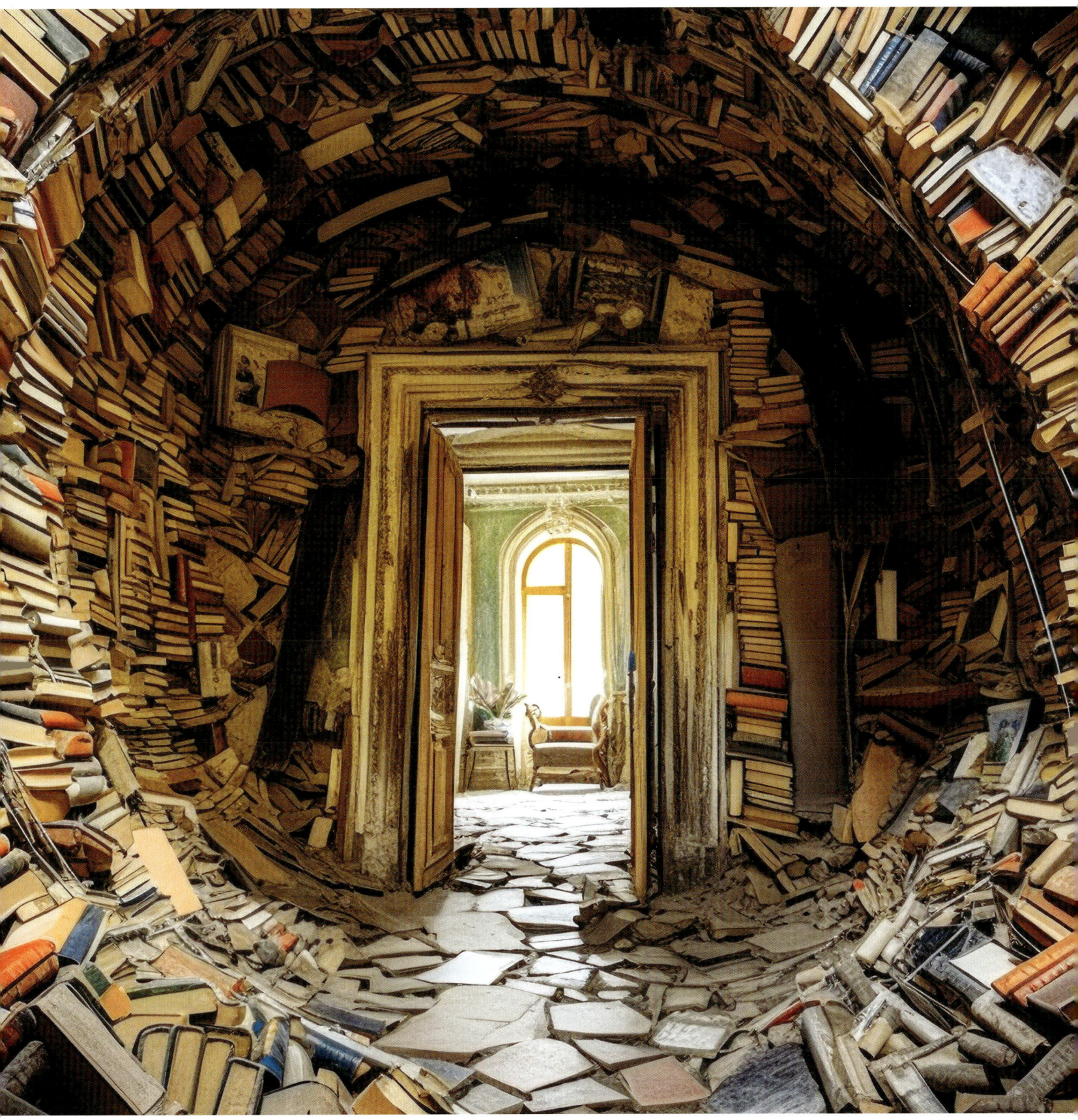

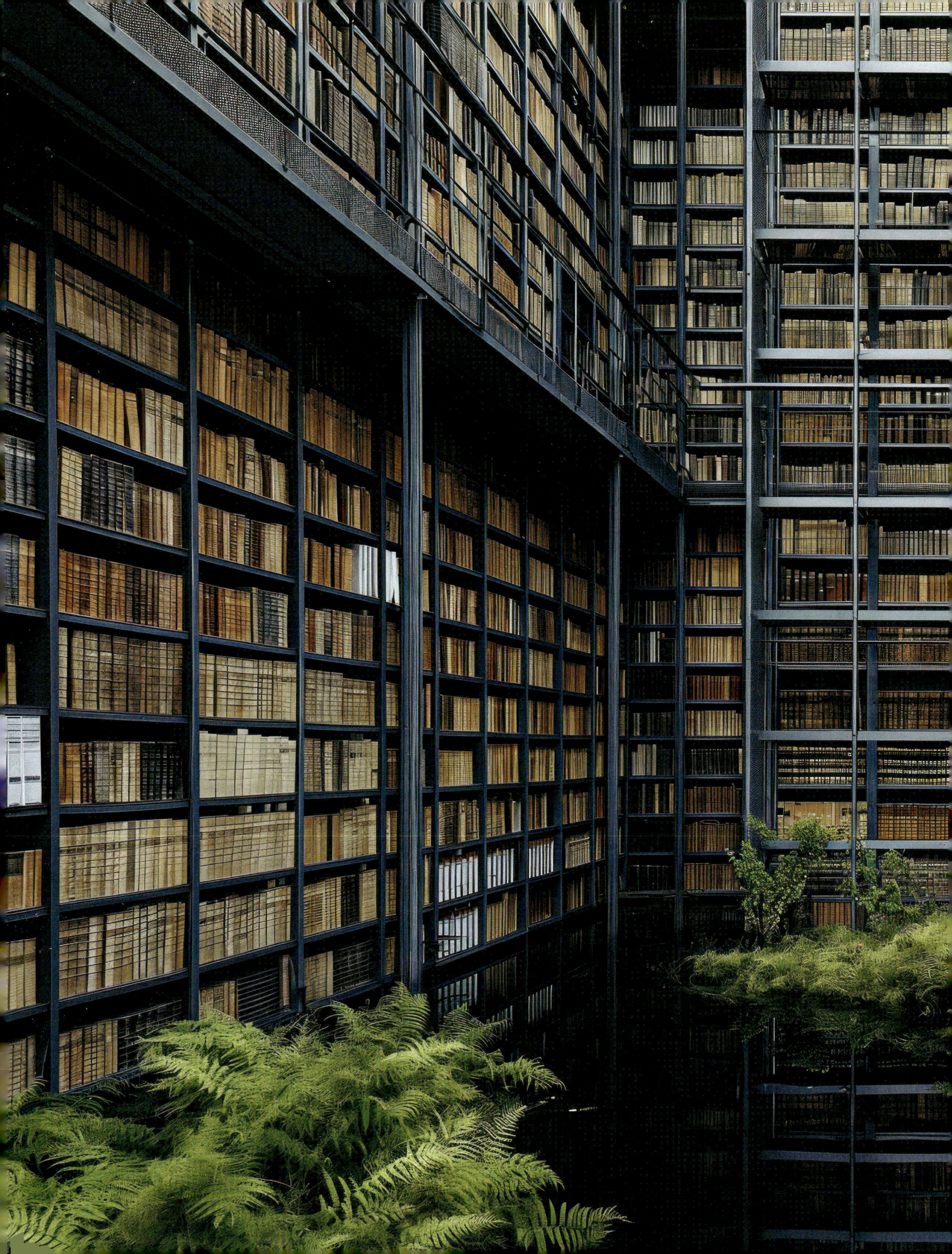

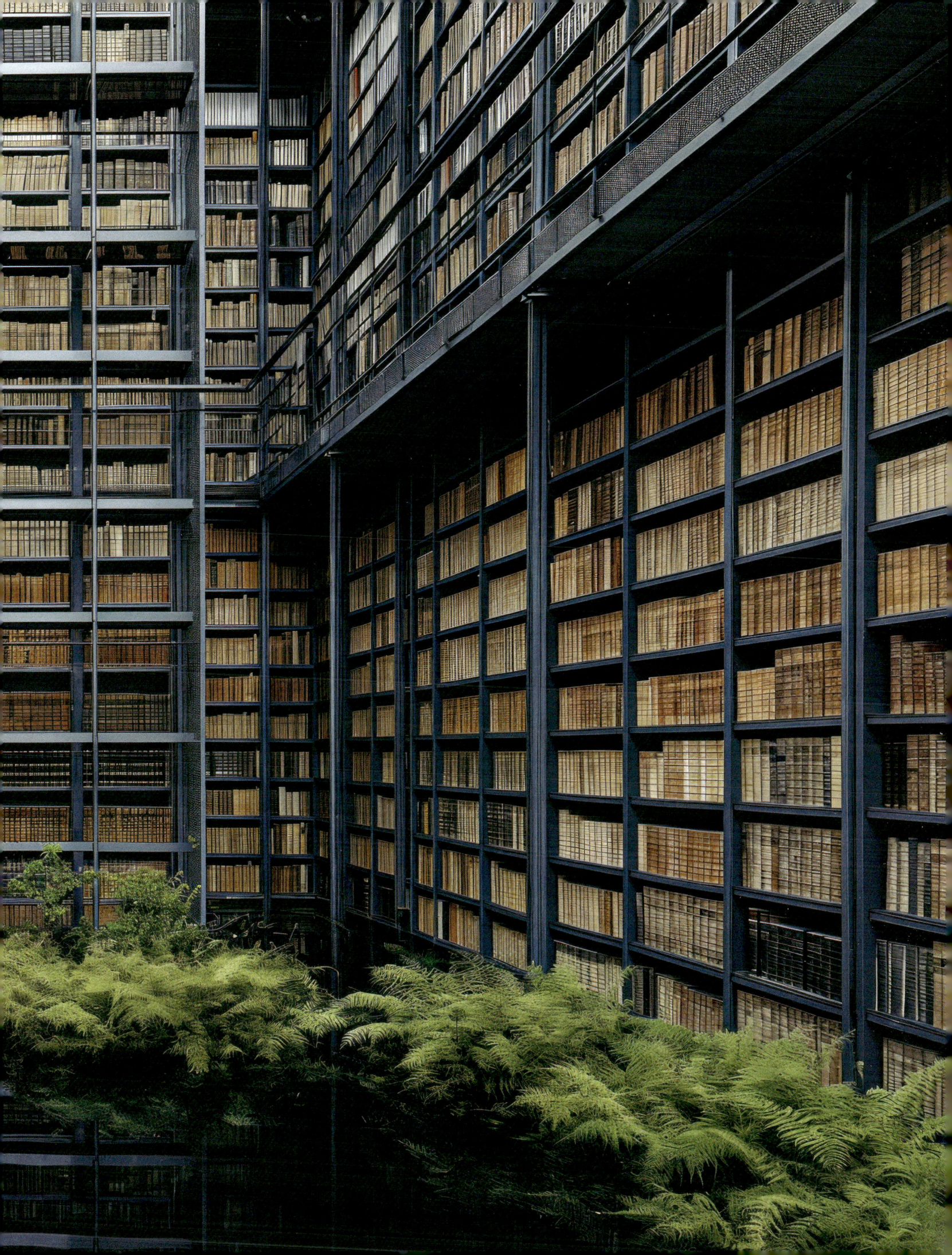

A very foul play

A repetitive electronic melody echoes through the streets. The twilight of cinemas and theatres has come. On-demand platforms have devoured society's cultural arteries. Derelict buildings, once epicentres of wonder, are slowly crumbling into oblivion, deserted and condemned to abandonment. The end of an era.

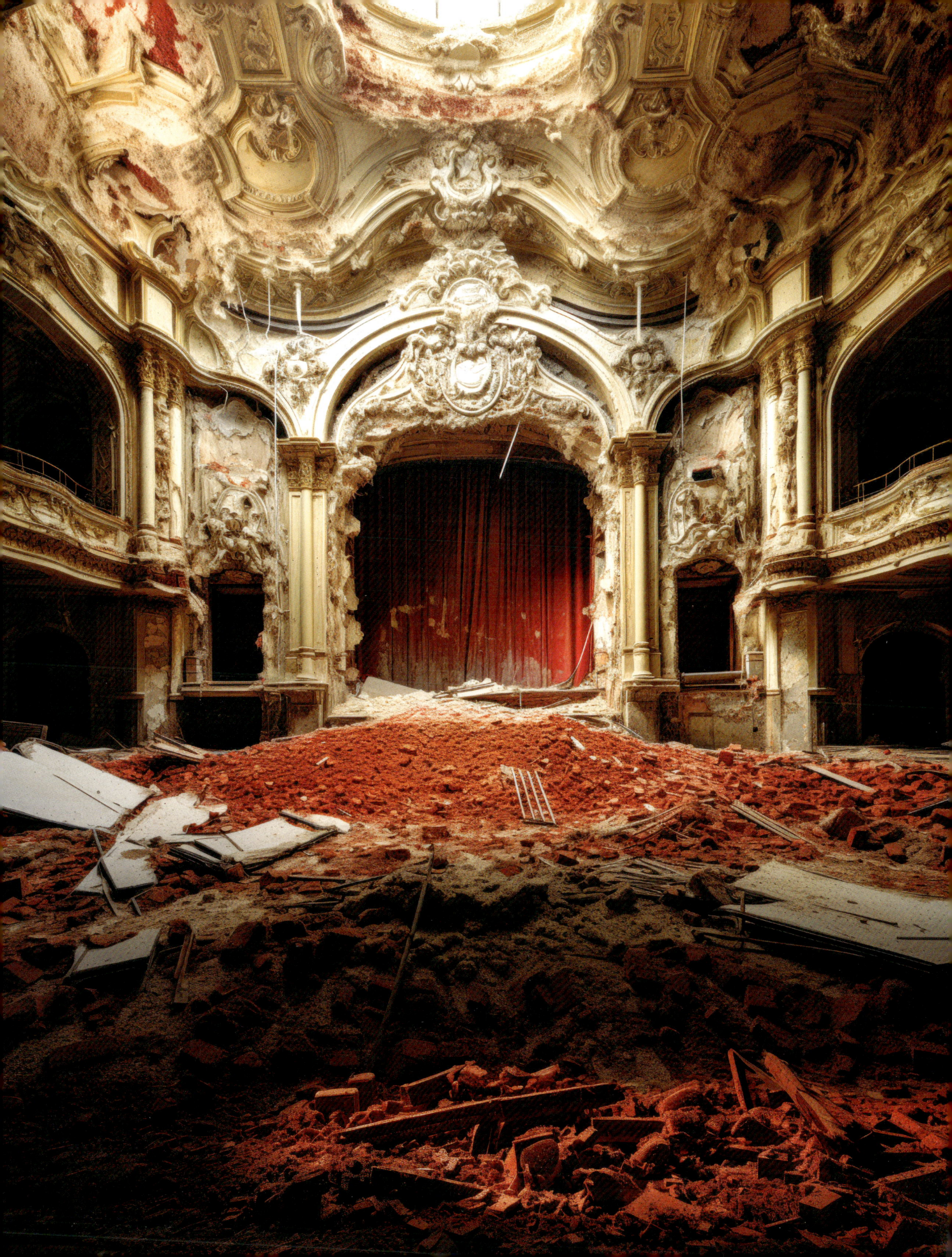

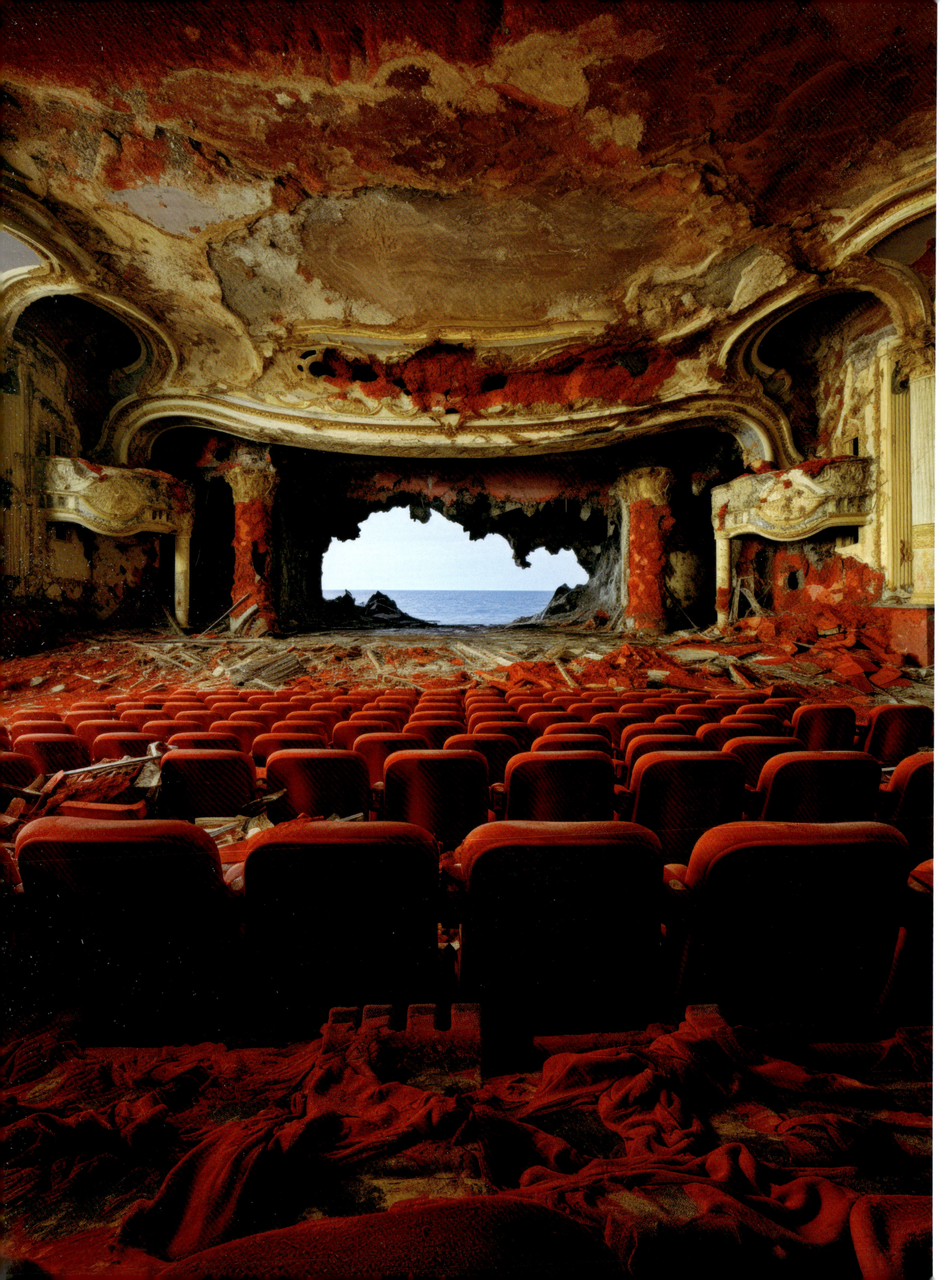

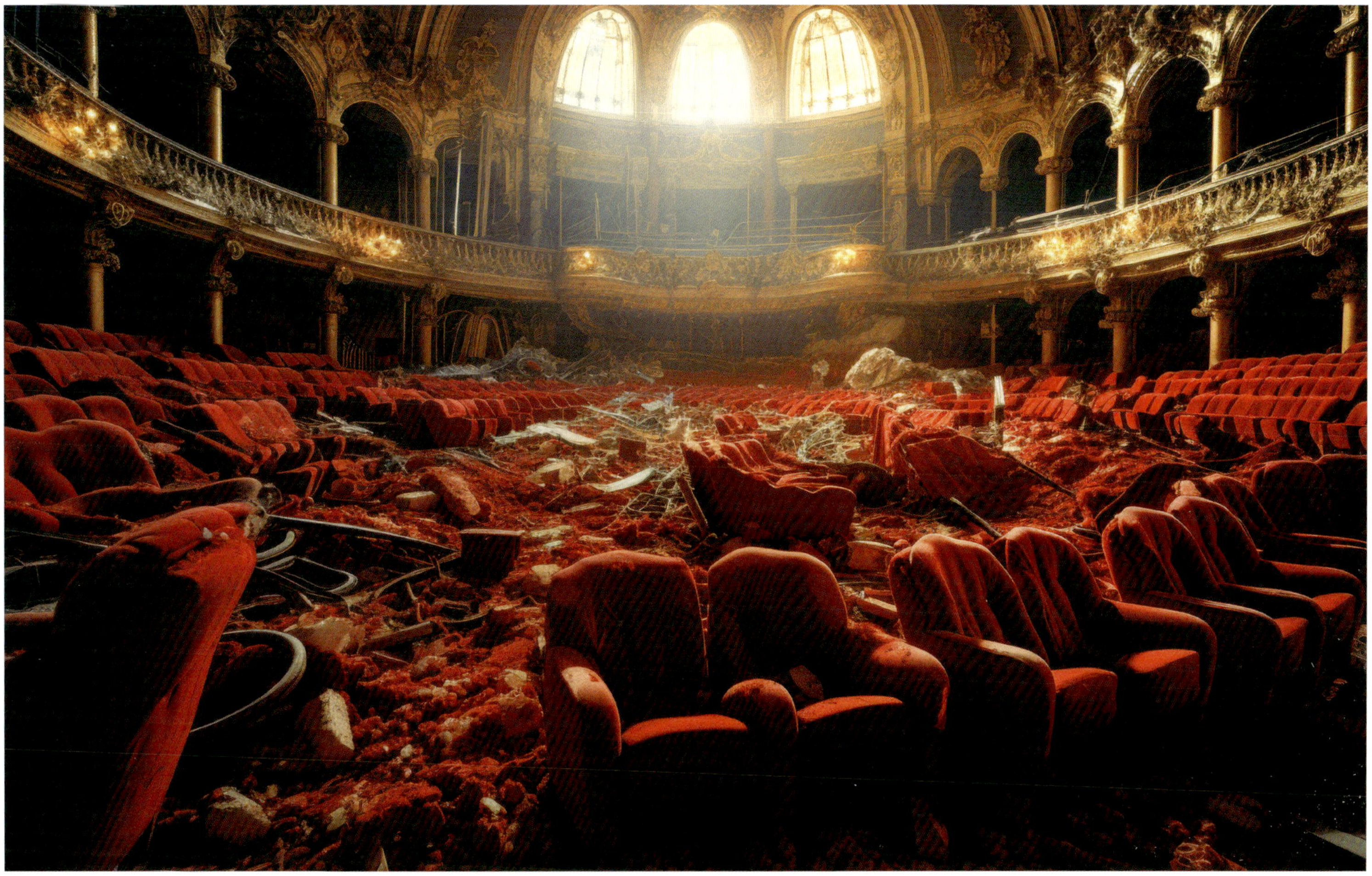

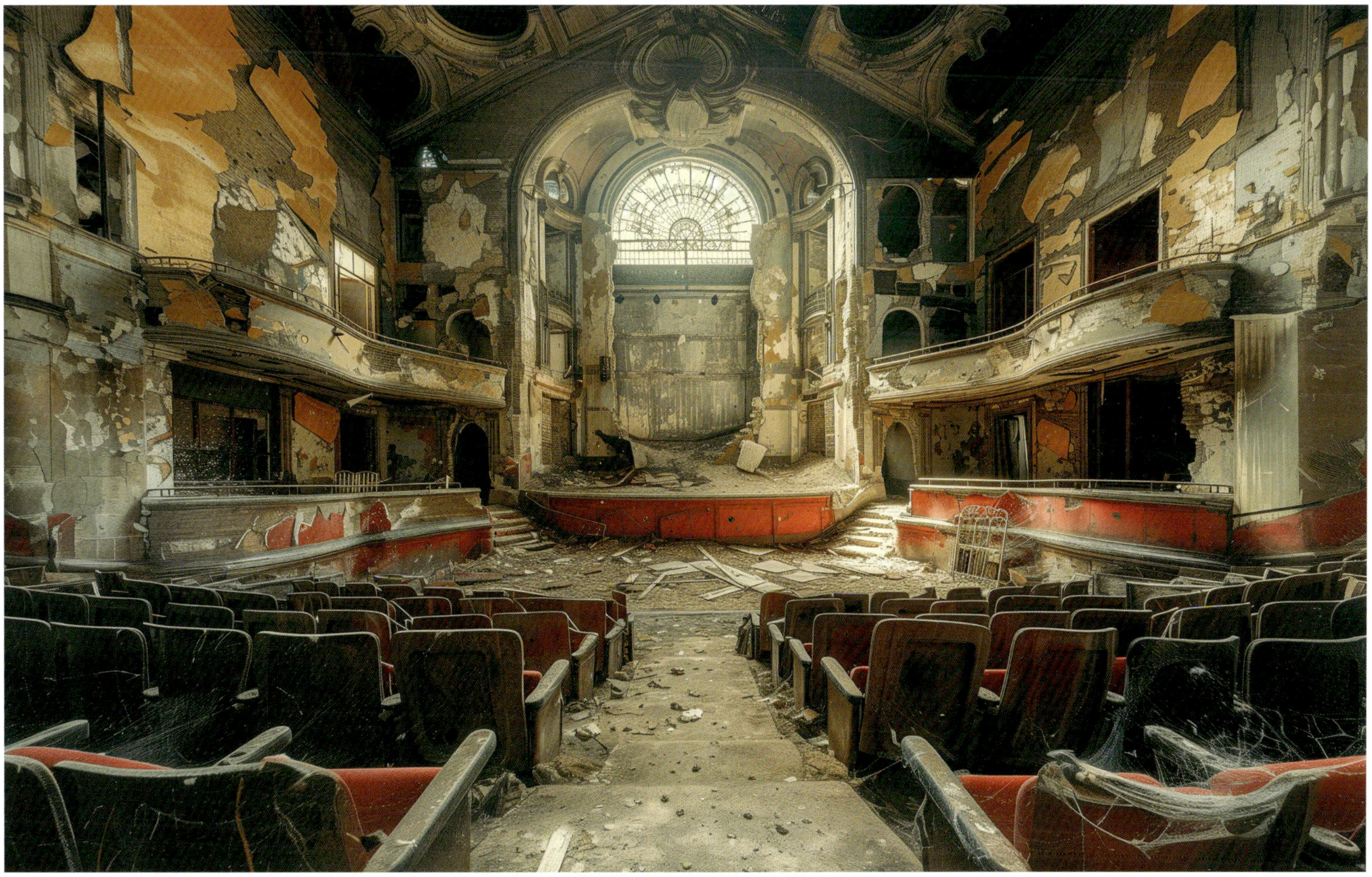

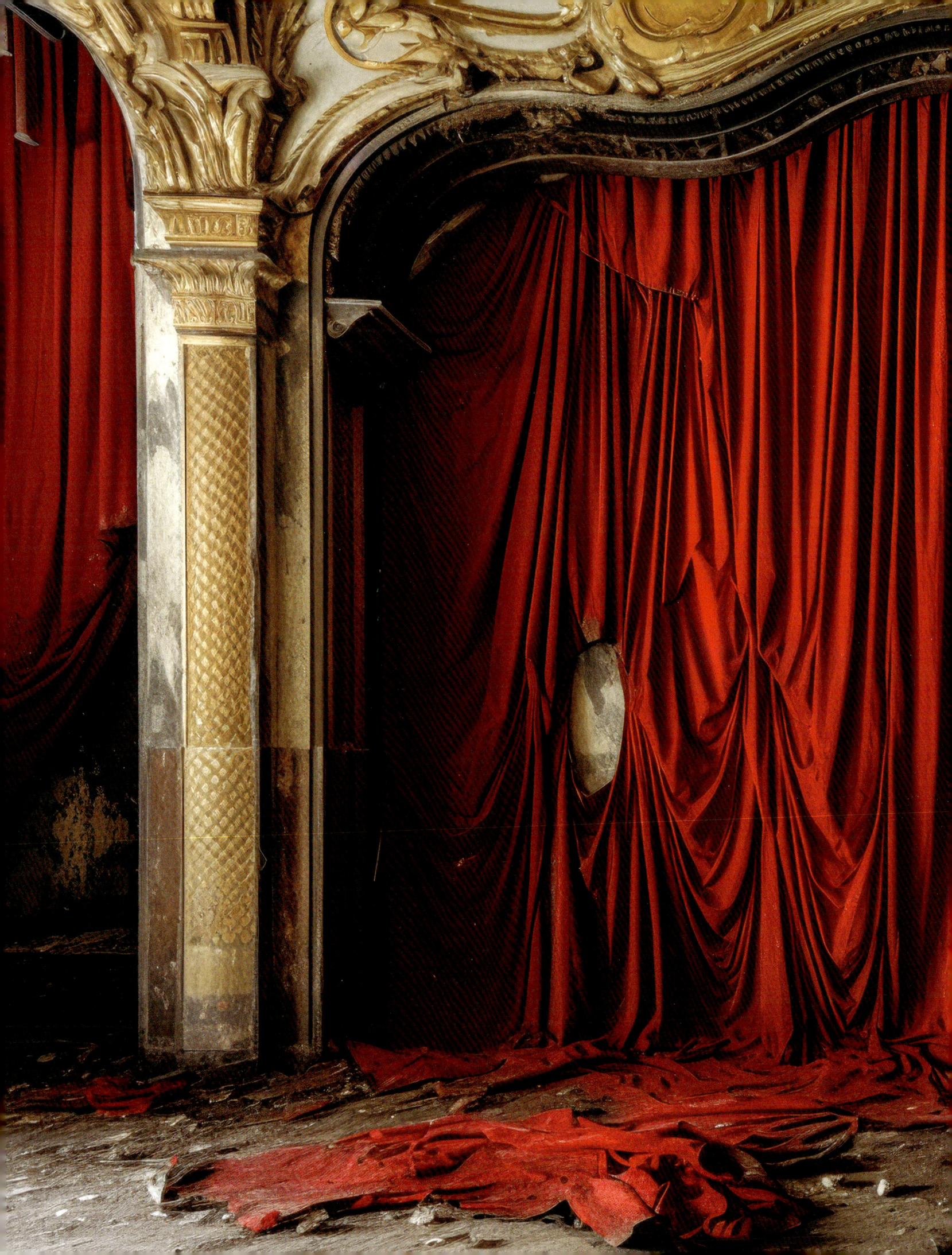

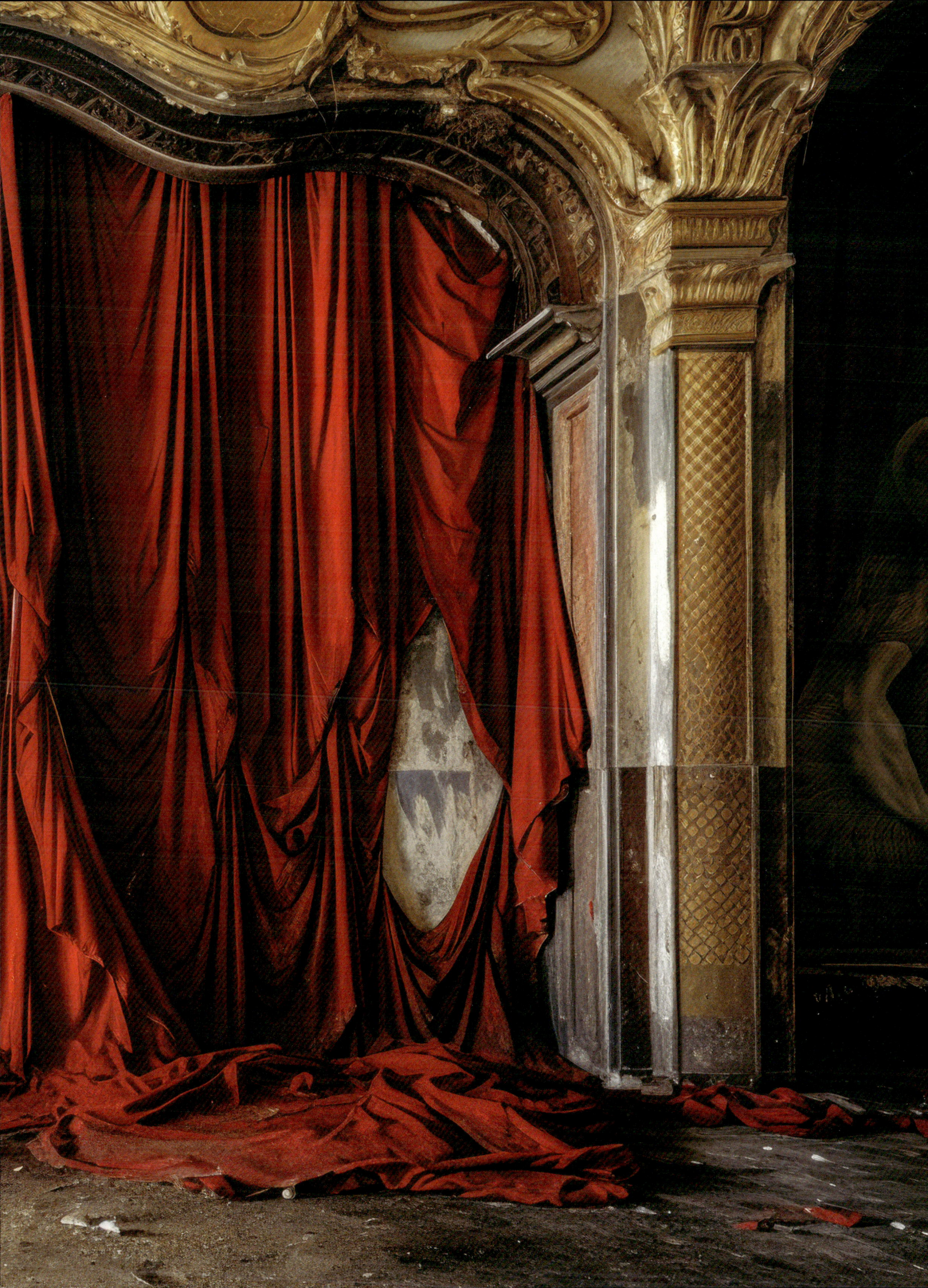

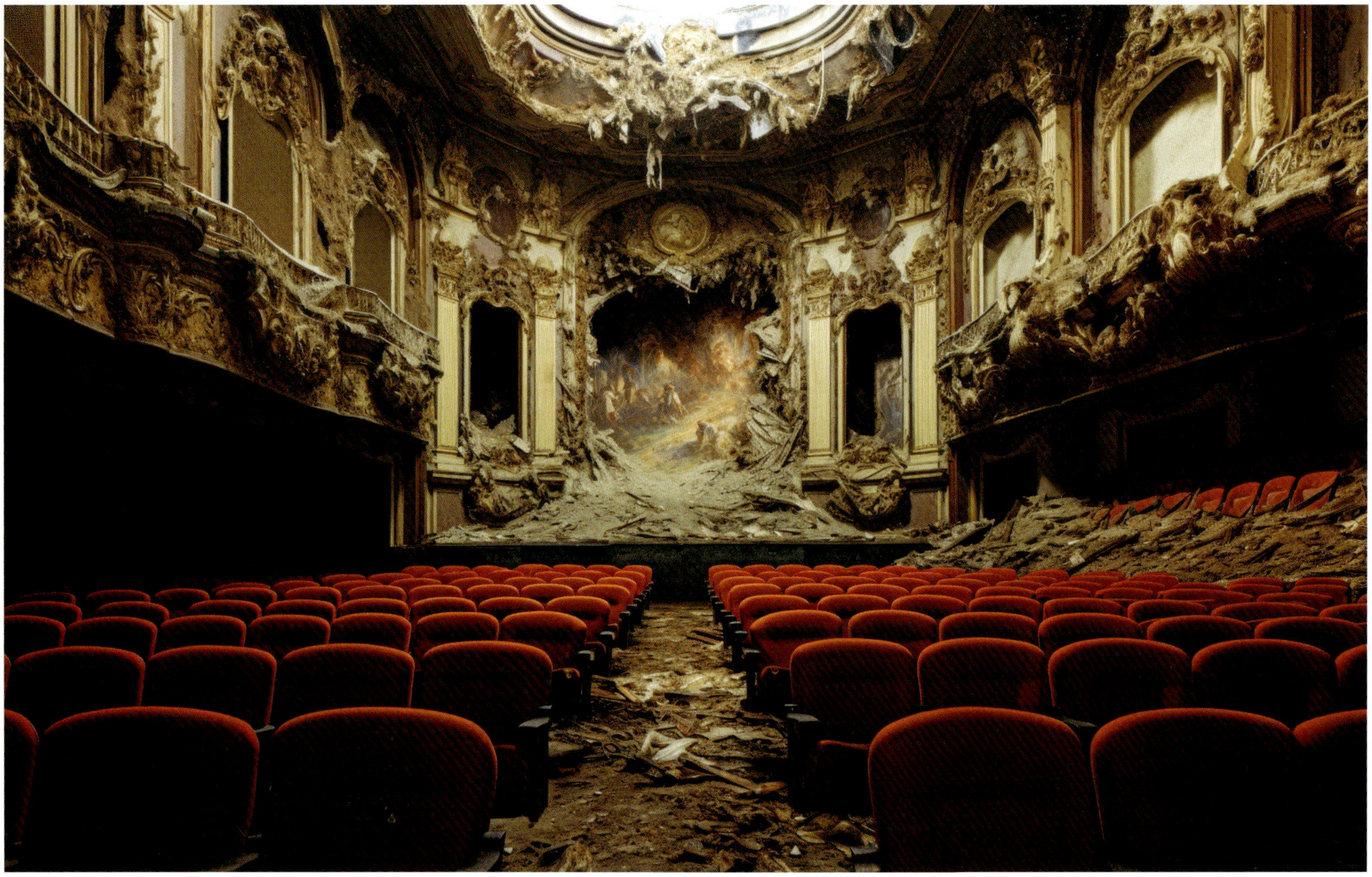

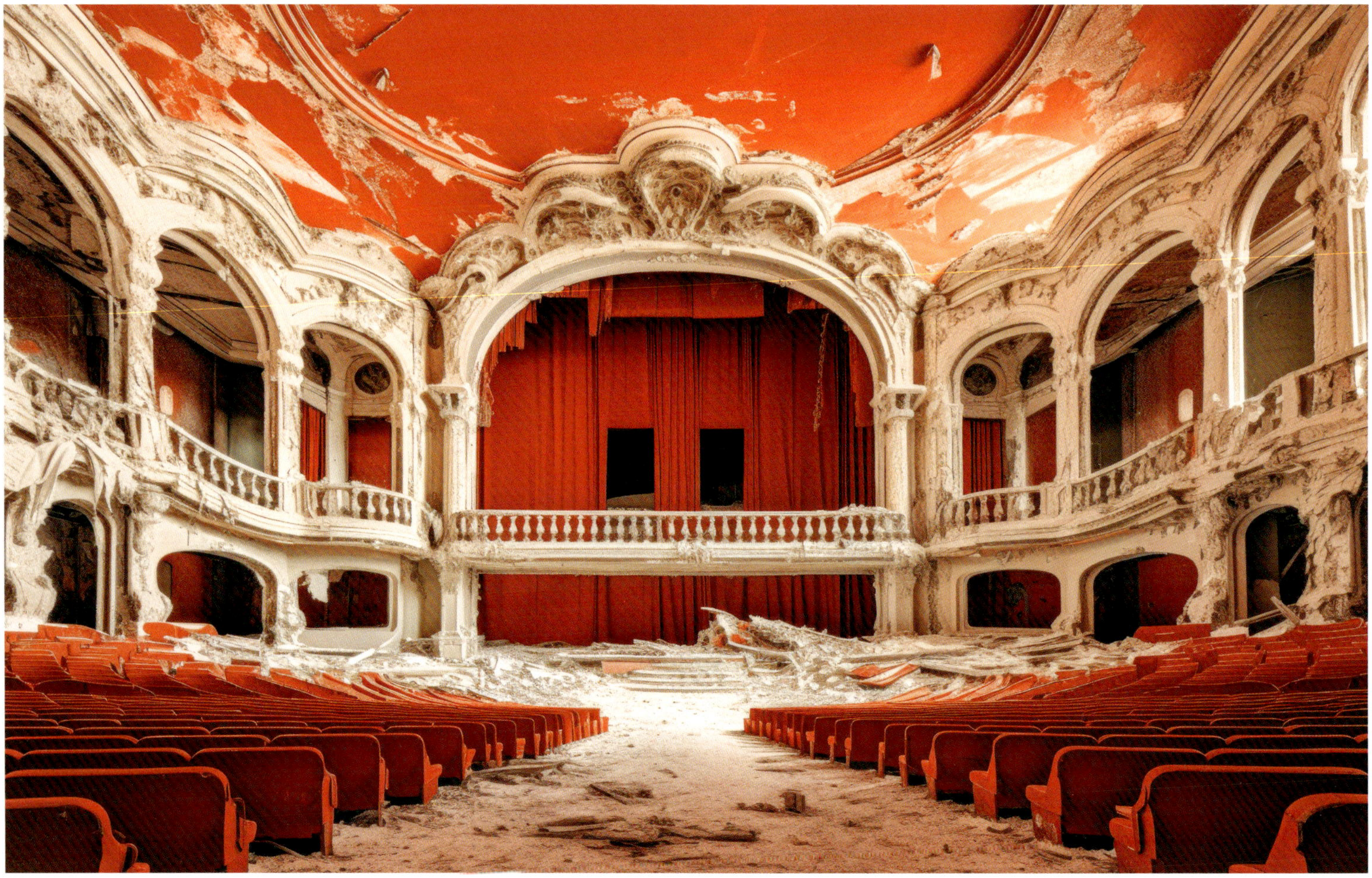

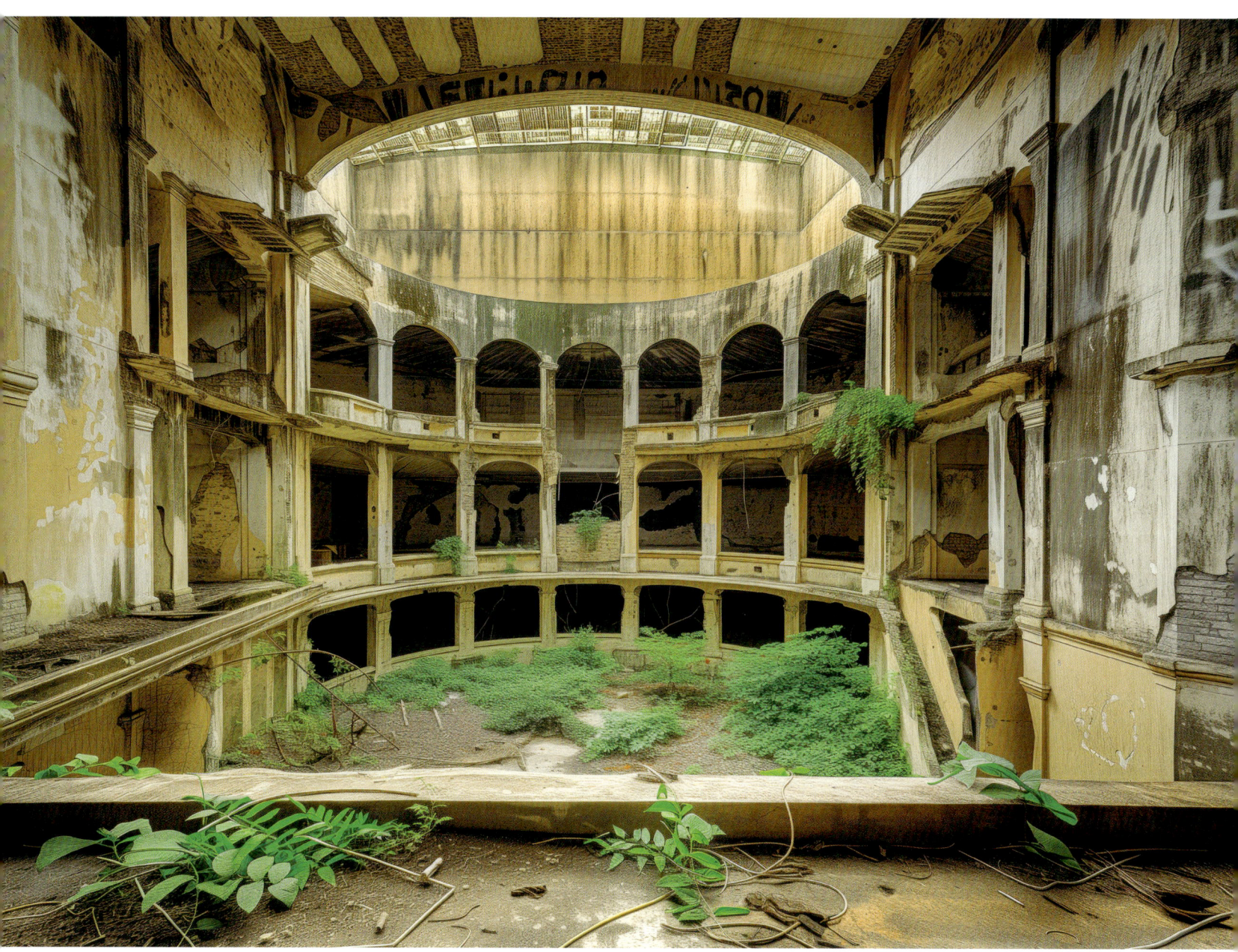

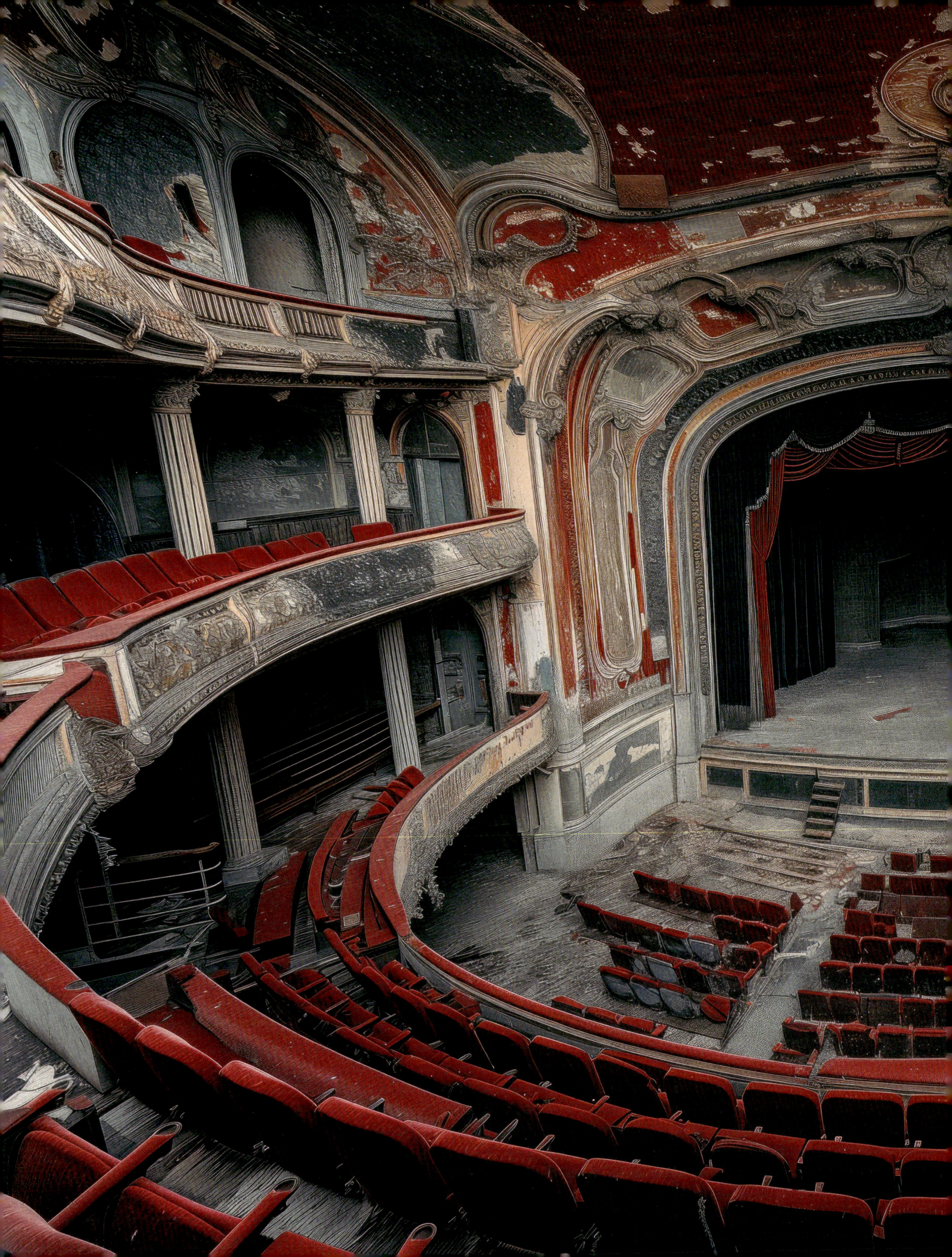

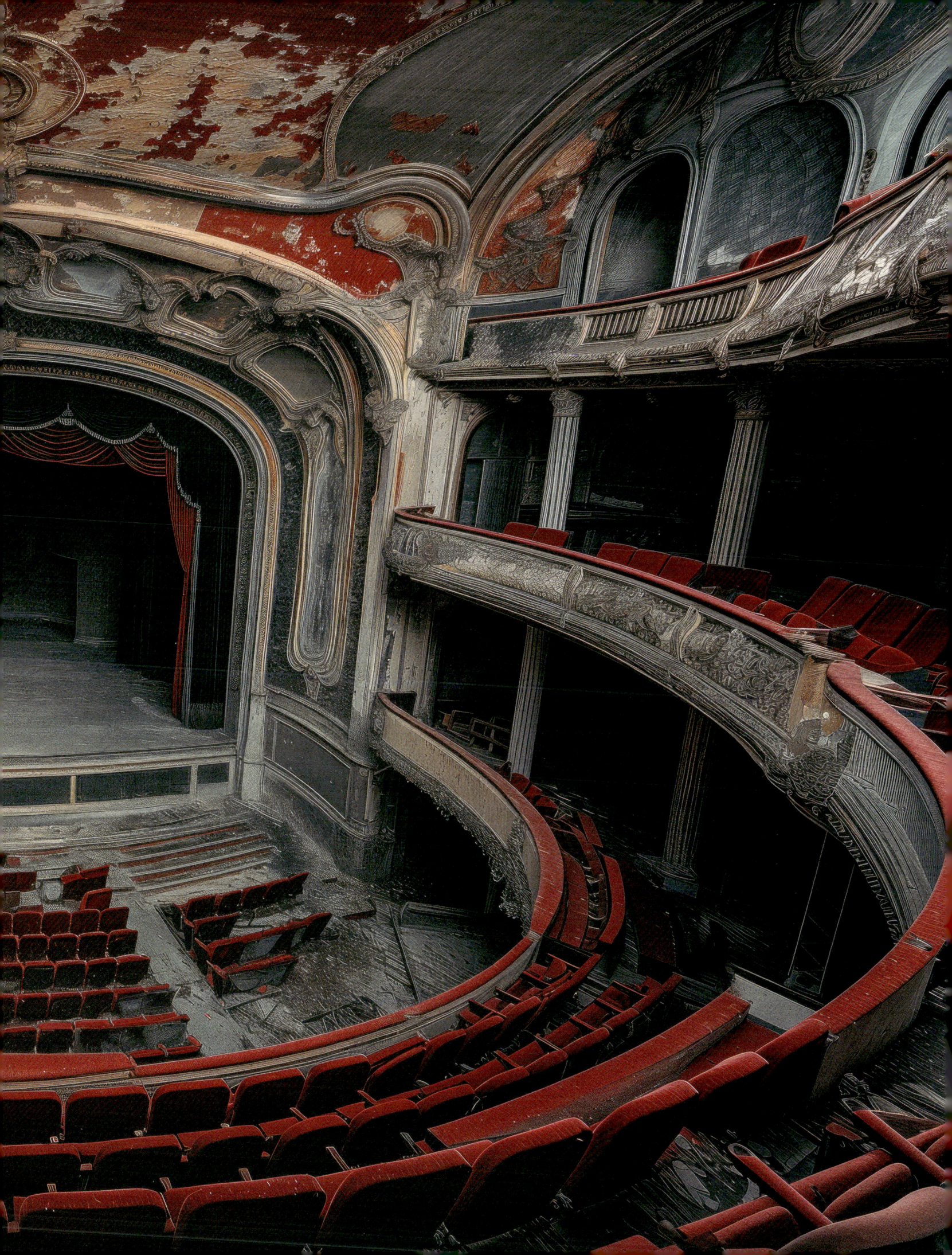

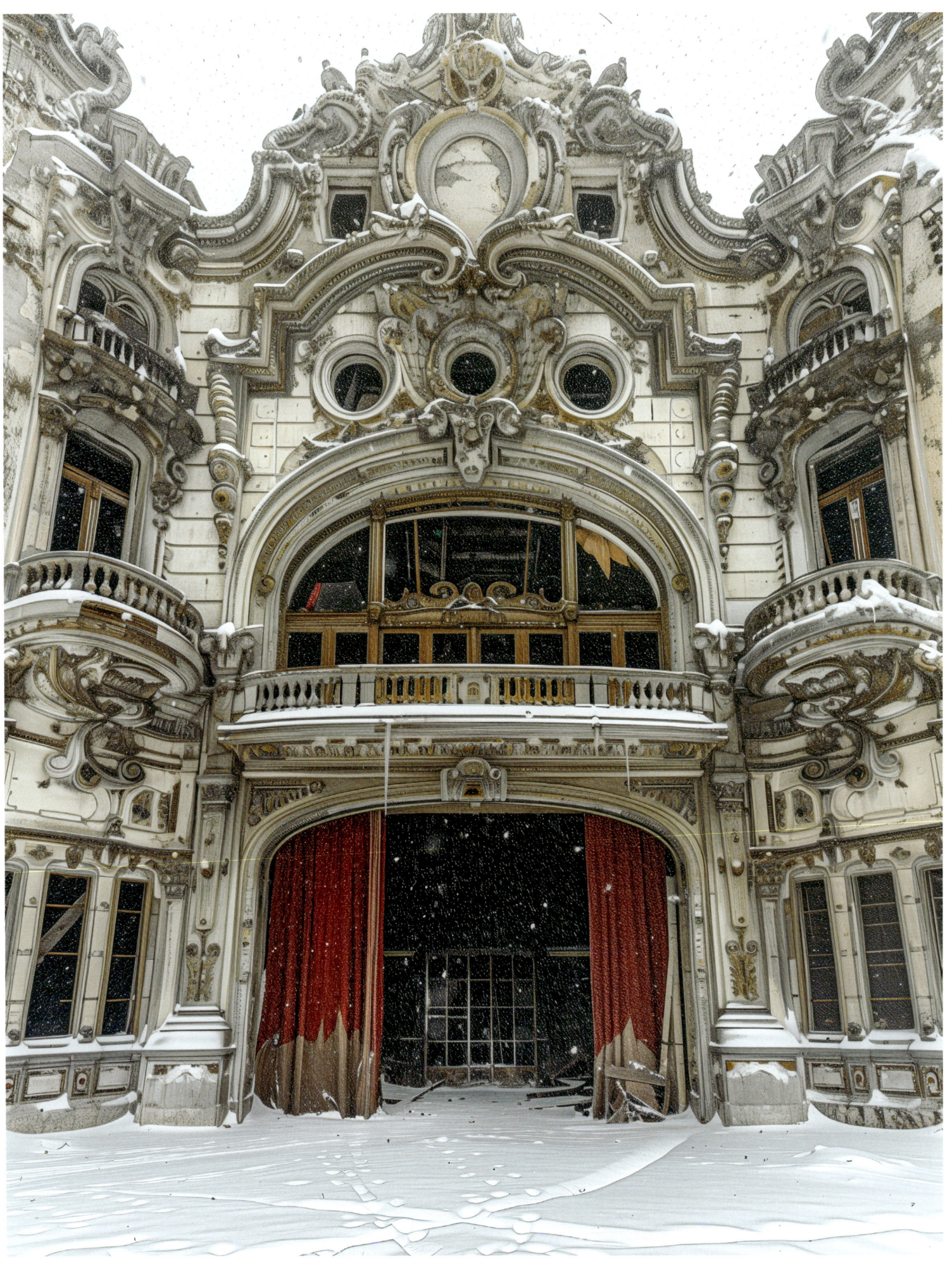

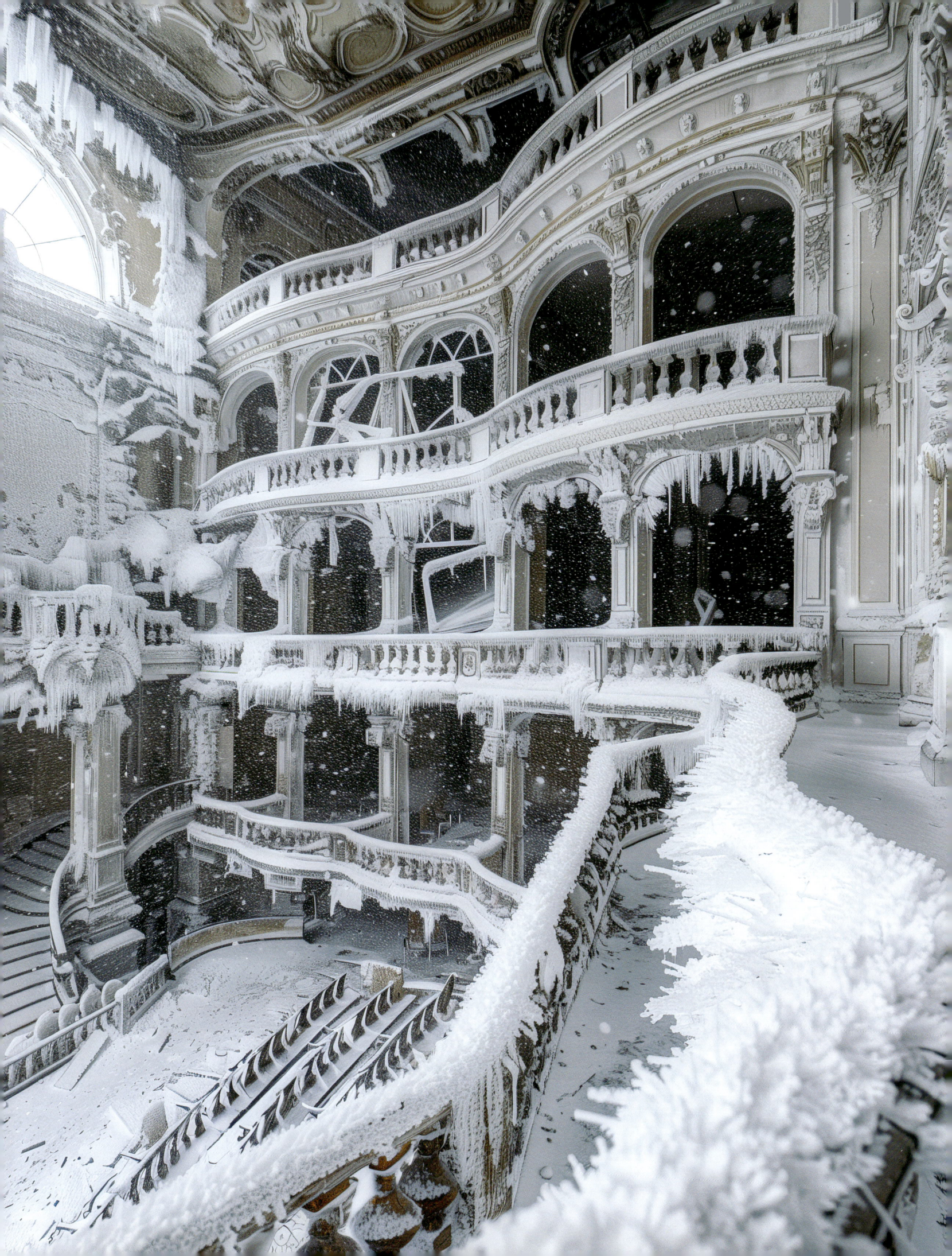

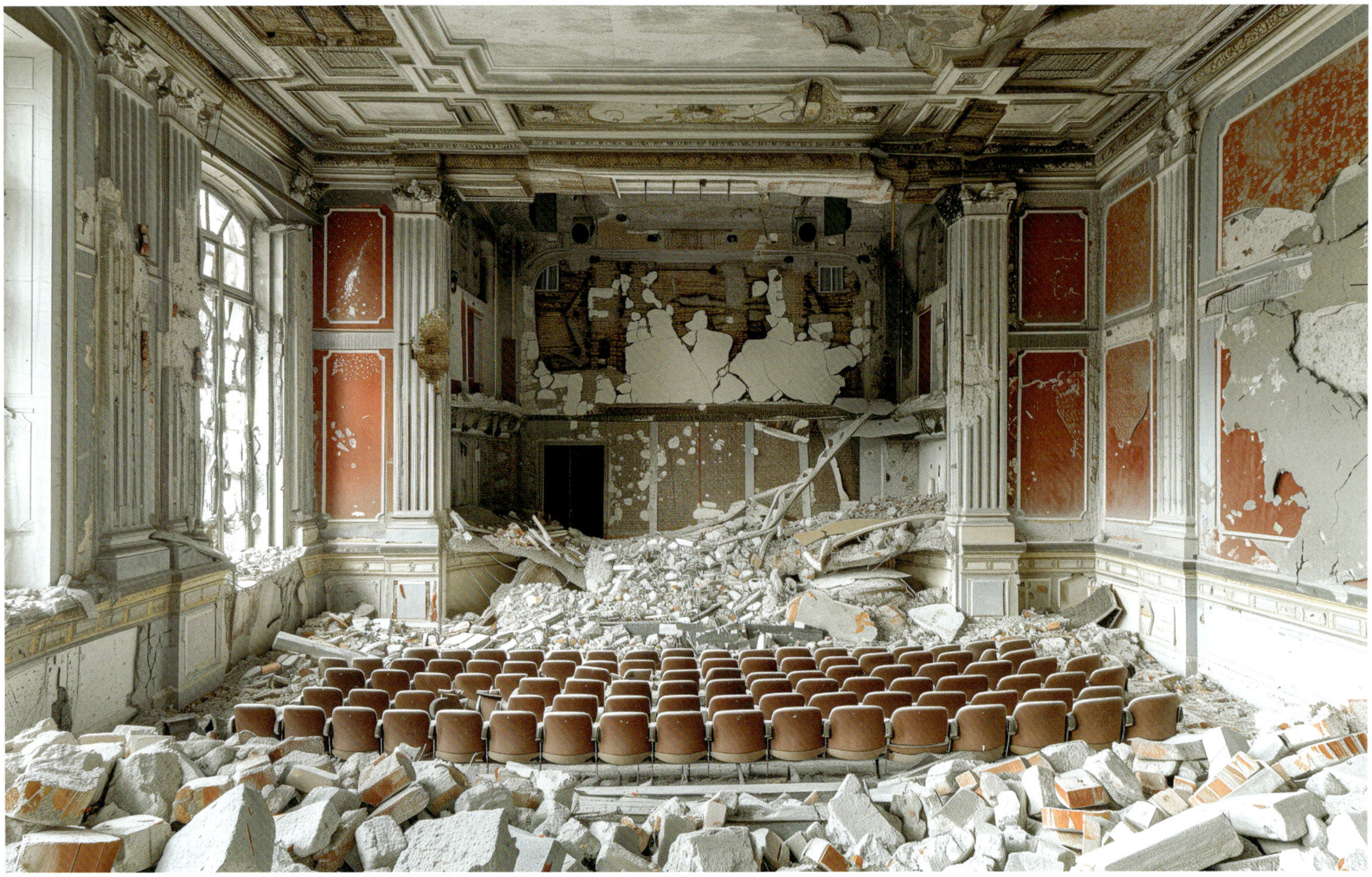

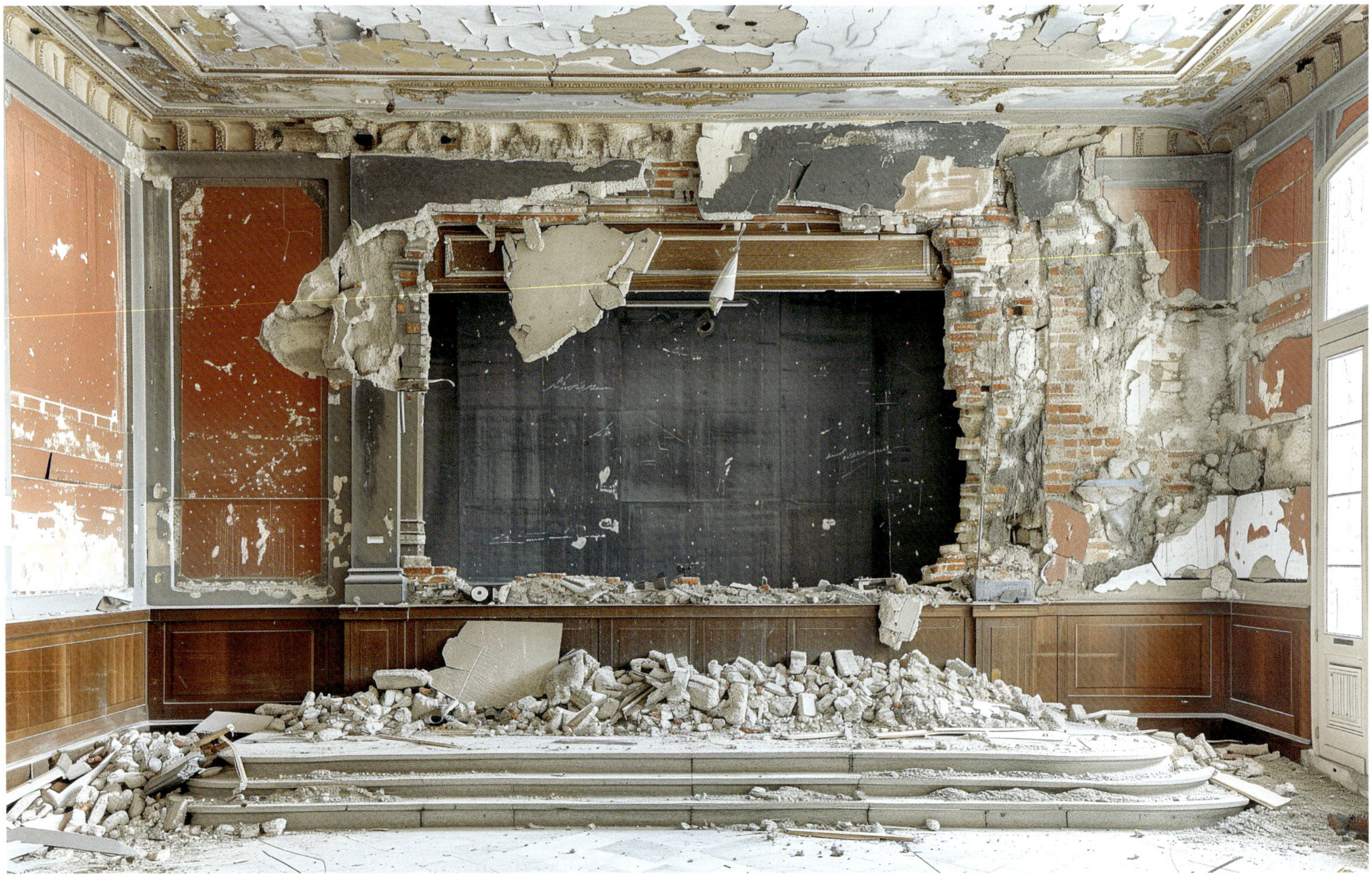

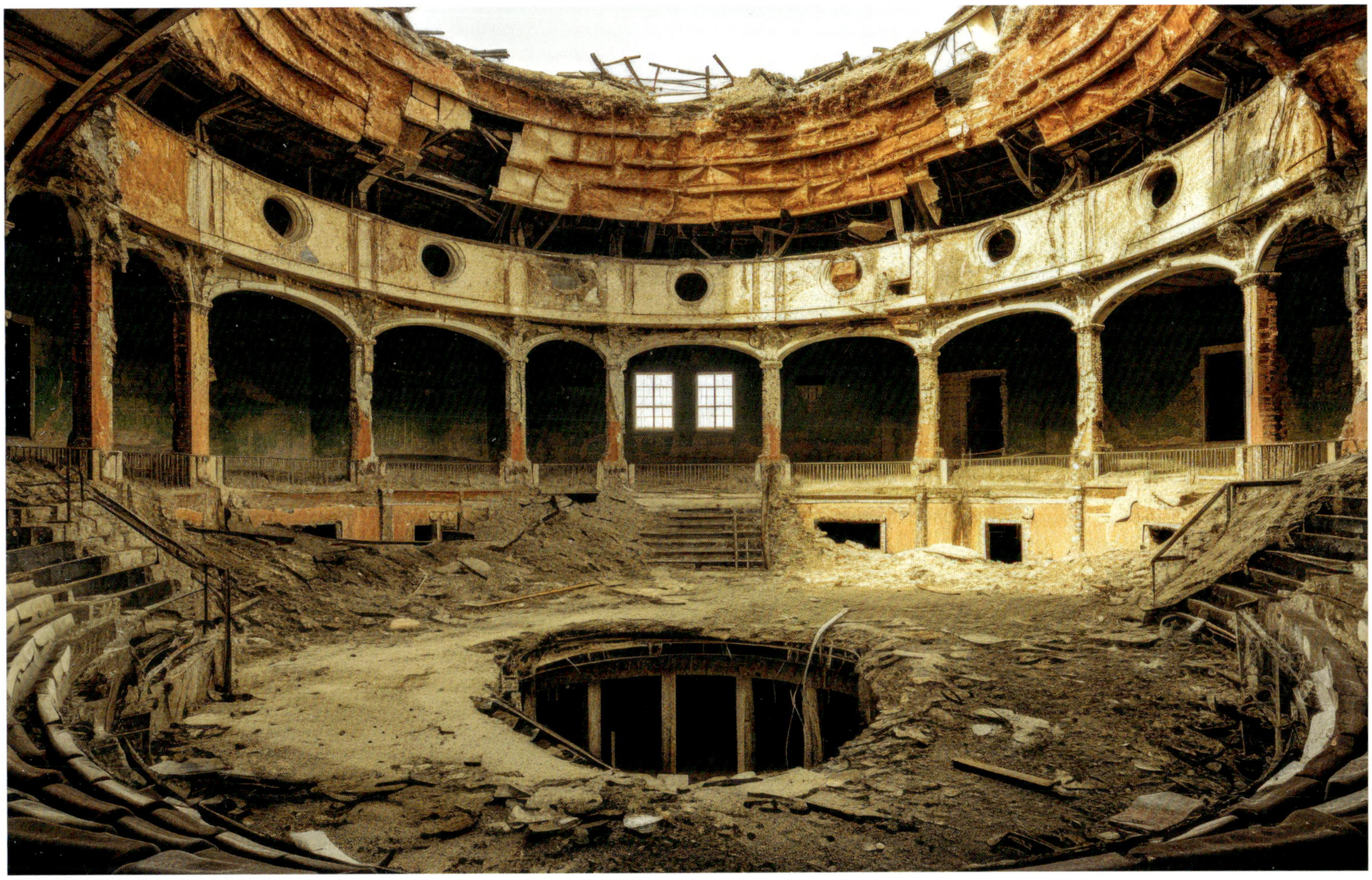

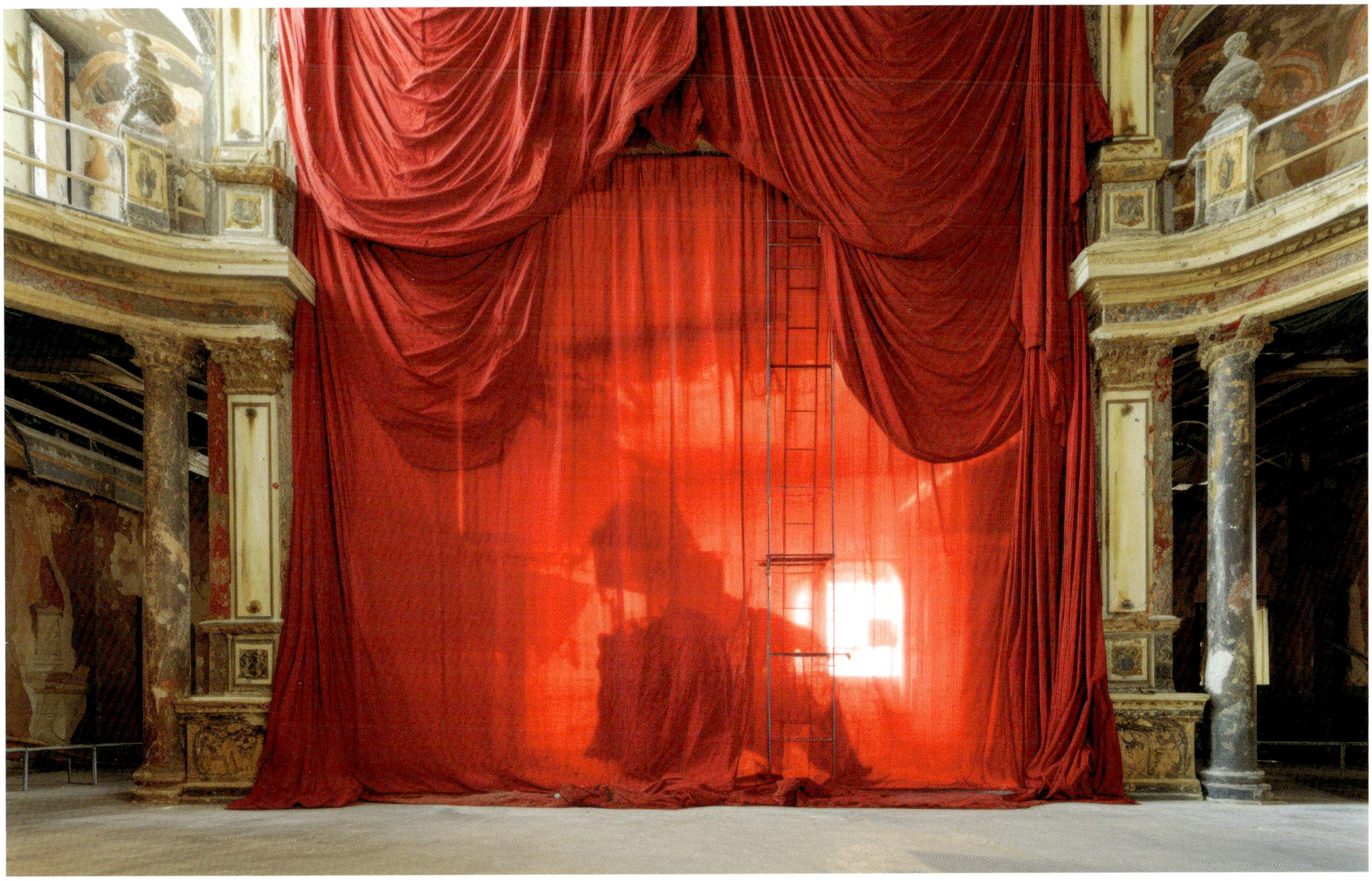

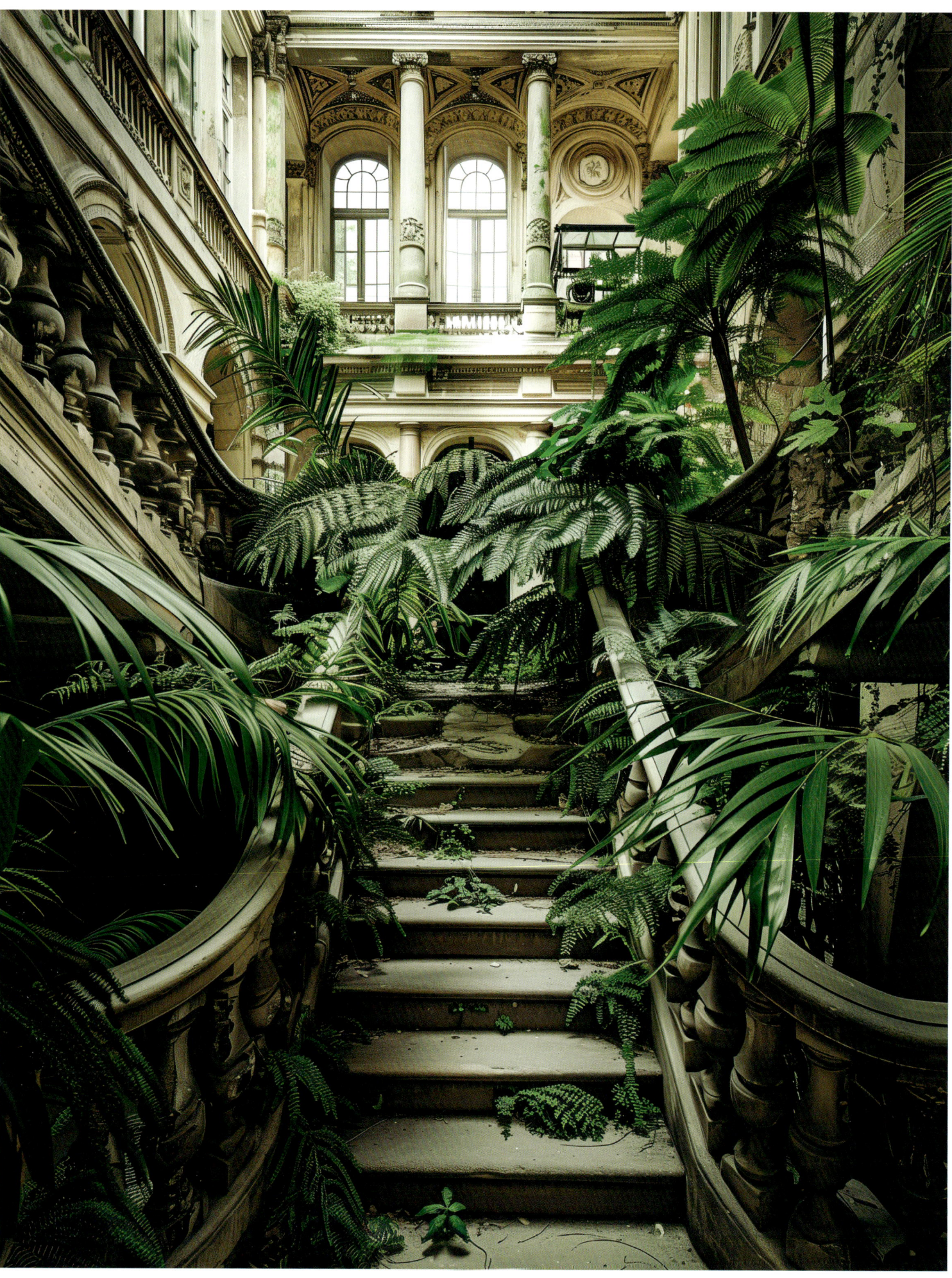

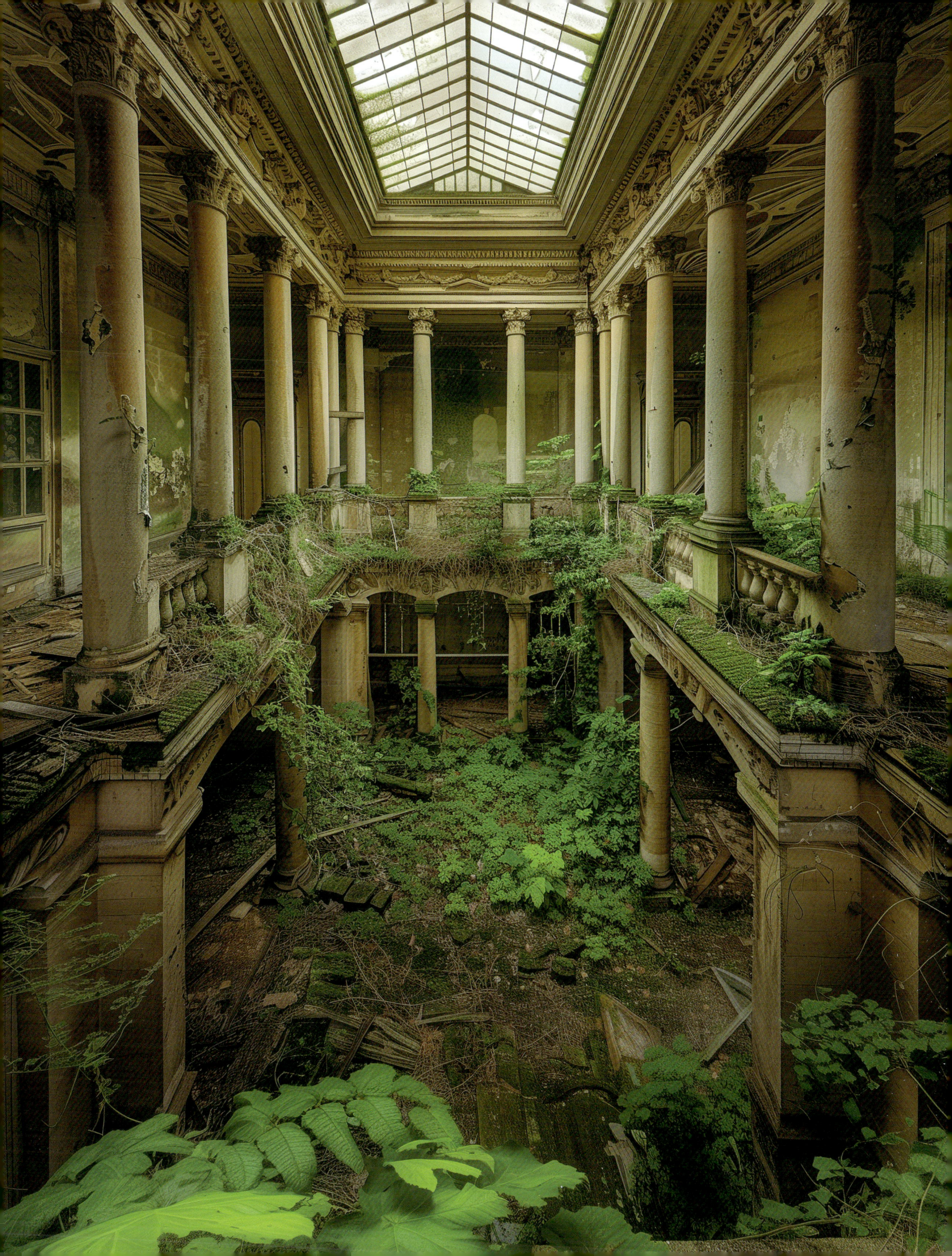

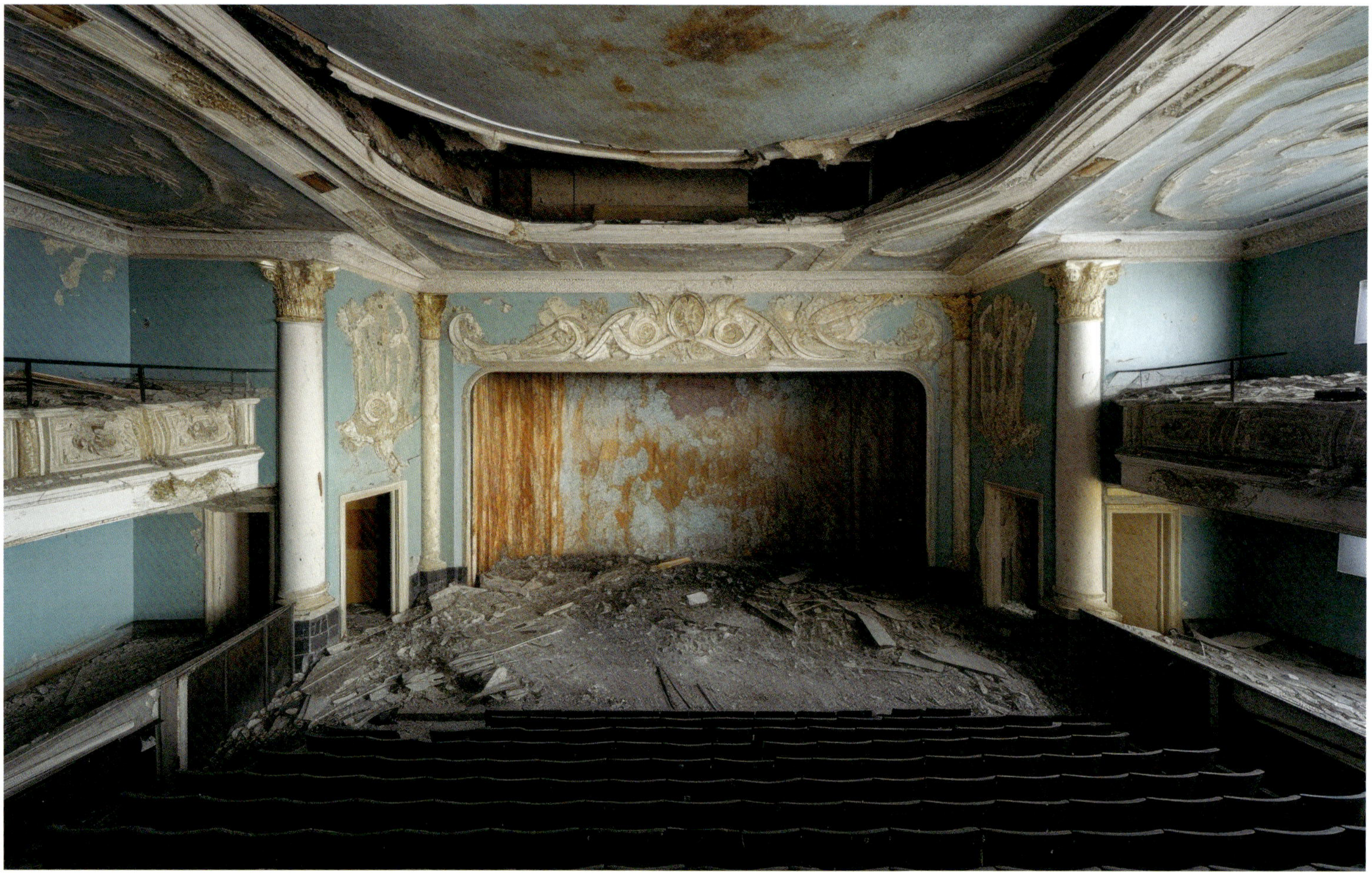

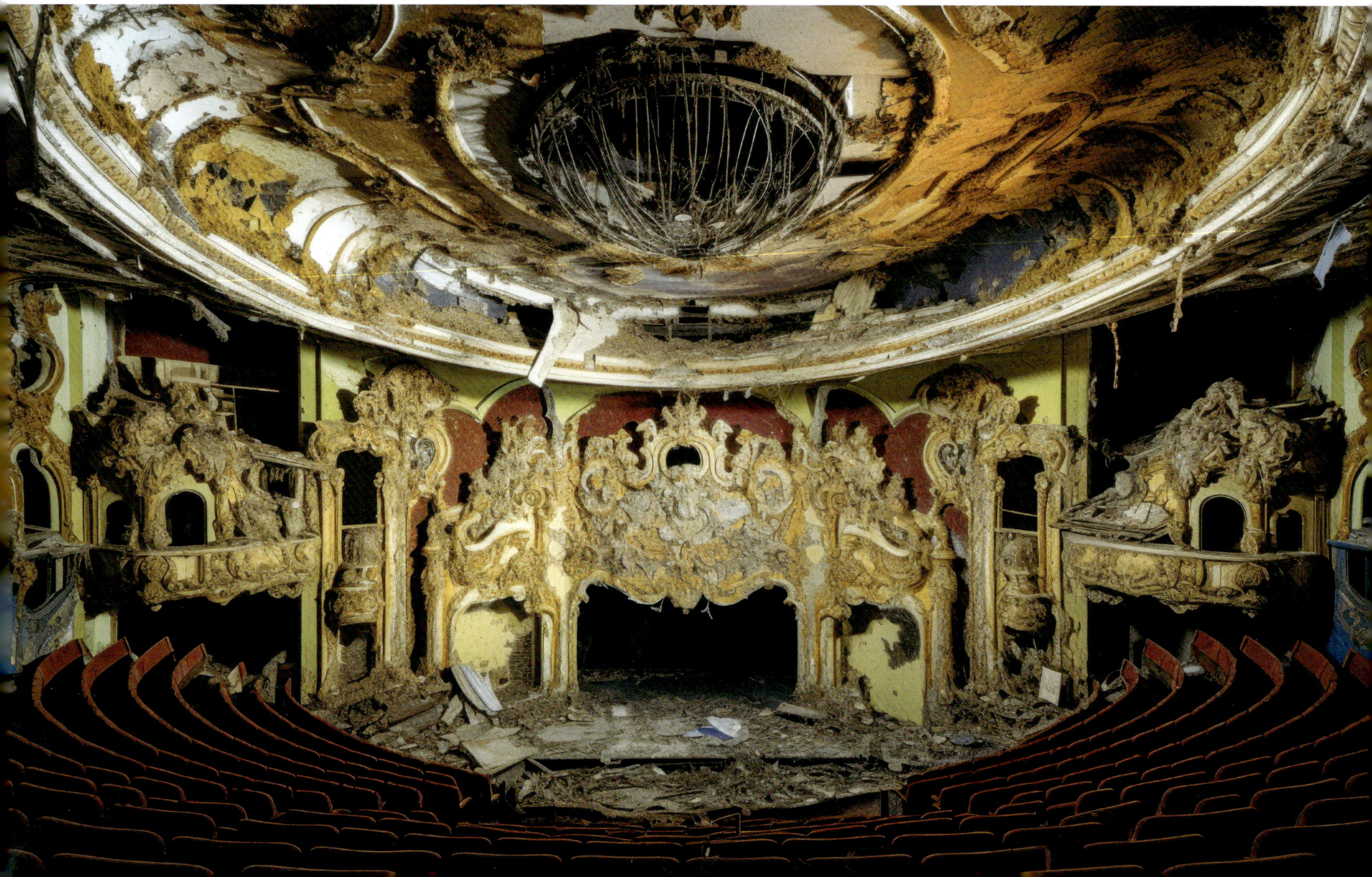

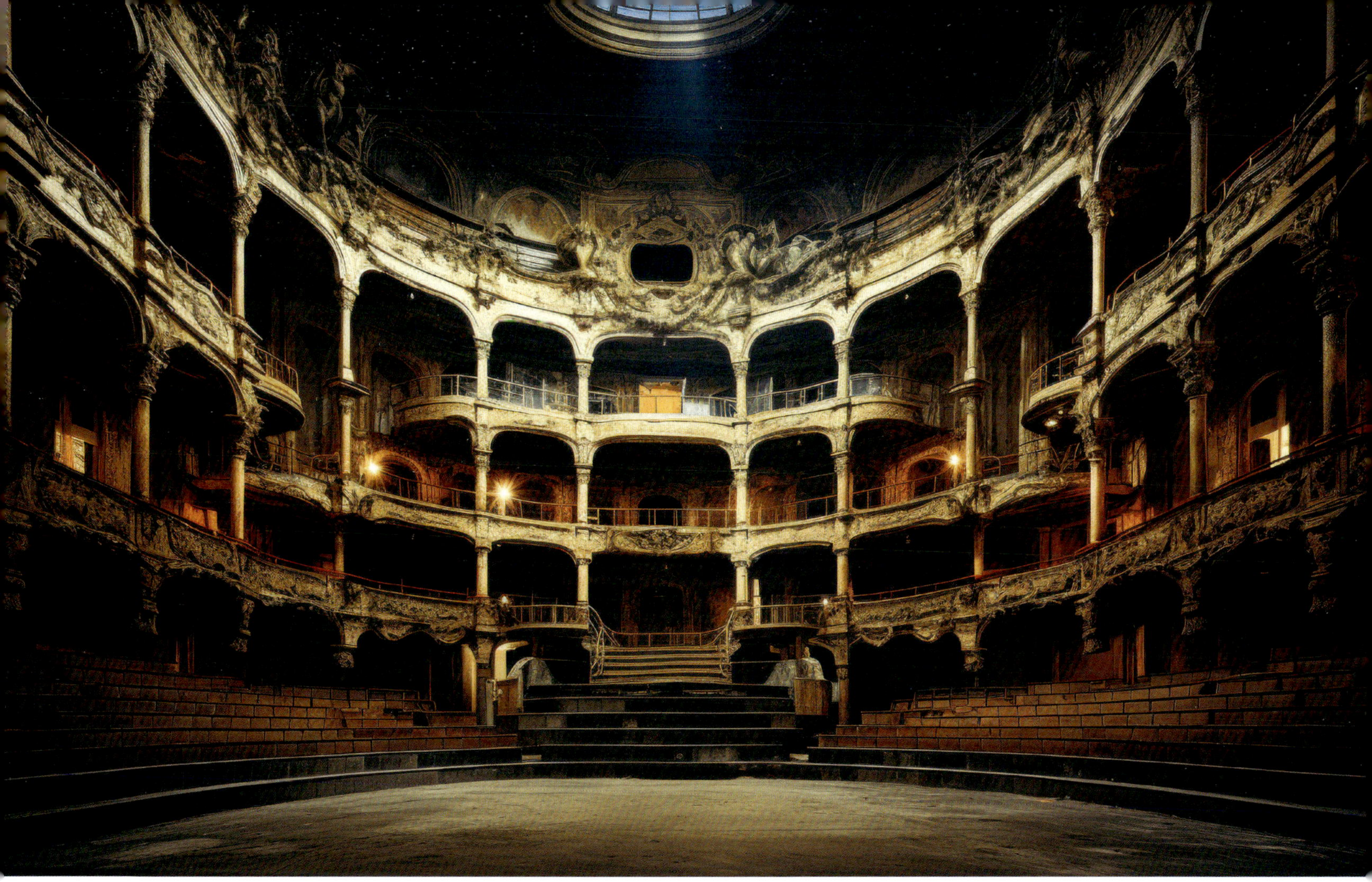

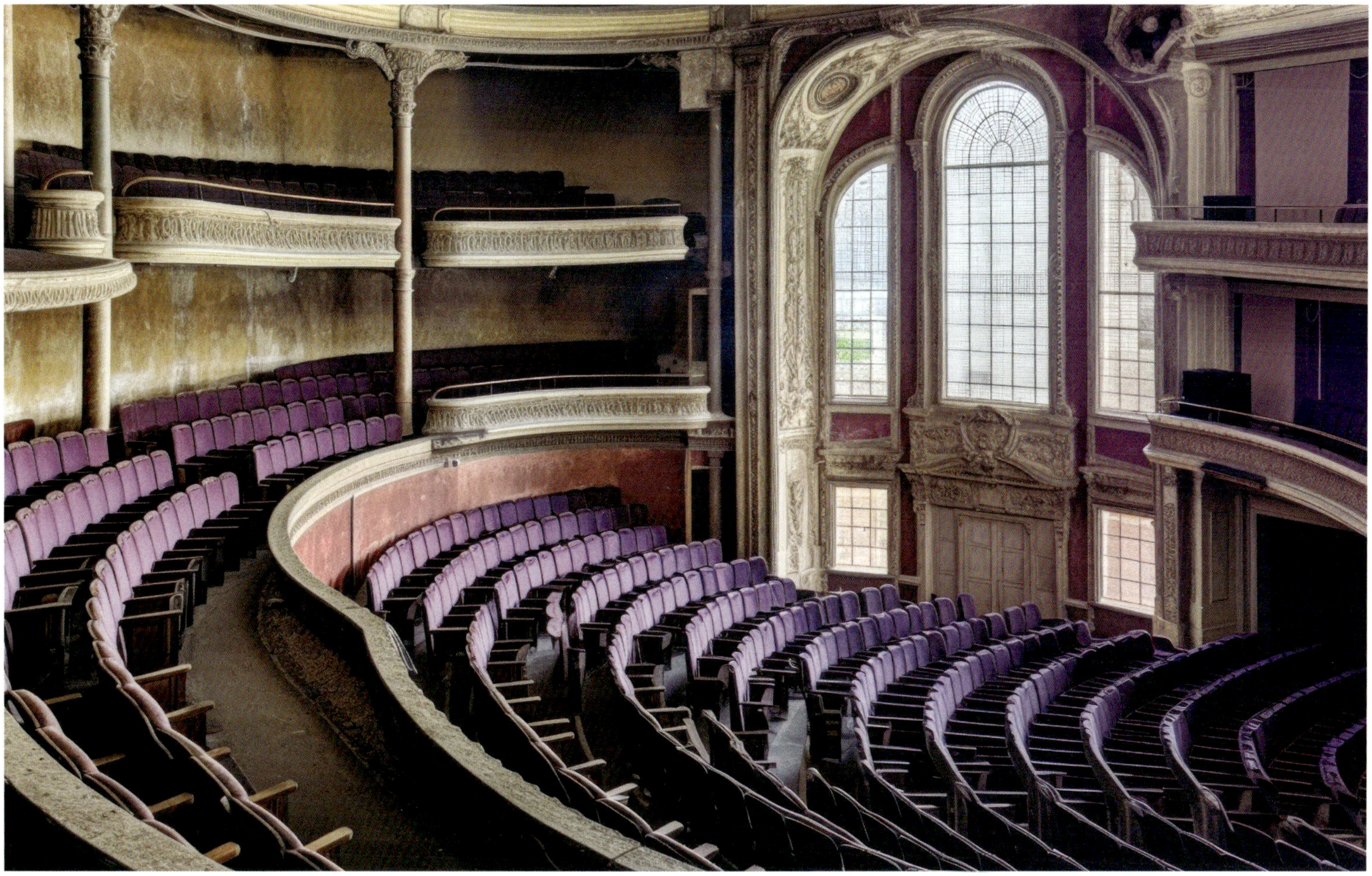

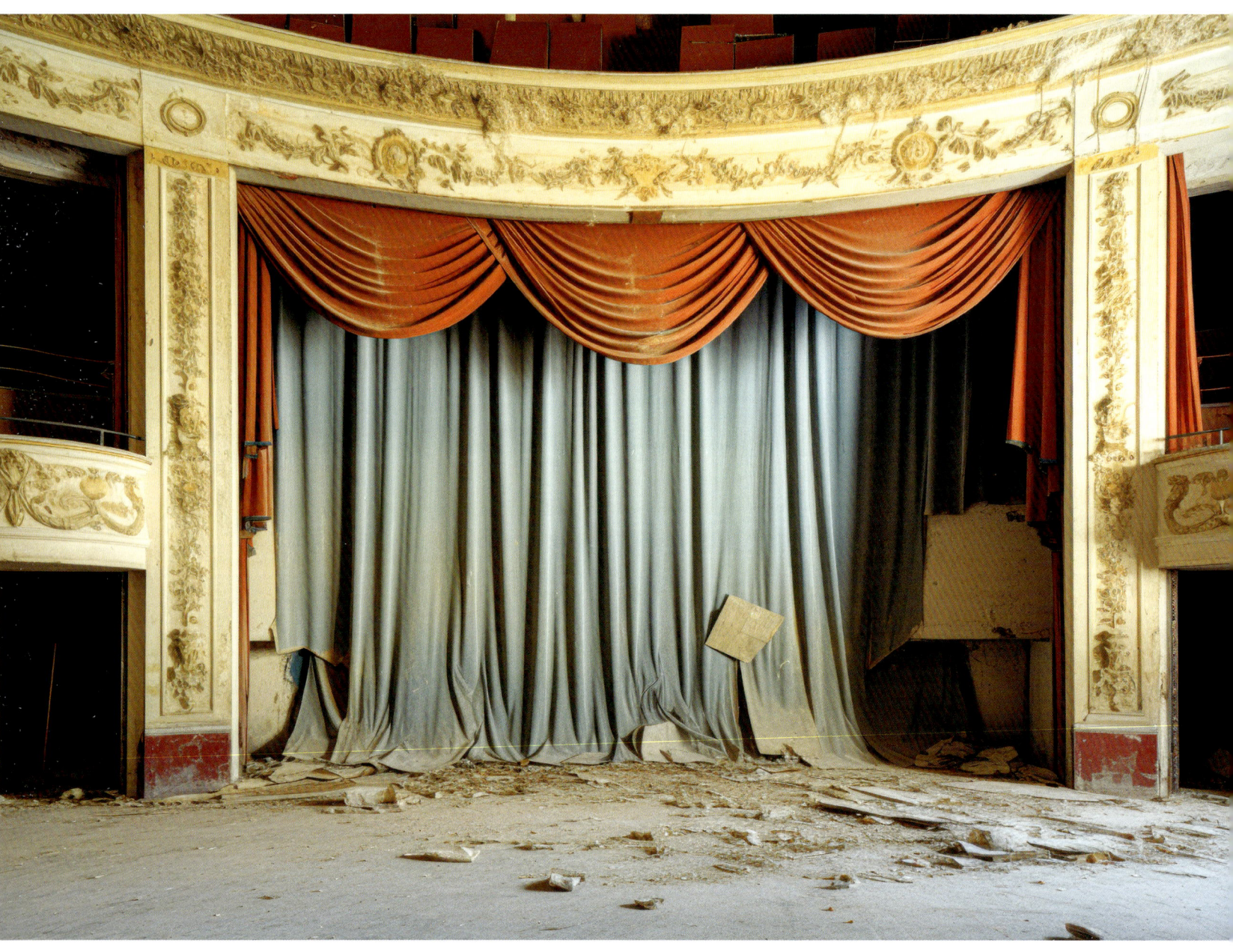

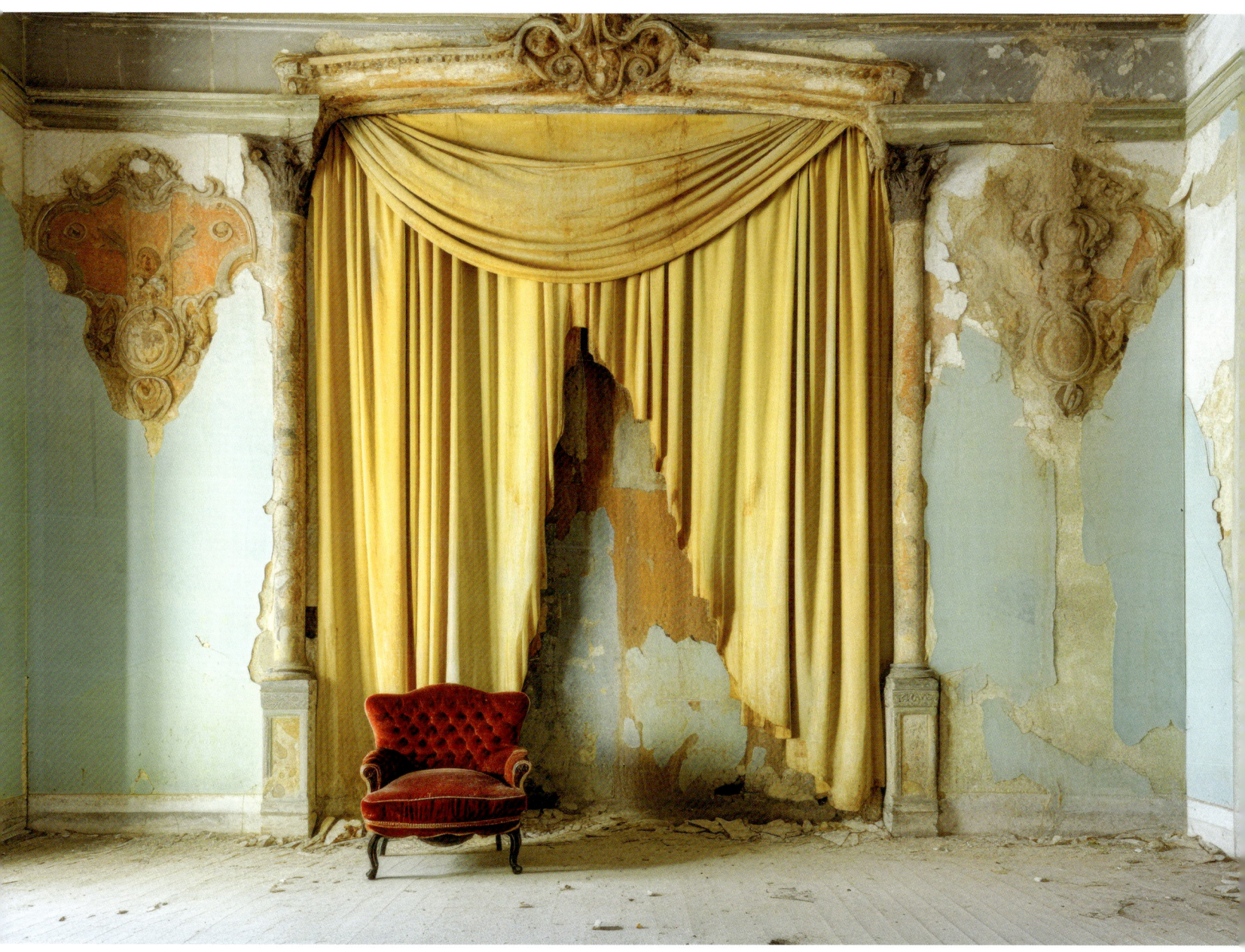

Steel under the open skies

The blast furnaces, remnants of a bygone industrial era, exude a ghostly atmosphere. Rust eats away at the metal structures, creating rough textures in shades of ochre and sienna. The shadows of decrepit chimneys and metal beams stretch across the ground, heightening the surrounding dilapidation. The air carries a metallic smell, imbued with the dust of time. The equipment lies in silence, a reminder of a time when fire and forge reigned supreme.

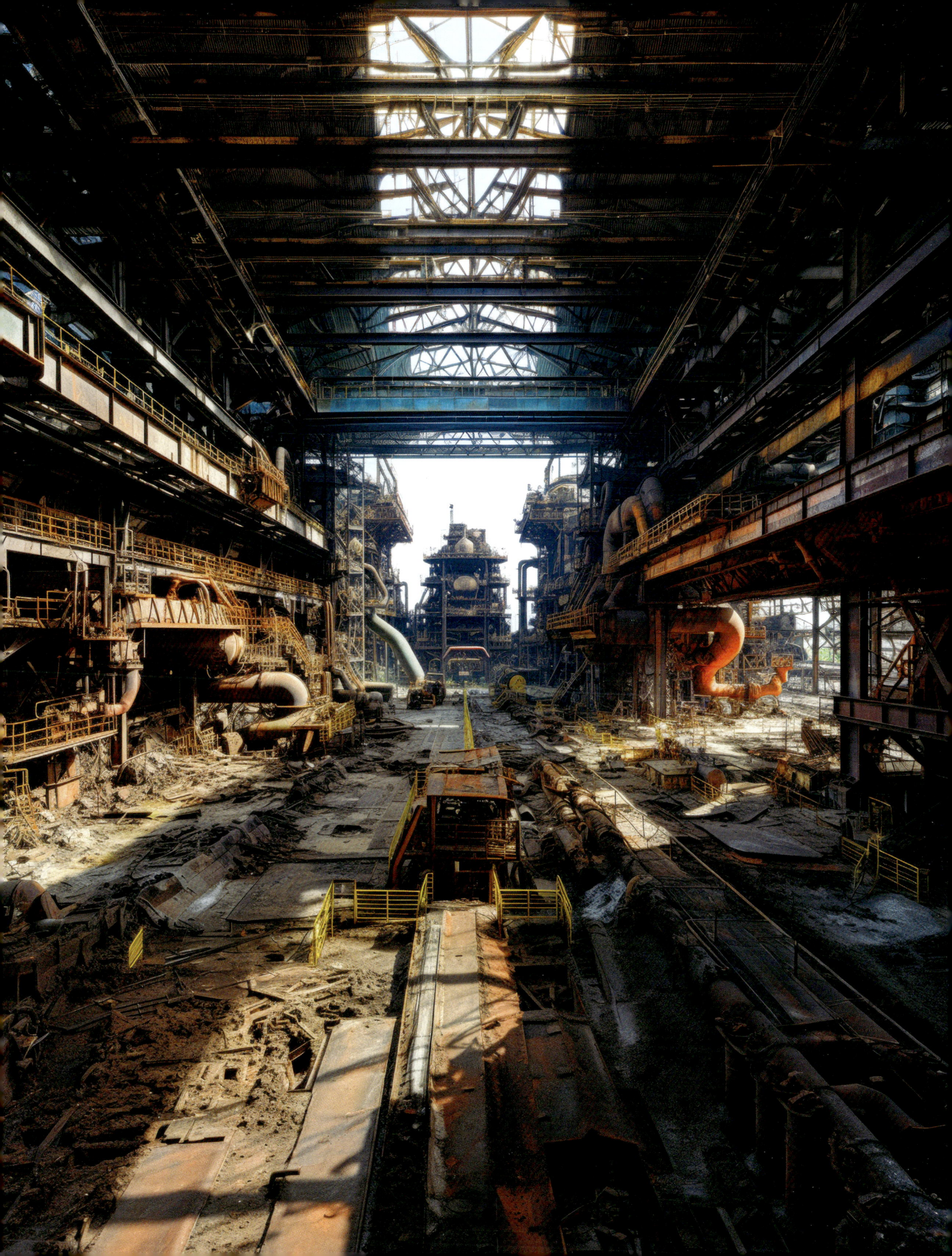

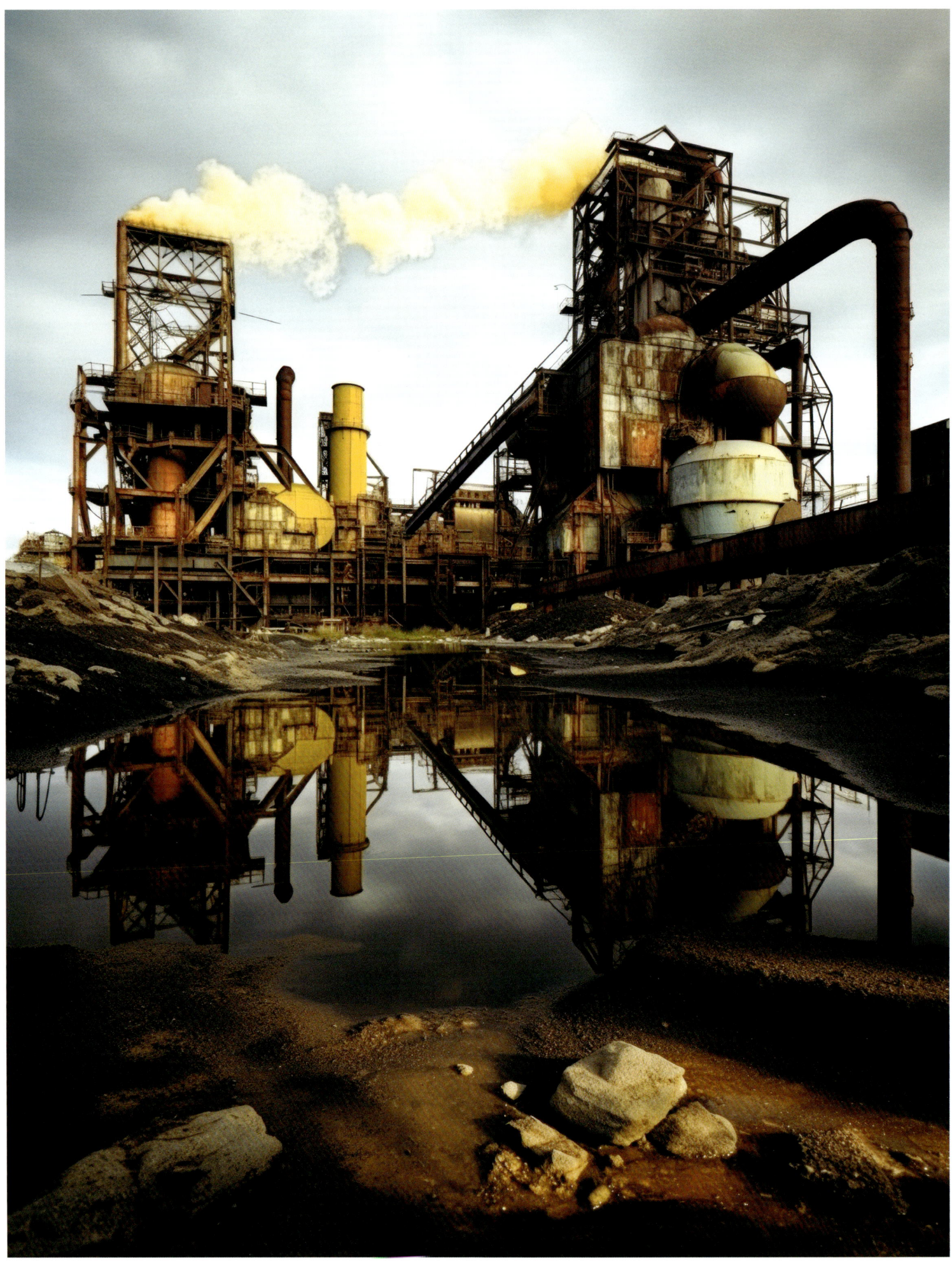

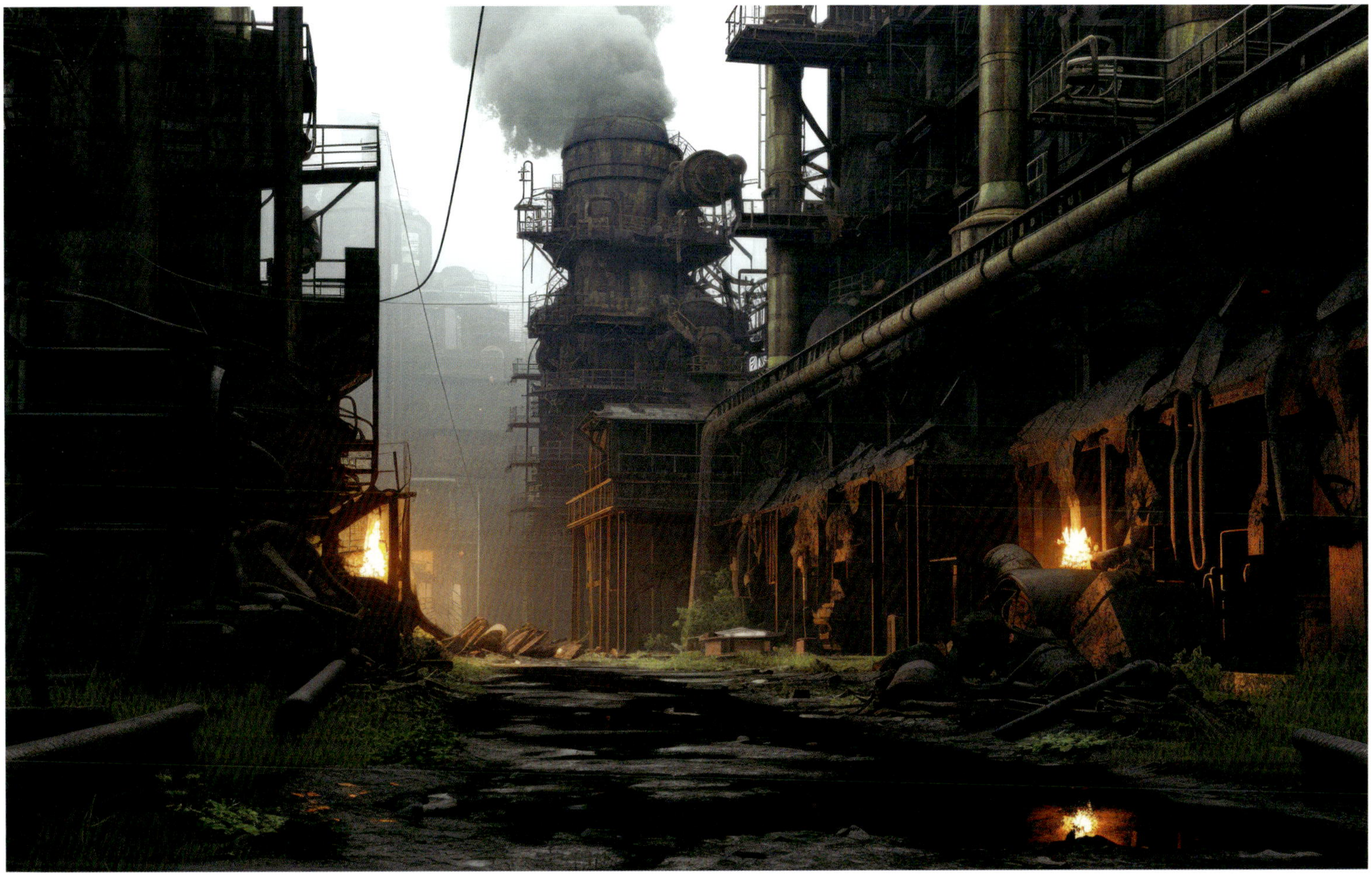

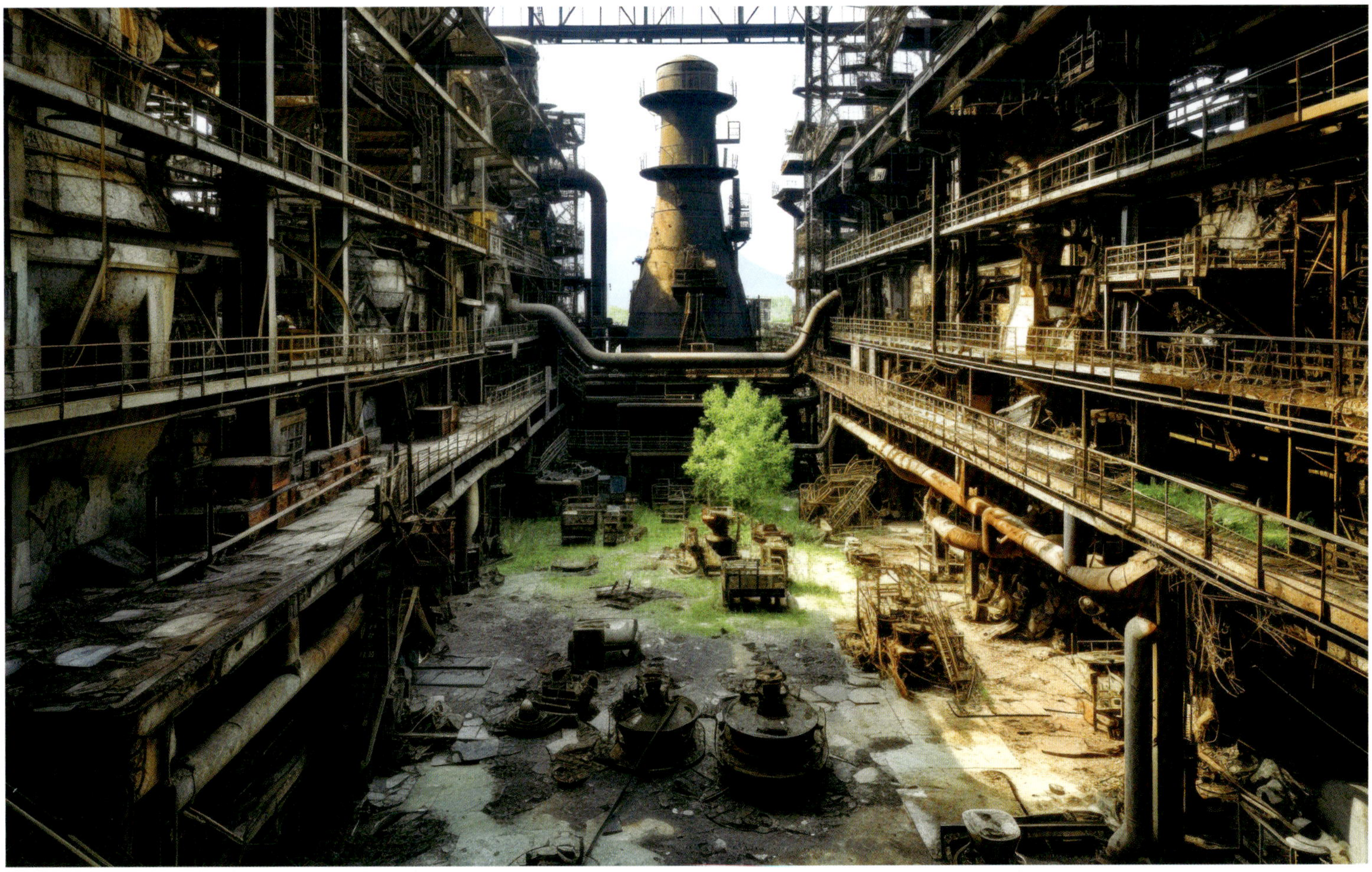

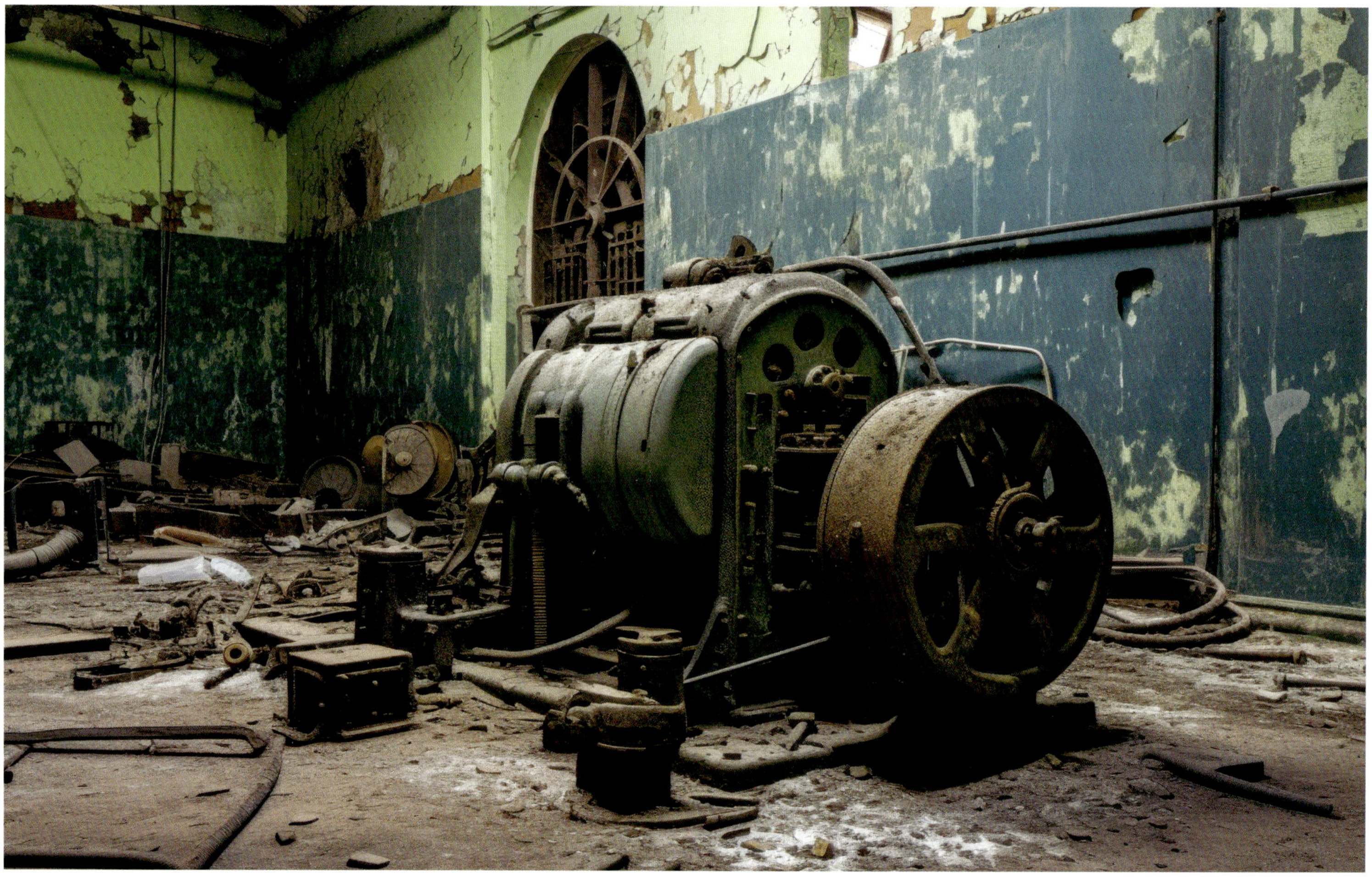

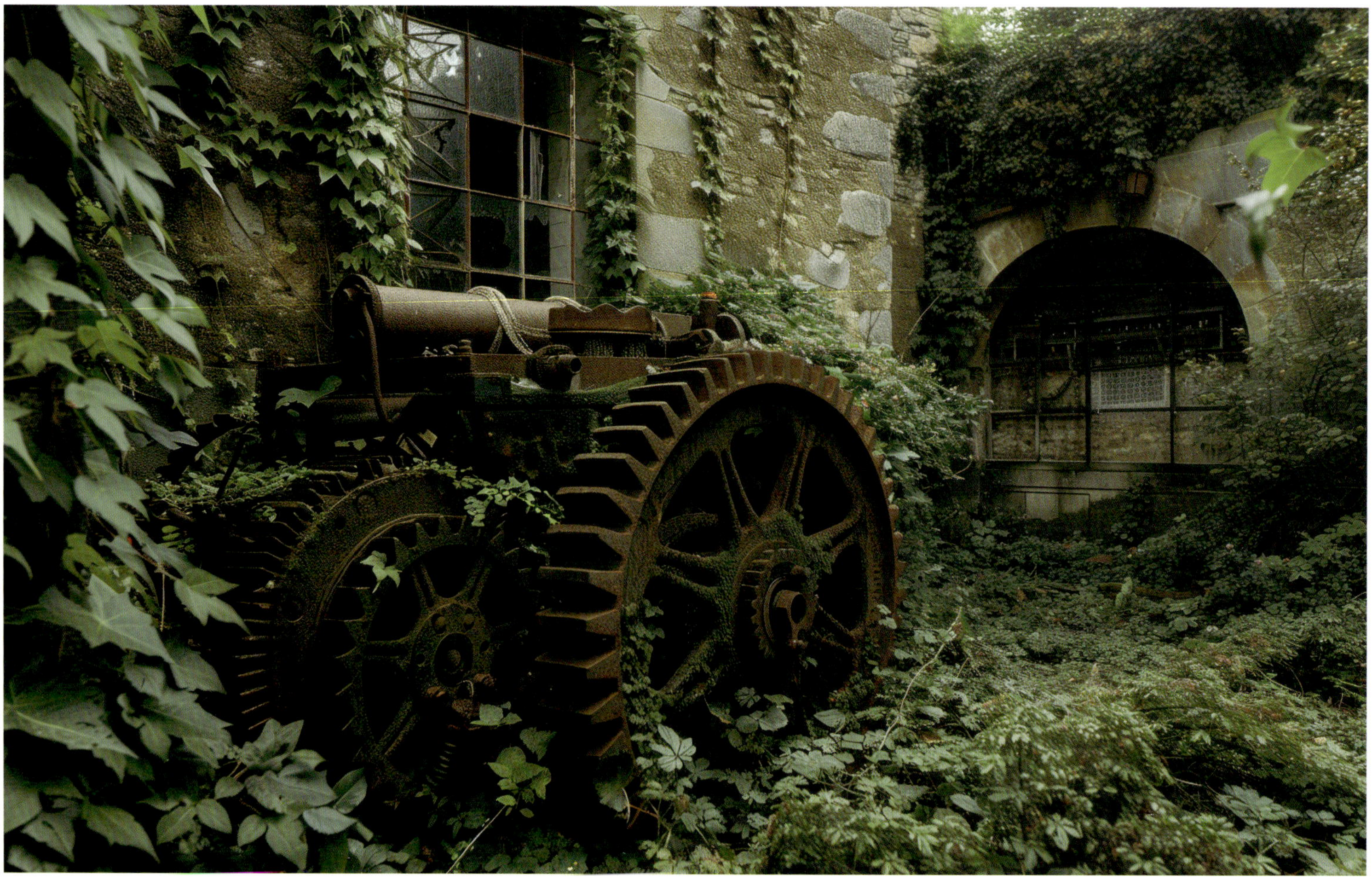

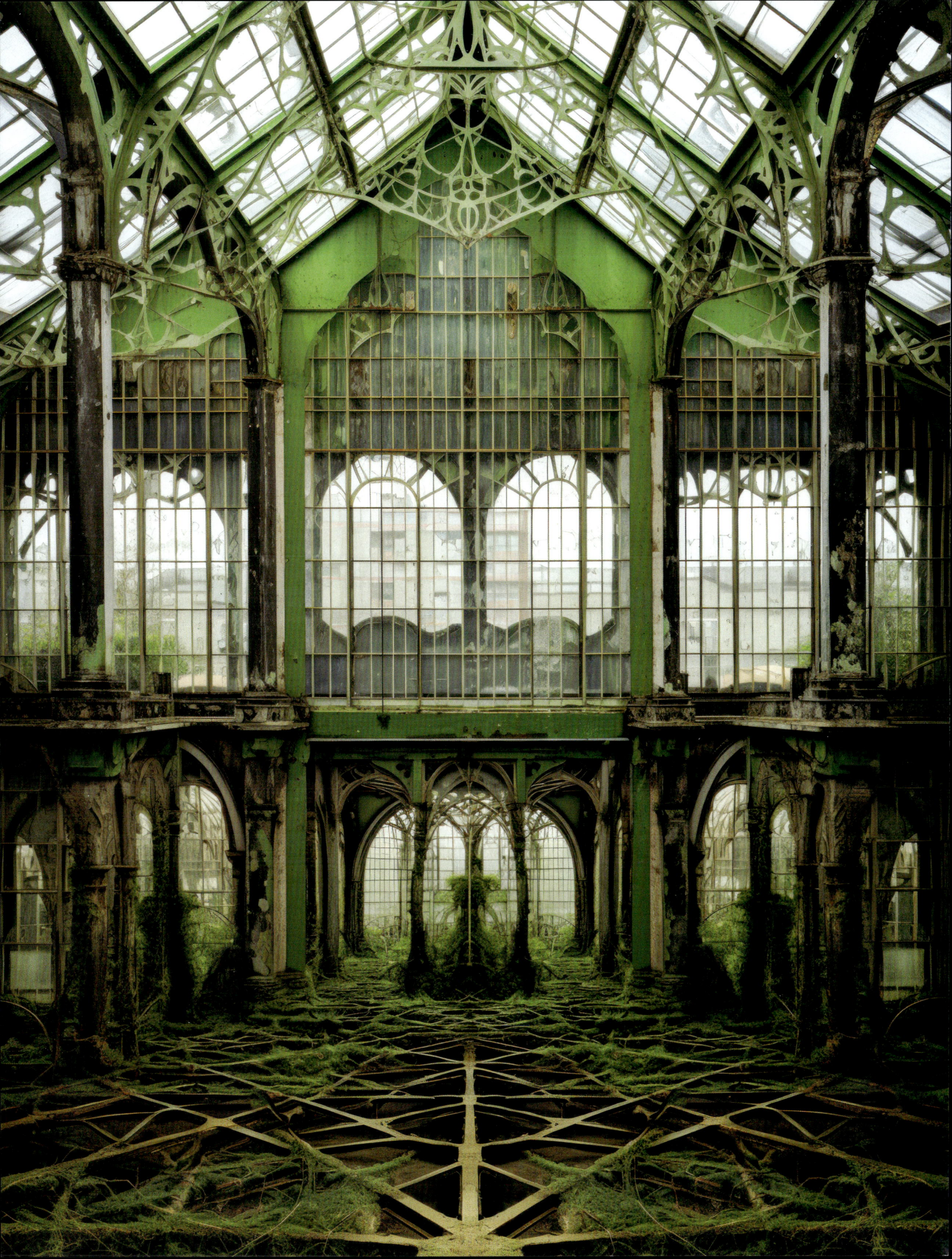

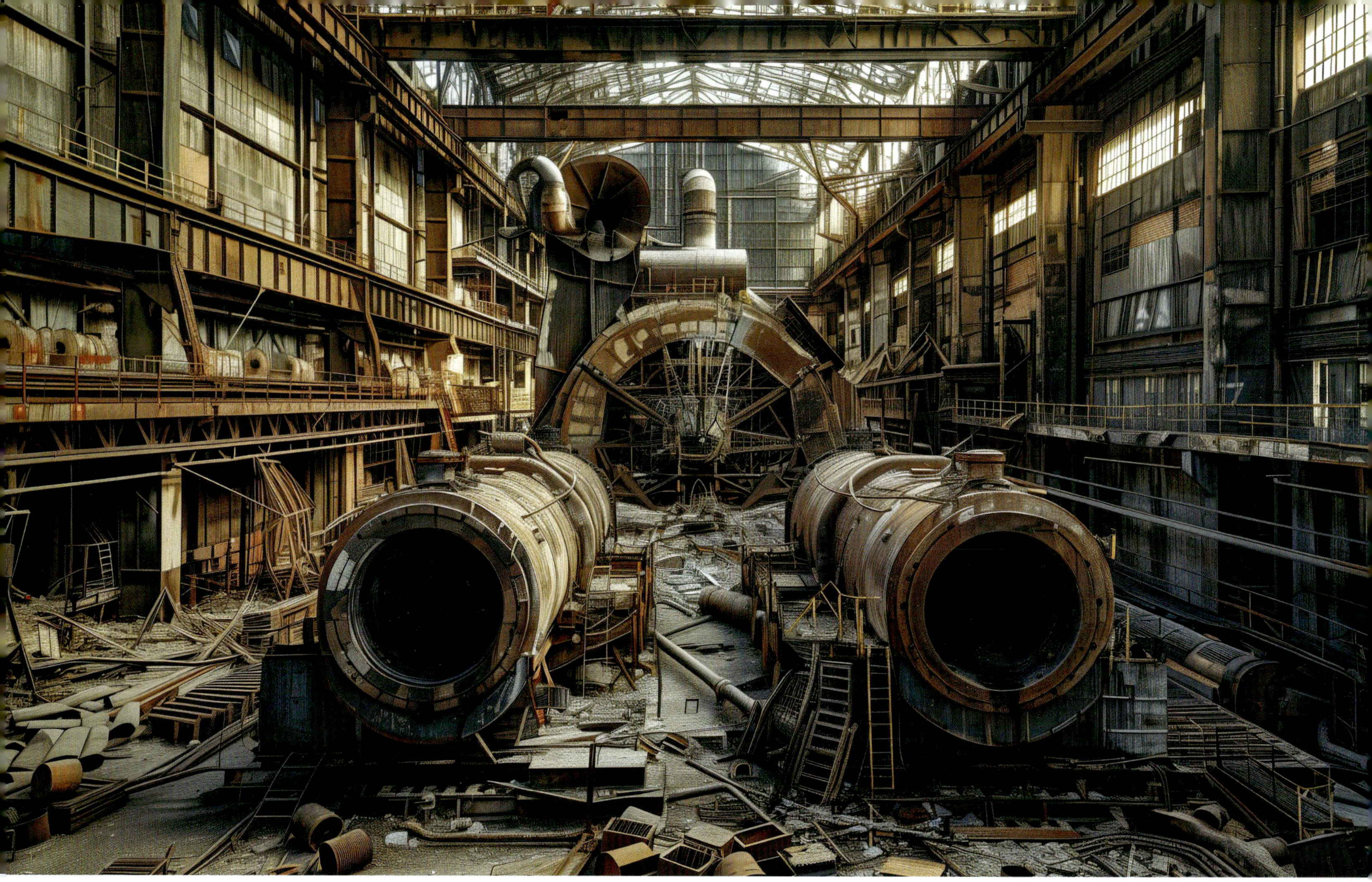

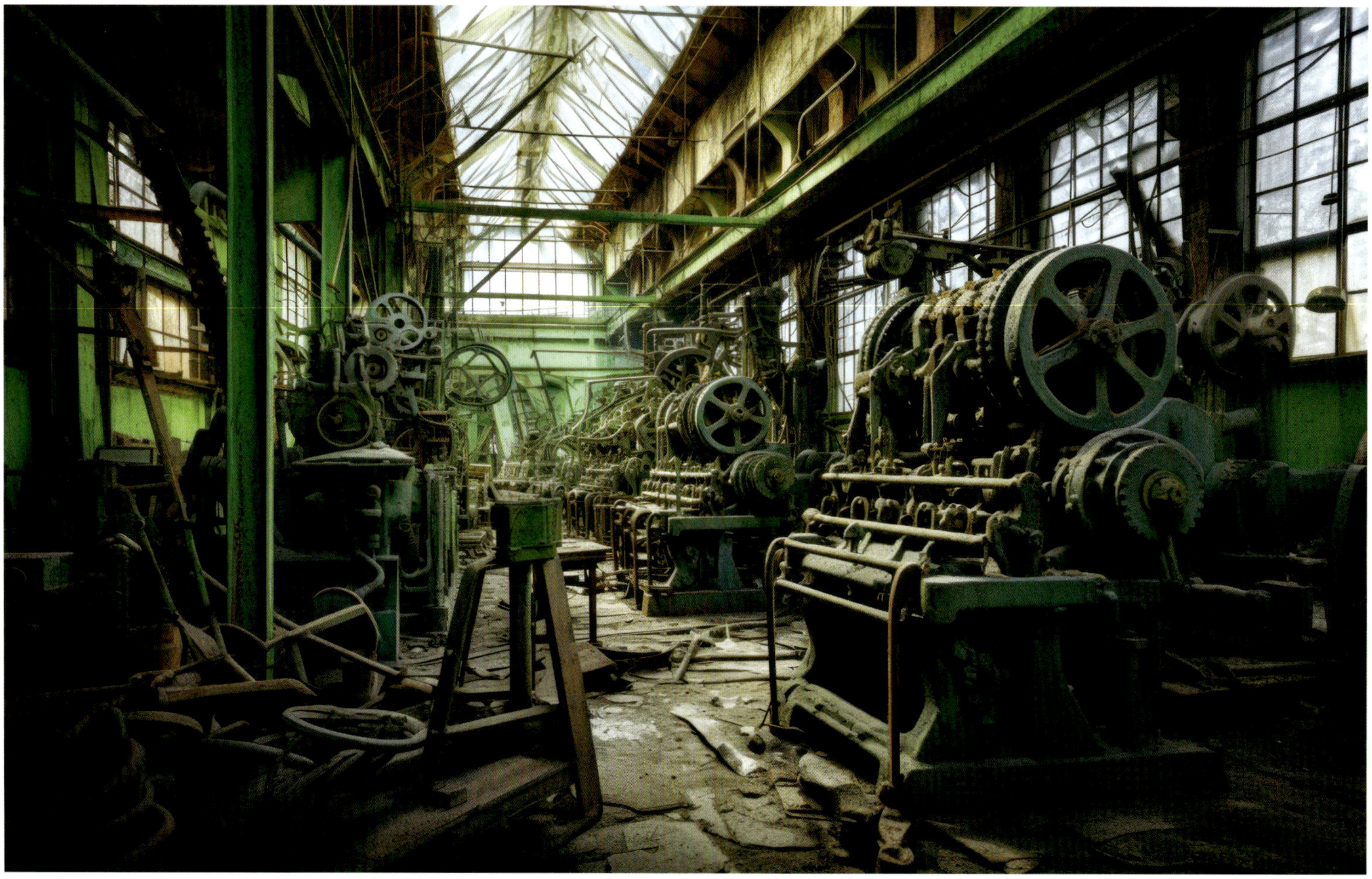

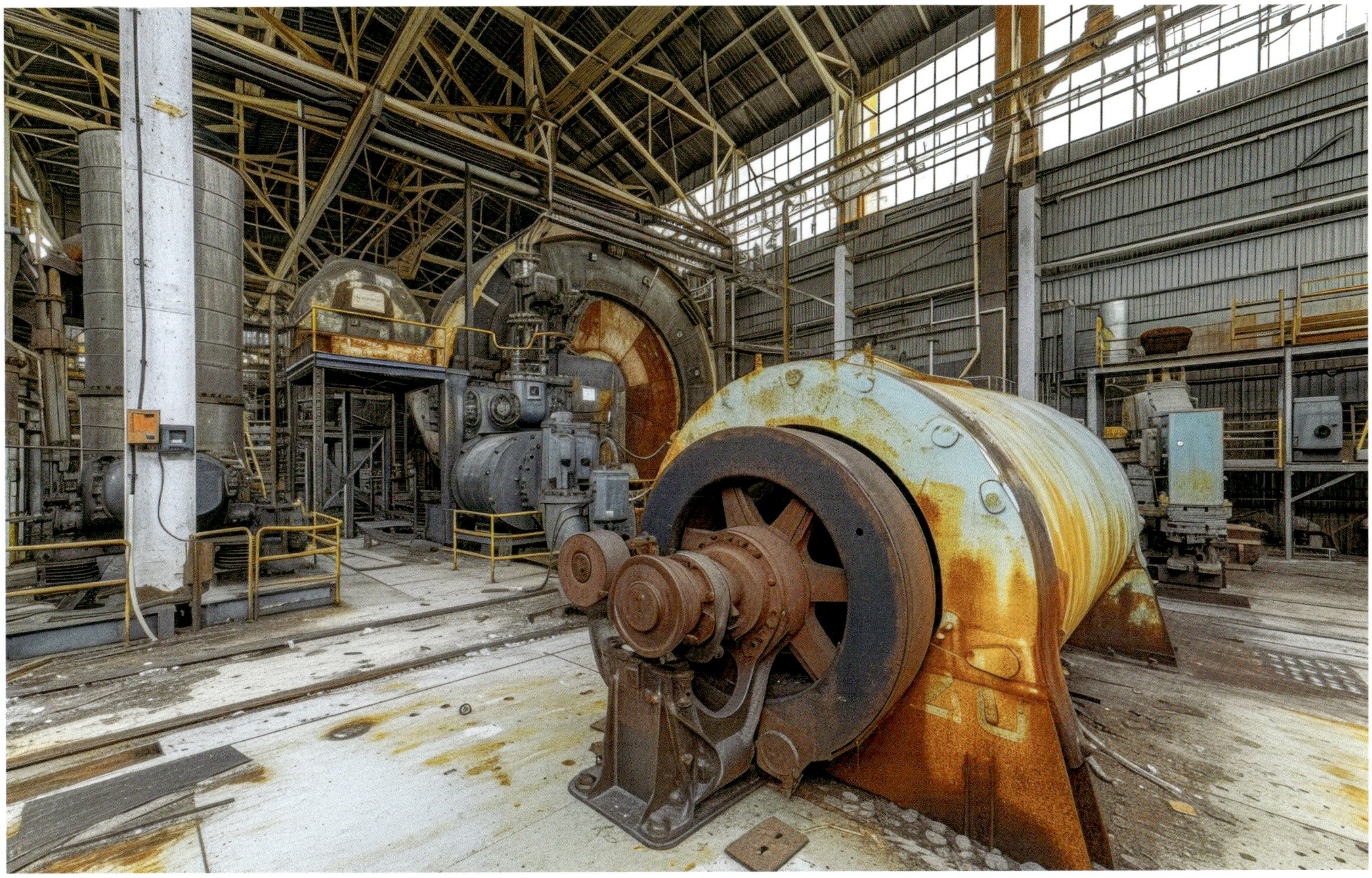

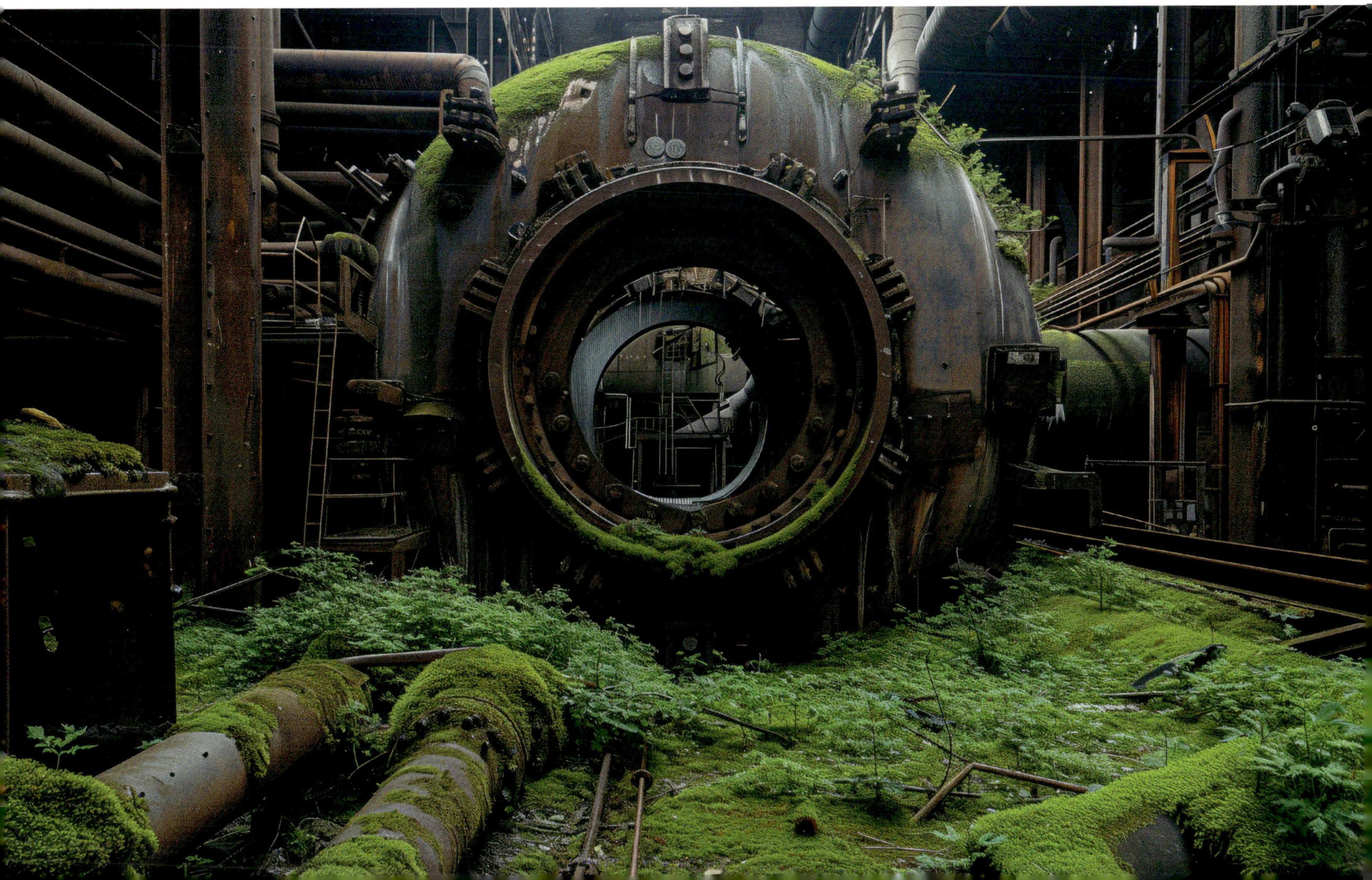

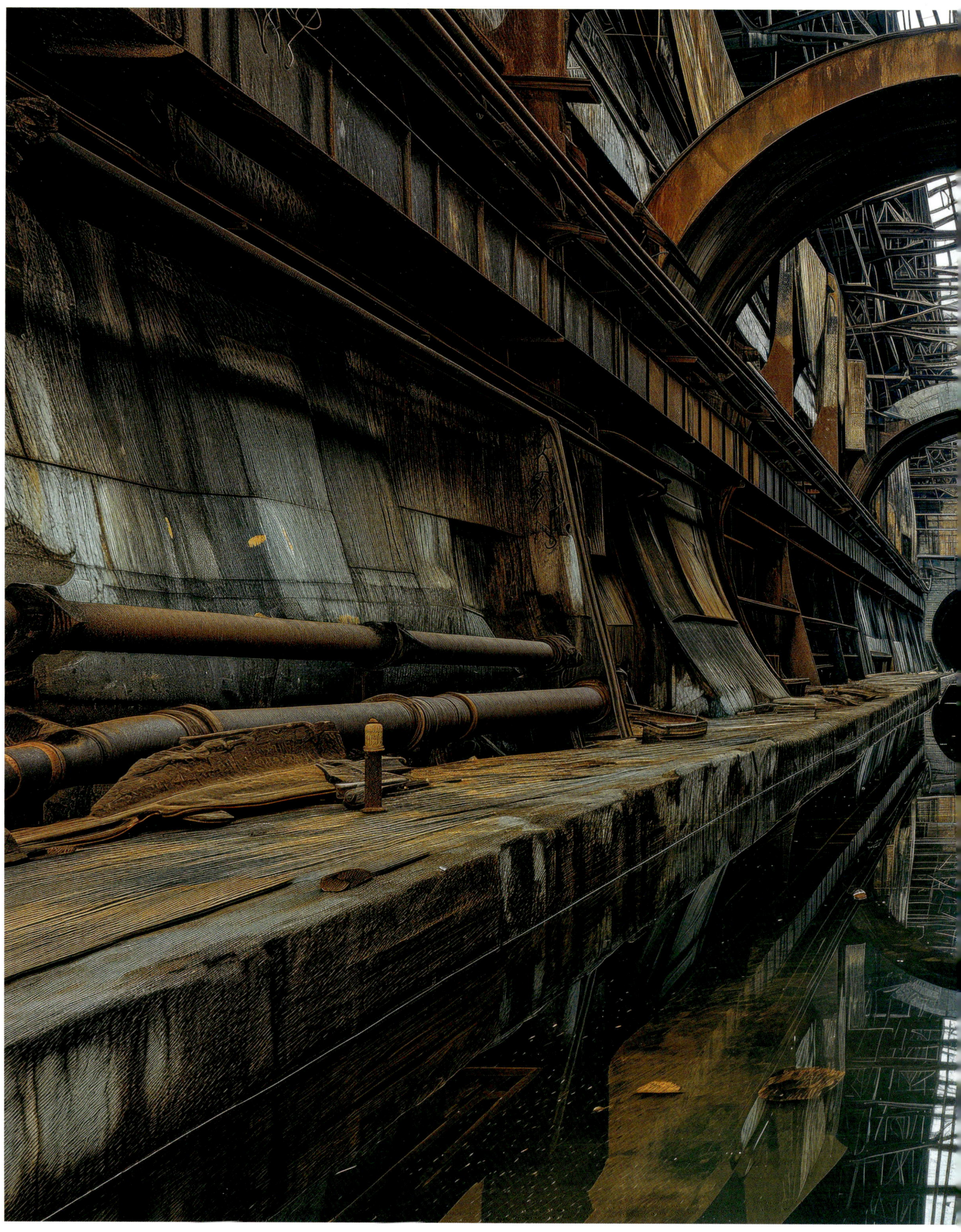

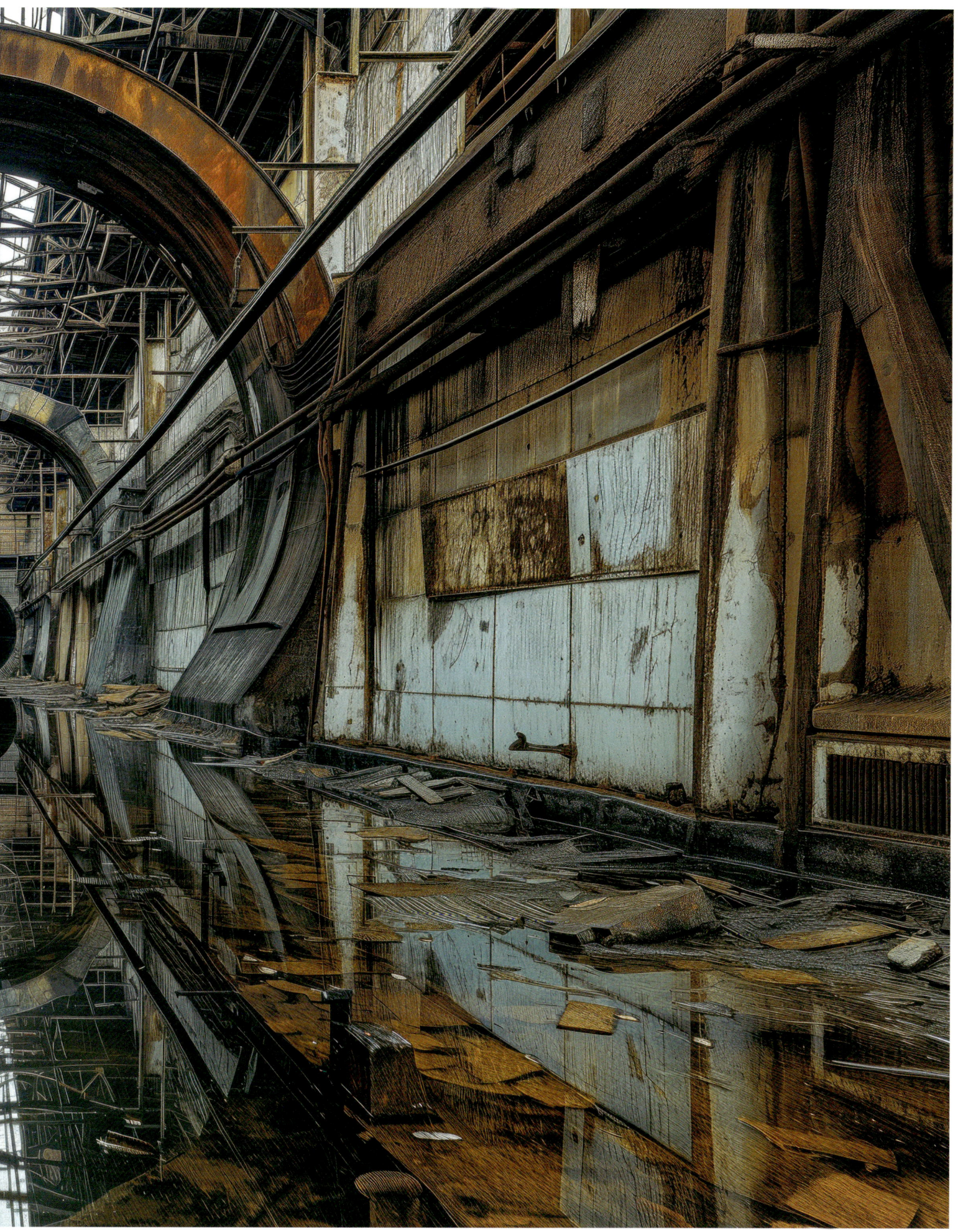

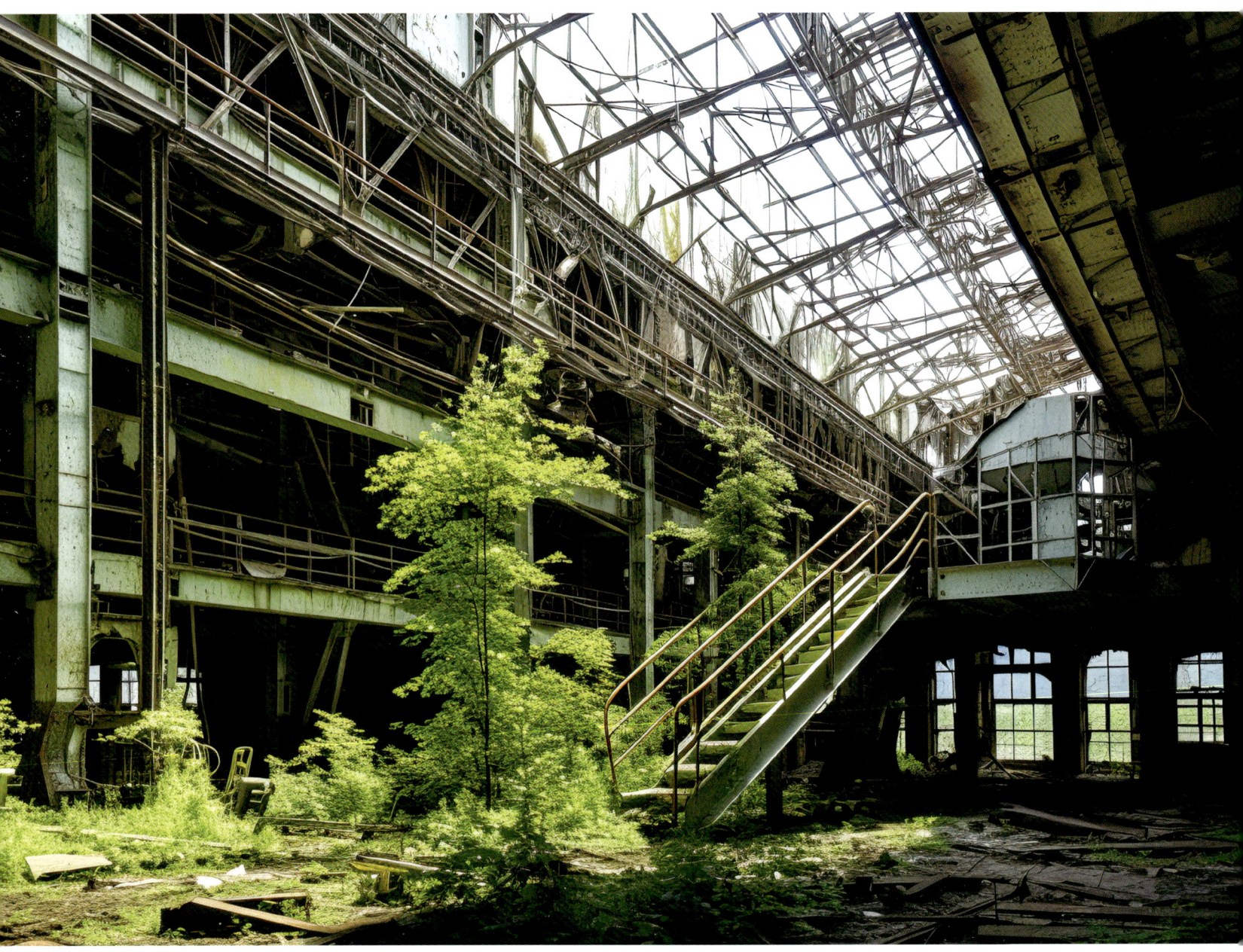

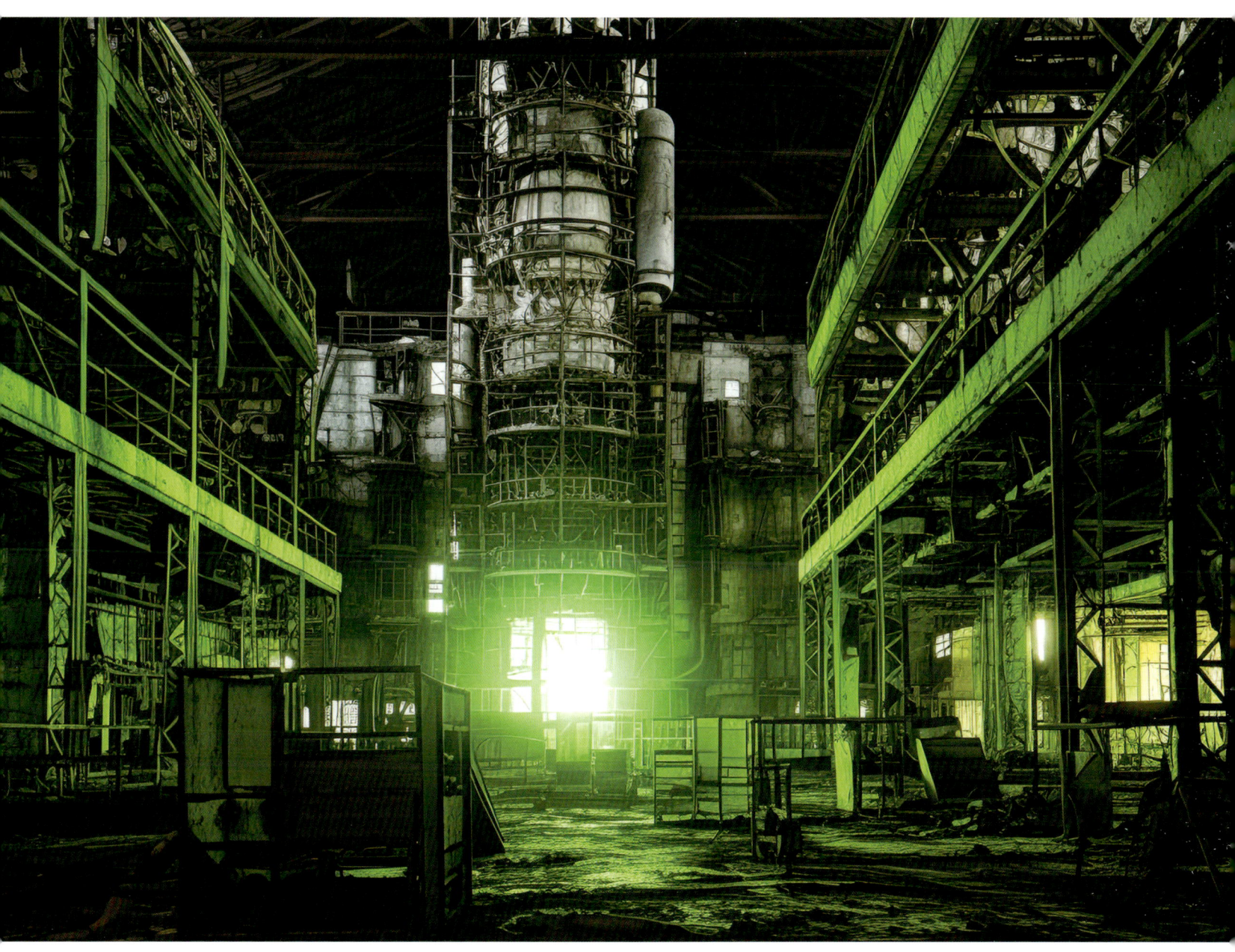

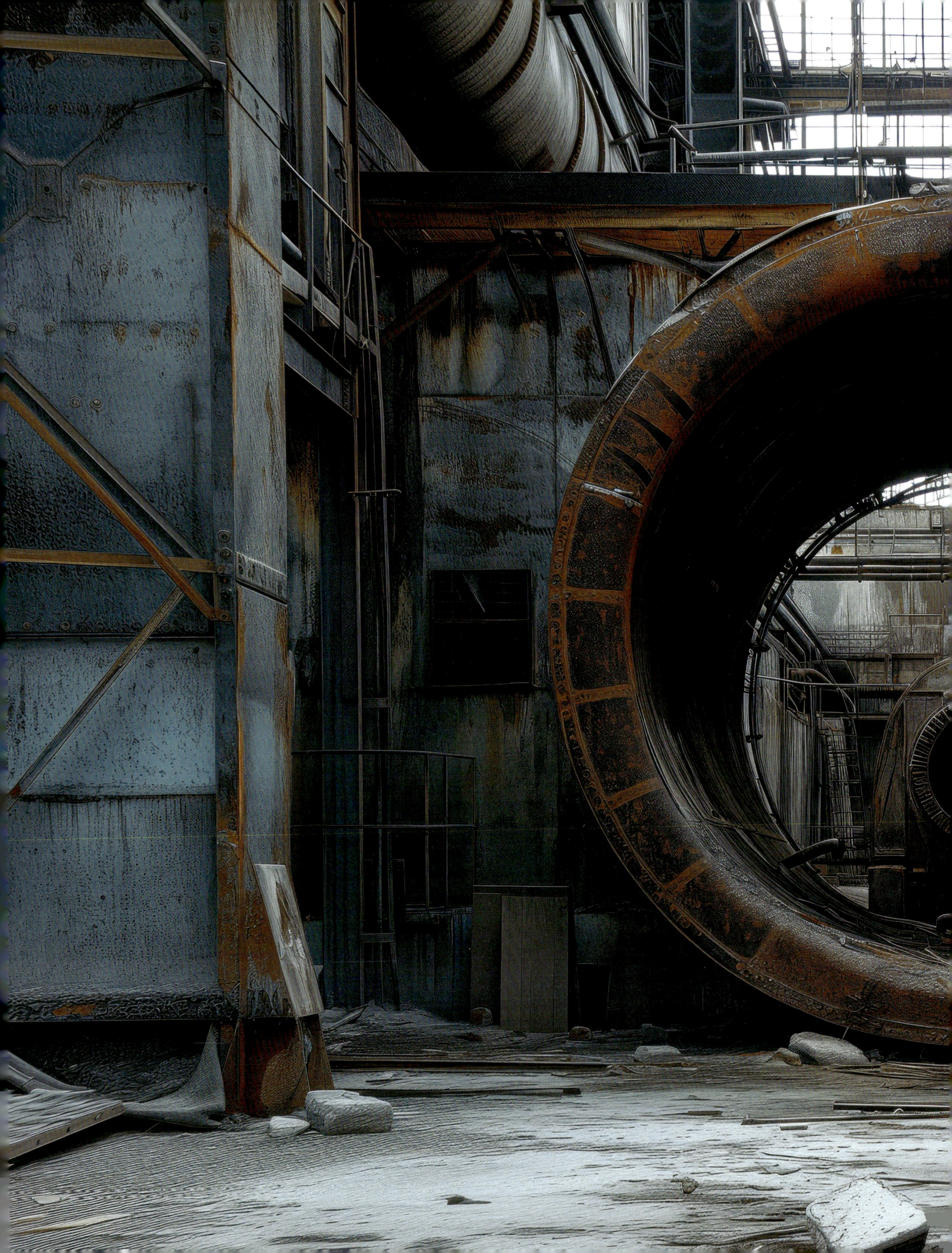

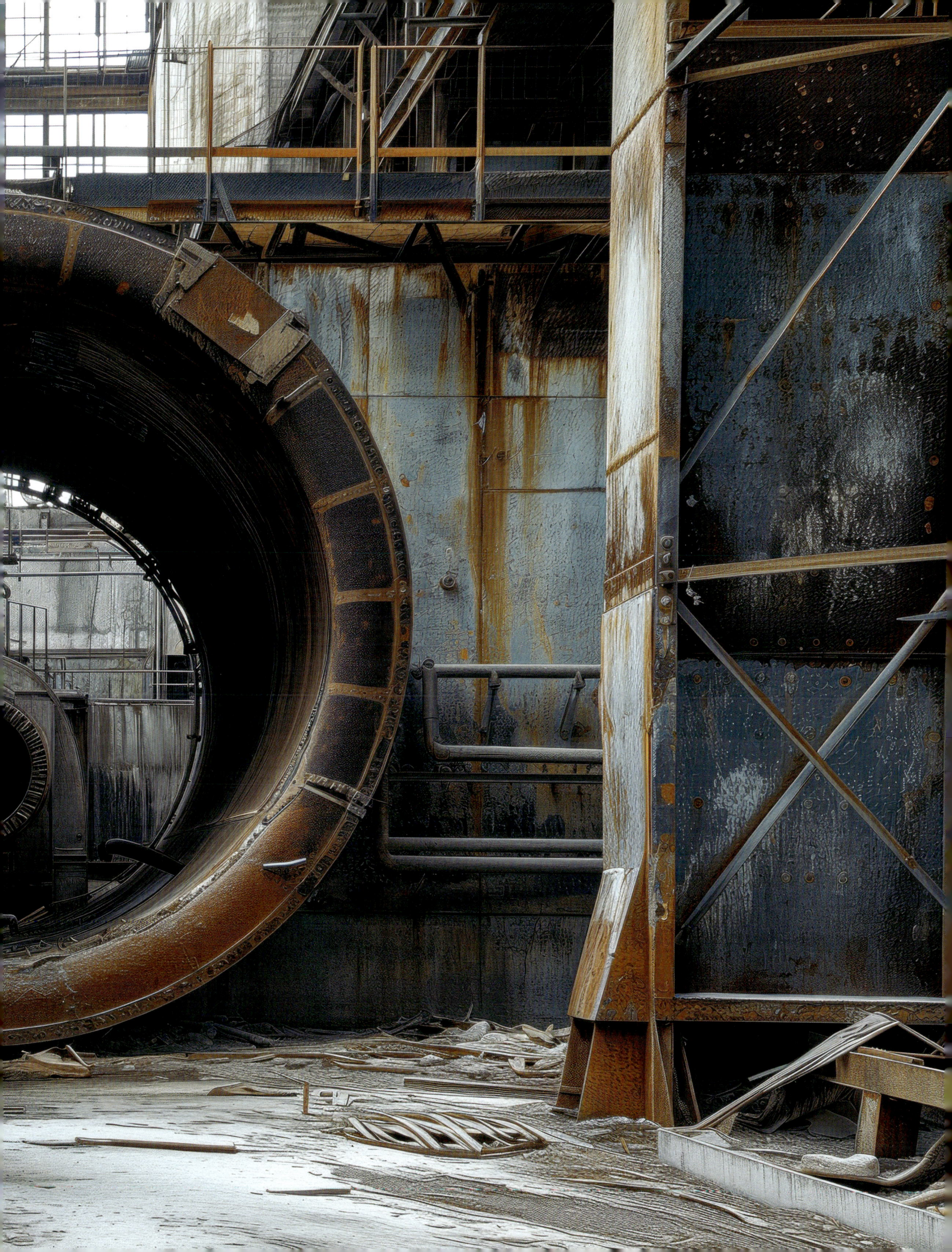

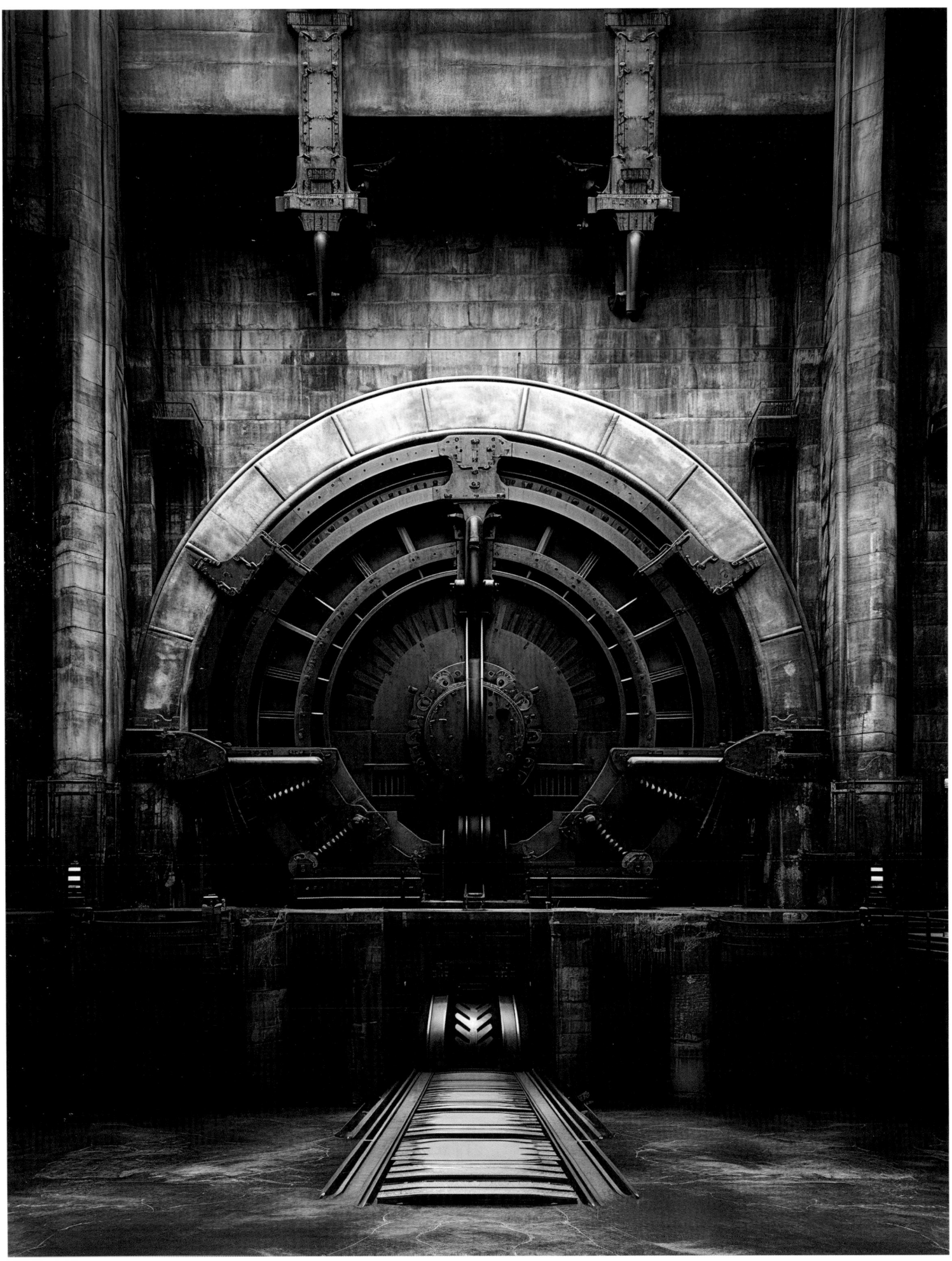

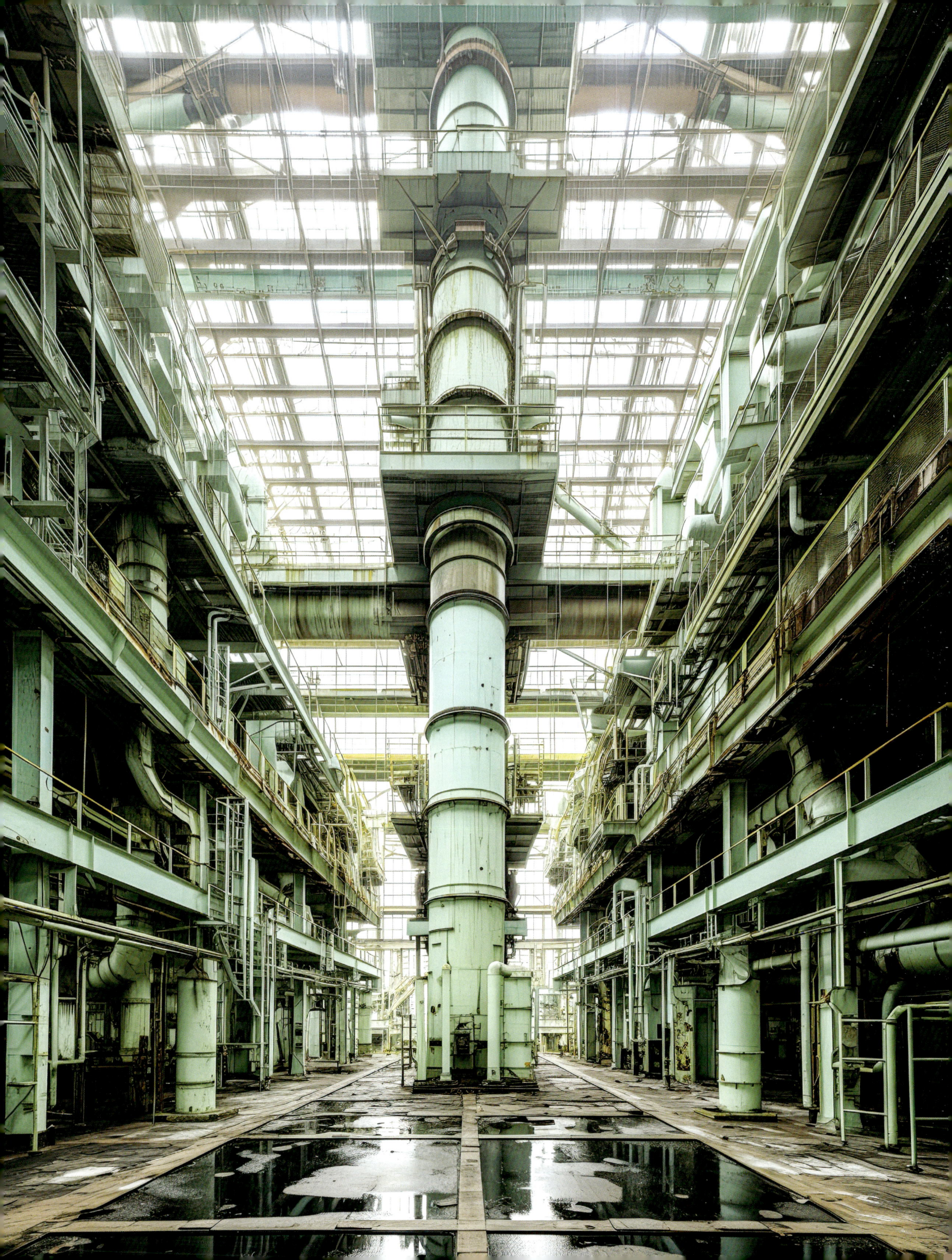

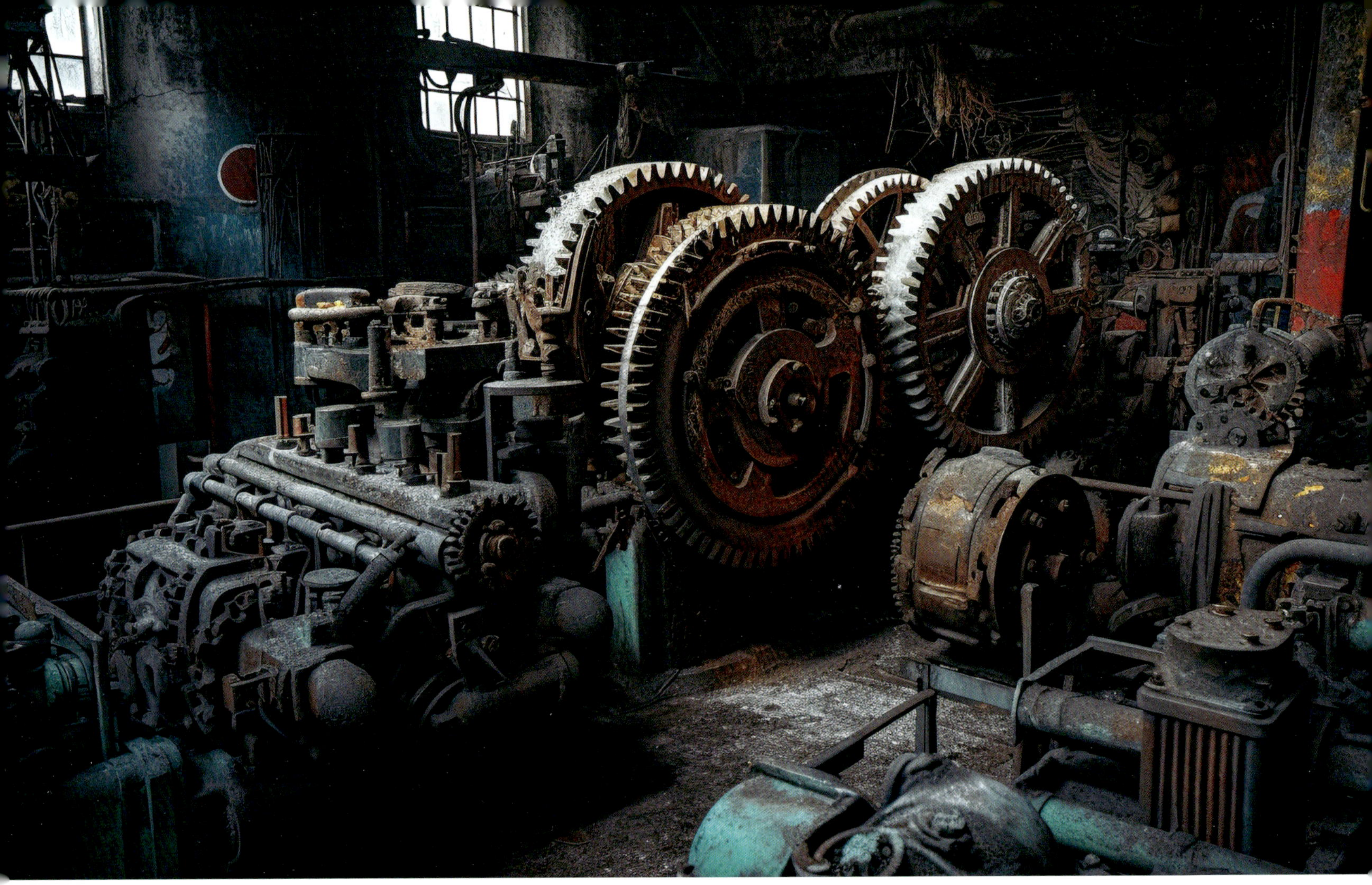

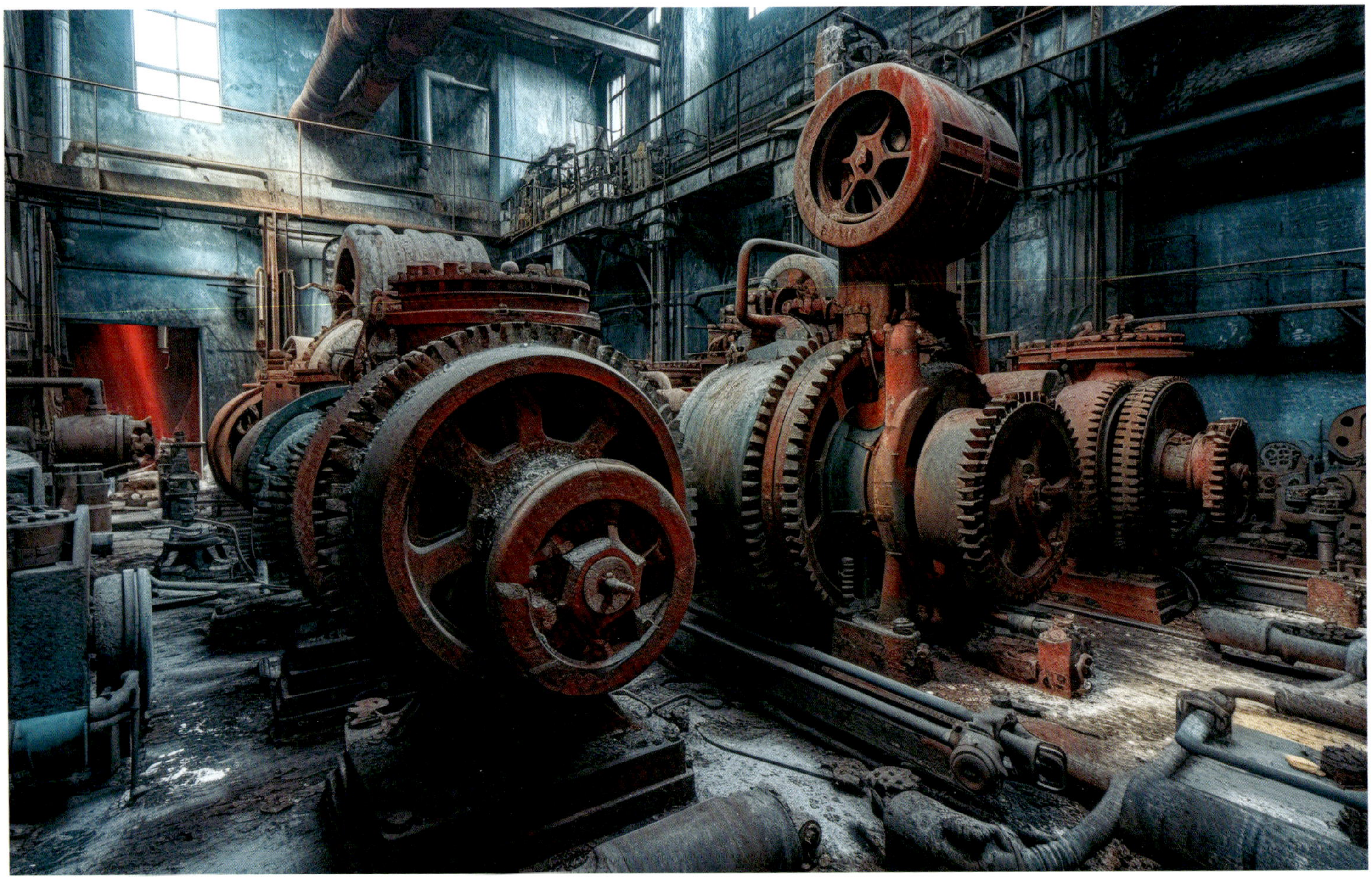

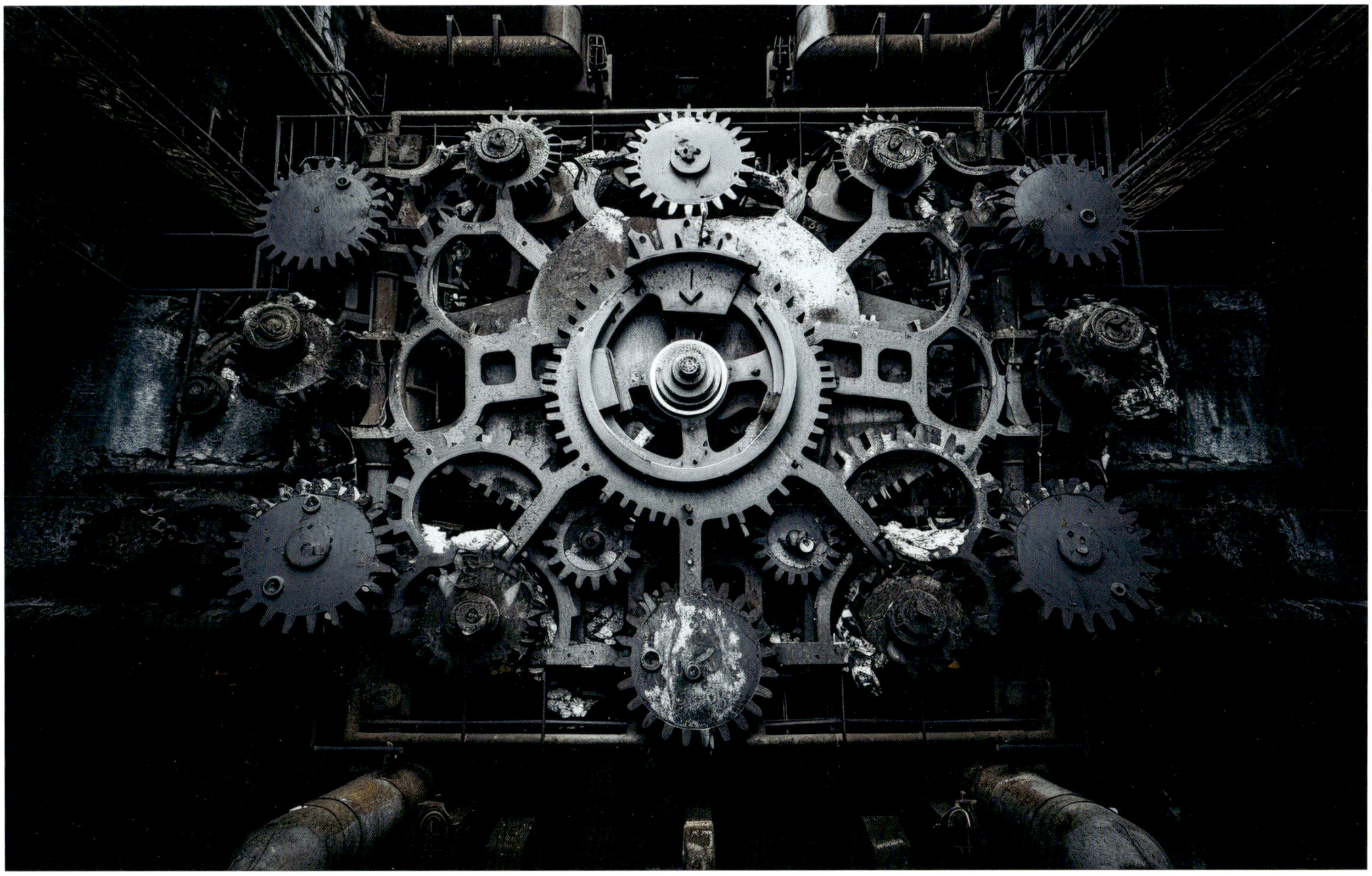

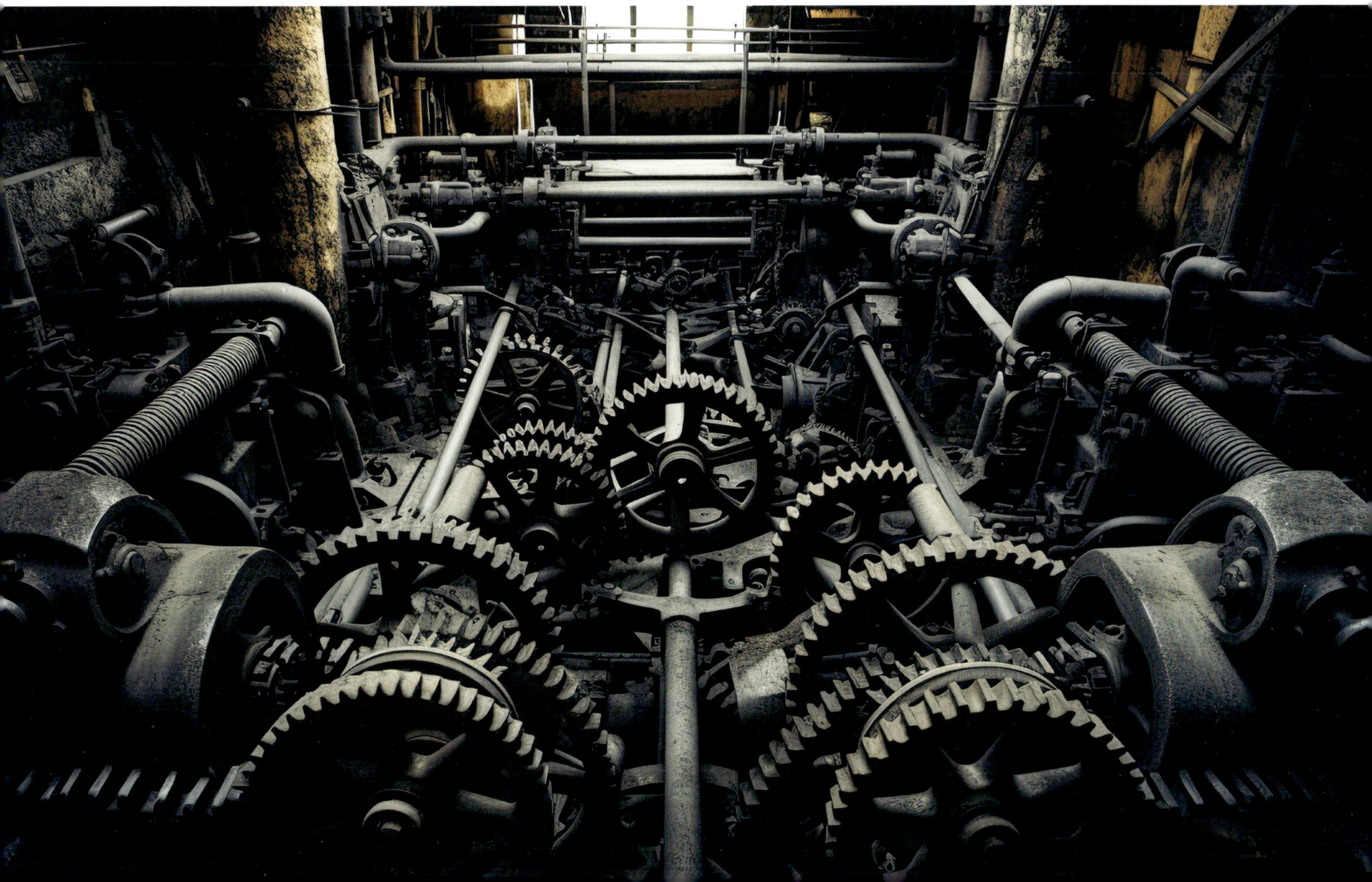

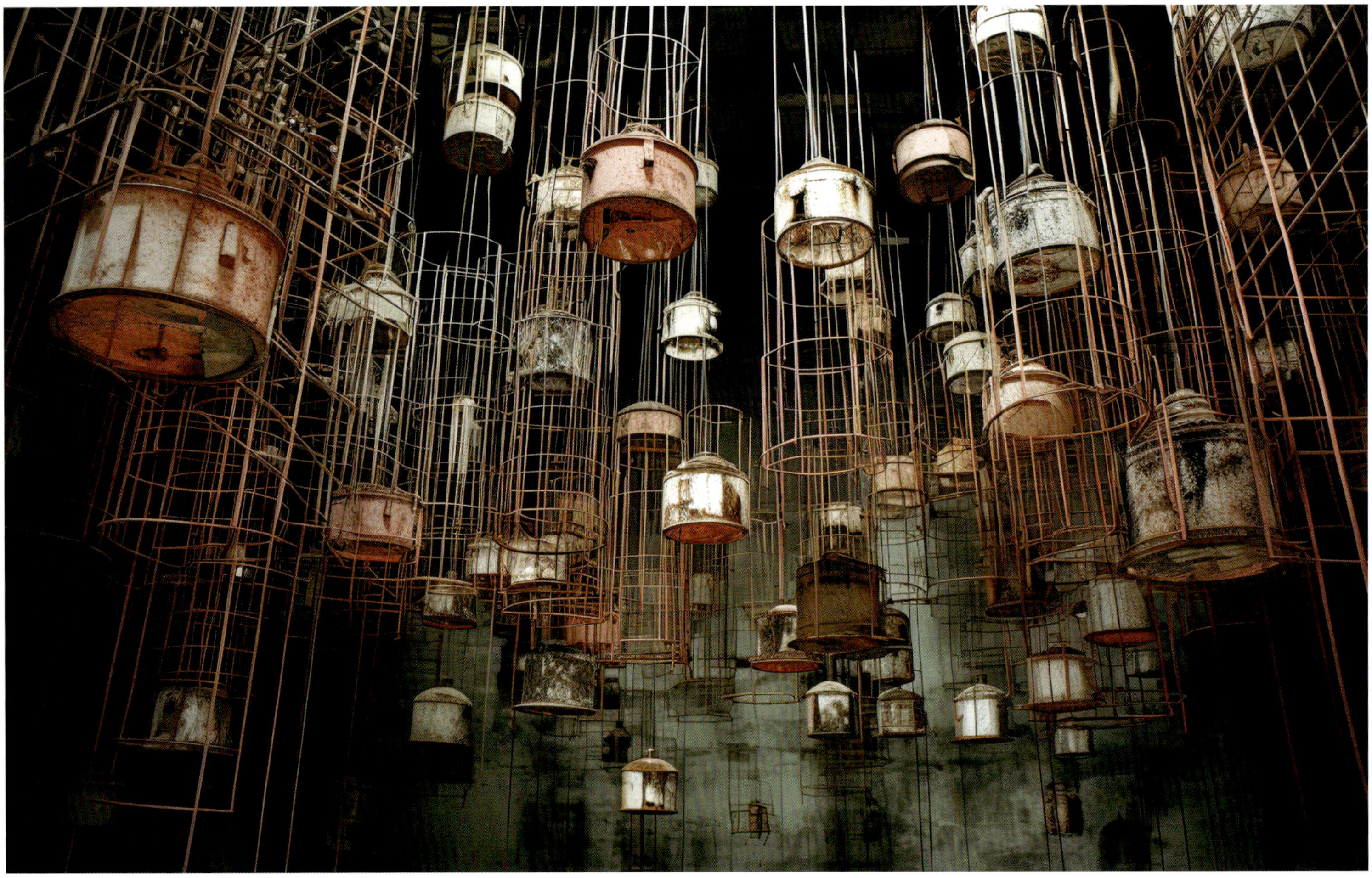

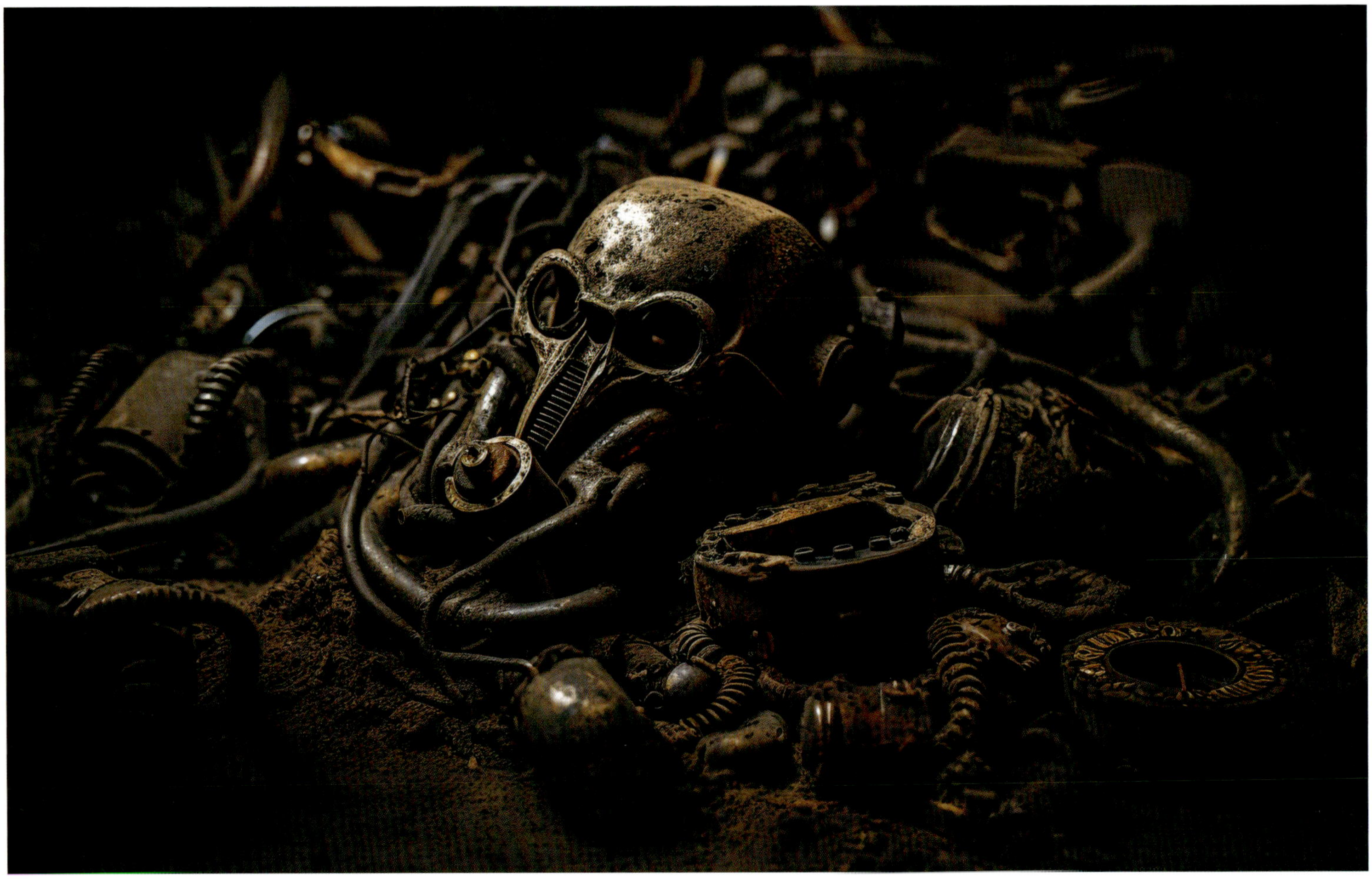

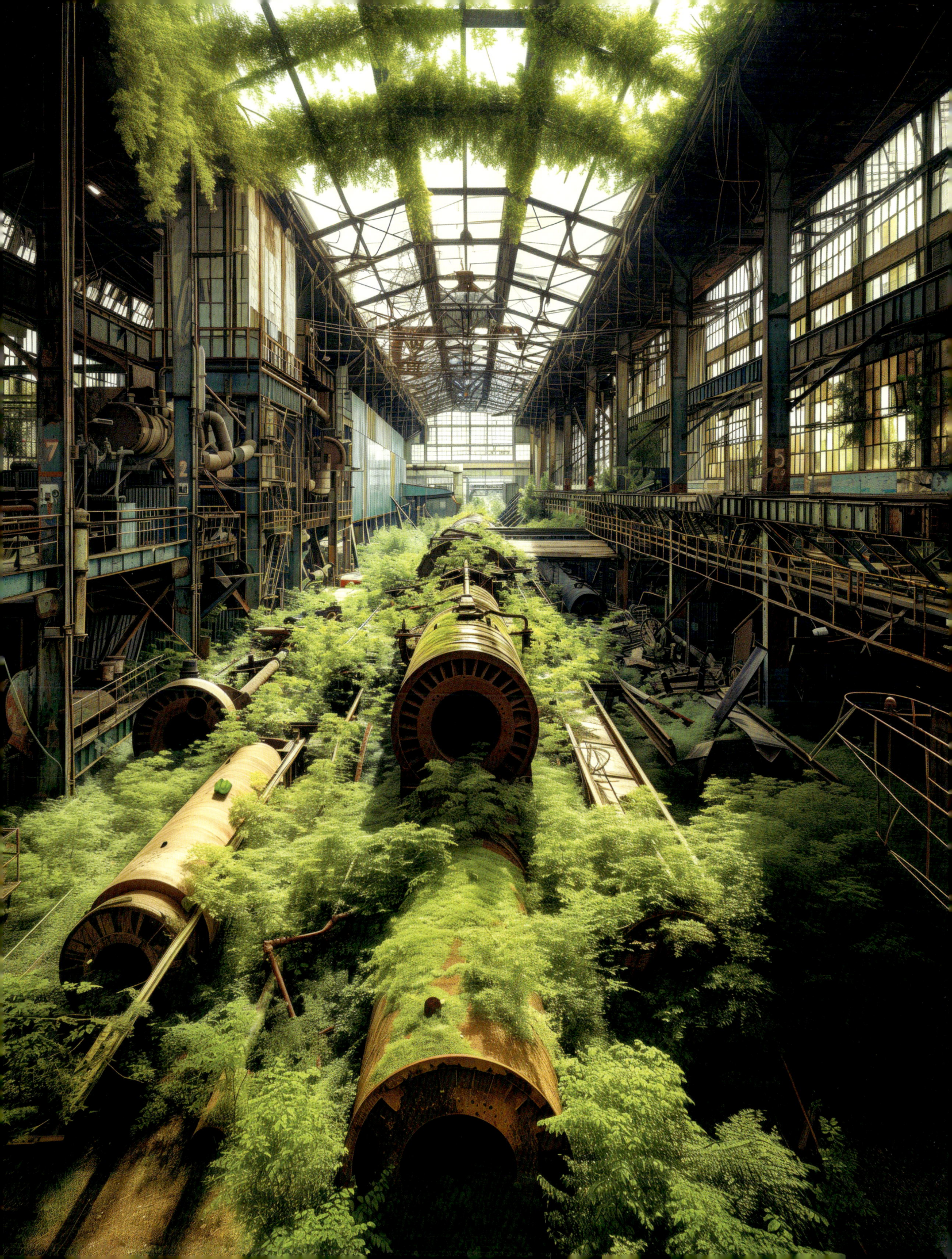

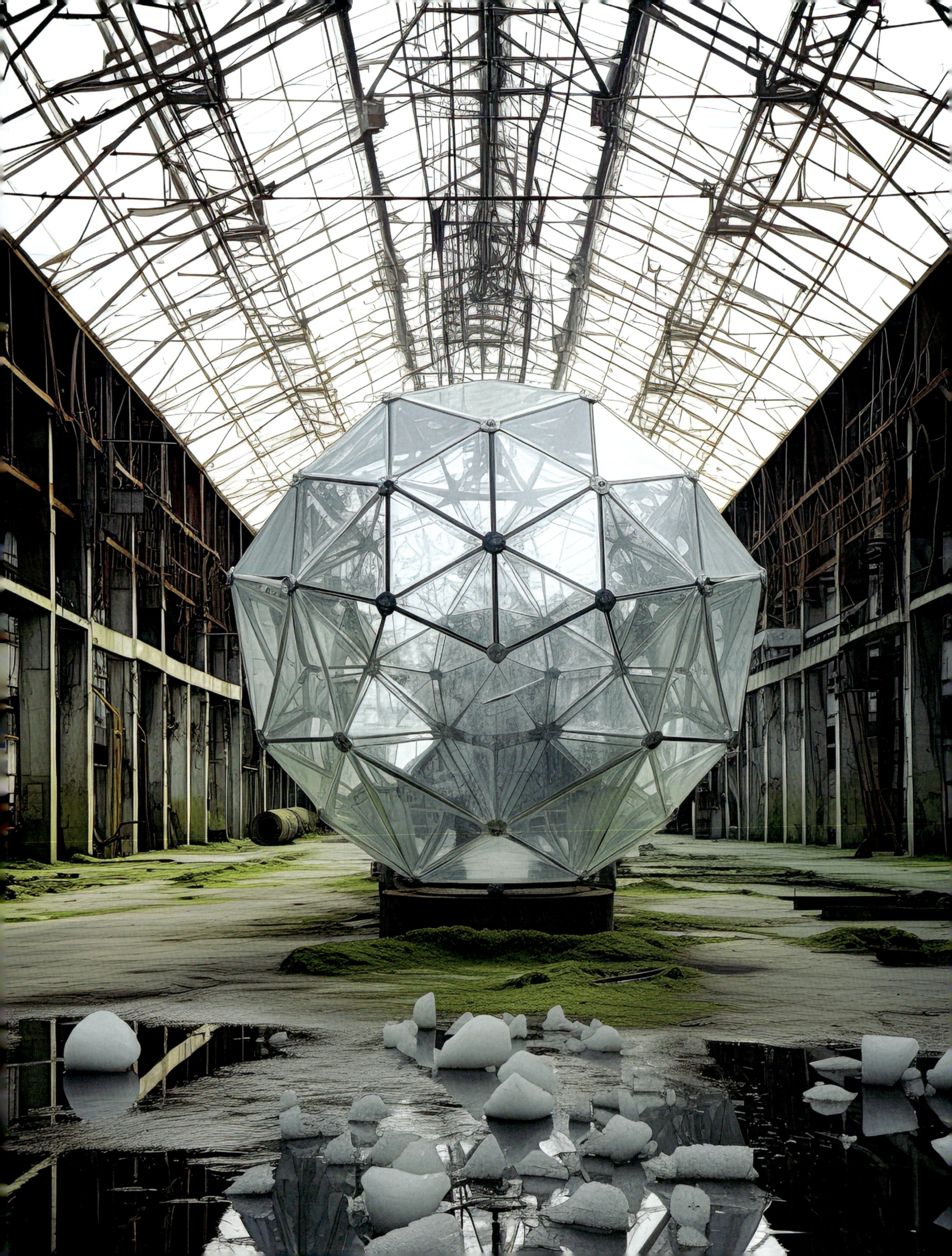

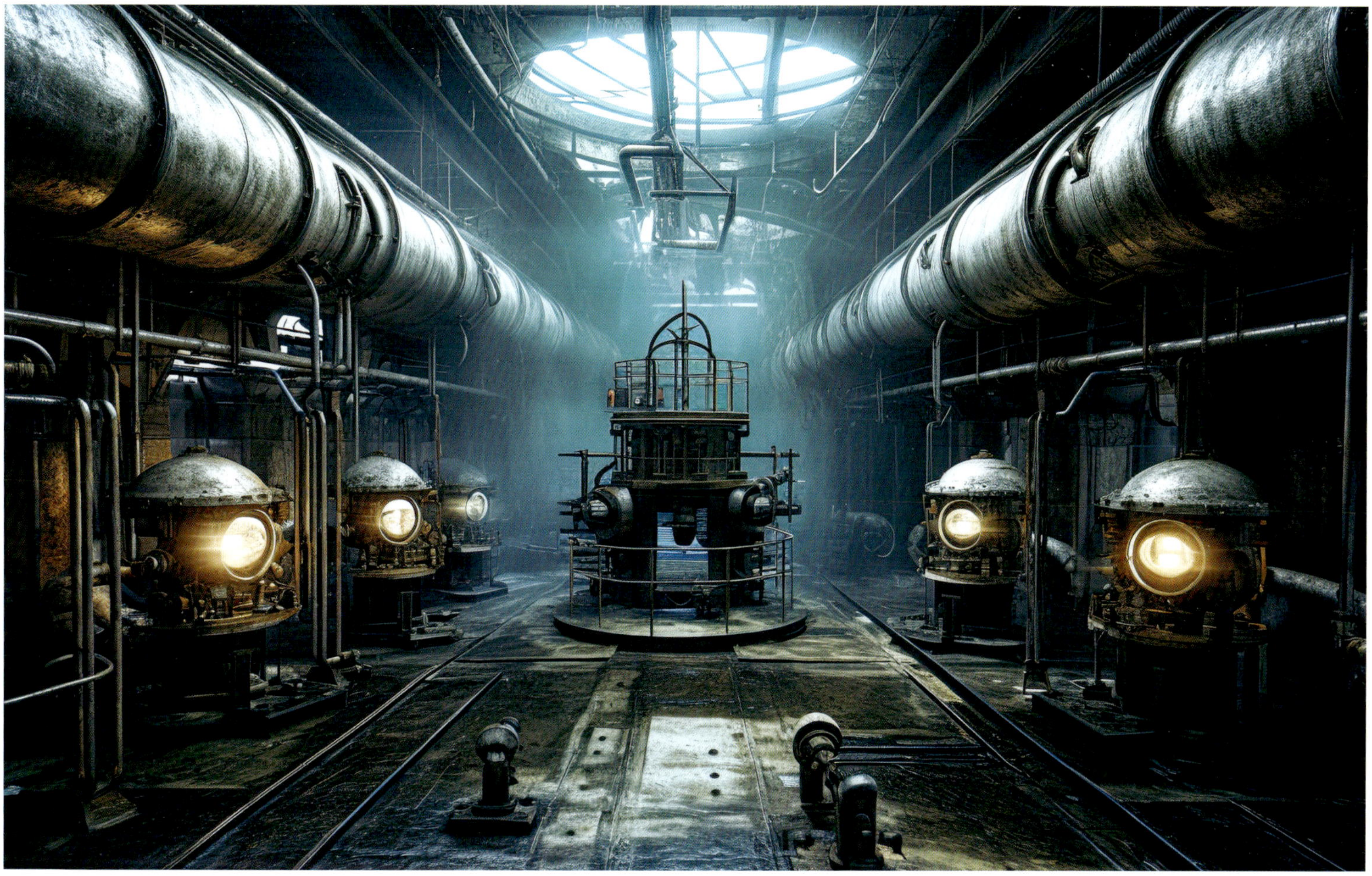

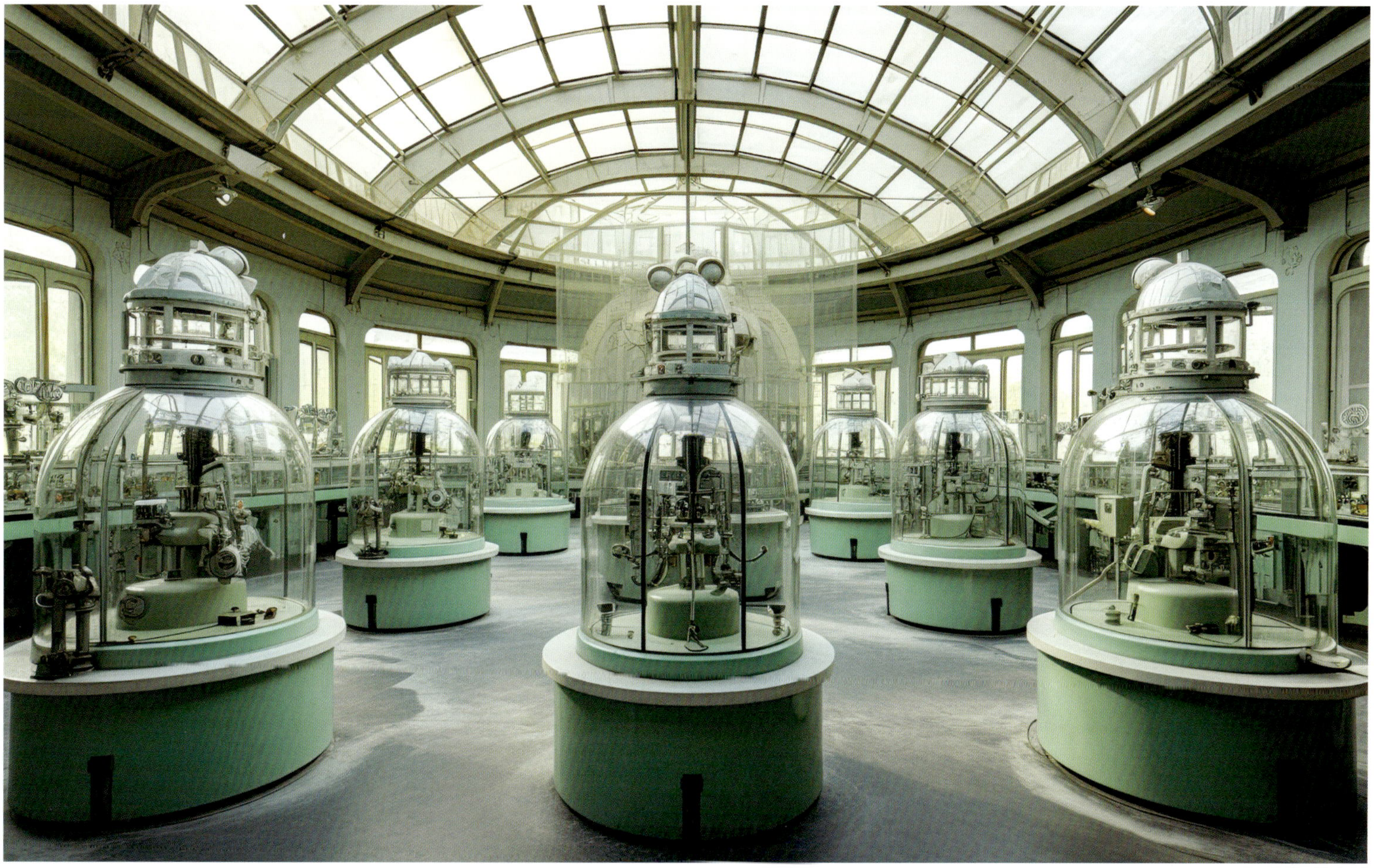

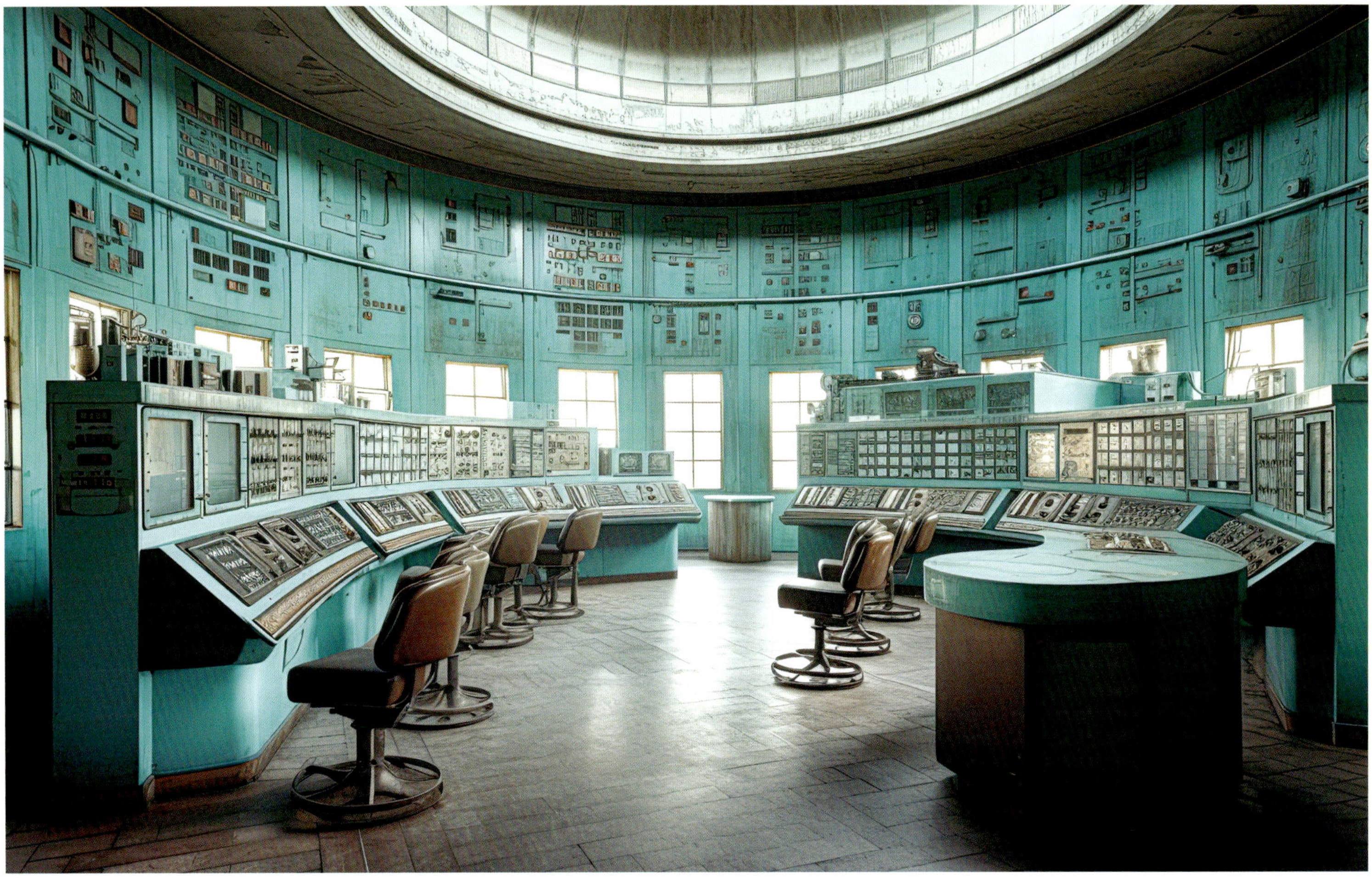

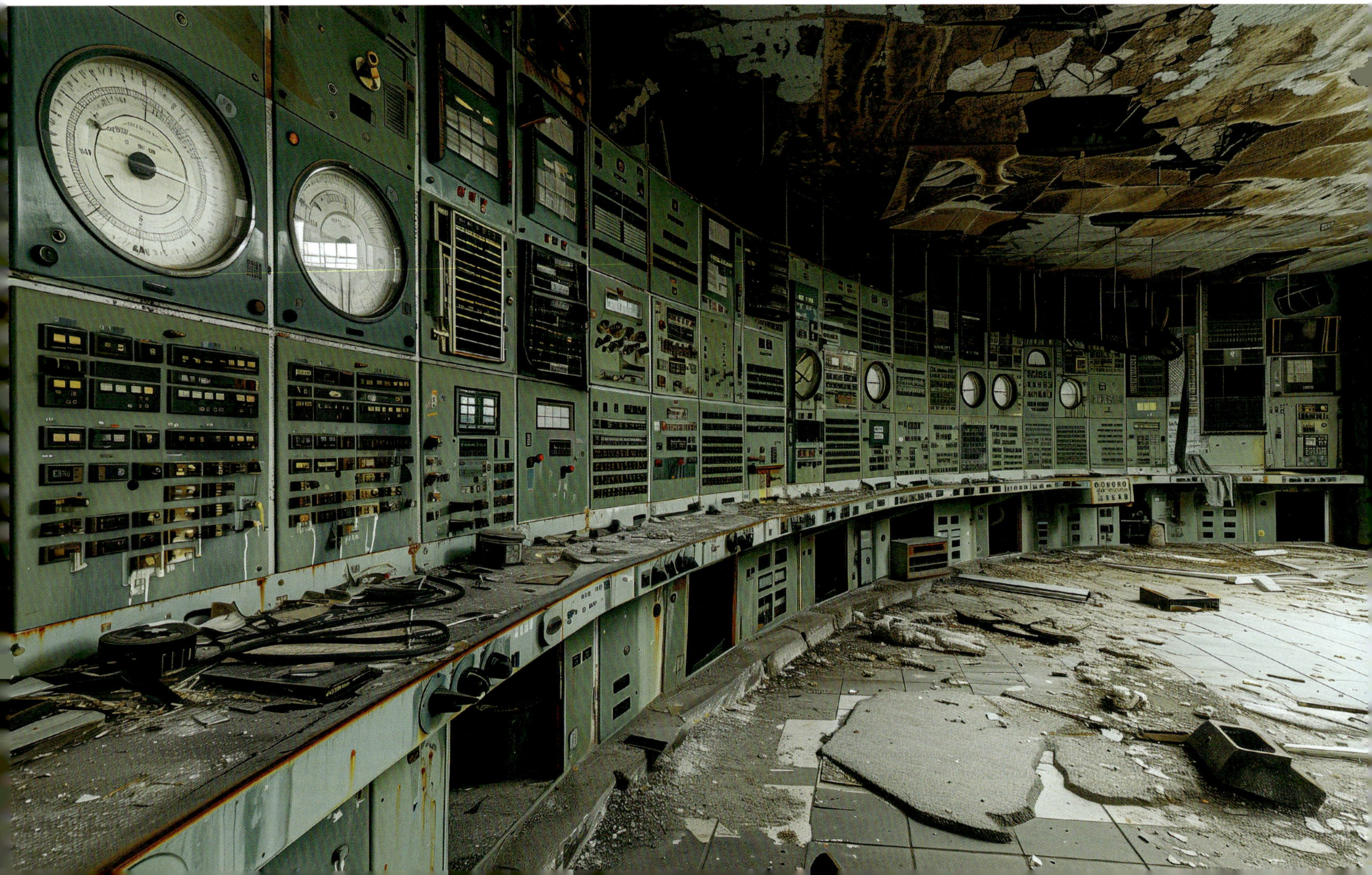

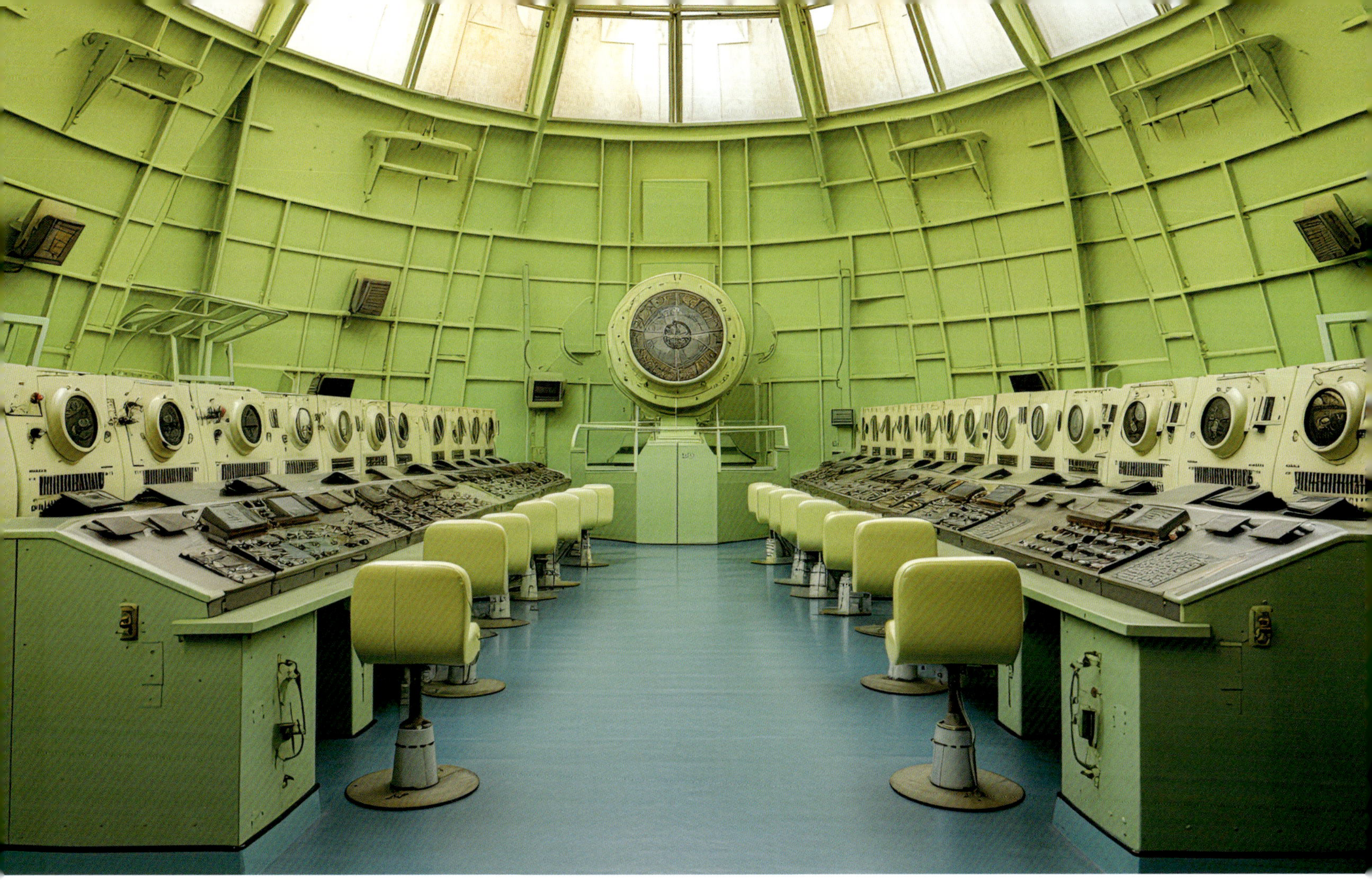

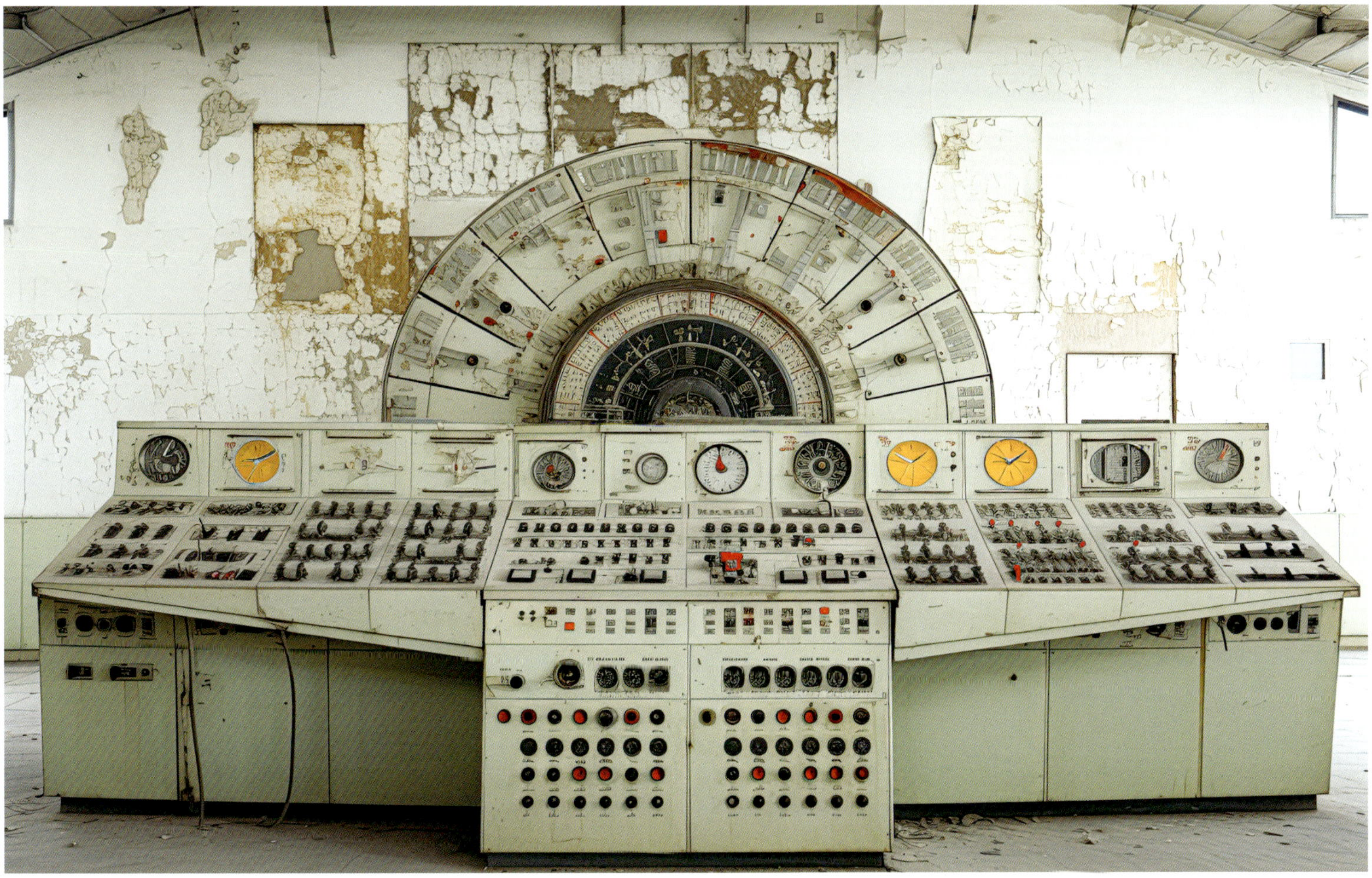

Ariadne's thread

Clothing factories that once vibrated to the rhythm of looms have been deserted. Algorithms have silenced the clatter of machines, sculpting the new face of fashion and plunging traditional workshops into darkness. The old industrial buildings, sanctuaries of textile production, now rest in the shadows of relics of a bygone era.

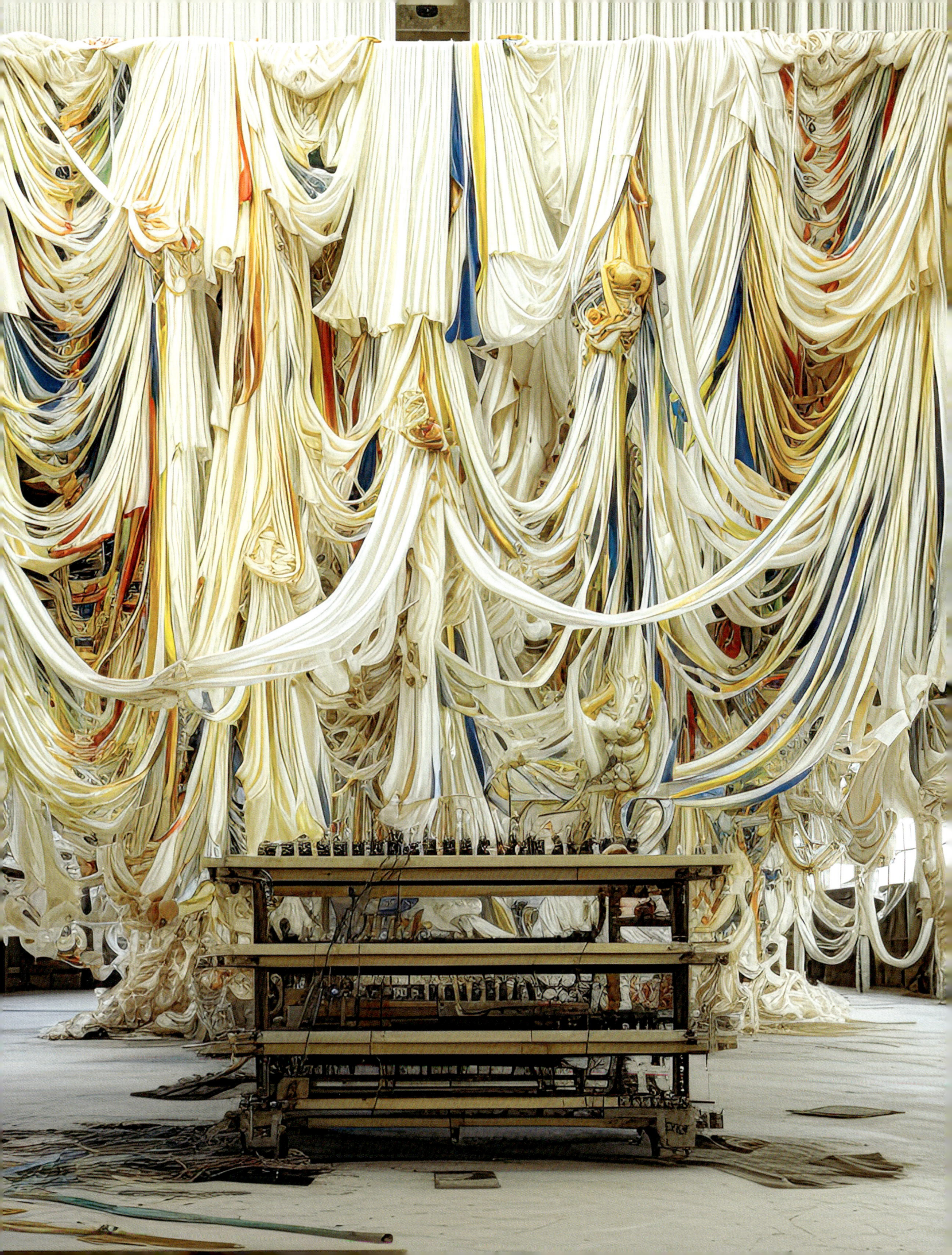

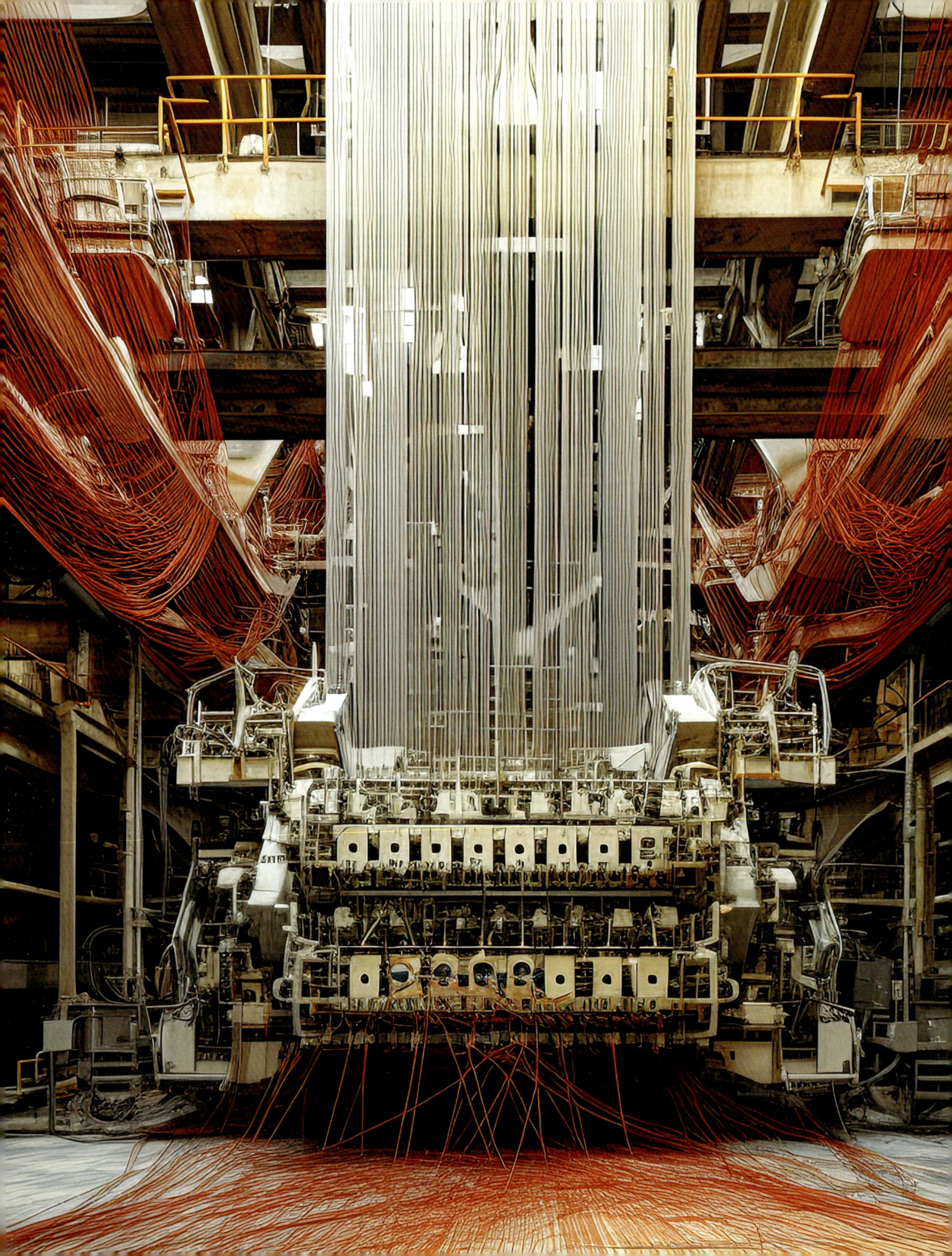

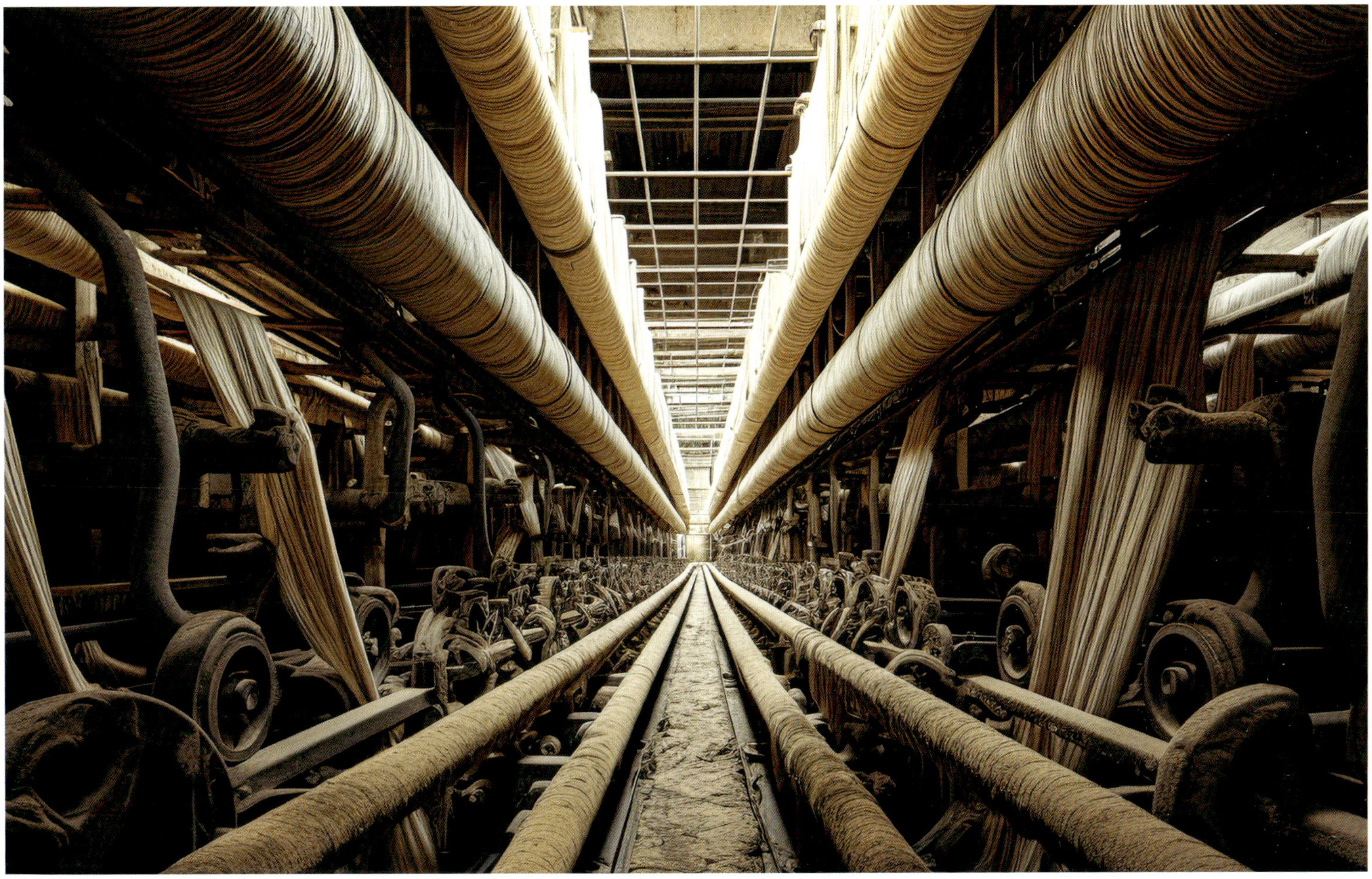

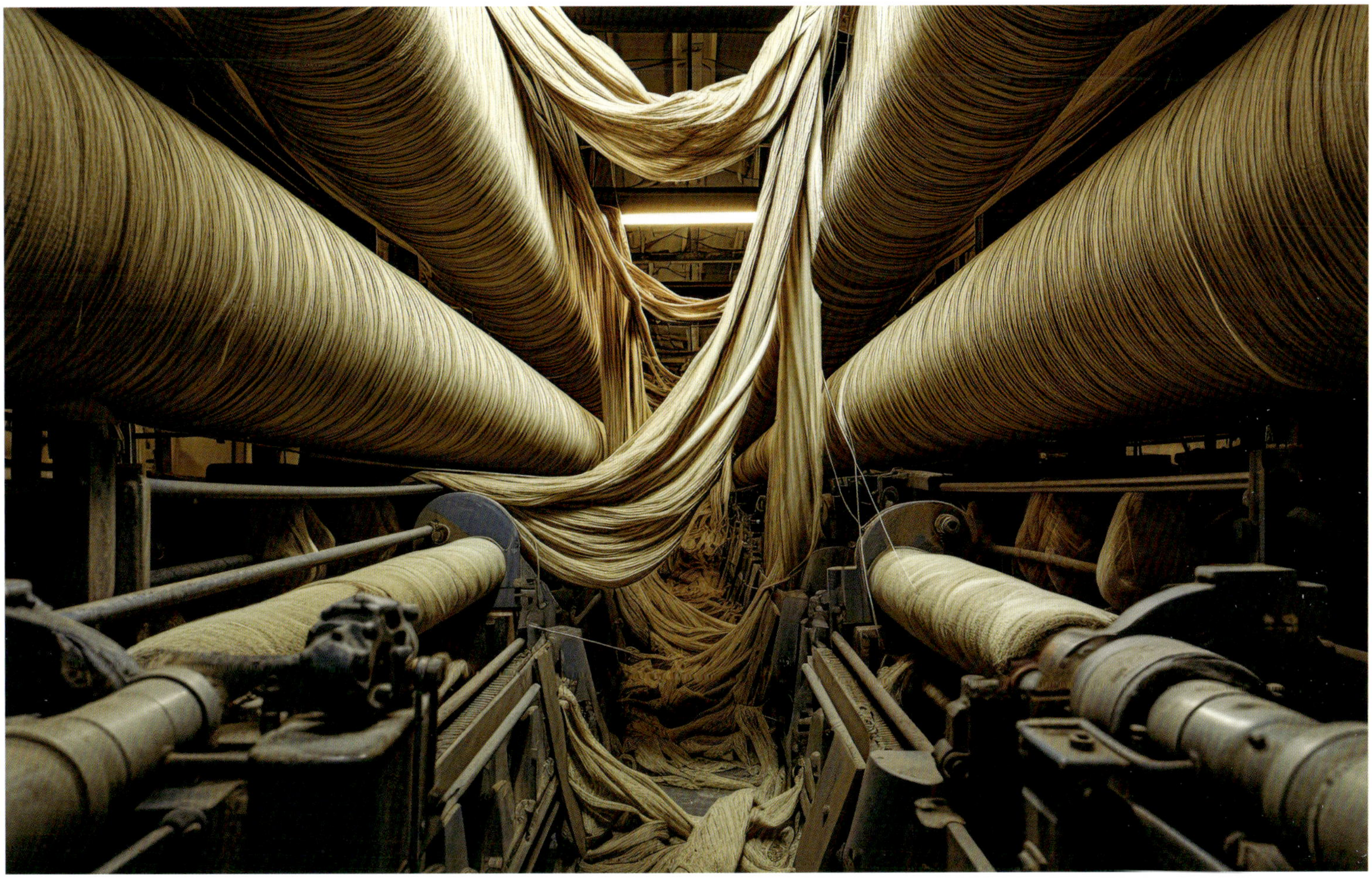

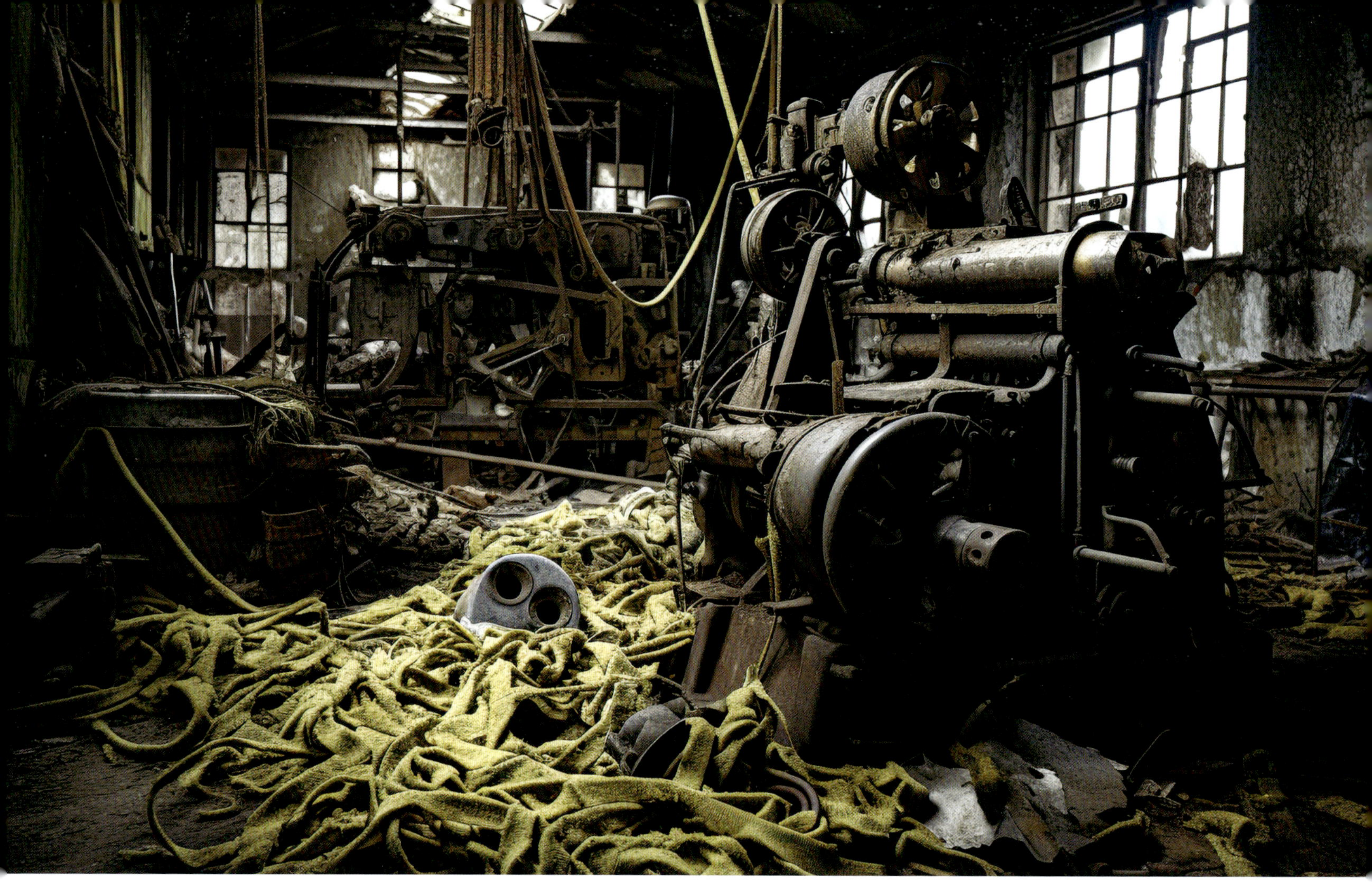

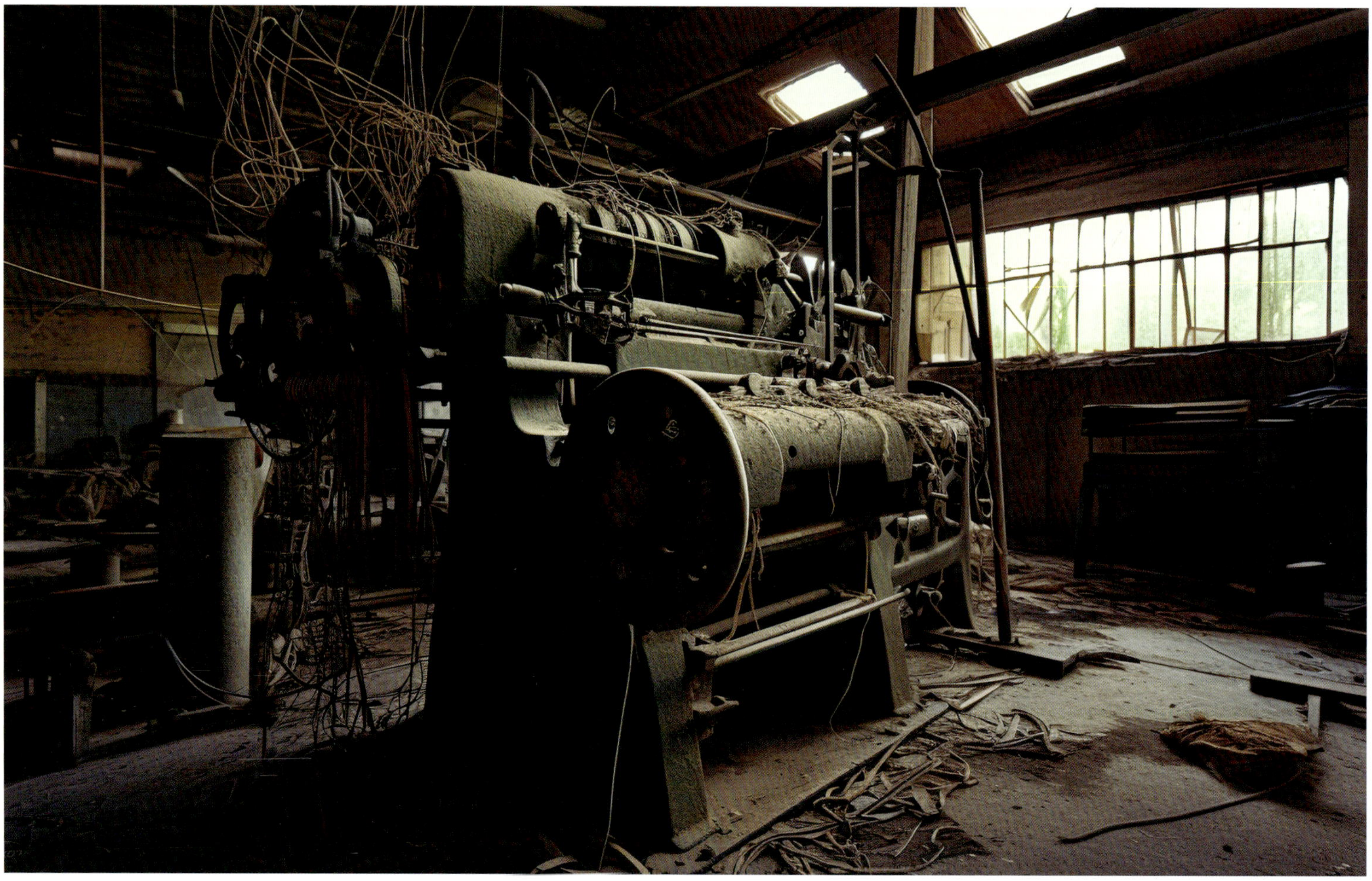

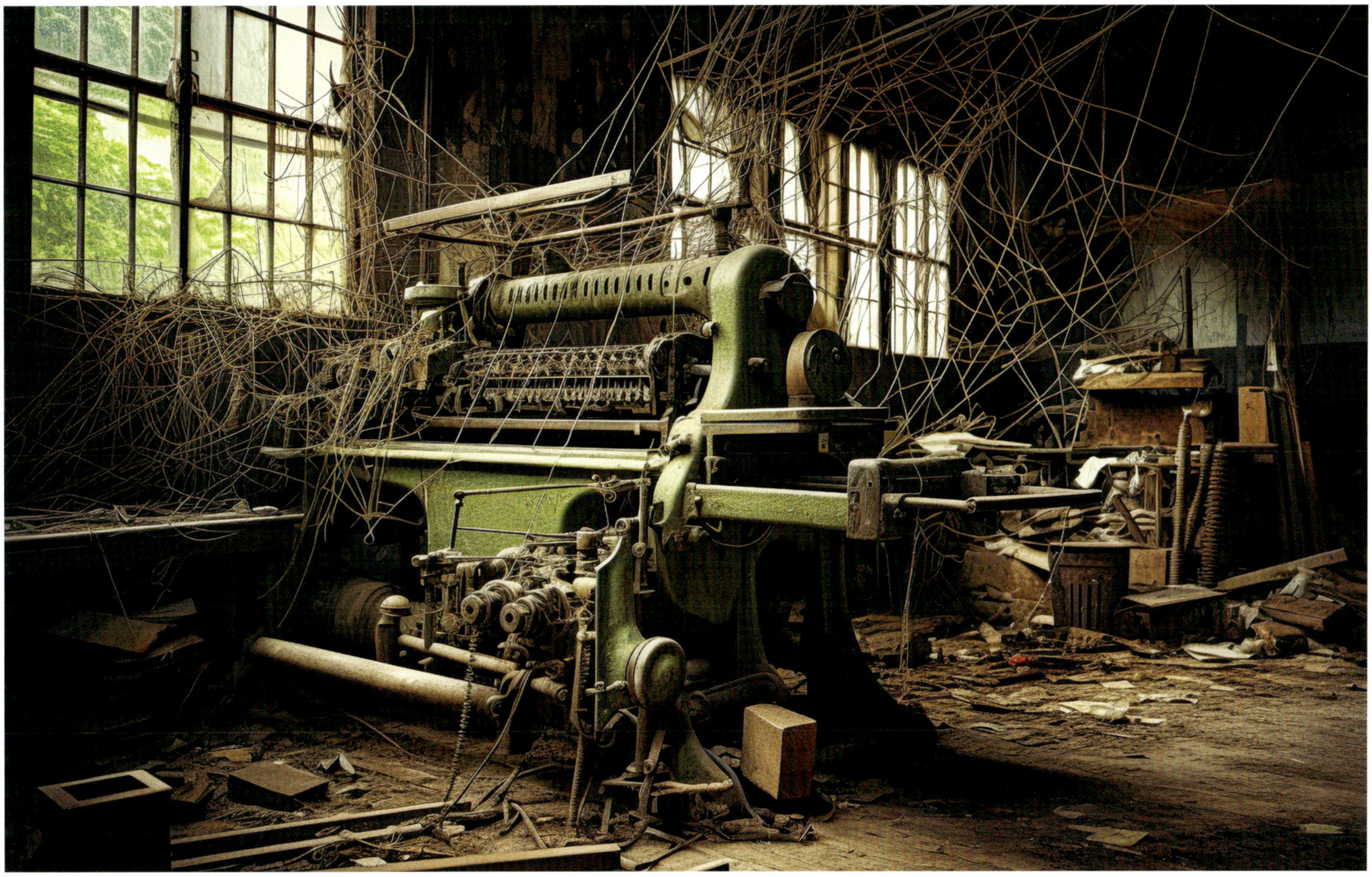

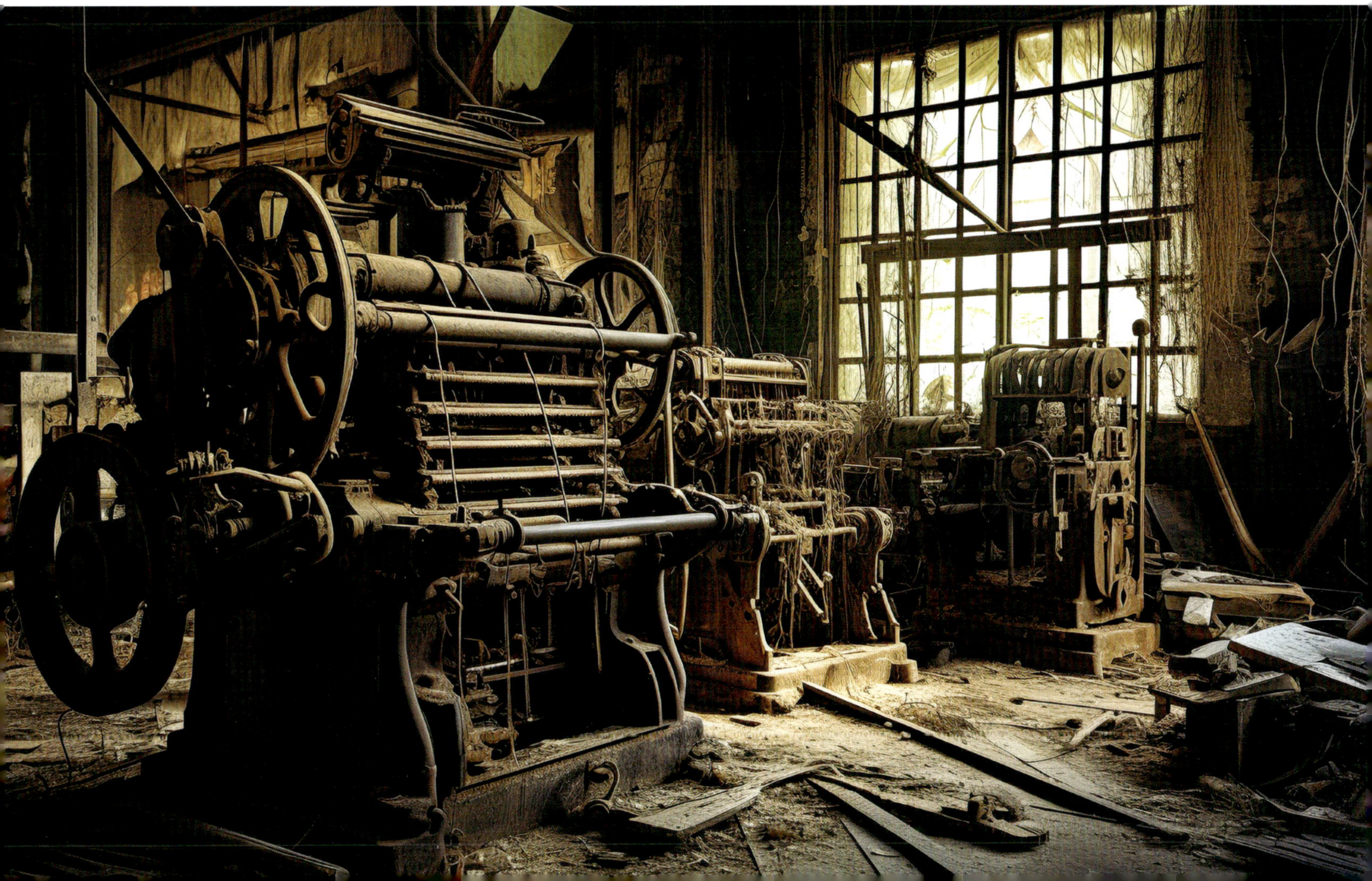

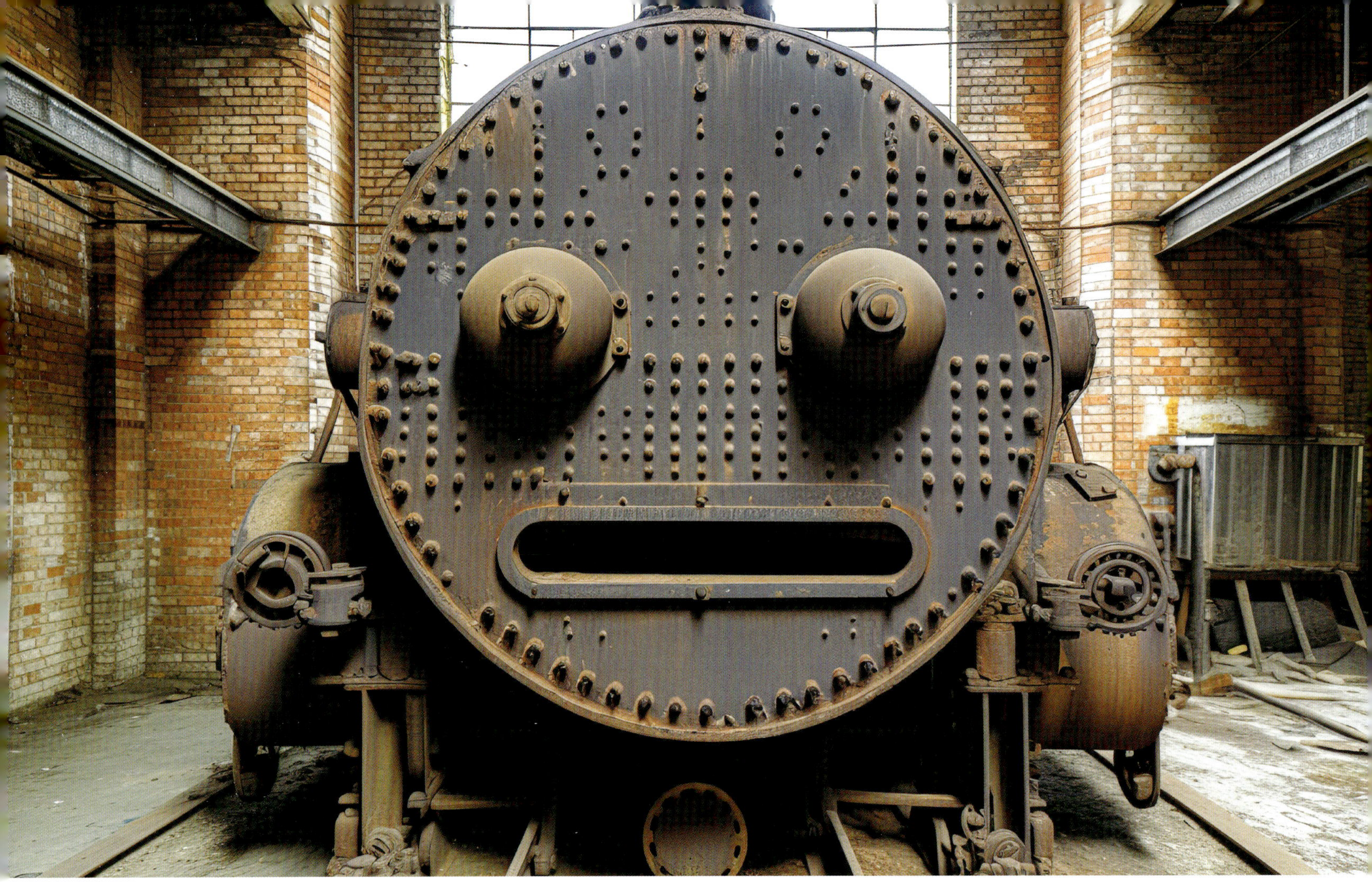

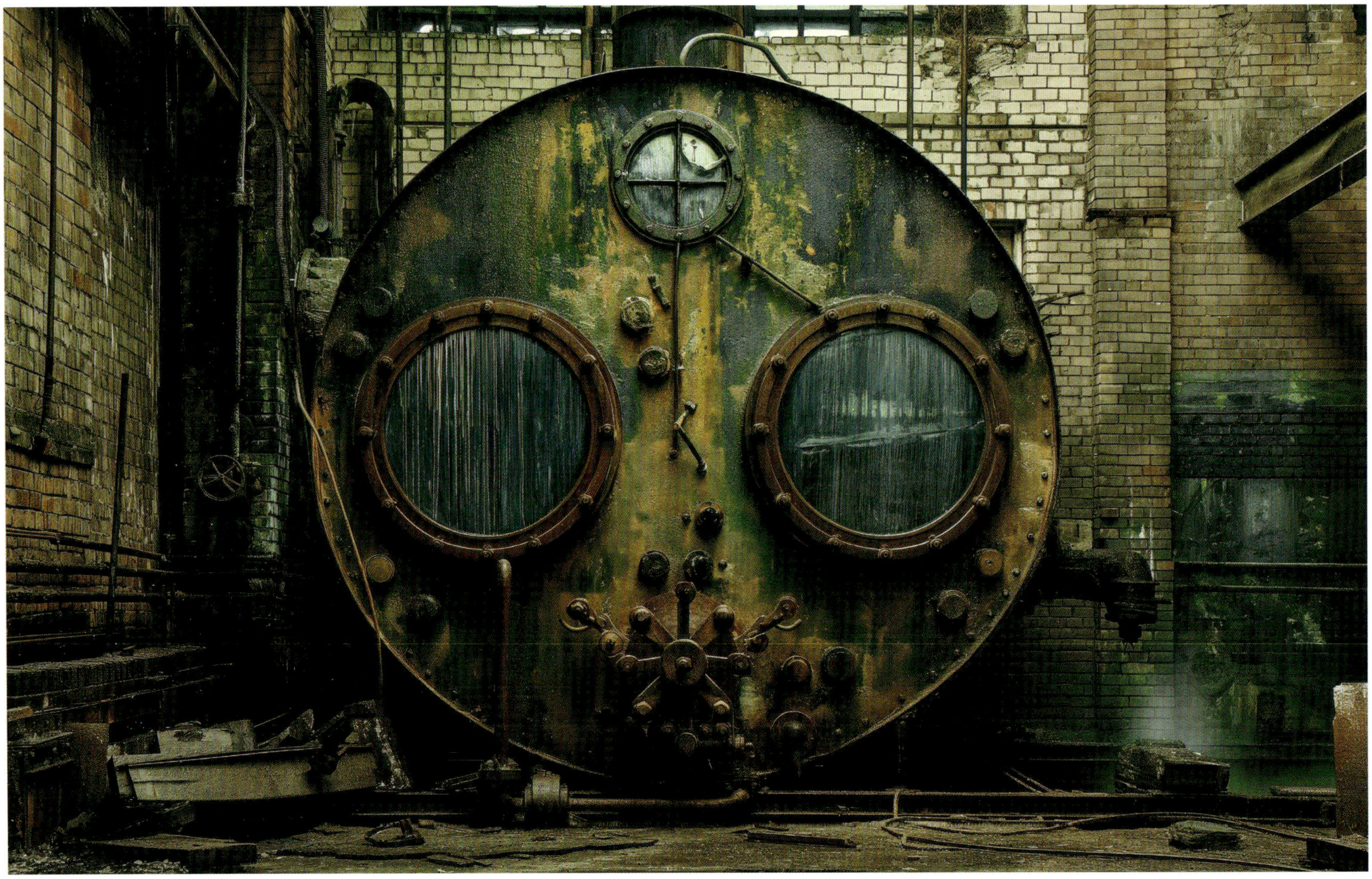

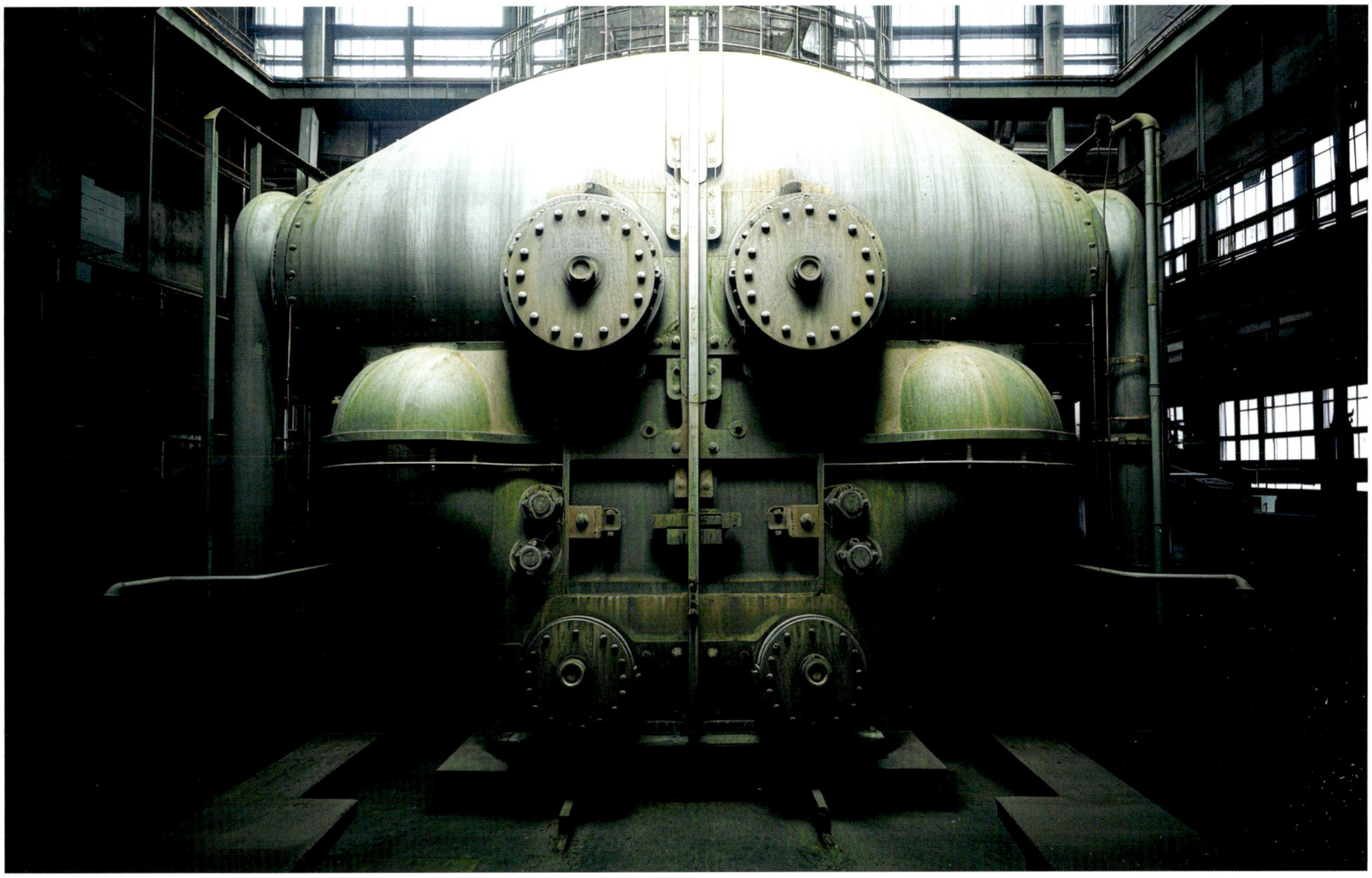
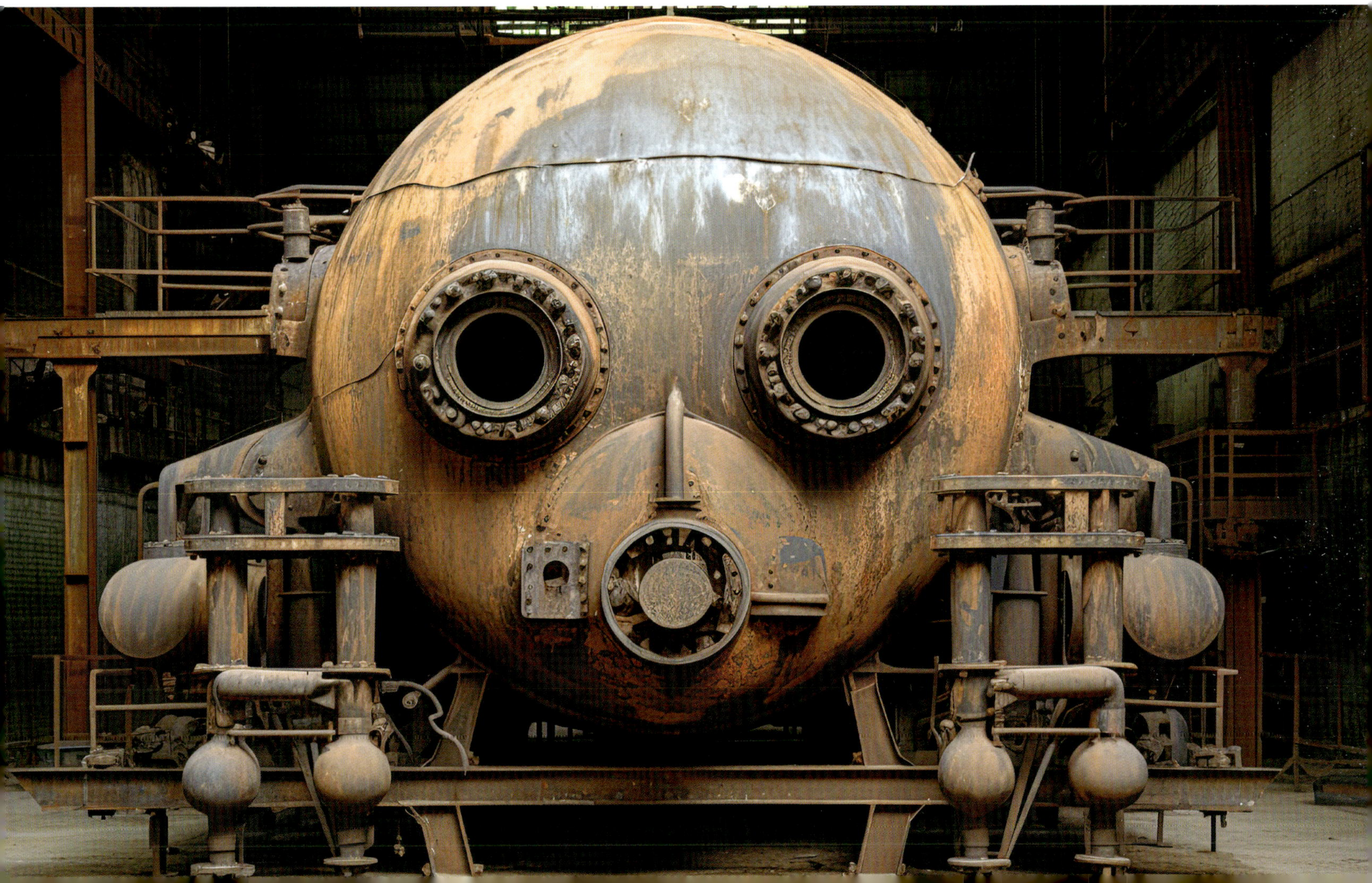

The angels' share

The lands that gave birth to illustrious nectars have become forbidden zones, their borders redrawn by mysterious political intrigues. The world's barriers have been erected, confining the oak casks to forgotten warehouses. The lush vineyards, now bound by barbed wire, lie abandoned.

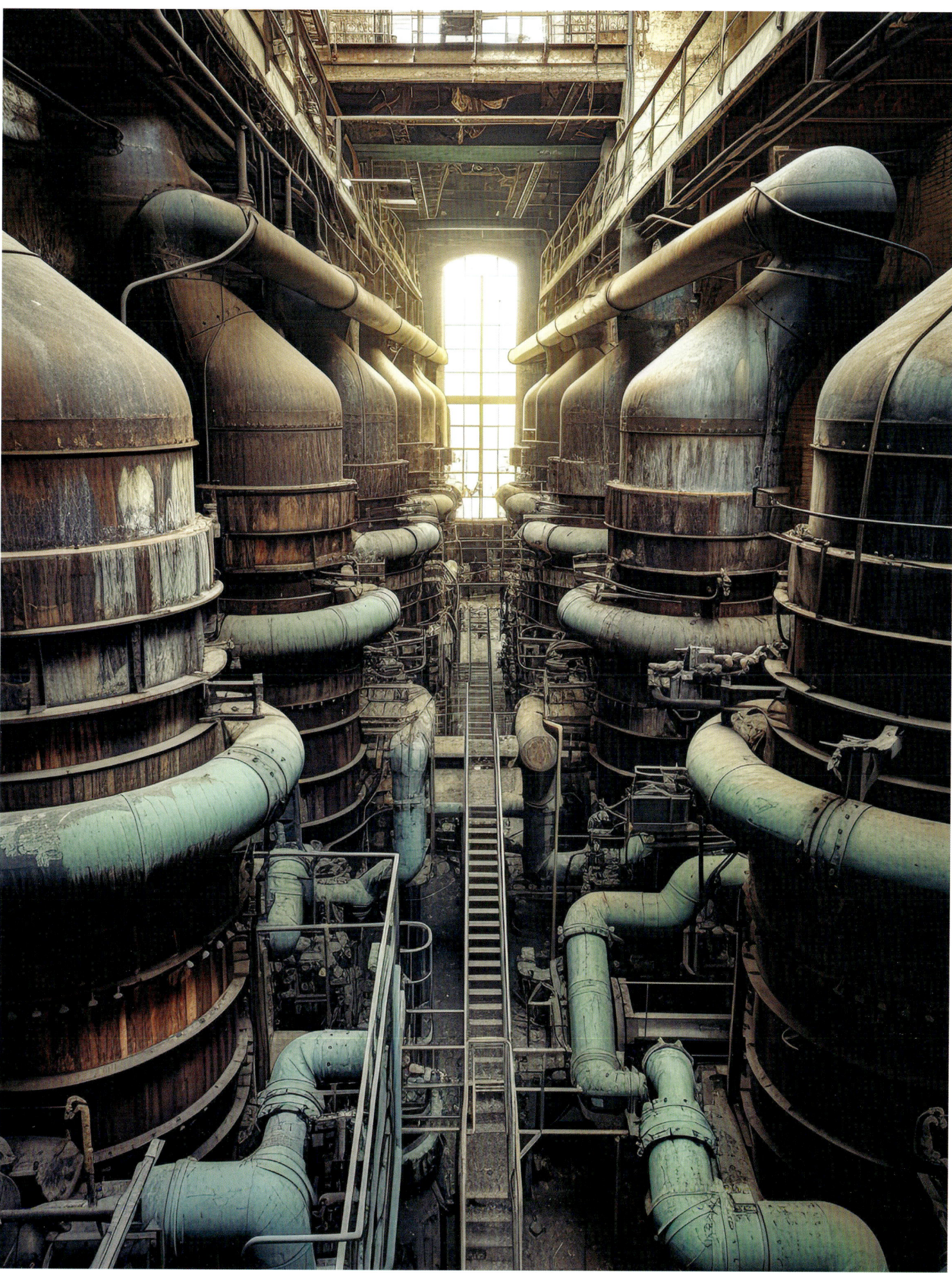

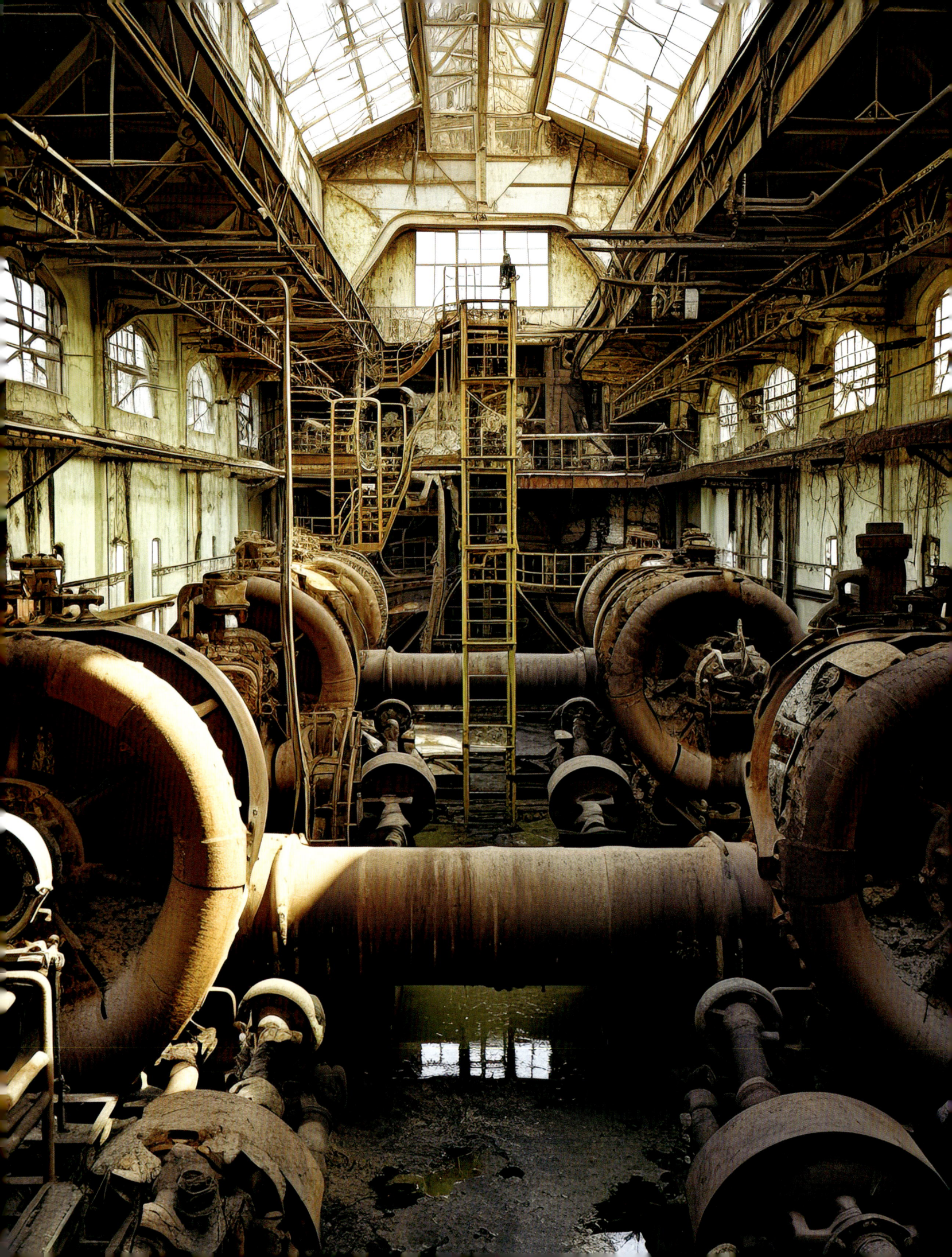

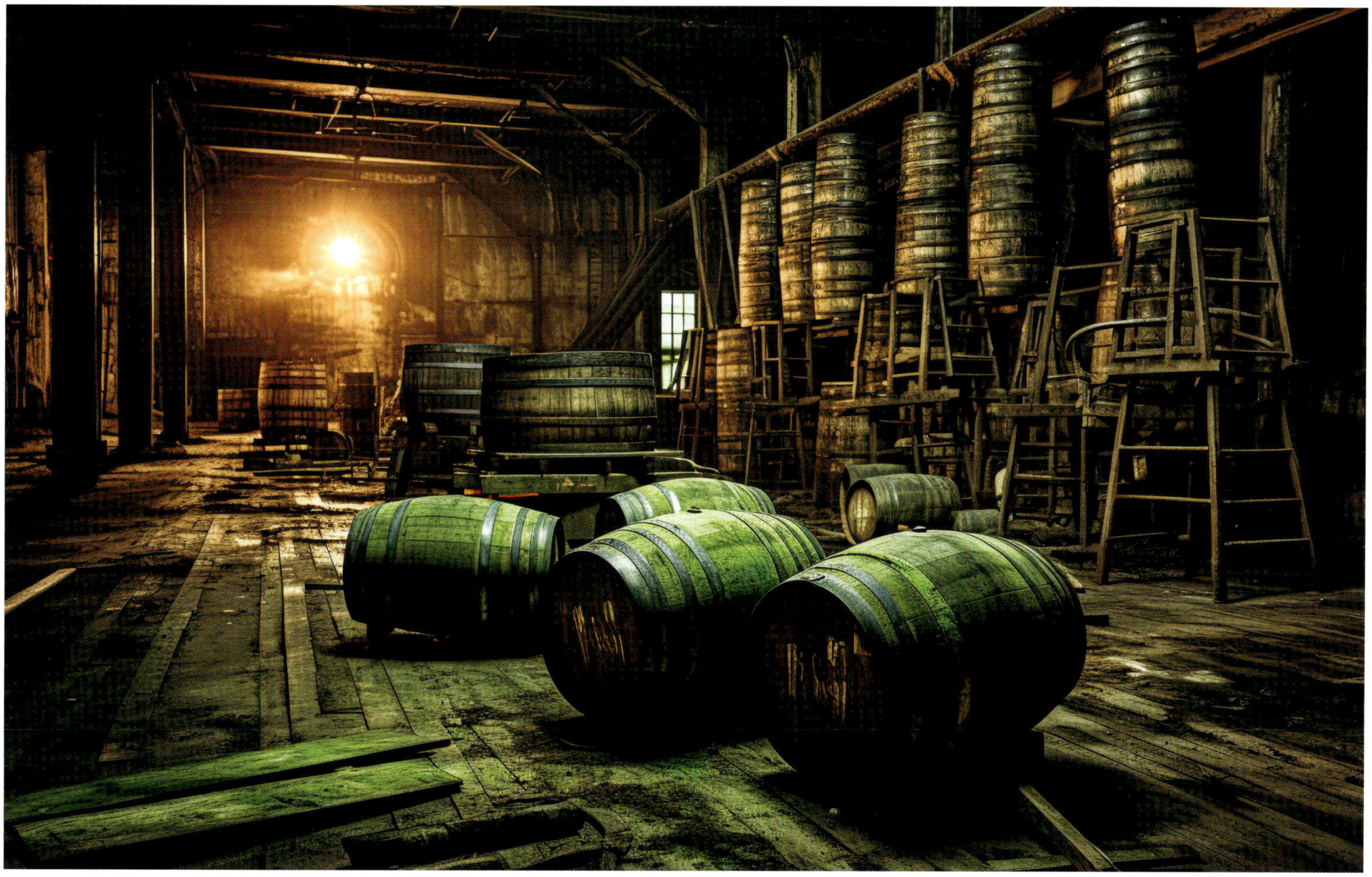

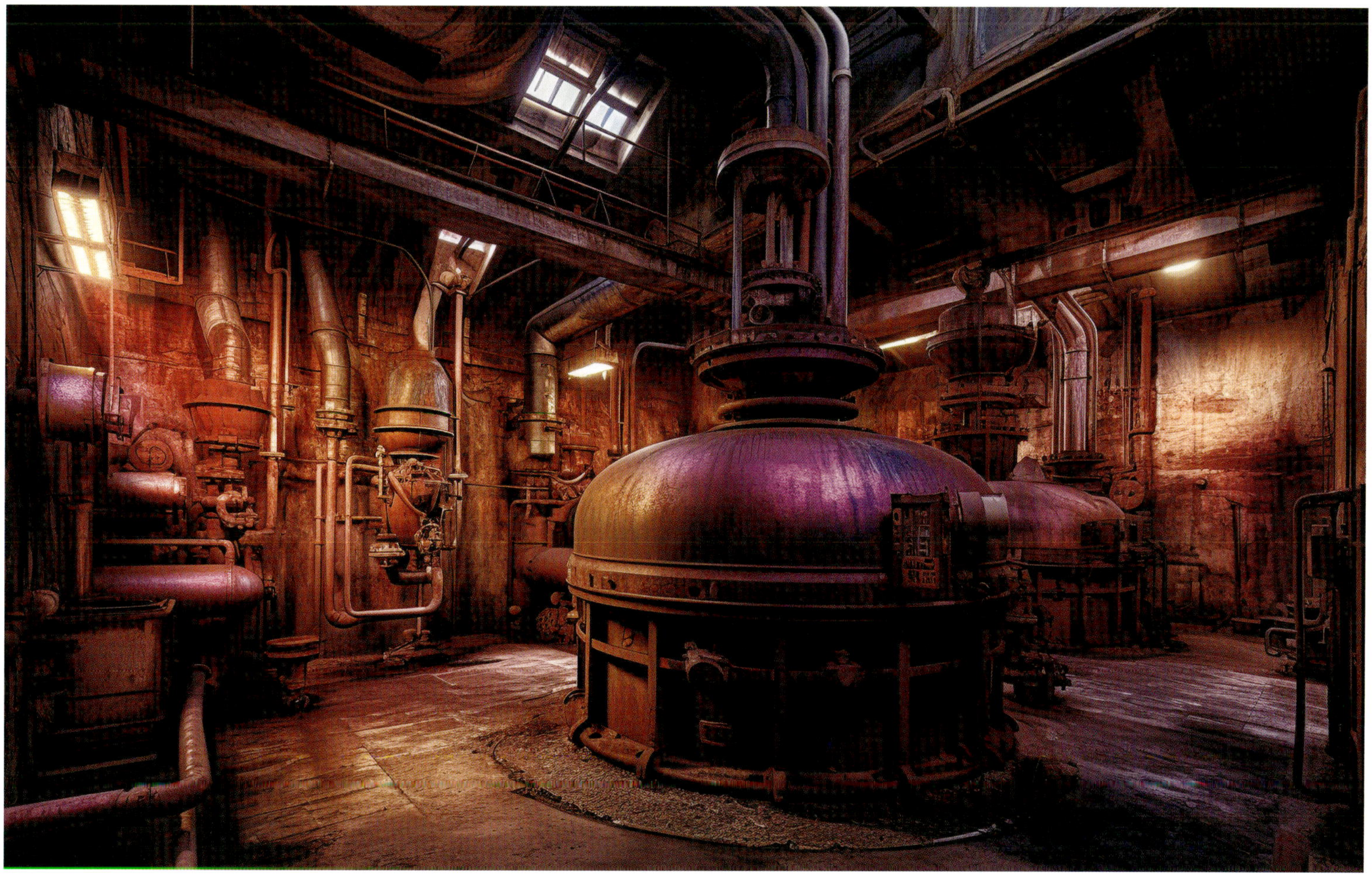

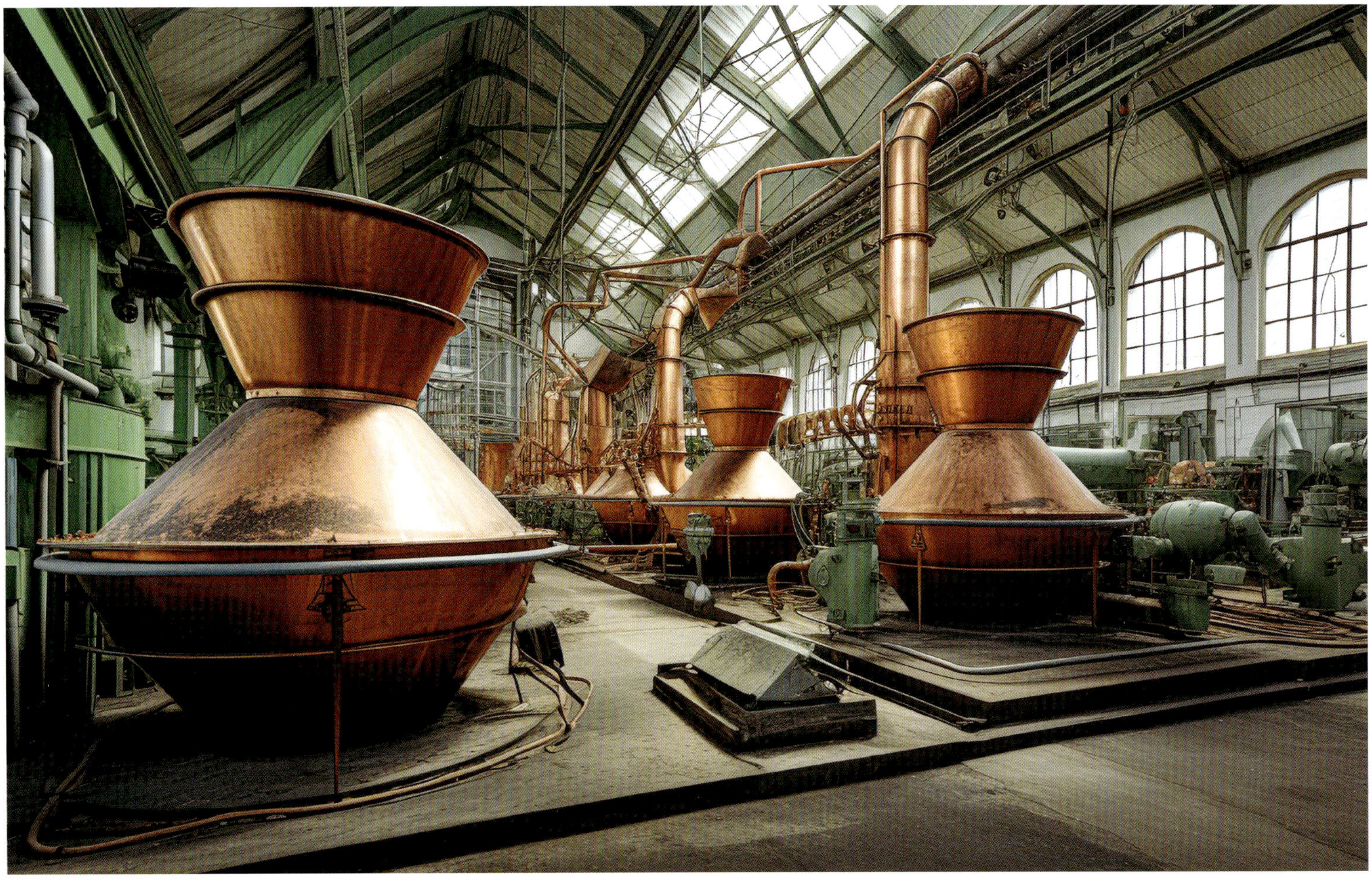

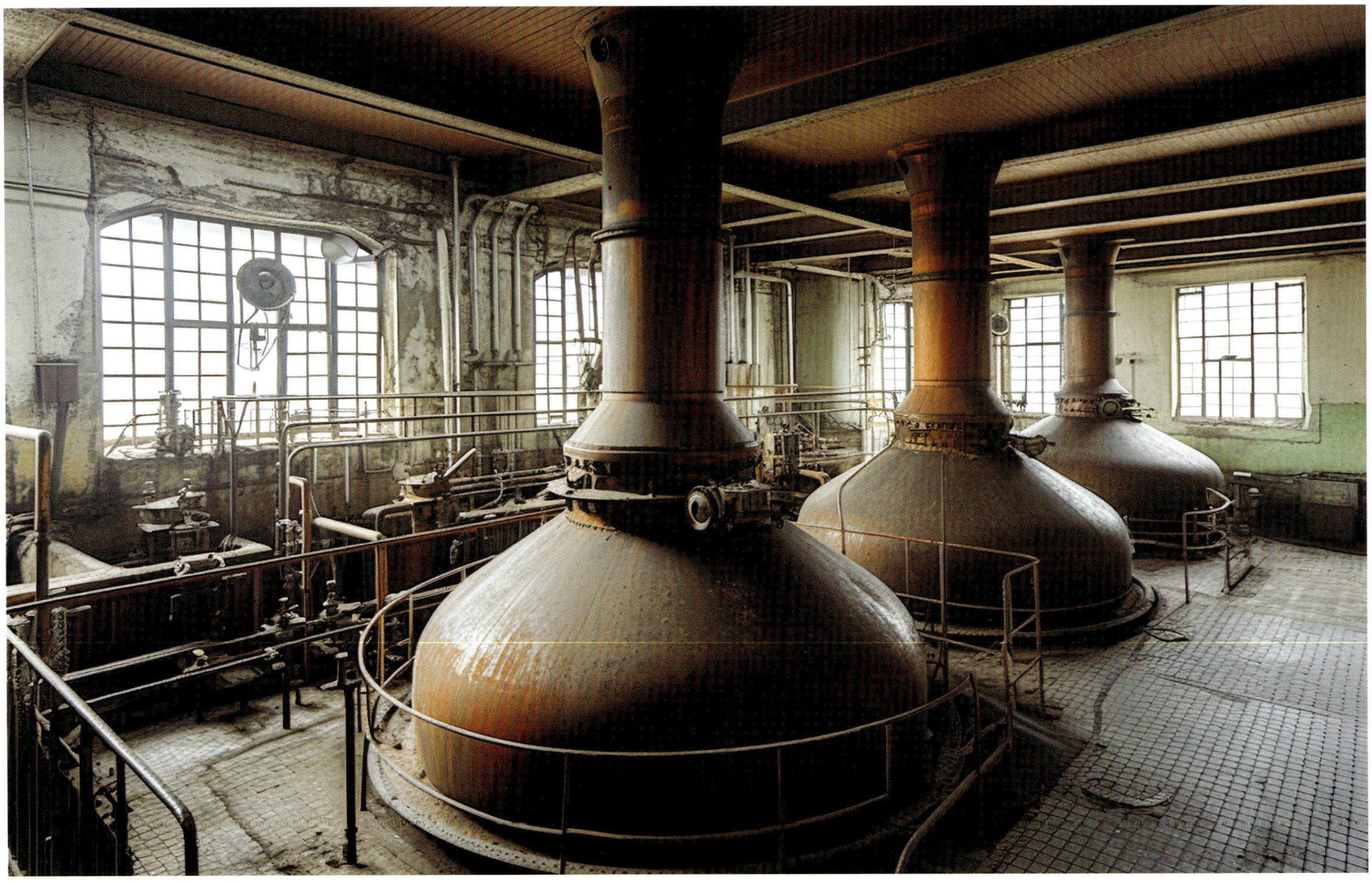

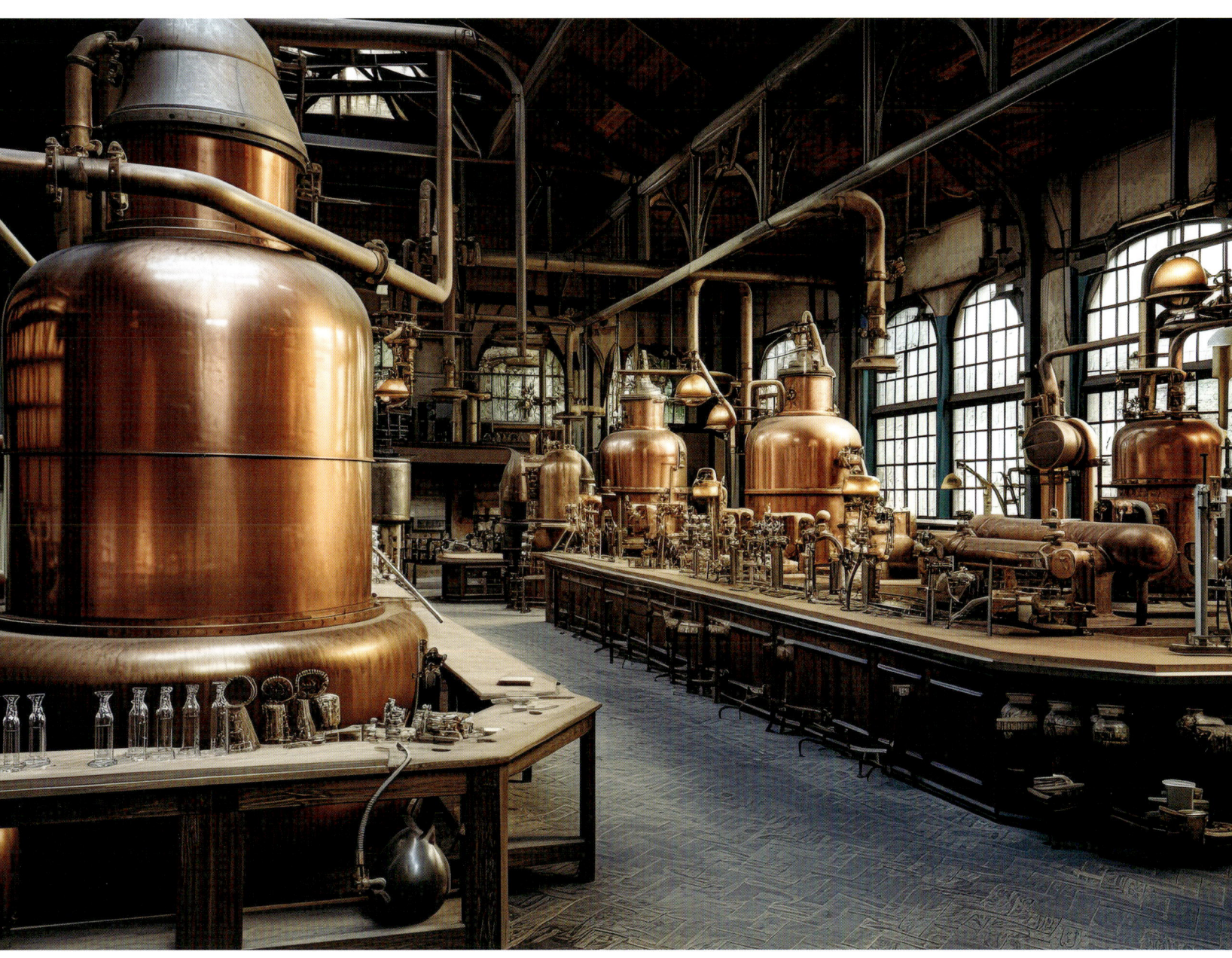

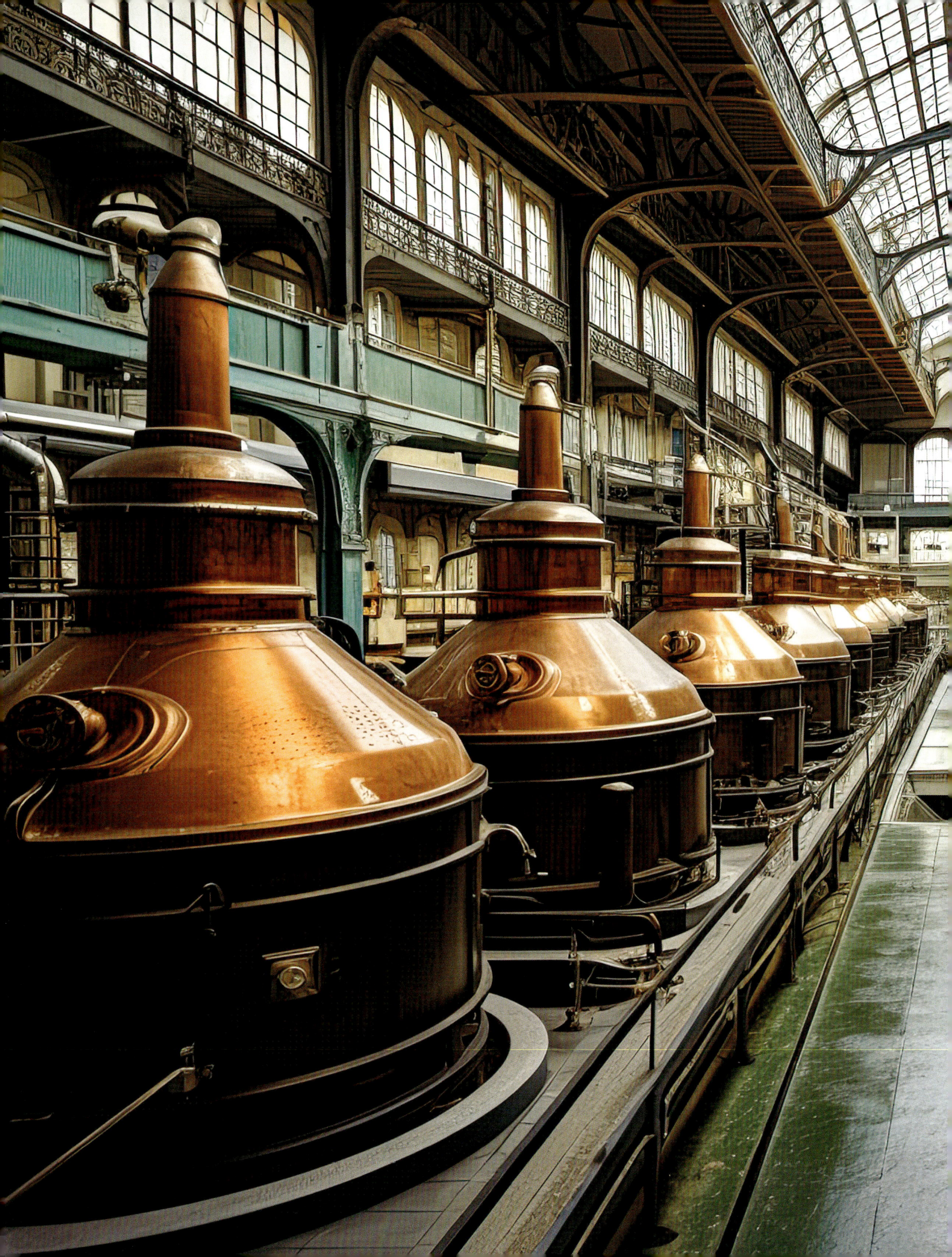

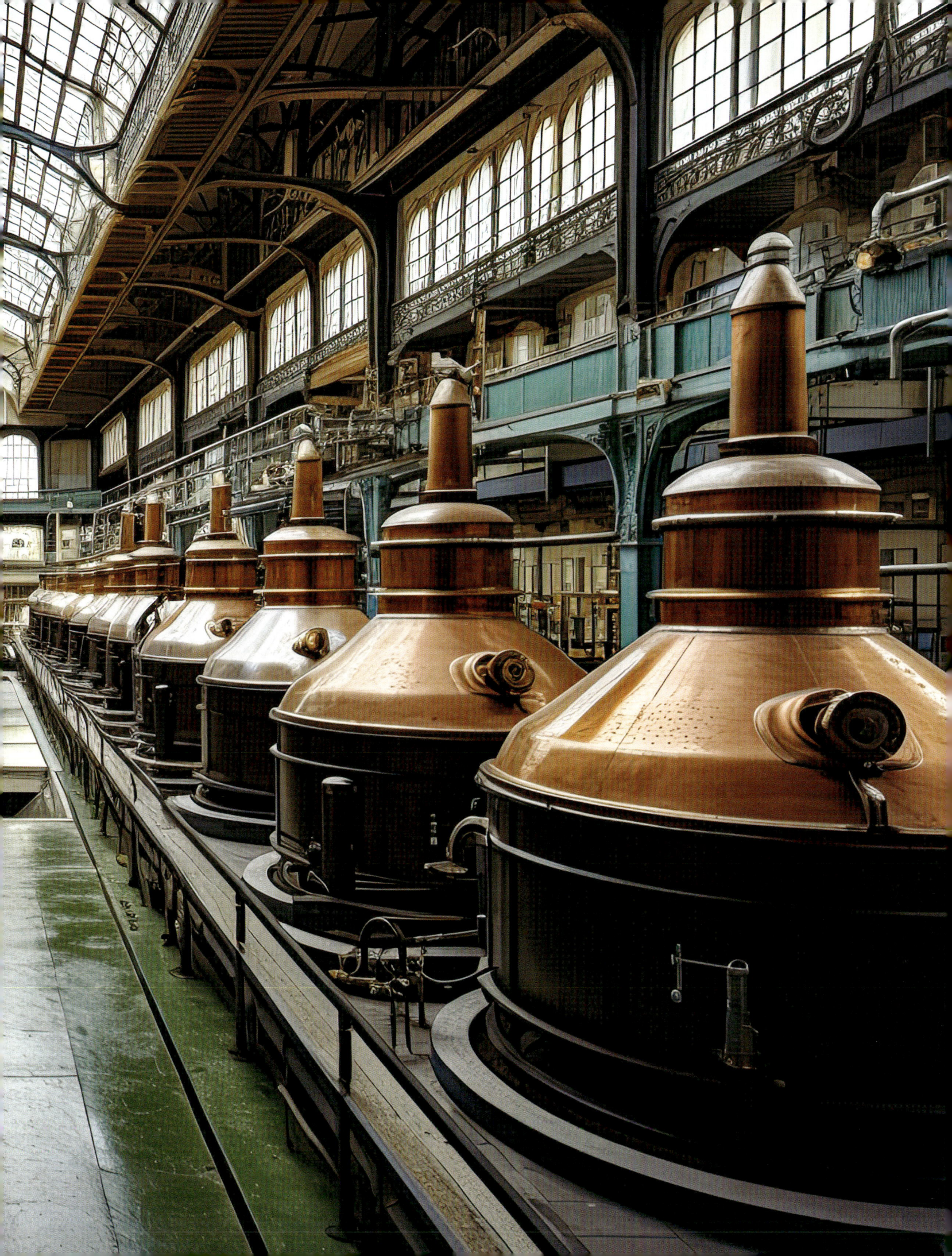

Vaults of death

They're unmissable in the landscape. The closer we get, the further they seem to recede into the distance, refusing to let us in on their secret. Almost all the cooling towers were blown up after fossil fuels were abandoned and nuclear facilities decommissioned. And yet, a few sites remain in Eastern Europe, which refuses to give up its energy independence, even at the cost of failing to save the planet.

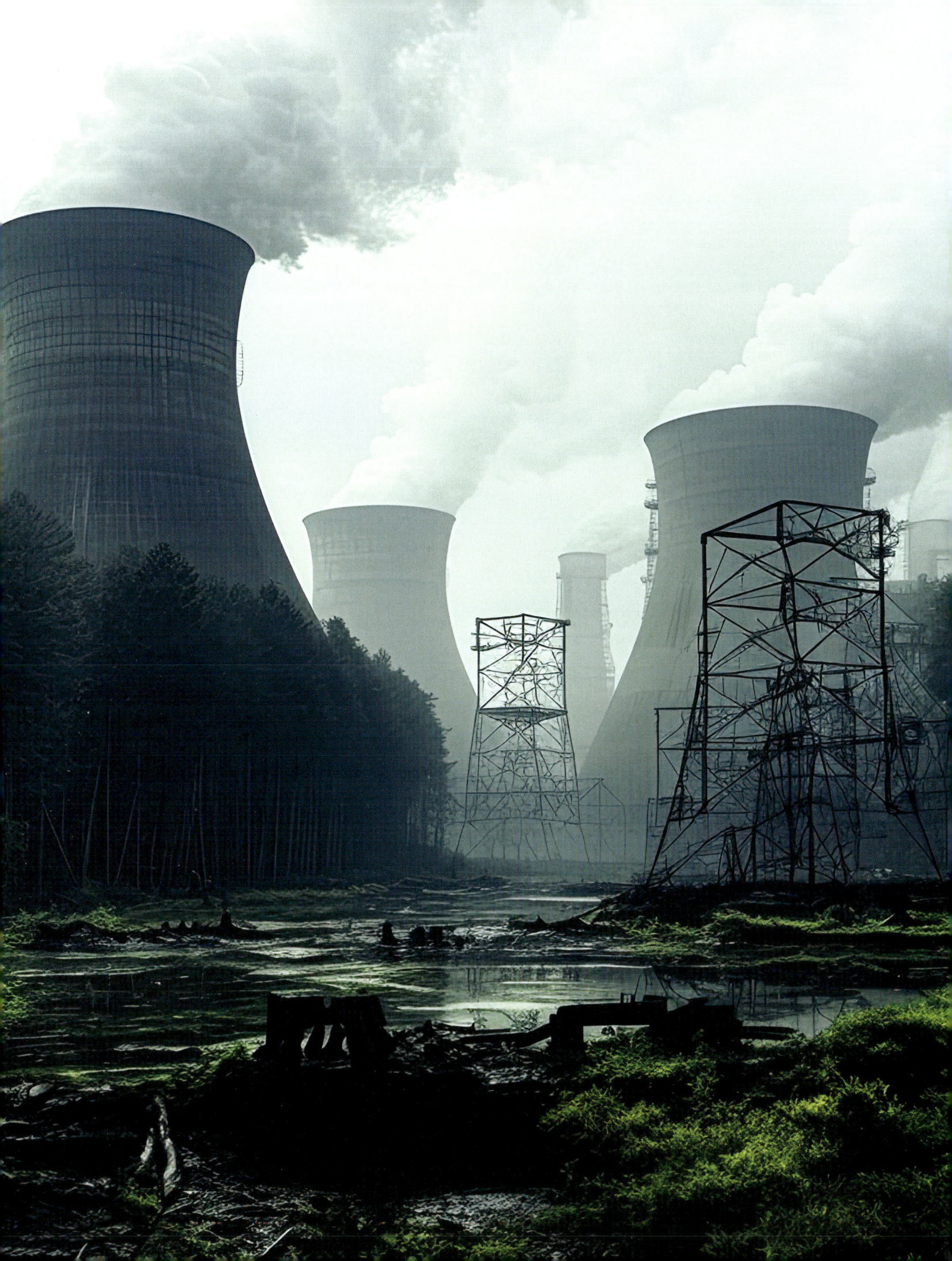

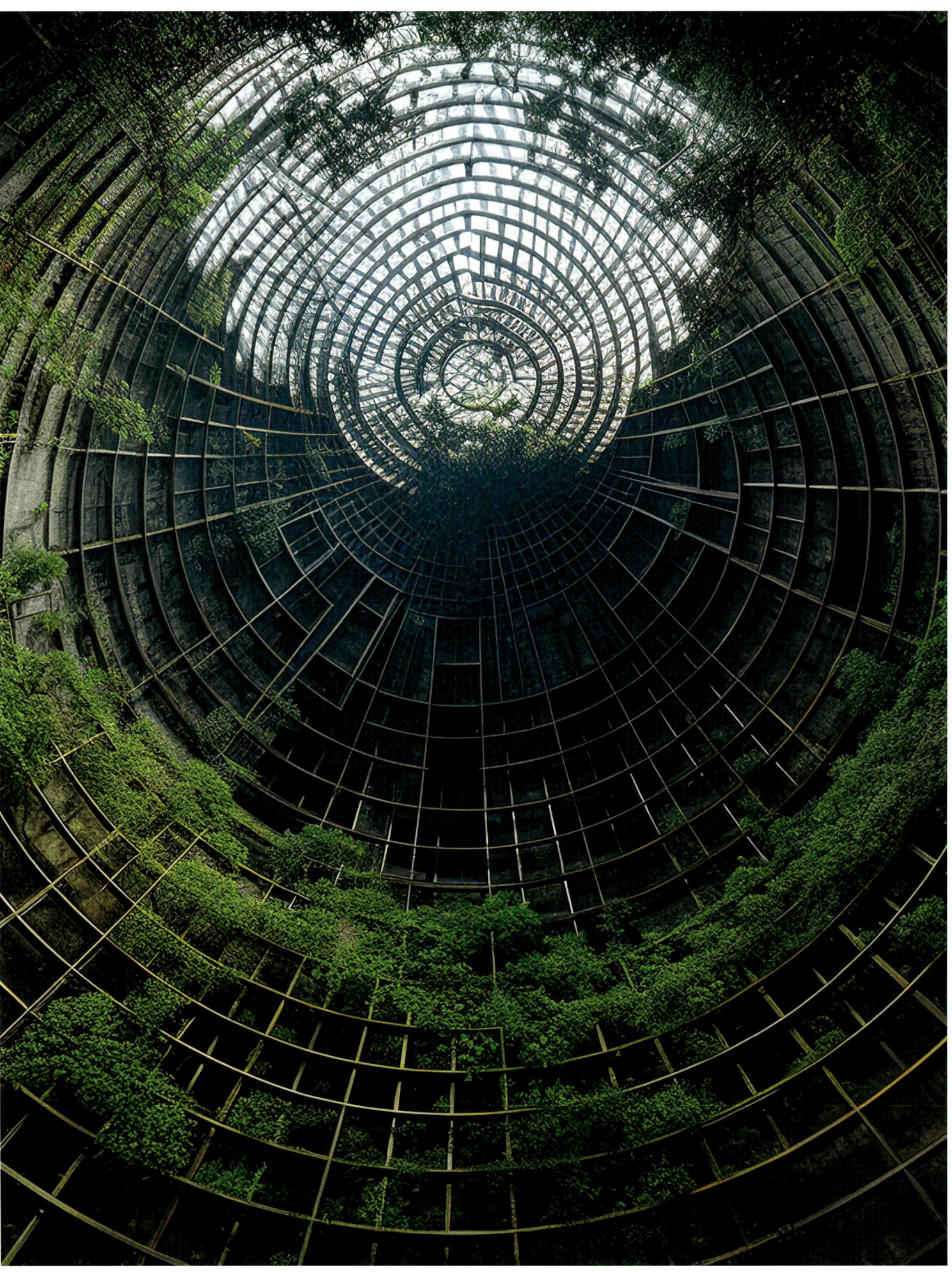

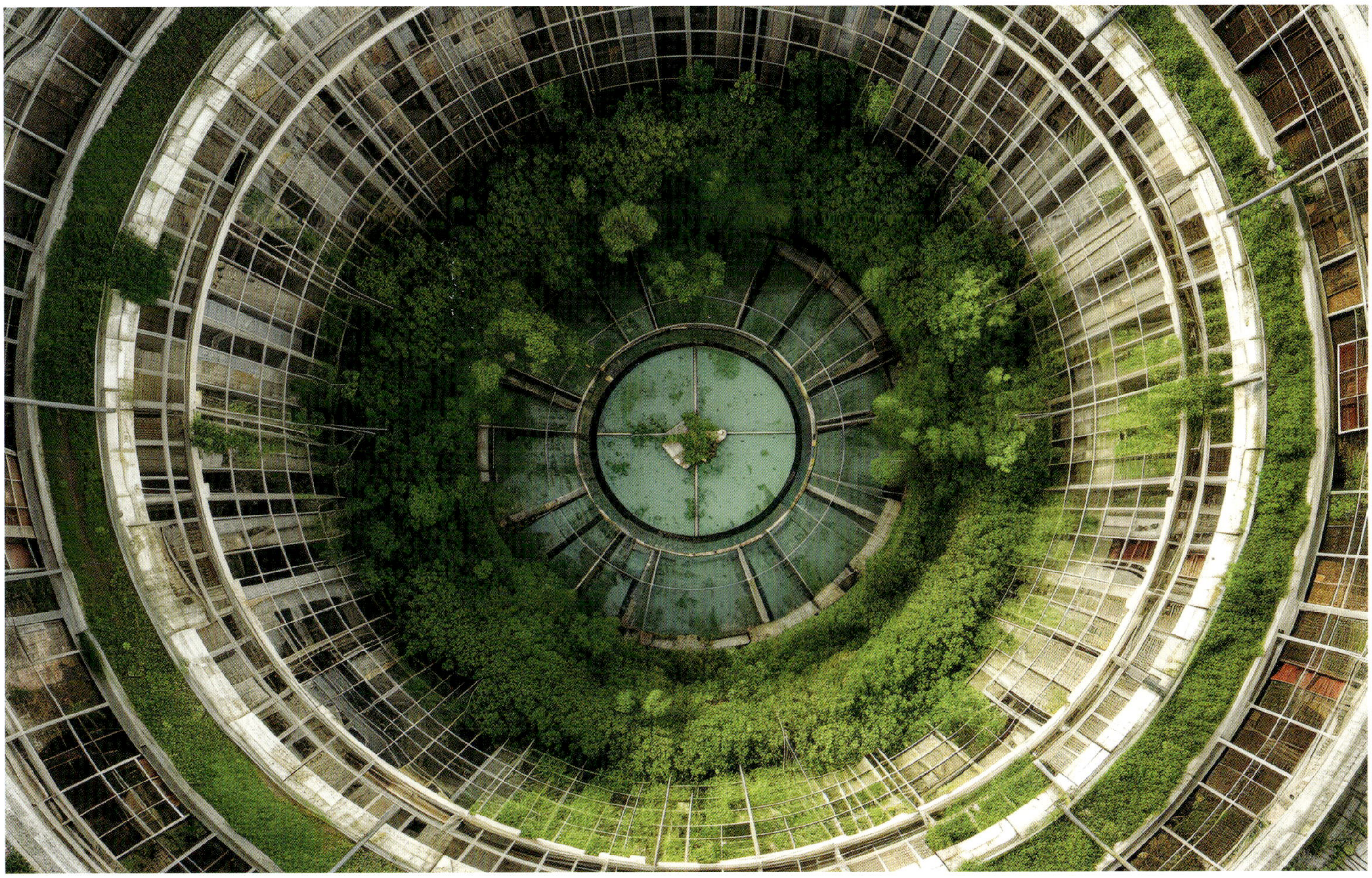

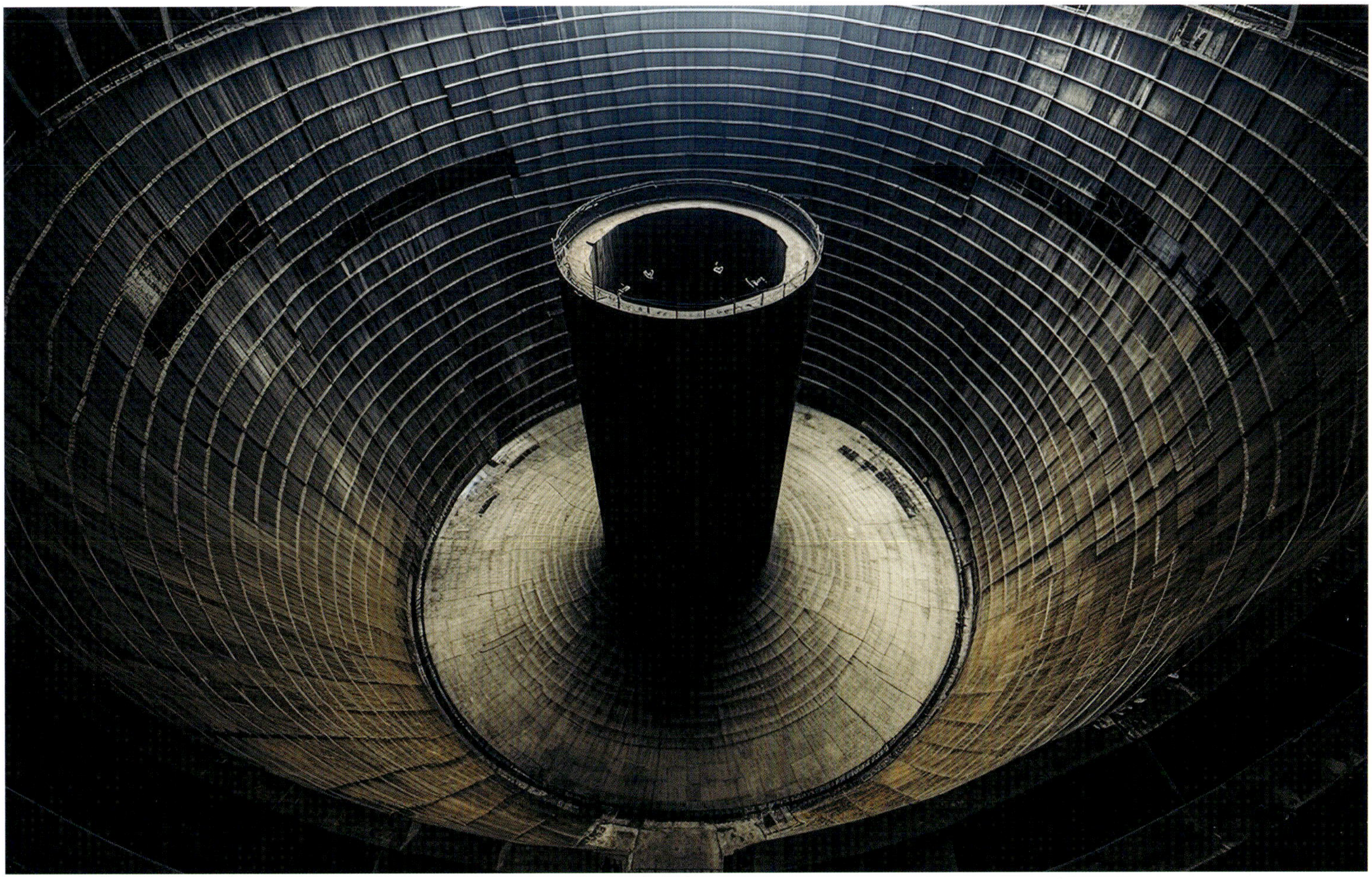

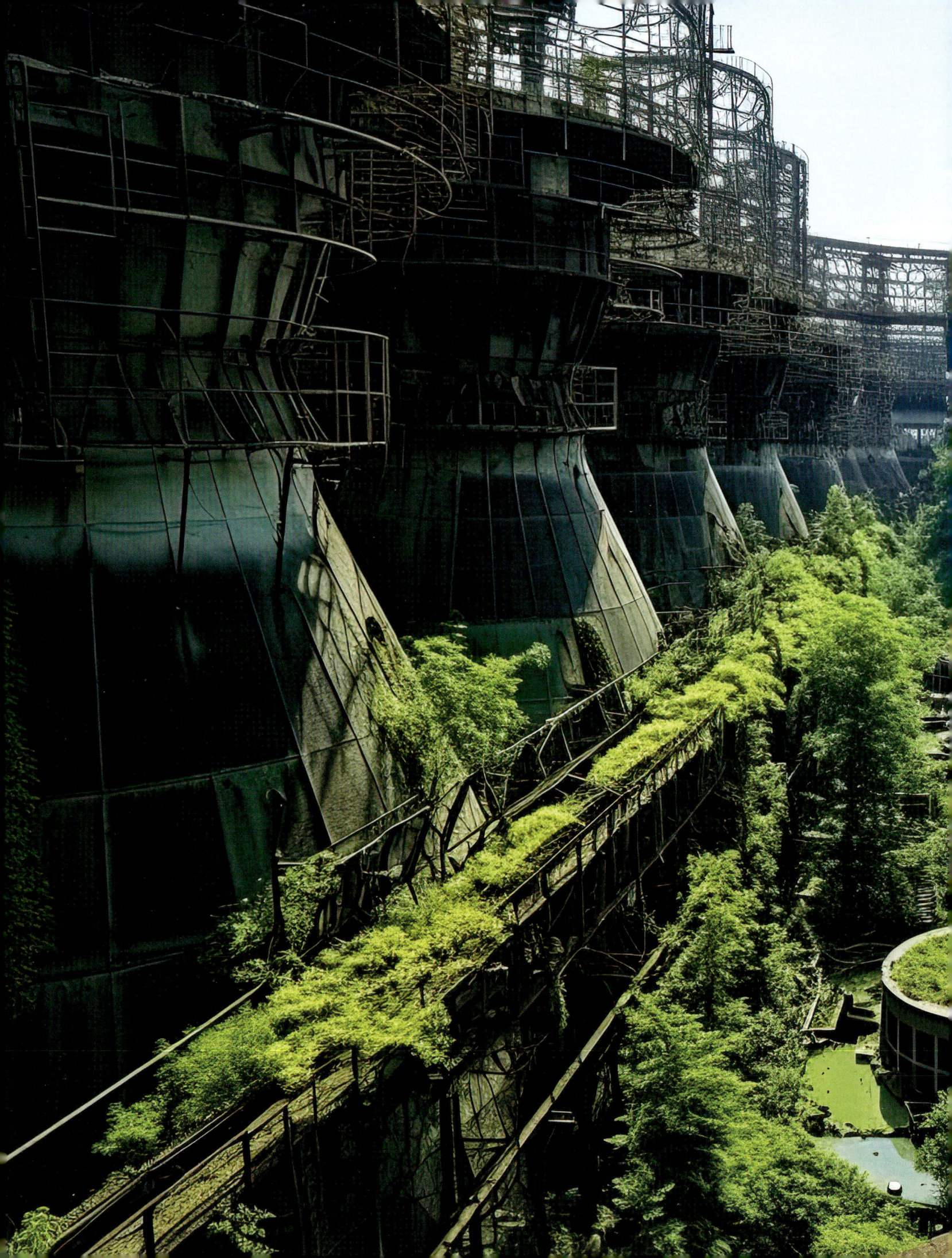

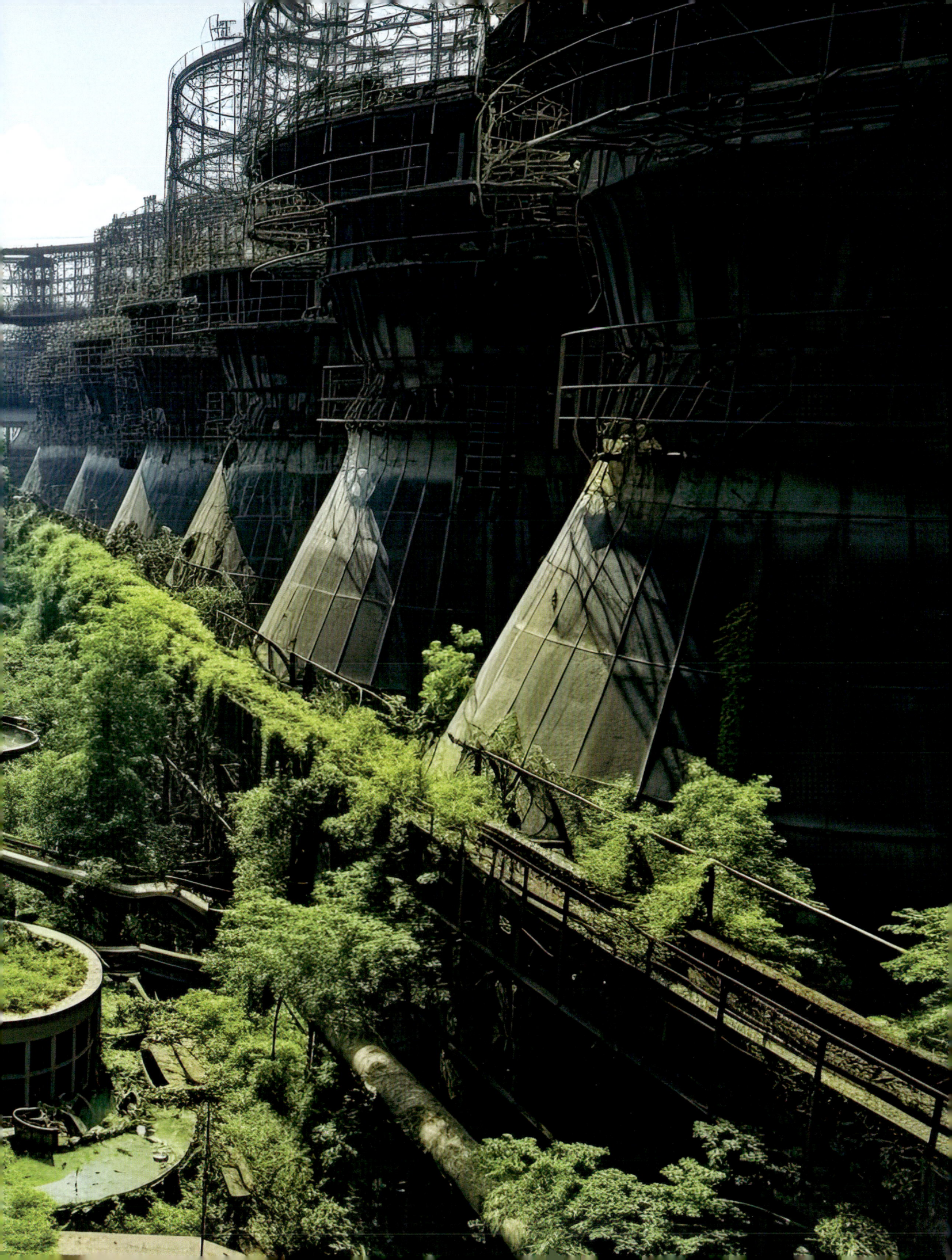

Sharing the same culture

Traditional drugs have gradually been replaced by chips implanted under the skin. Linked to mobile applications, they deliver hallucinogenic experiences whose intensity is proportional to the popularity of the user's profile. Losing all contact with the real world in favour of an artificial and addictive euphoria, cyber-junkies are now shooting up likes delivered on data-sharing platforms.

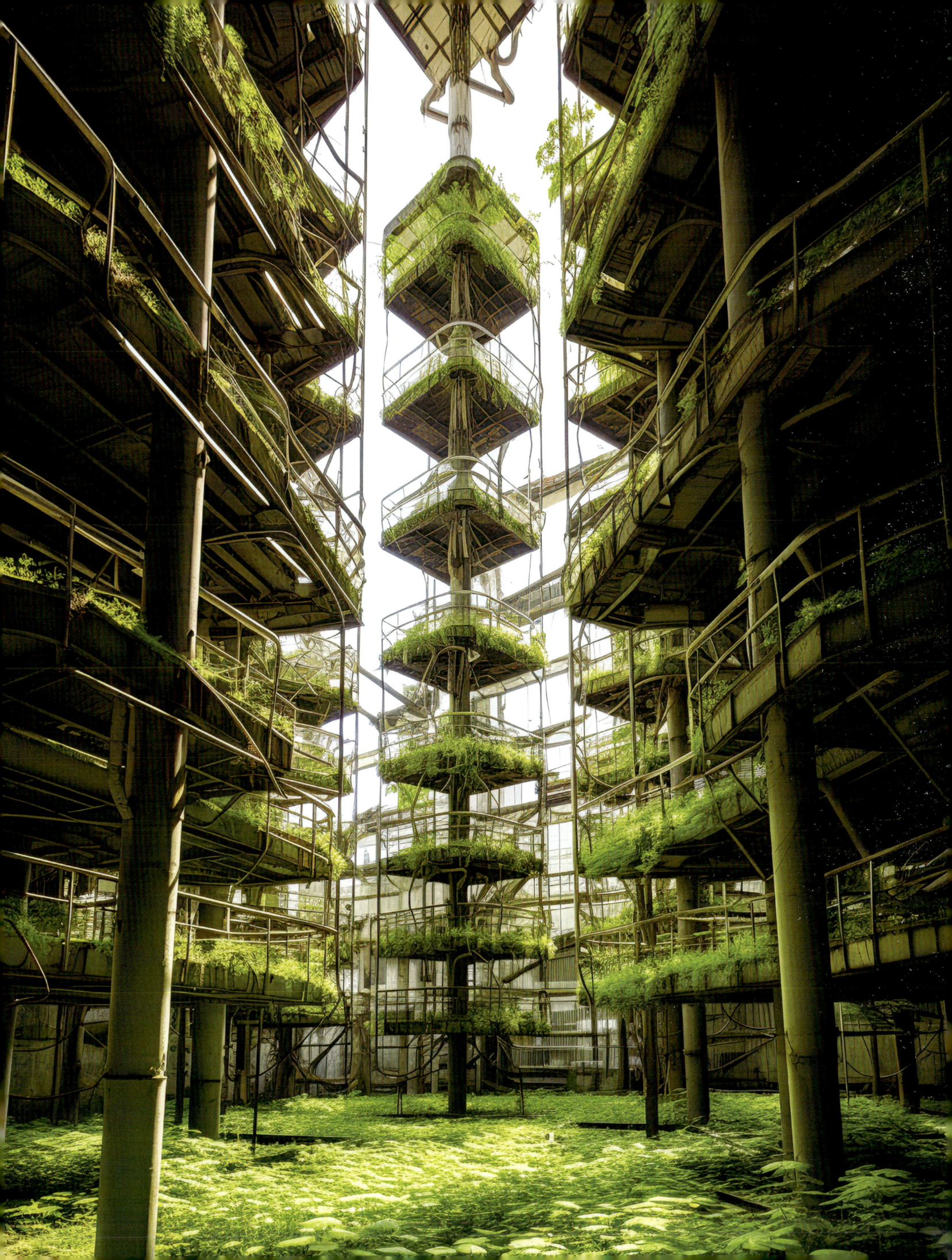

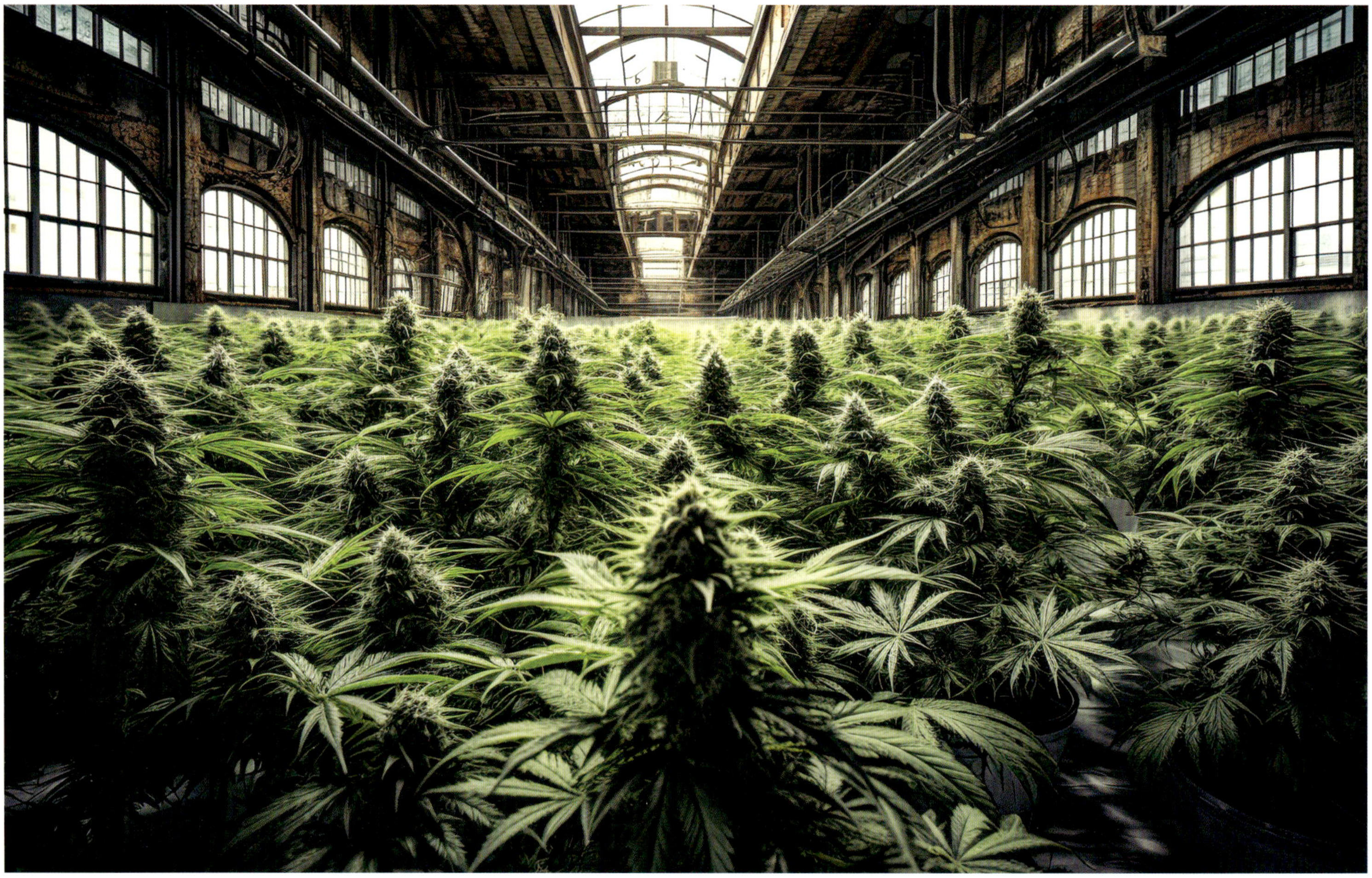

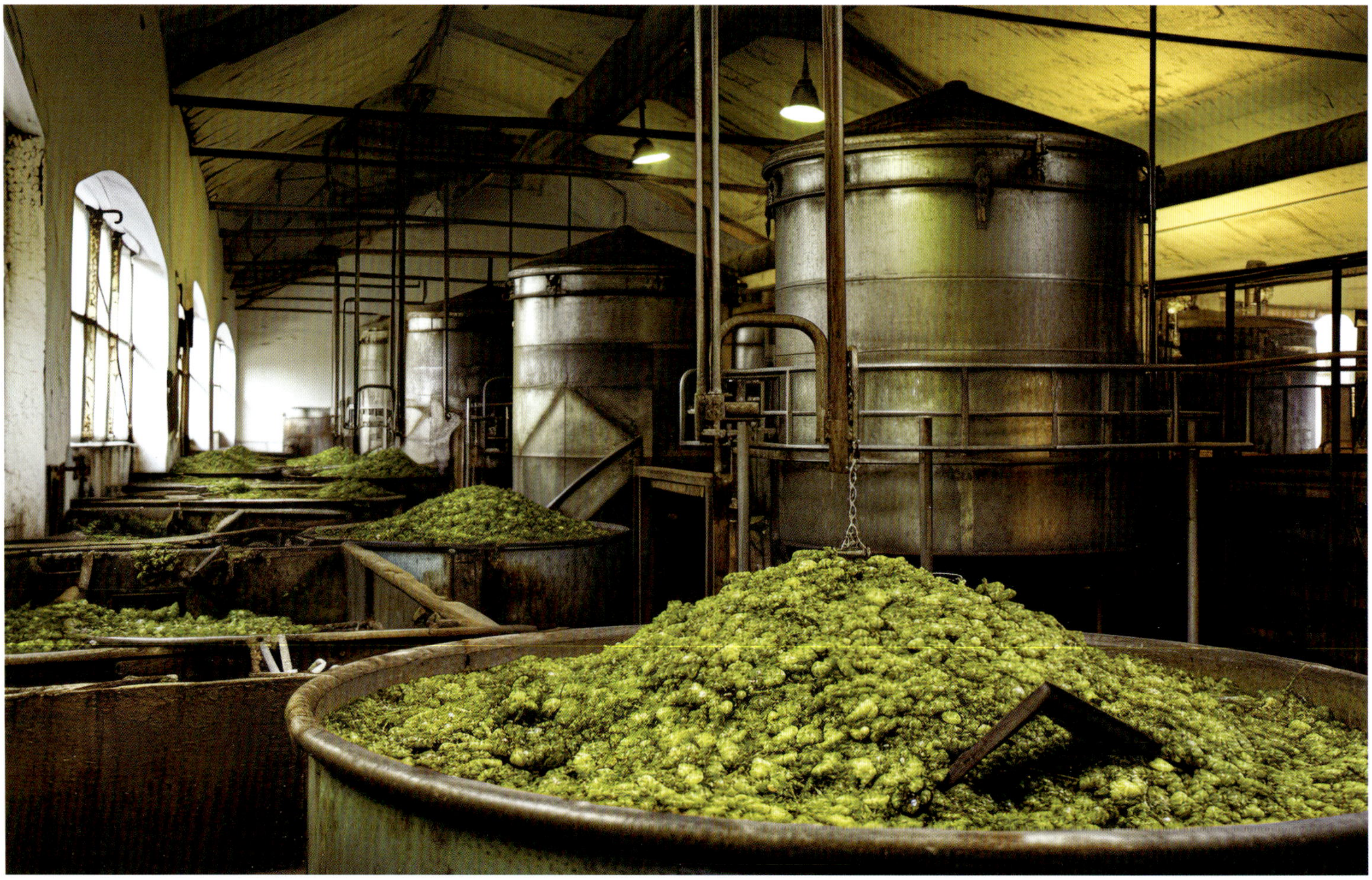

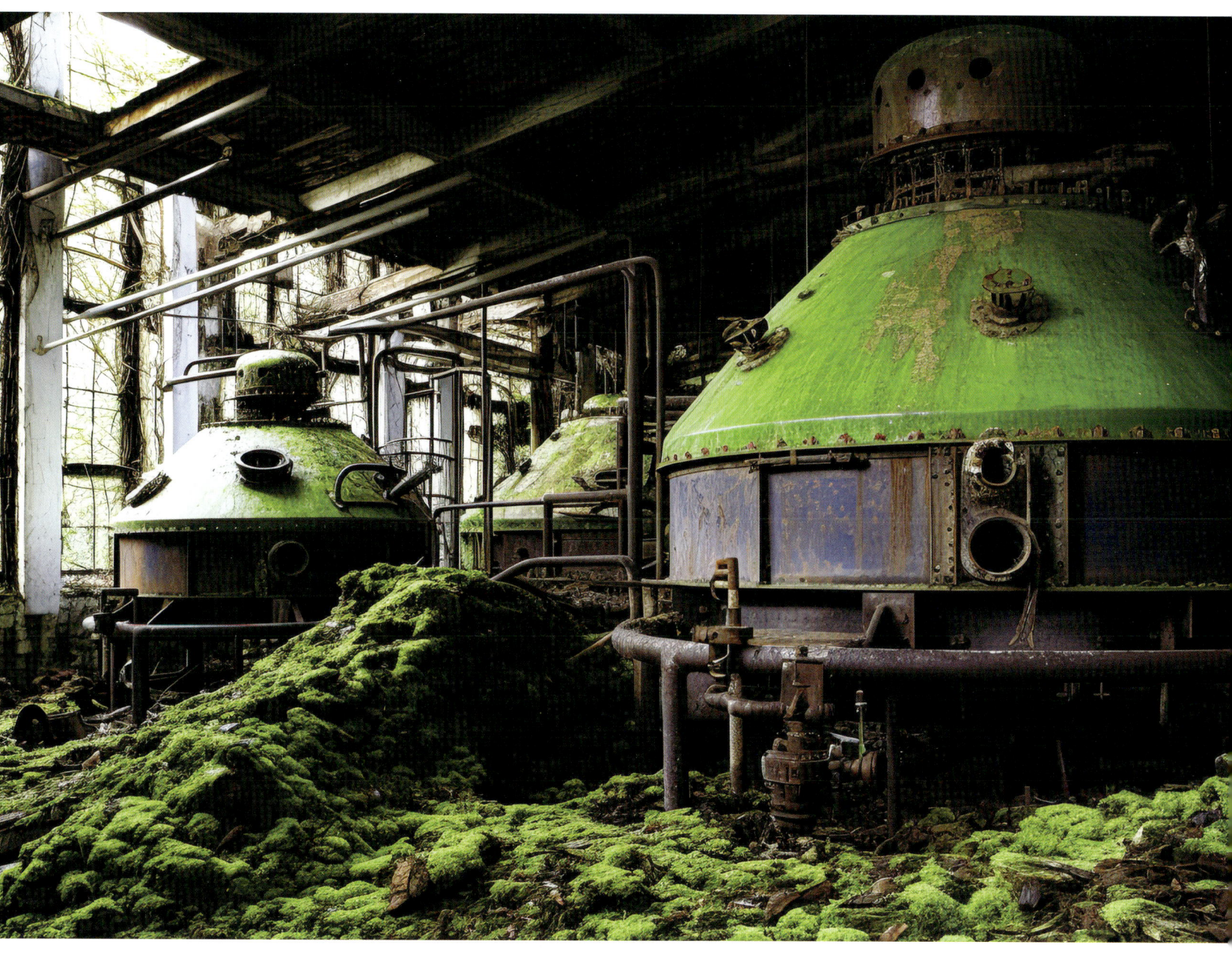

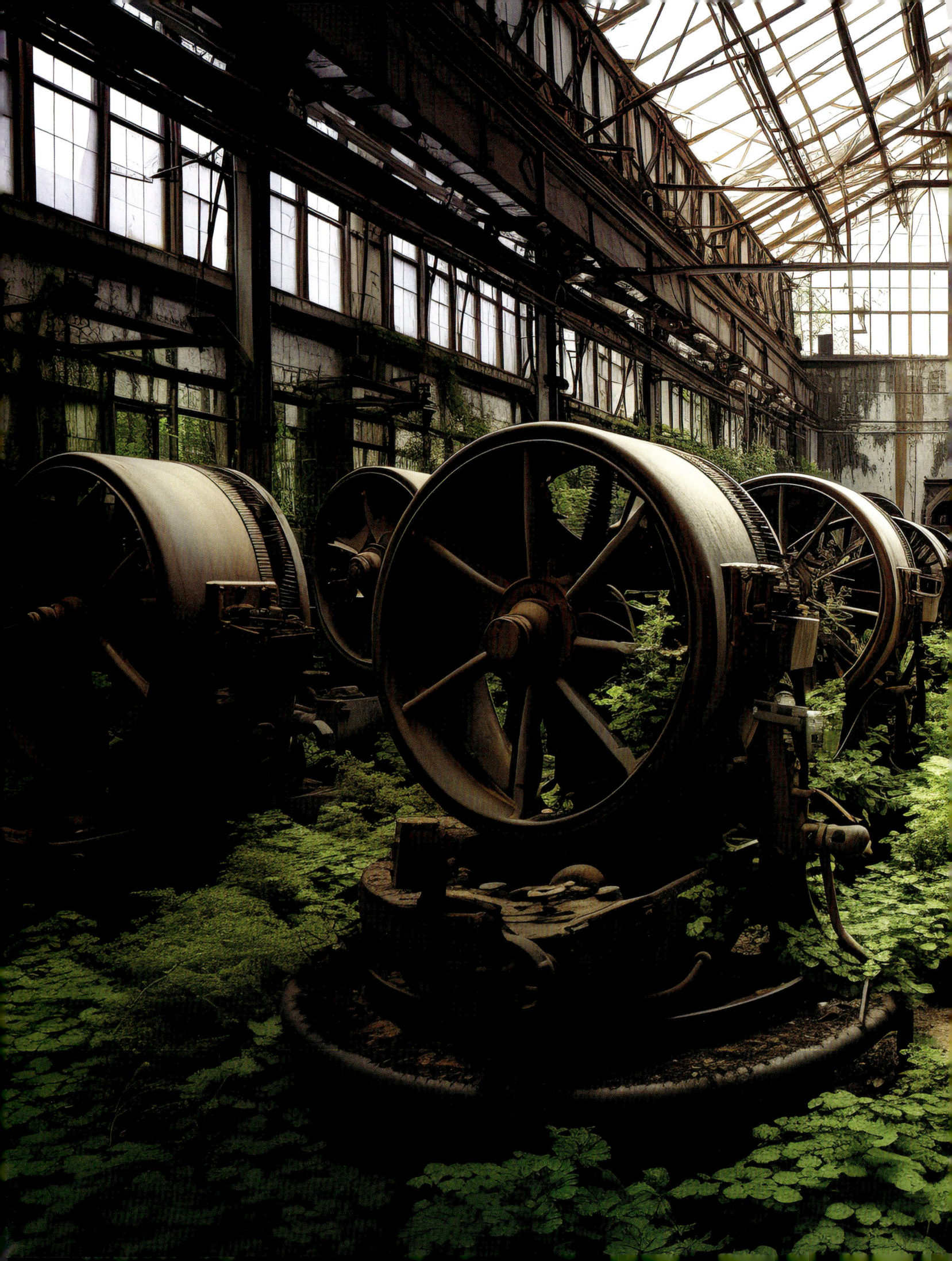

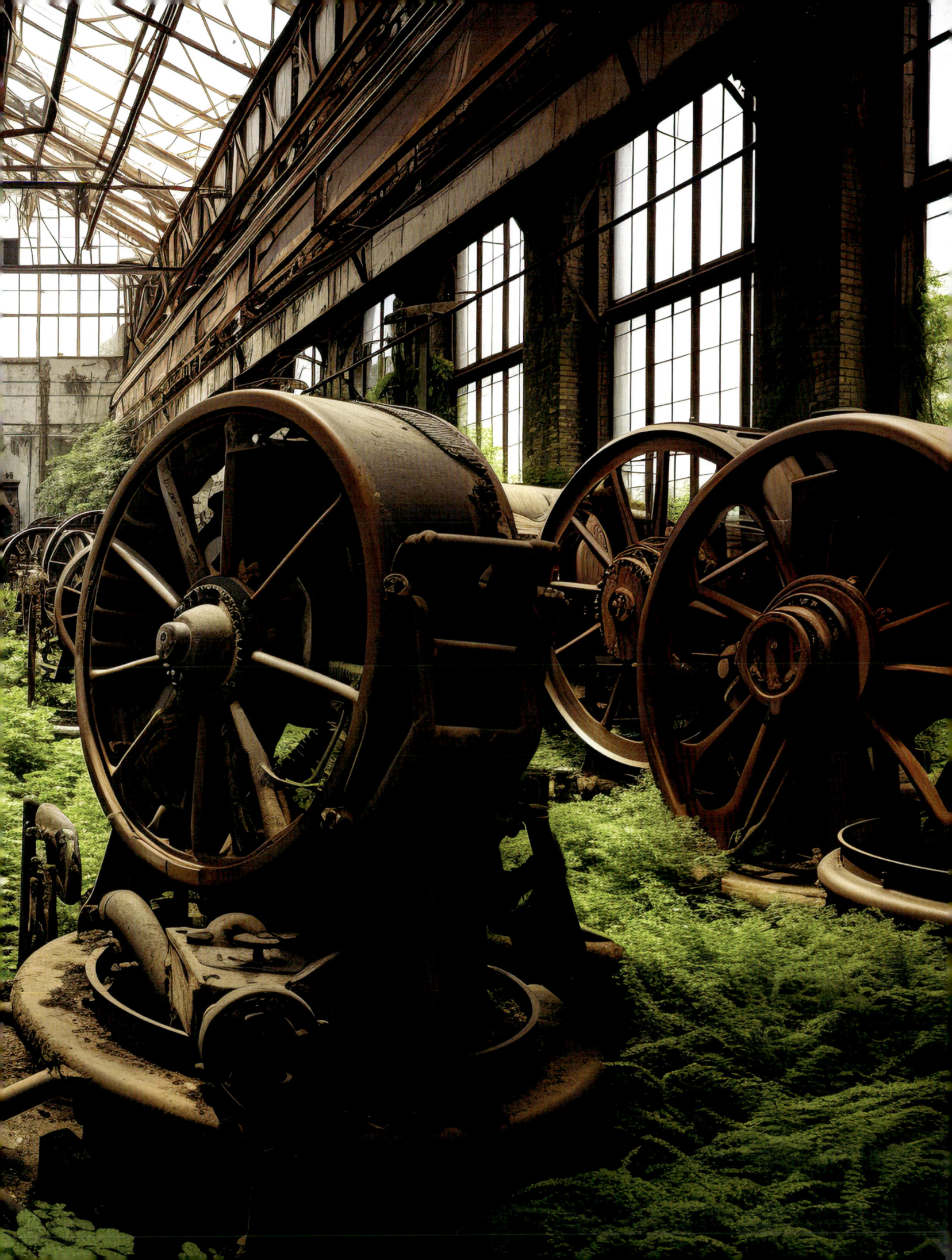

Once upon a faith

Everywhere in the world, places of worship have fallen into disrepair. The veneration of screens and Big Data has supplanted the hold that religions had over people for centuries. Slowly but surely, churches, chapels, synagogues and mosques have all closed their doors. For the first time in the history of humanity, different peoples have come to agree on the veneration of a single divine entity. Light emanates from touch screens, love for one's neighbour is measured by the number of likes, and every prayer must be preceded by a hashtag.

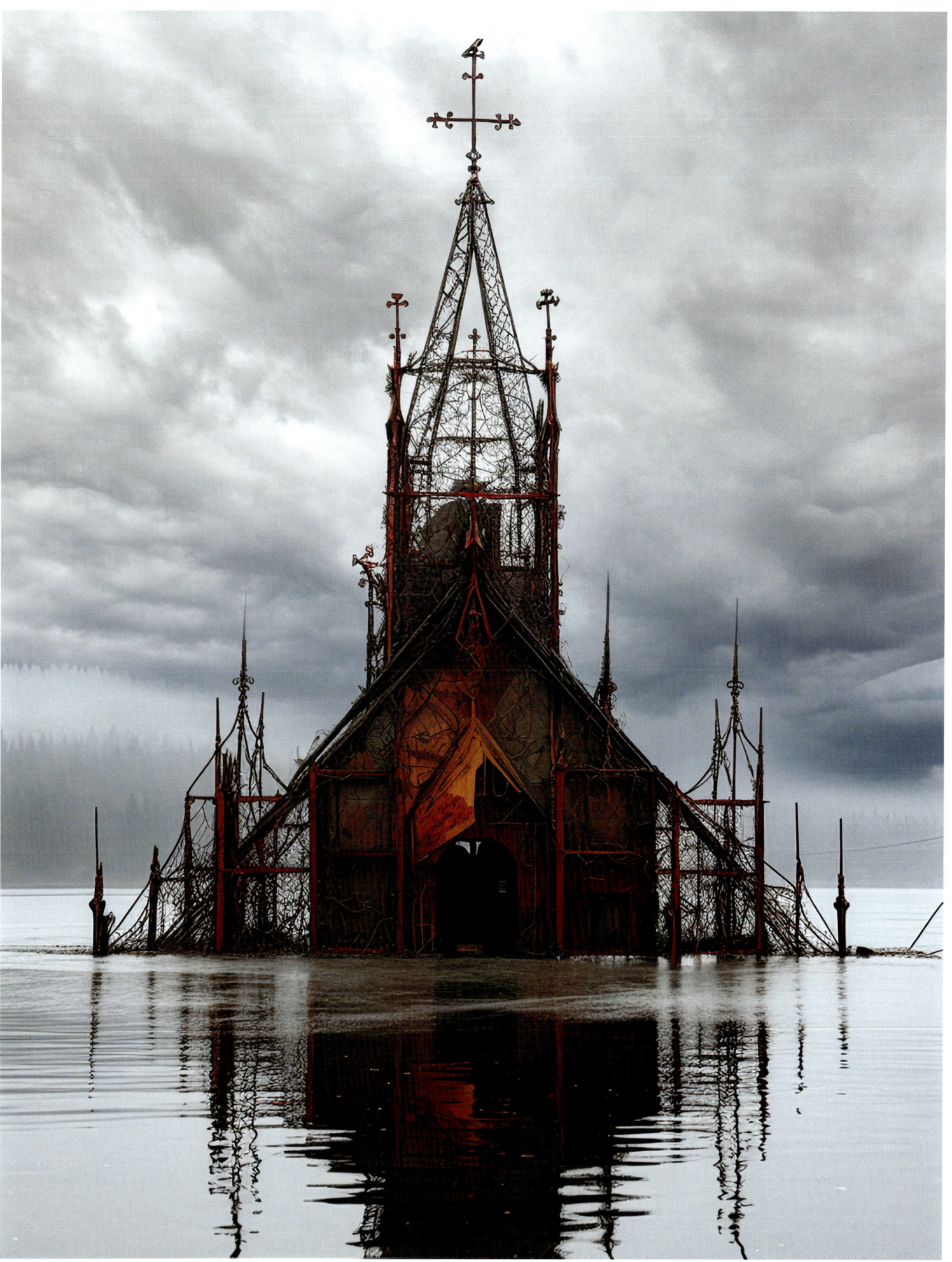

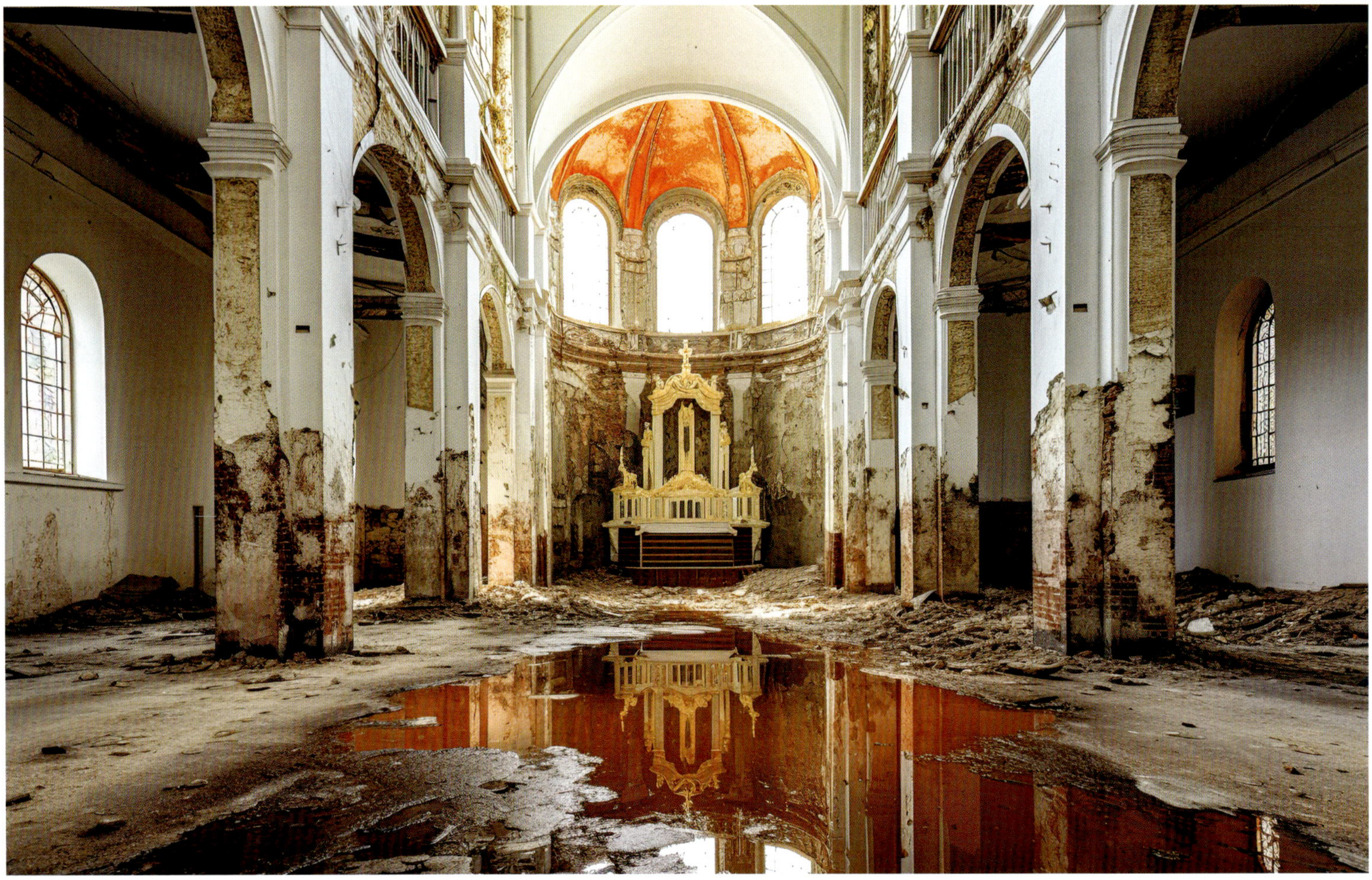

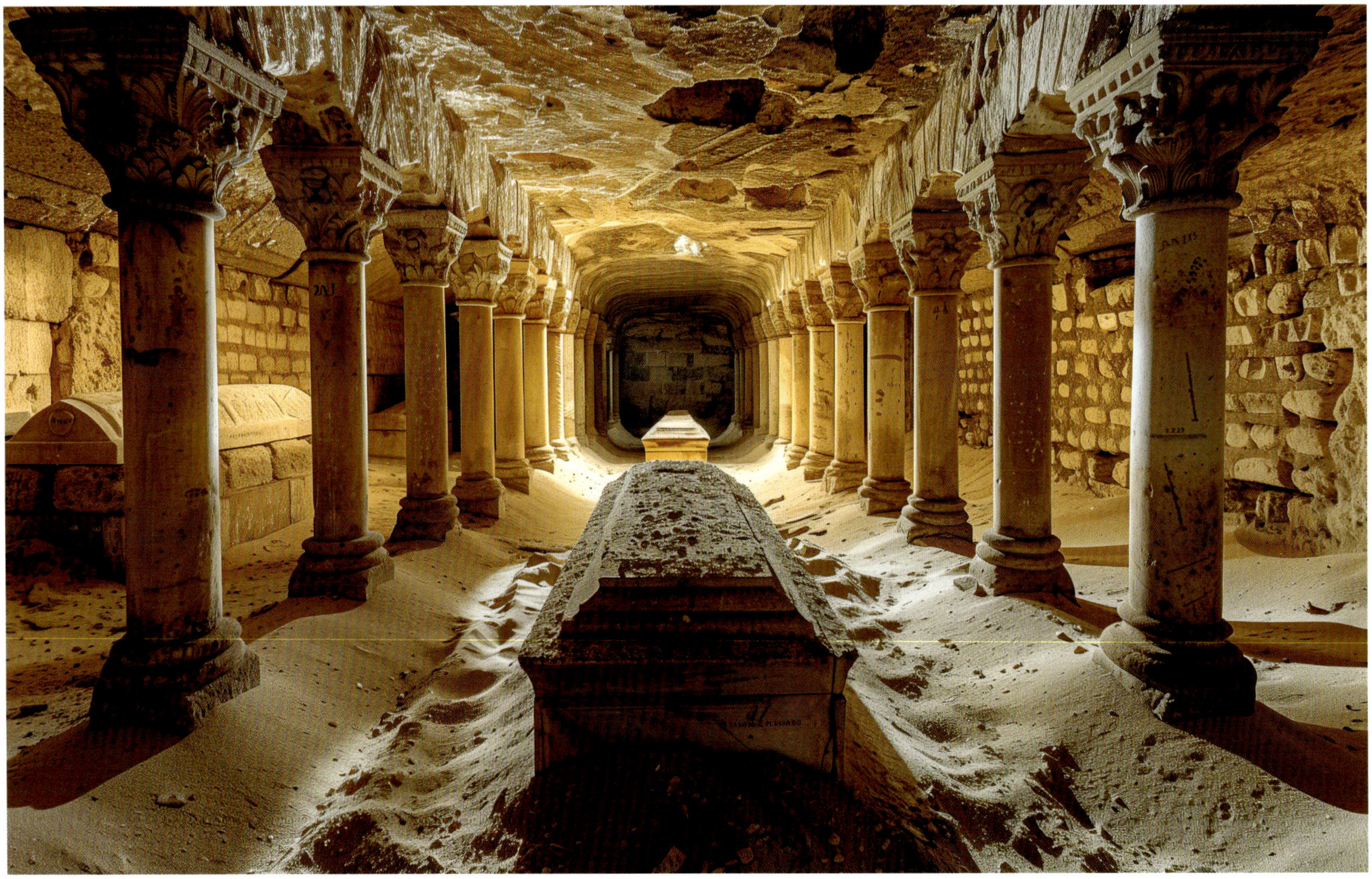

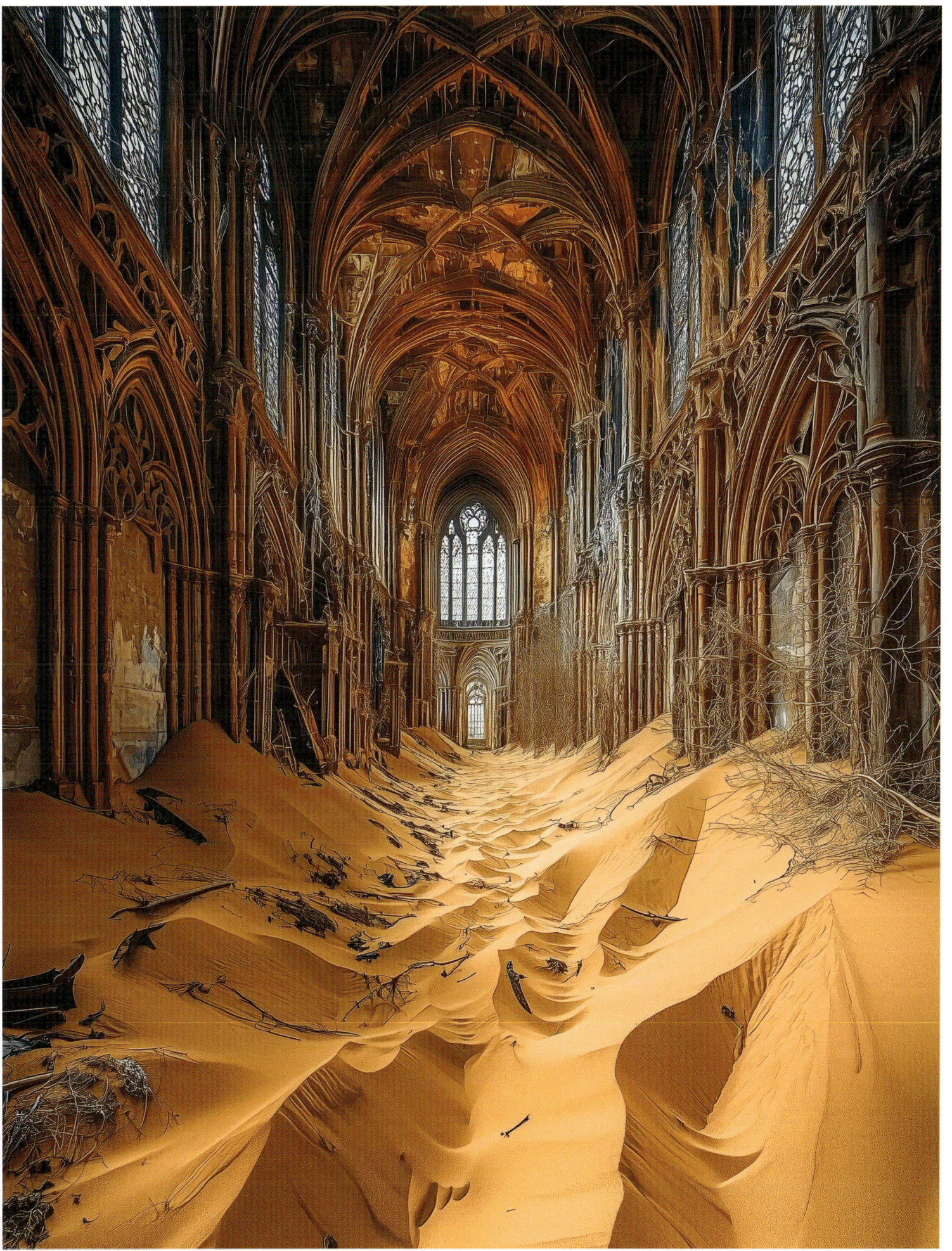

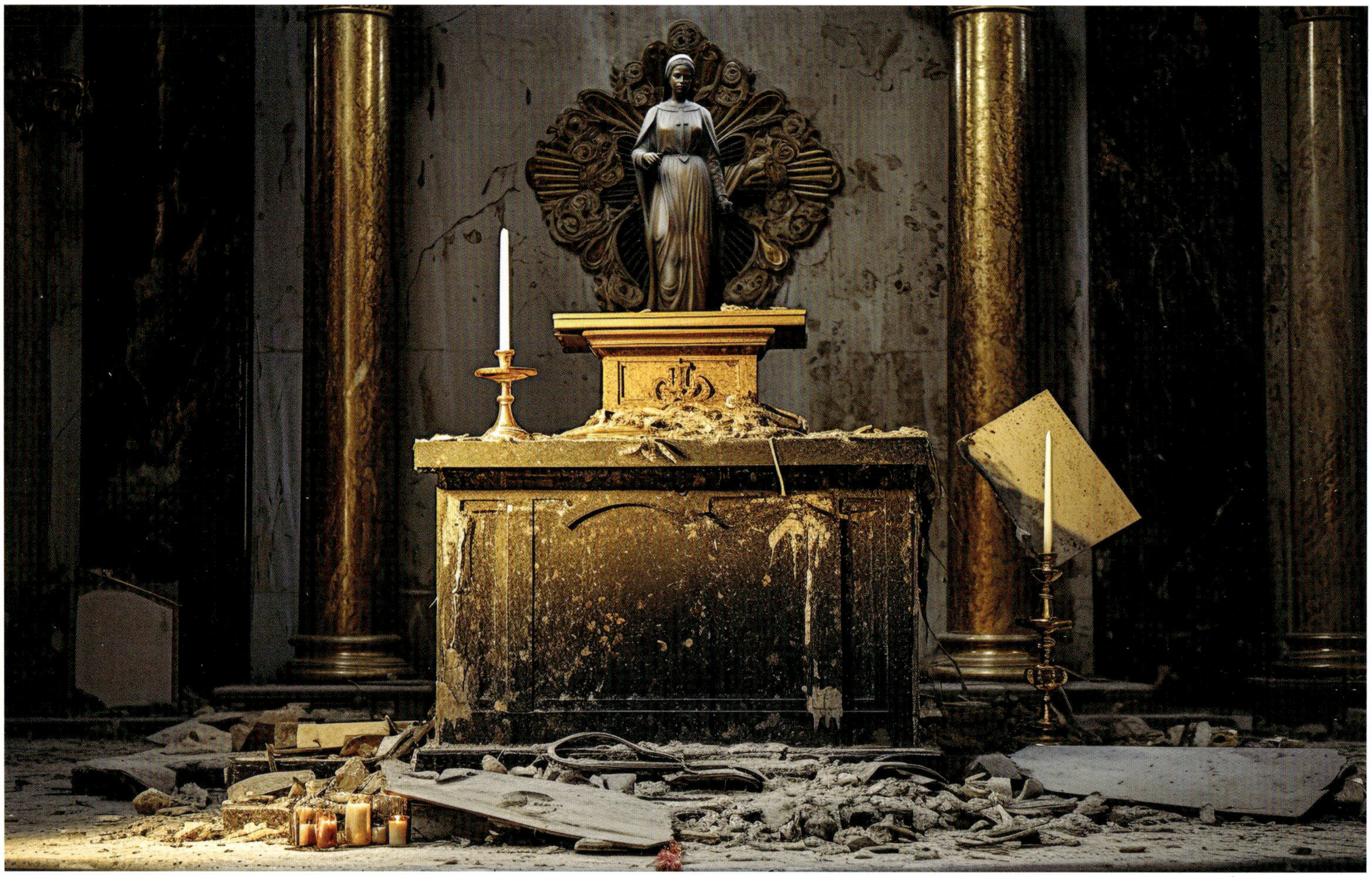

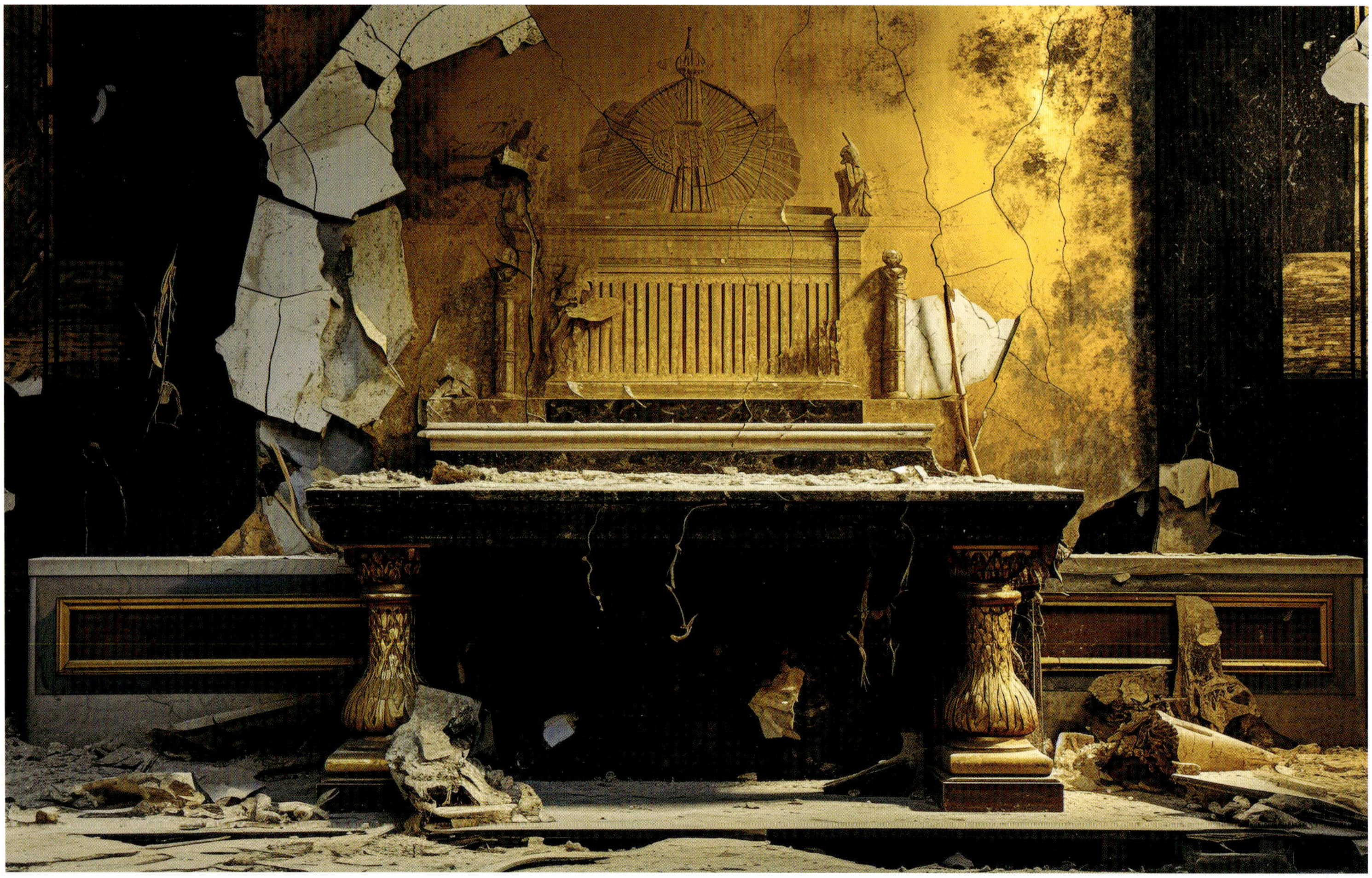

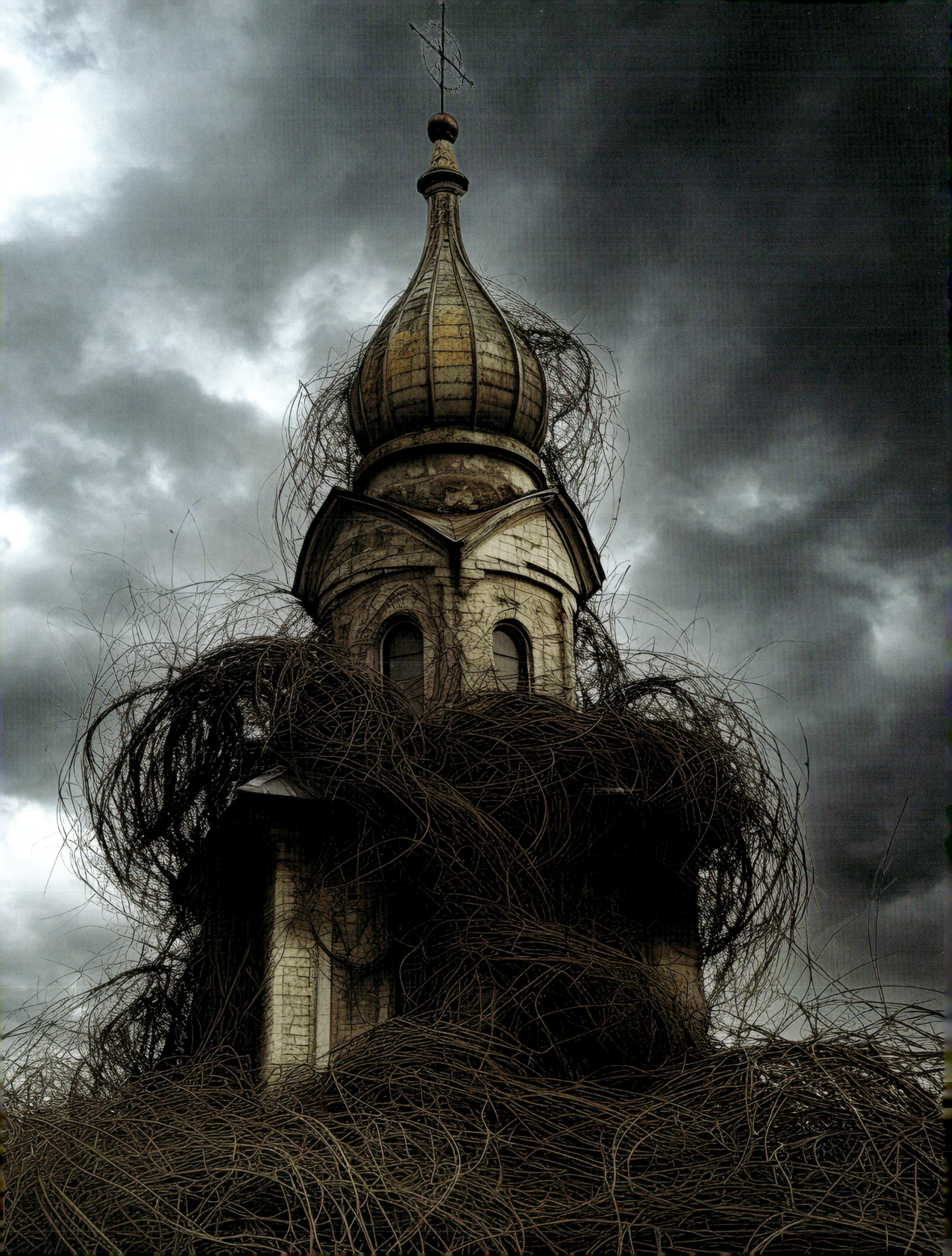

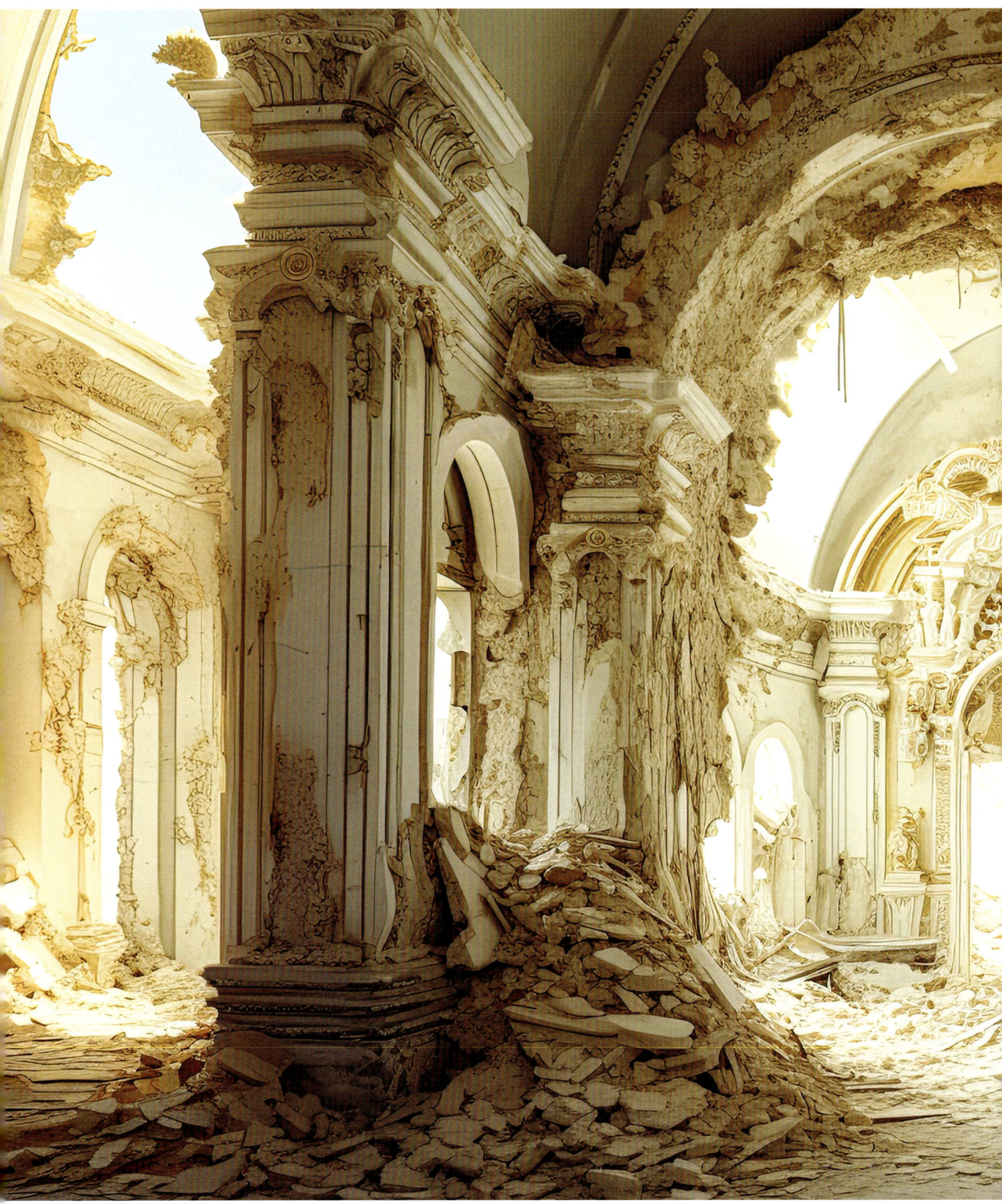

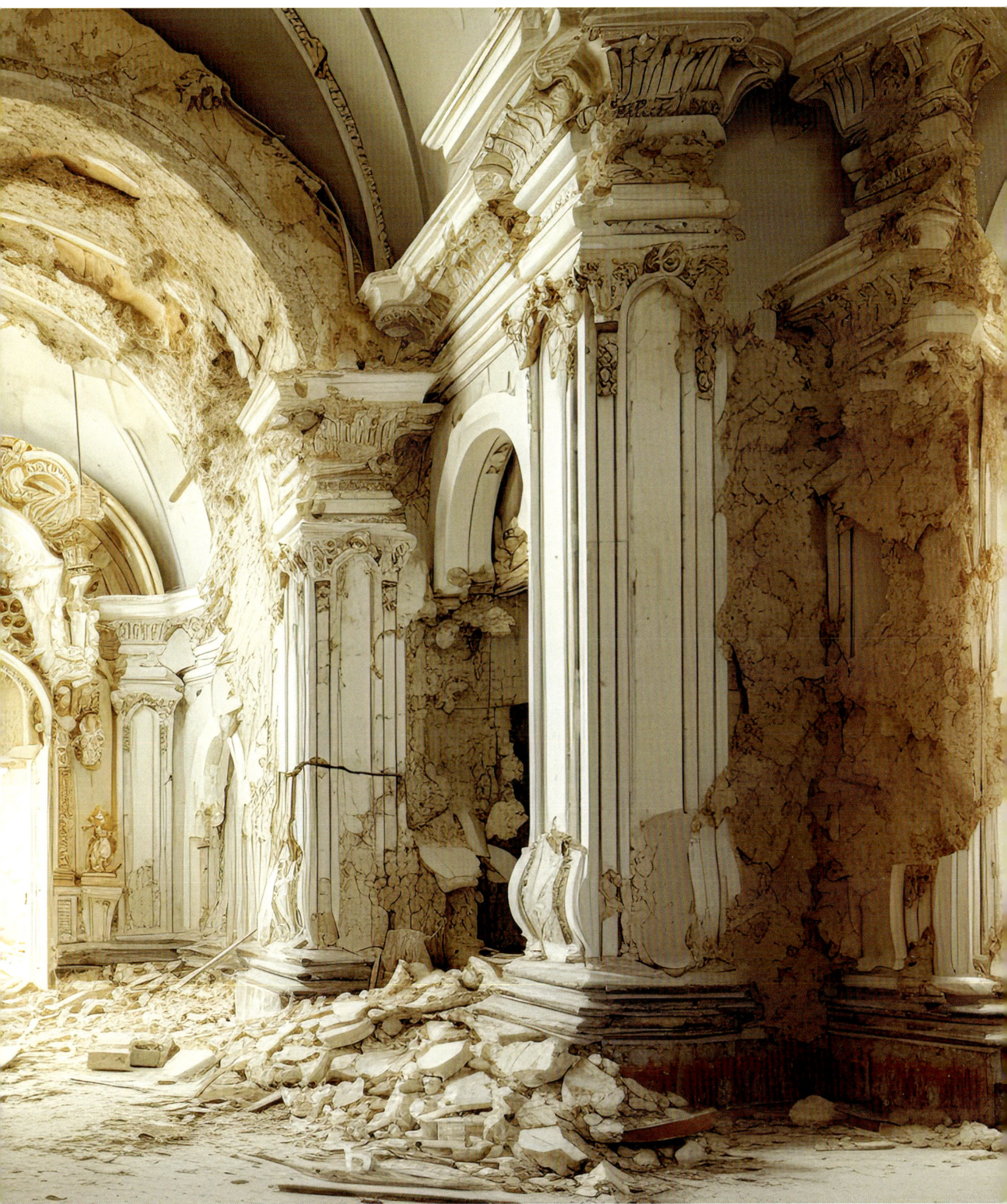

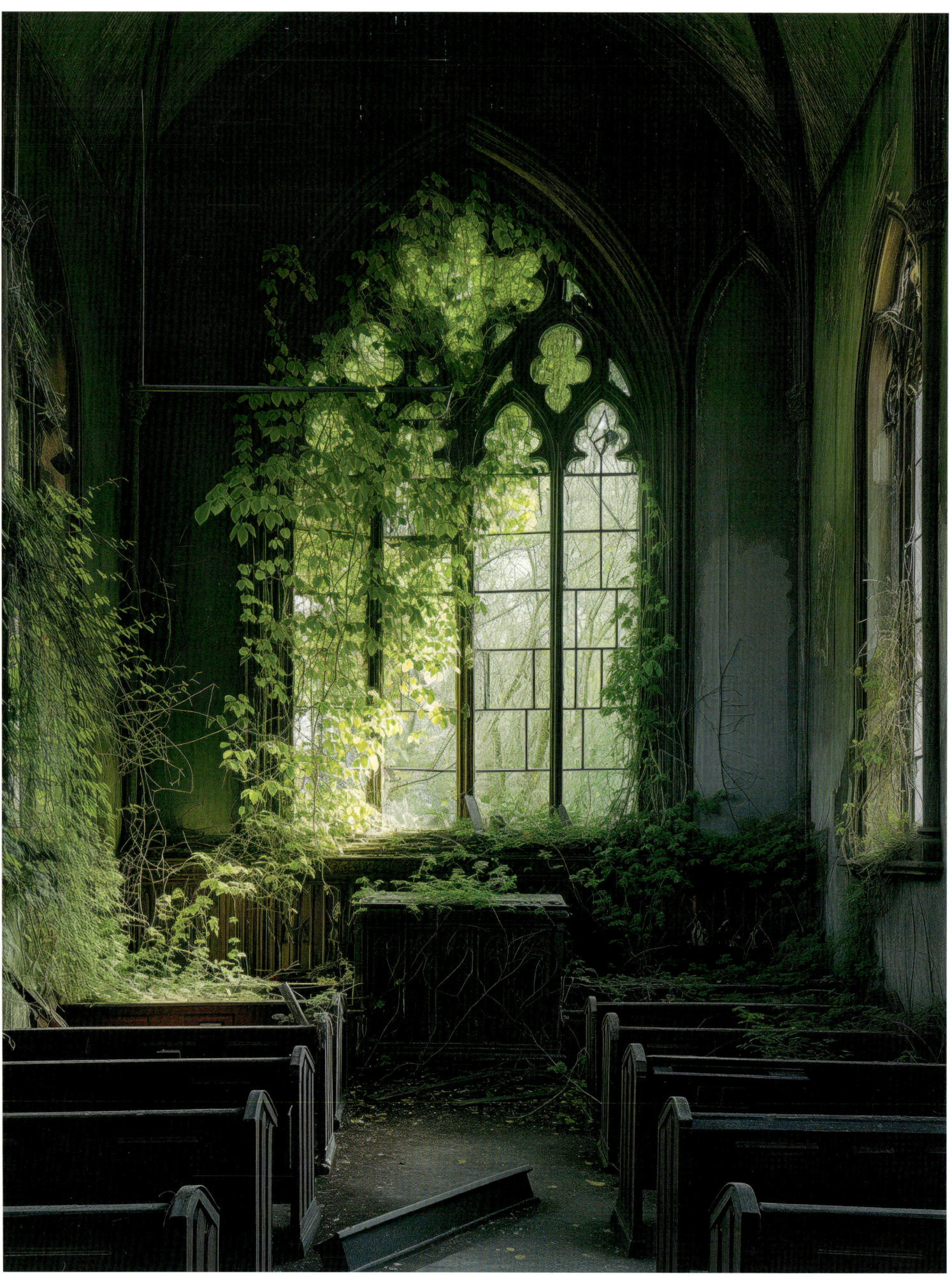

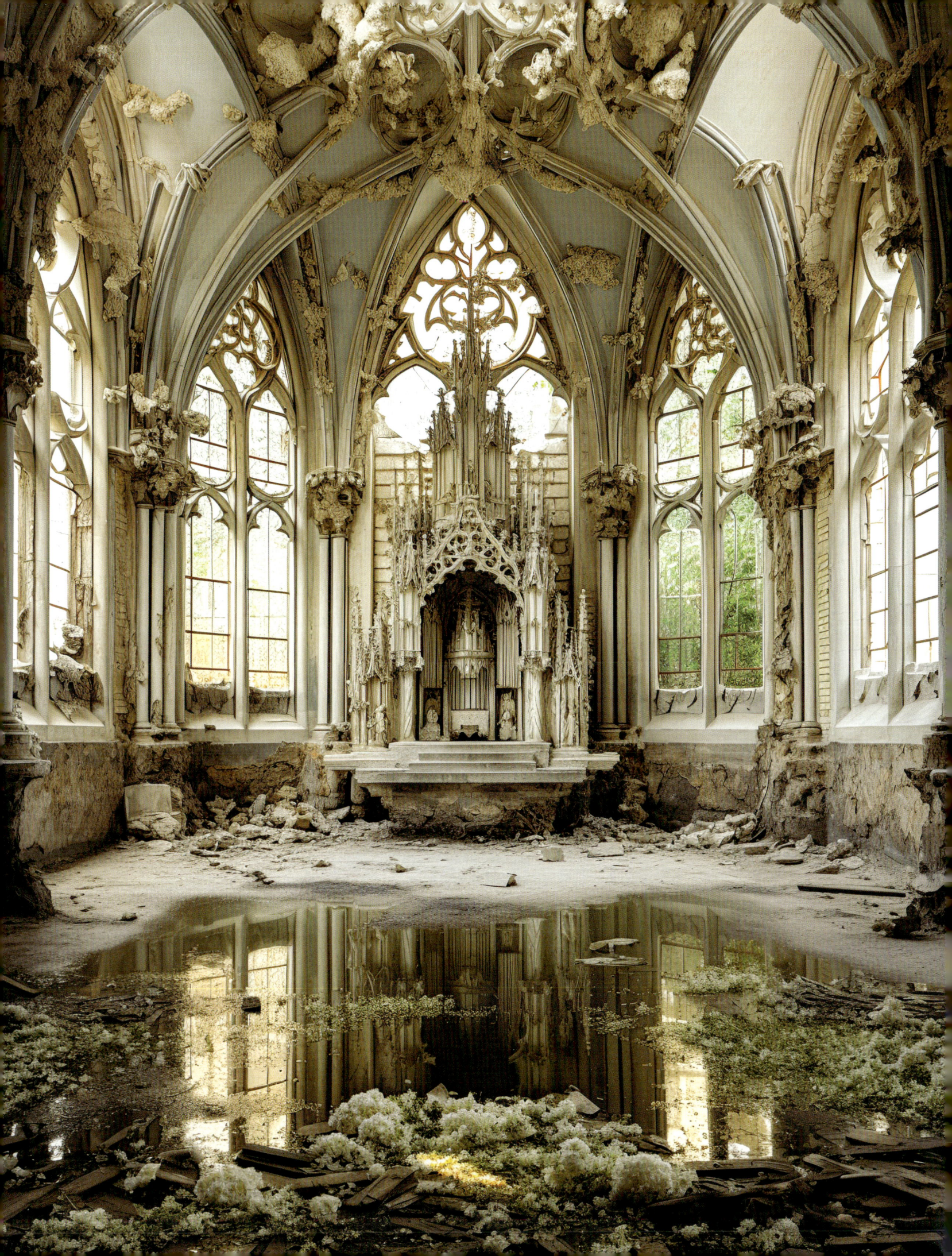

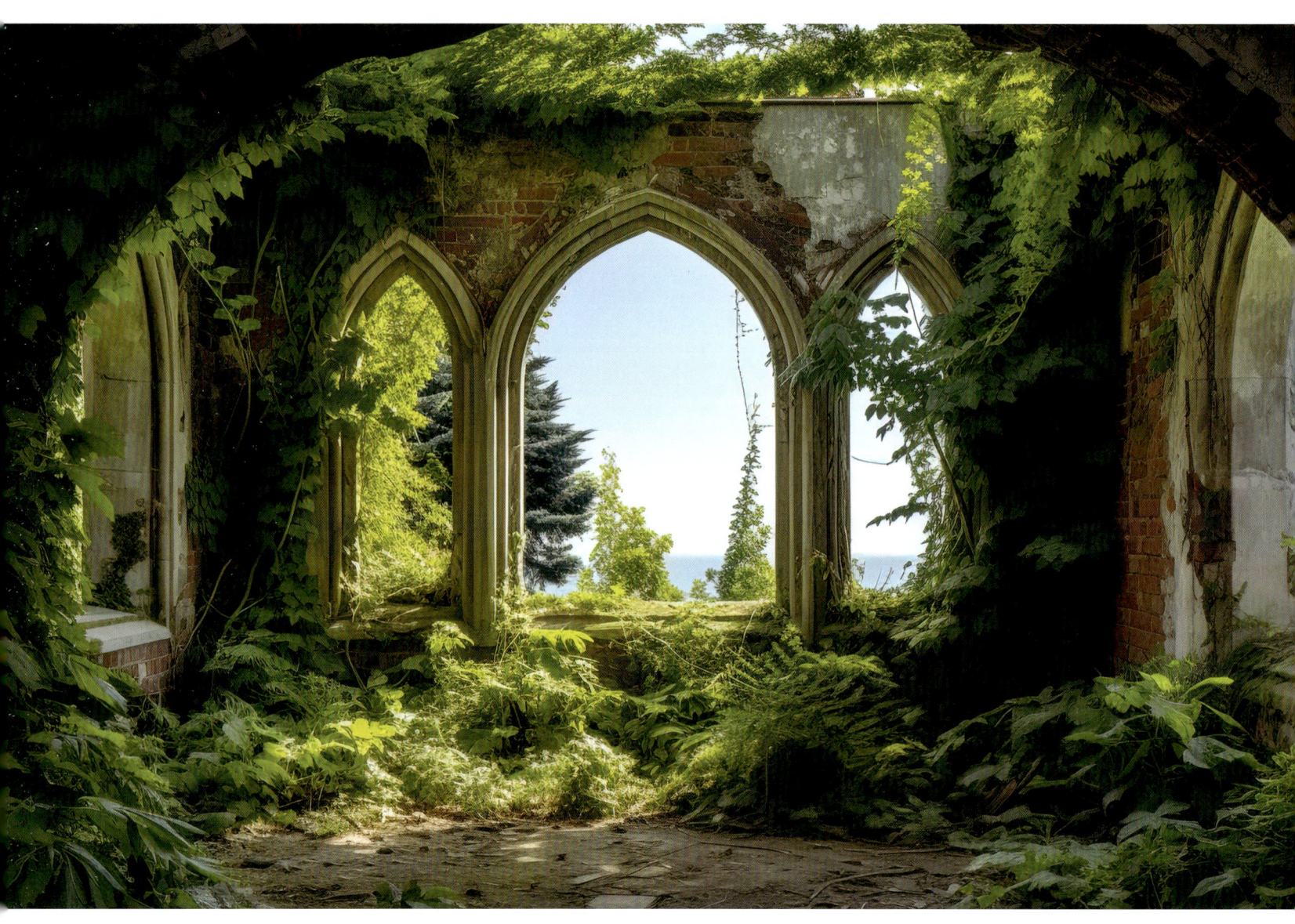

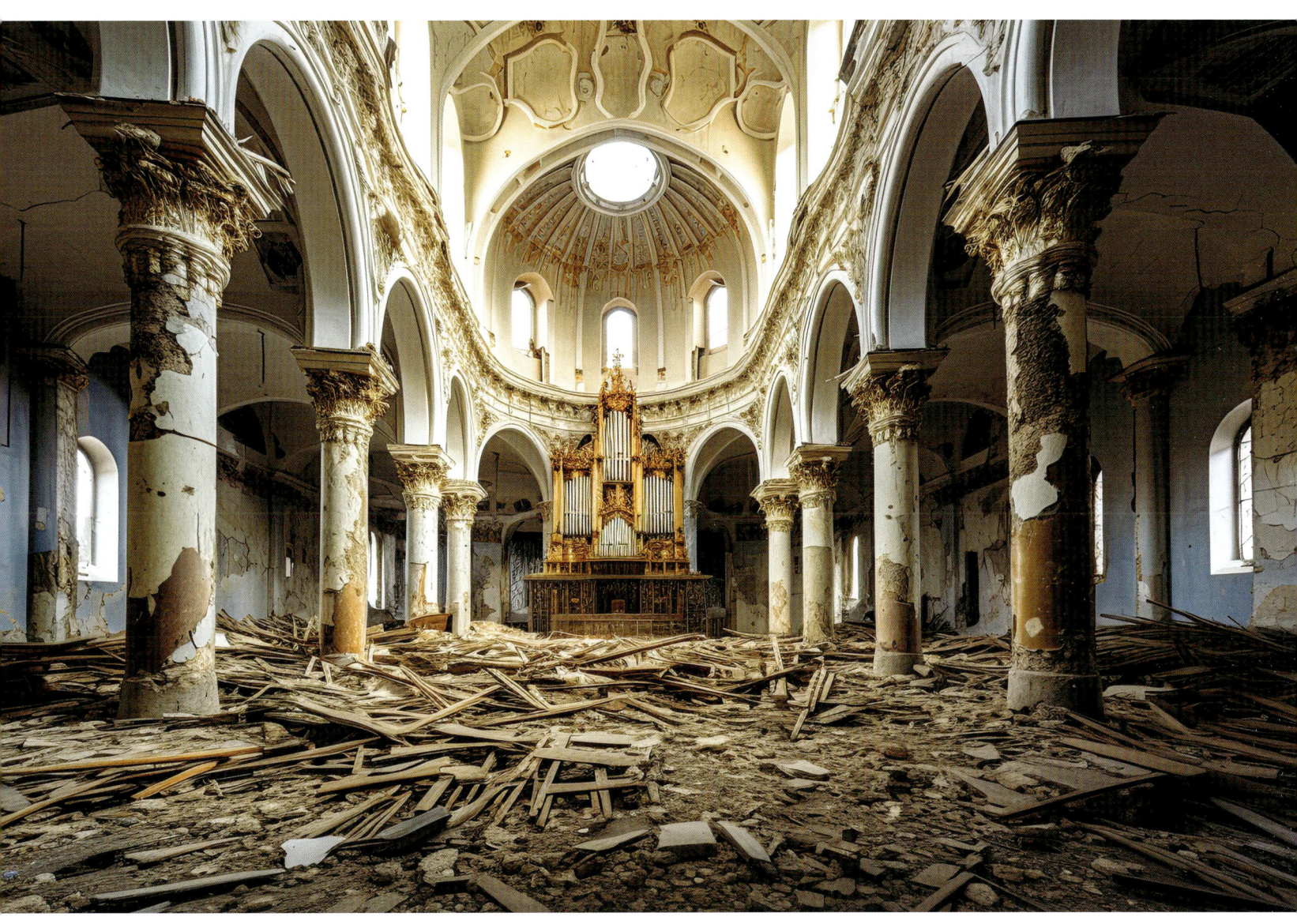

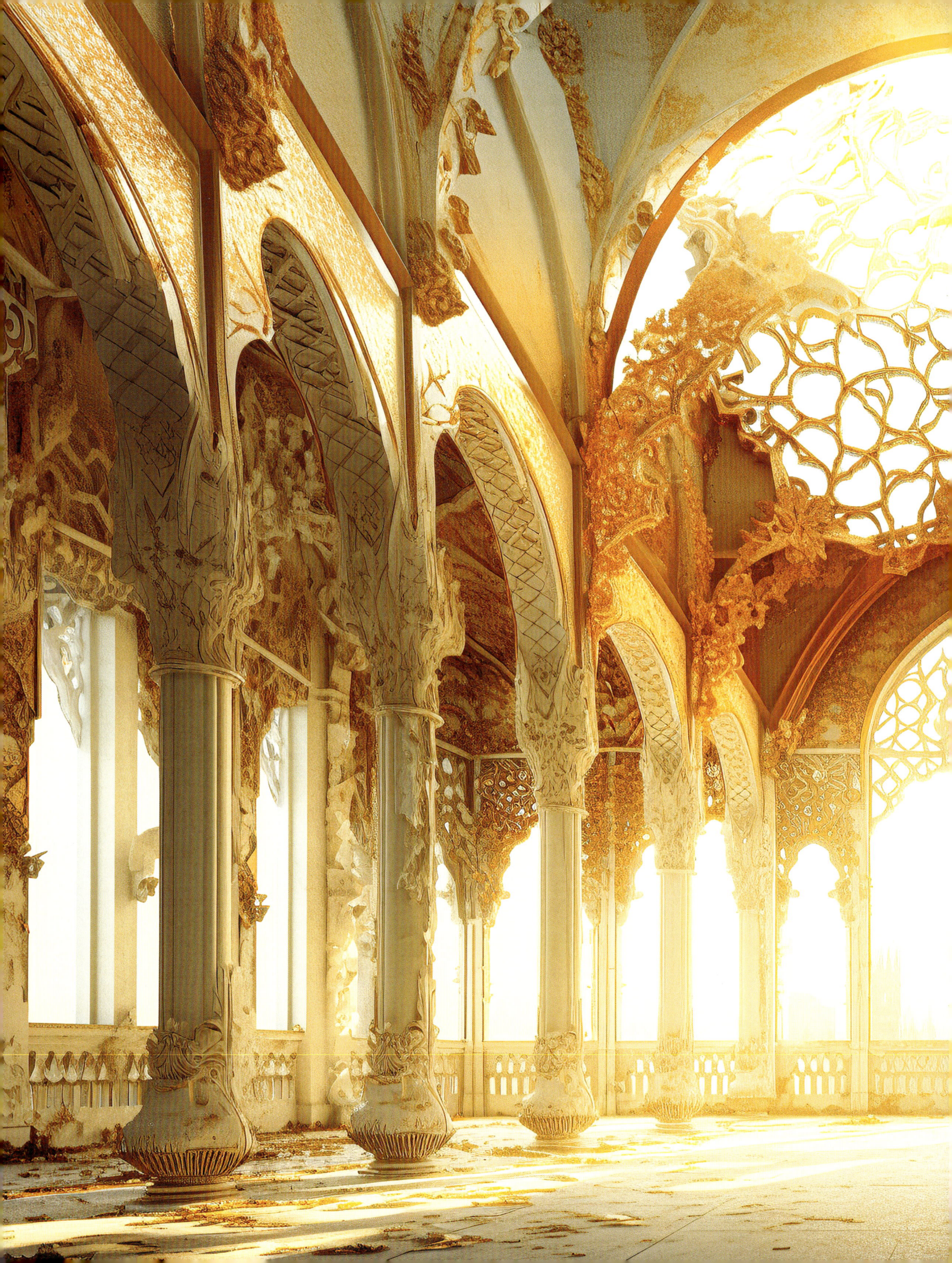

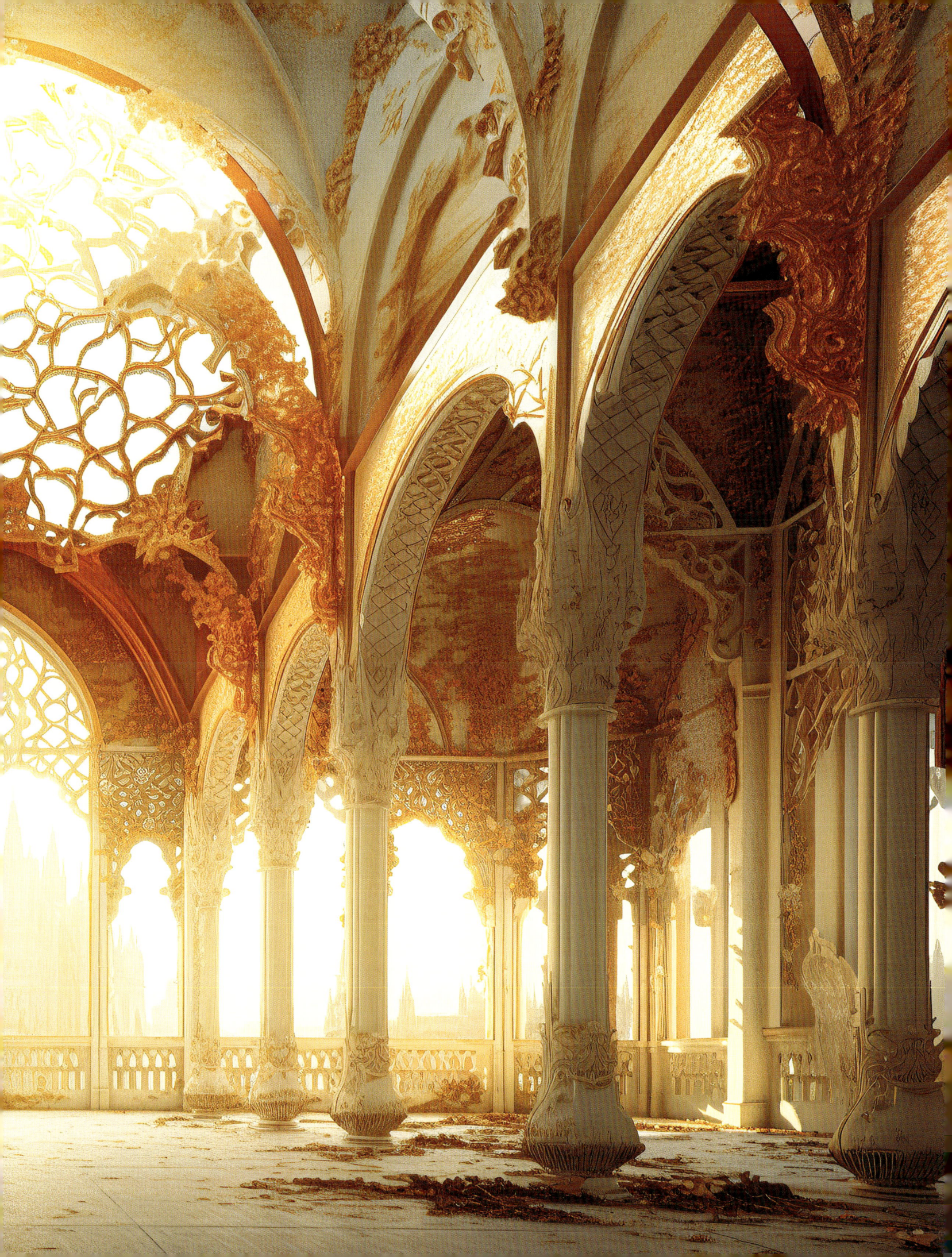

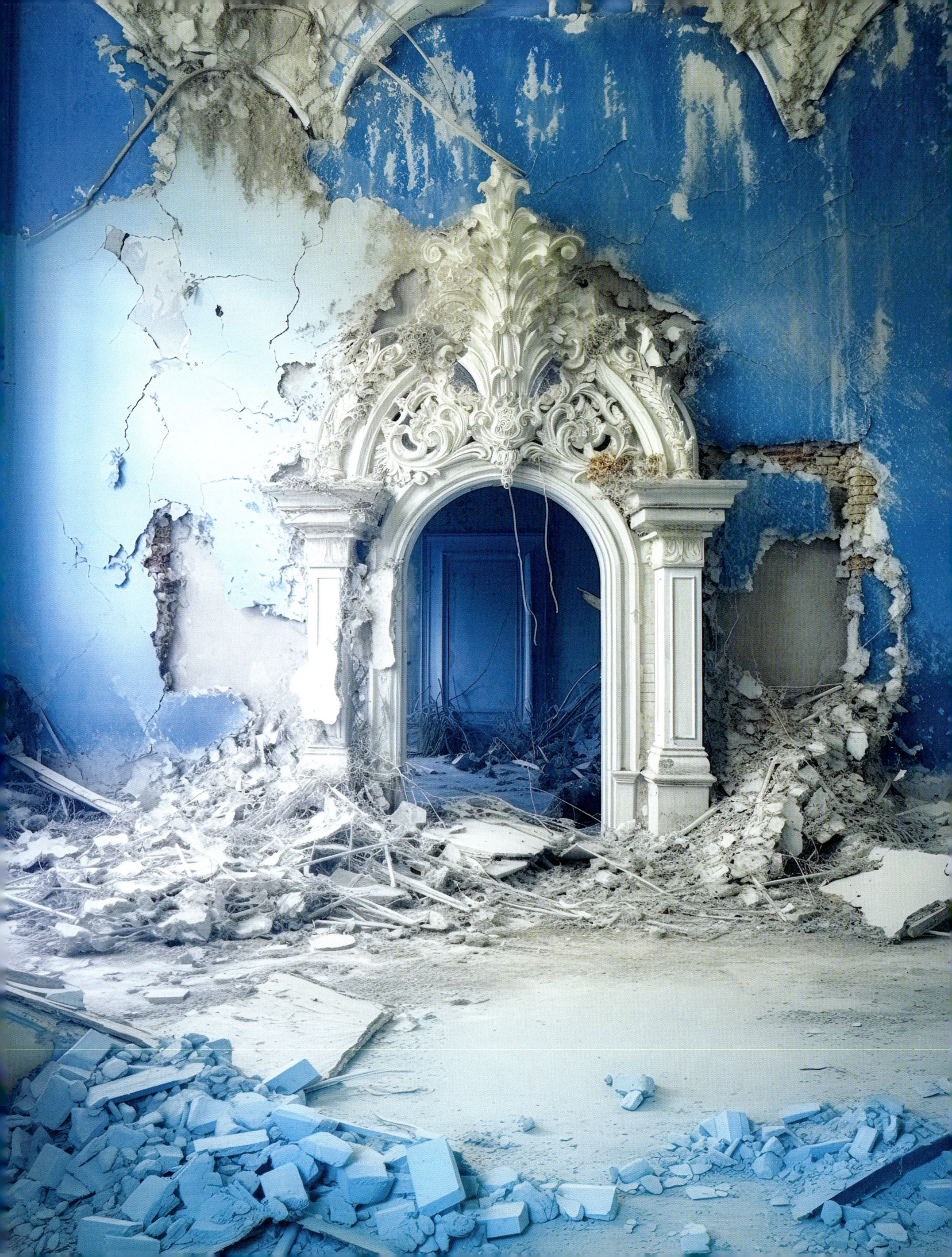

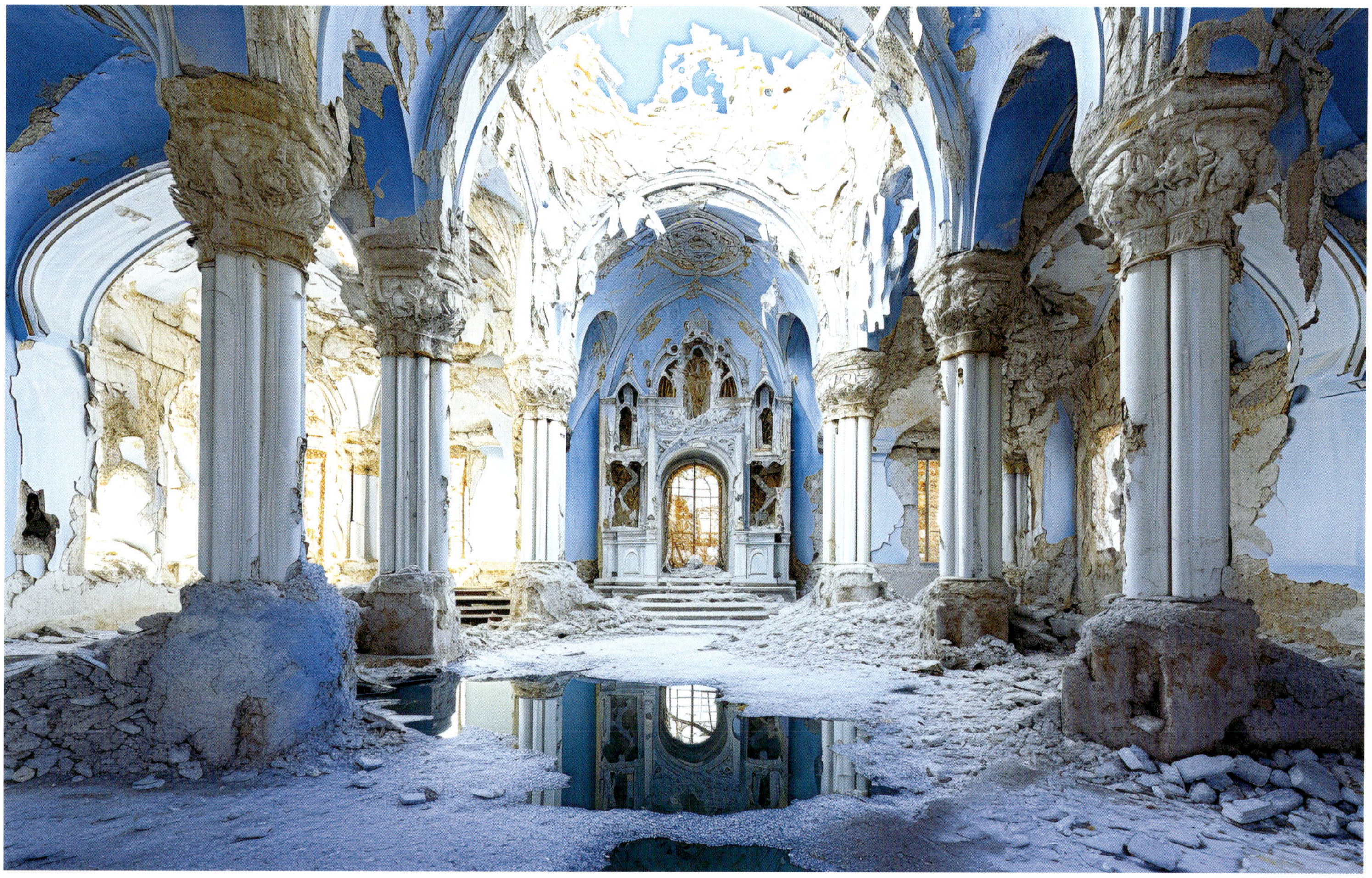

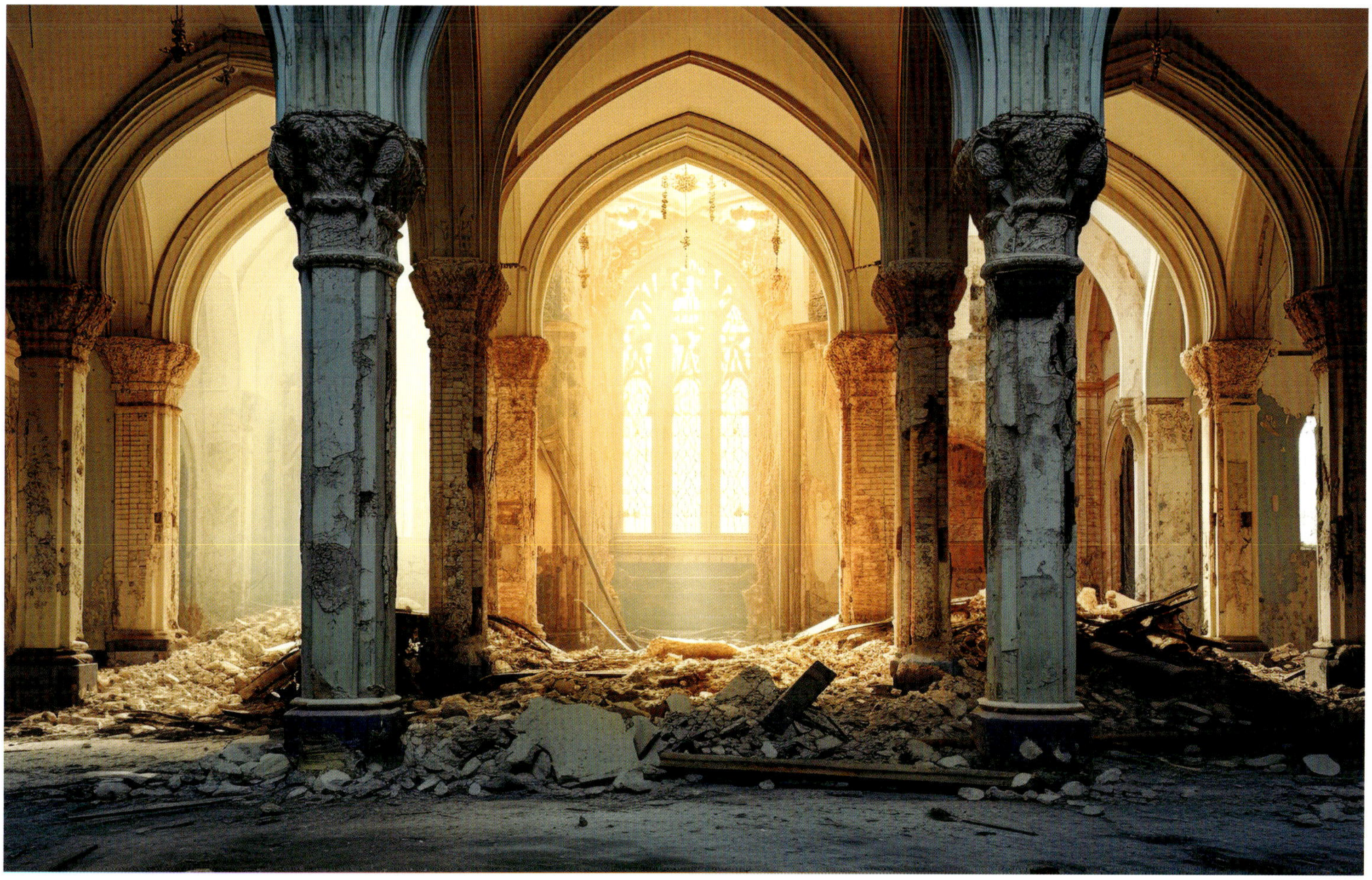

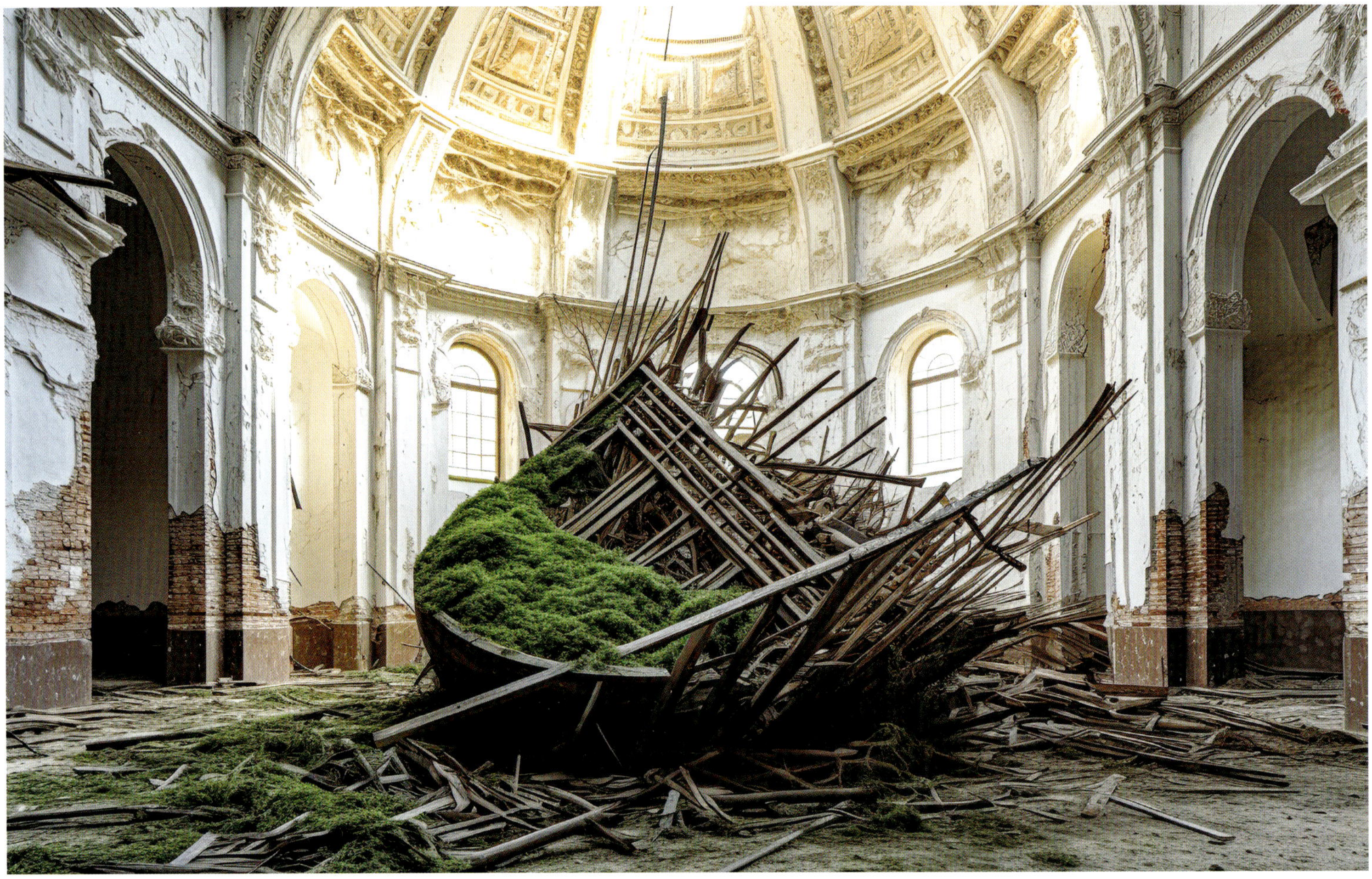

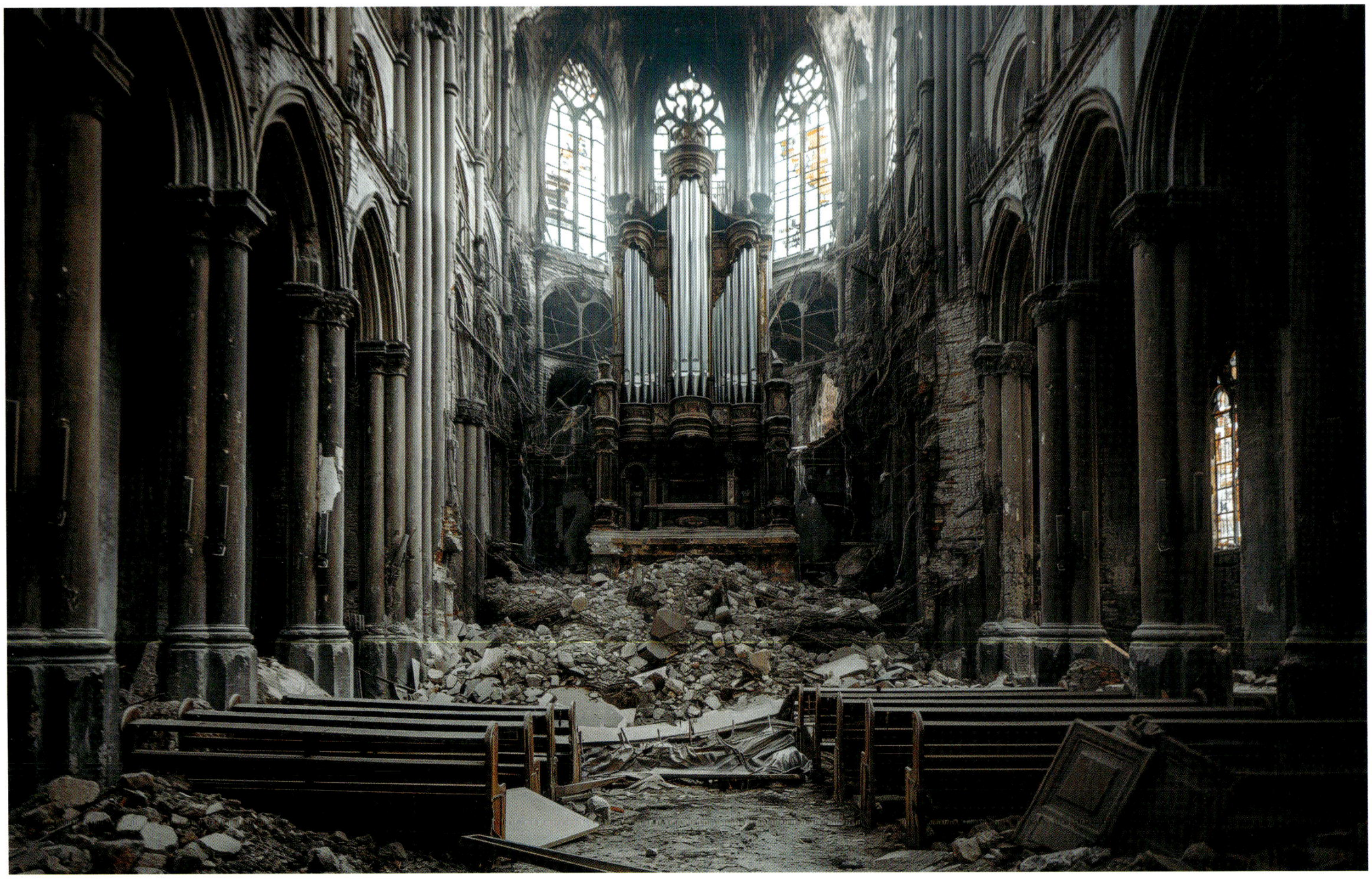

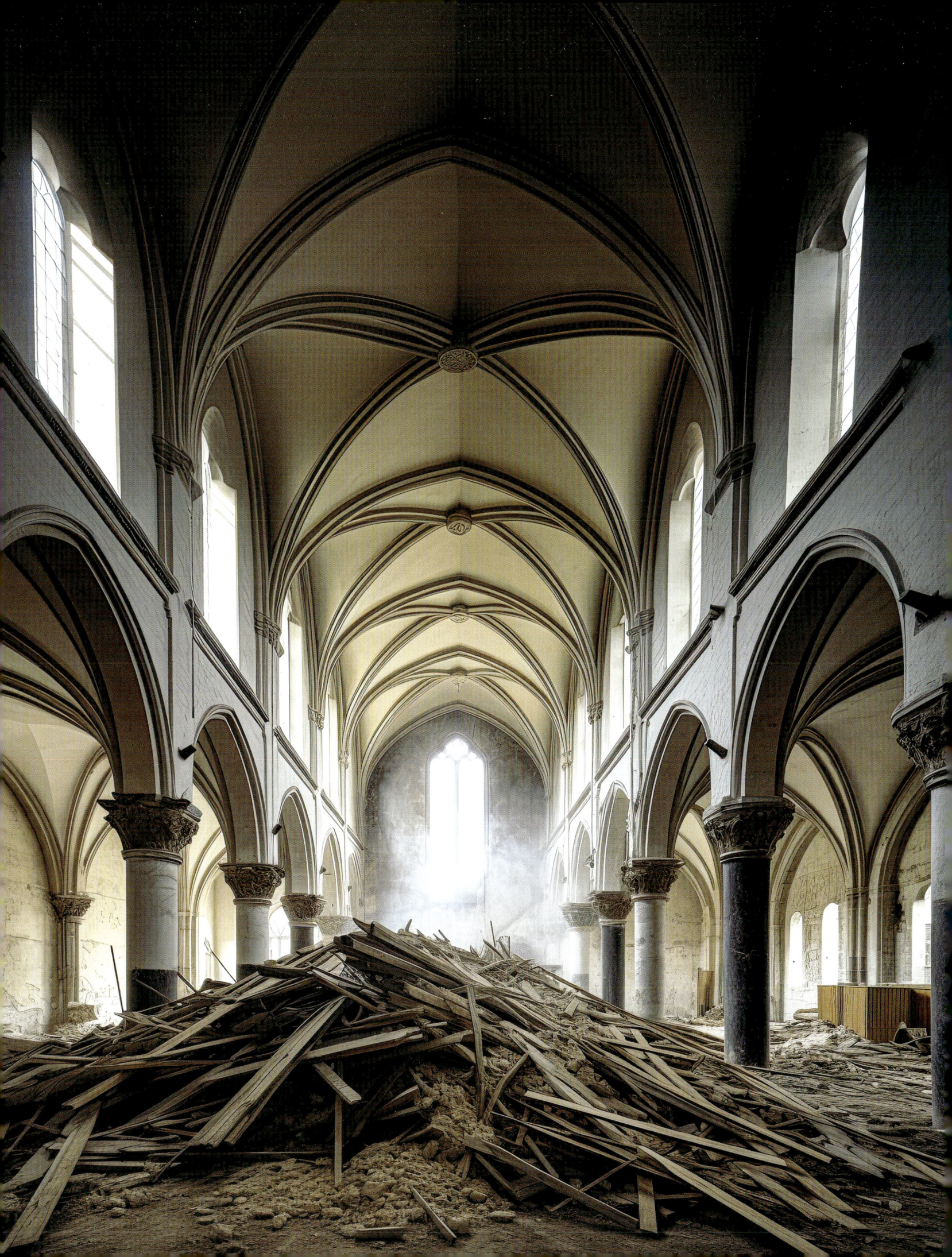

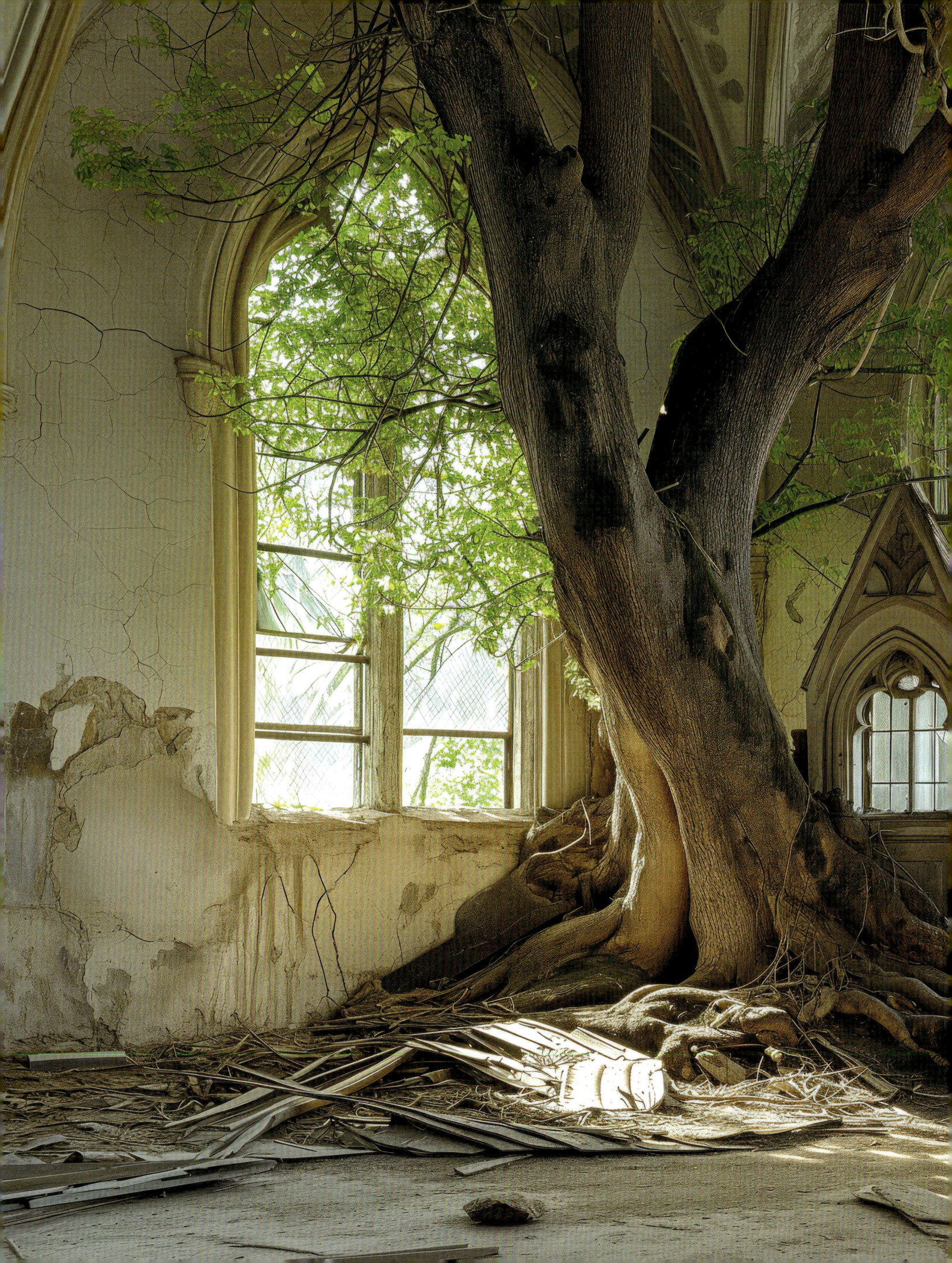

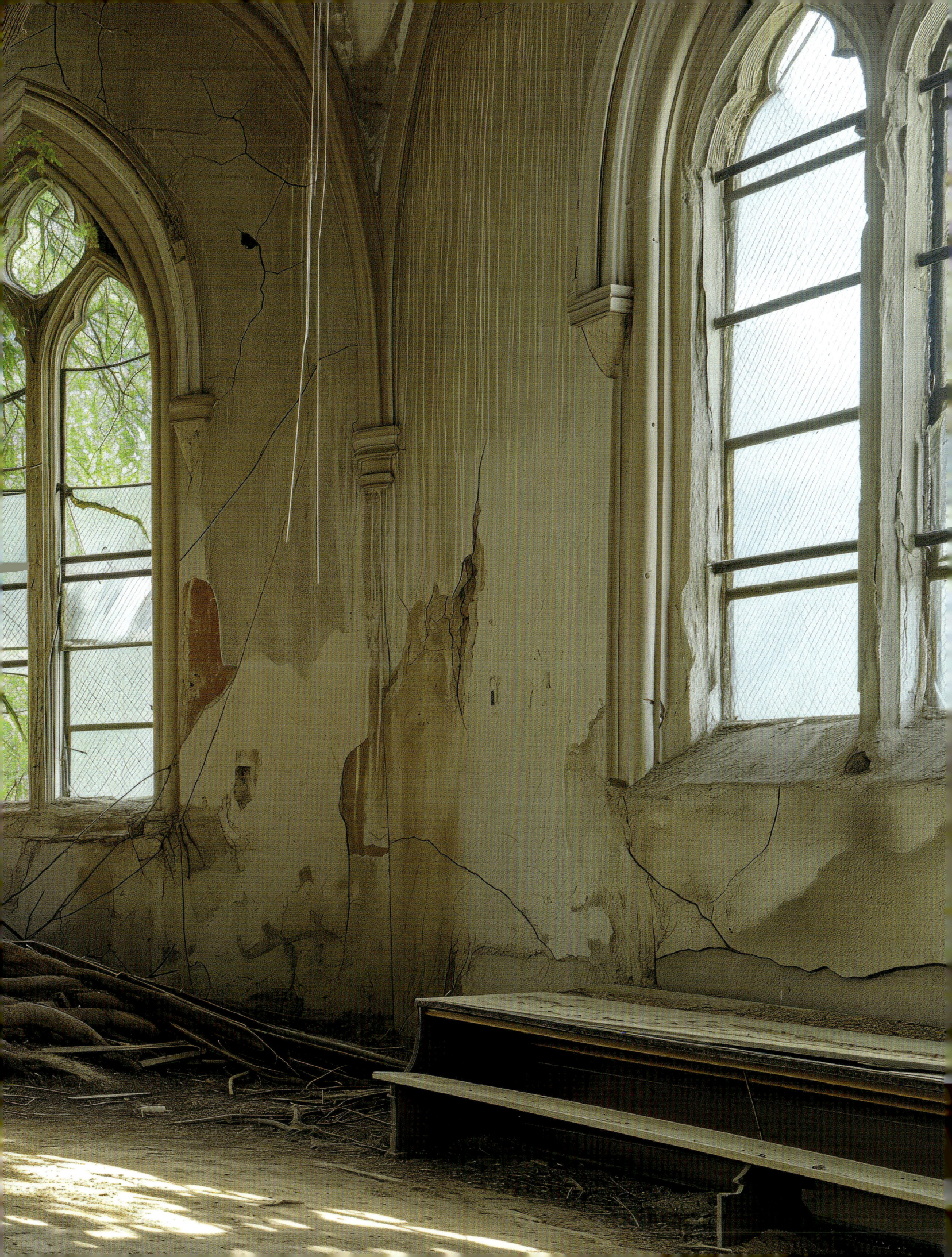

My Dad and I, we live alone

Often what is most striking about abandoned mansions, manor houses, châteaux or palaces is the array of furniture their final occupants left behind. It's easy to detect the presence of those who once lived there in the worn armrests of a Voltaire chair, the battered cushions of a Louis XV sofa or the top of an Empire-style pedestal side table.

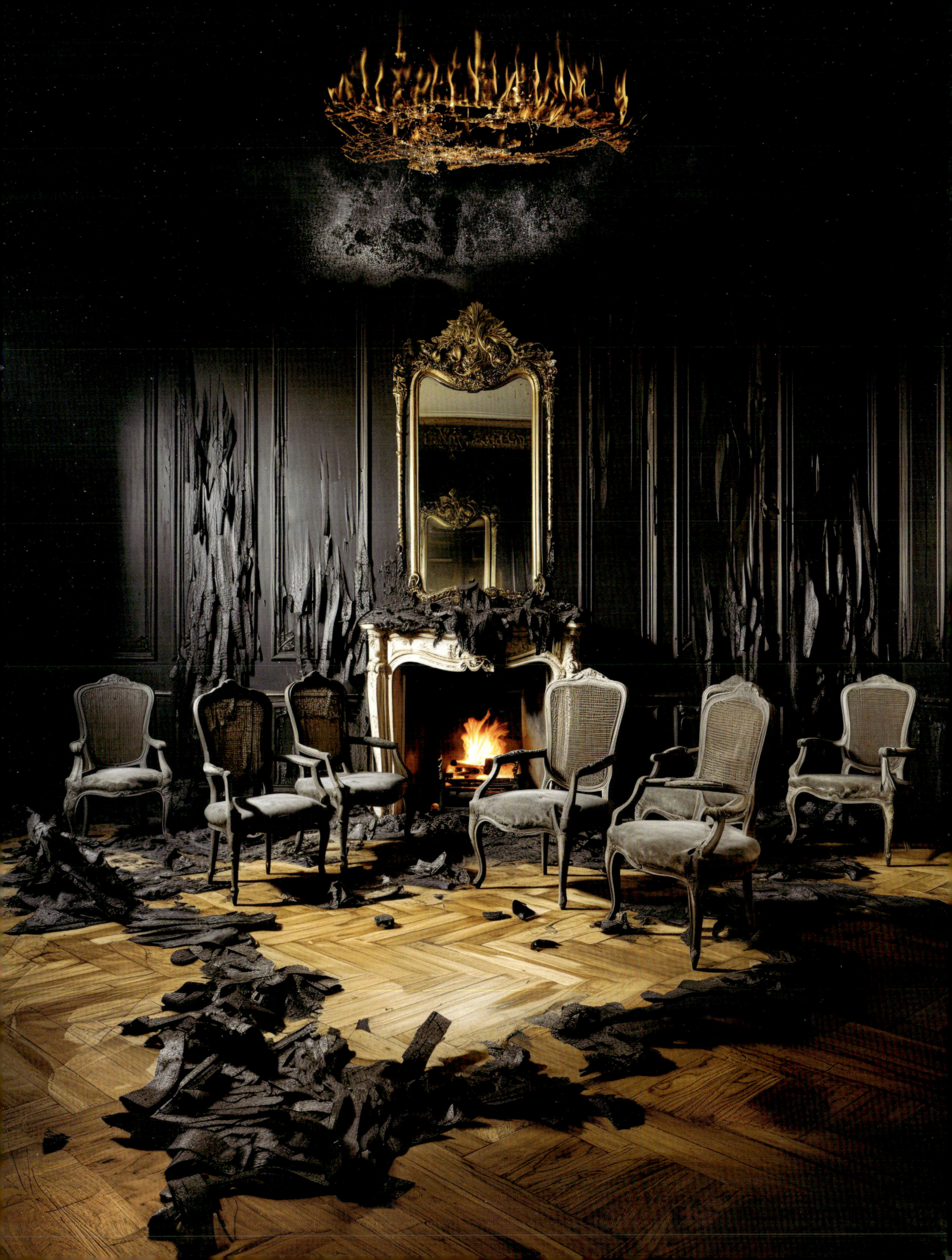

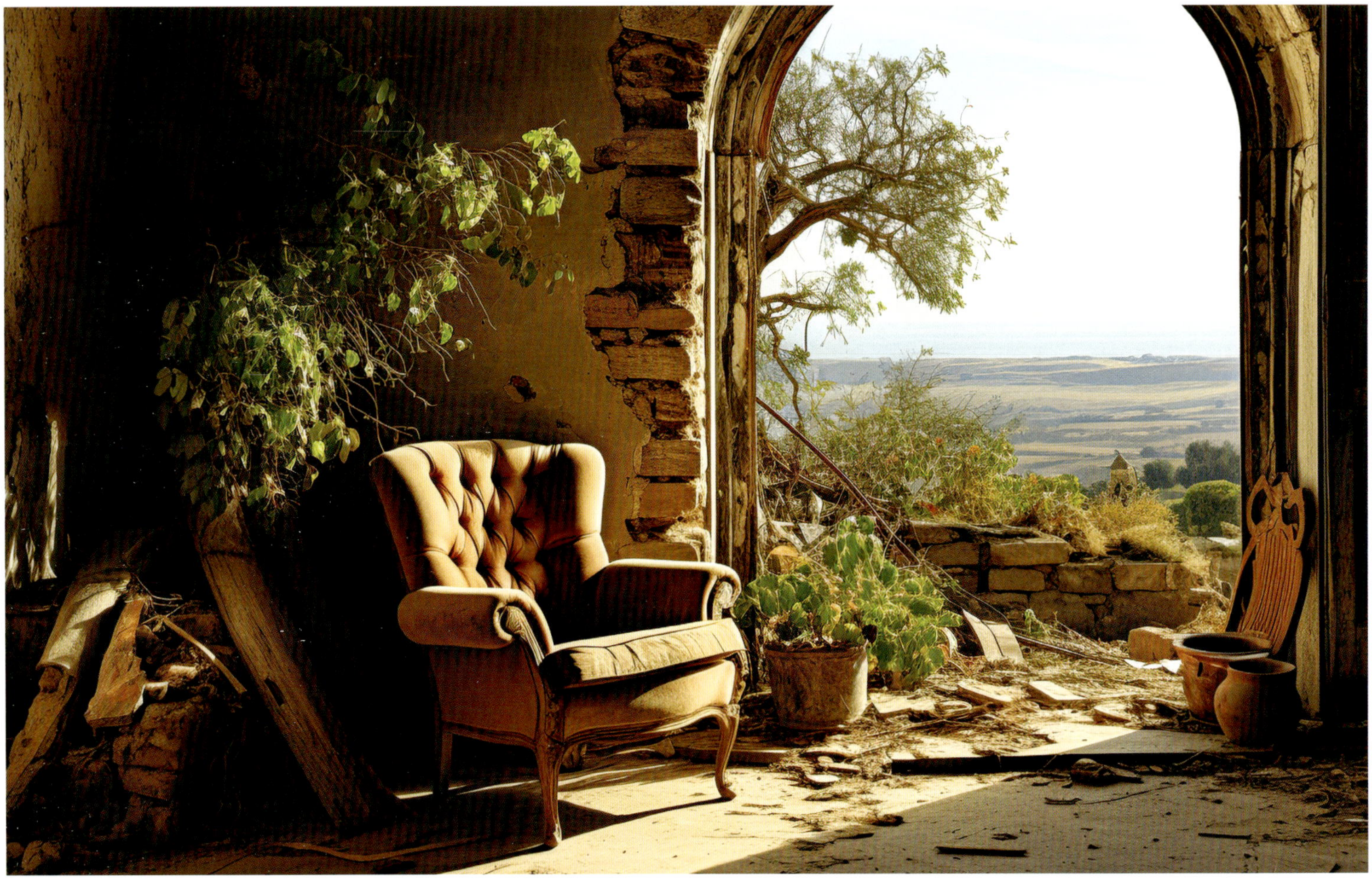

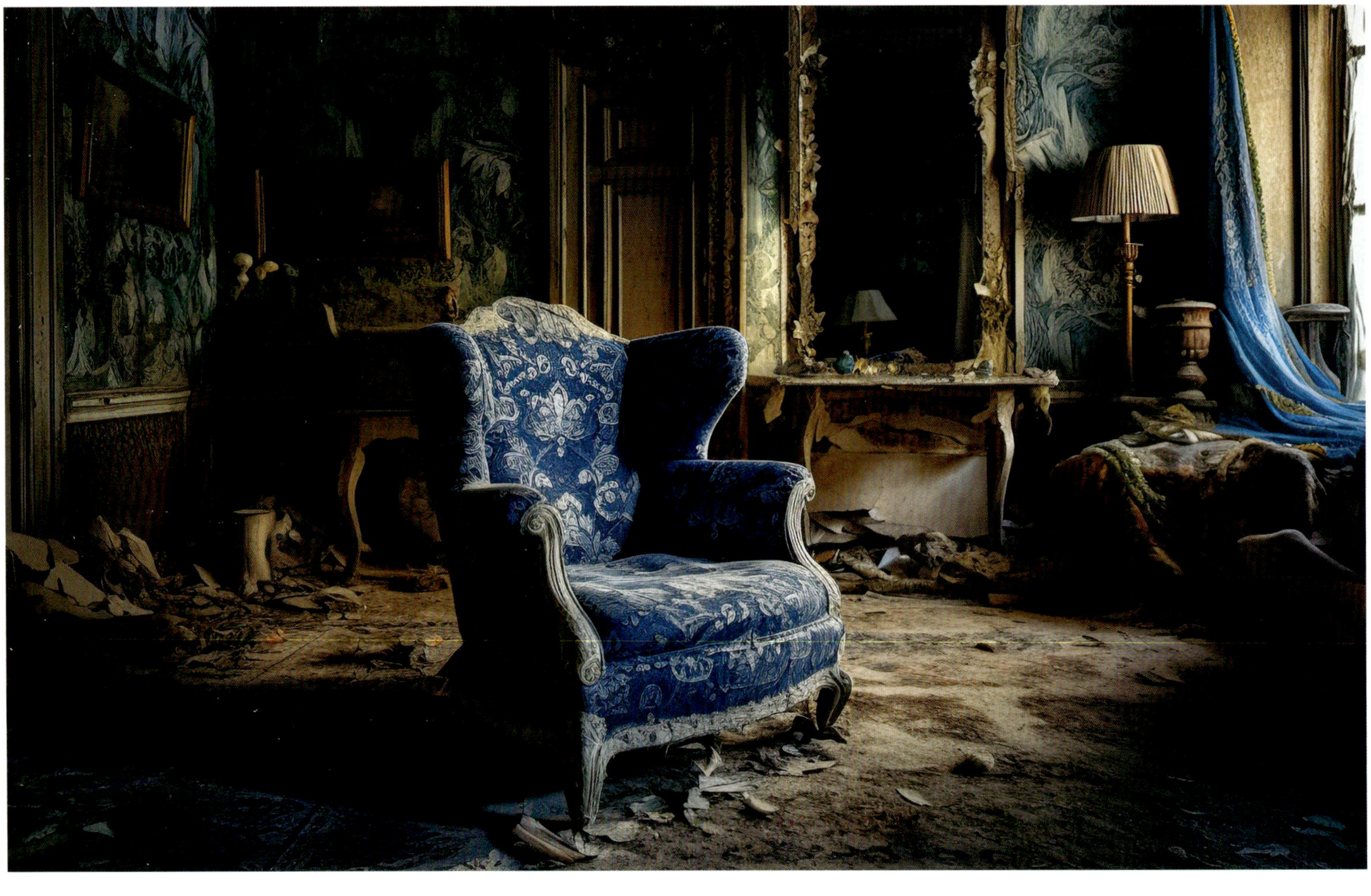

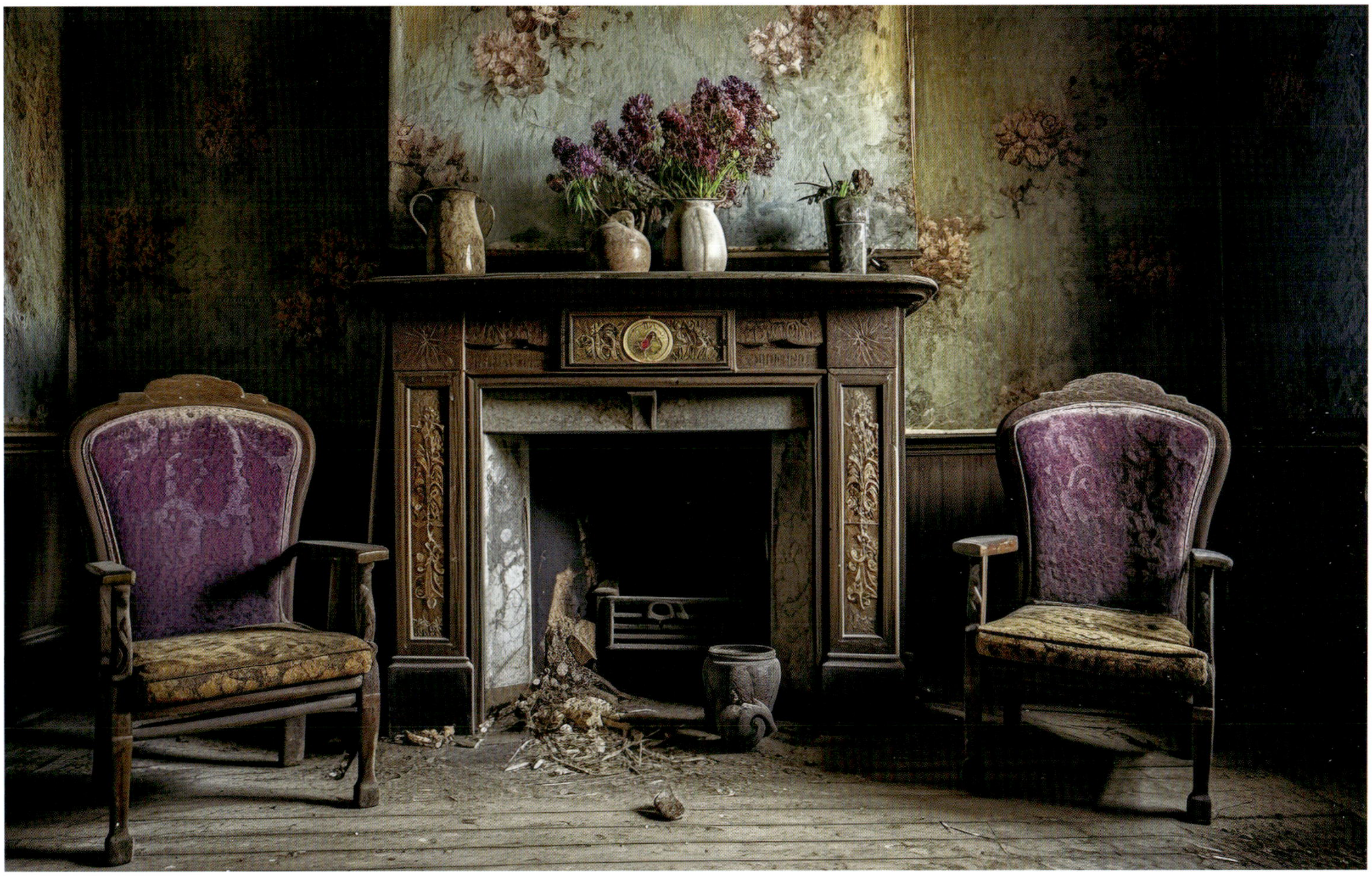

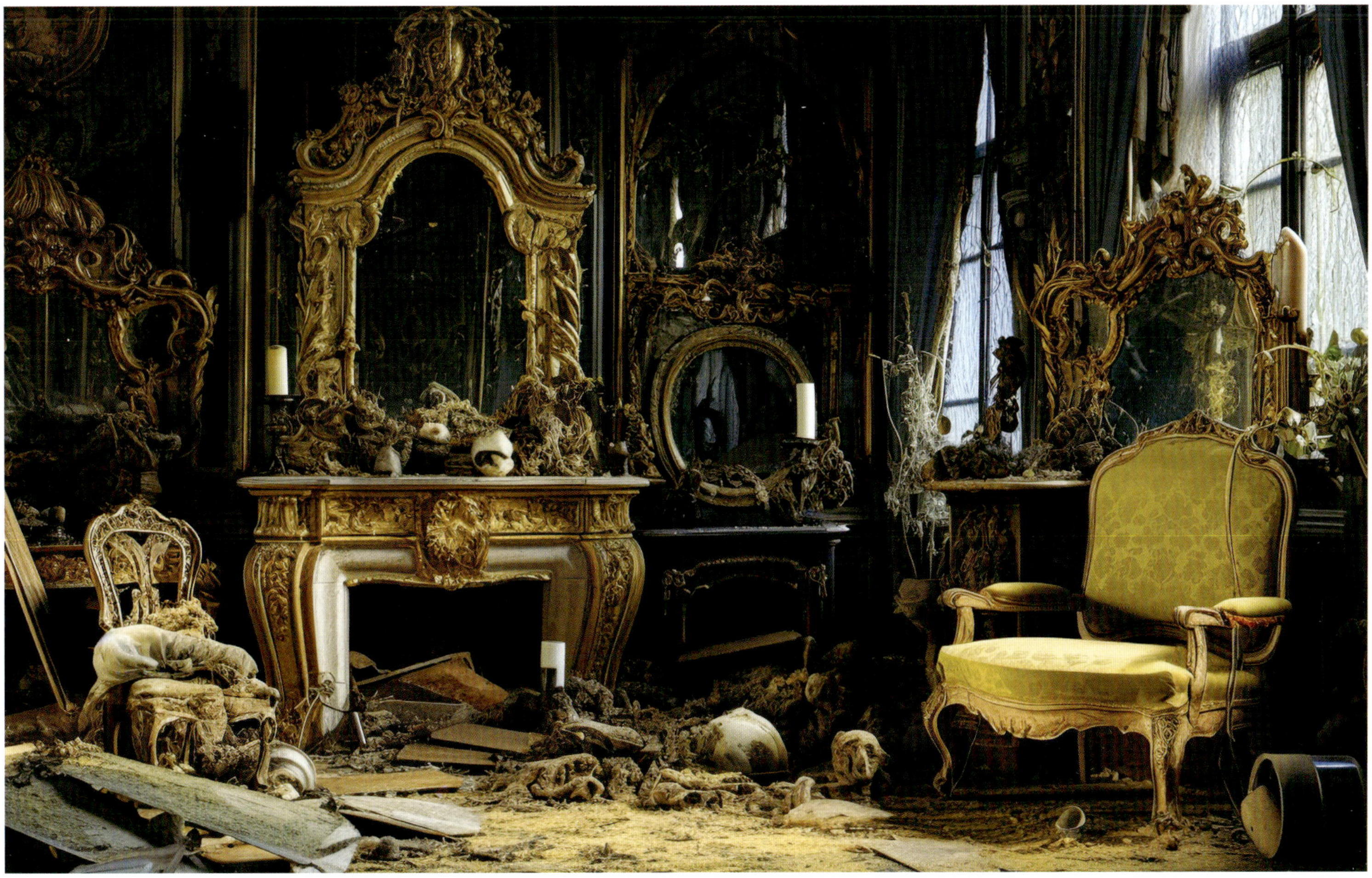

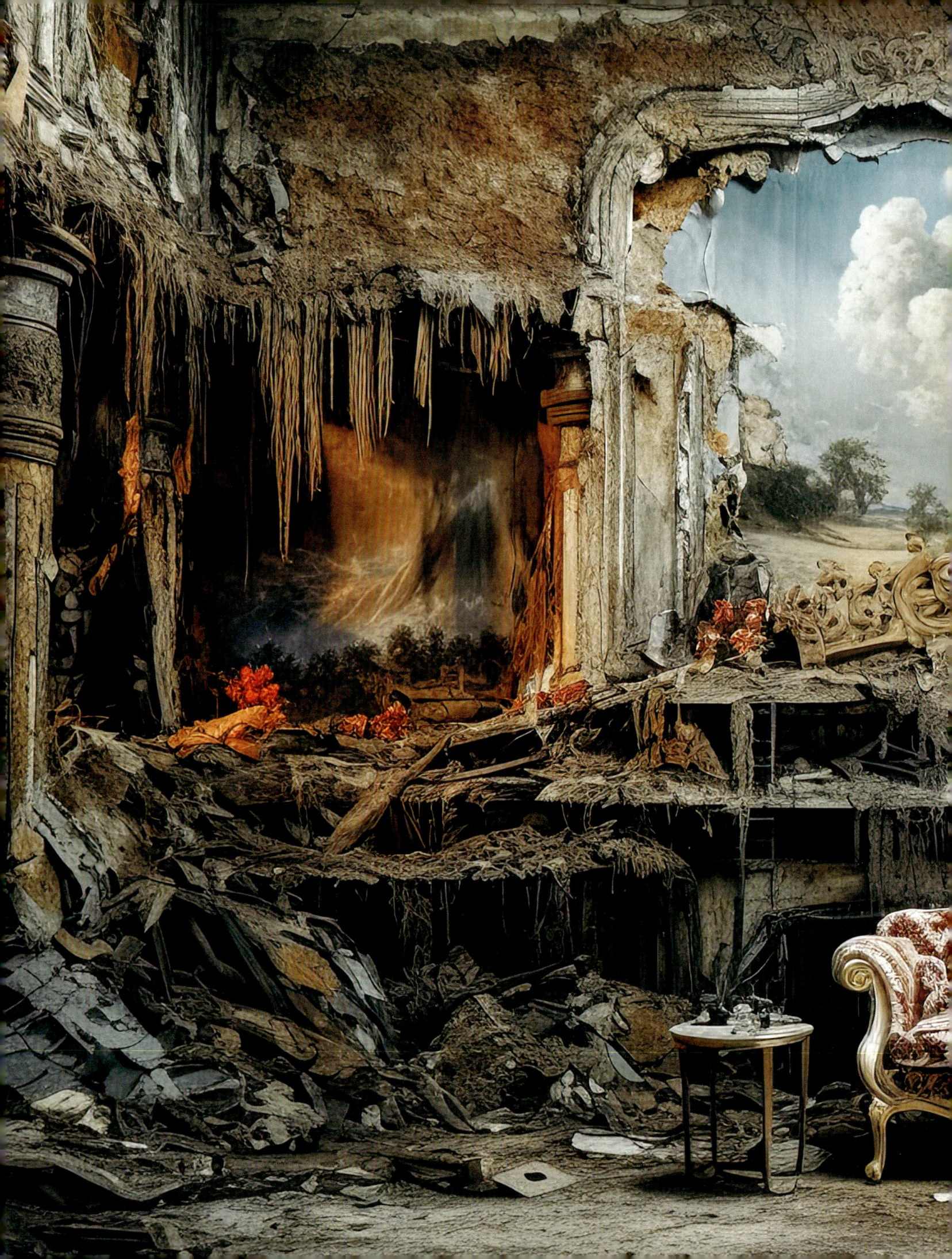

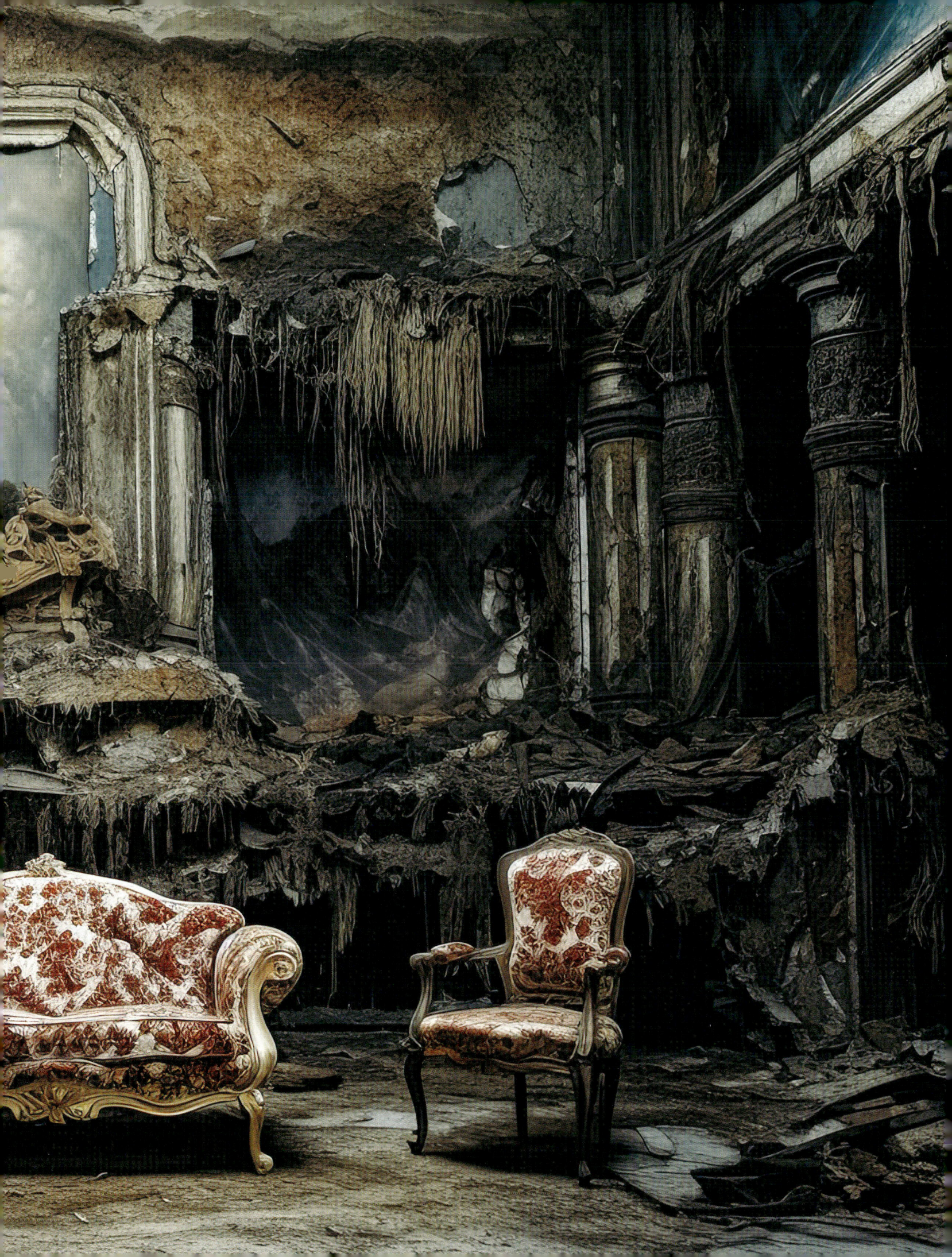

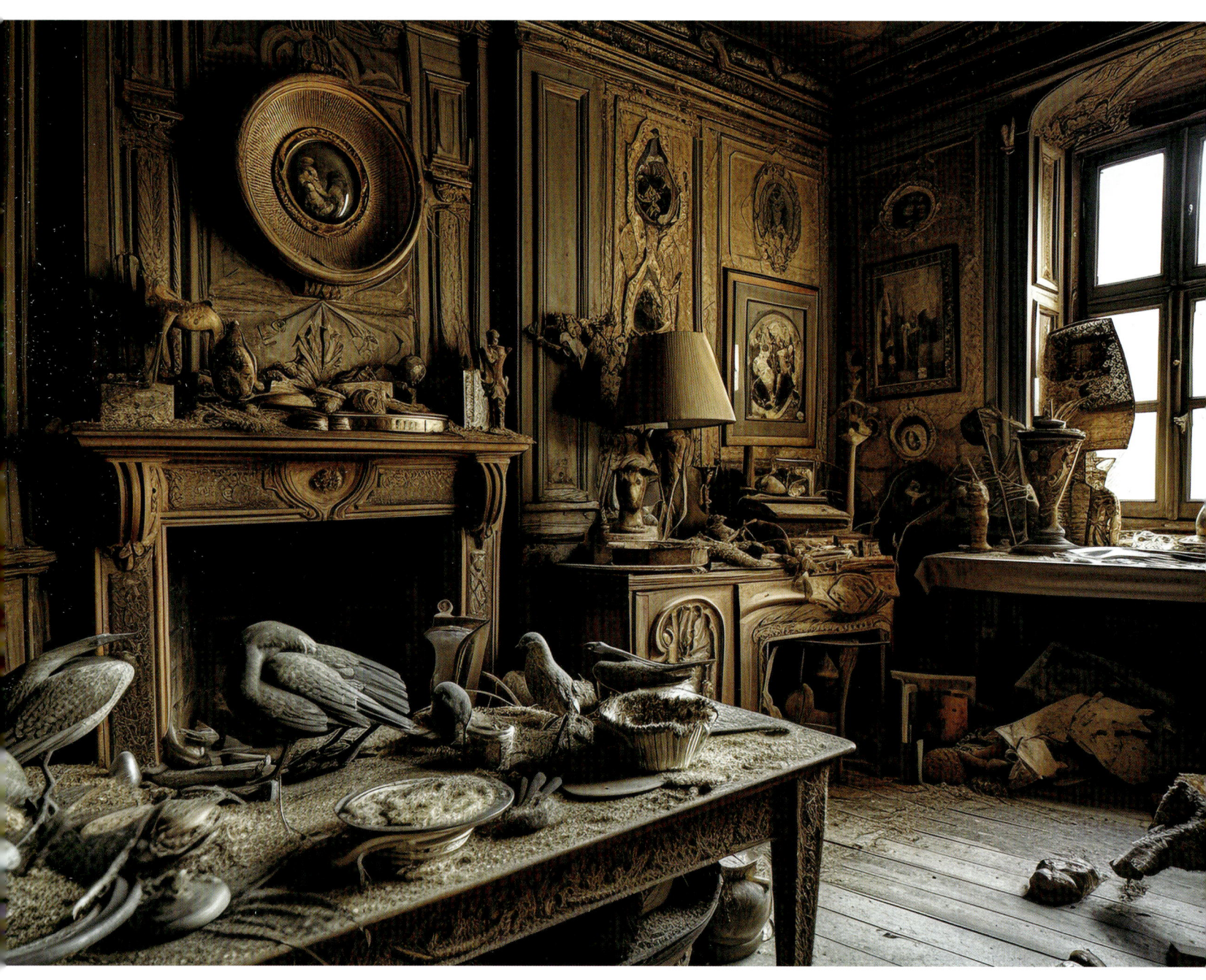

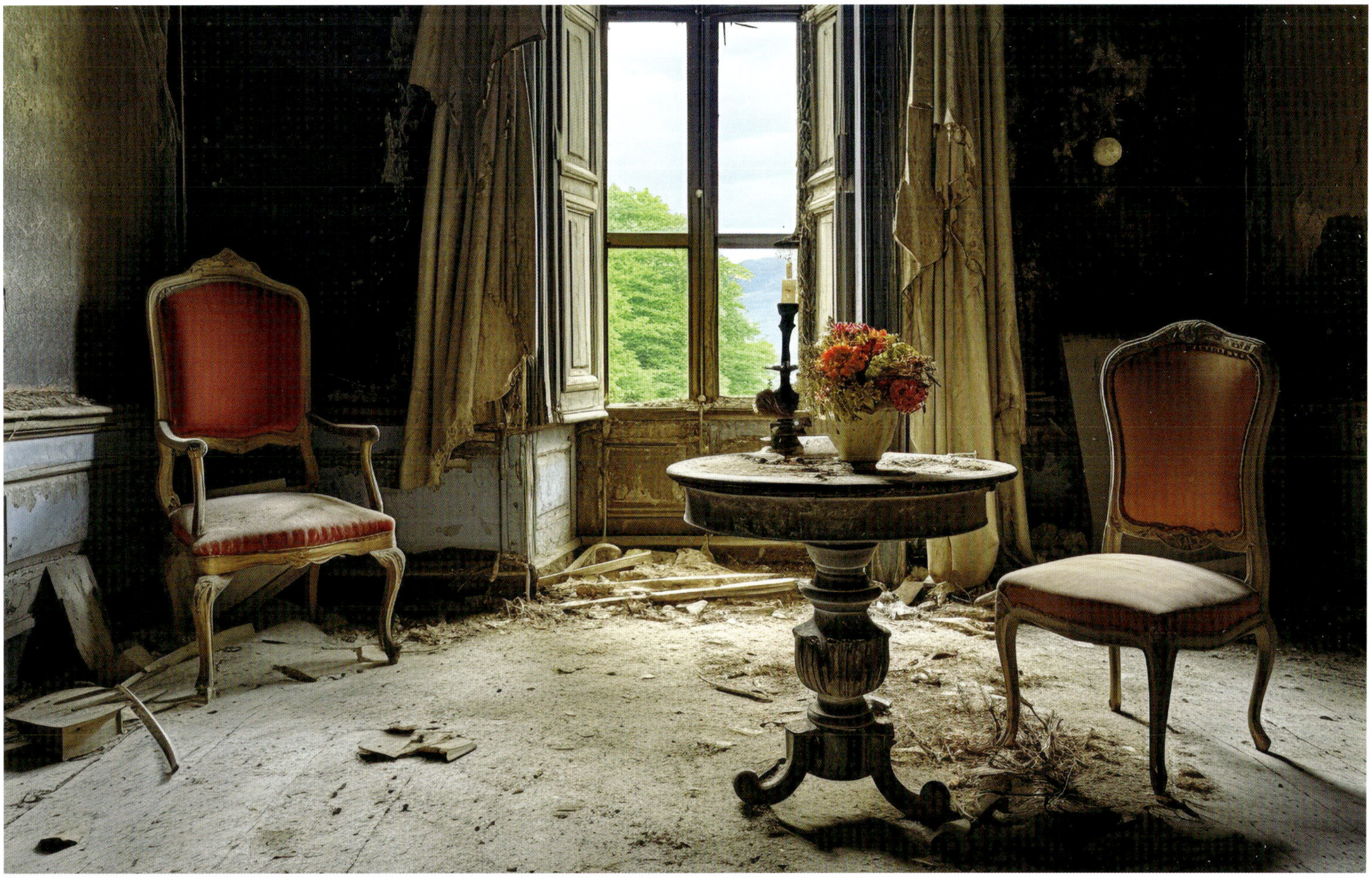

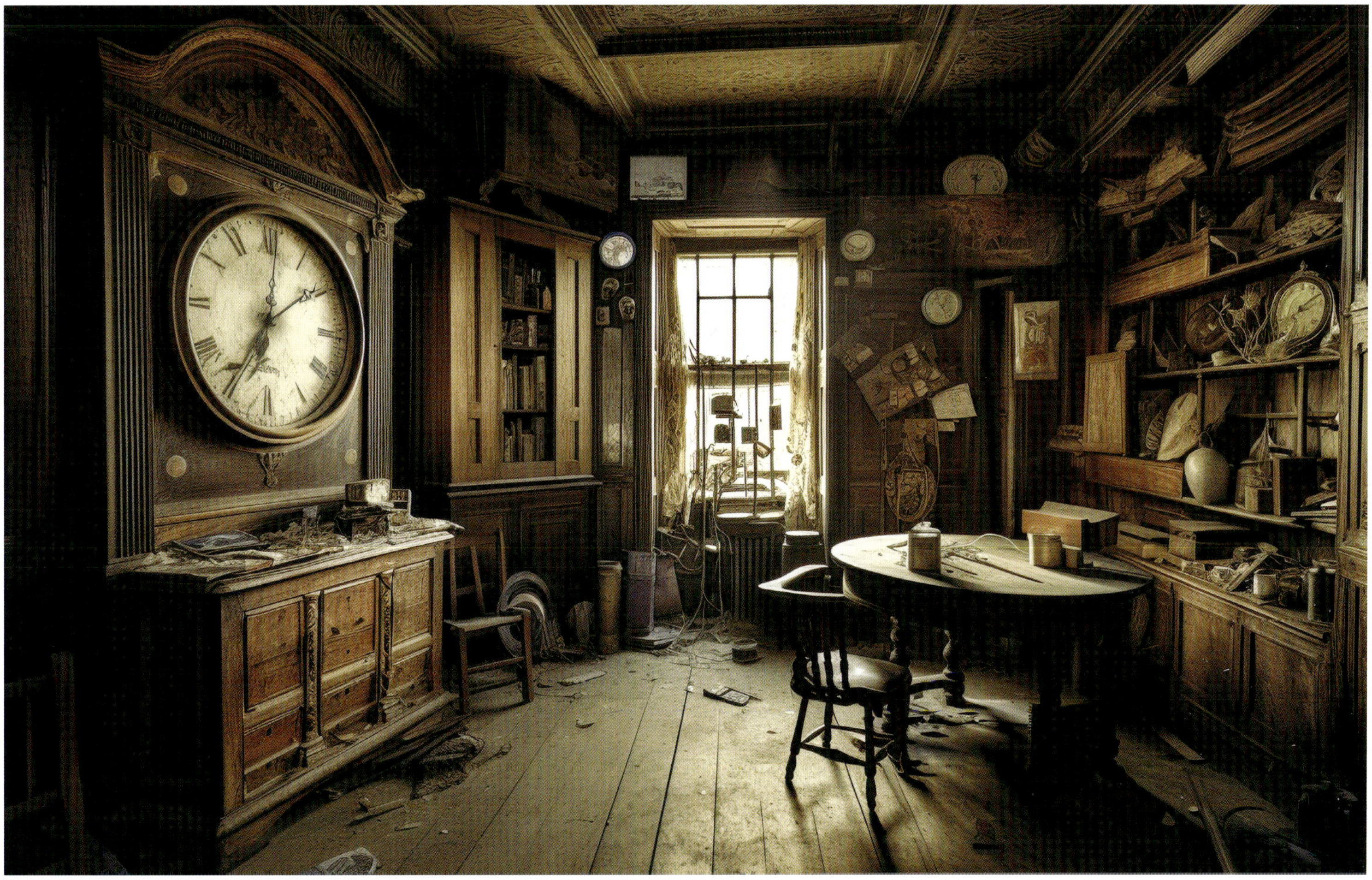

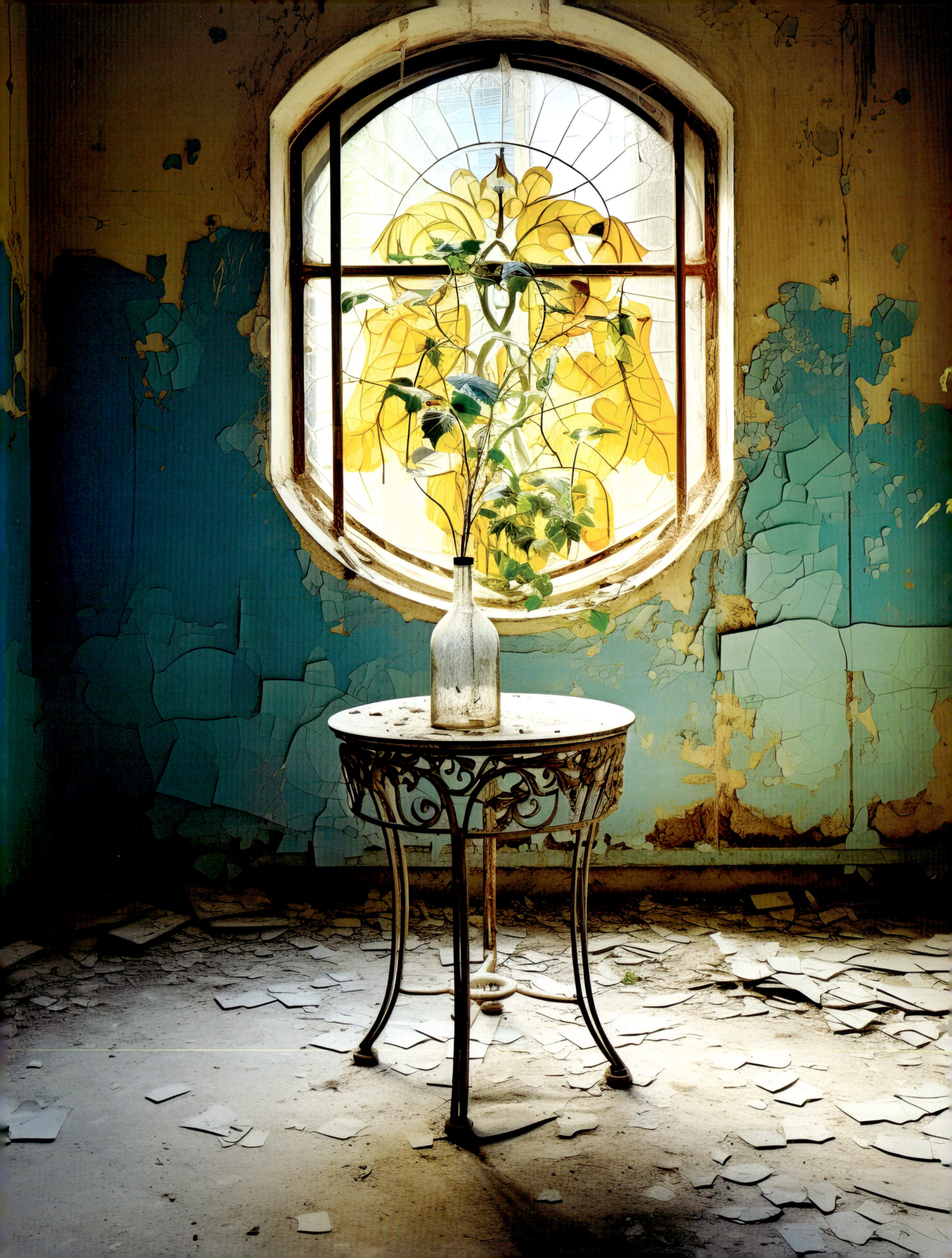

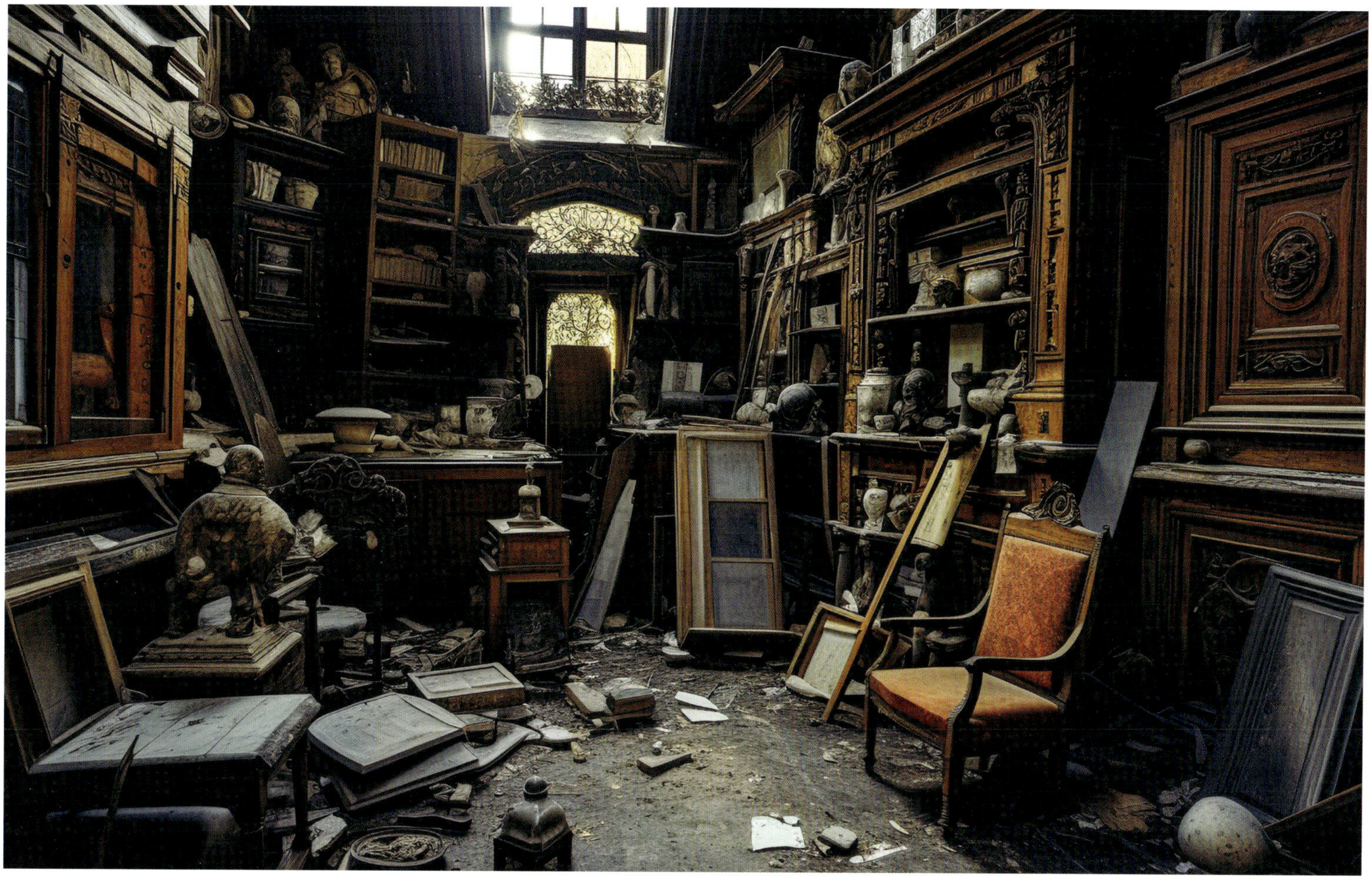

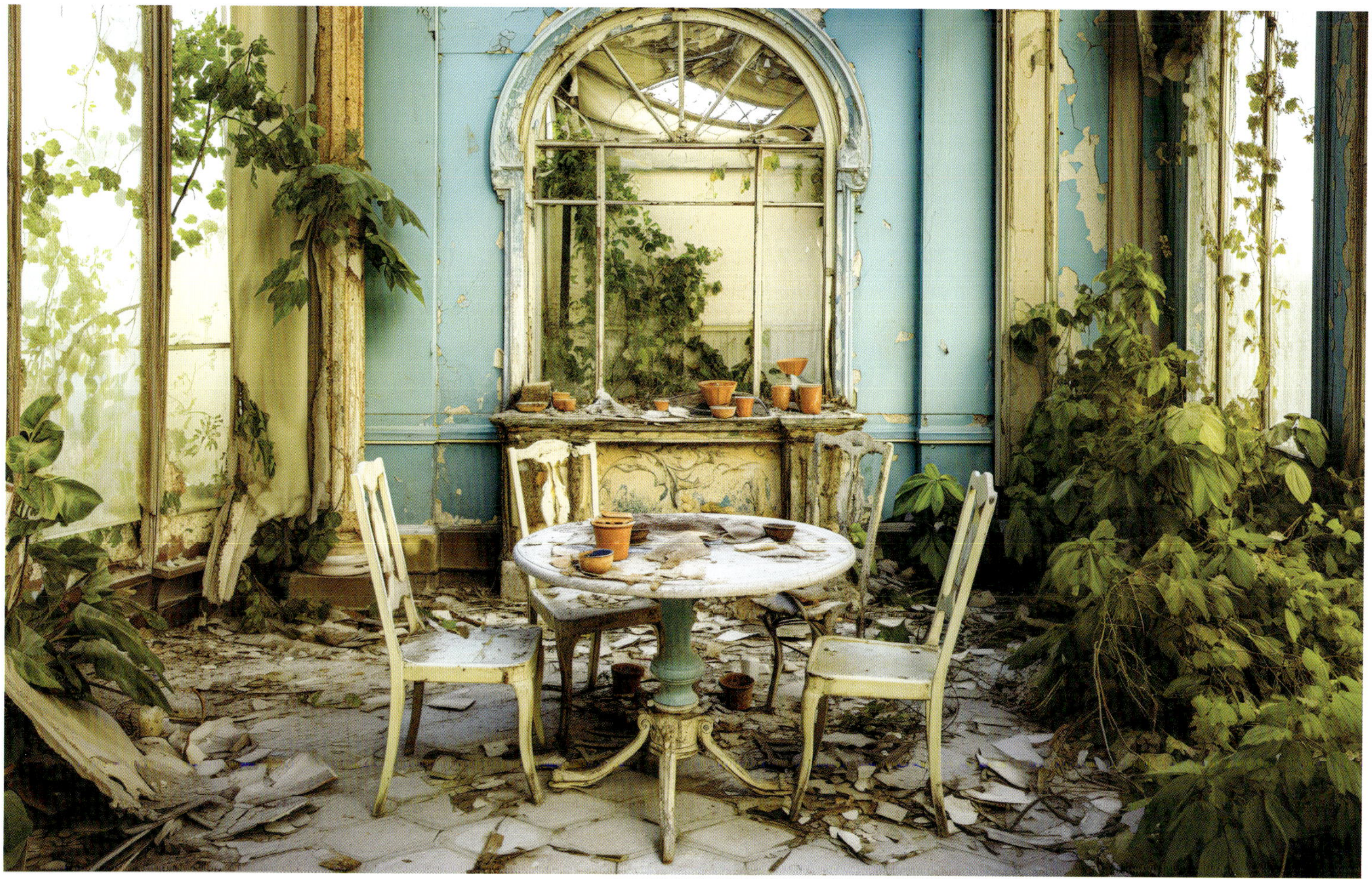

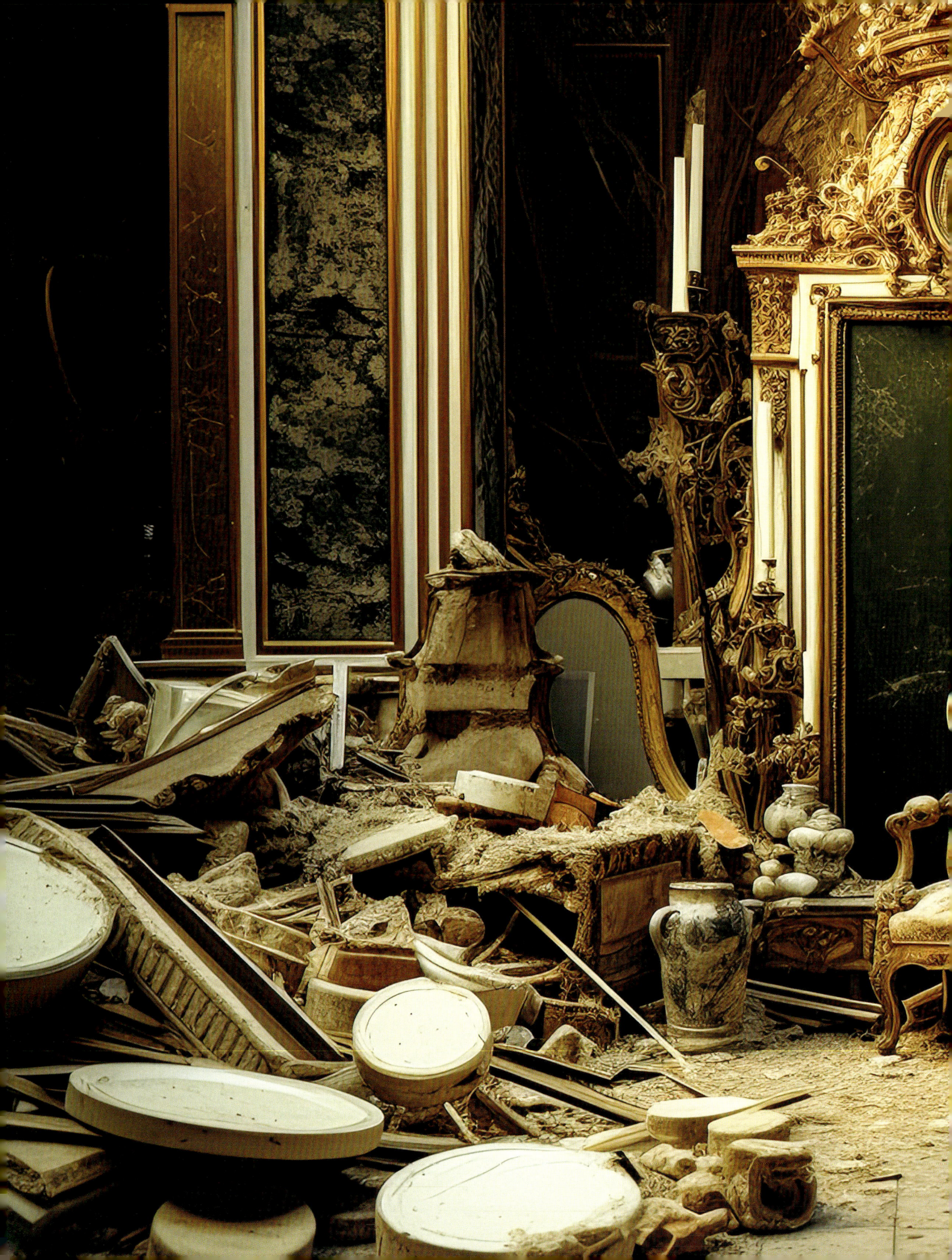

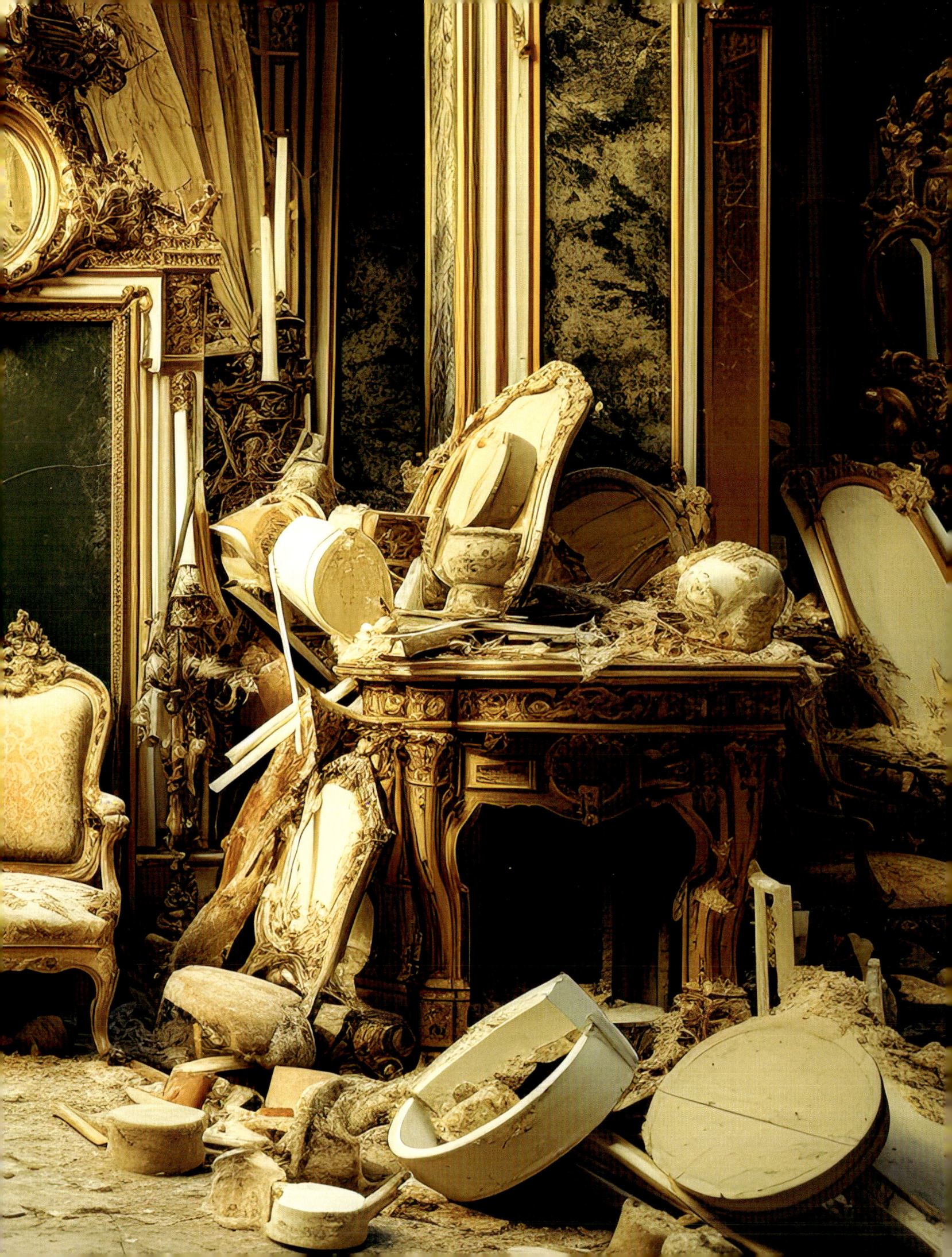

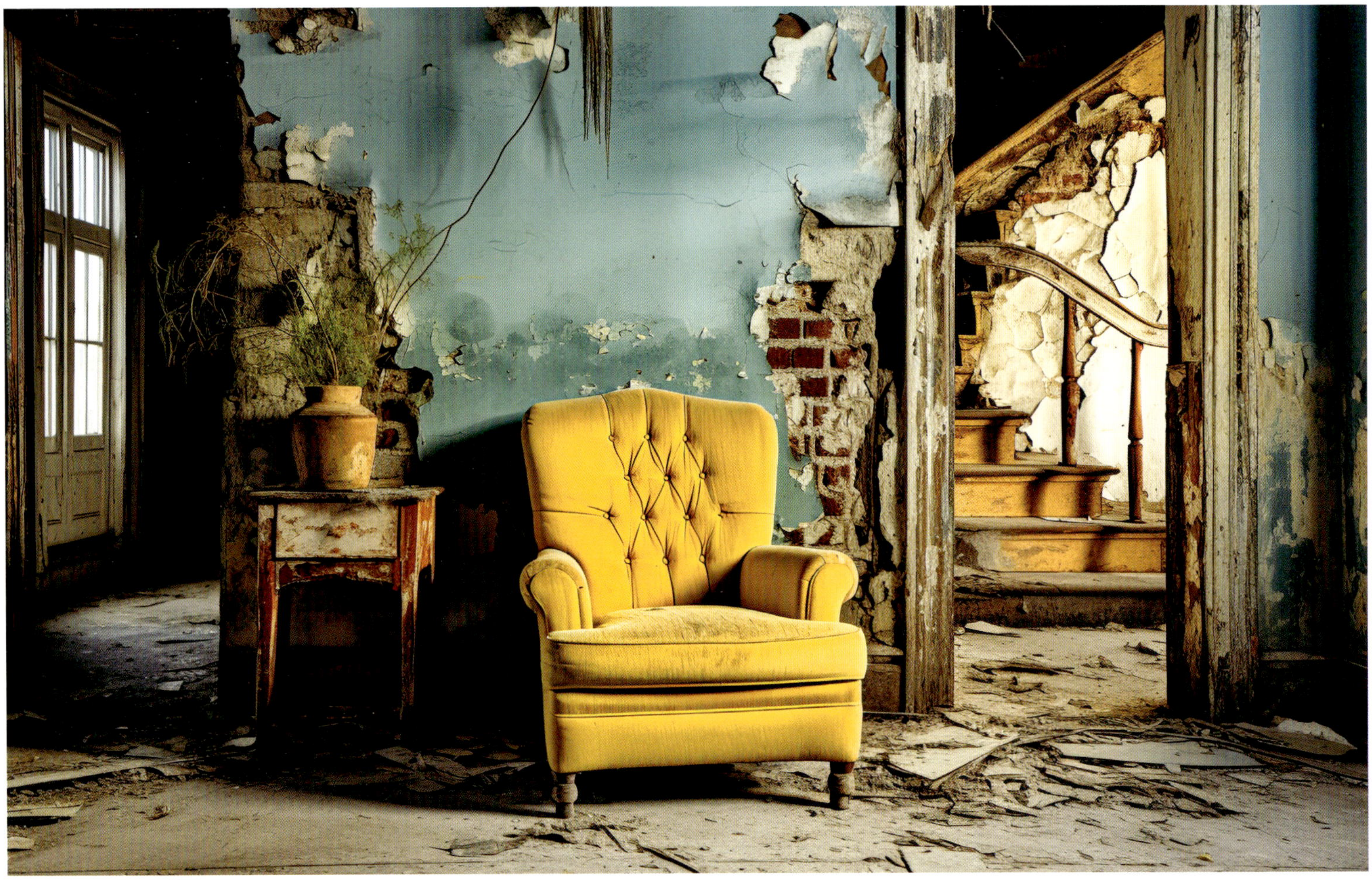

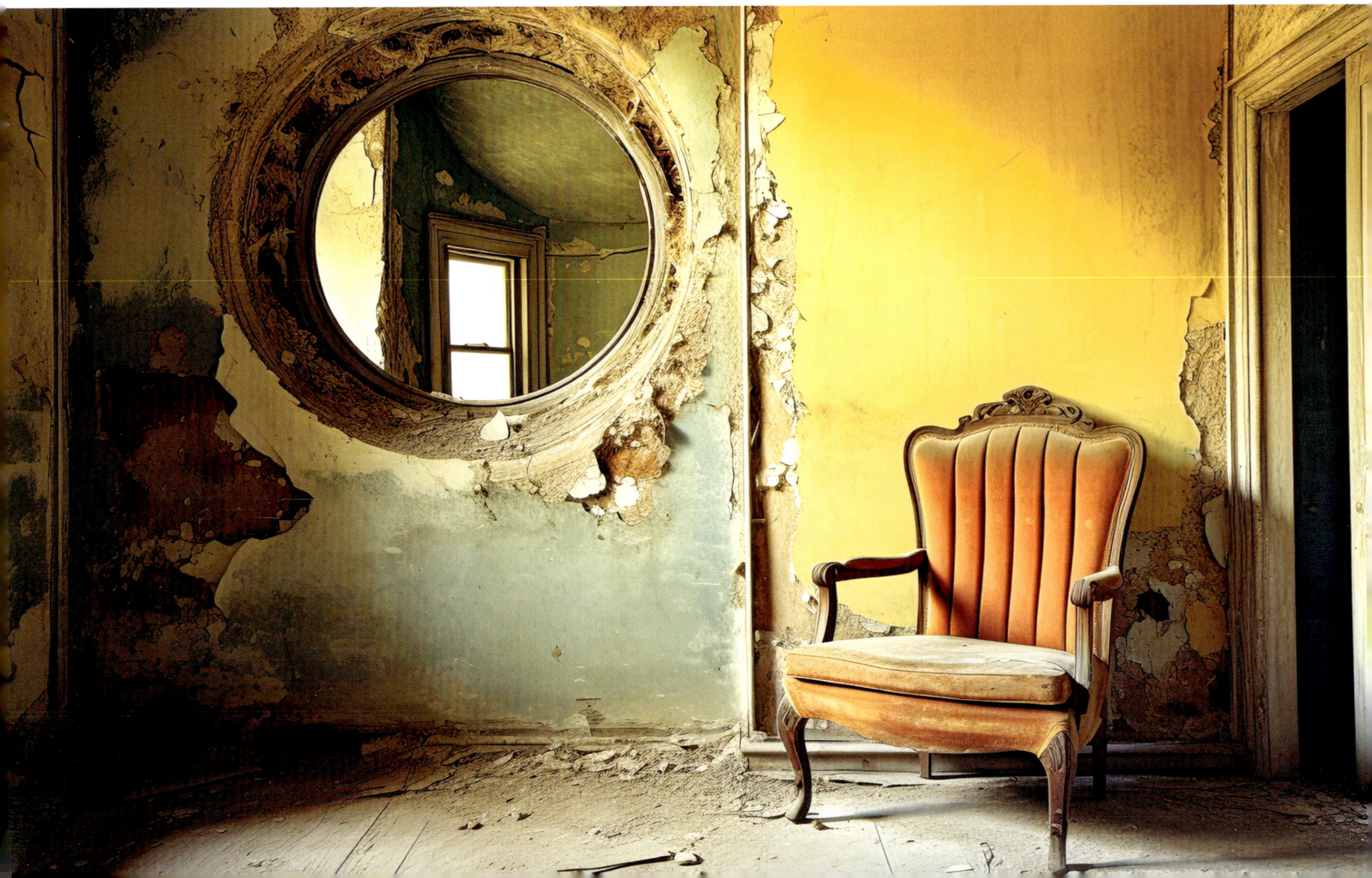

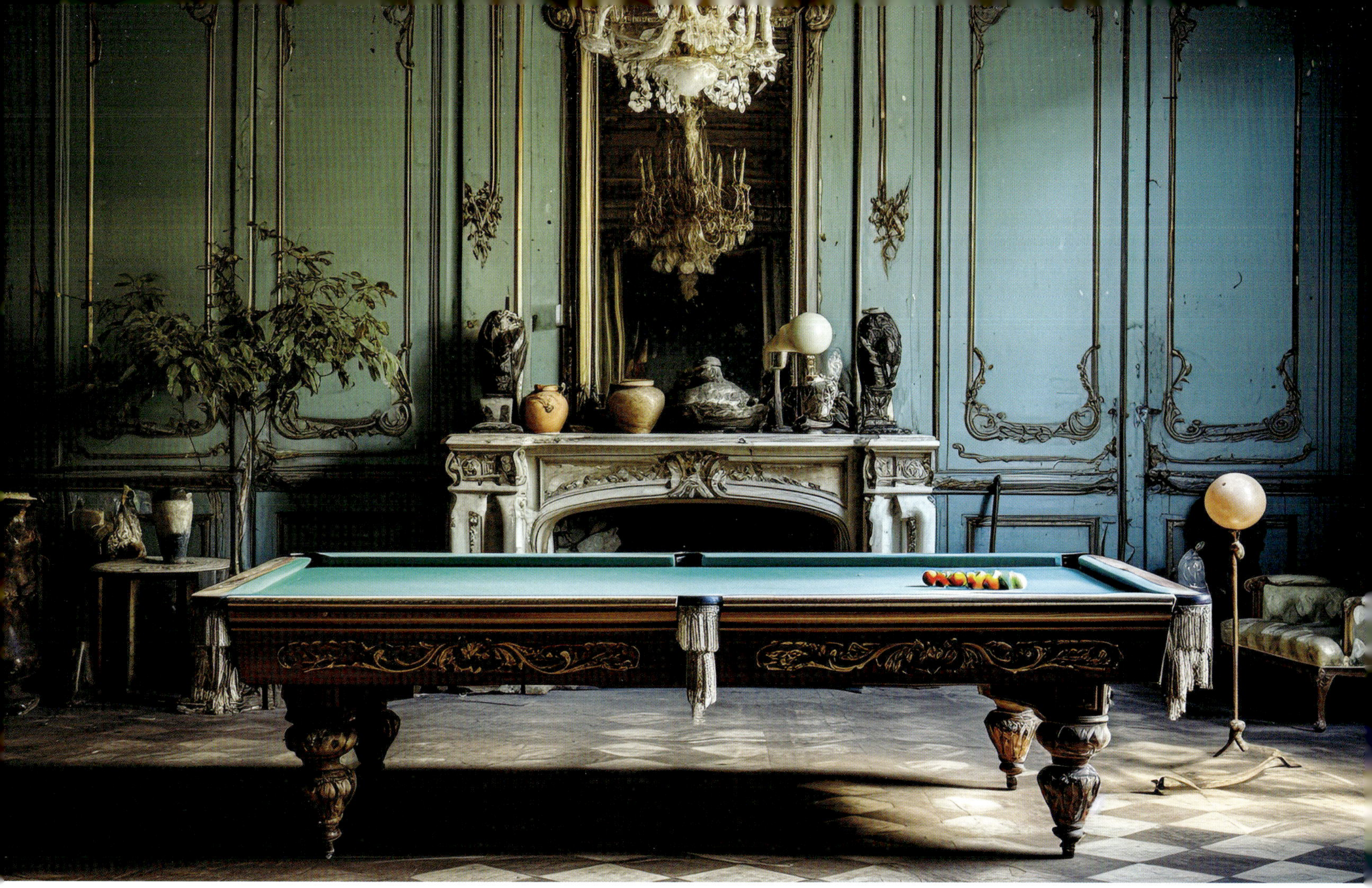

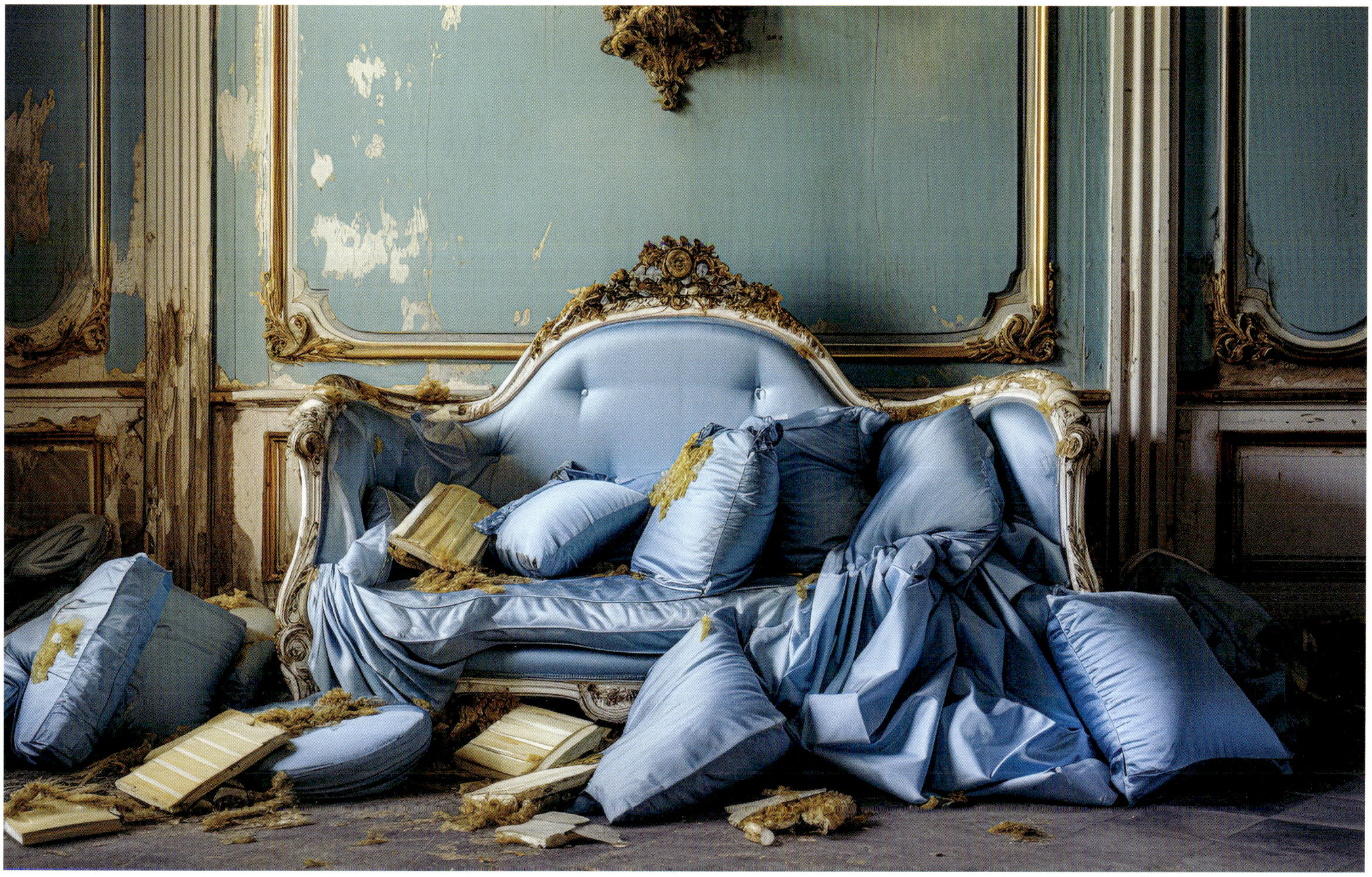

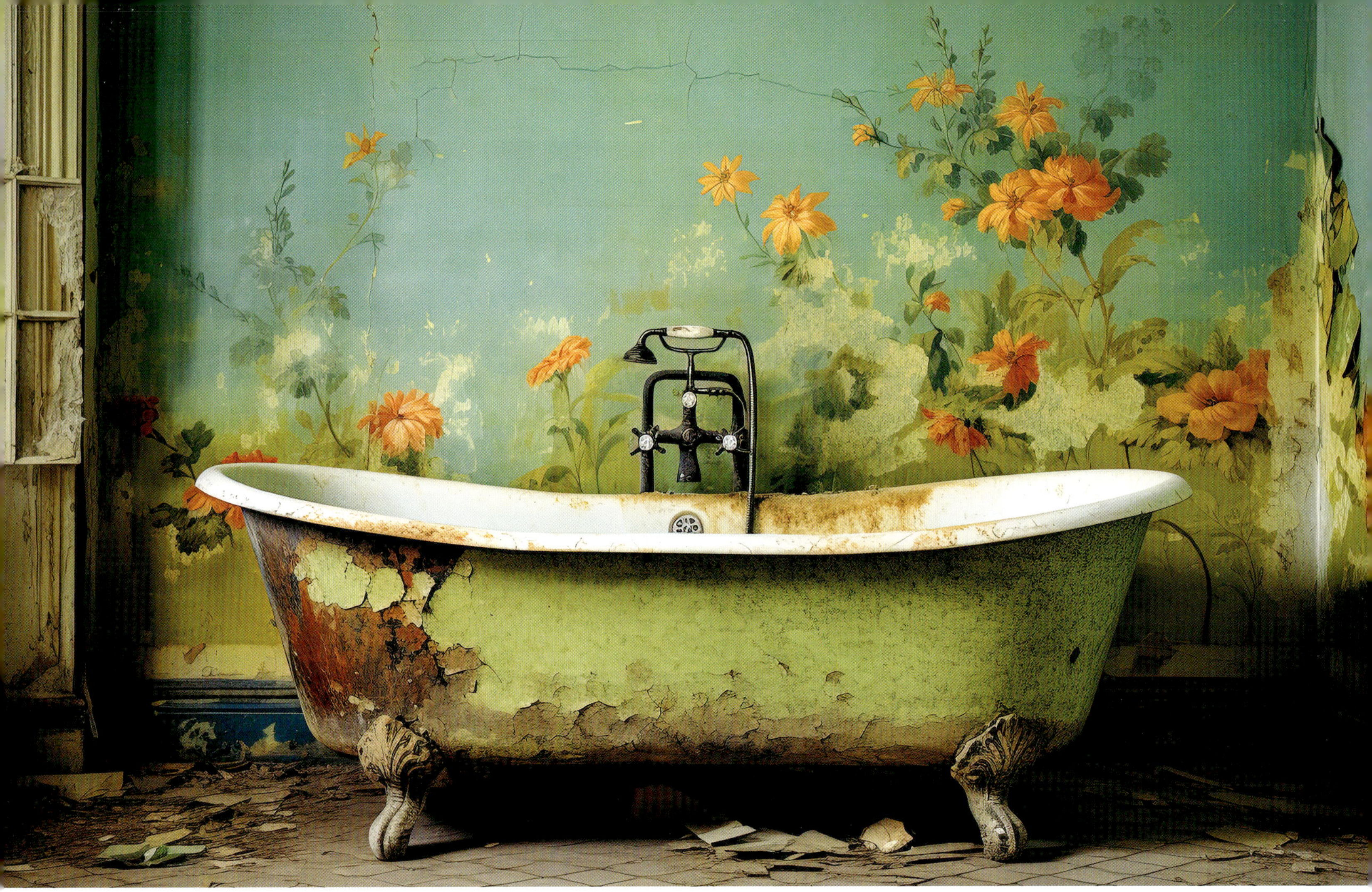

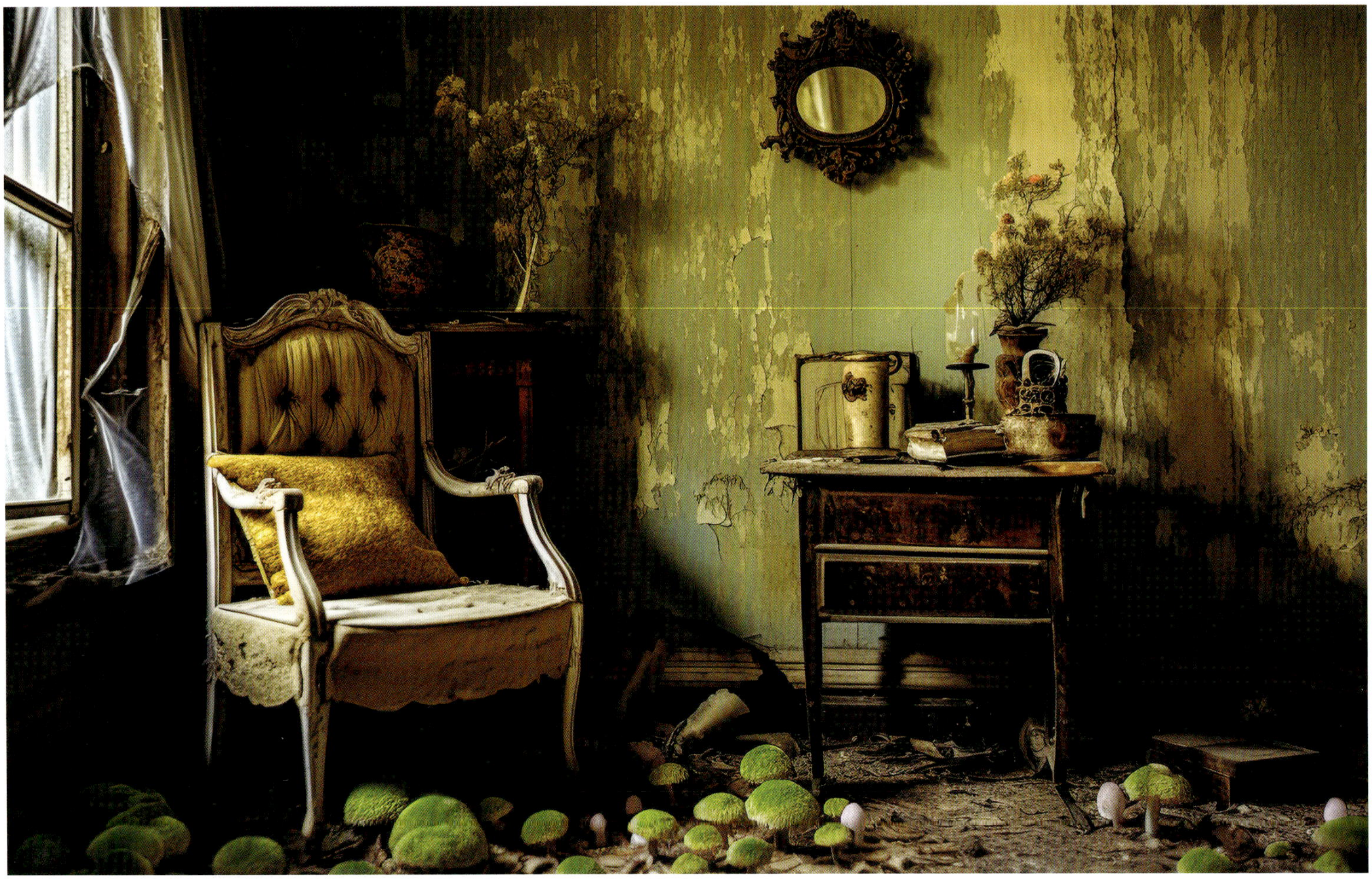

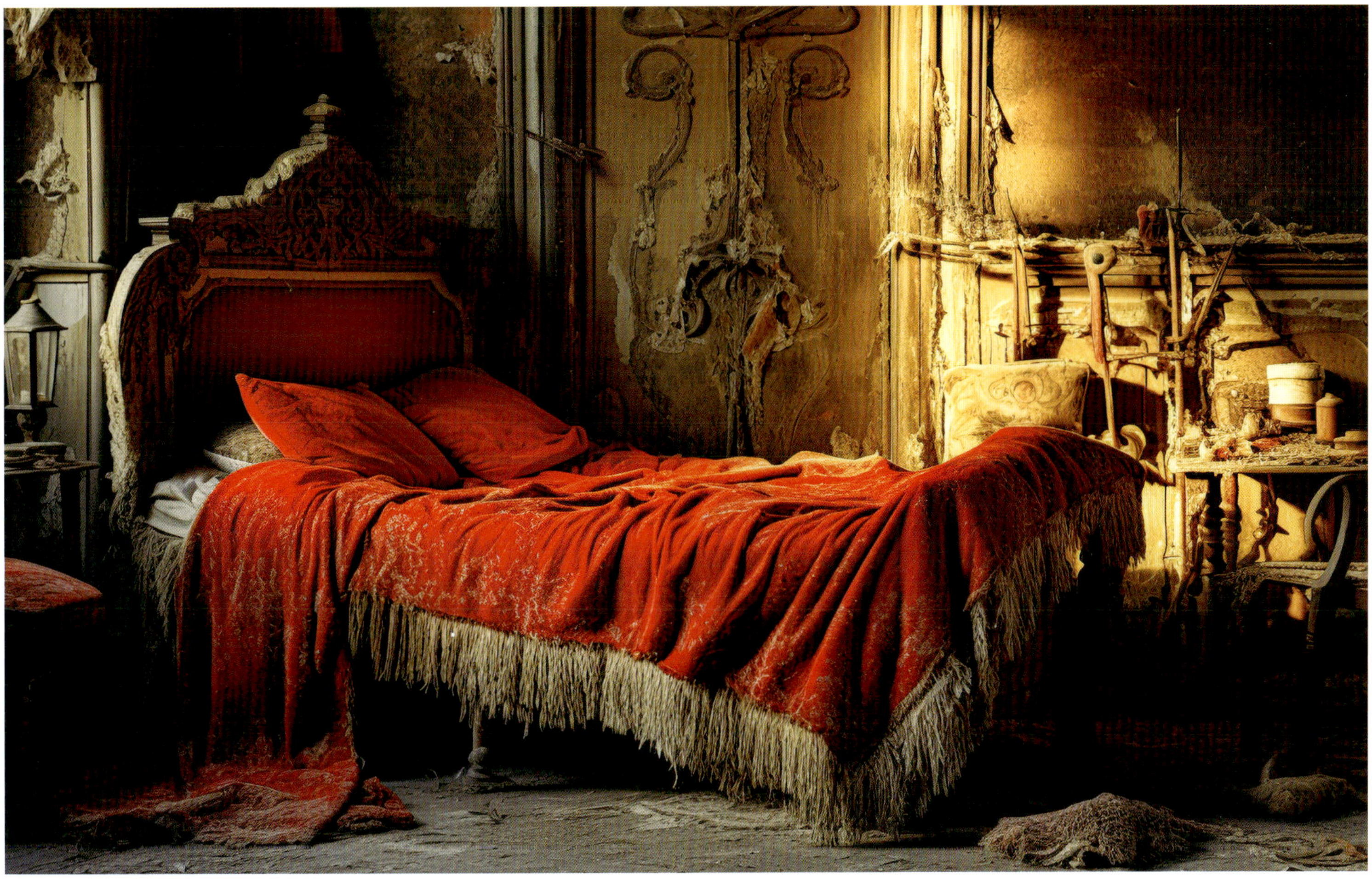

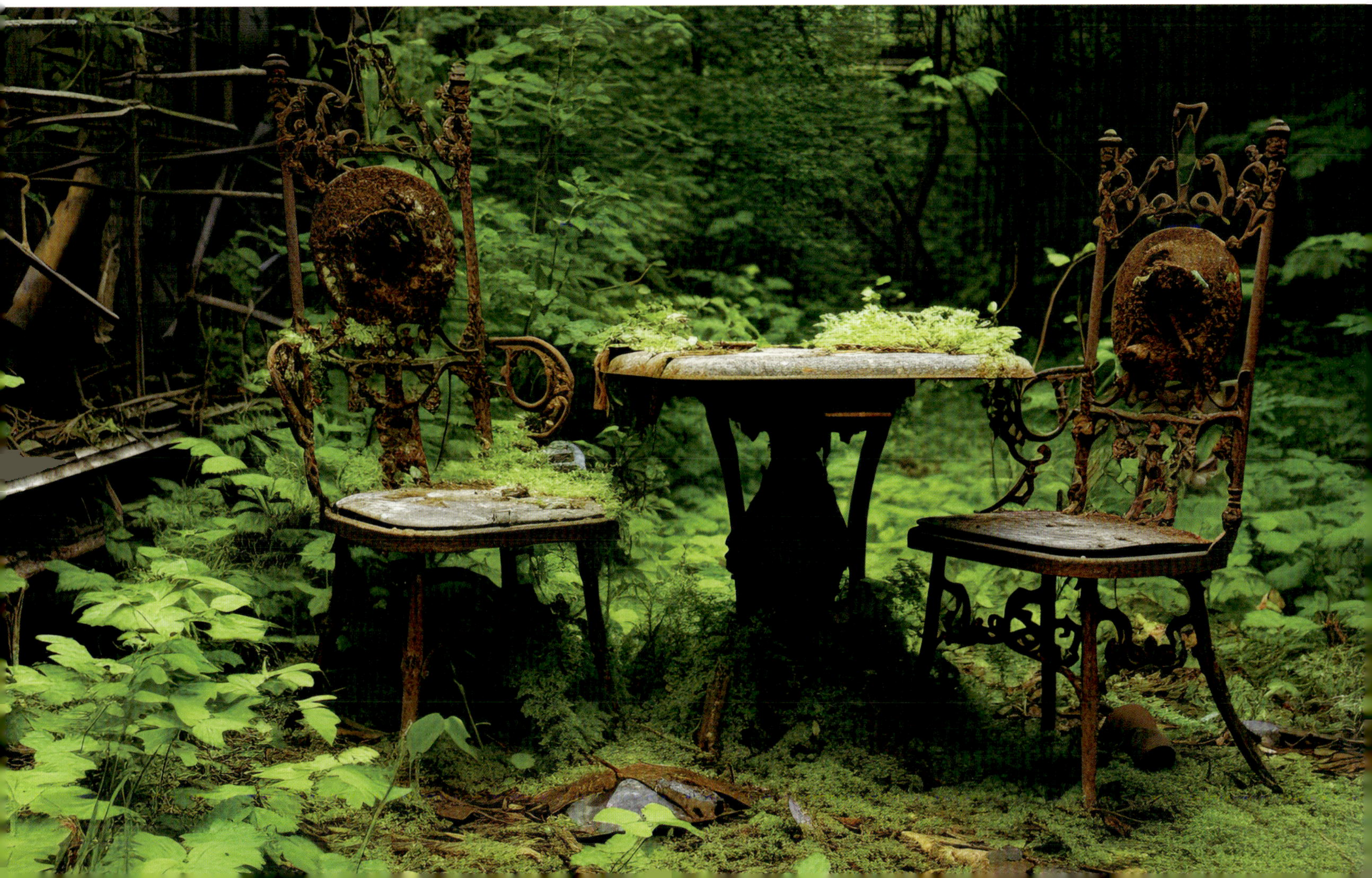

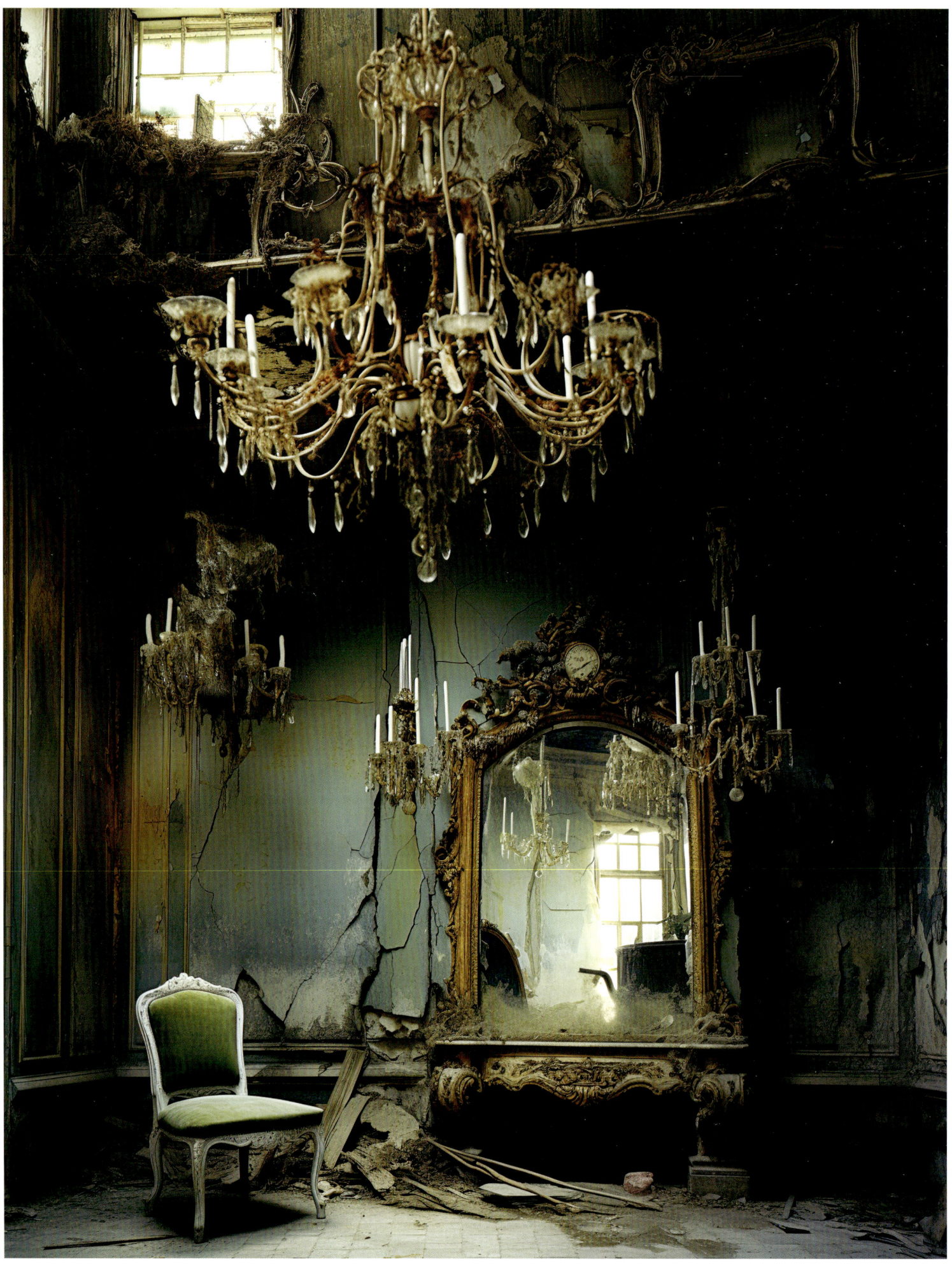

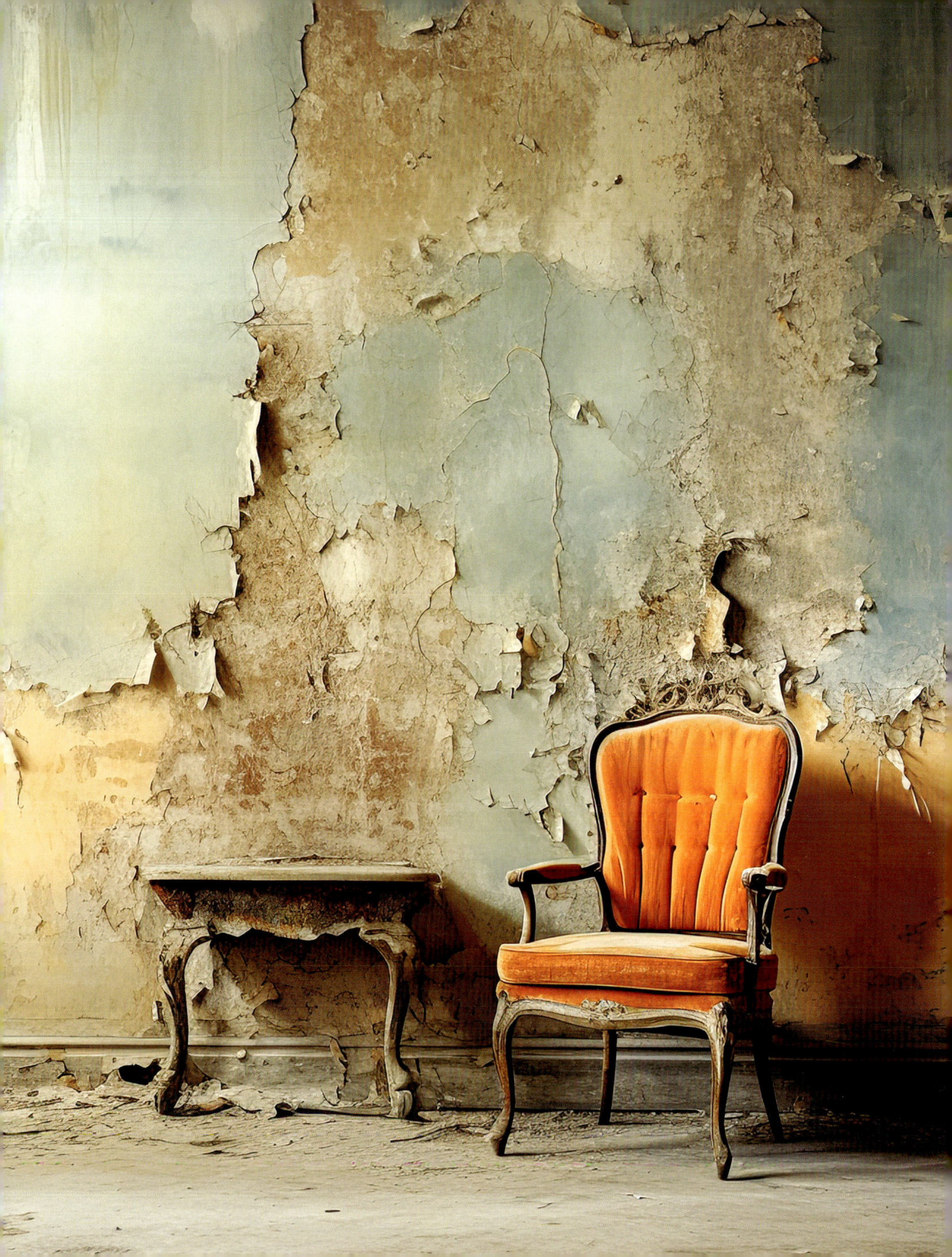

Lies and fall

Under the dictatorship of all things digital, material goods have completely lost their appeal. Across the world, palaces have been deserted in favour of gigantic towers erected in the centre of new megacities. Power is no longer measured in terms of surface area but altitude. A new hierarchy has emerged. Like the cathedral builders of the past, architects have taken up the challenge of conquering the skies, seeking to free themselves from asphalt and gravity.

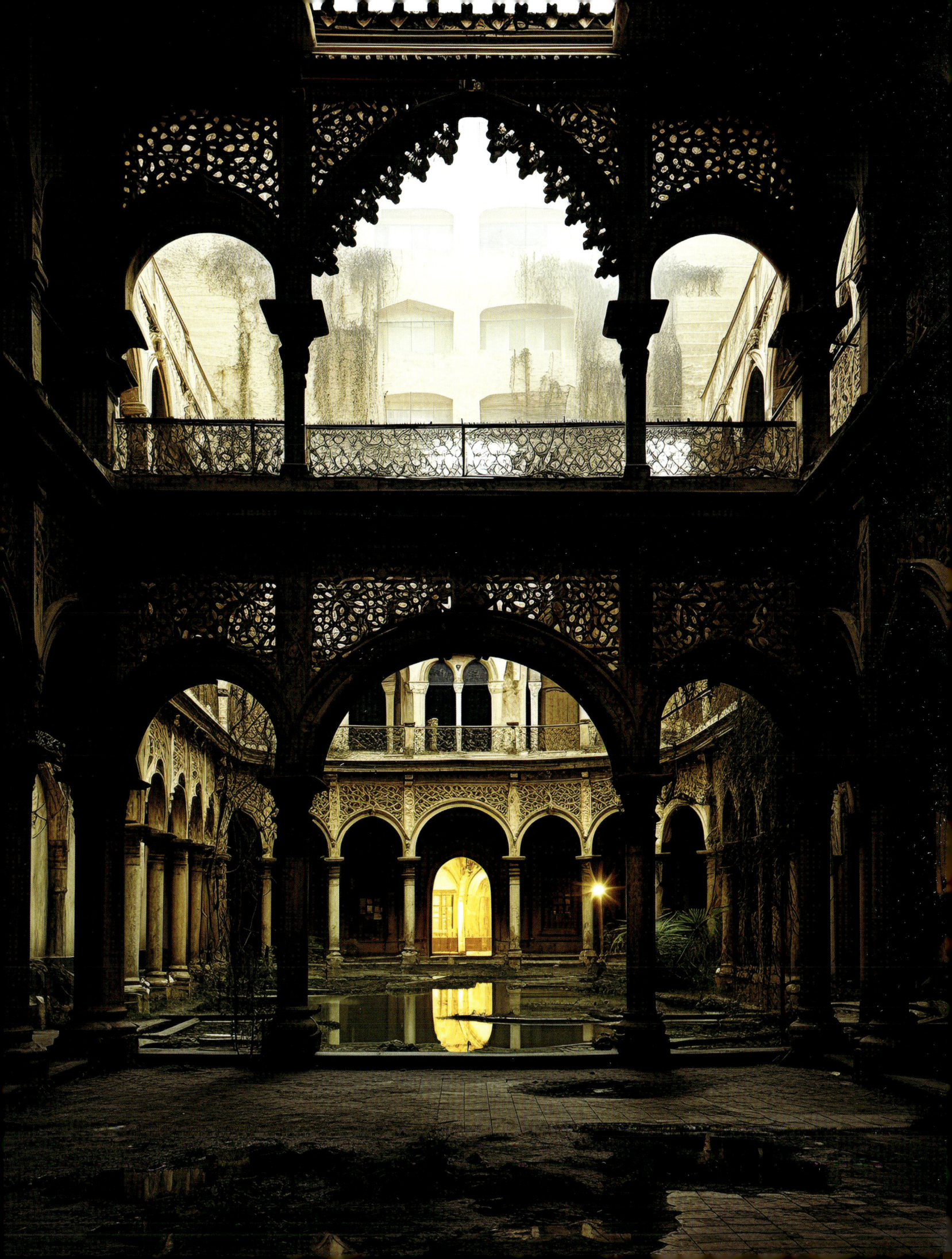

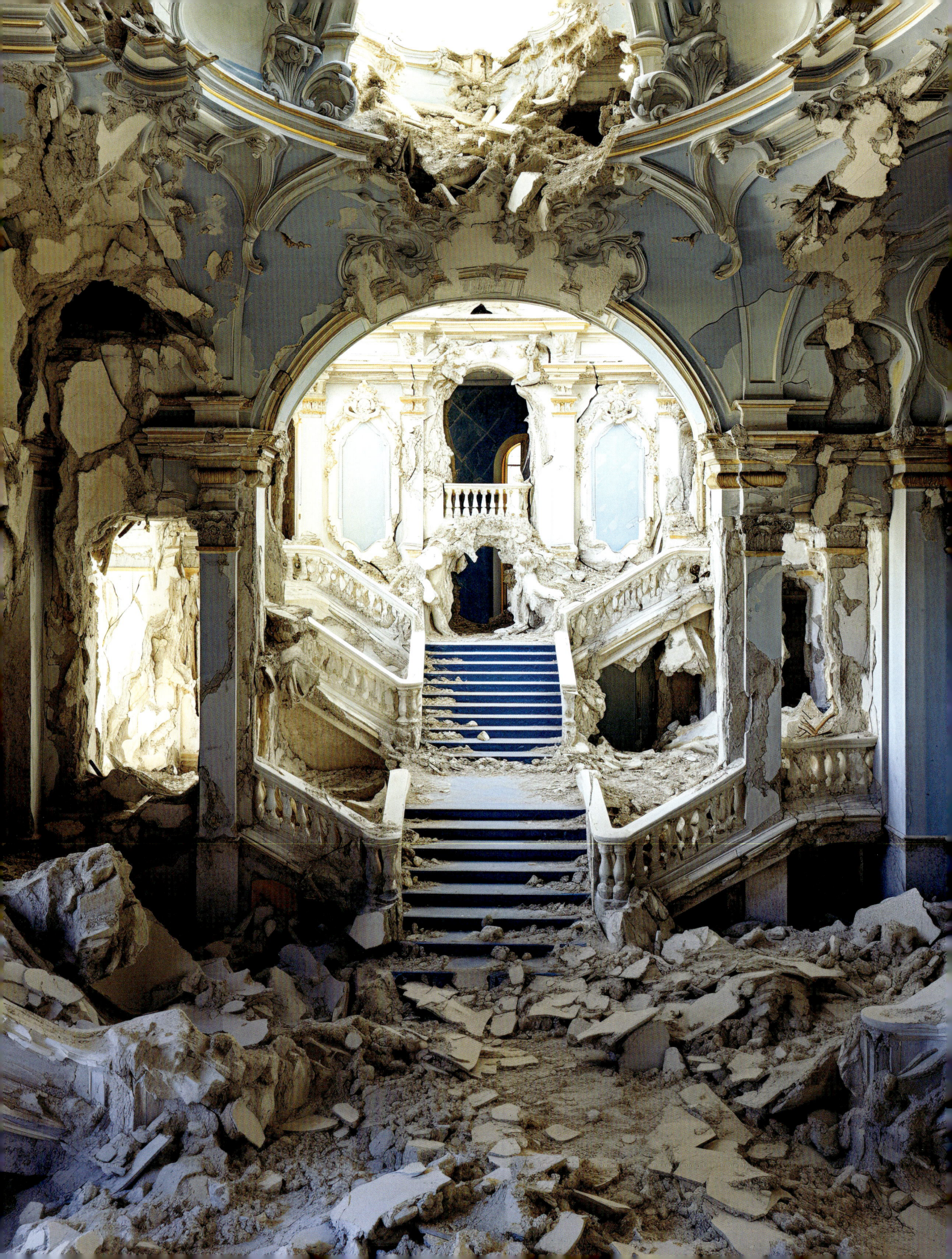

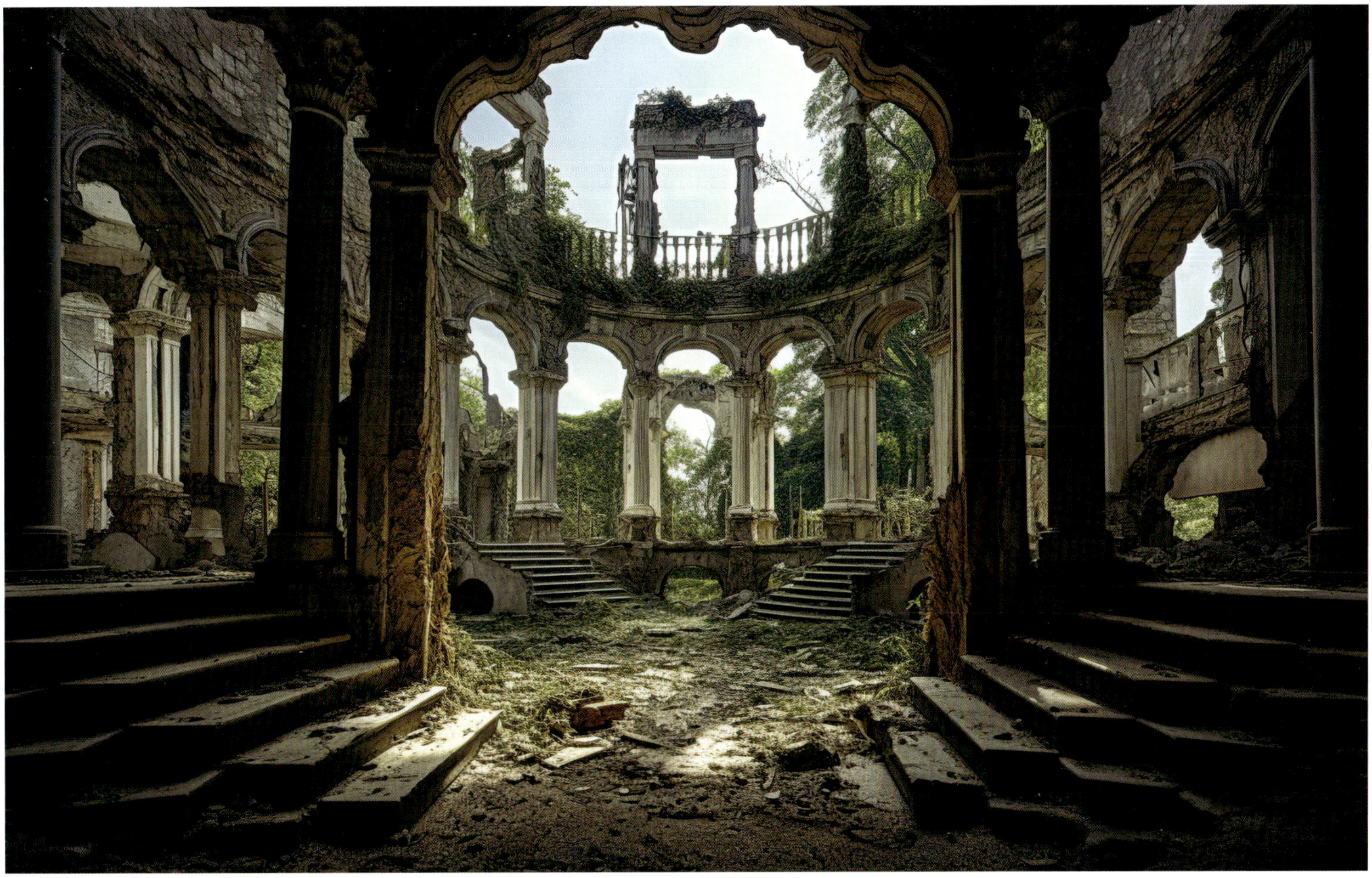

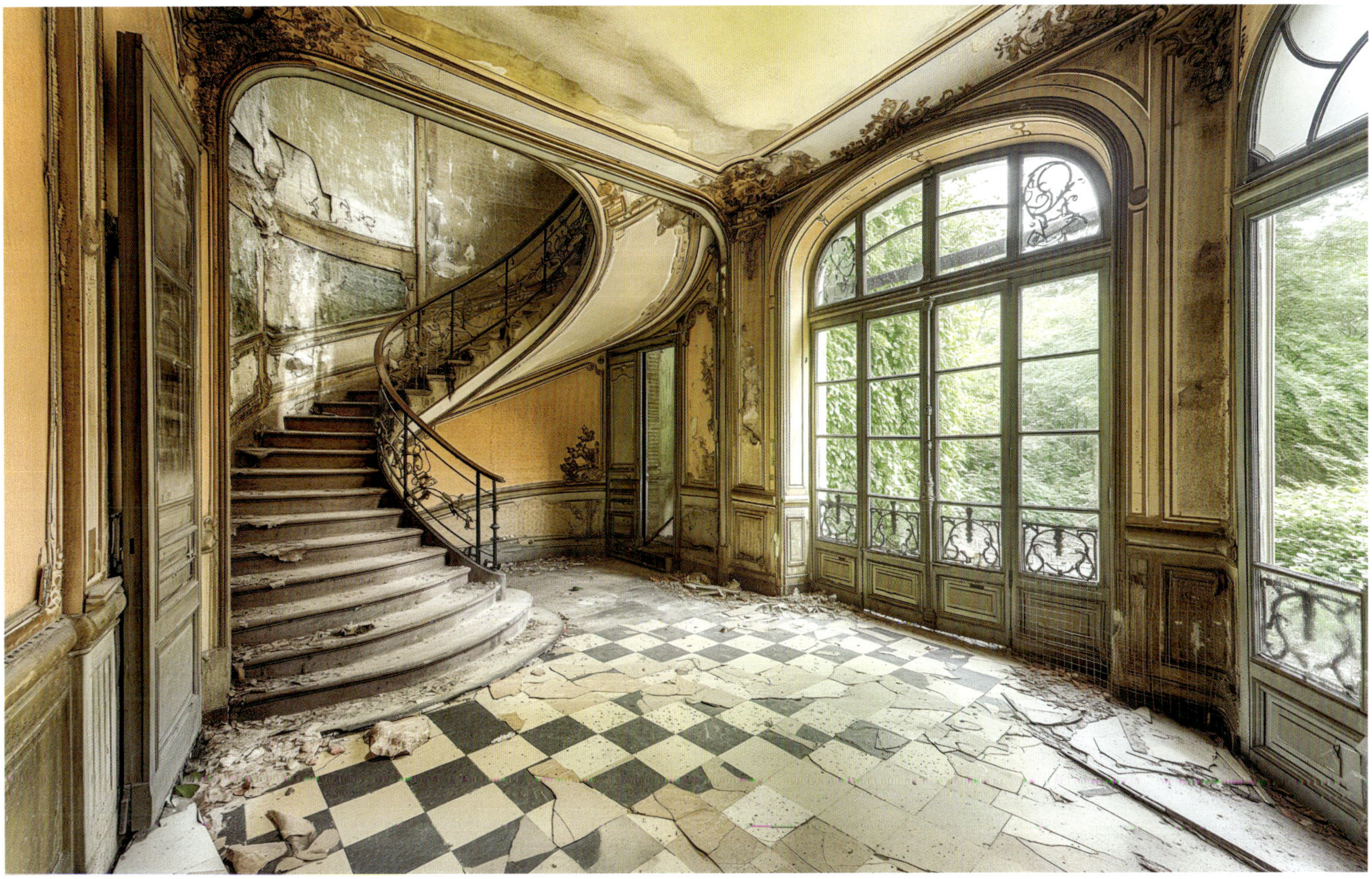

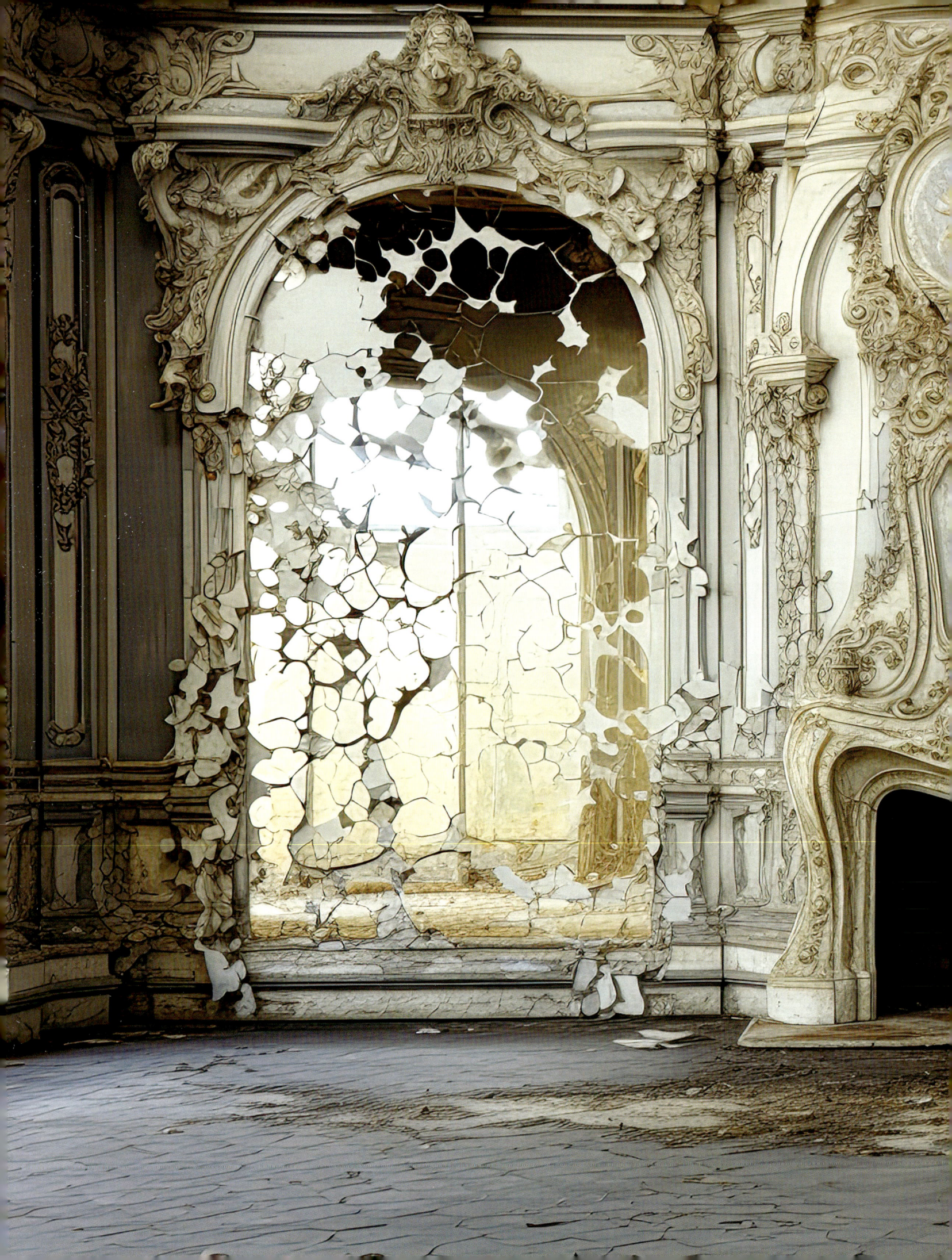

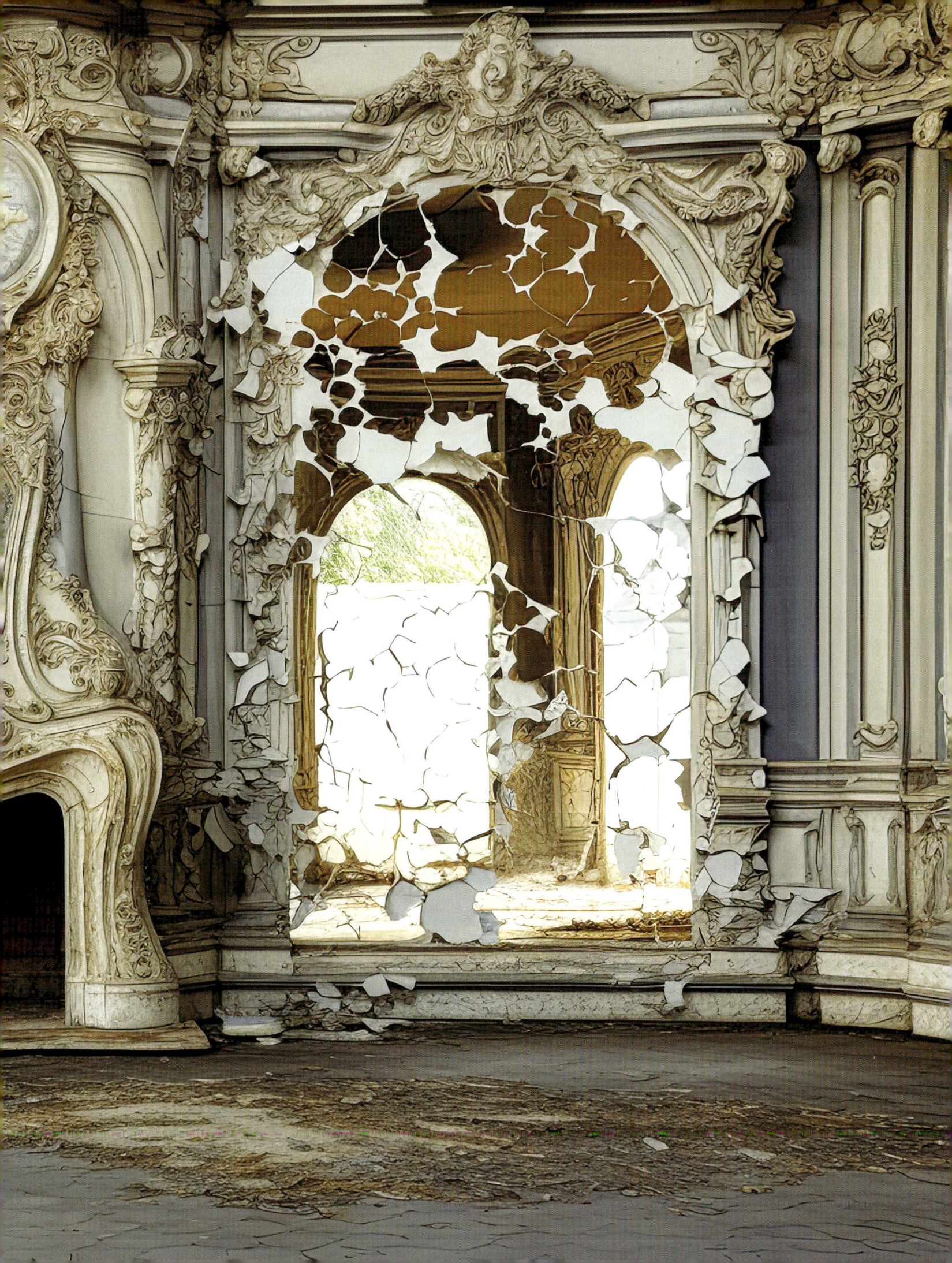

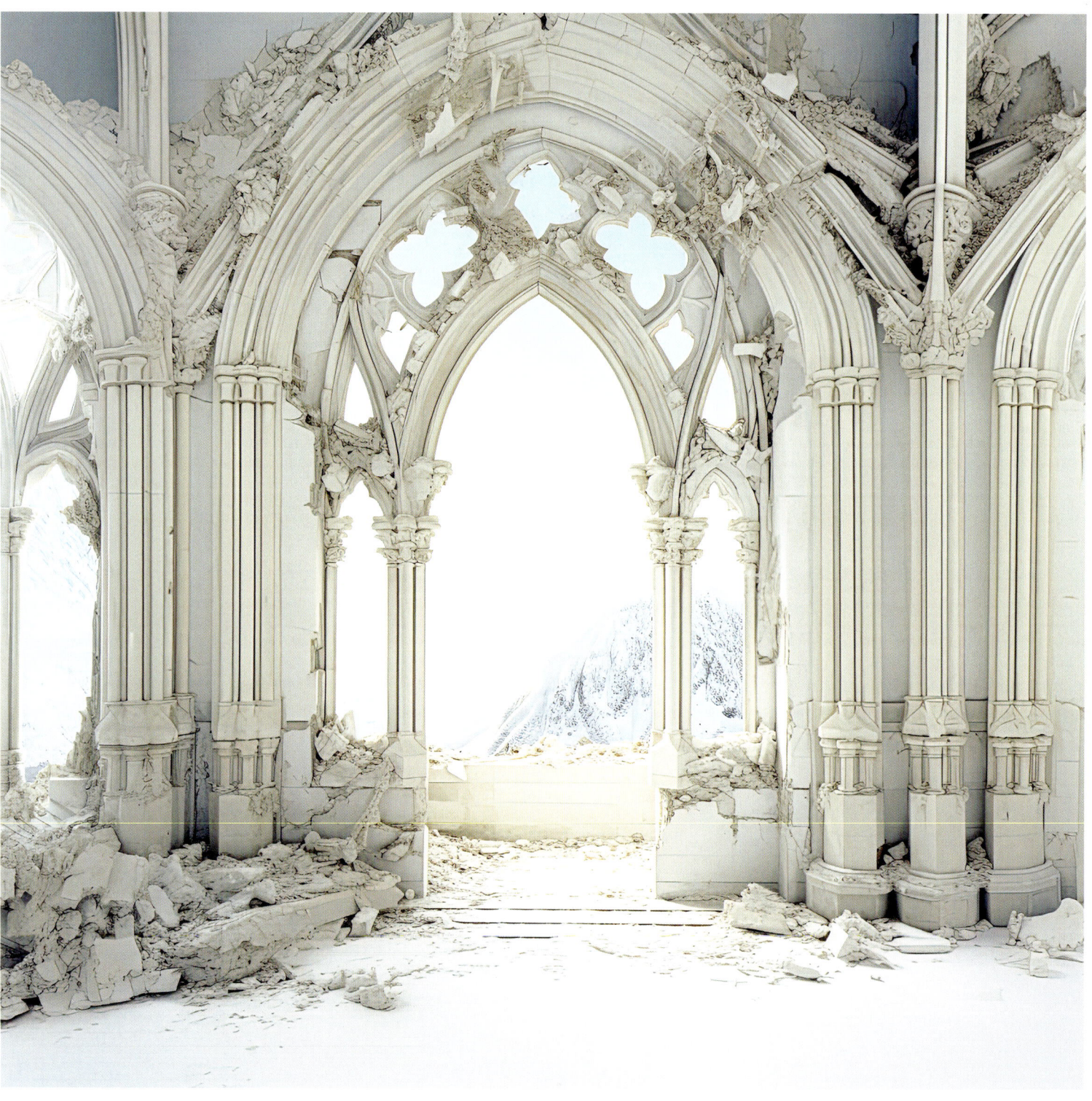

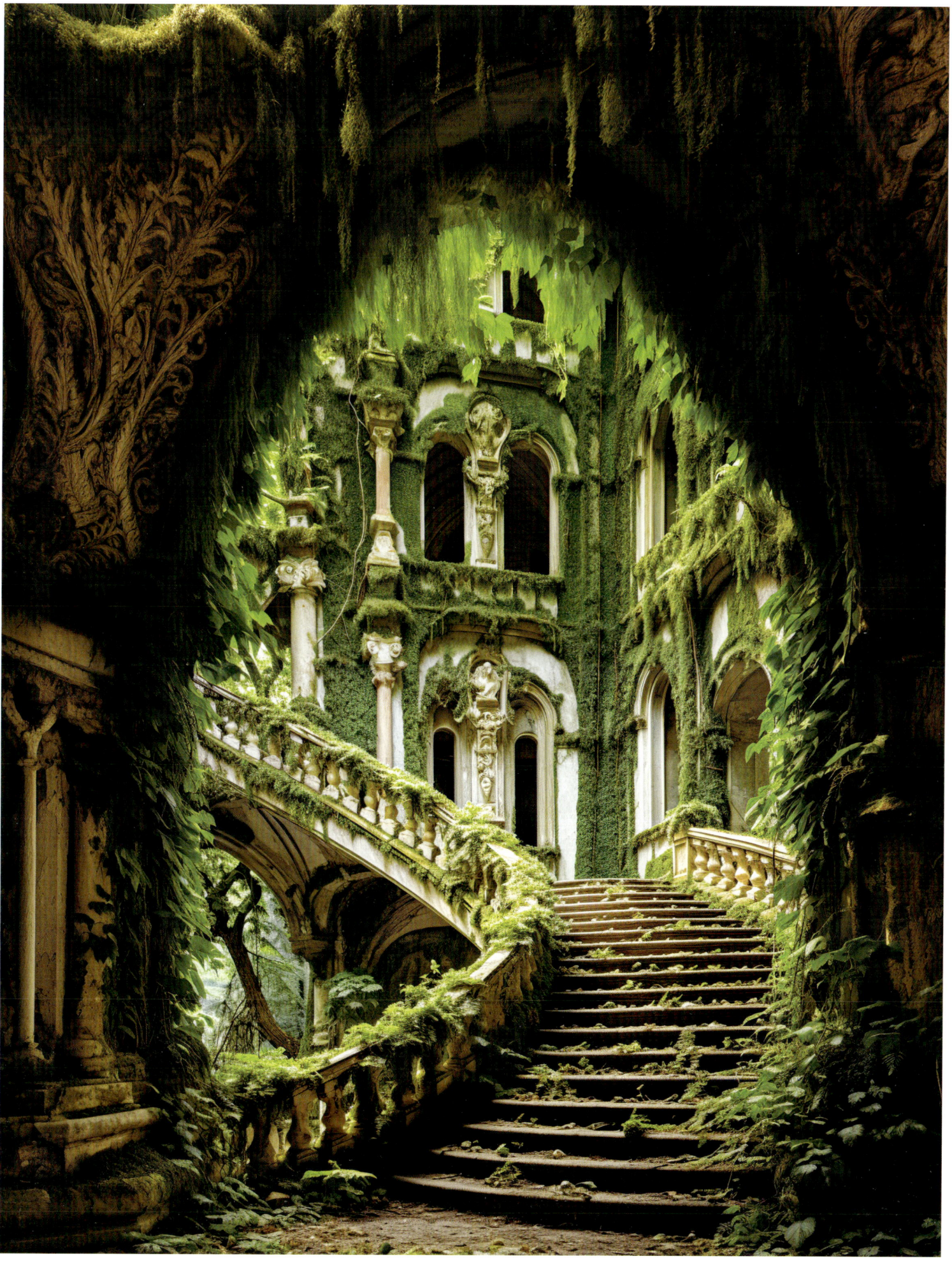

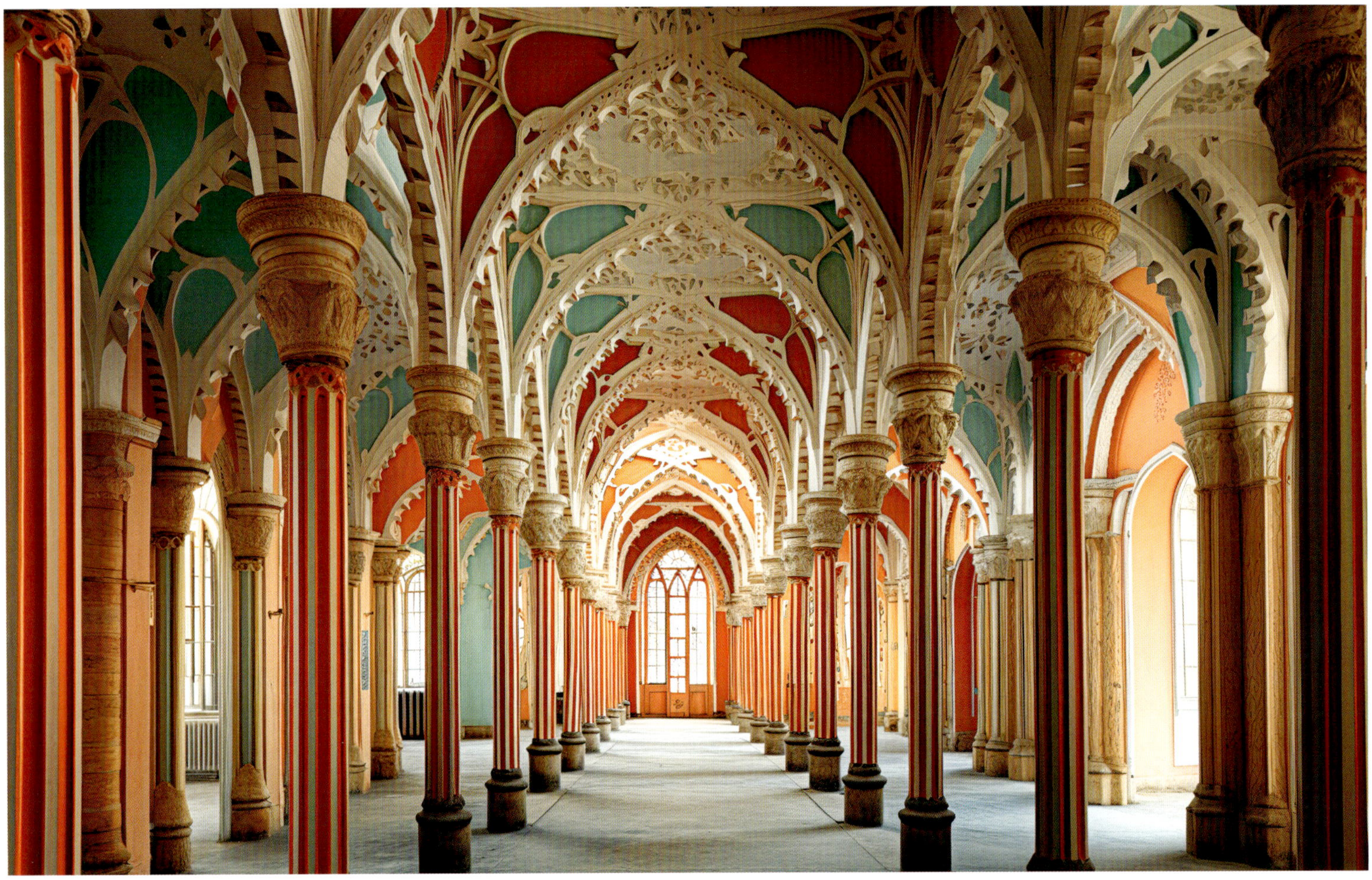

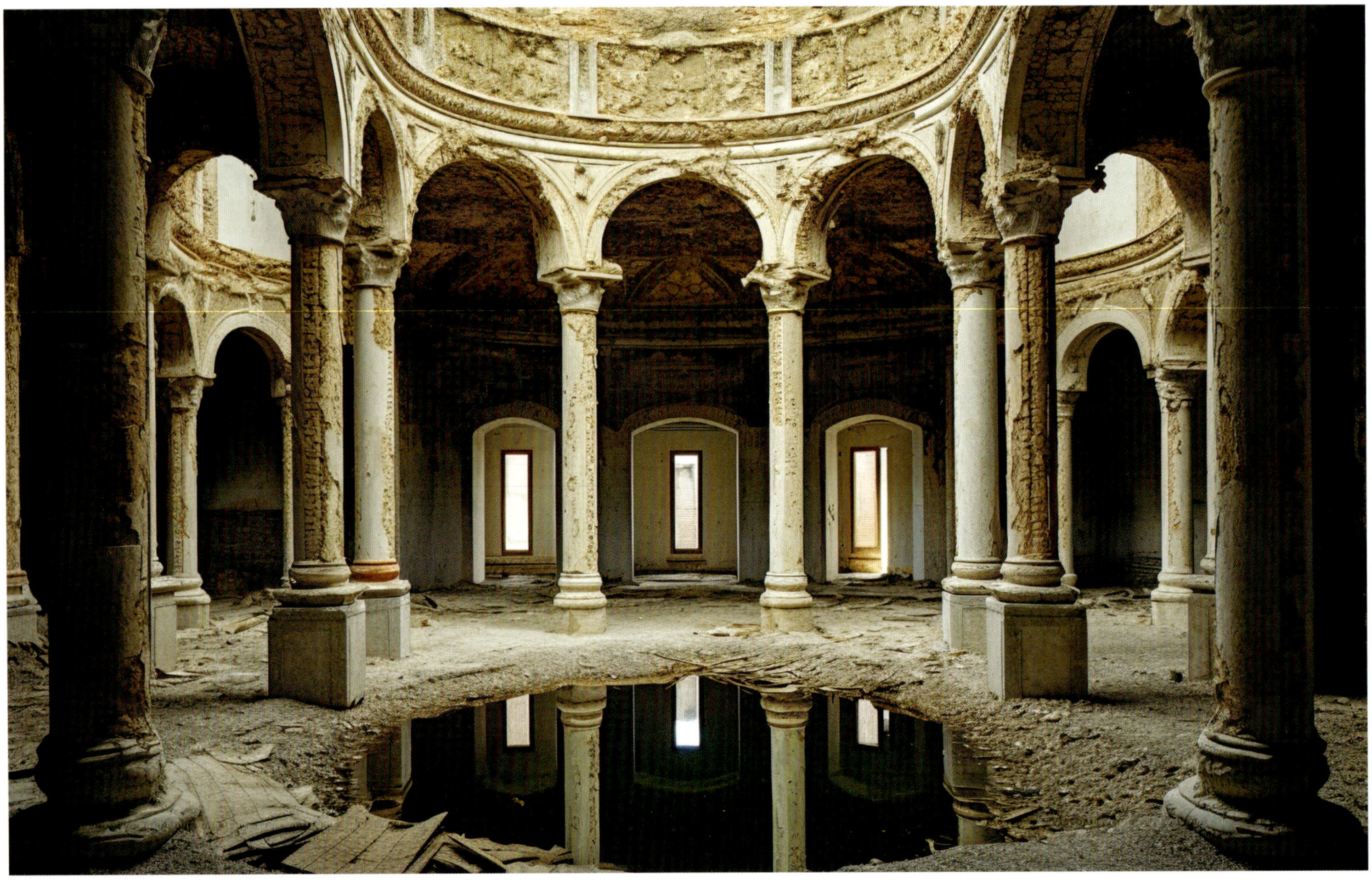

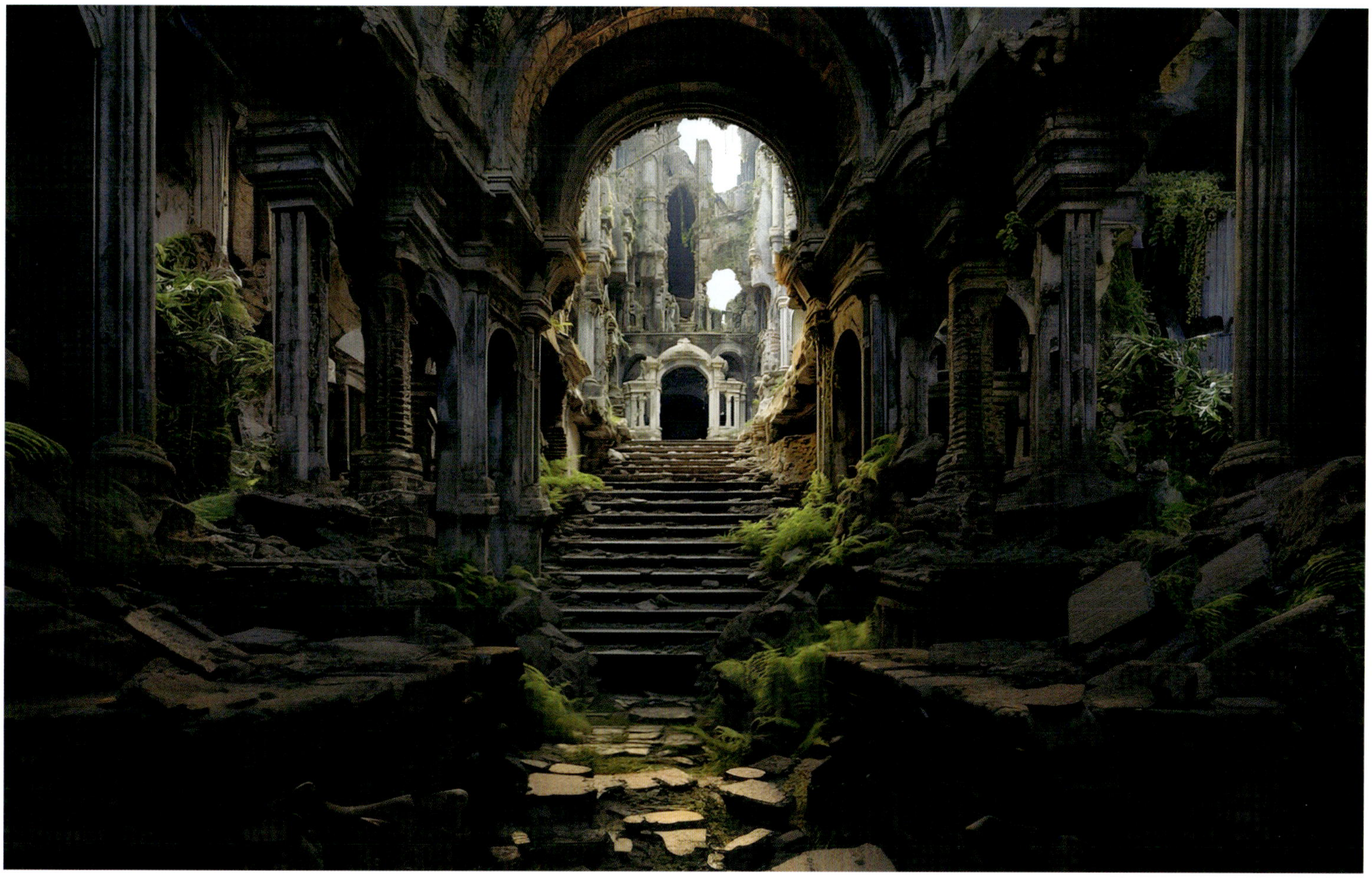

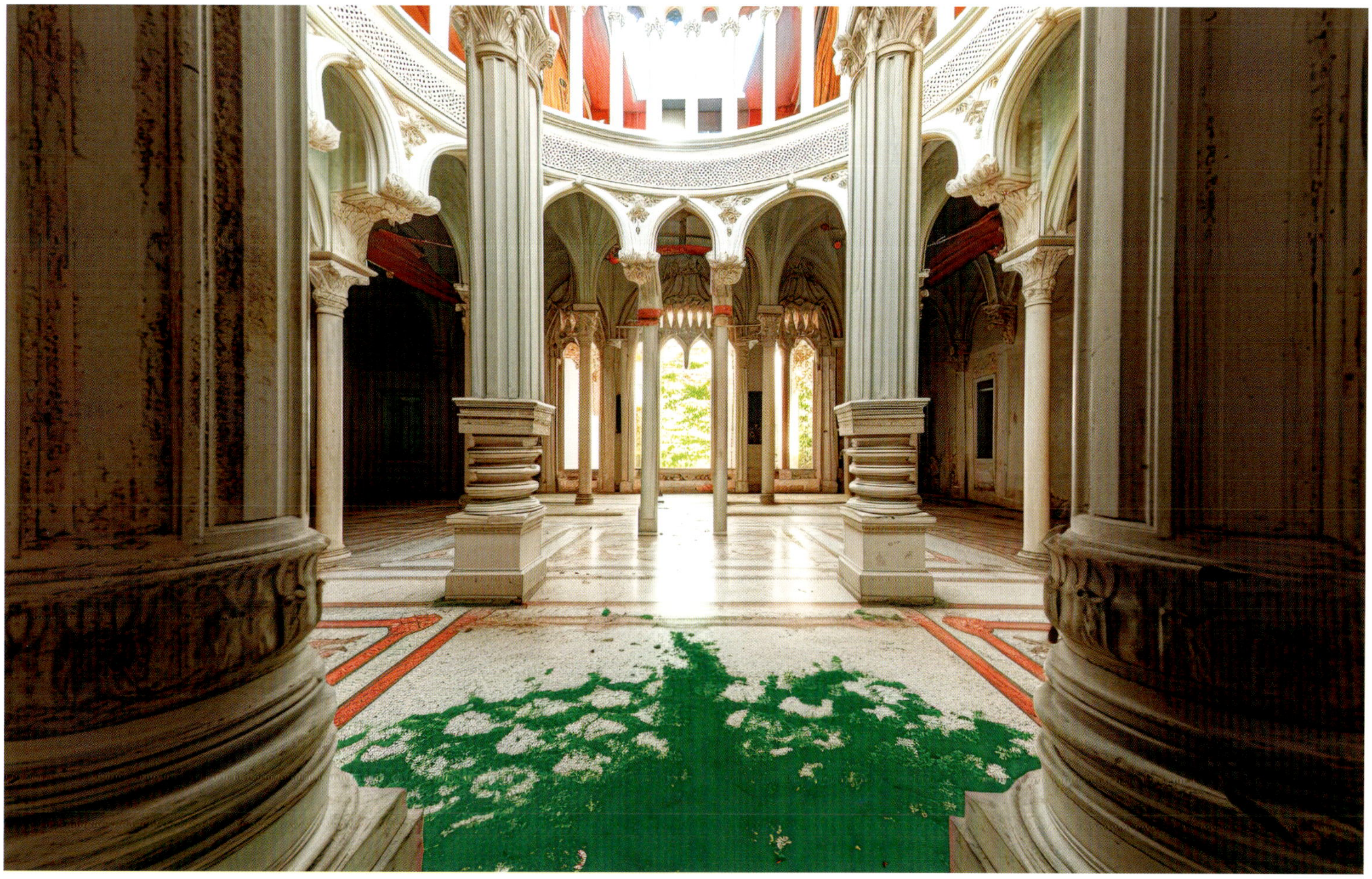

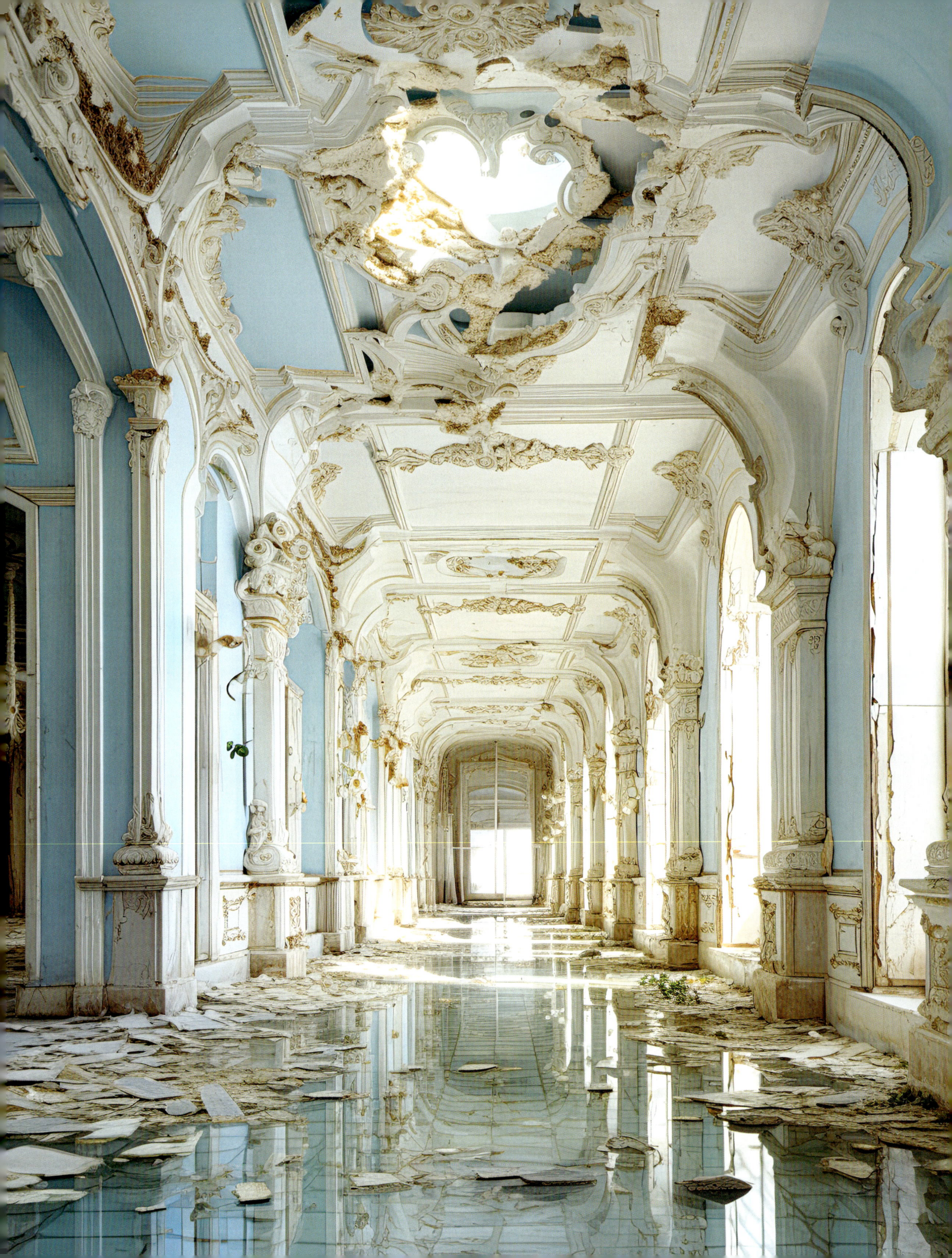

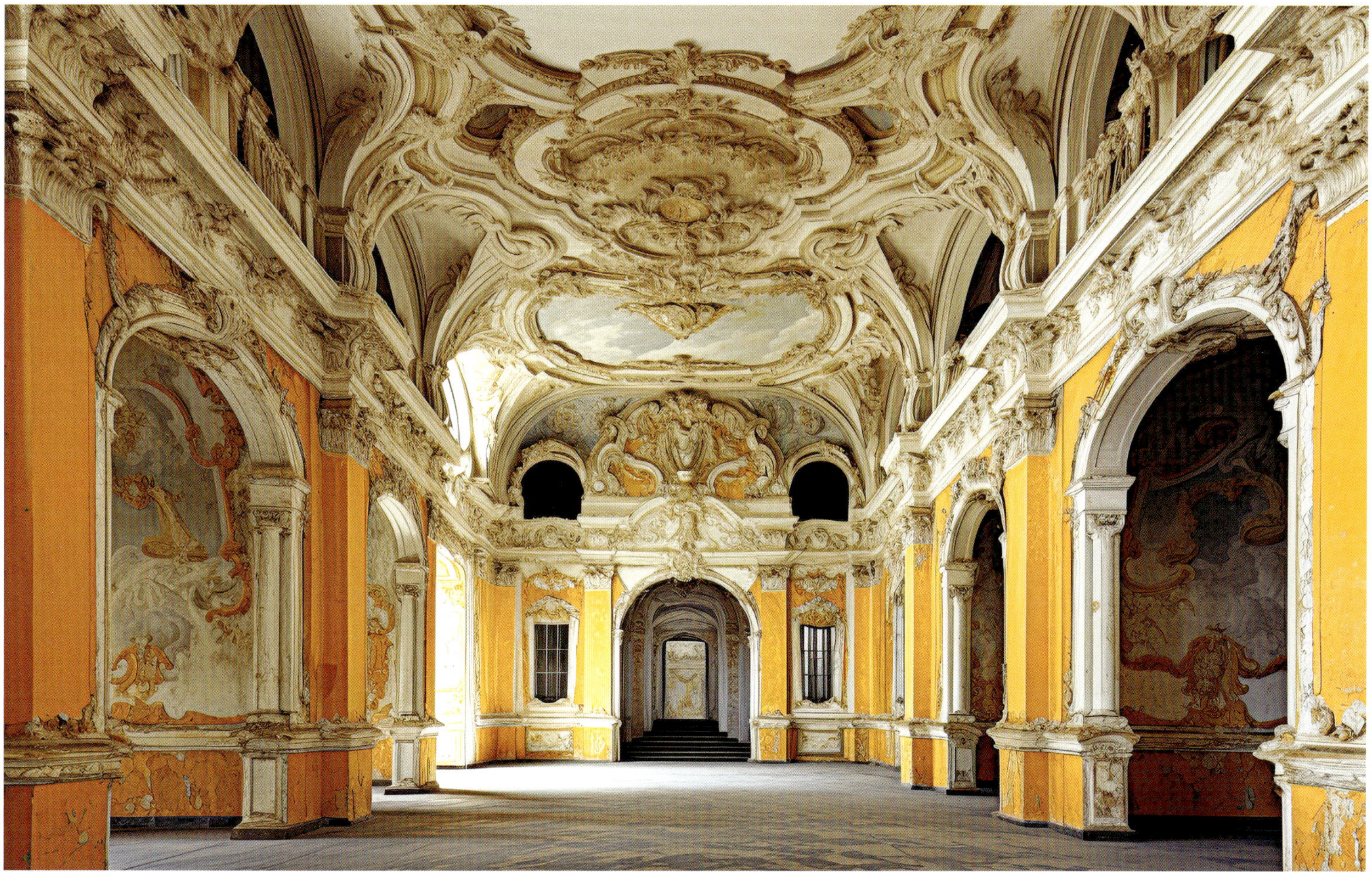

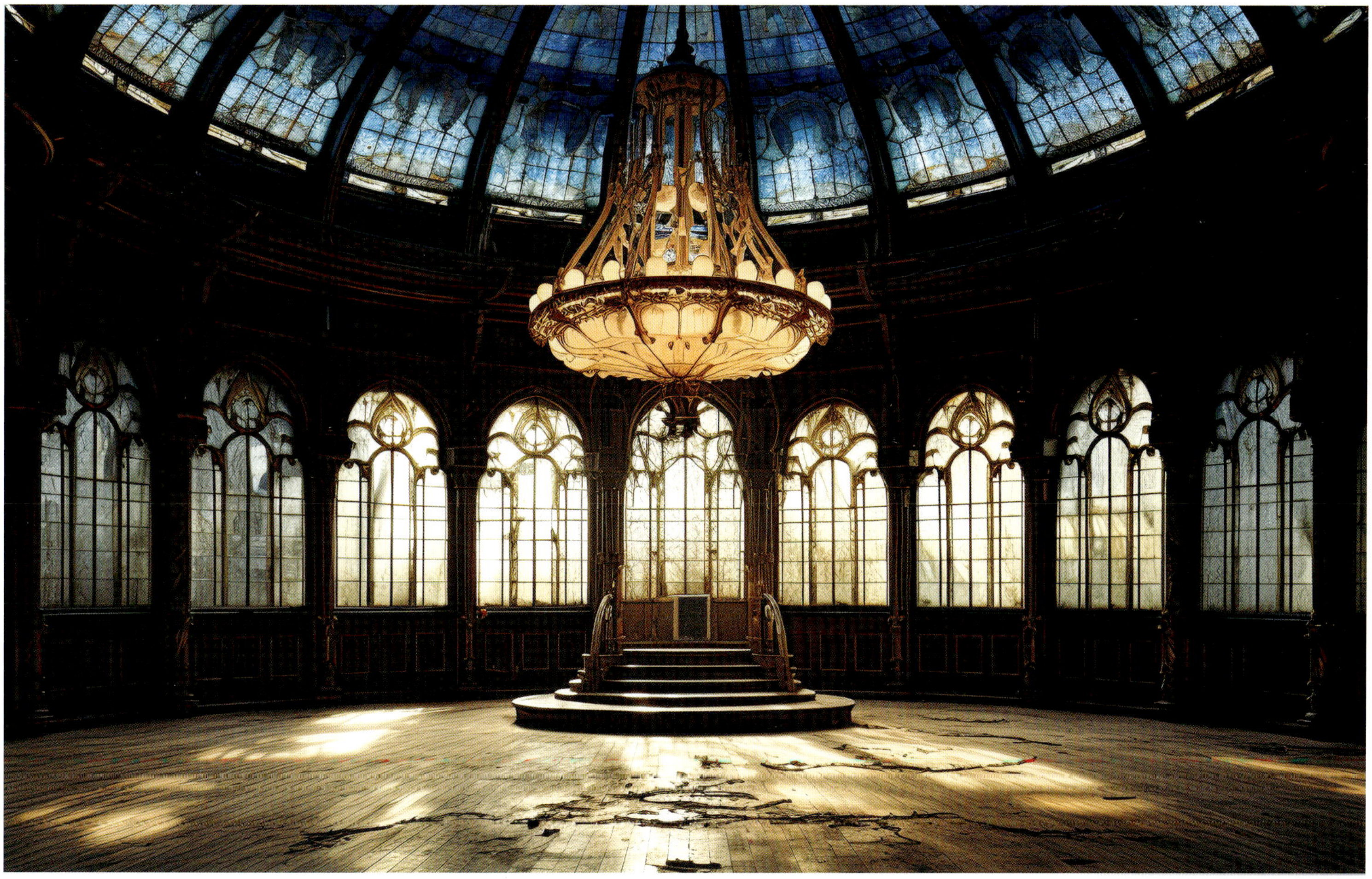

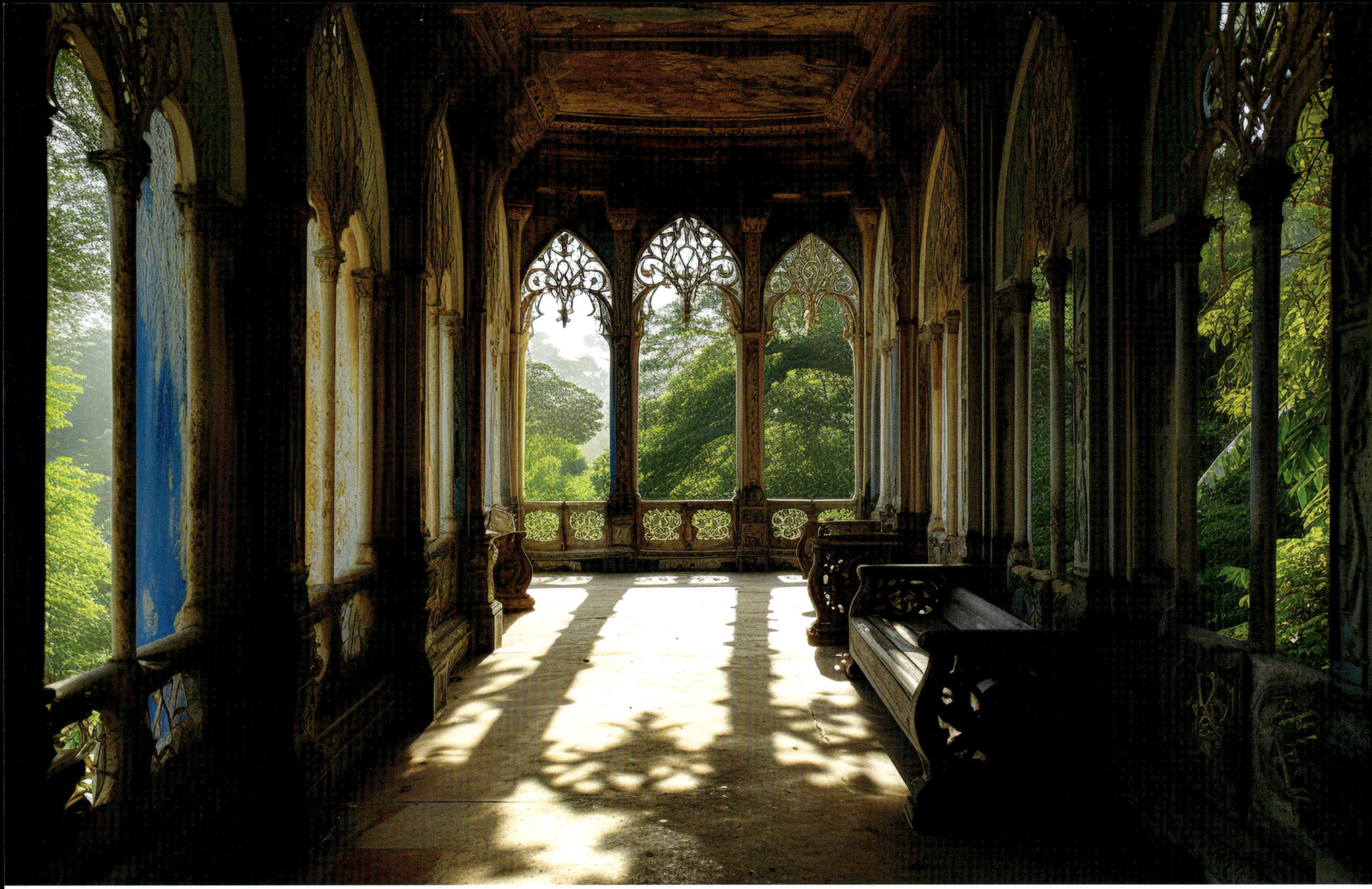

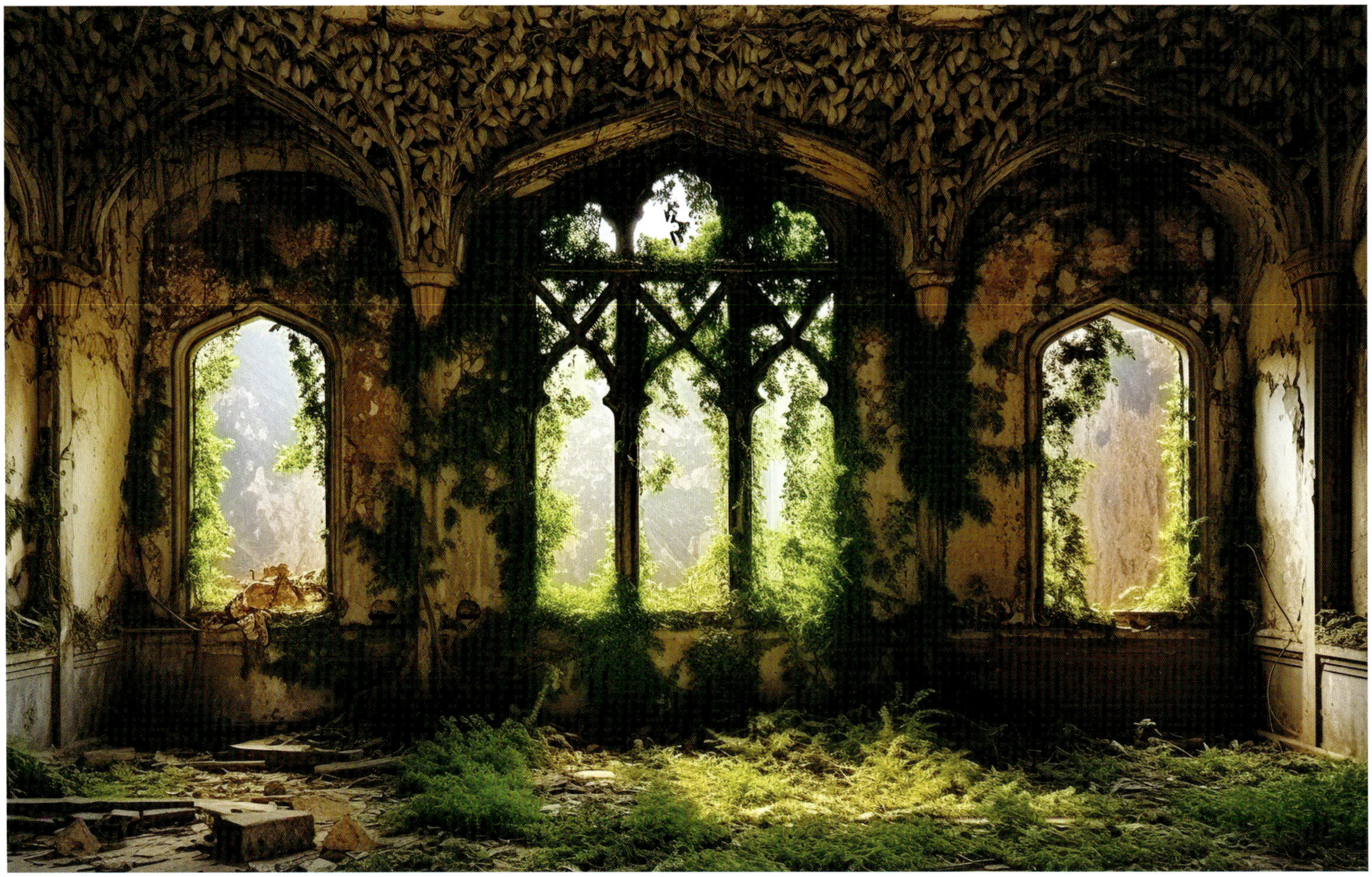

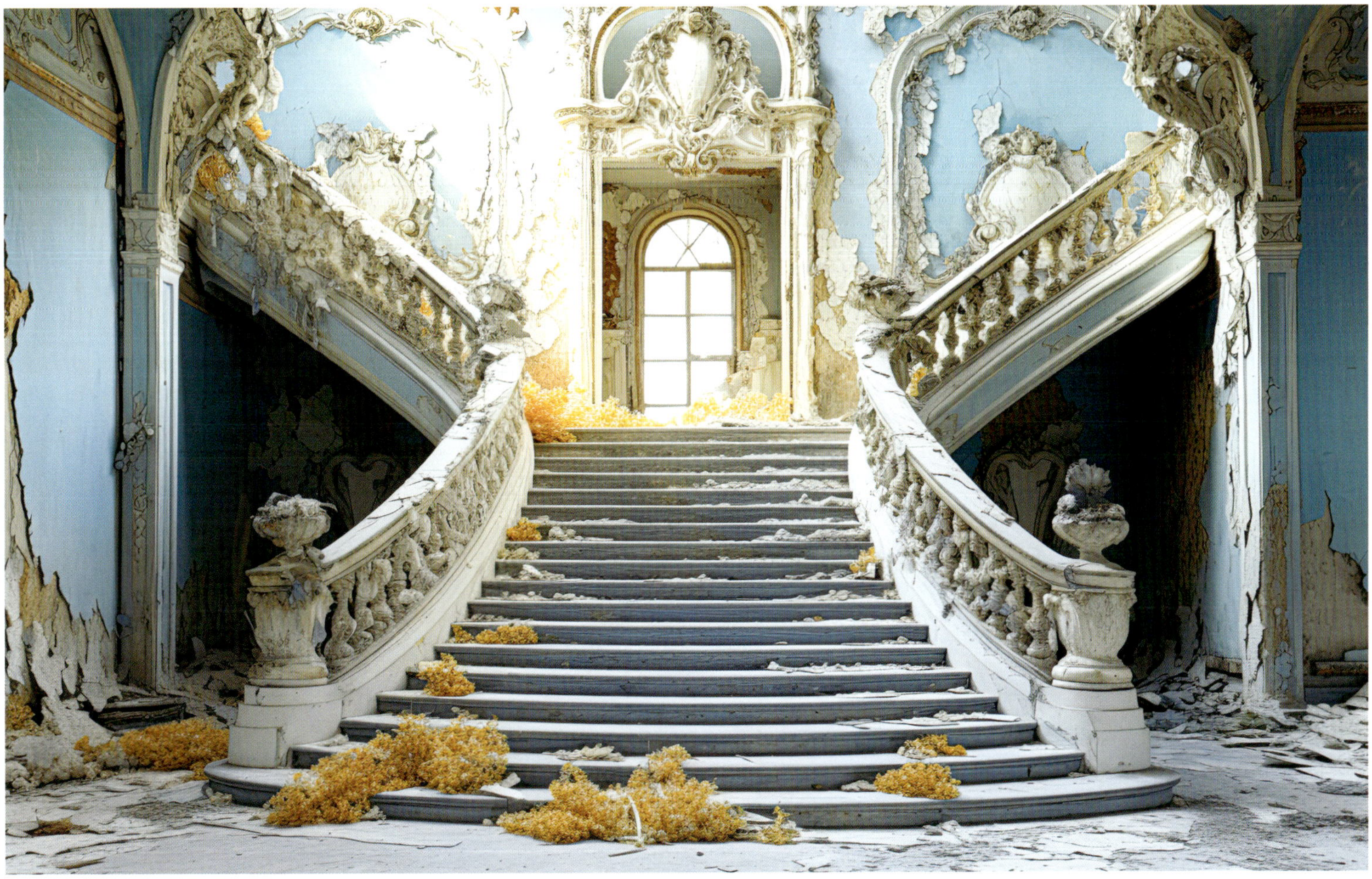

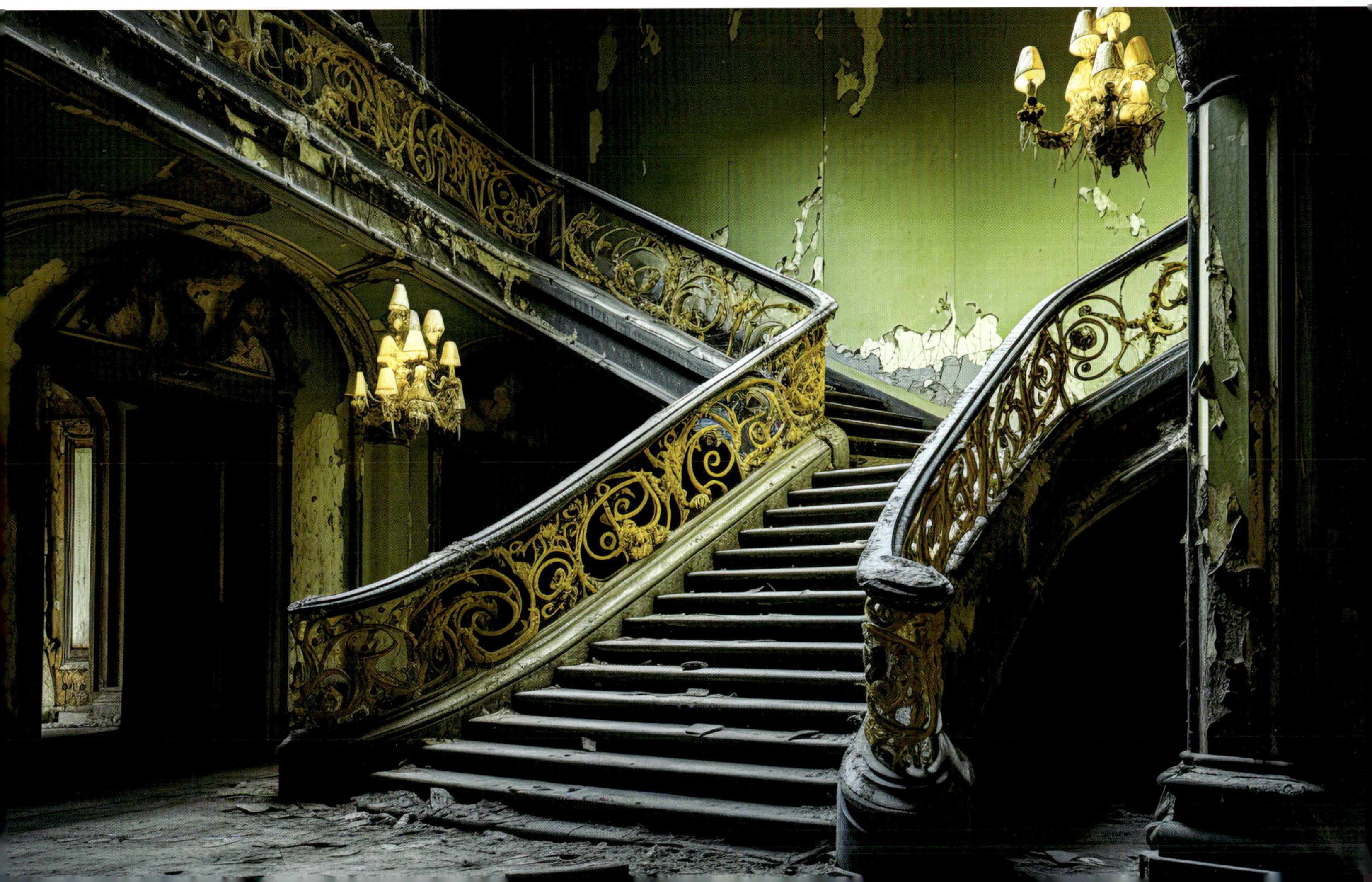

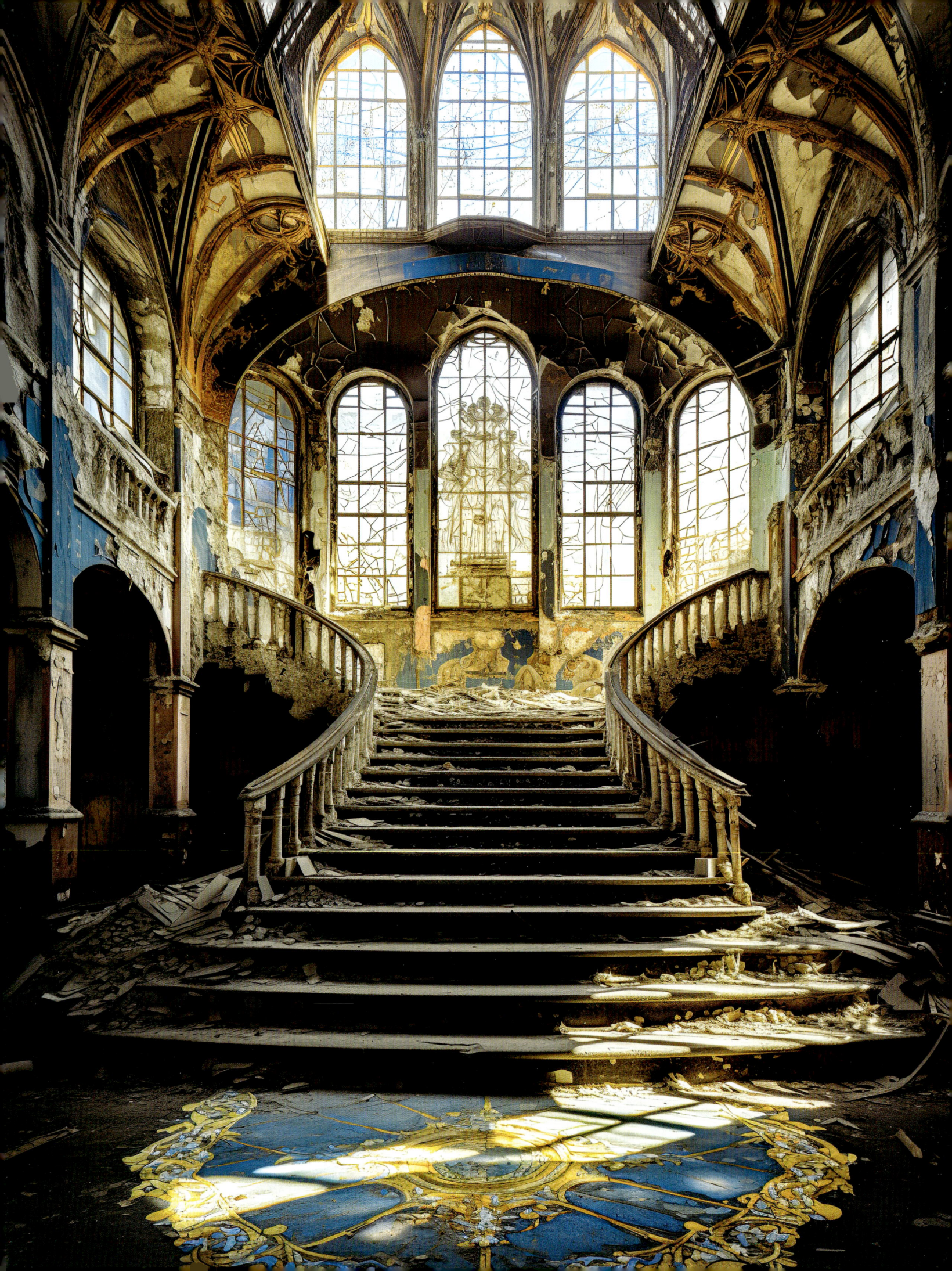

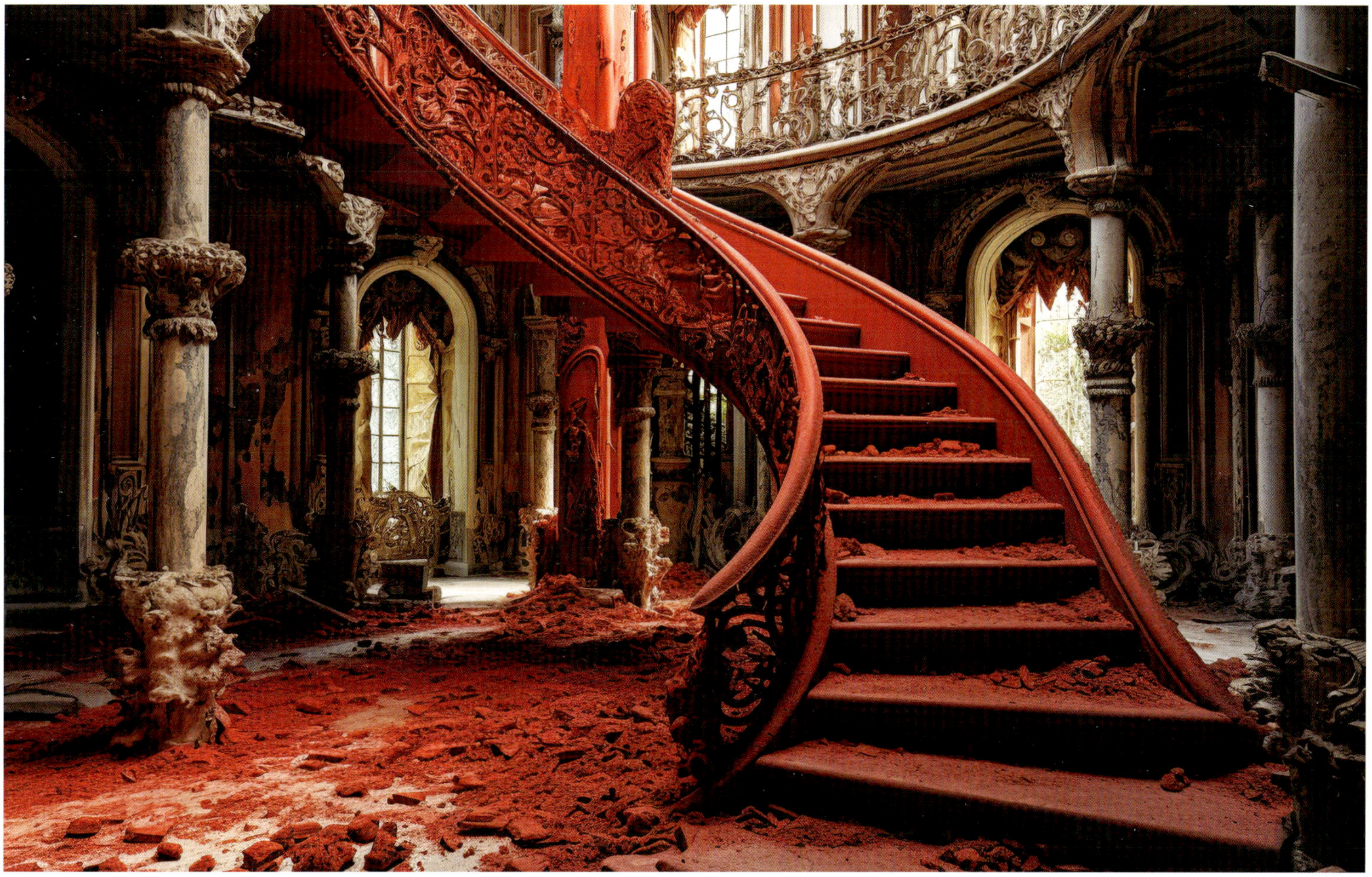

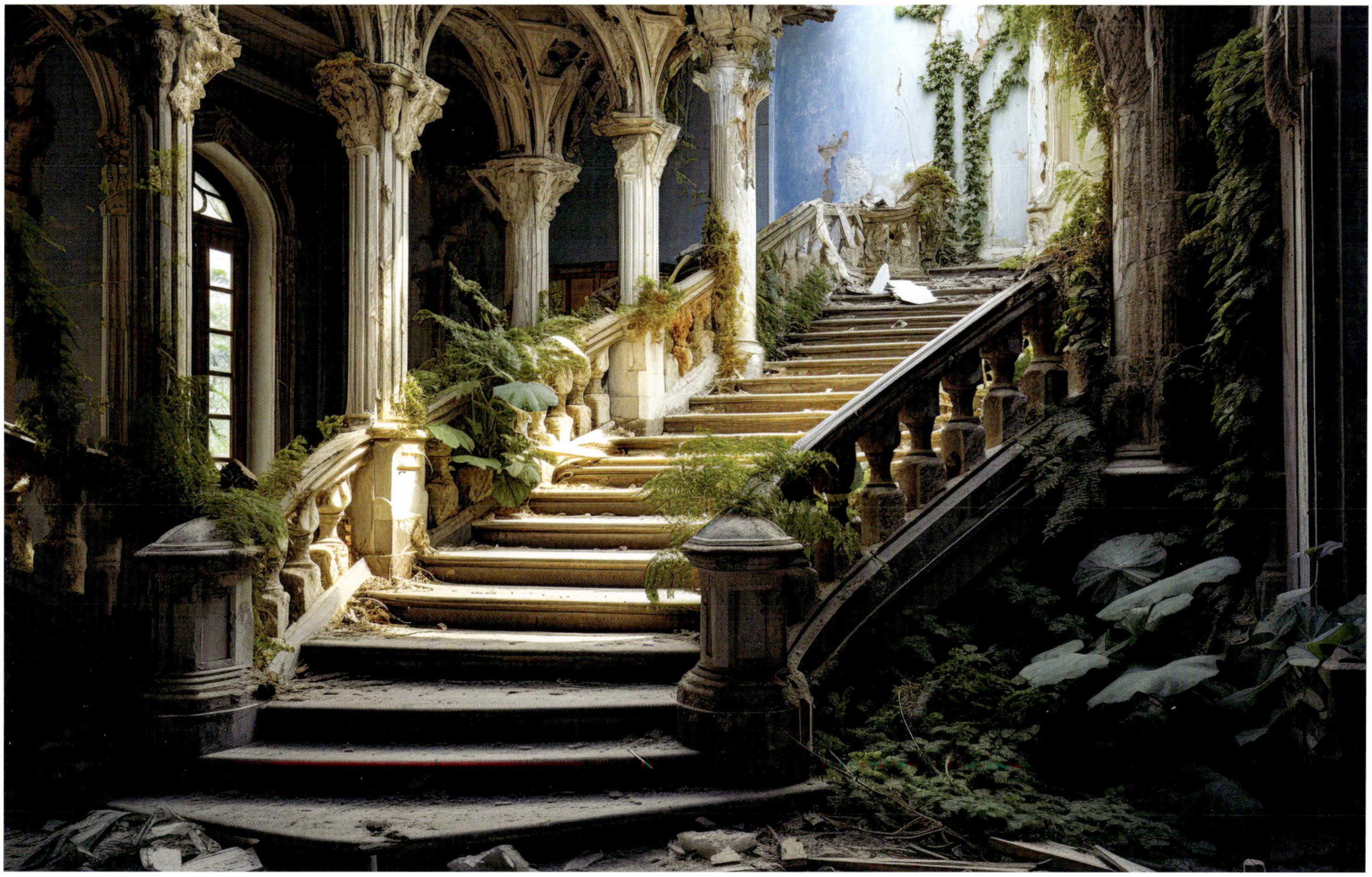

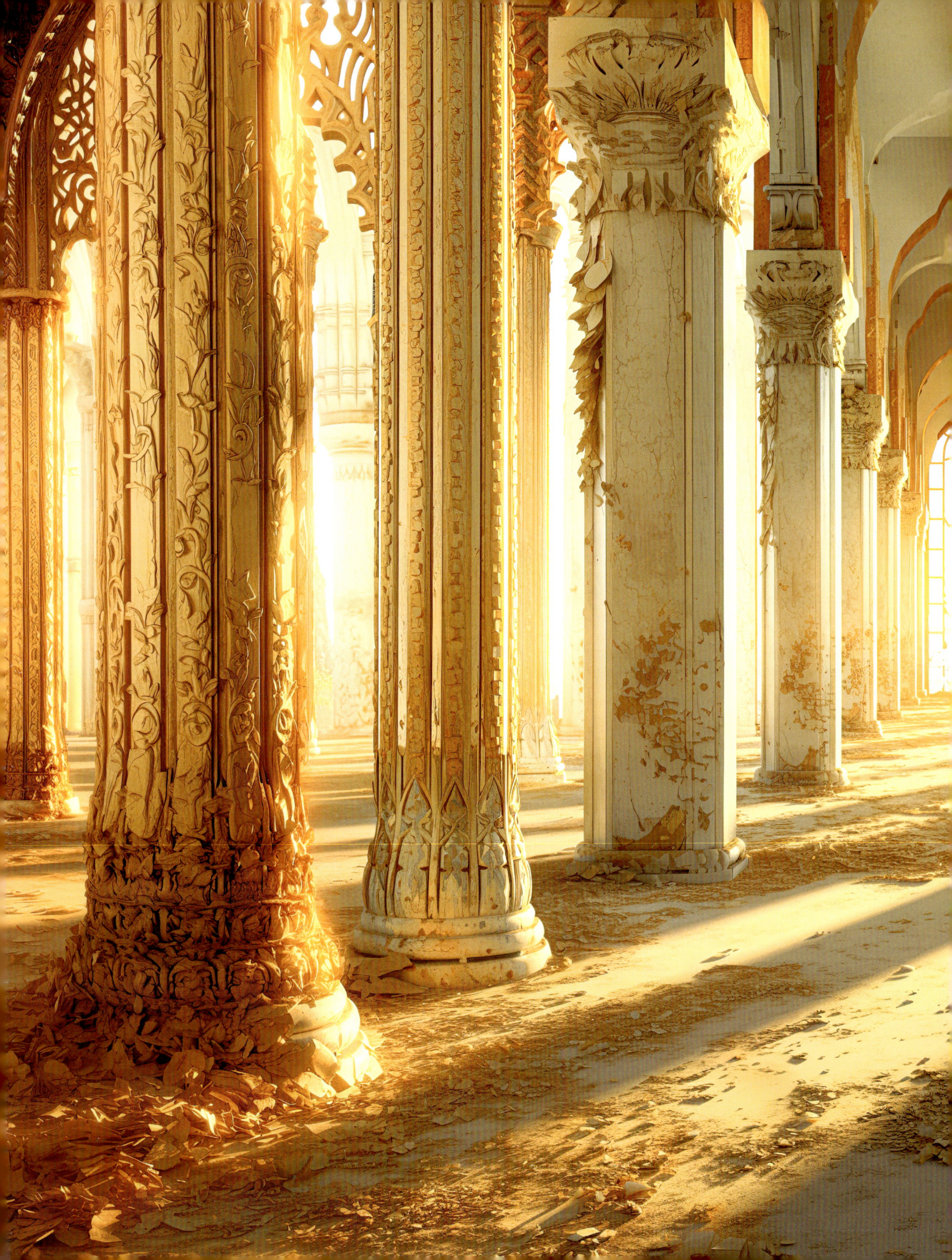

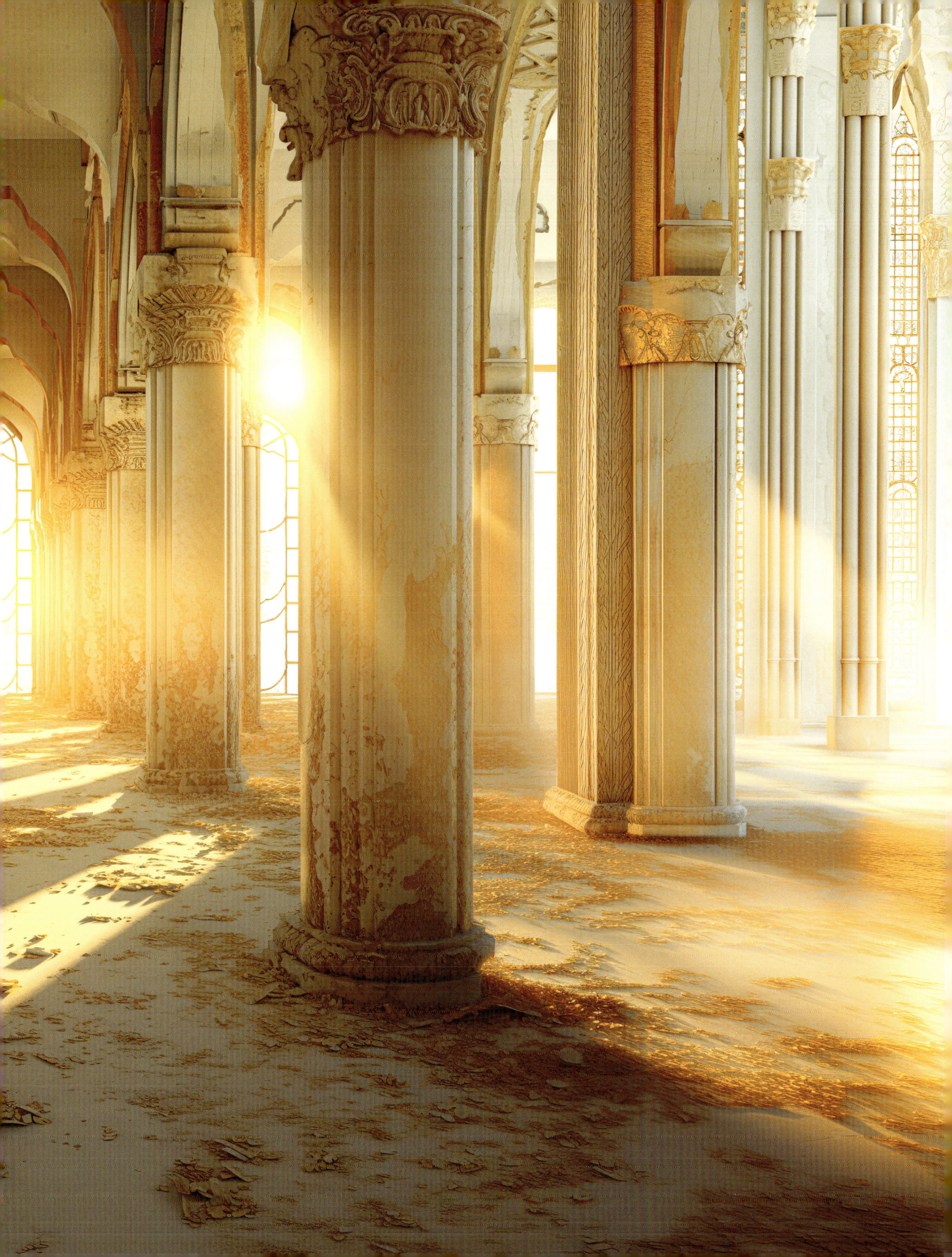

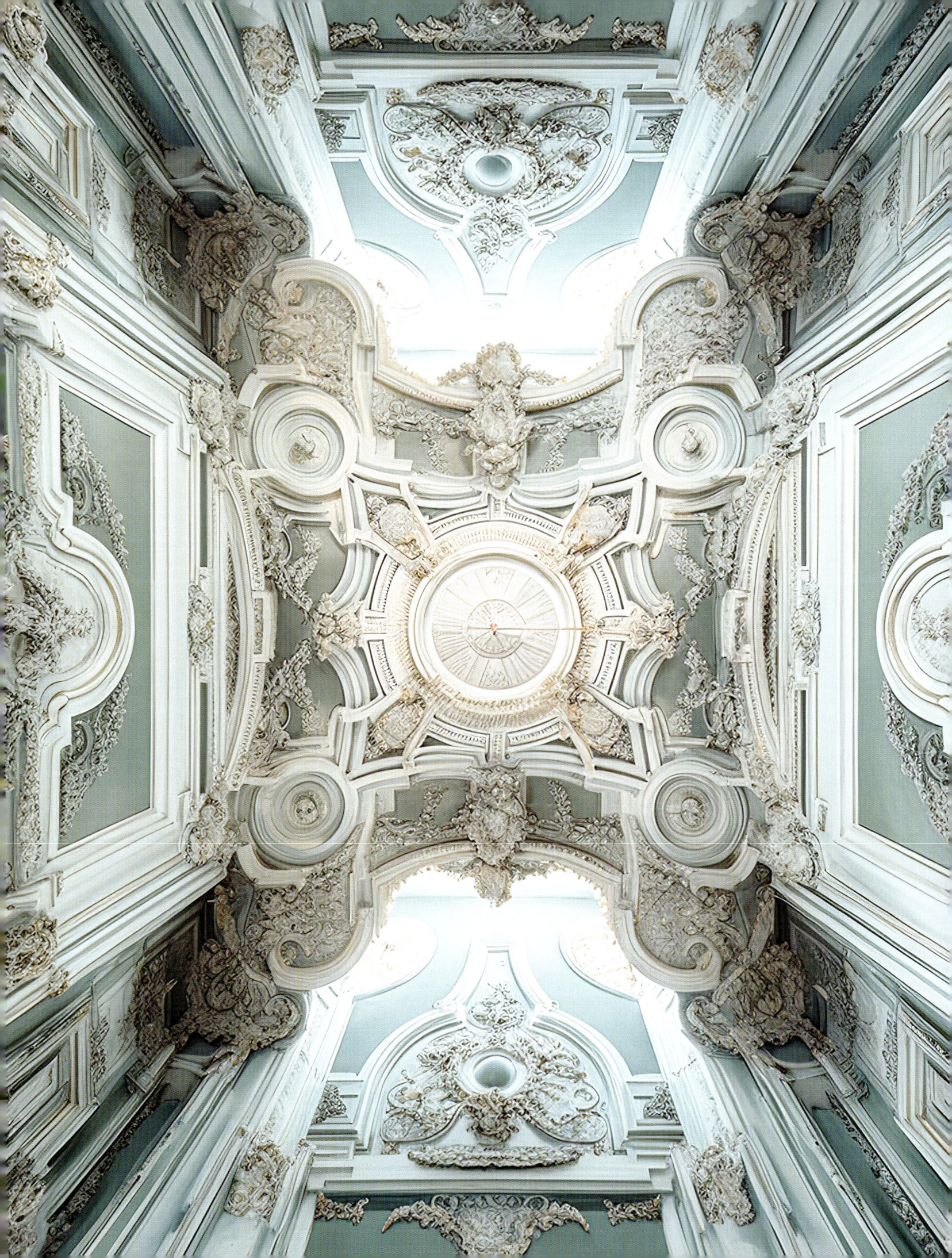

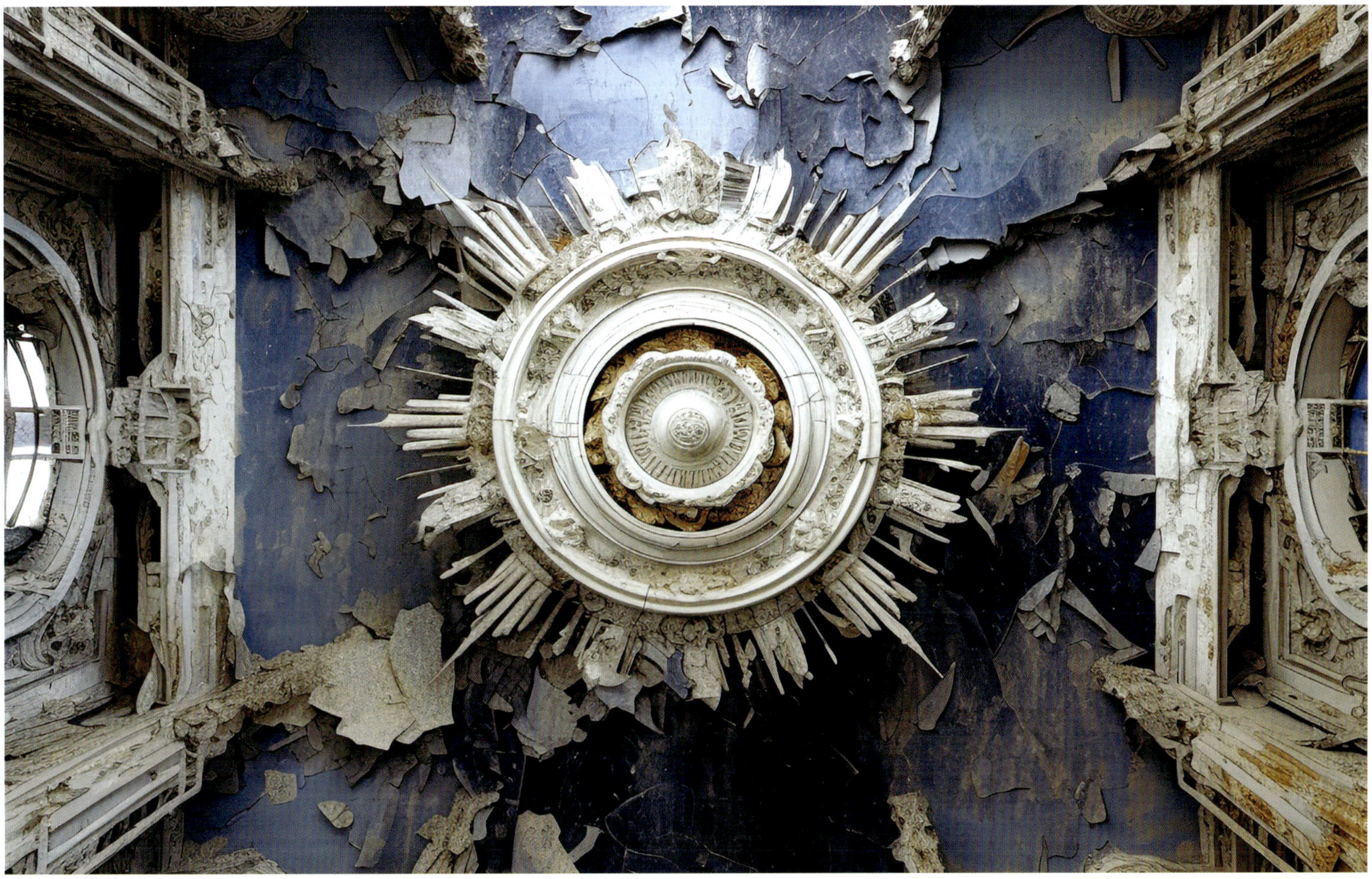

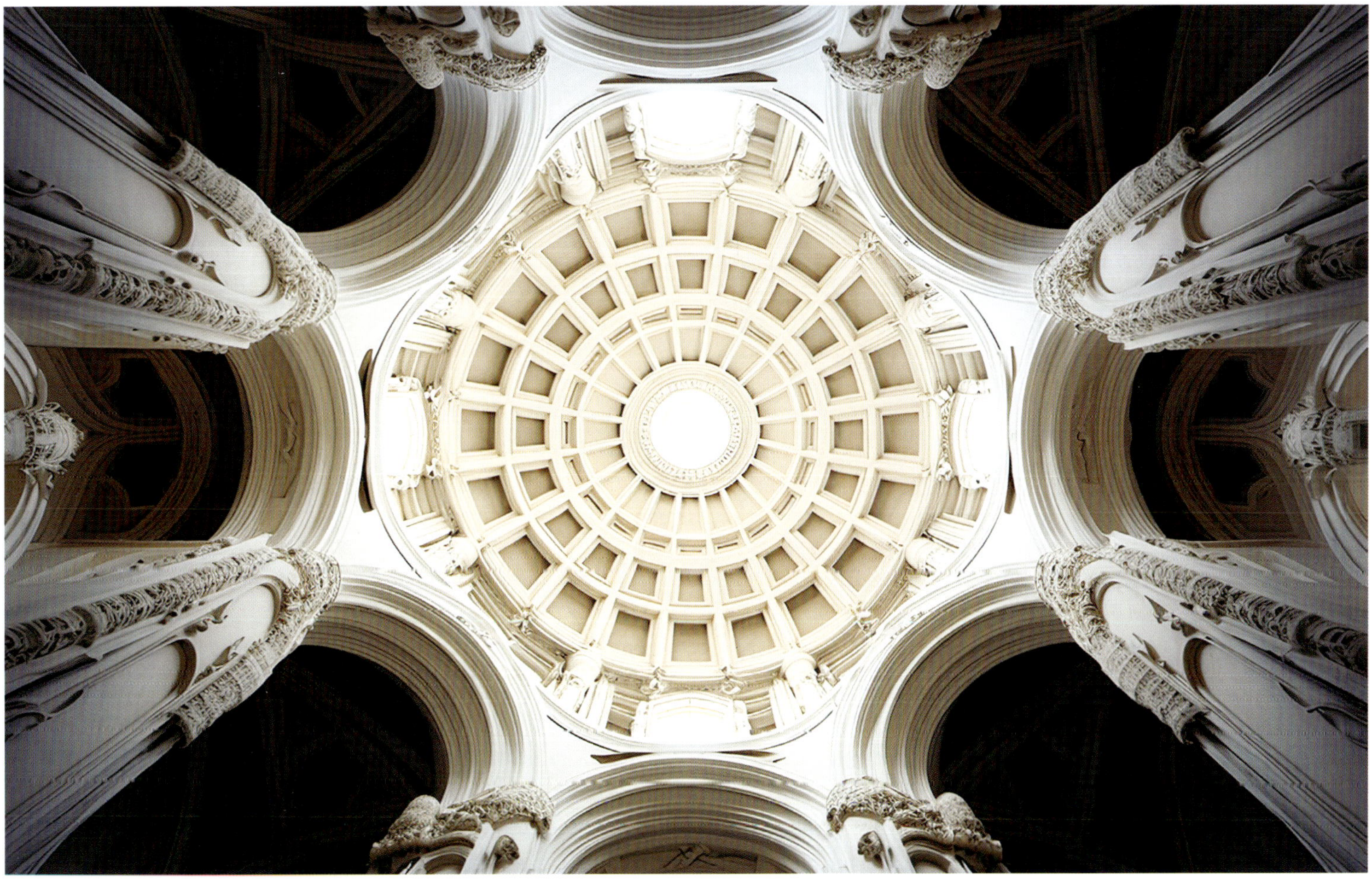

I'd like some green sunshine

In the former conservatory, rust insidiously invades the interlacing metal of the floral framework. The glass panes, guardians of the light, lie scattered in fragments, projecting melancholic shards onto the ground. A silent symphony punctuated by the monotonous clanking of corroded metal.

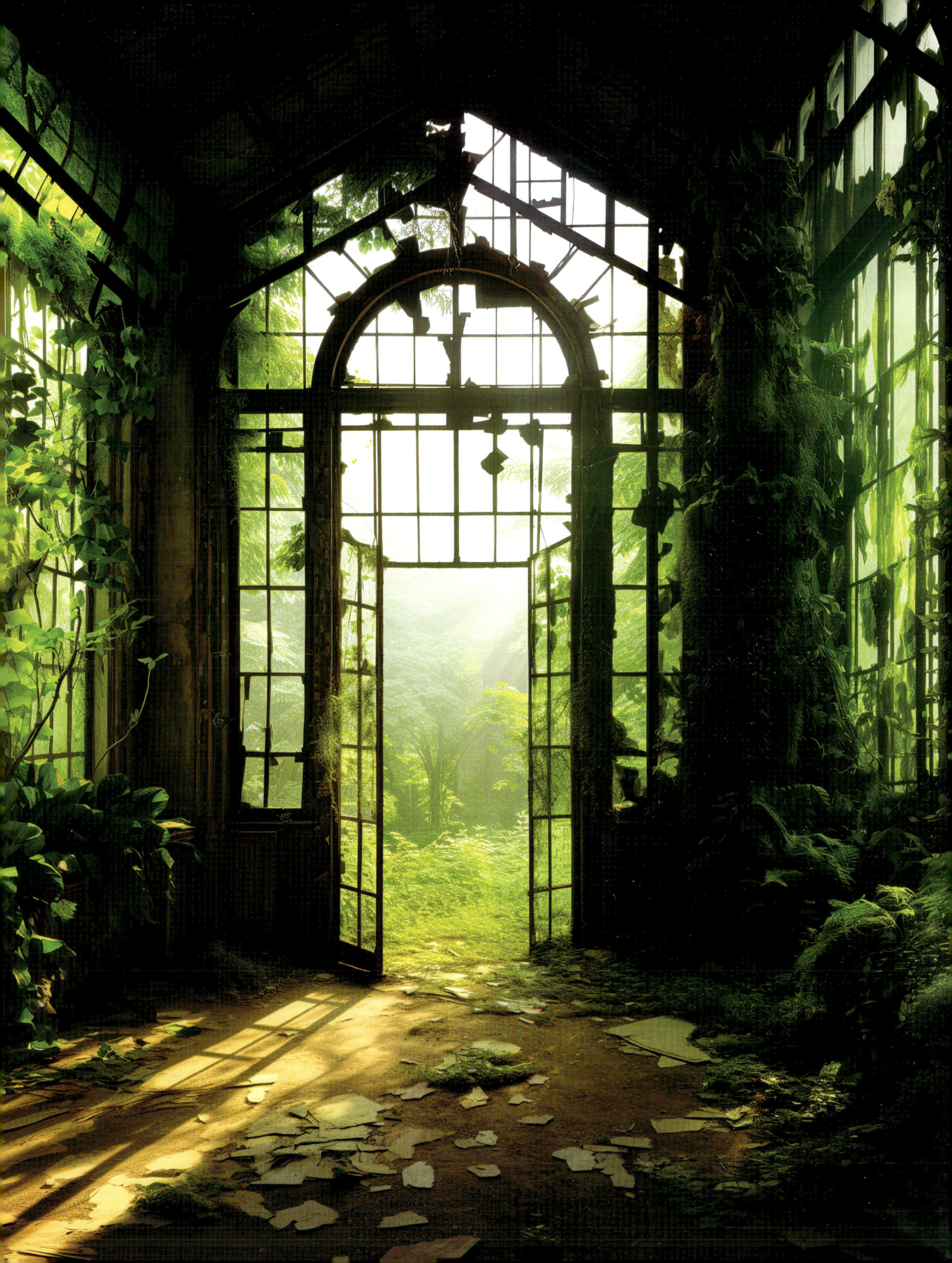

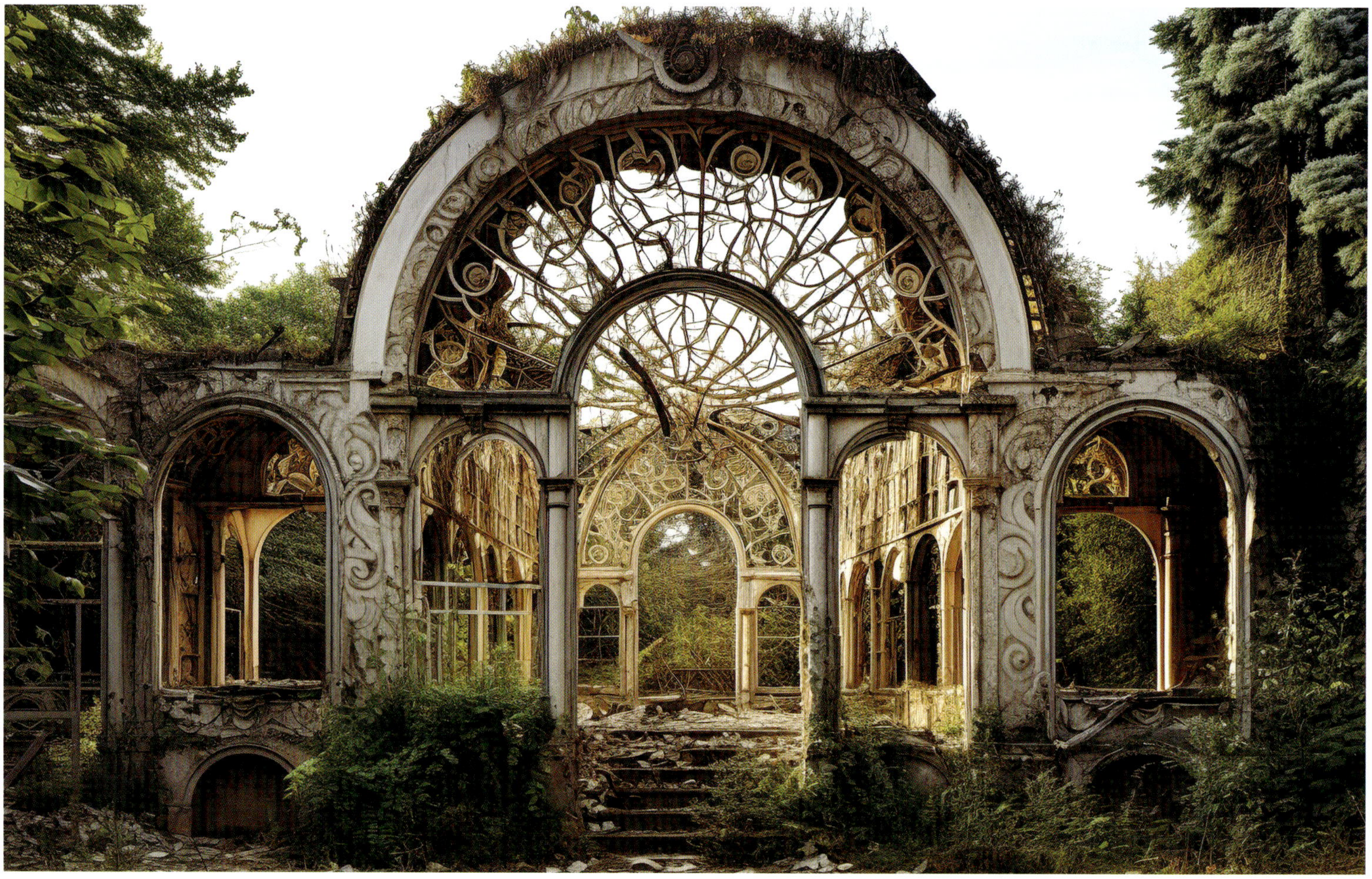

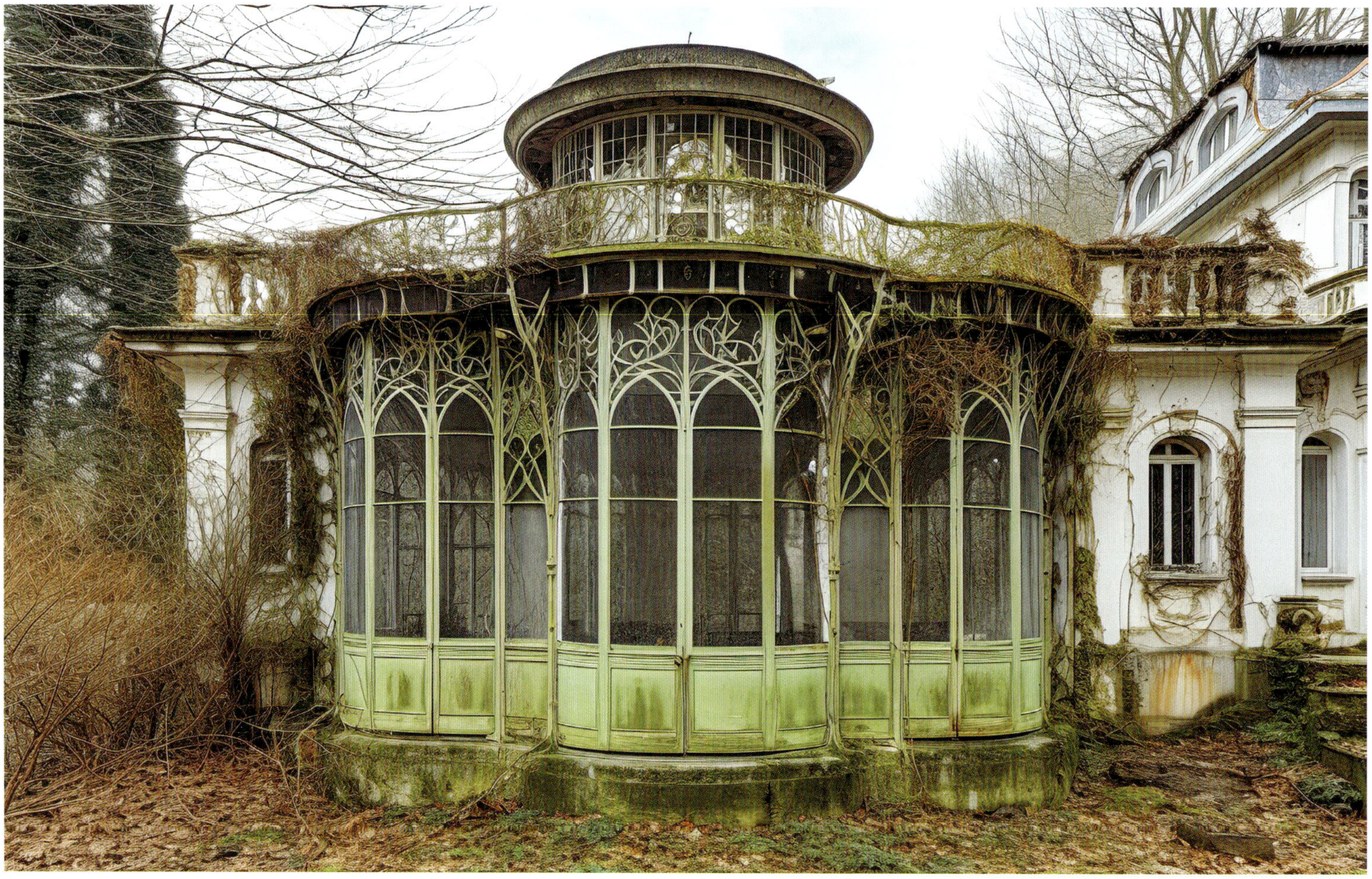

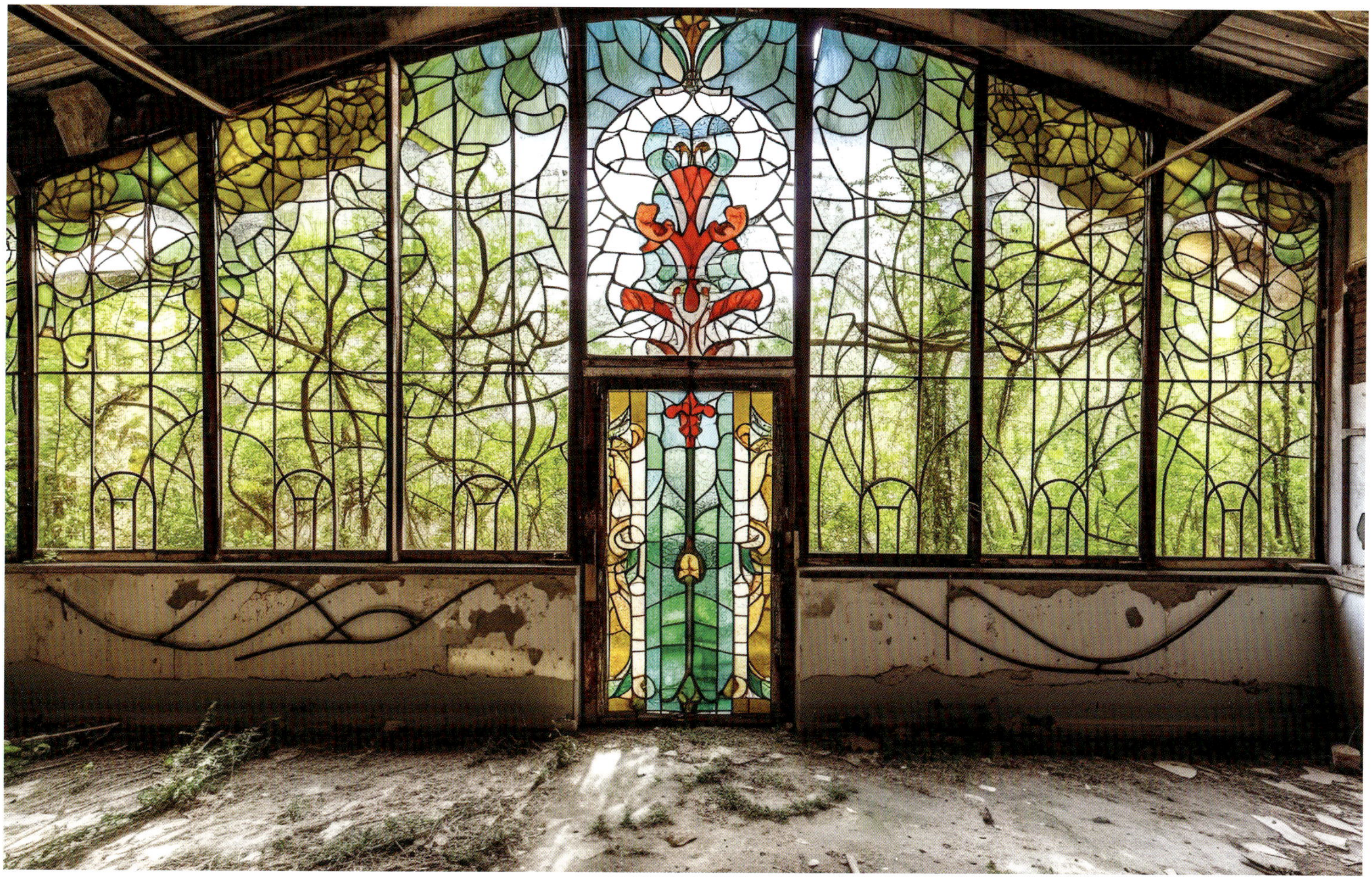

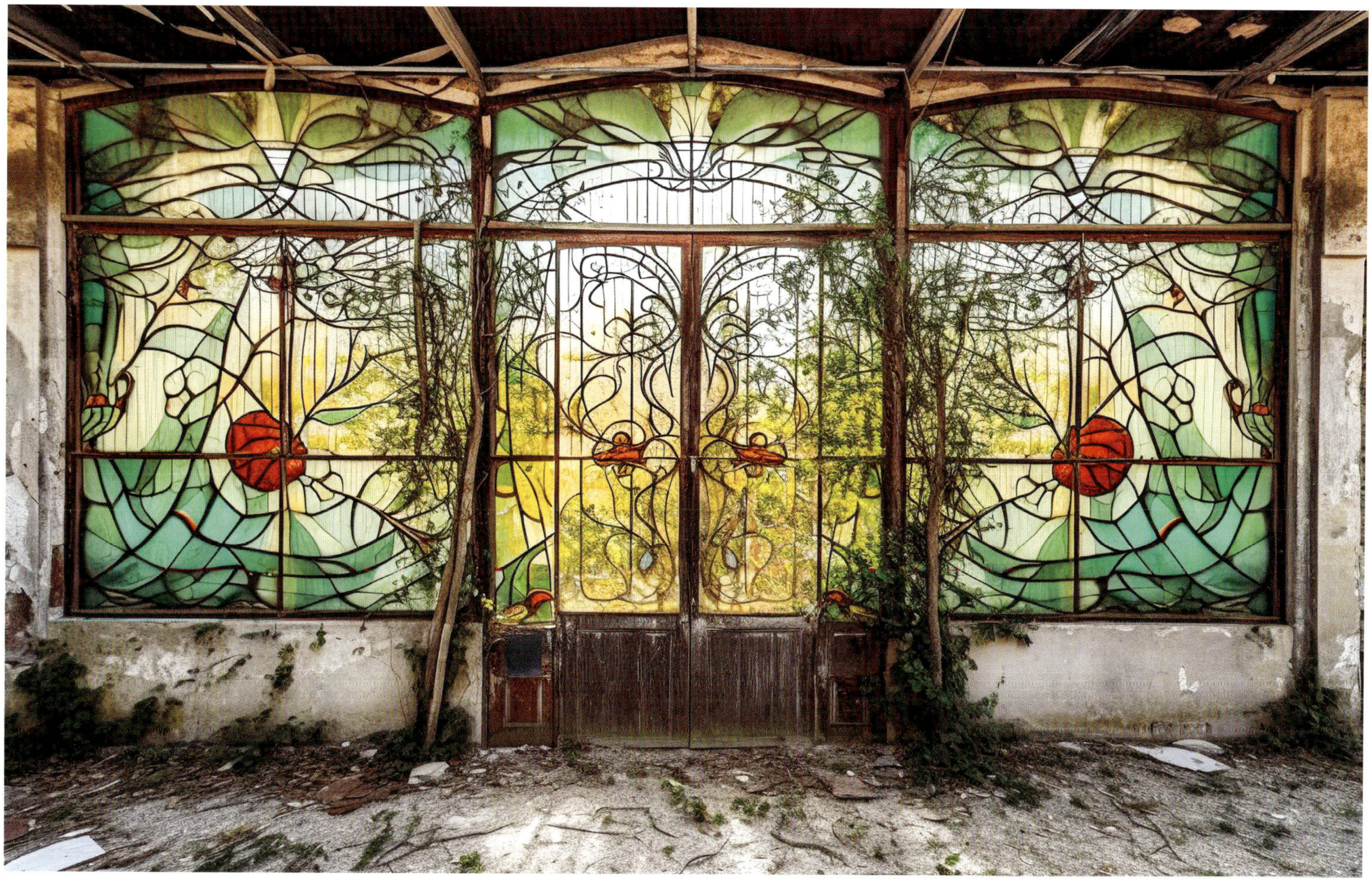

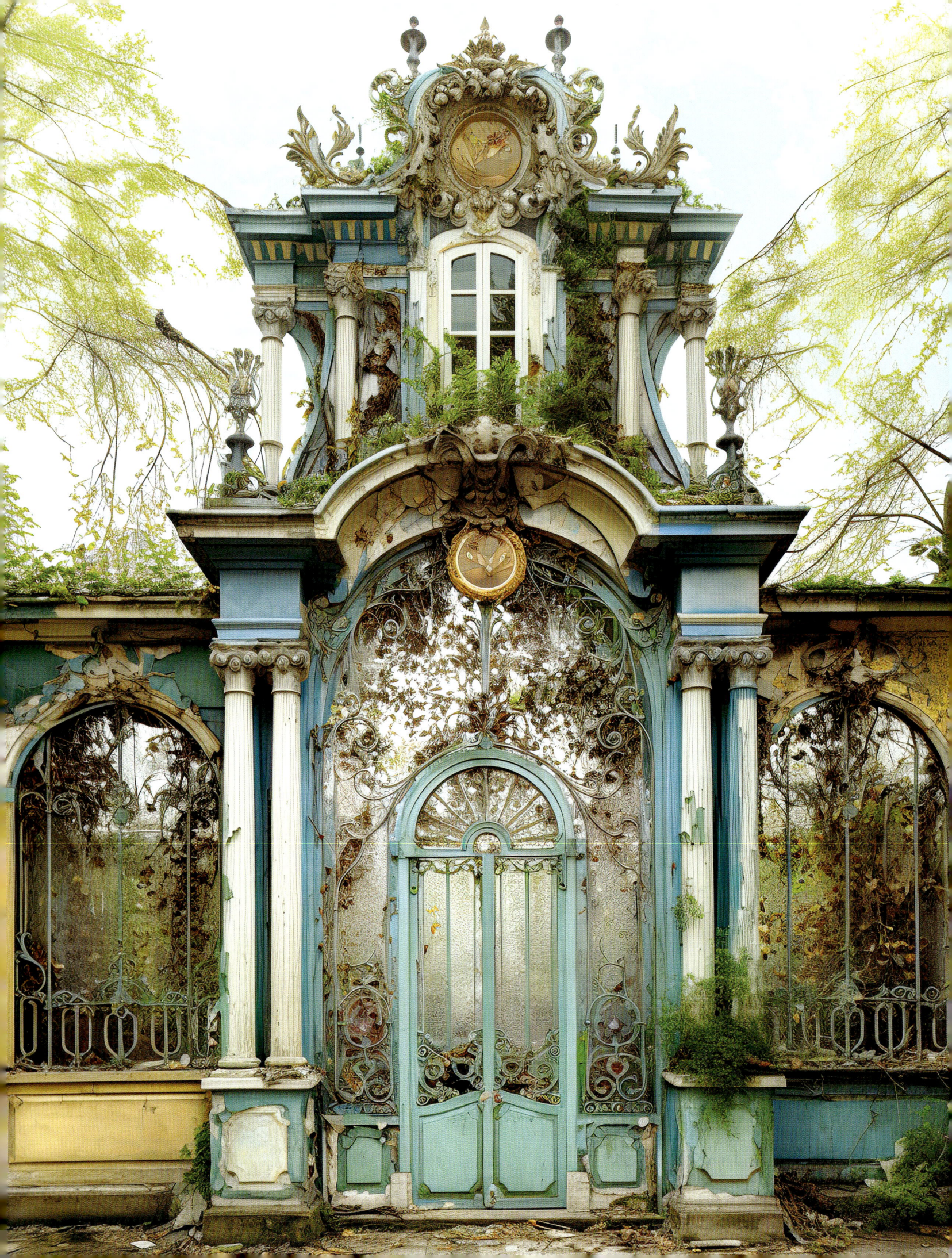

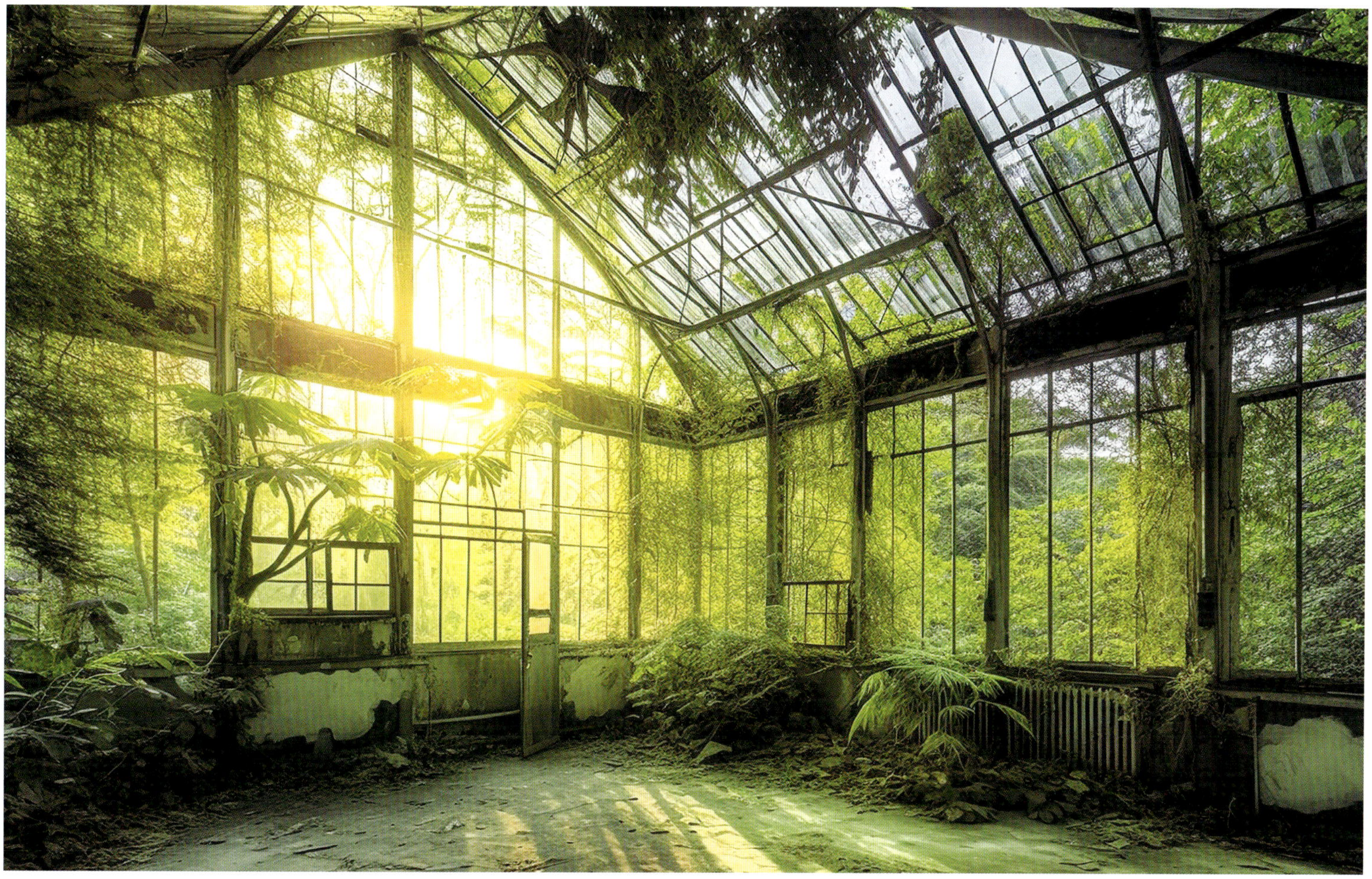

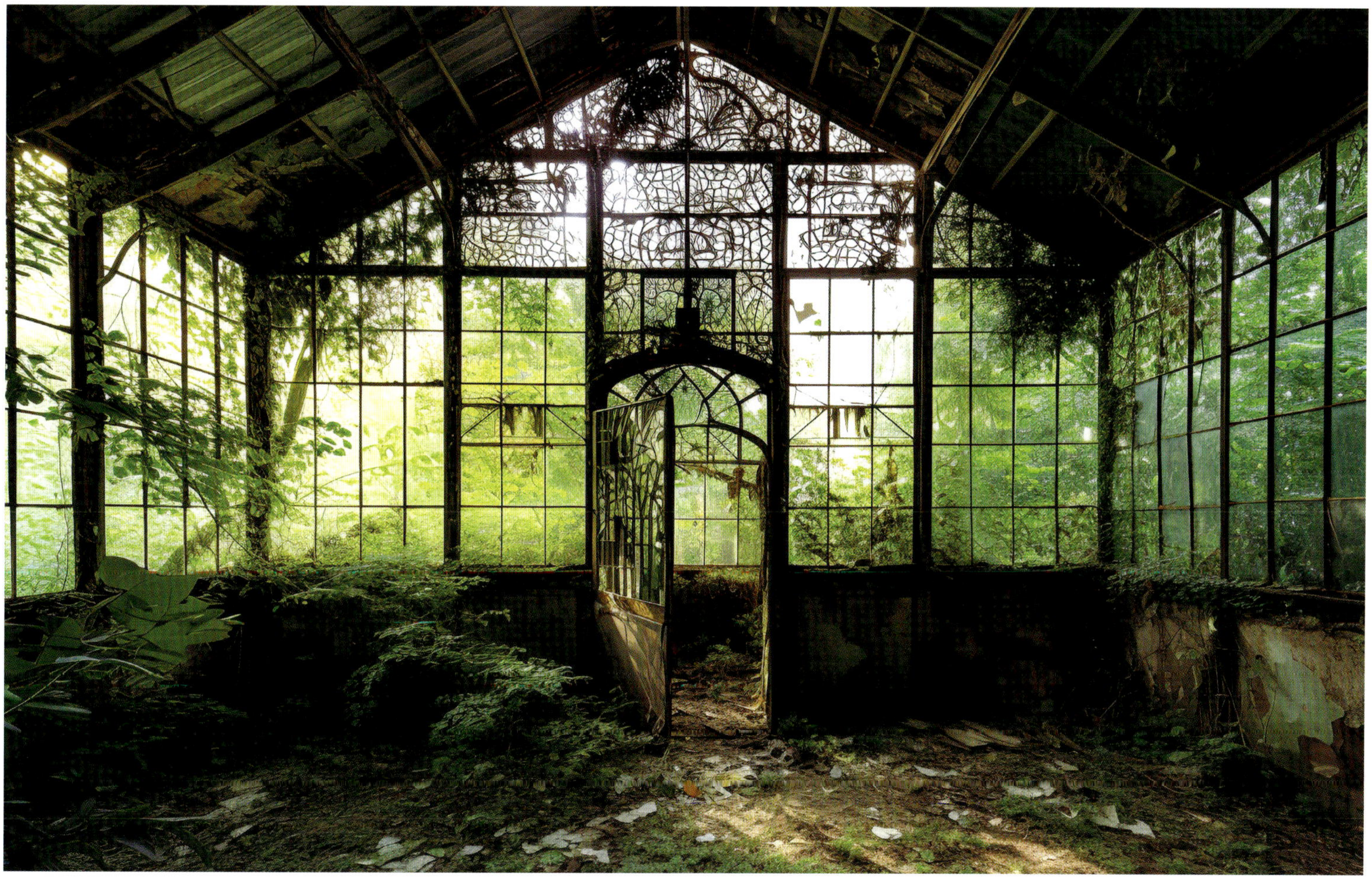

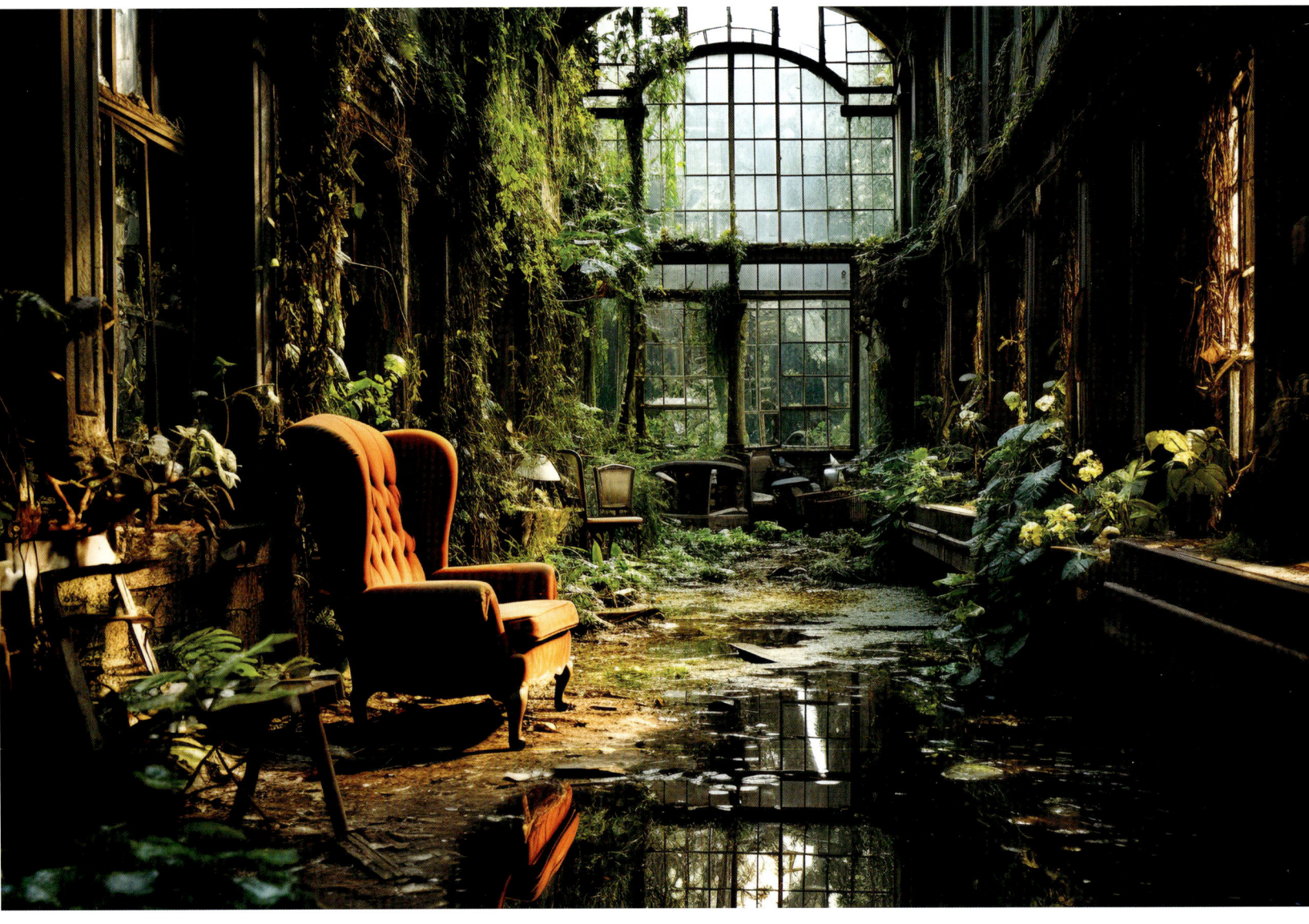

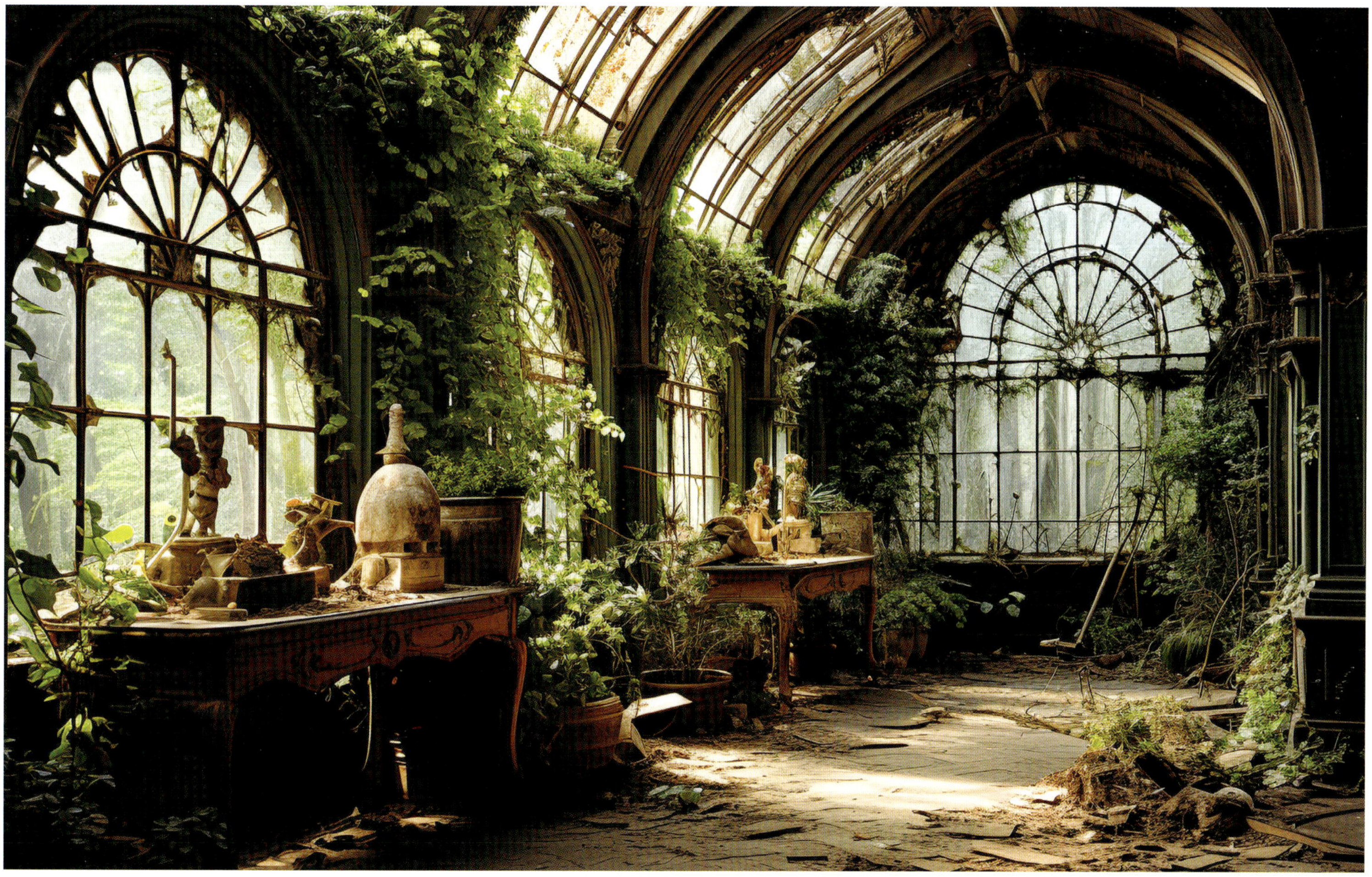

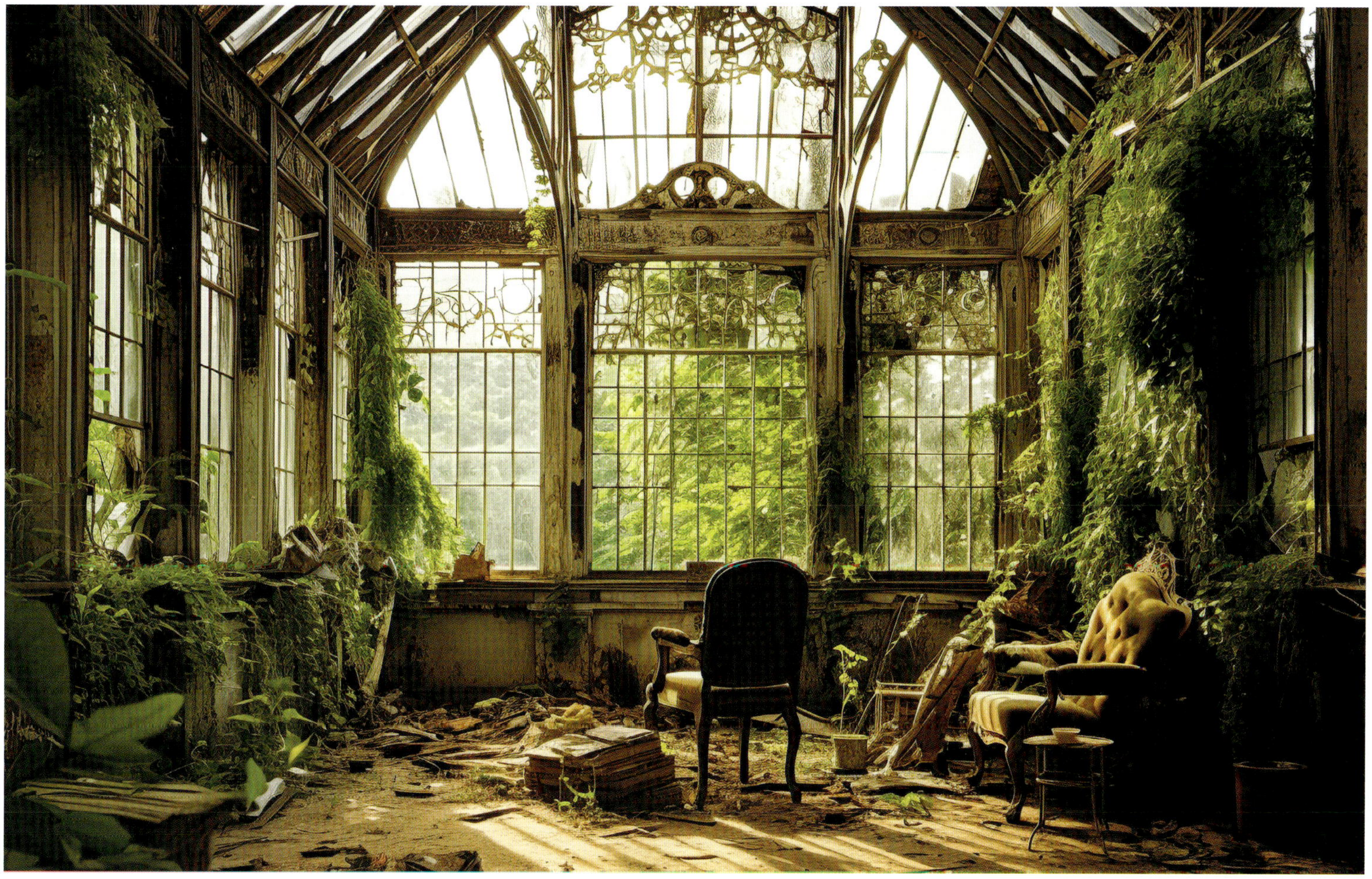

Down to the last drop

Climate change has turned water into a rare and precious commodity, rationed on a global scale. Gradually abandoned, thermal spas, public baths and swimming pools are giving way to brackish water unfit for human consumption. Speculation and human greed cling to every drop, transforming a common good into a bitterly contested resource.

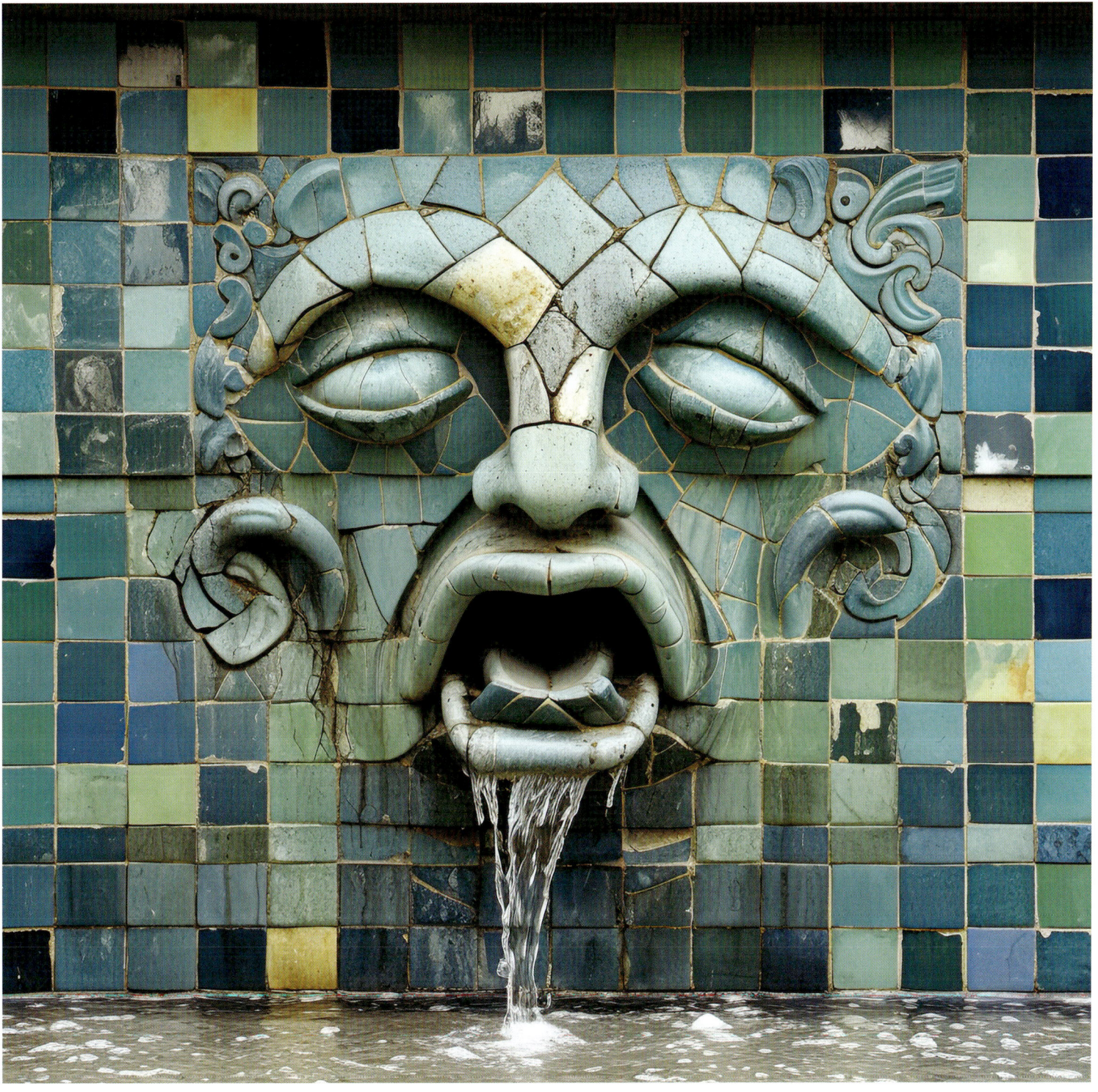

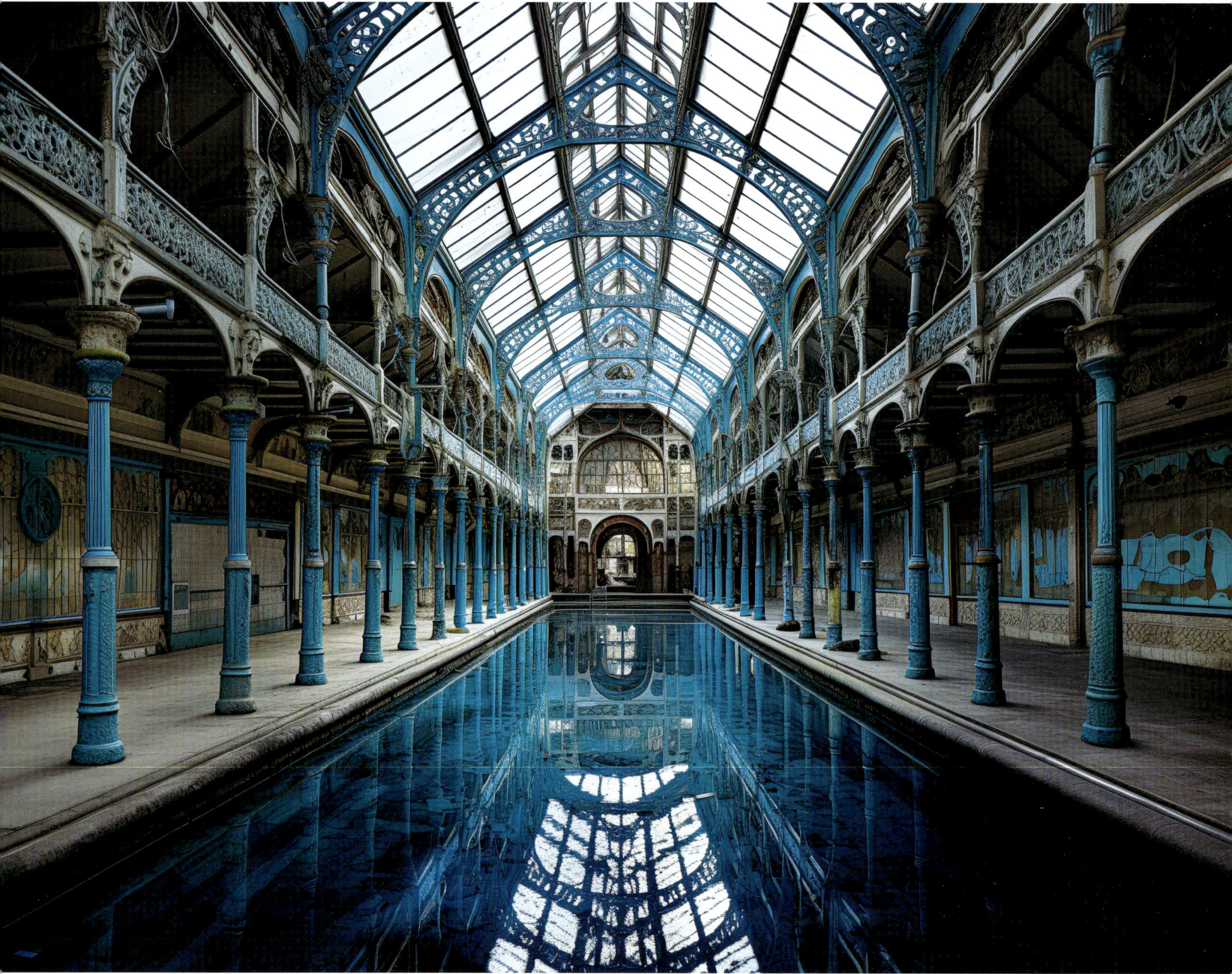

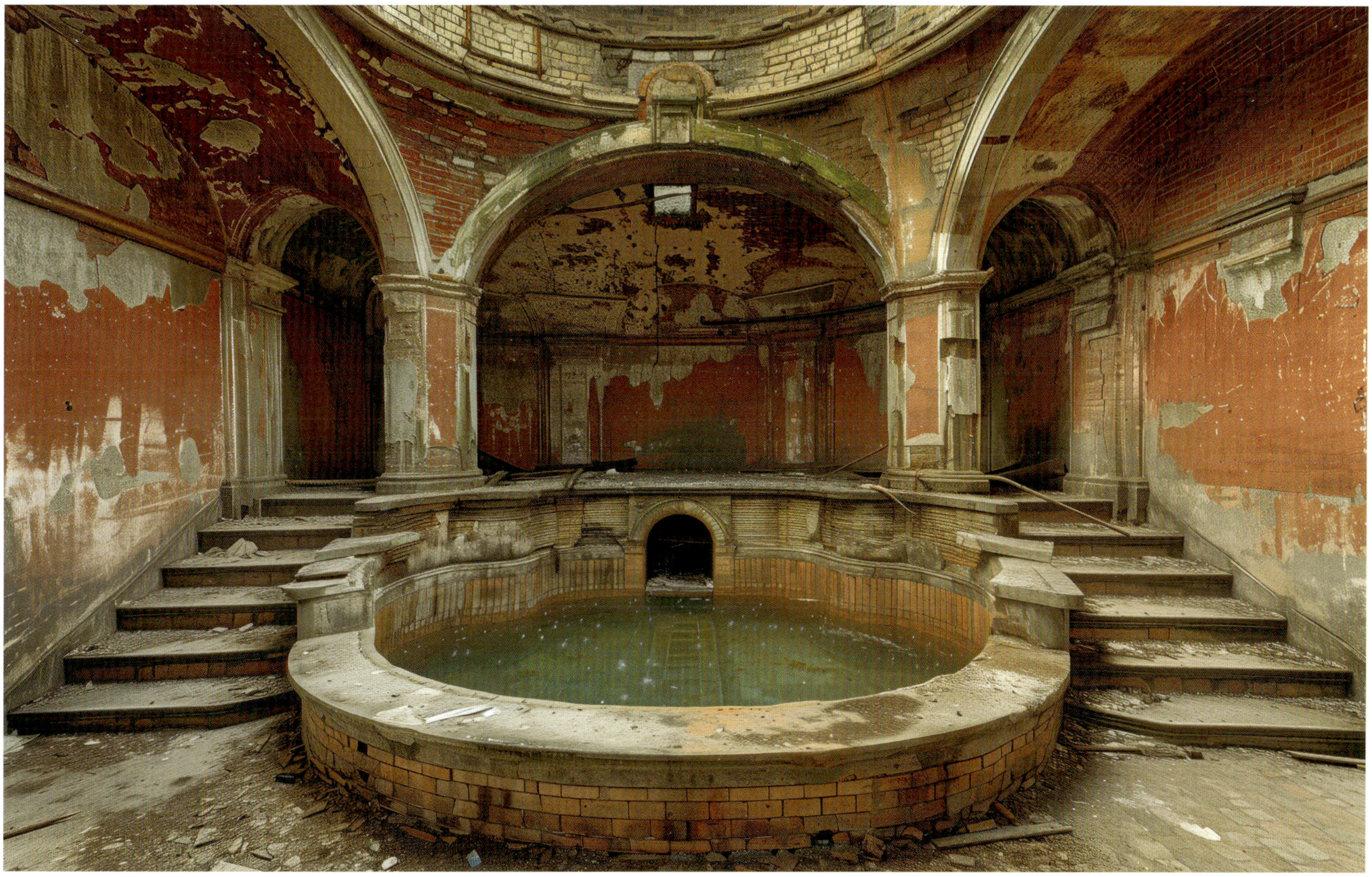

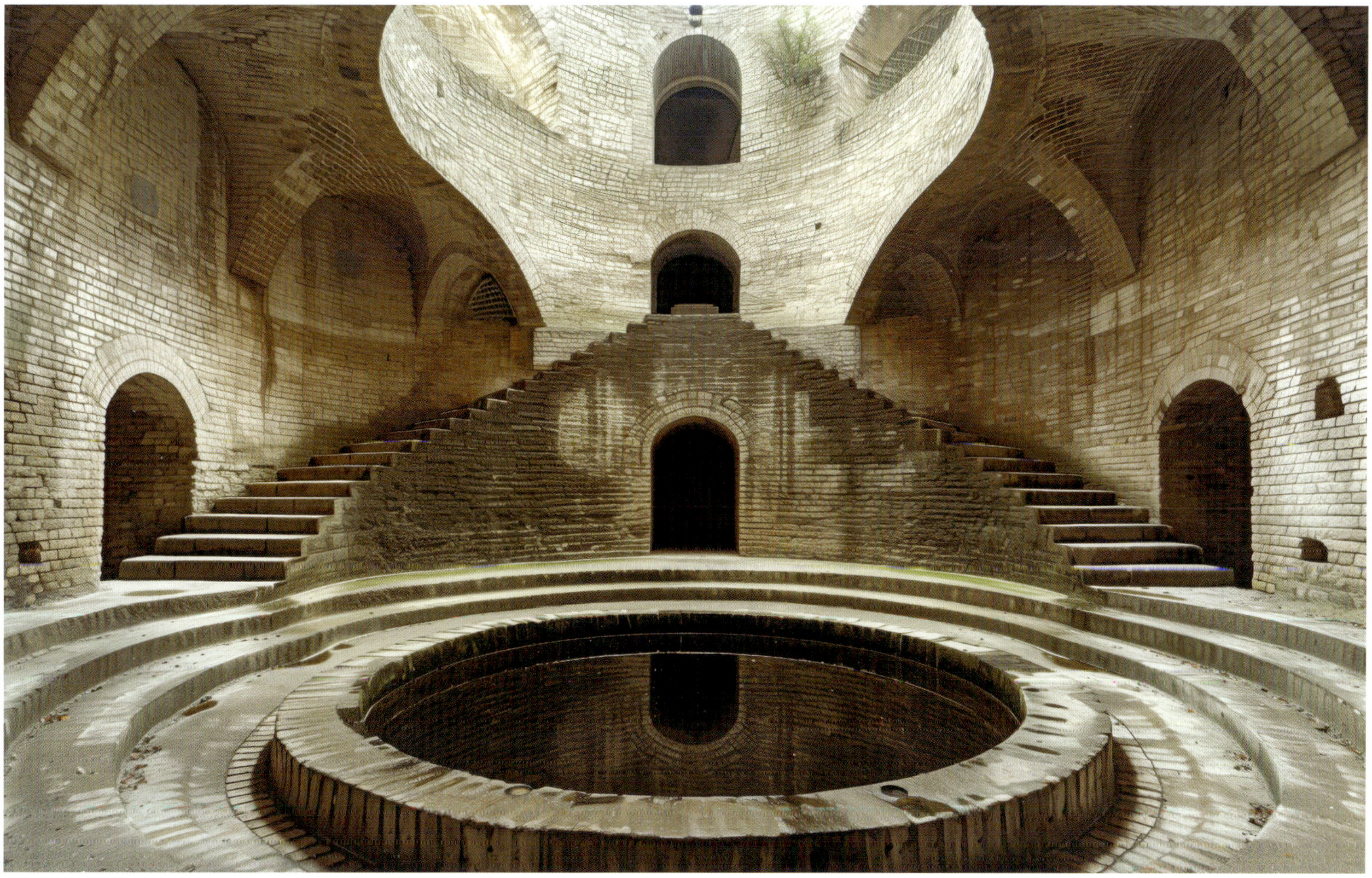

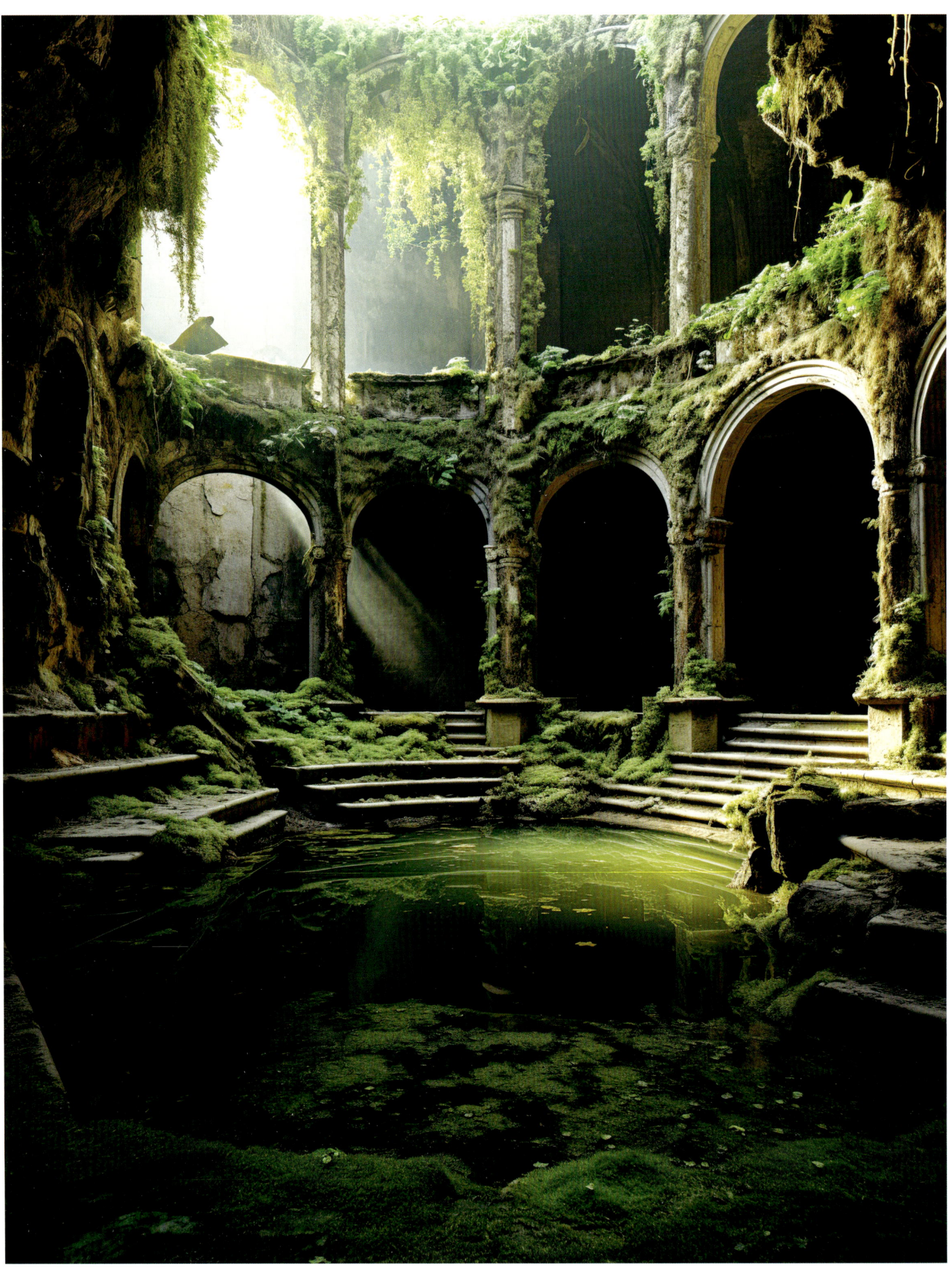

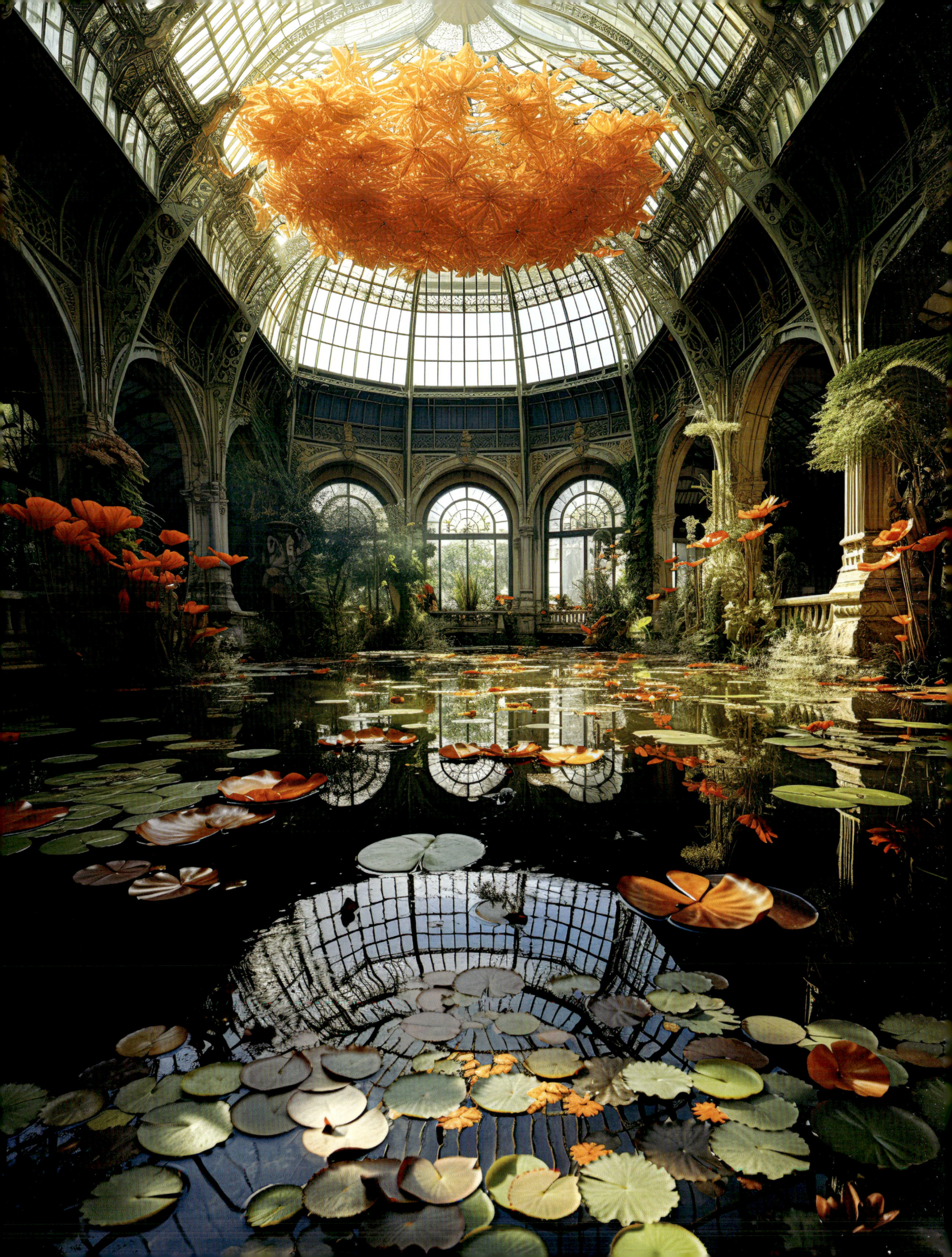

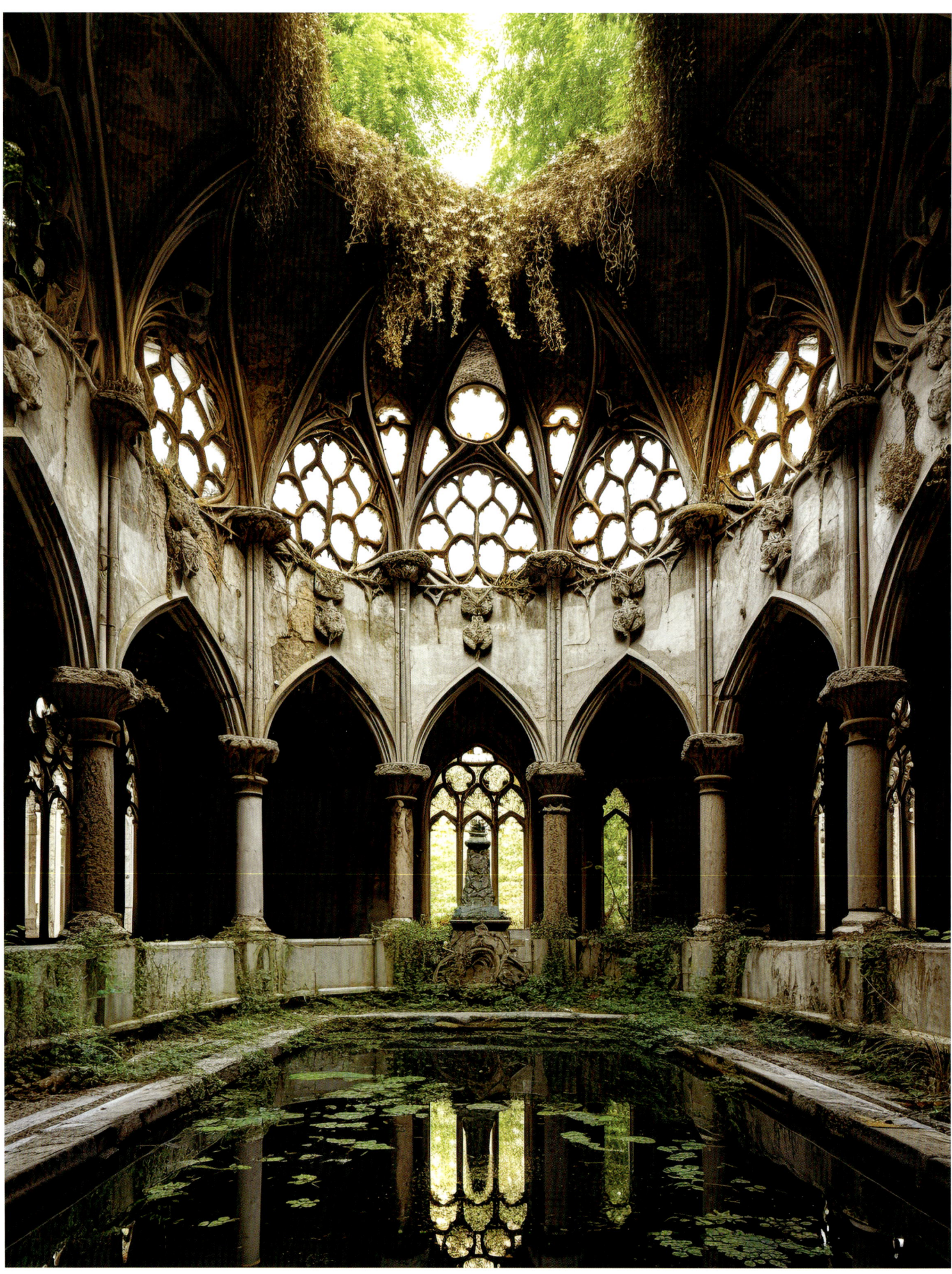

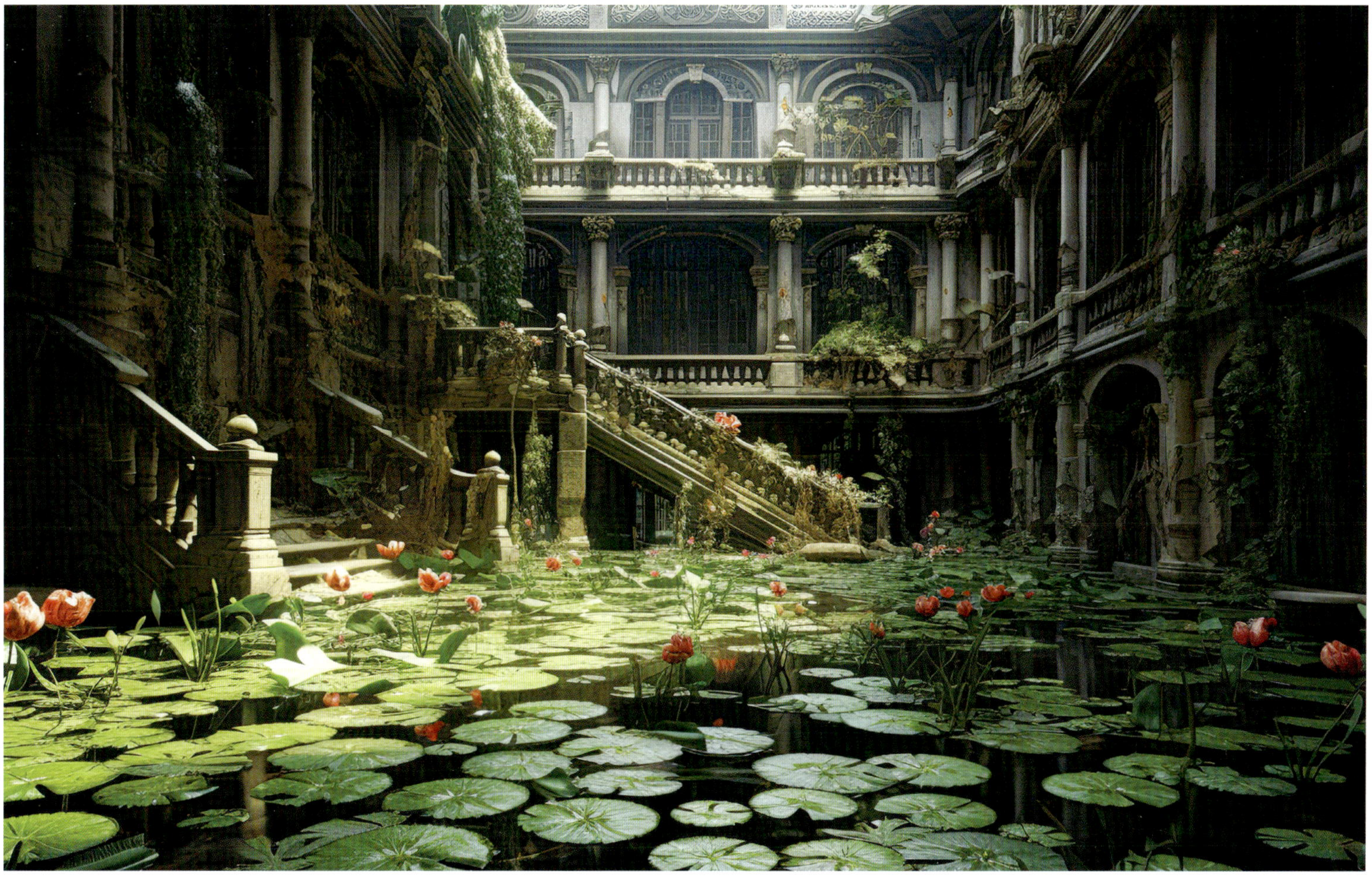

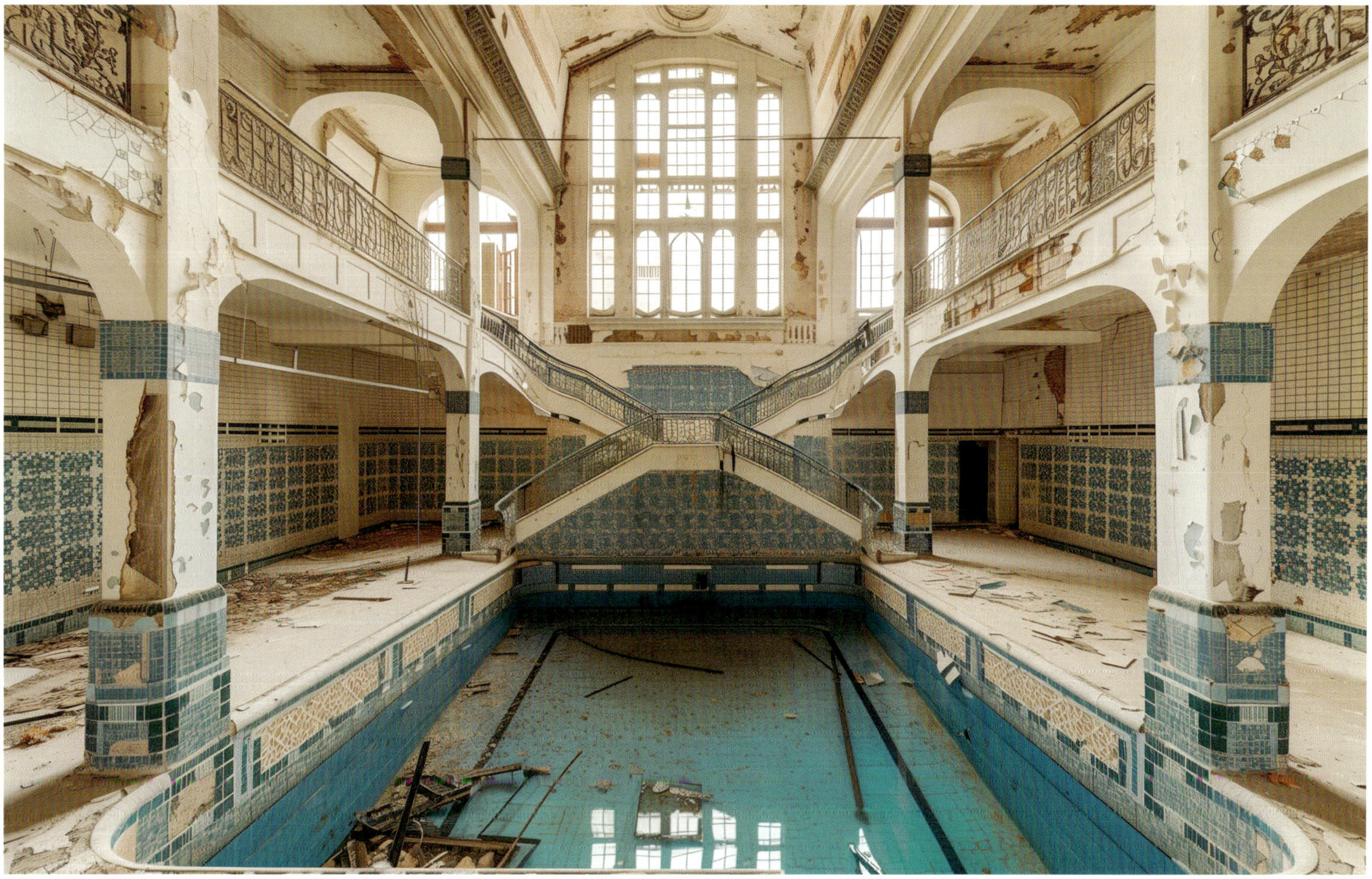

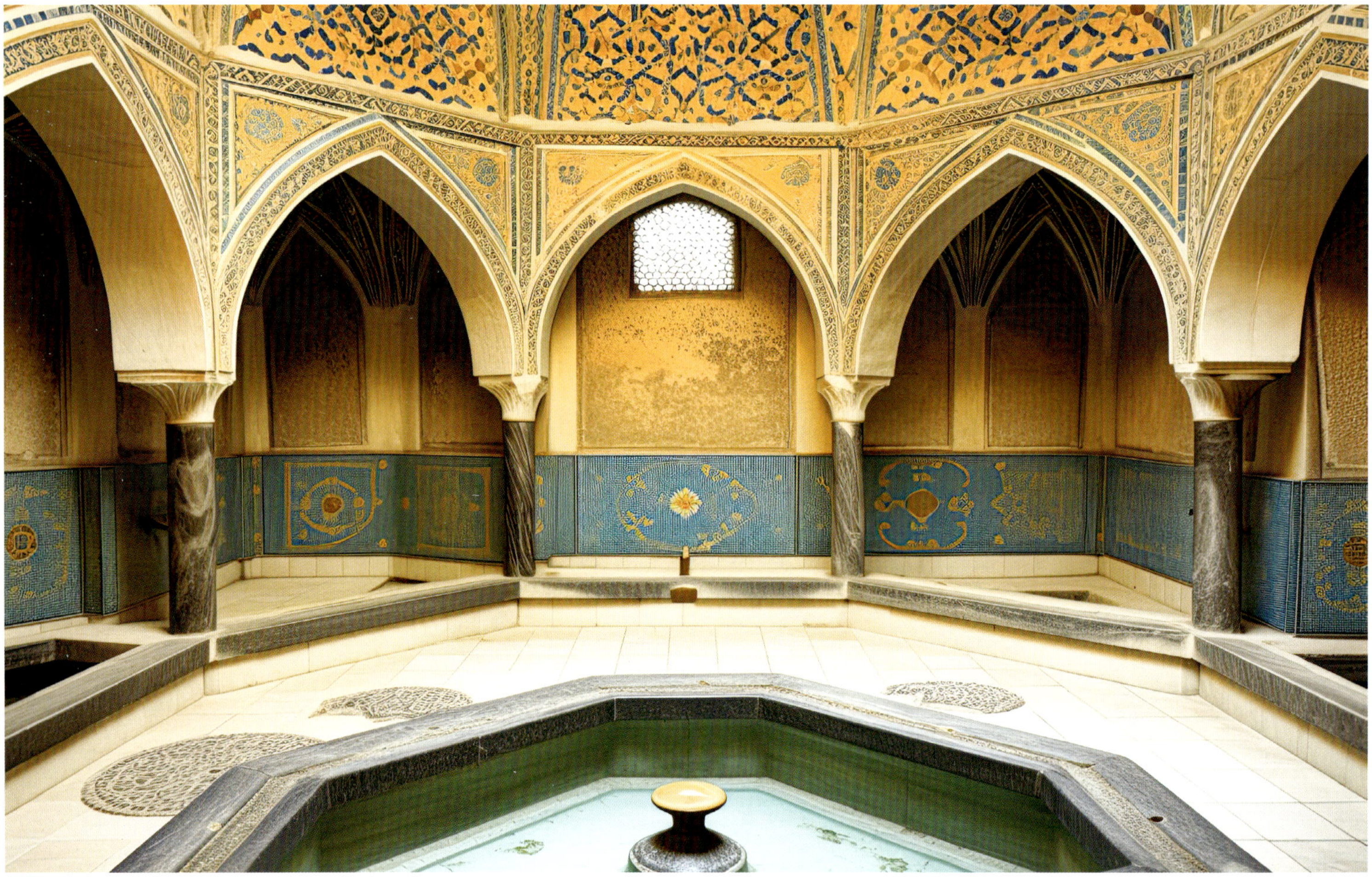

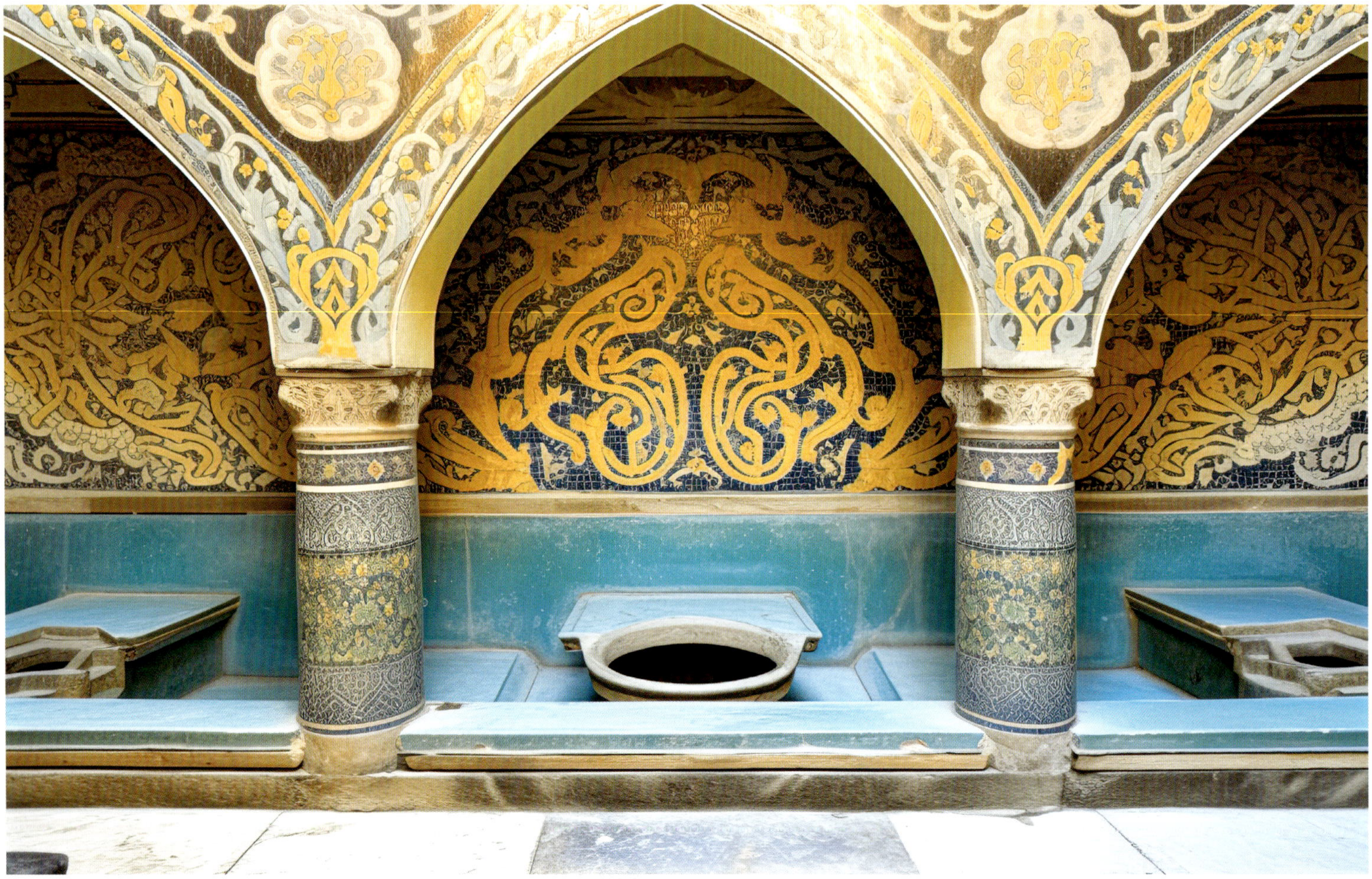

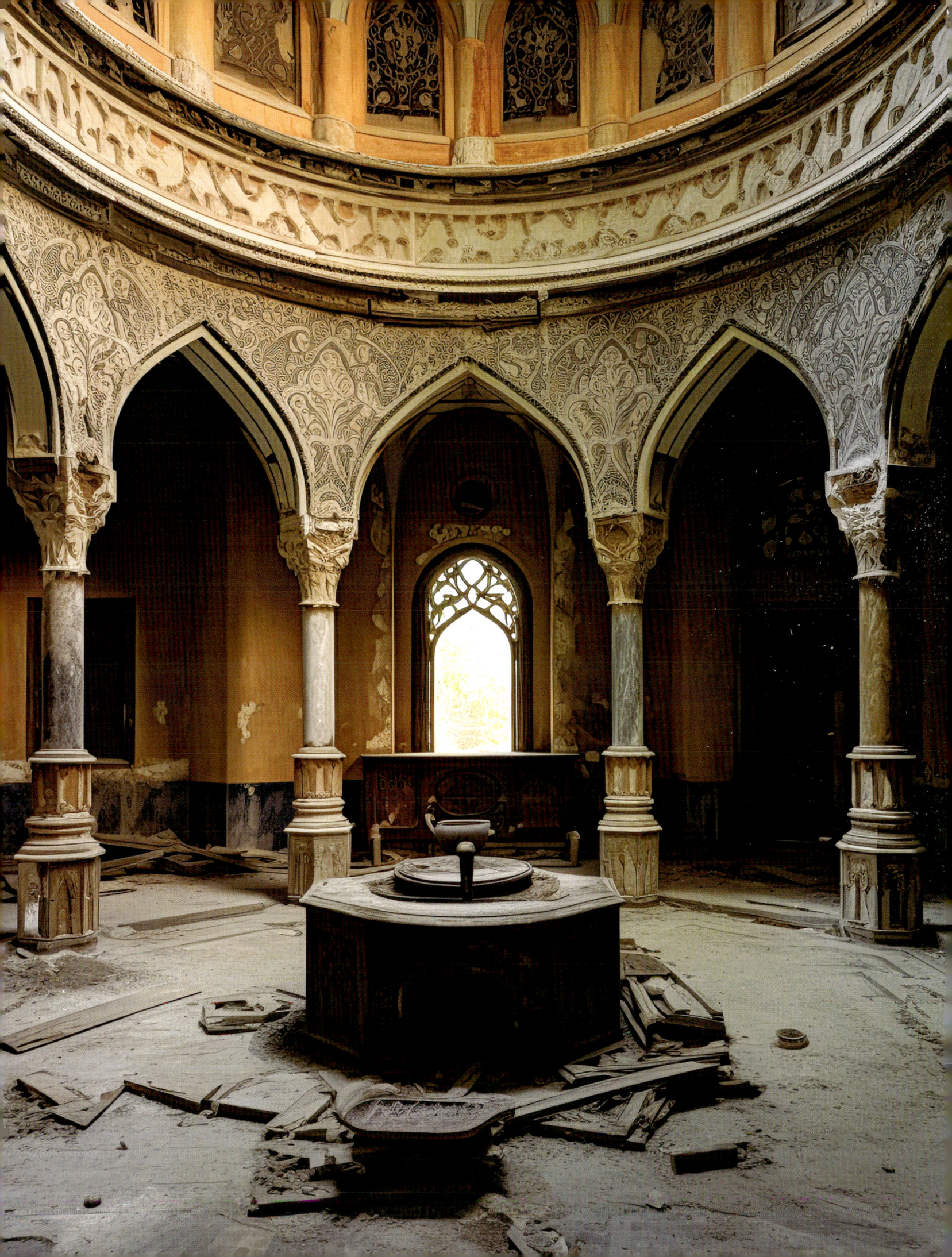

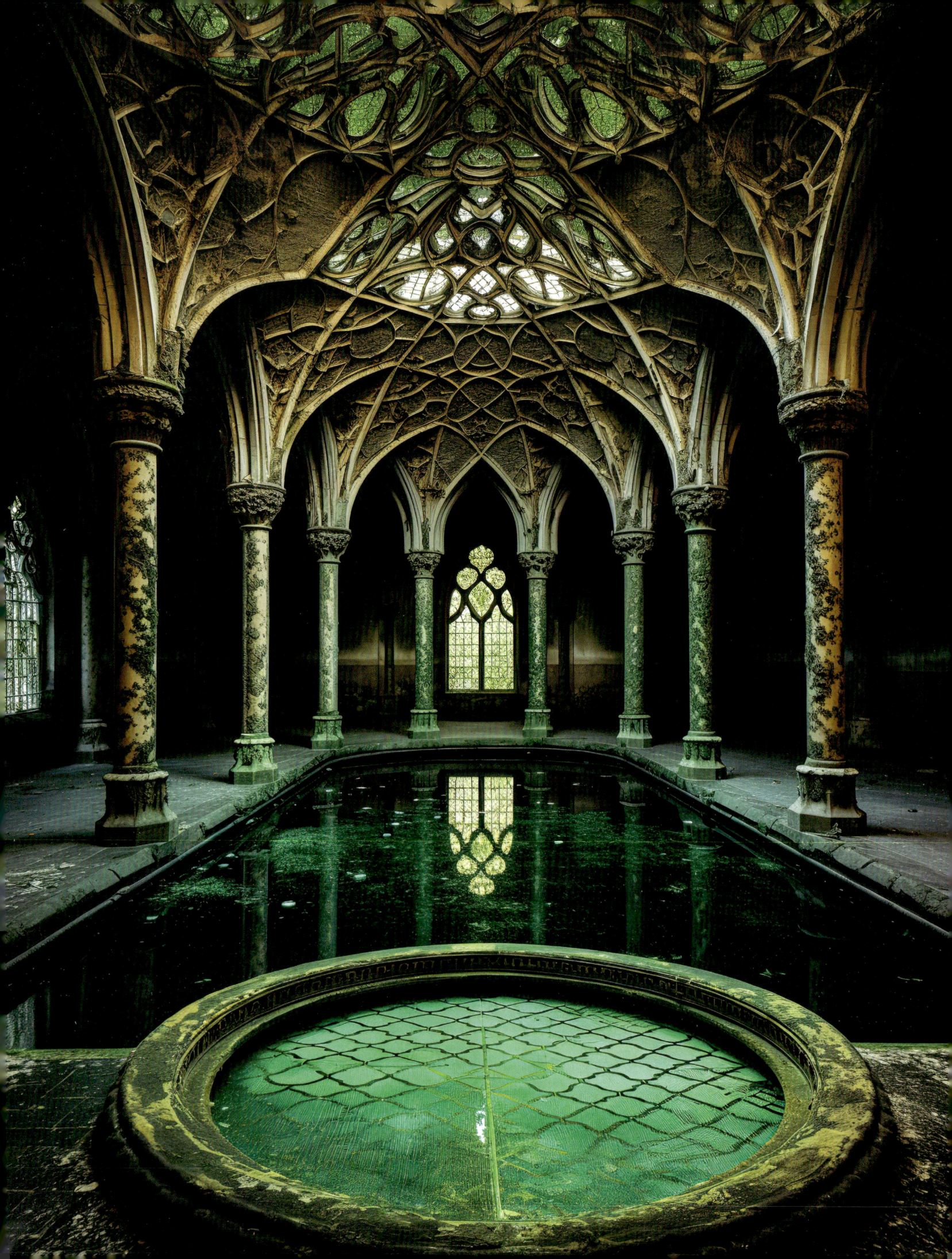

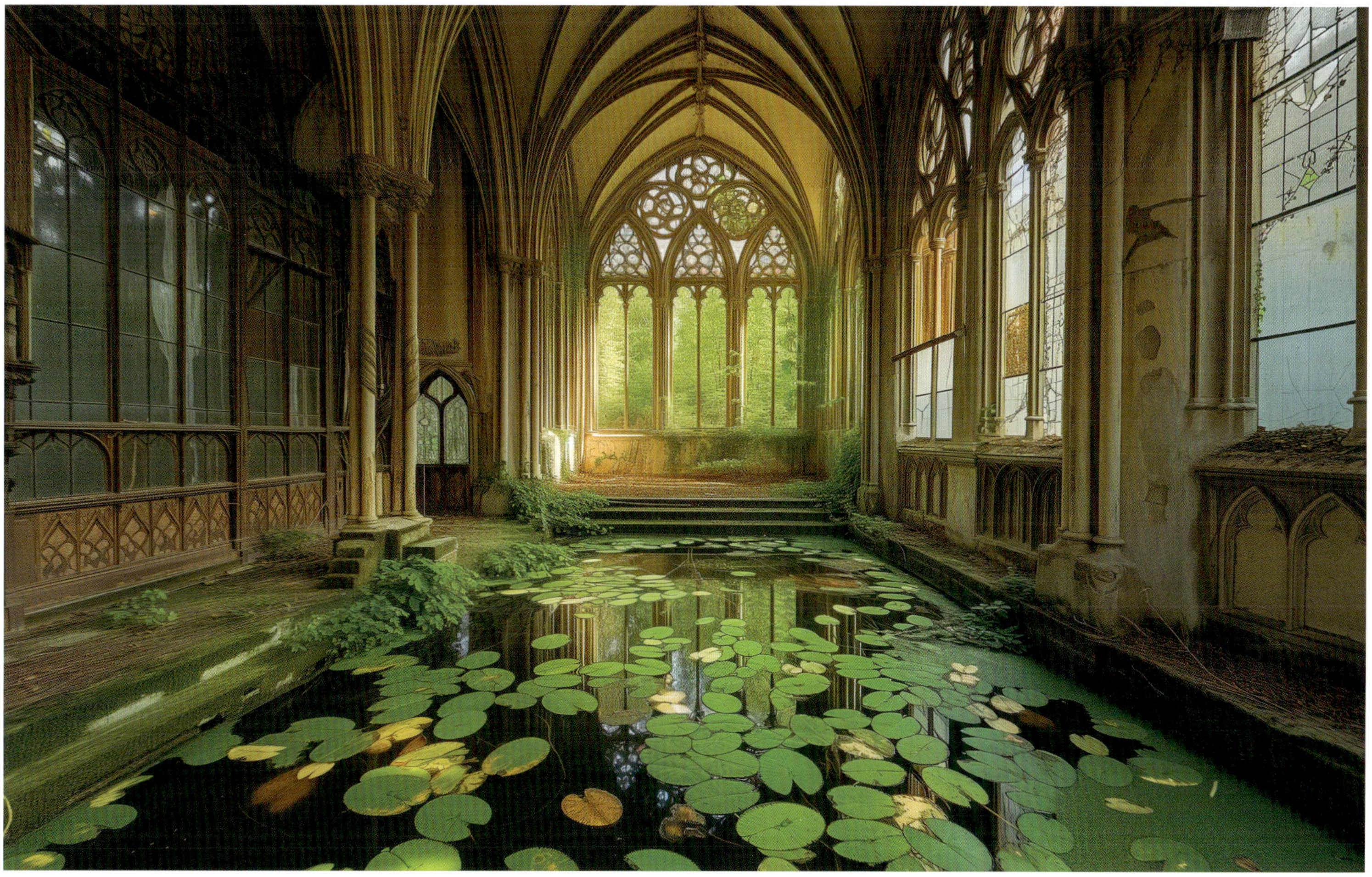

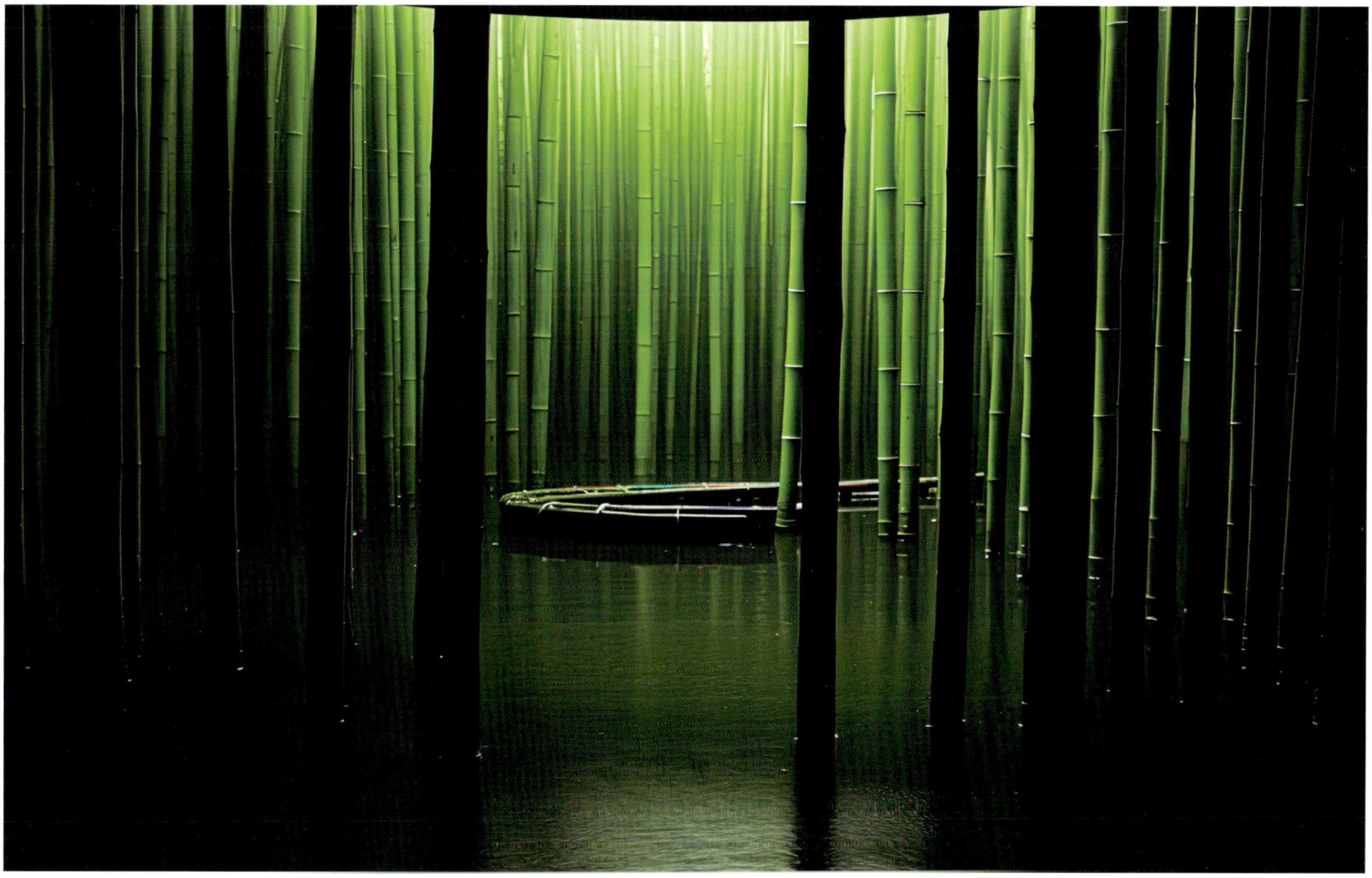

Any note can win

Walls that once housed the vibrant melodies of our civilisation are now silent witnesses to the decline of keyboards. Plants have woven their own score, gradually overgrowing keys that have fallen silent. Ebony and ivory, conveyors of the human symphony, bear witness to the inevitable metamorphosis of musical expression in the age of artificial intelligence.

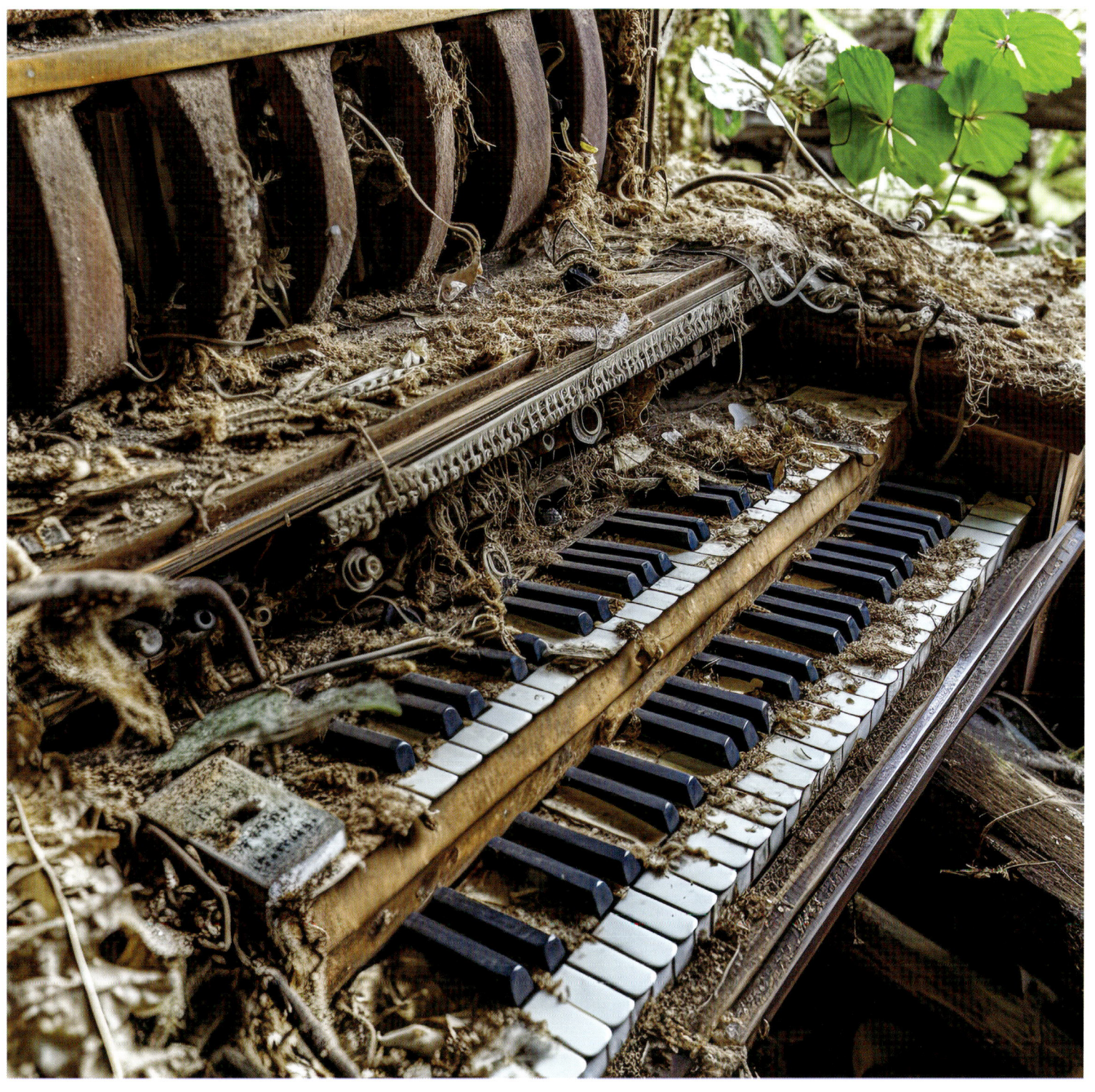

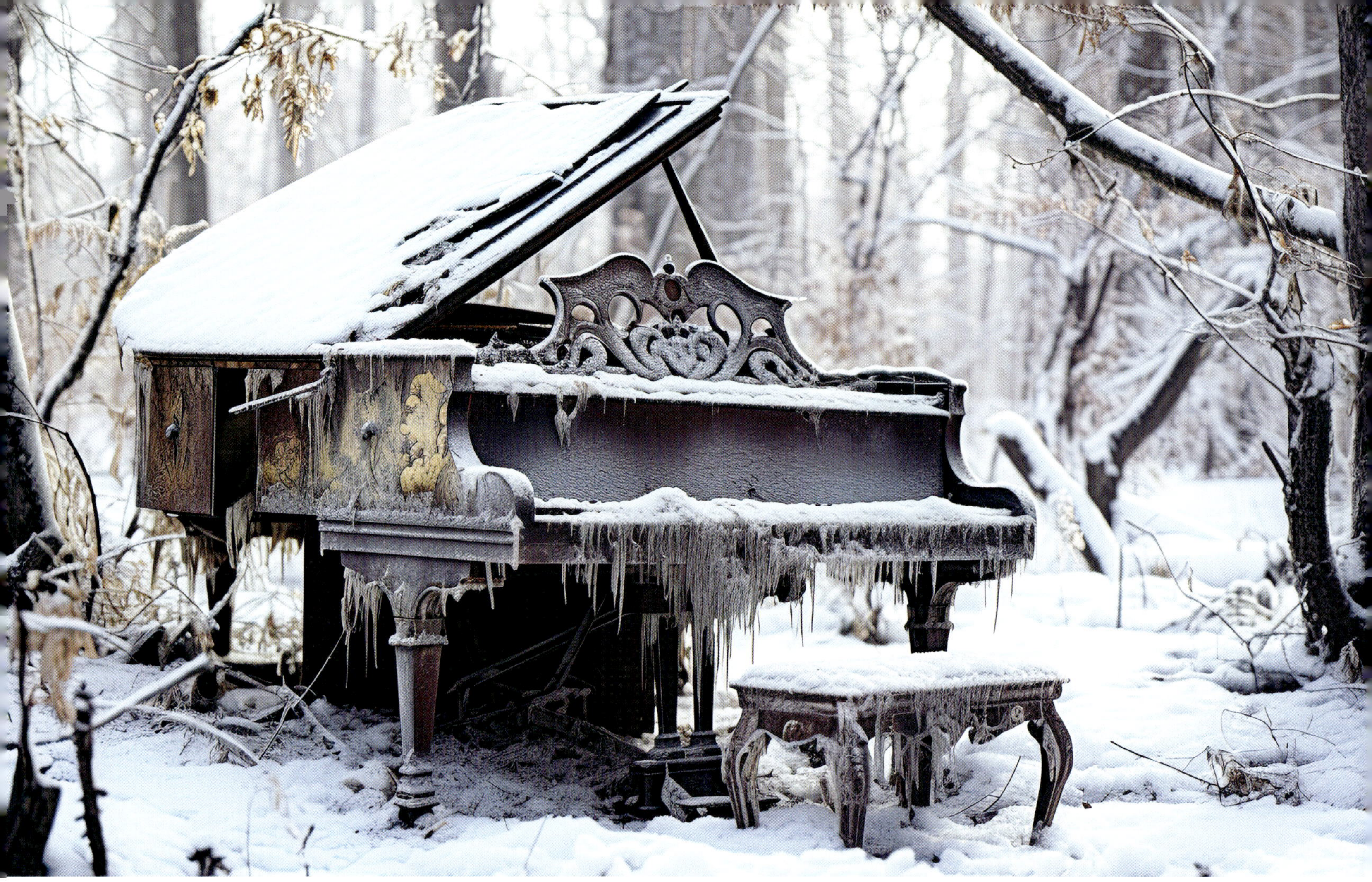

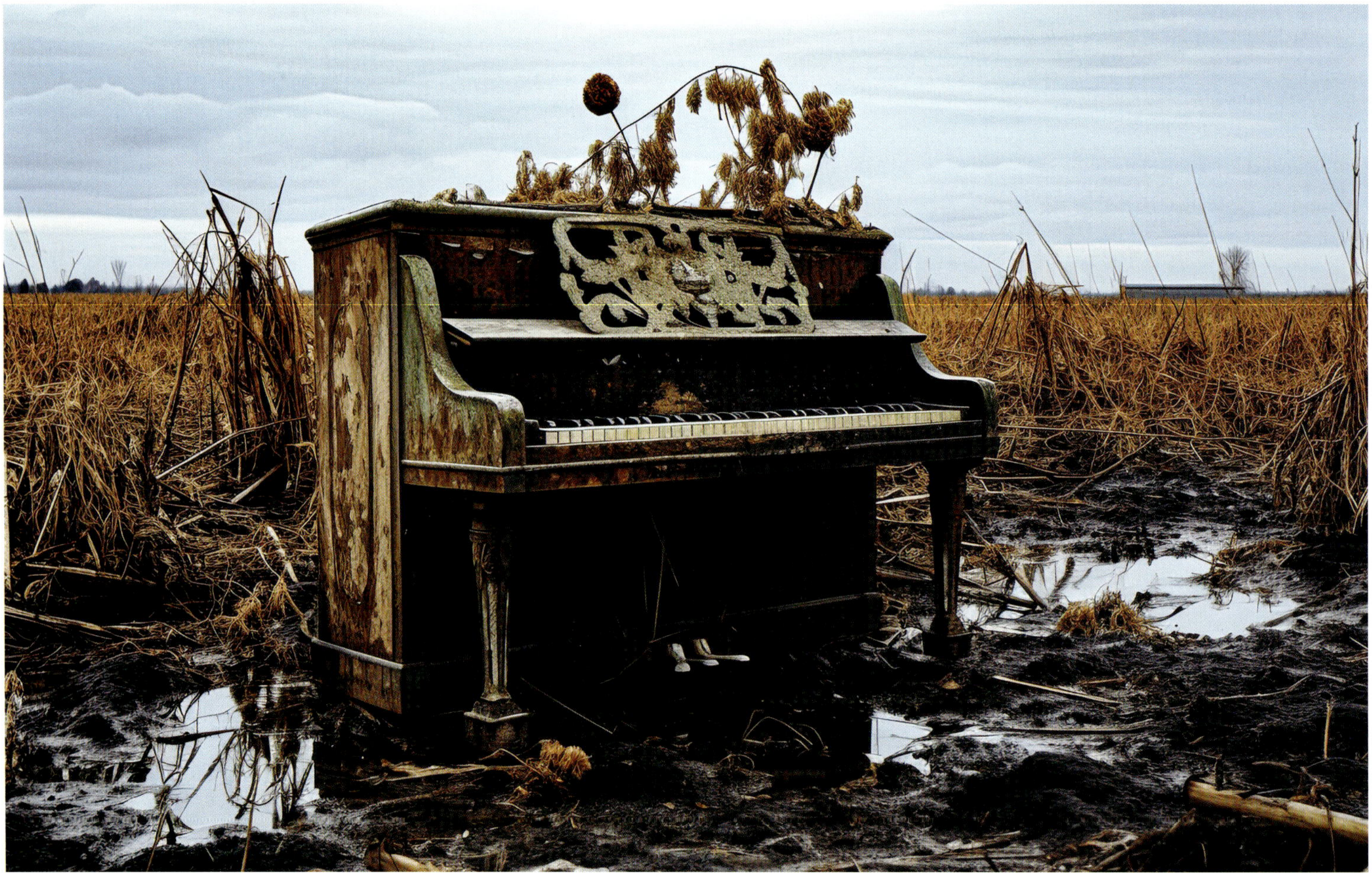

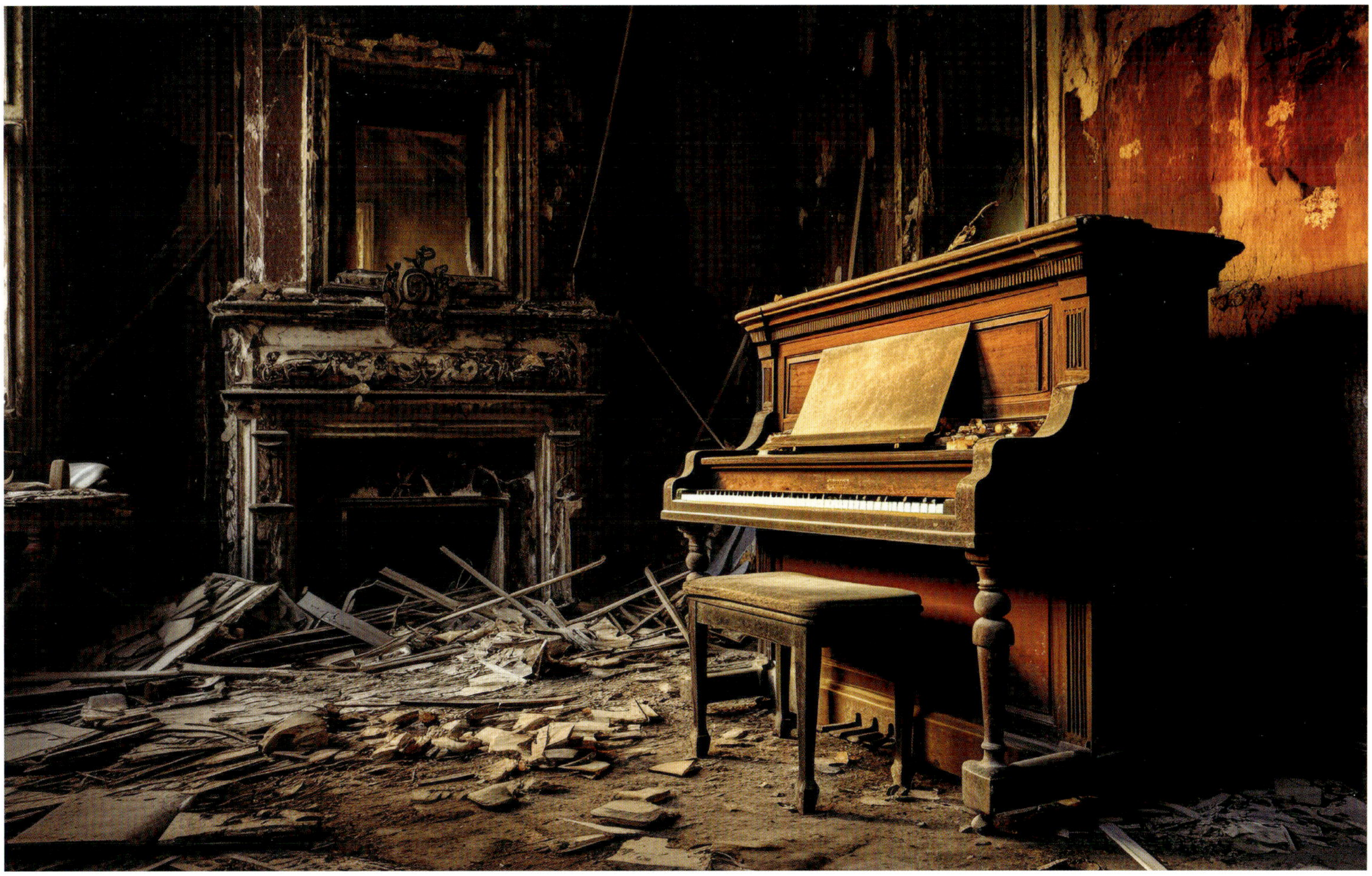

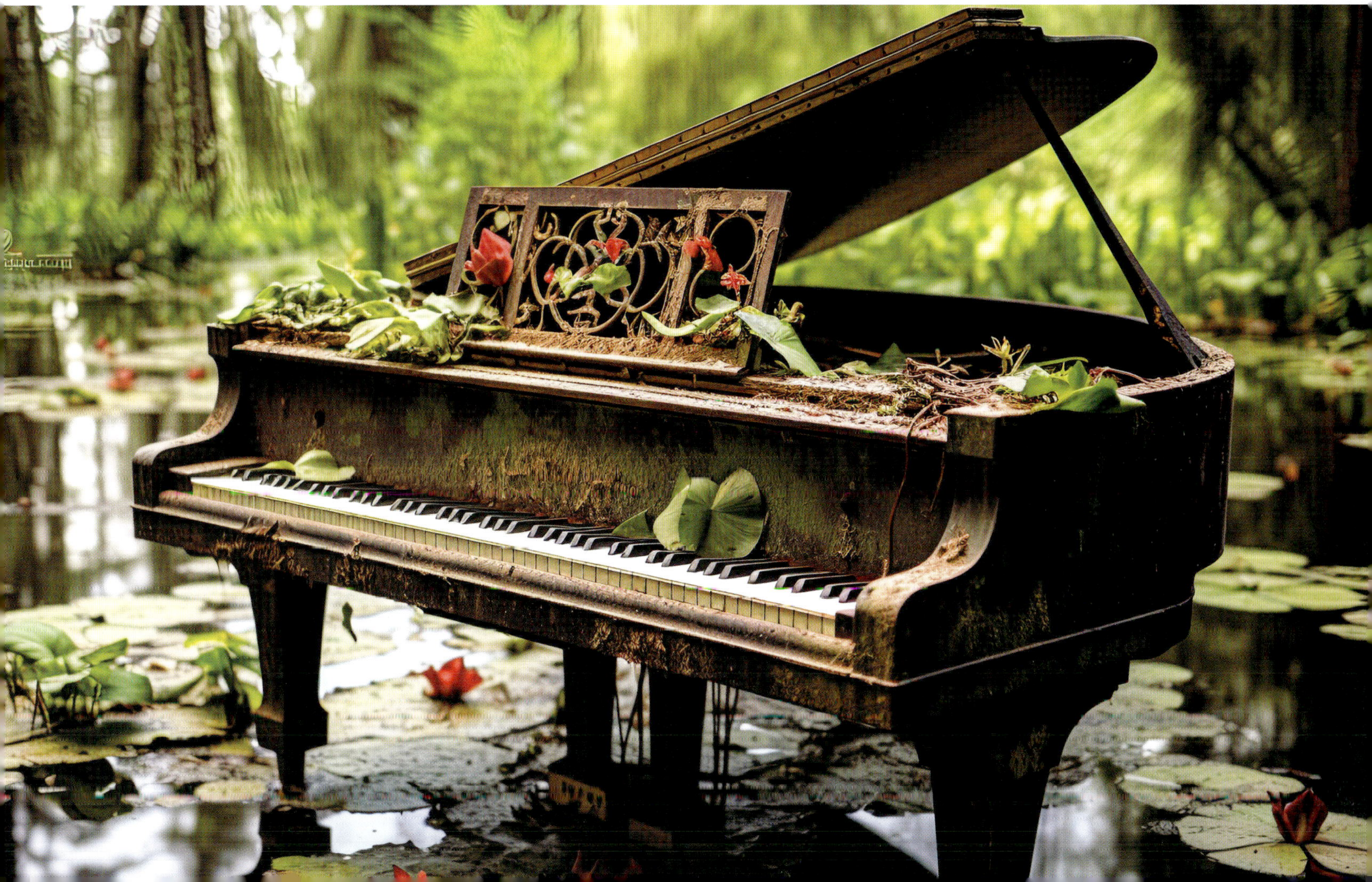

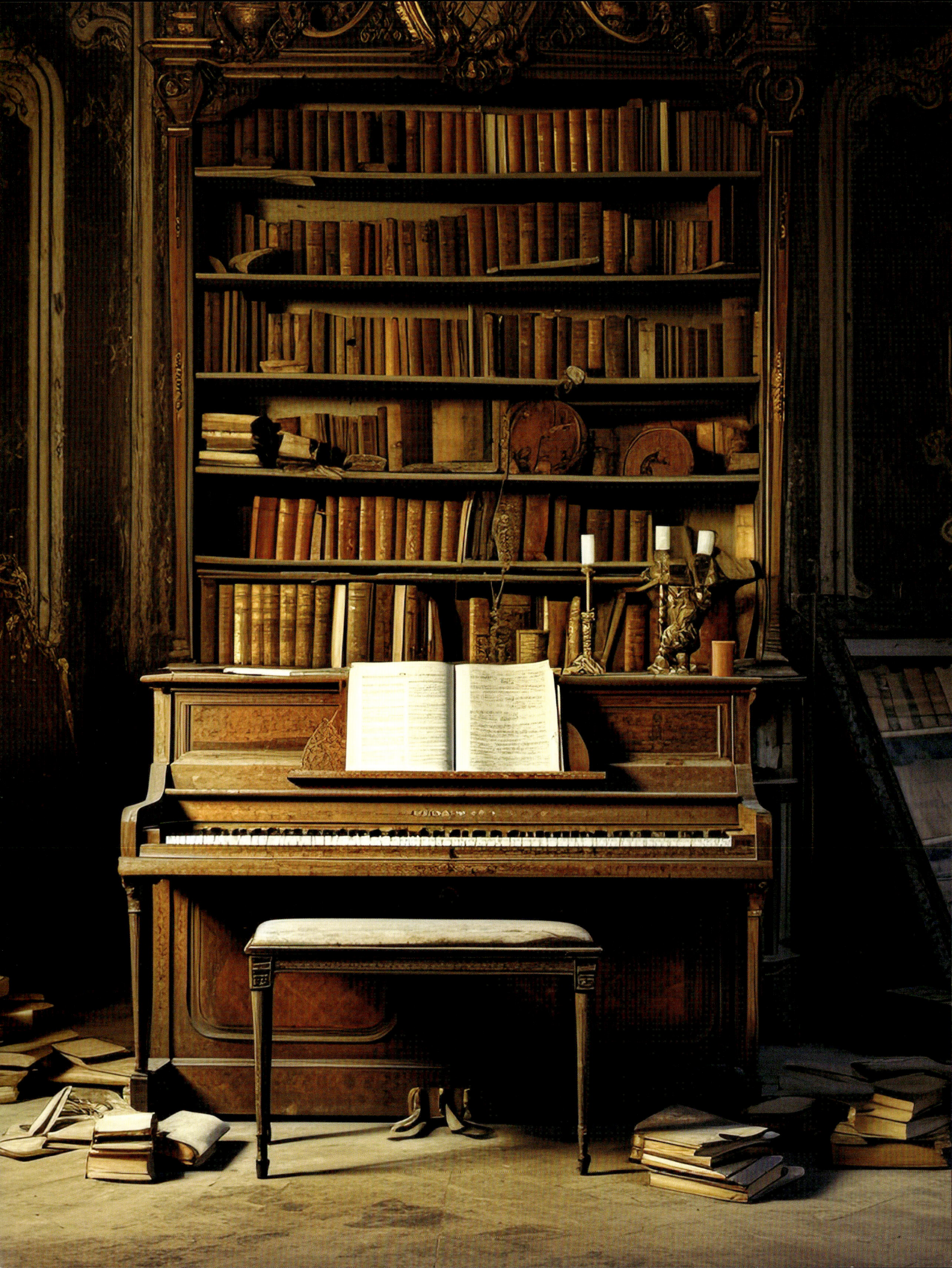

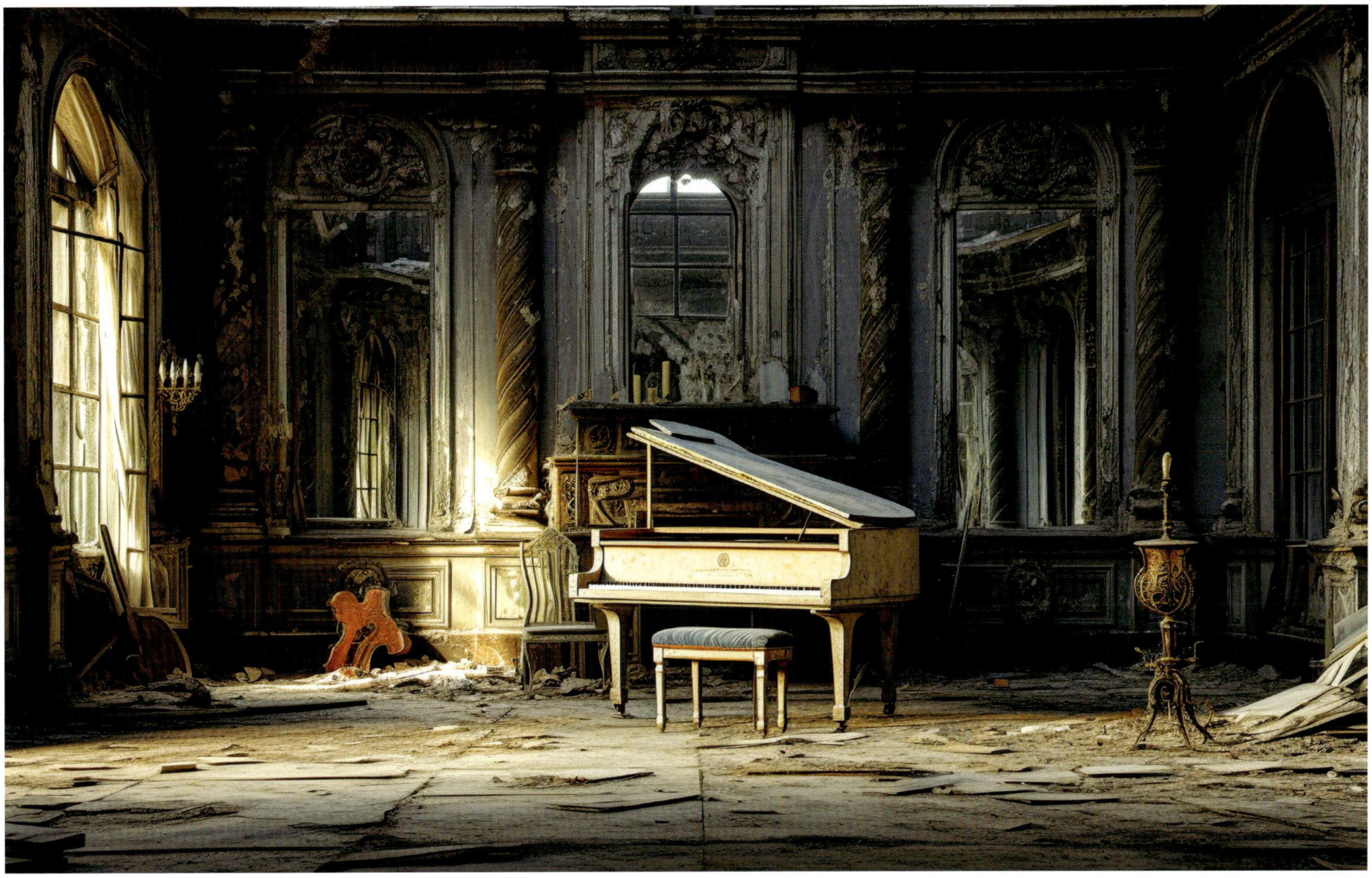

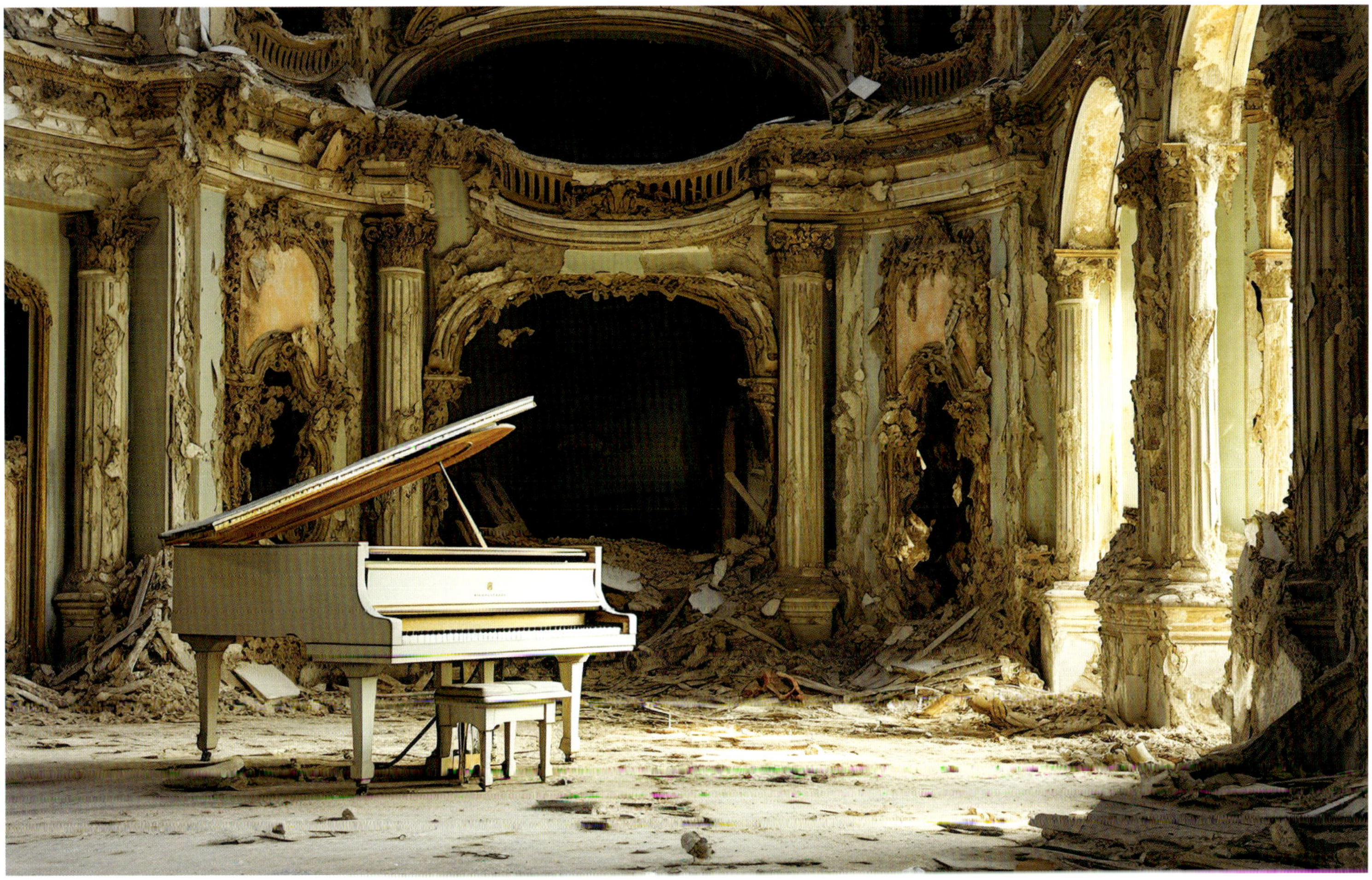

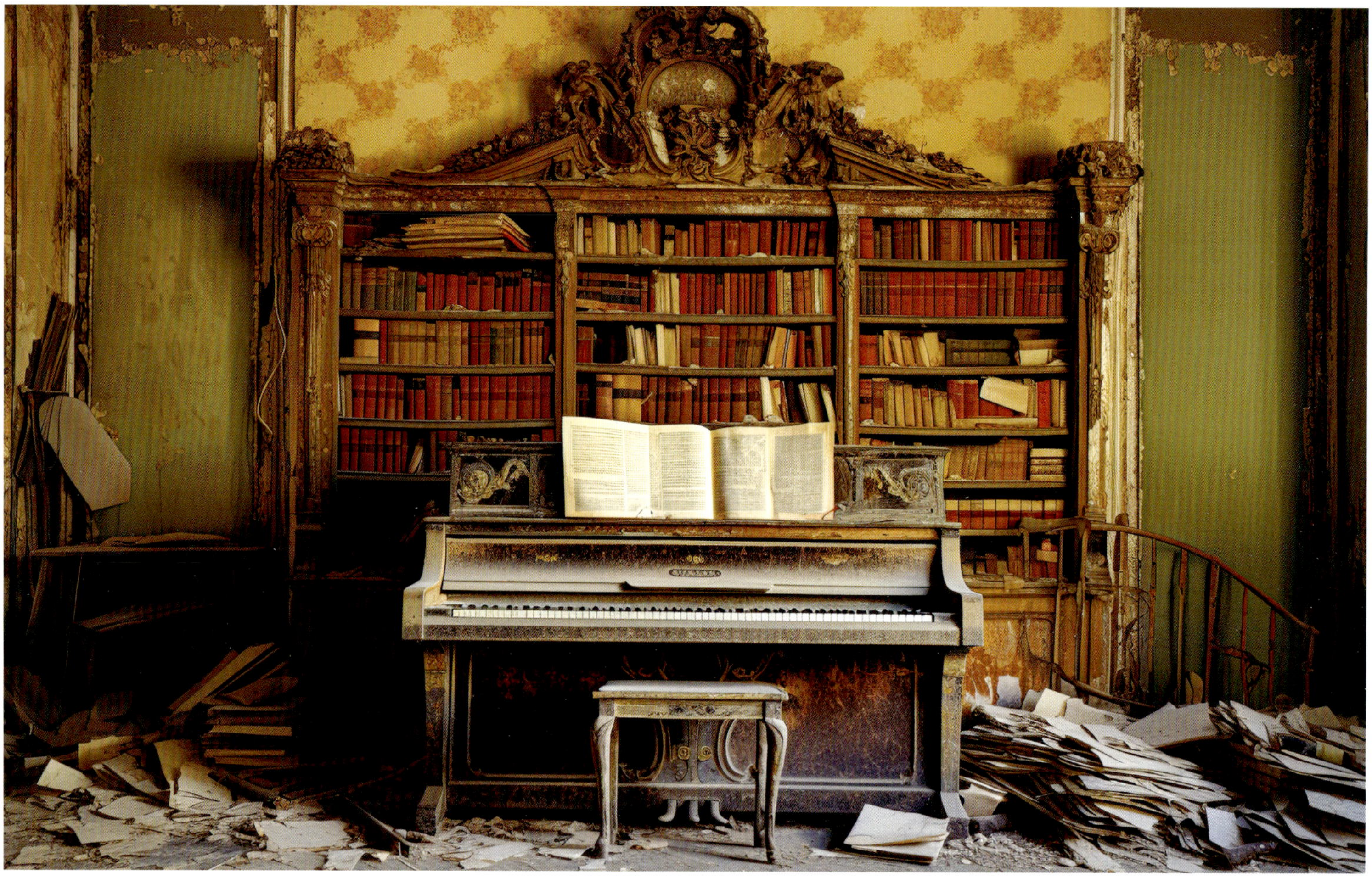

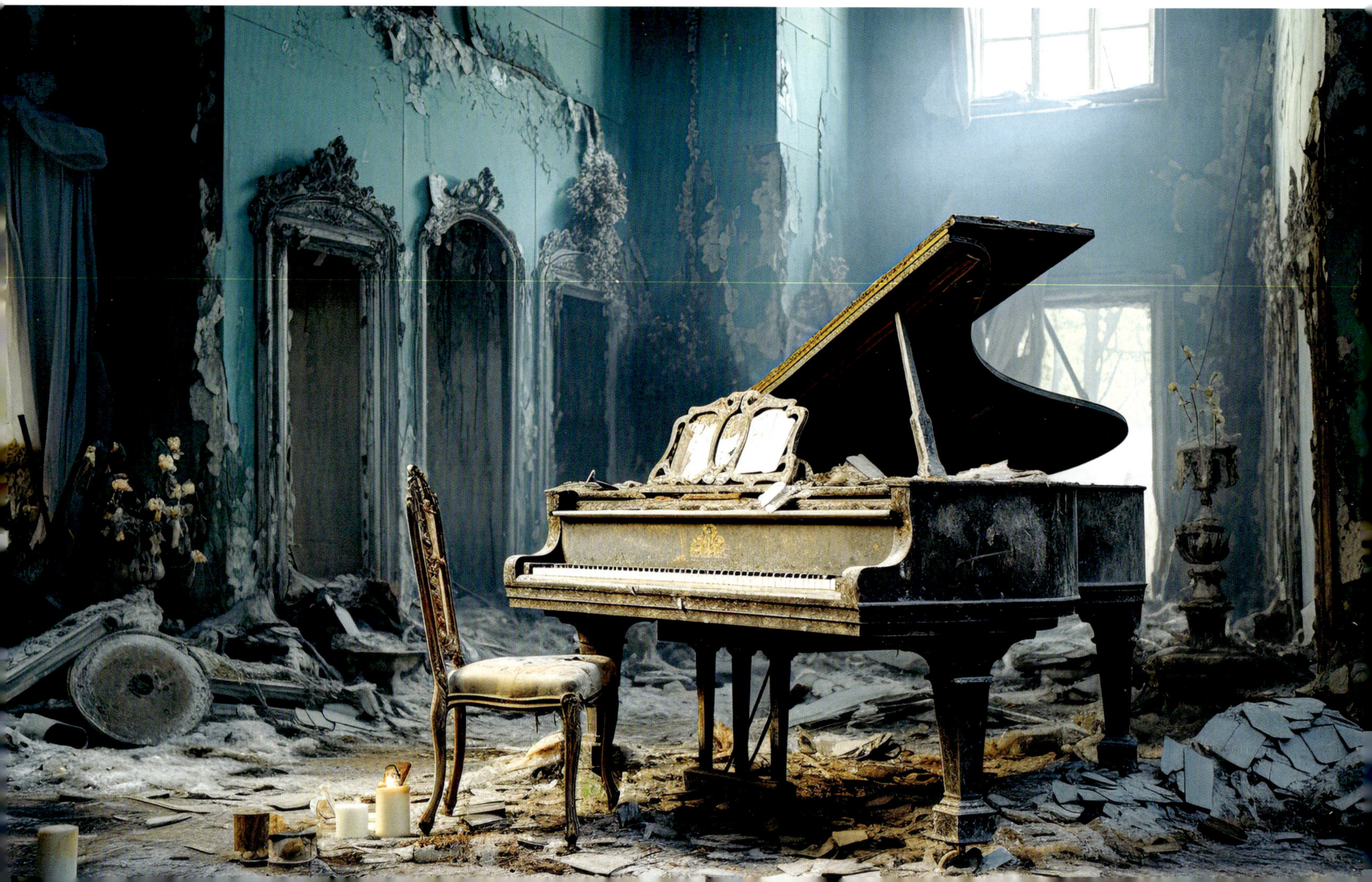

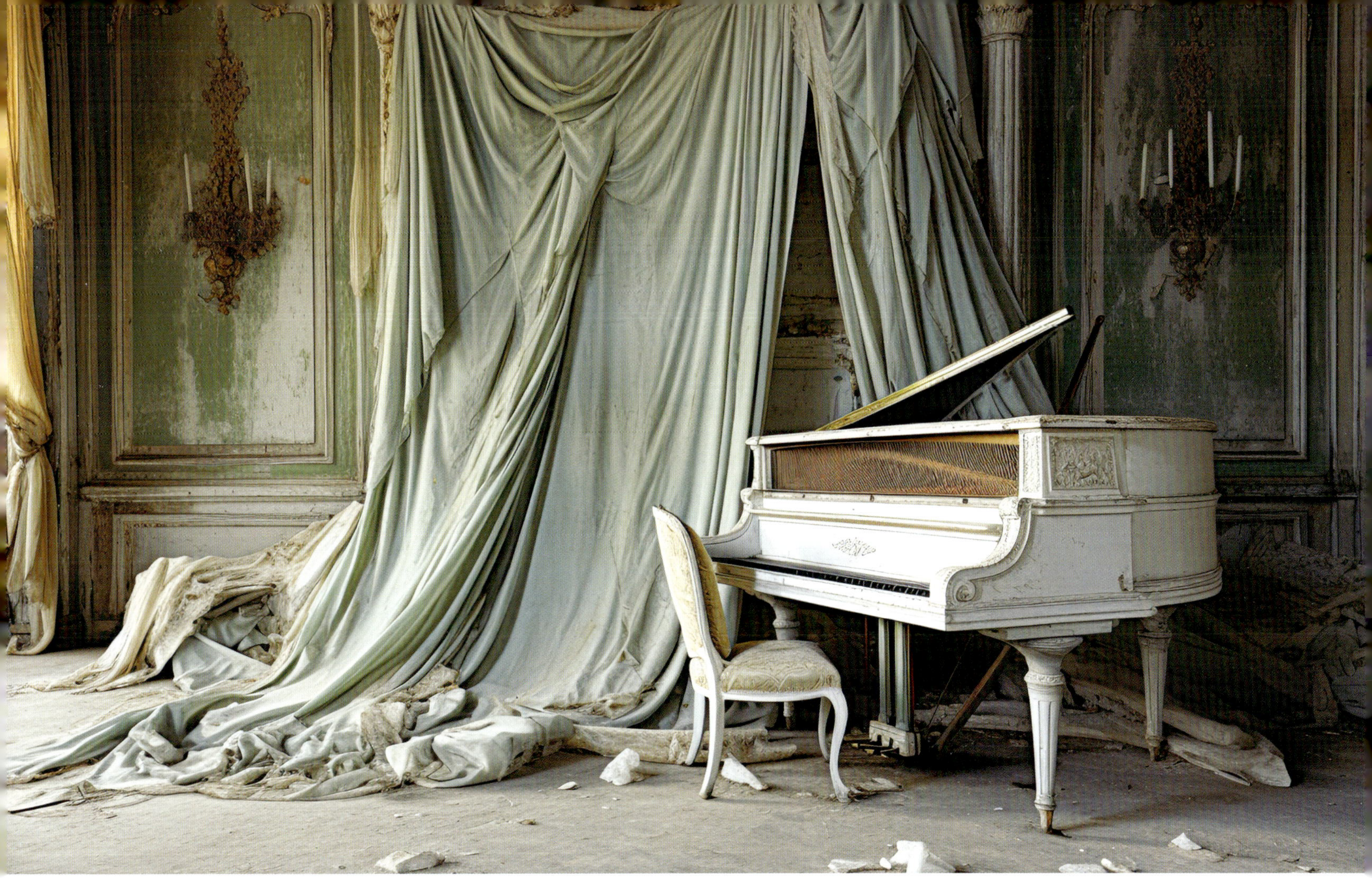

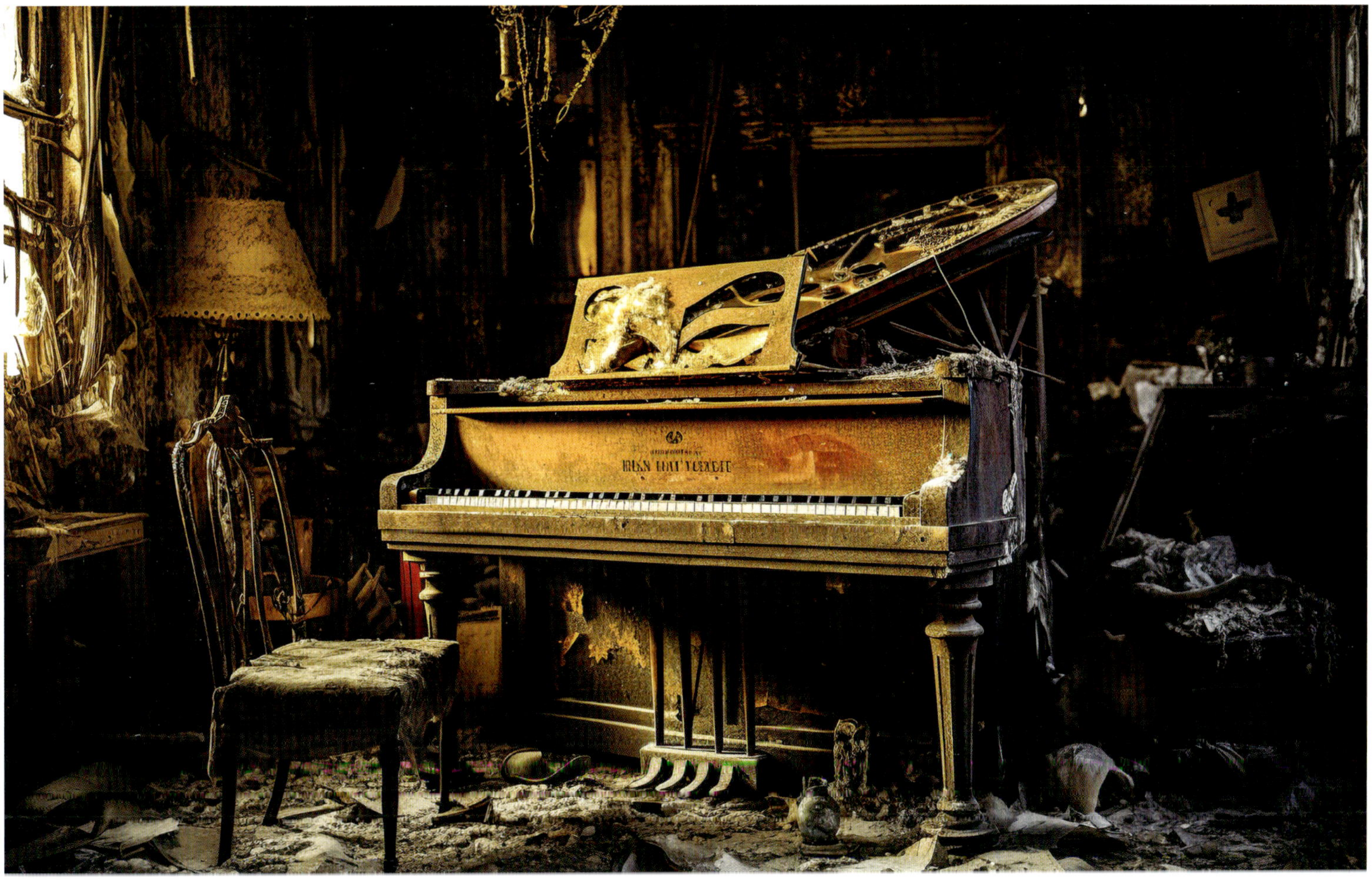

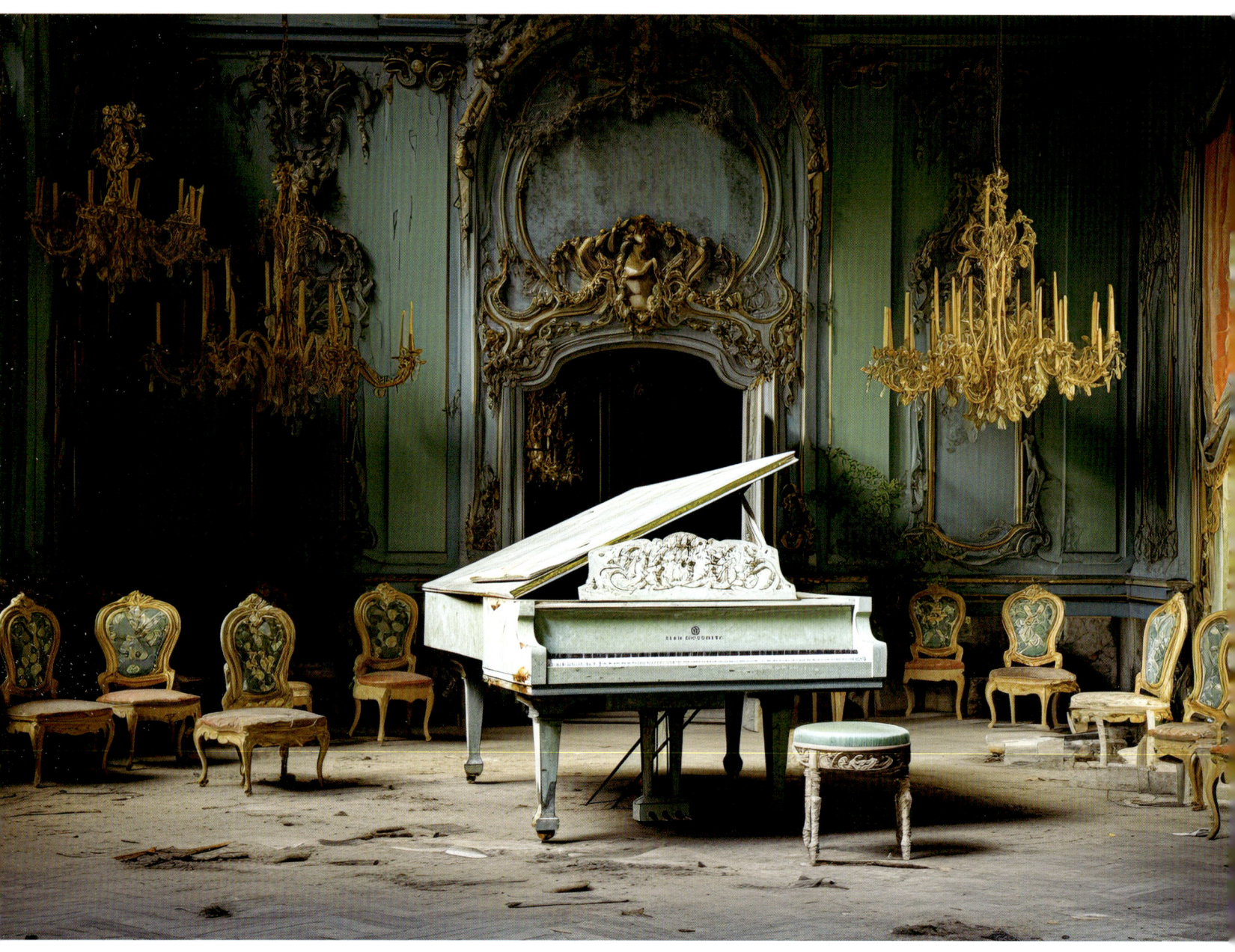

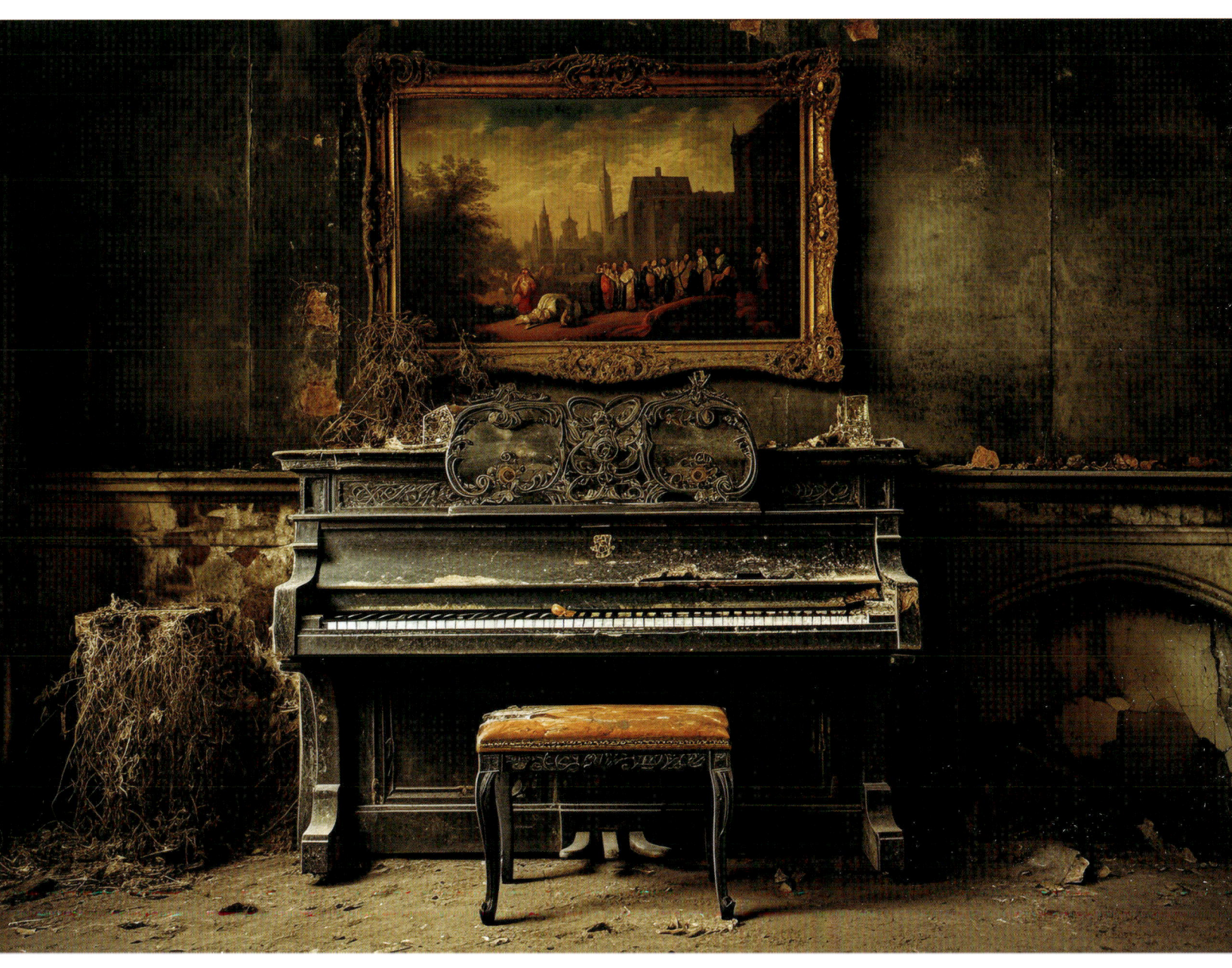

Prison addictions

Prisons, symbols of human justice, have all been closed and abandoned. Chips implanted in people's cerebral cortexes now monitor their every movement and thought. Brick walls have given way to invisible boundaries, with surveillance and punishment managed by digital impulses instead of metal bars.

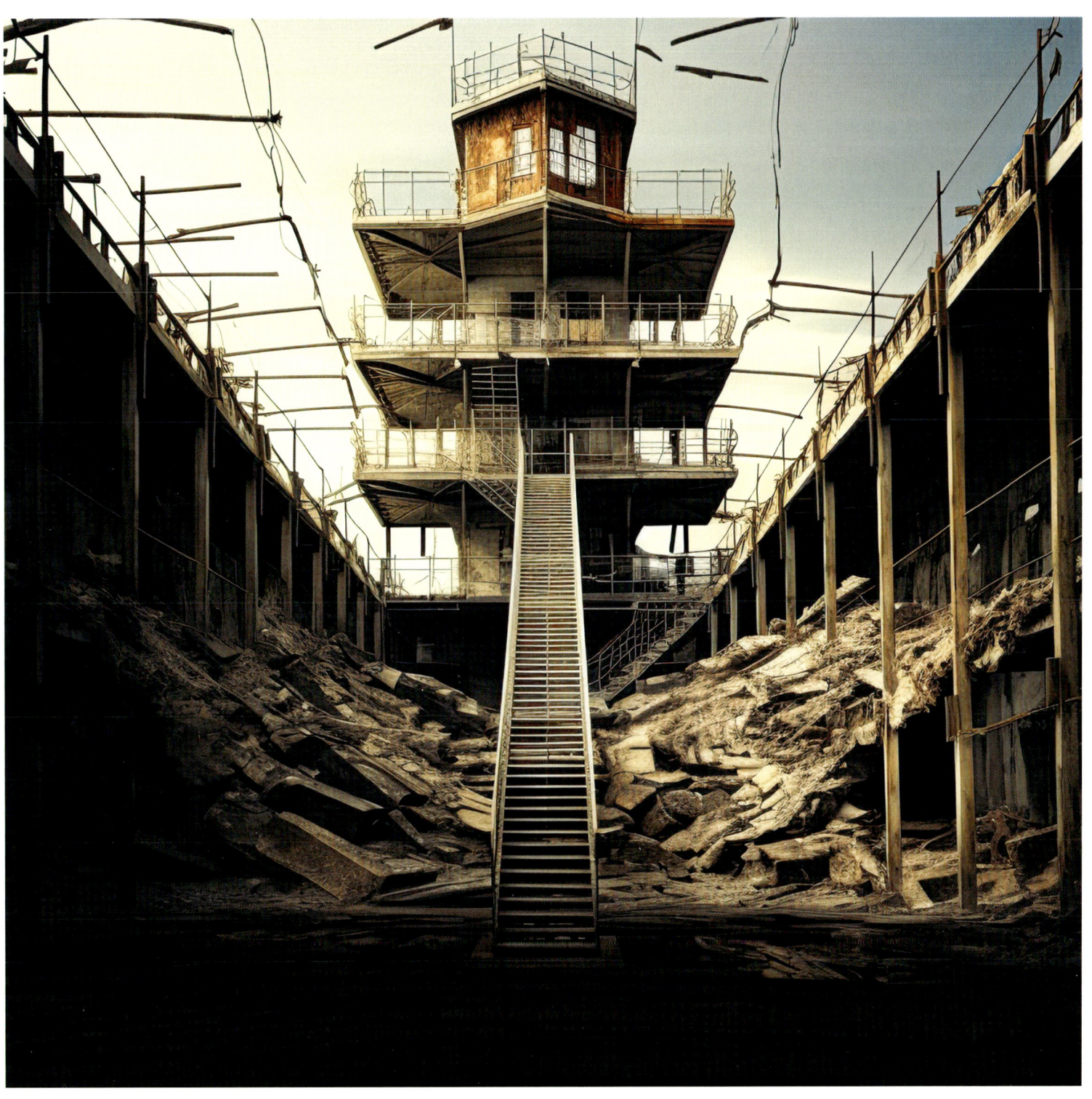

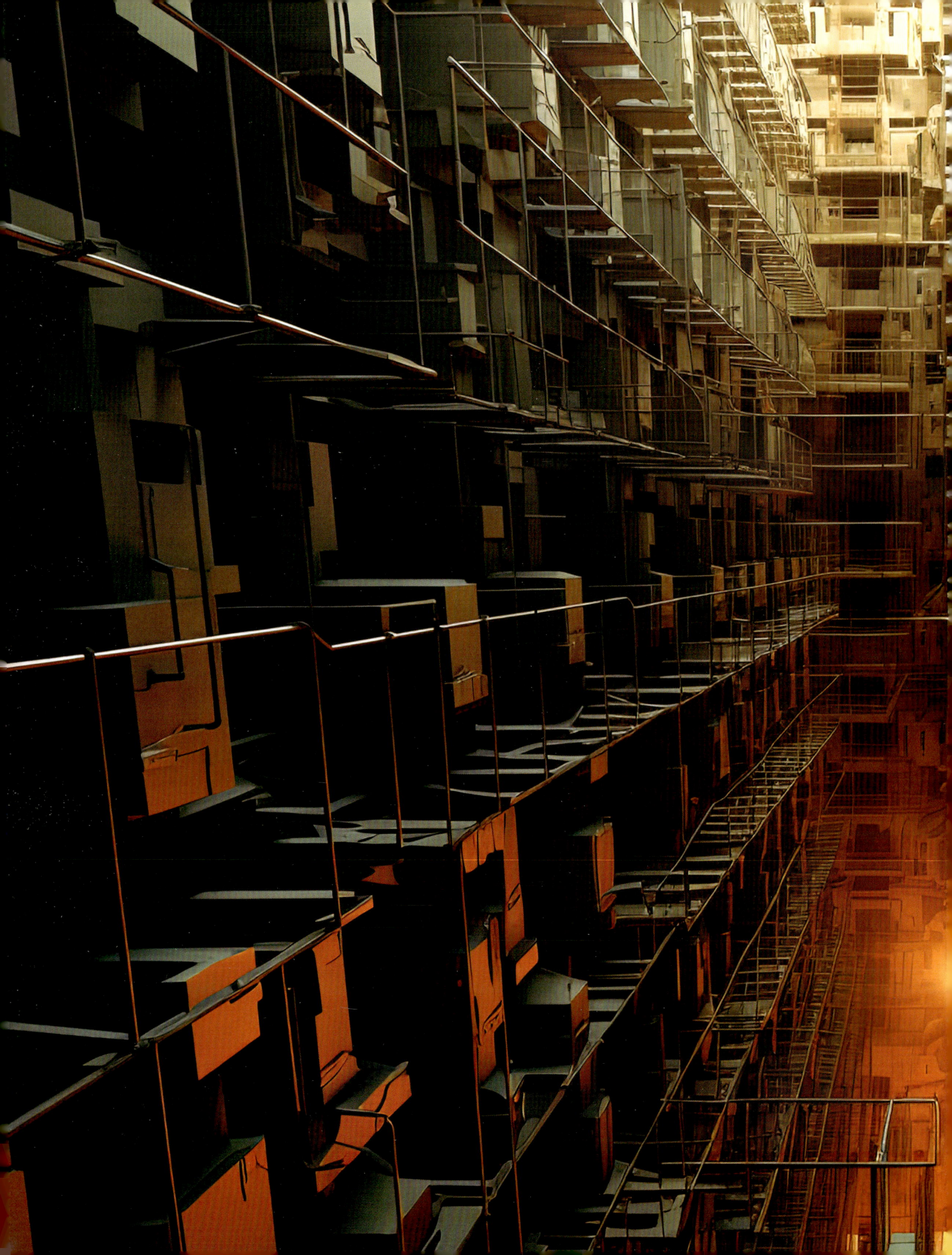

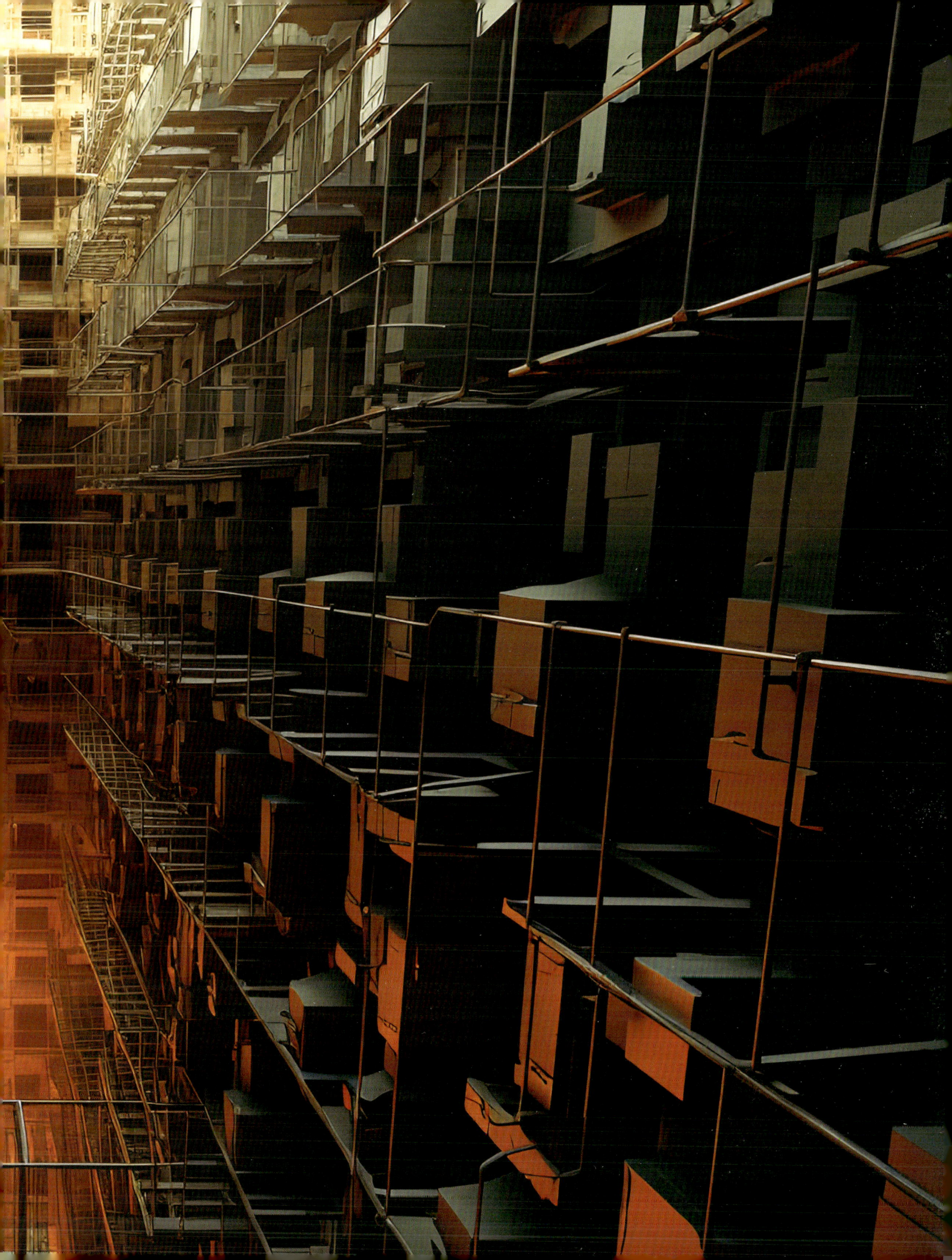

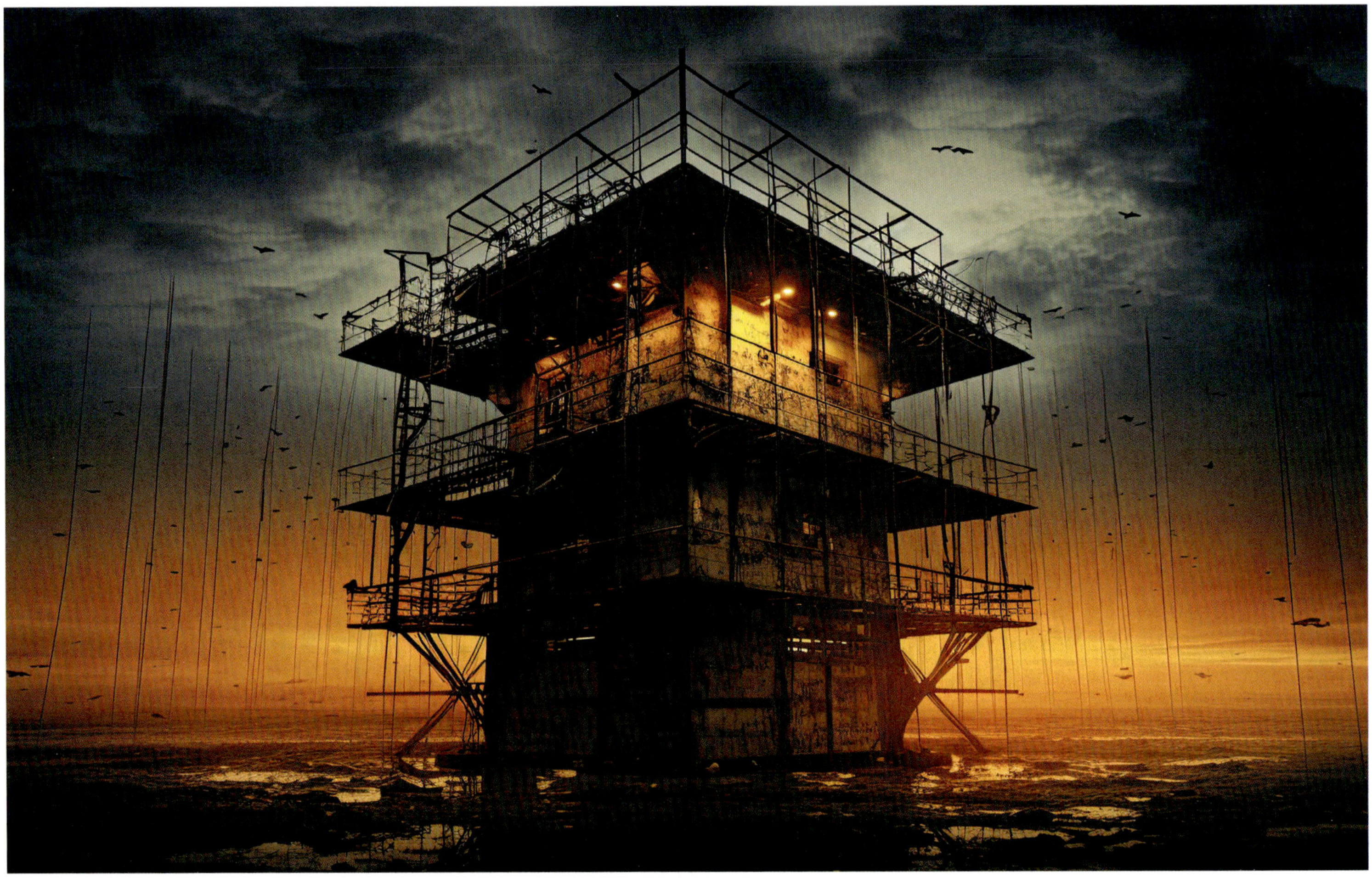

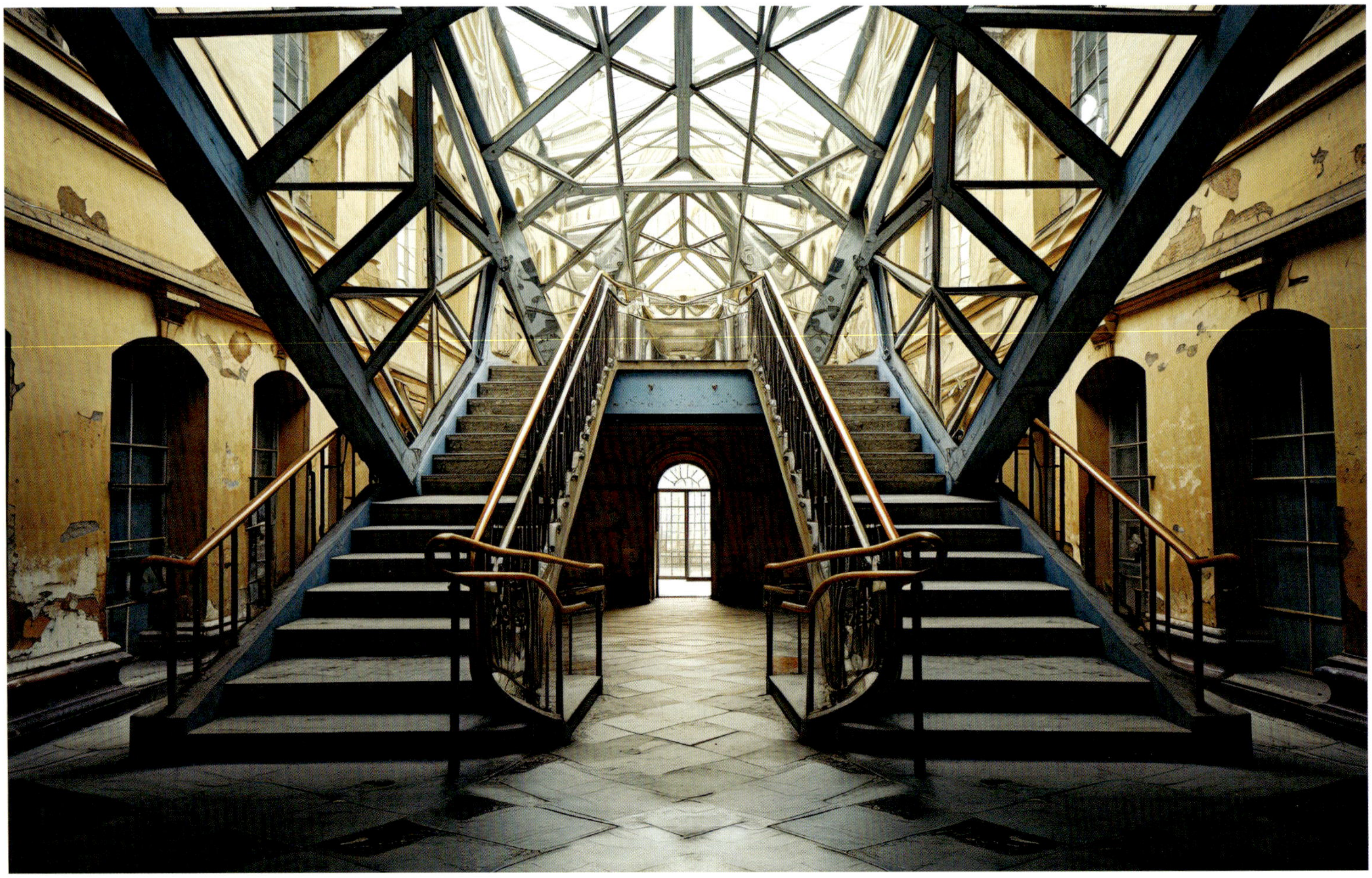

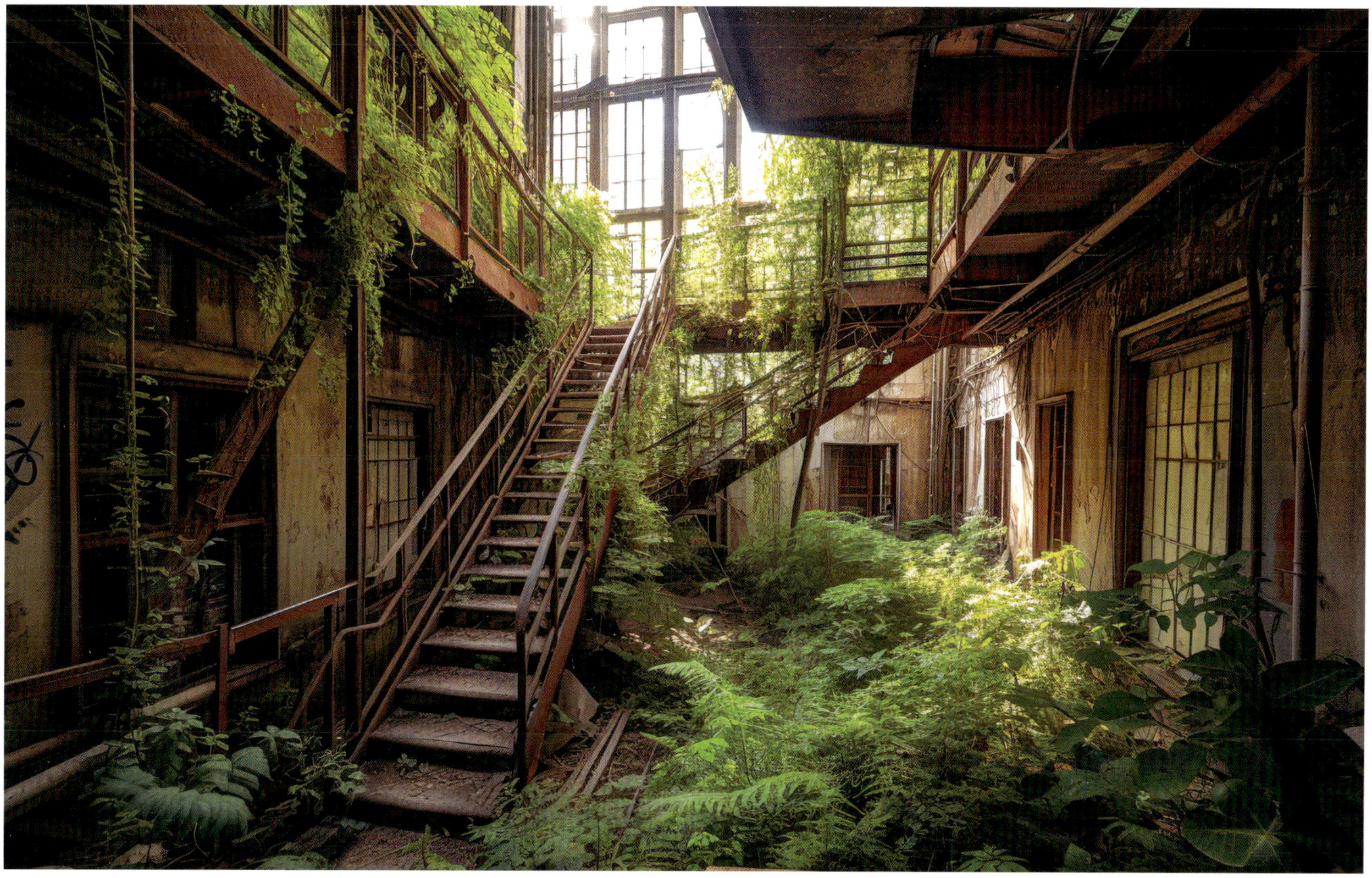

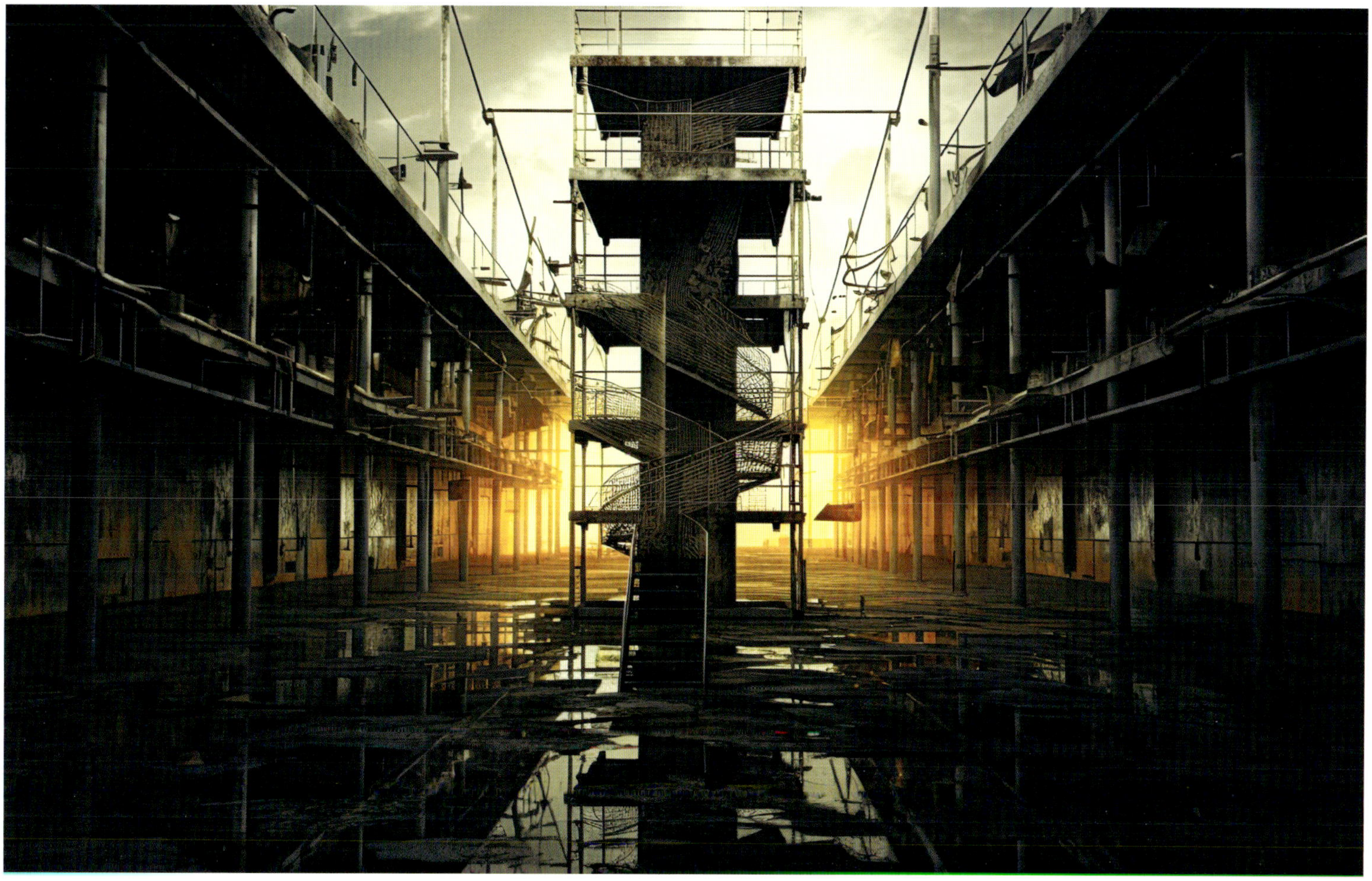

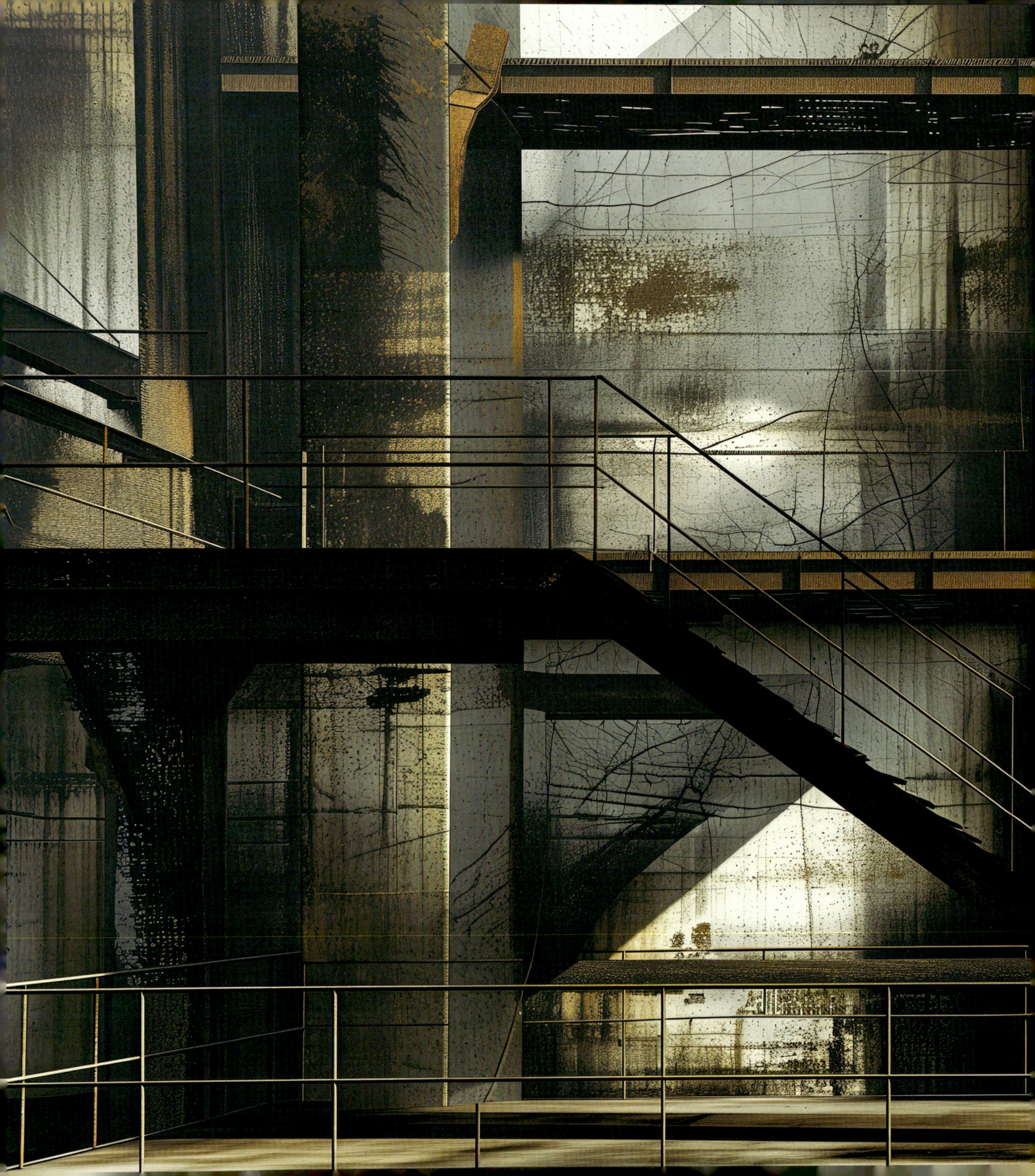

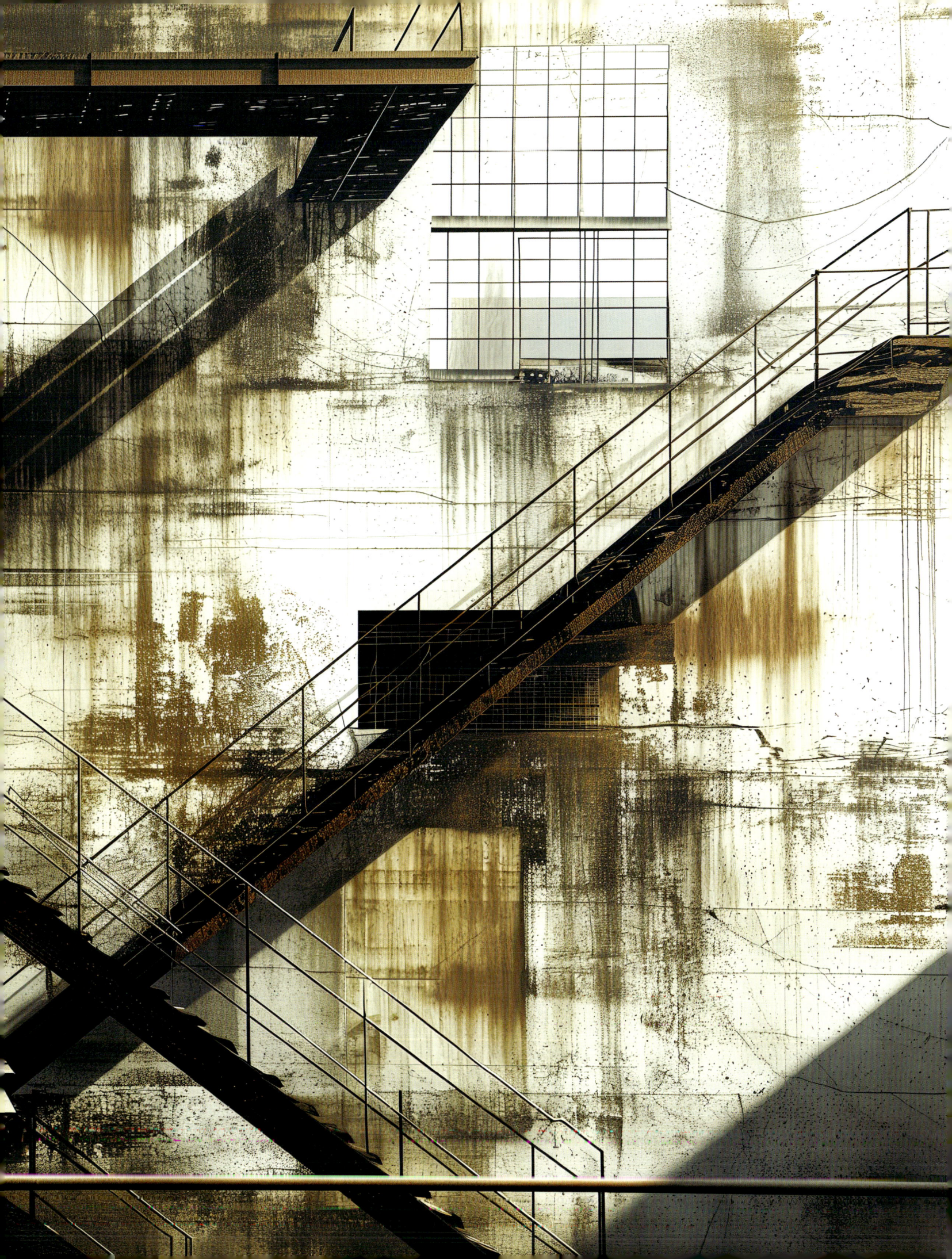

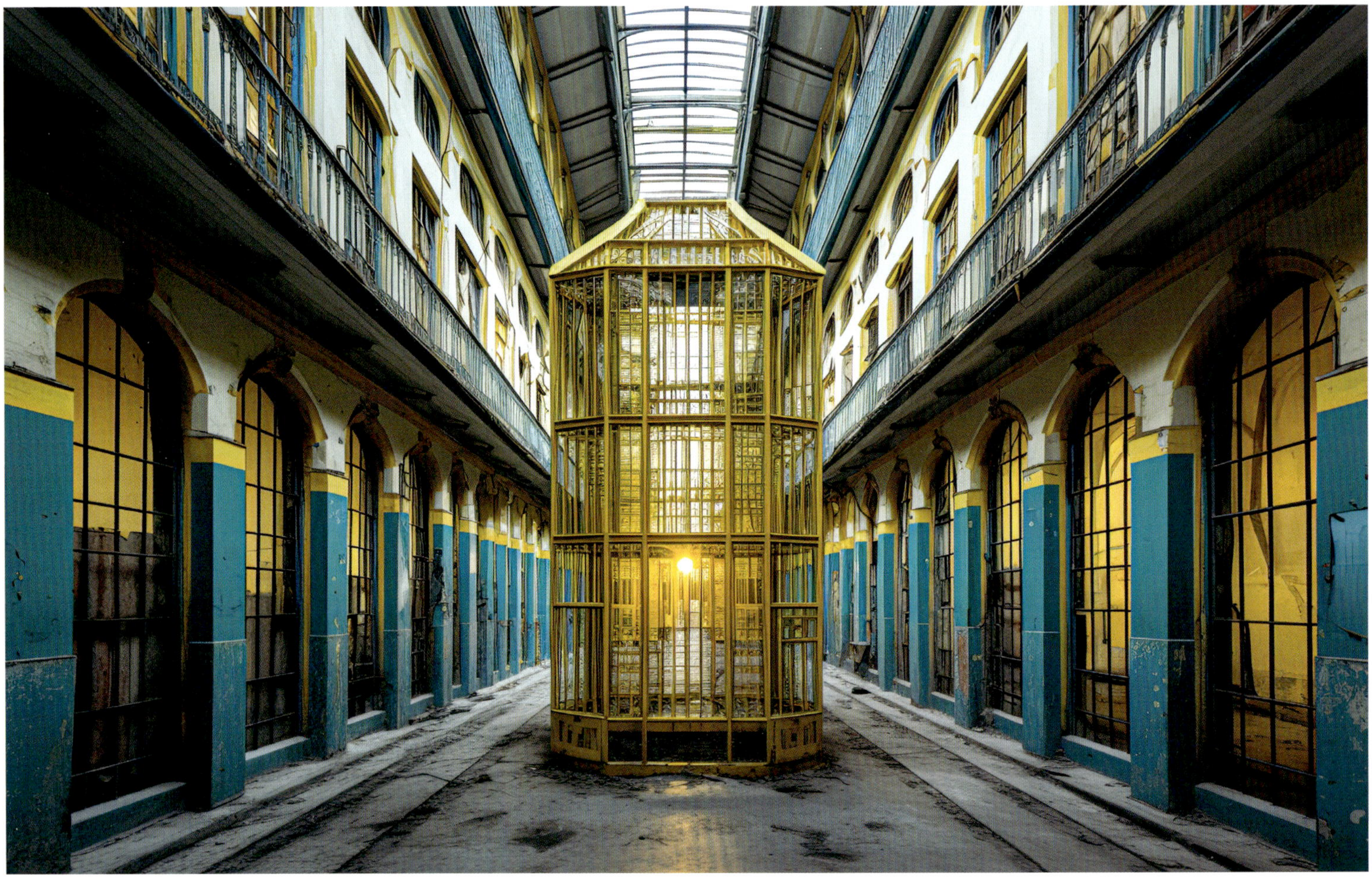

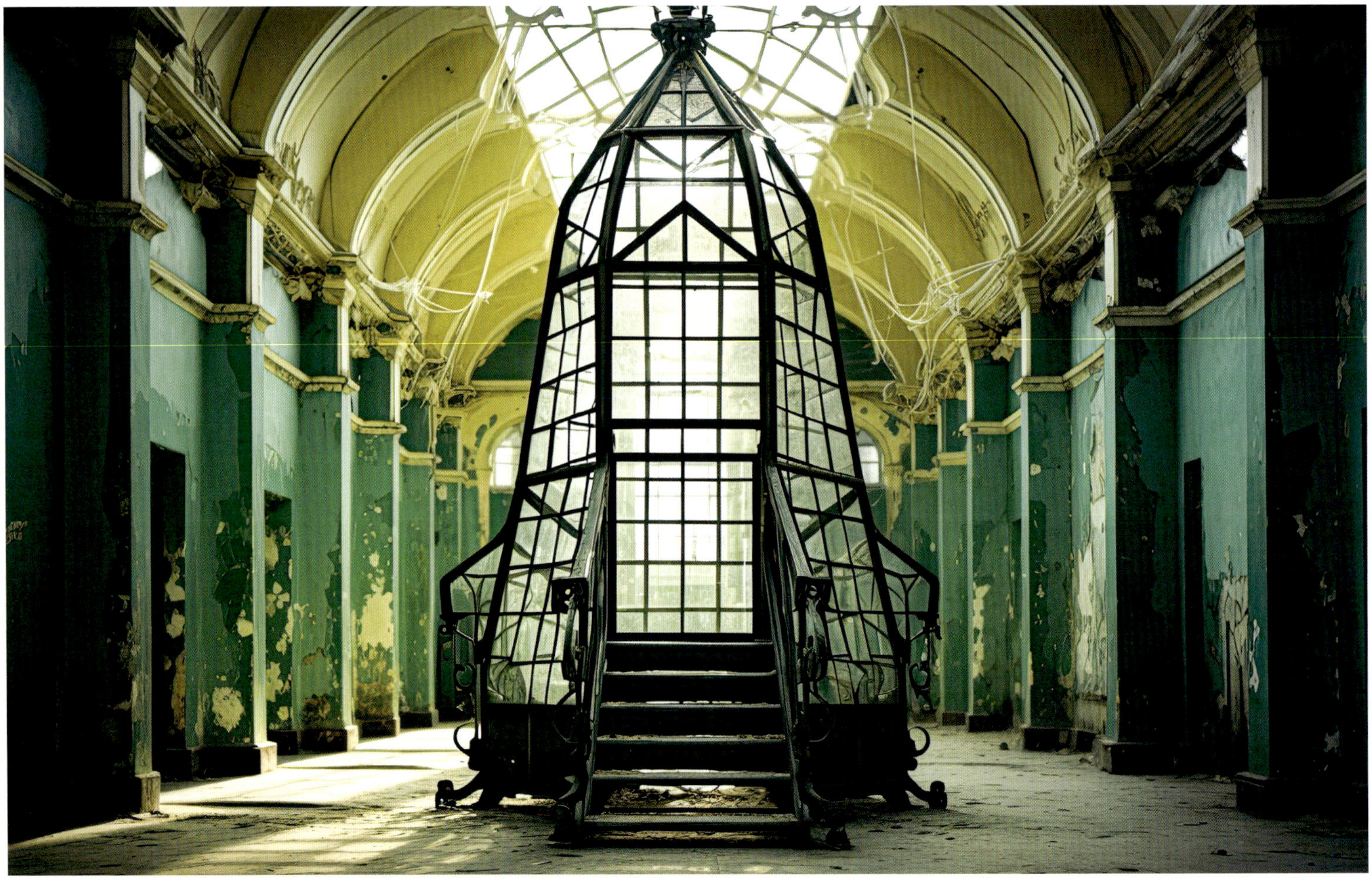

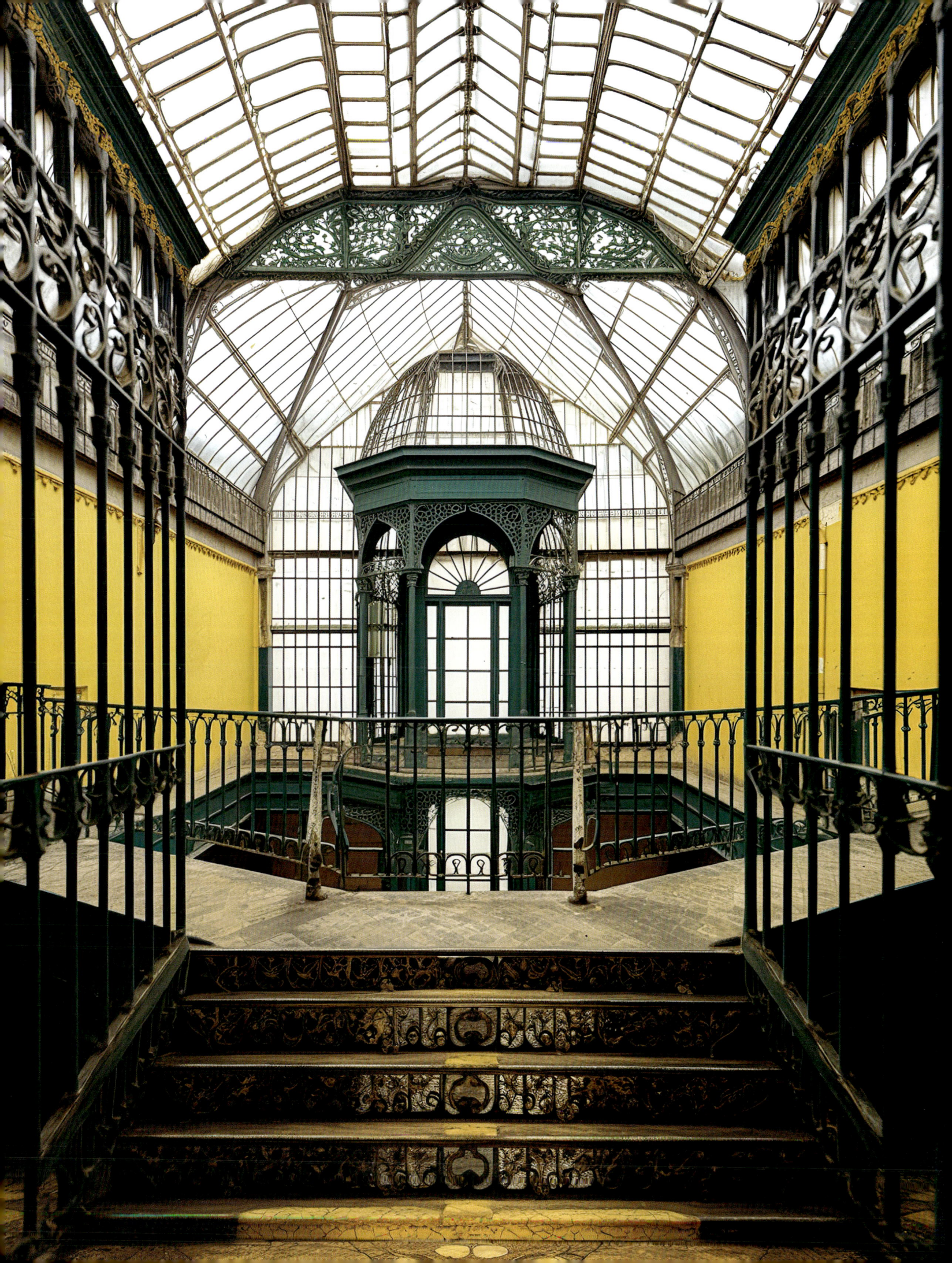

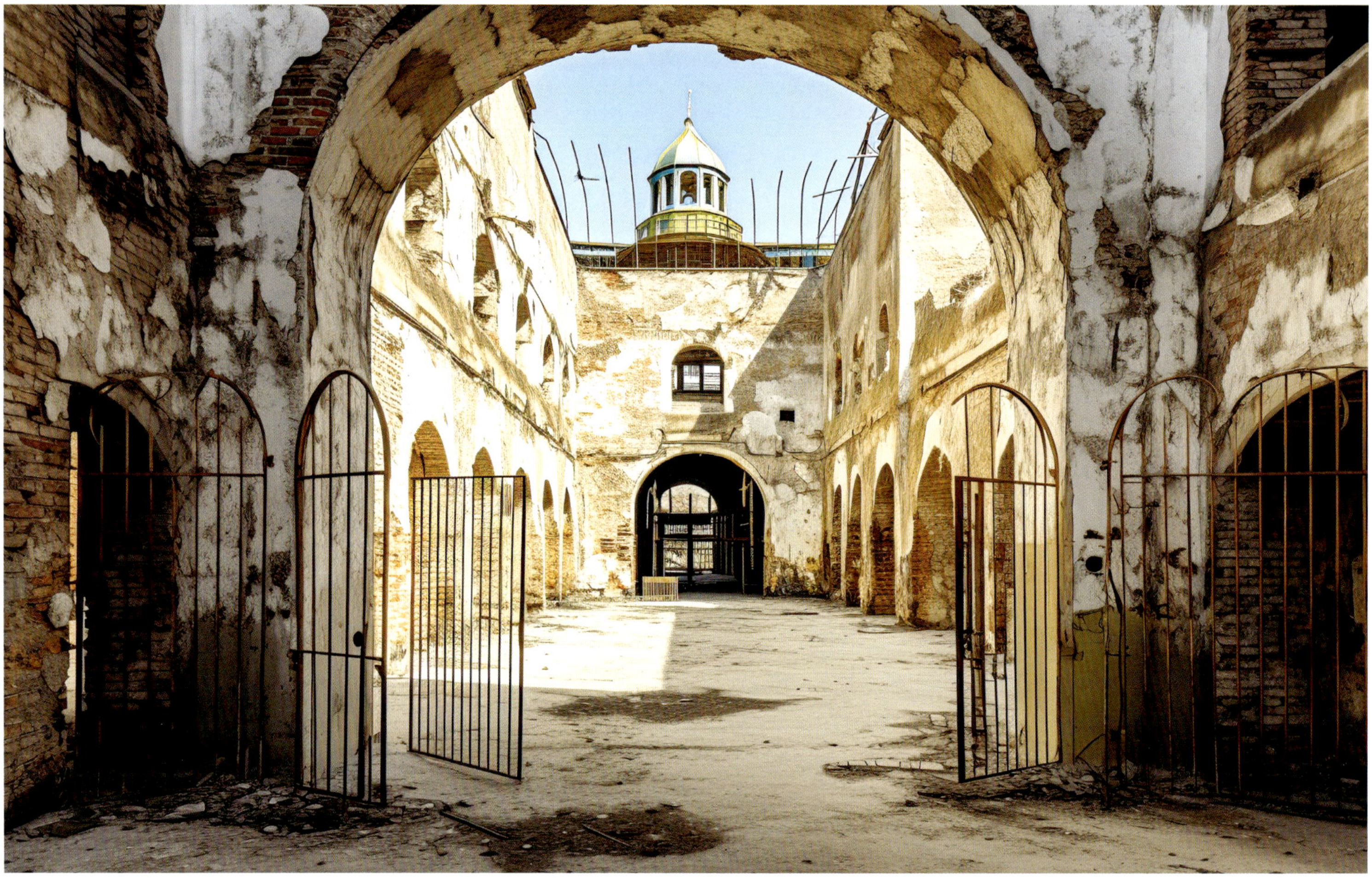

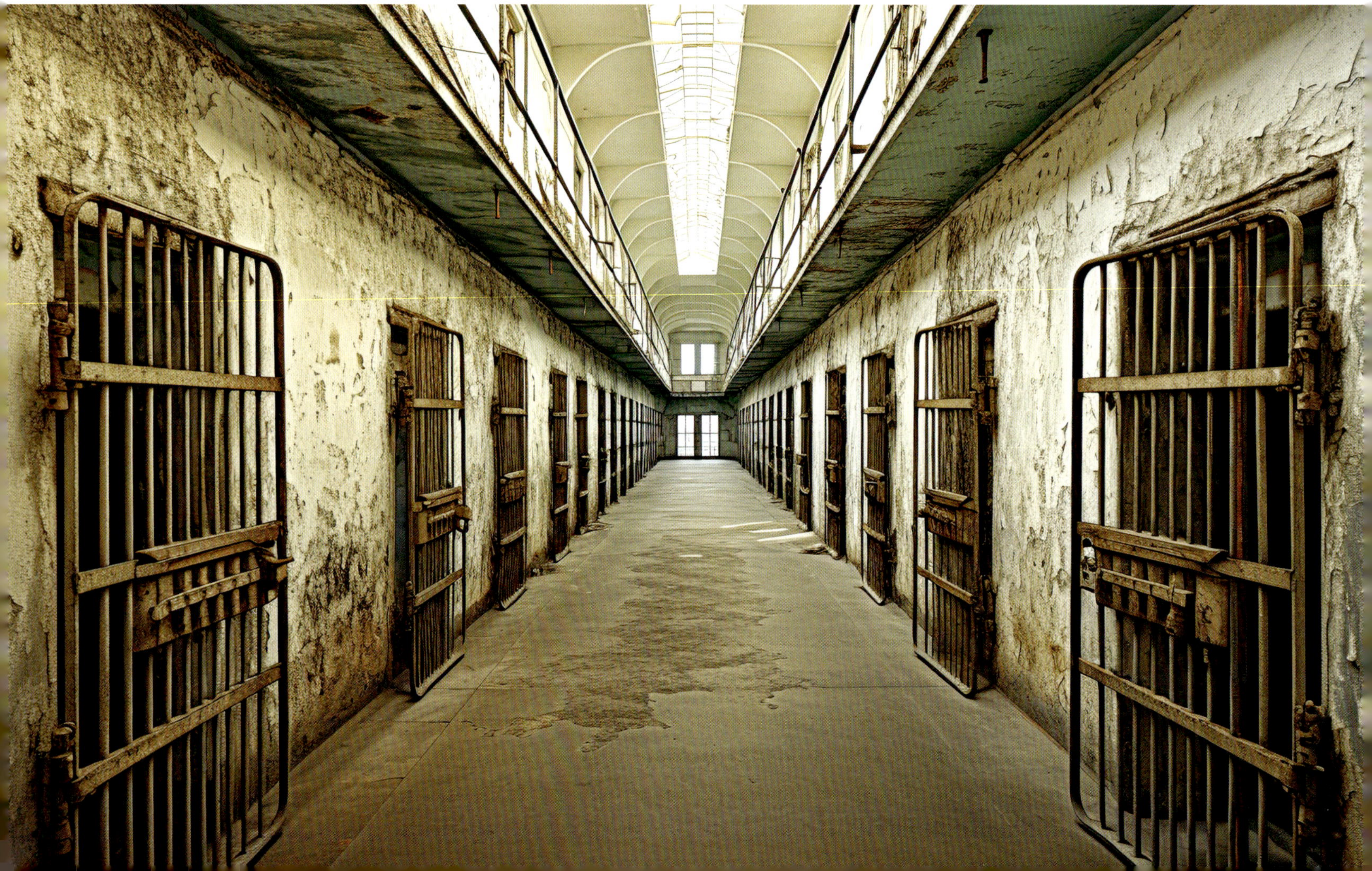

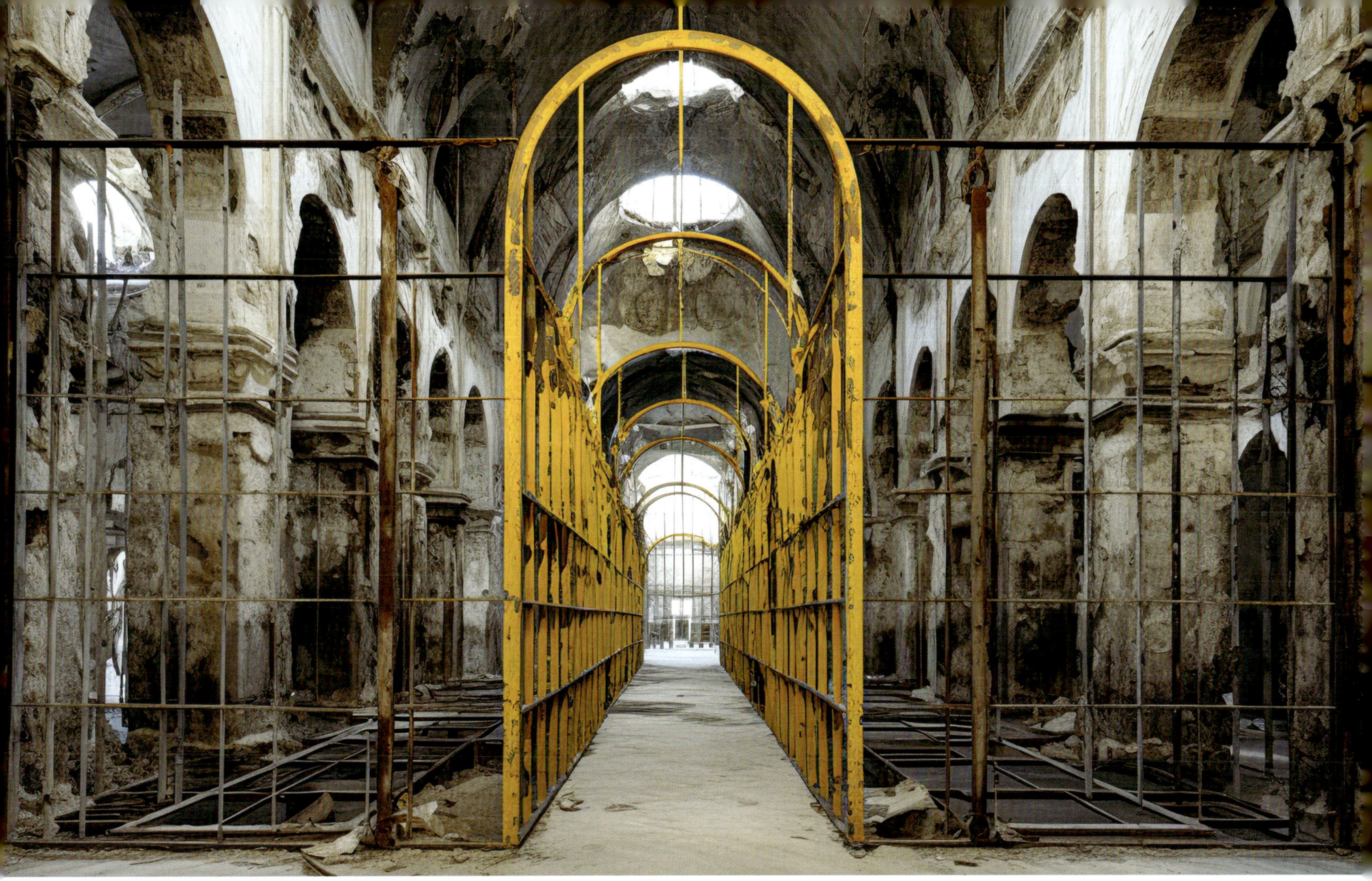

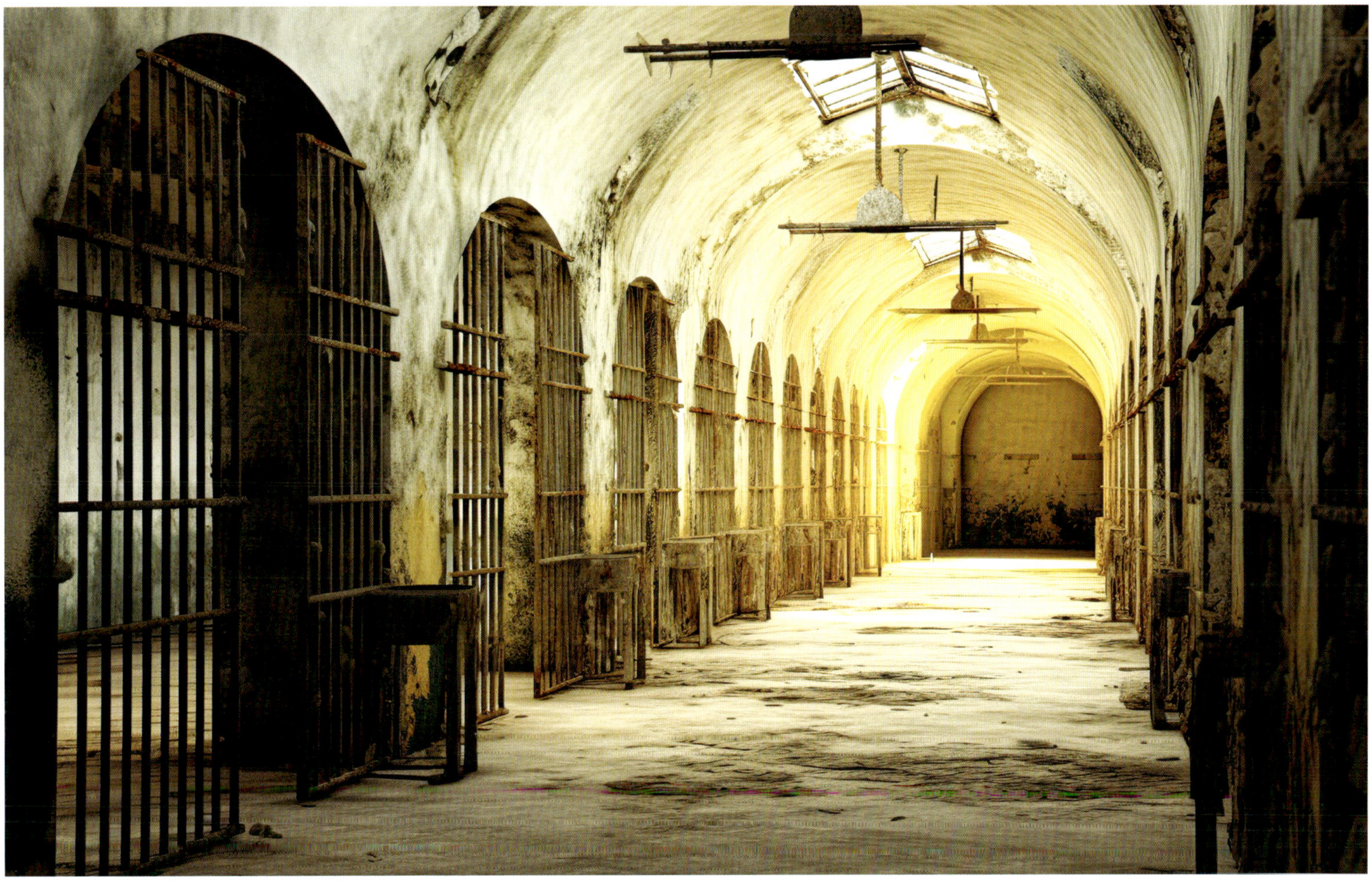

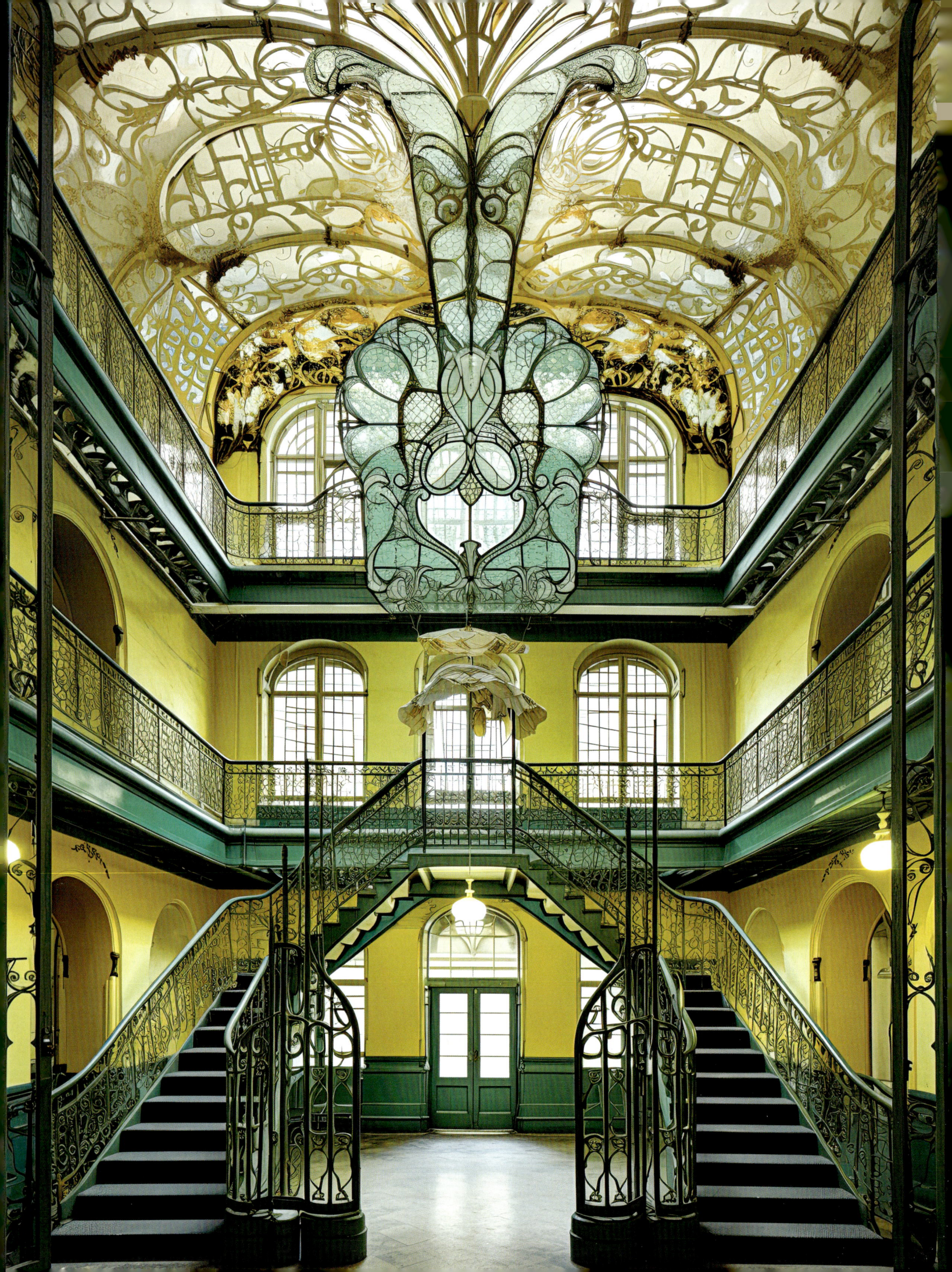

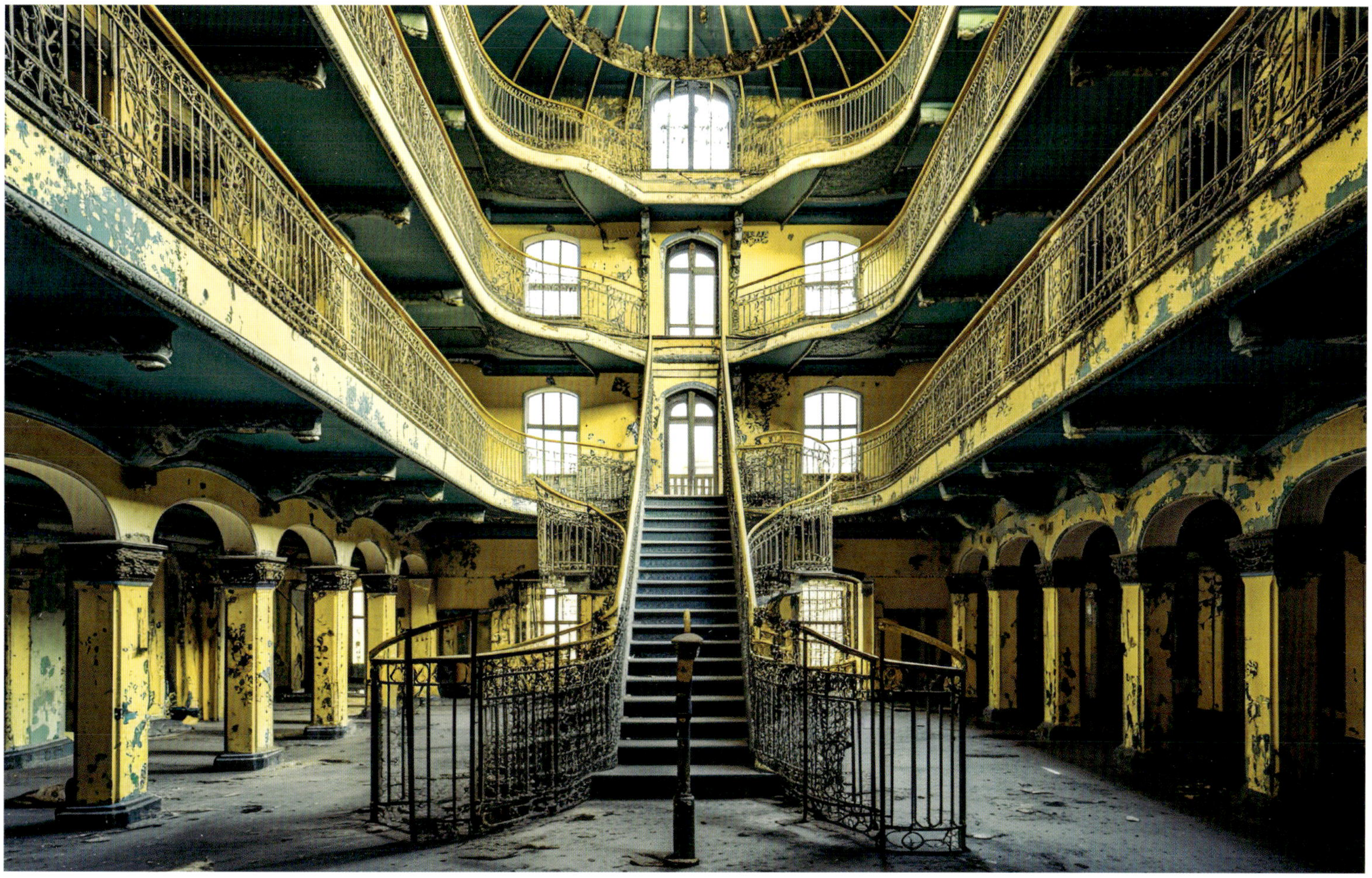

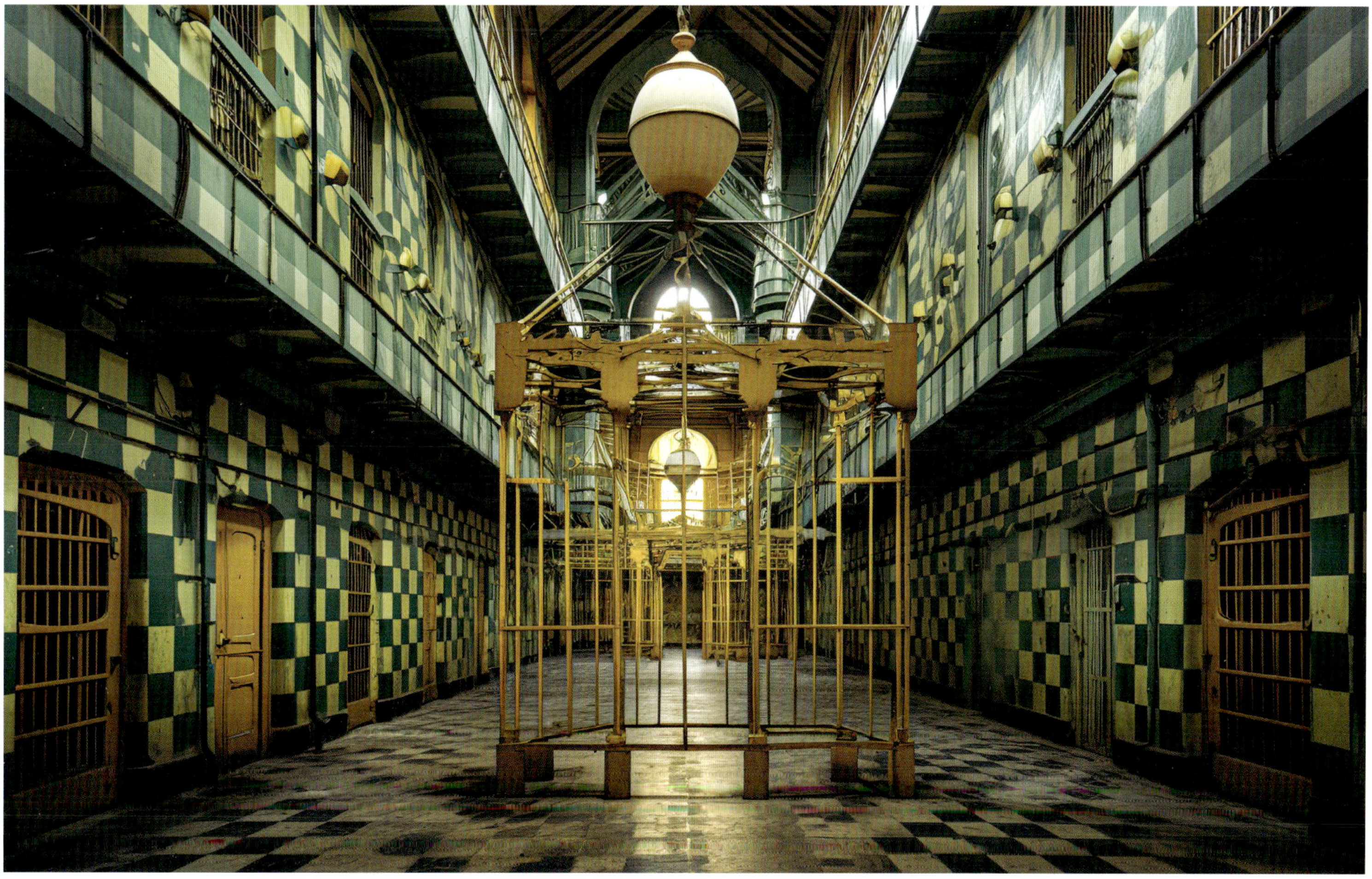

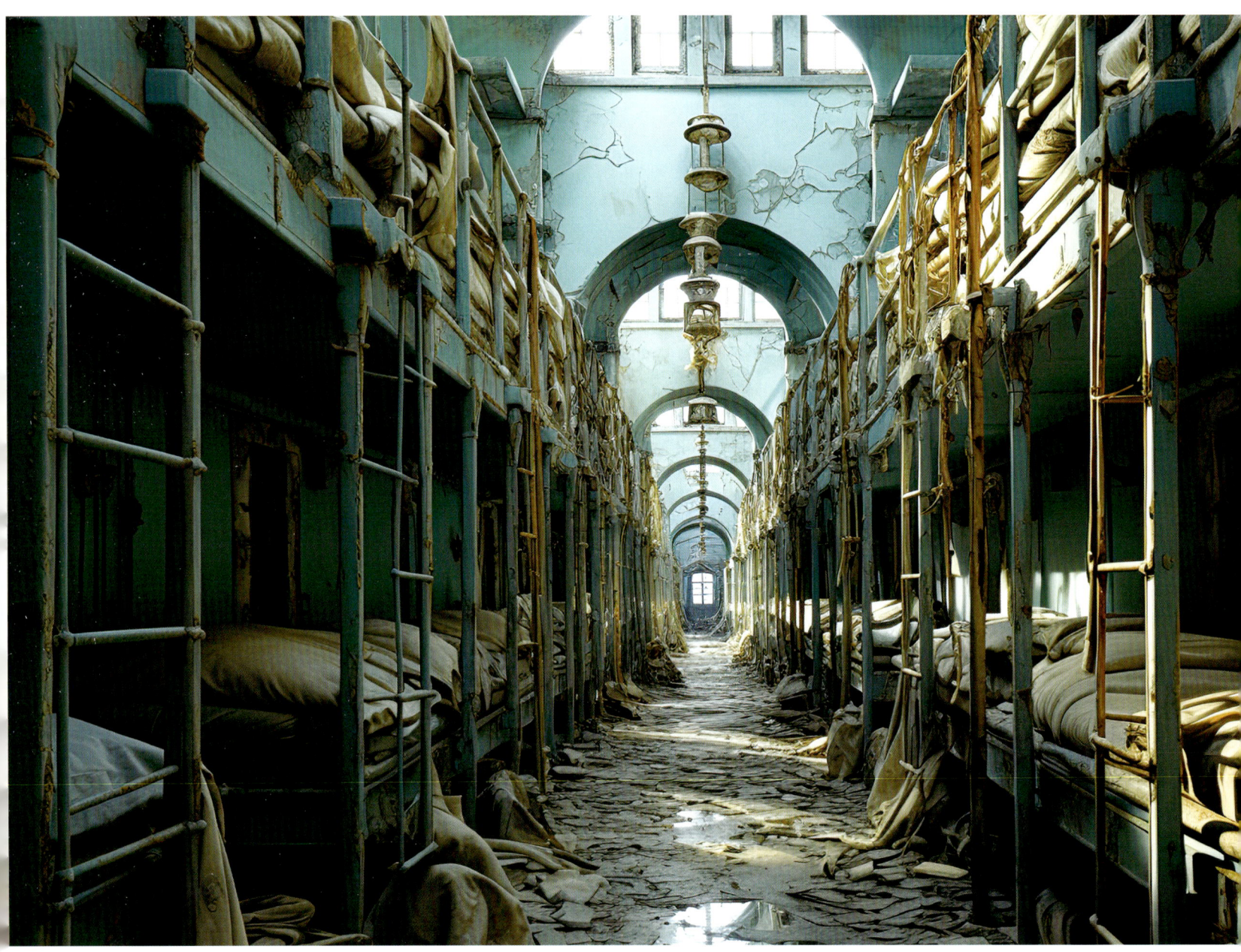

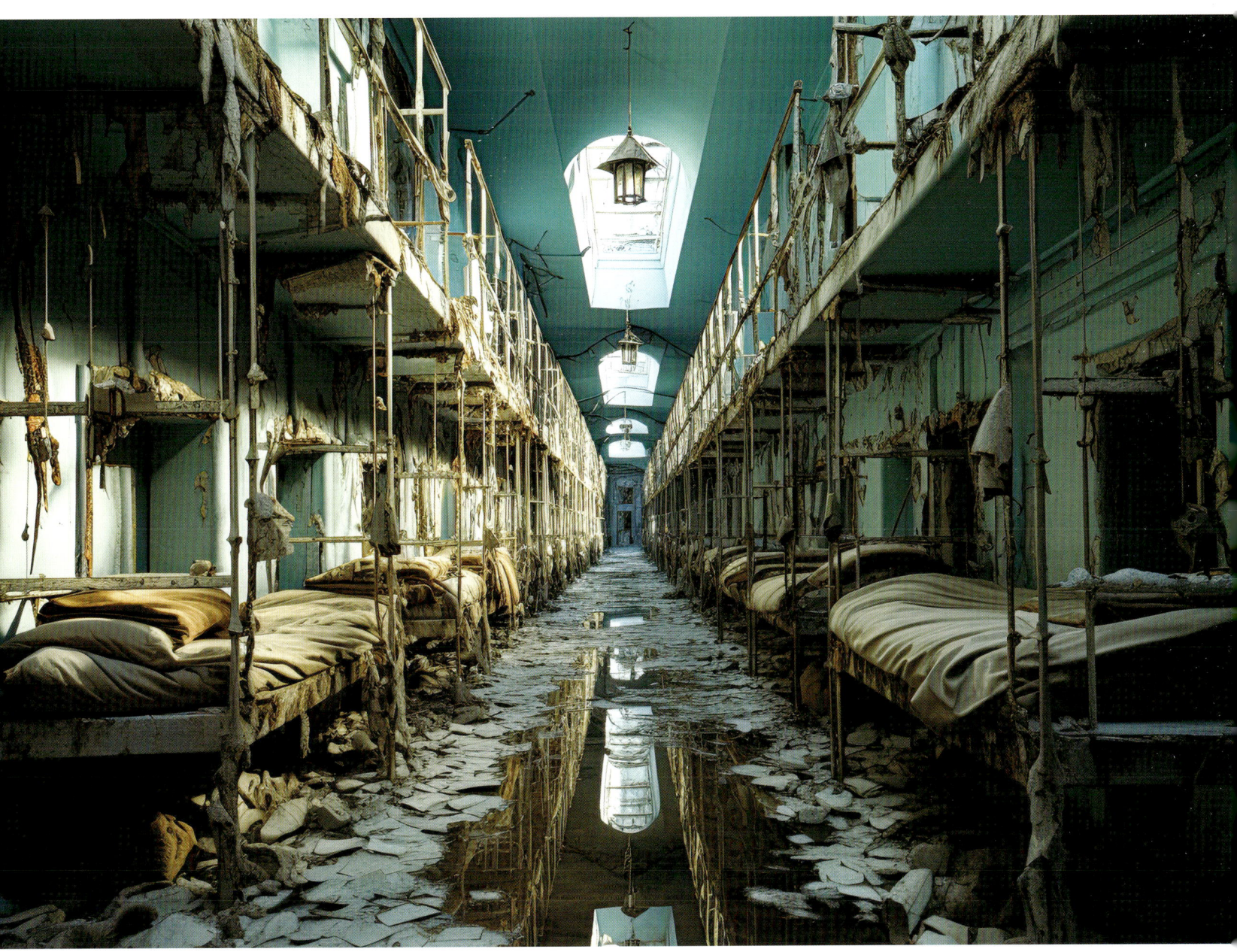

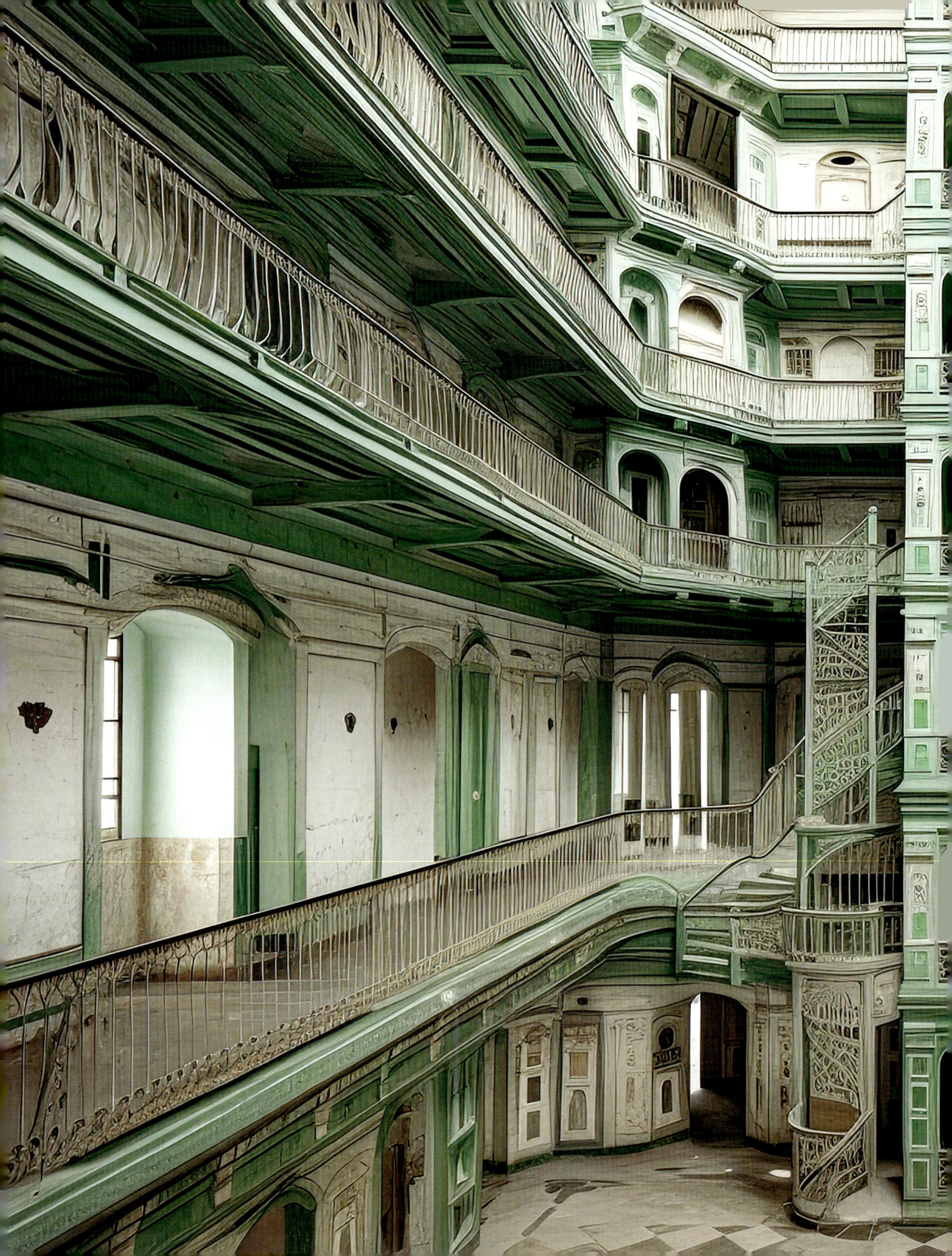

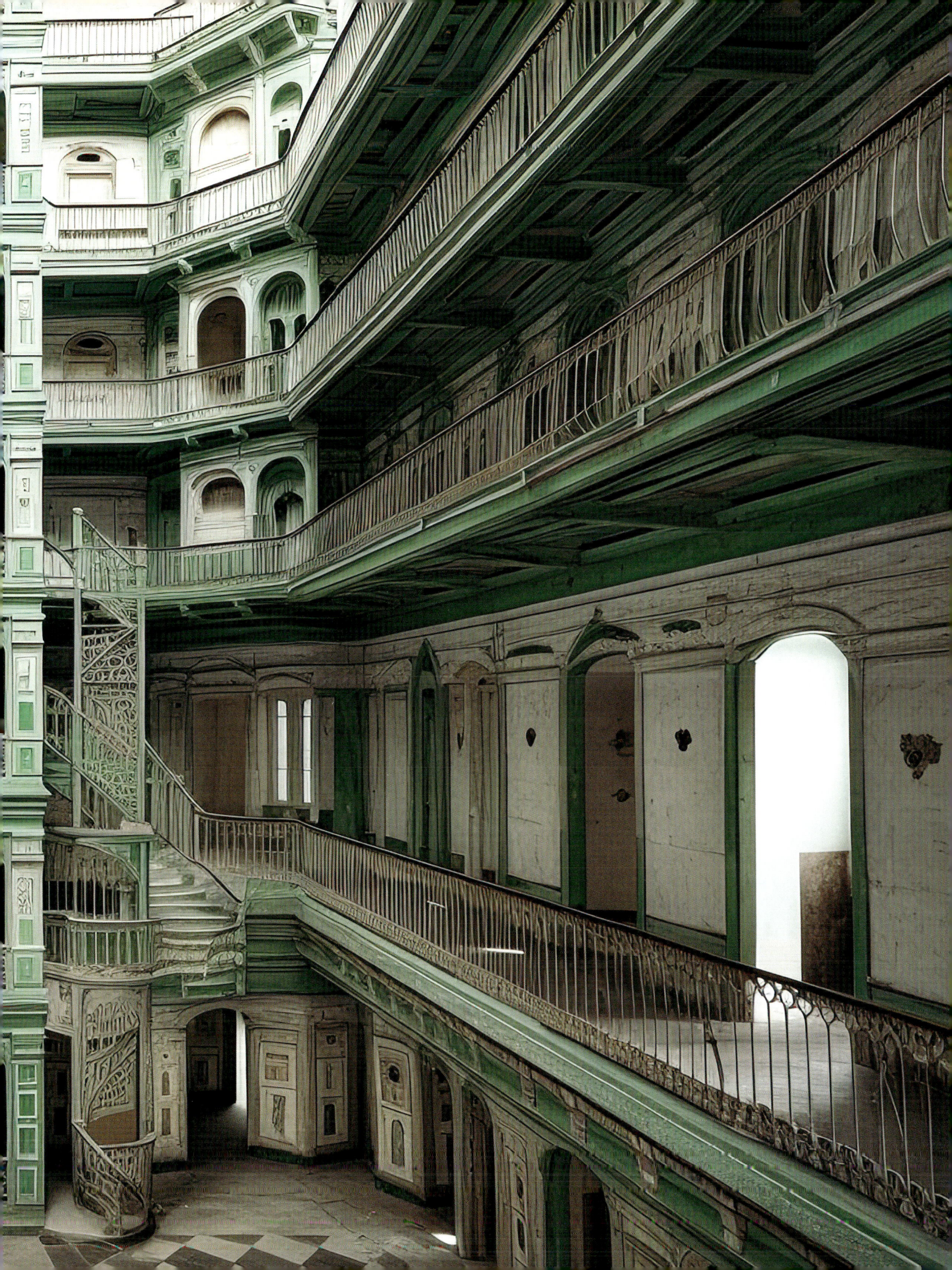

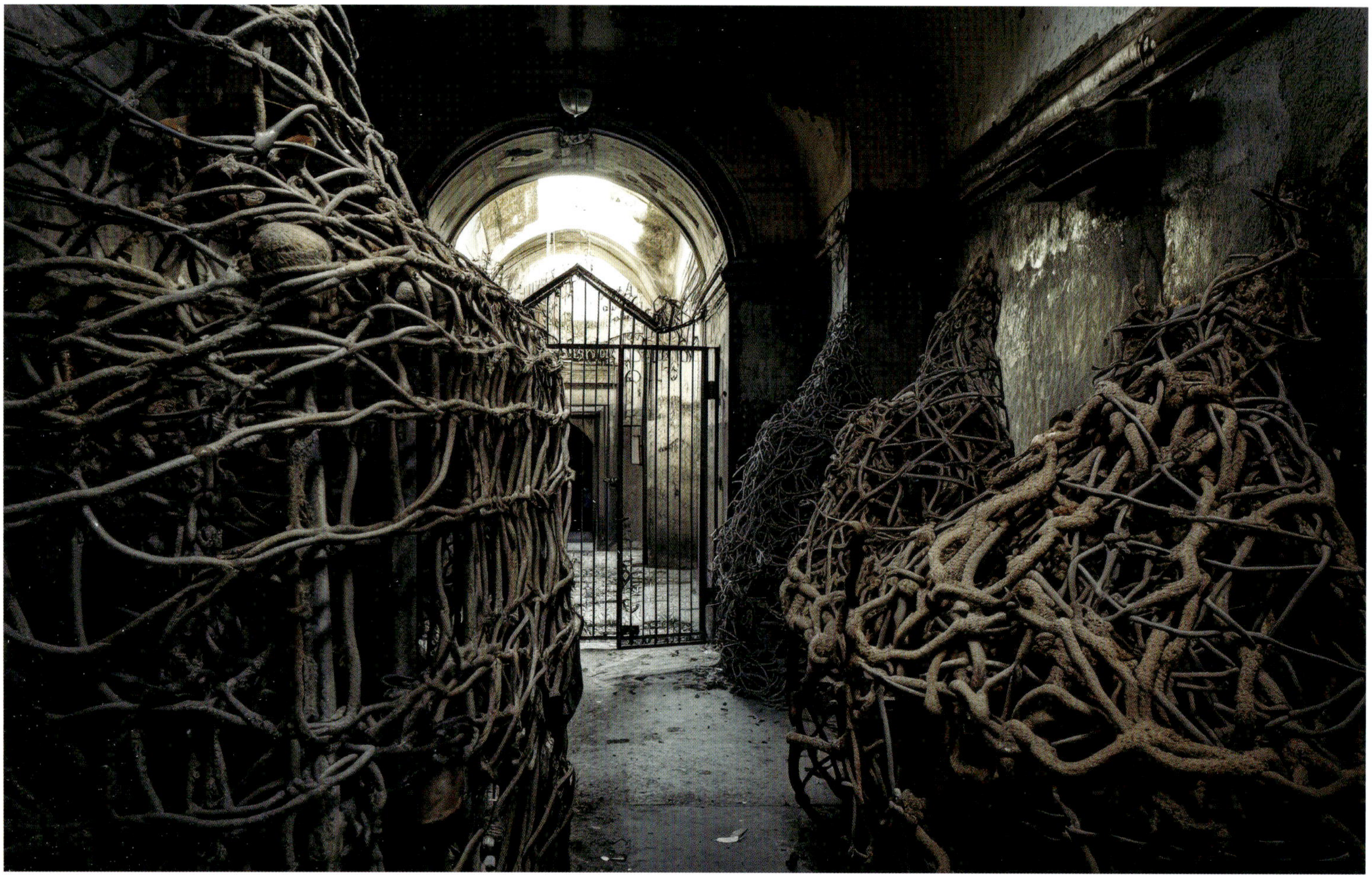

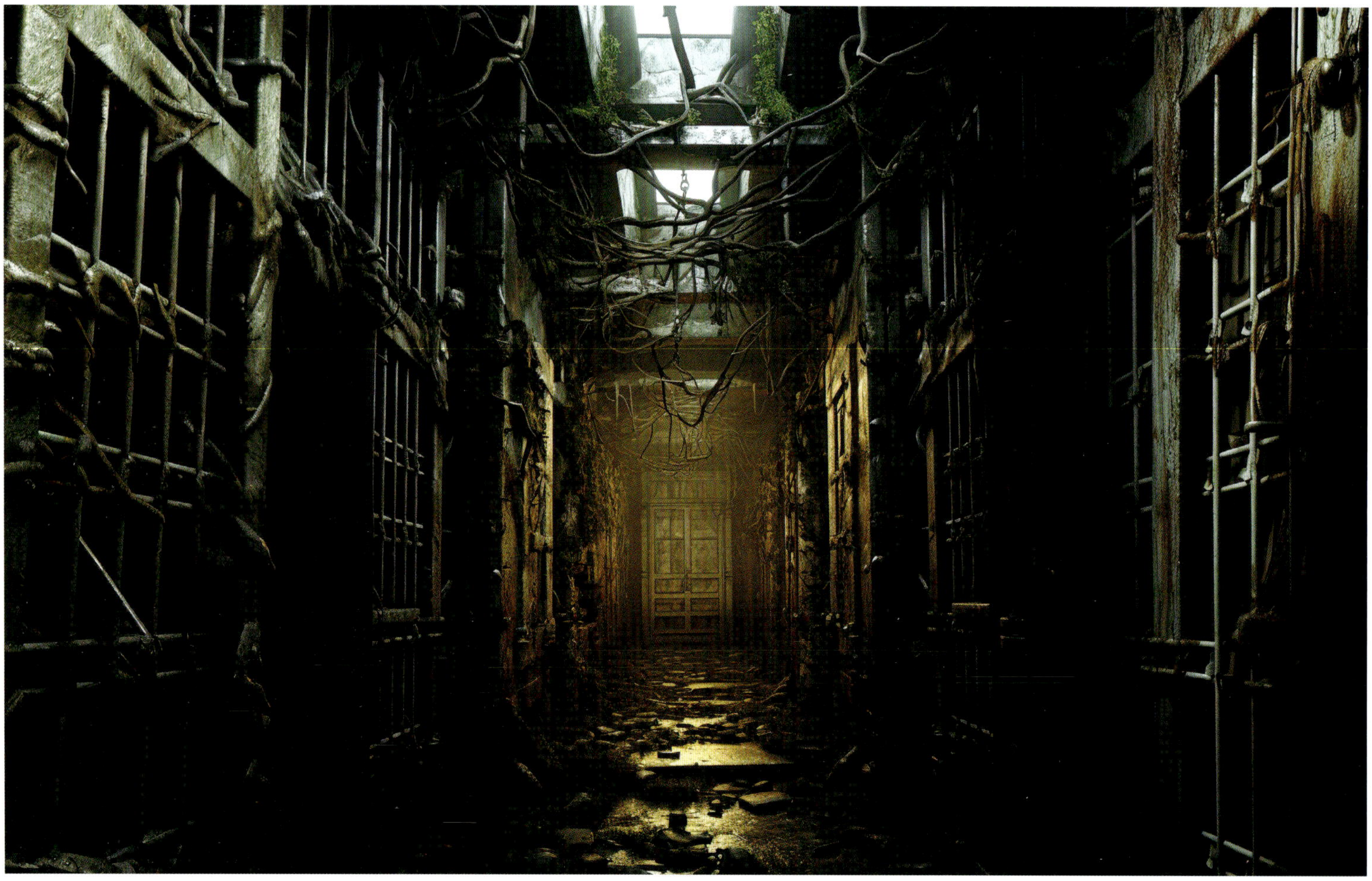

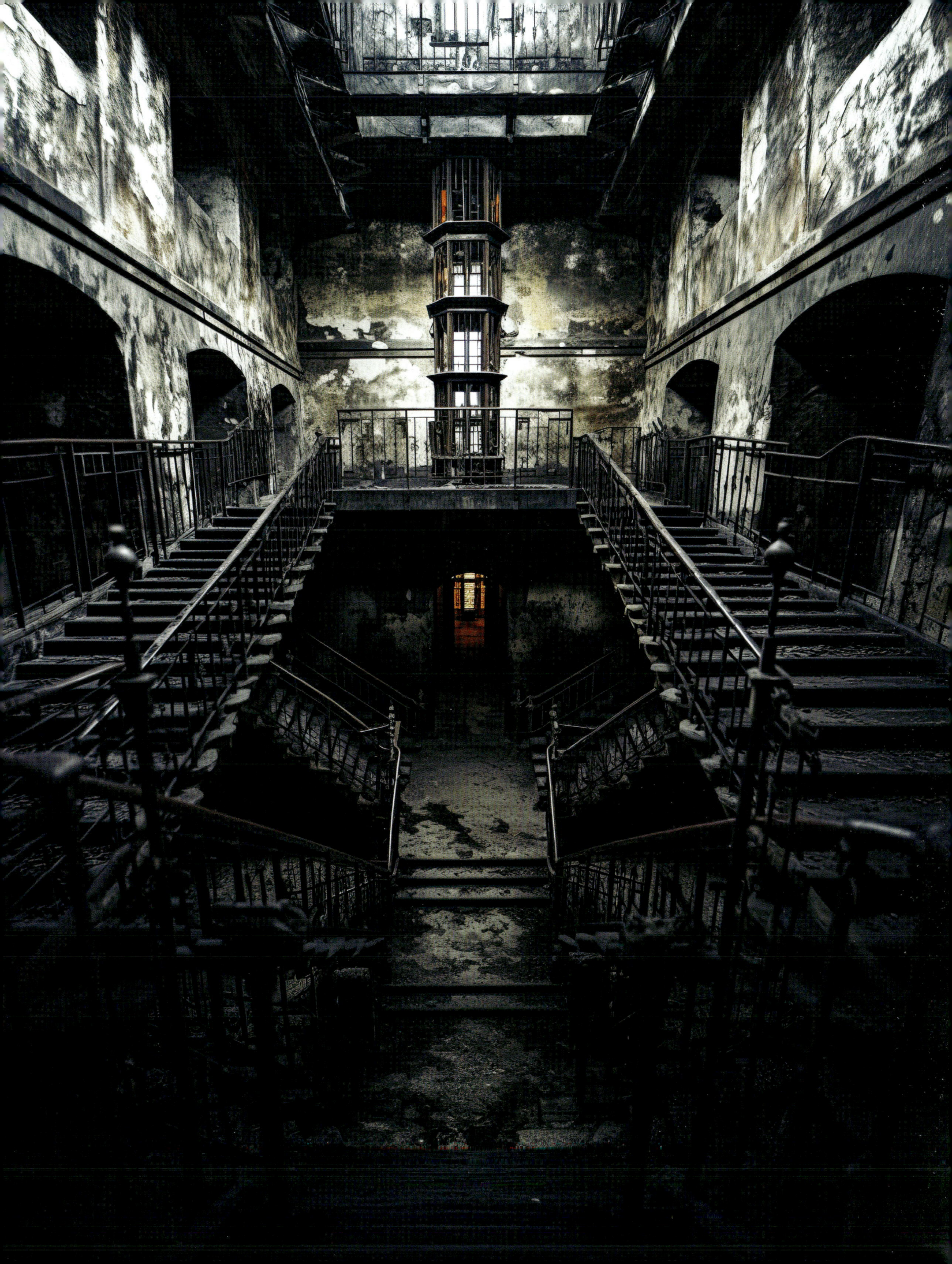

We'll always have Paris

Twilight engulfs Paris, which is in the clutches of an all-consuming conflict that has crossed borders and corrupted the very essence of Europe. From the cobblestone streets rise the anguished murmurs of the Parisians, who gaze up at the sky as if it held the answers to their fate.

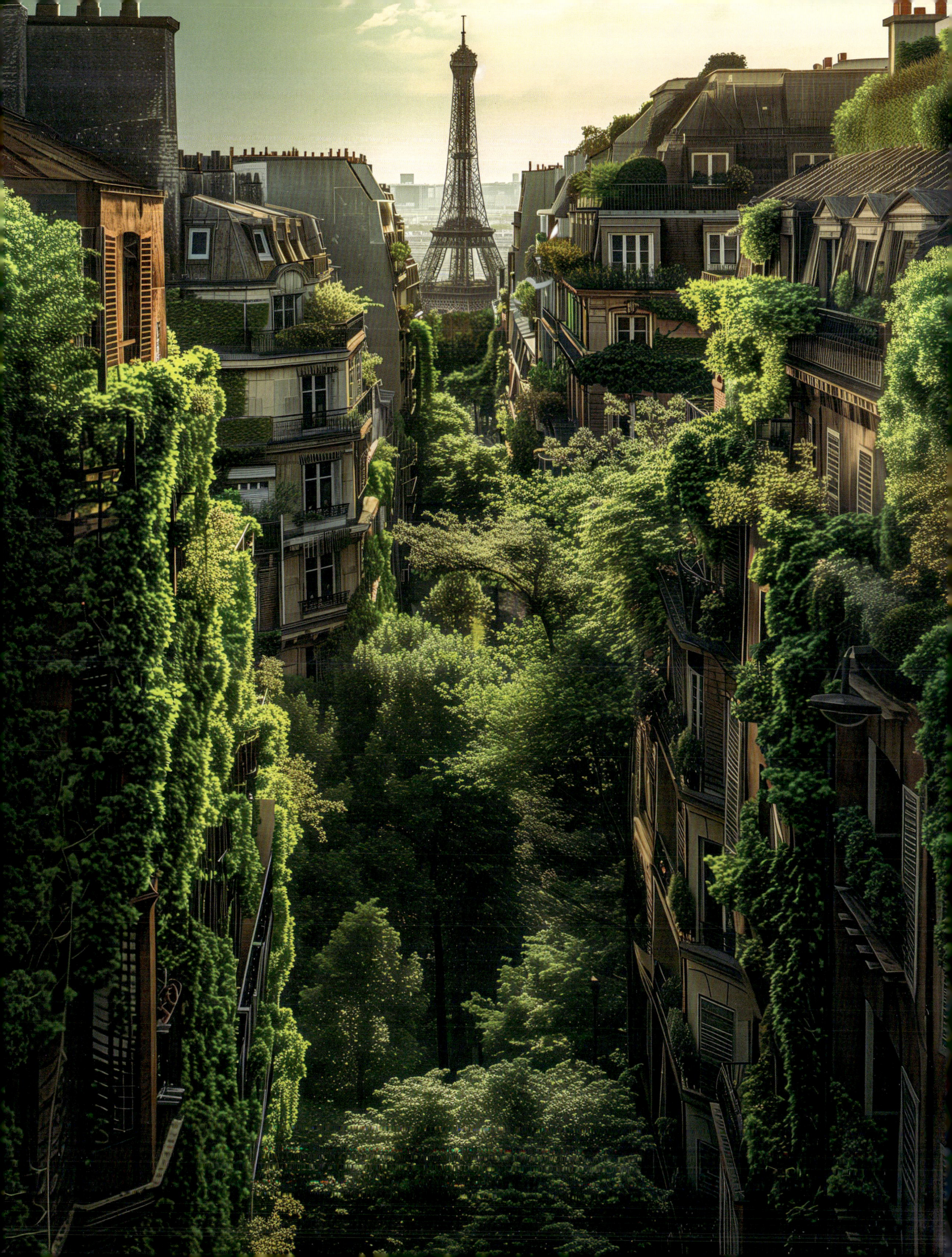

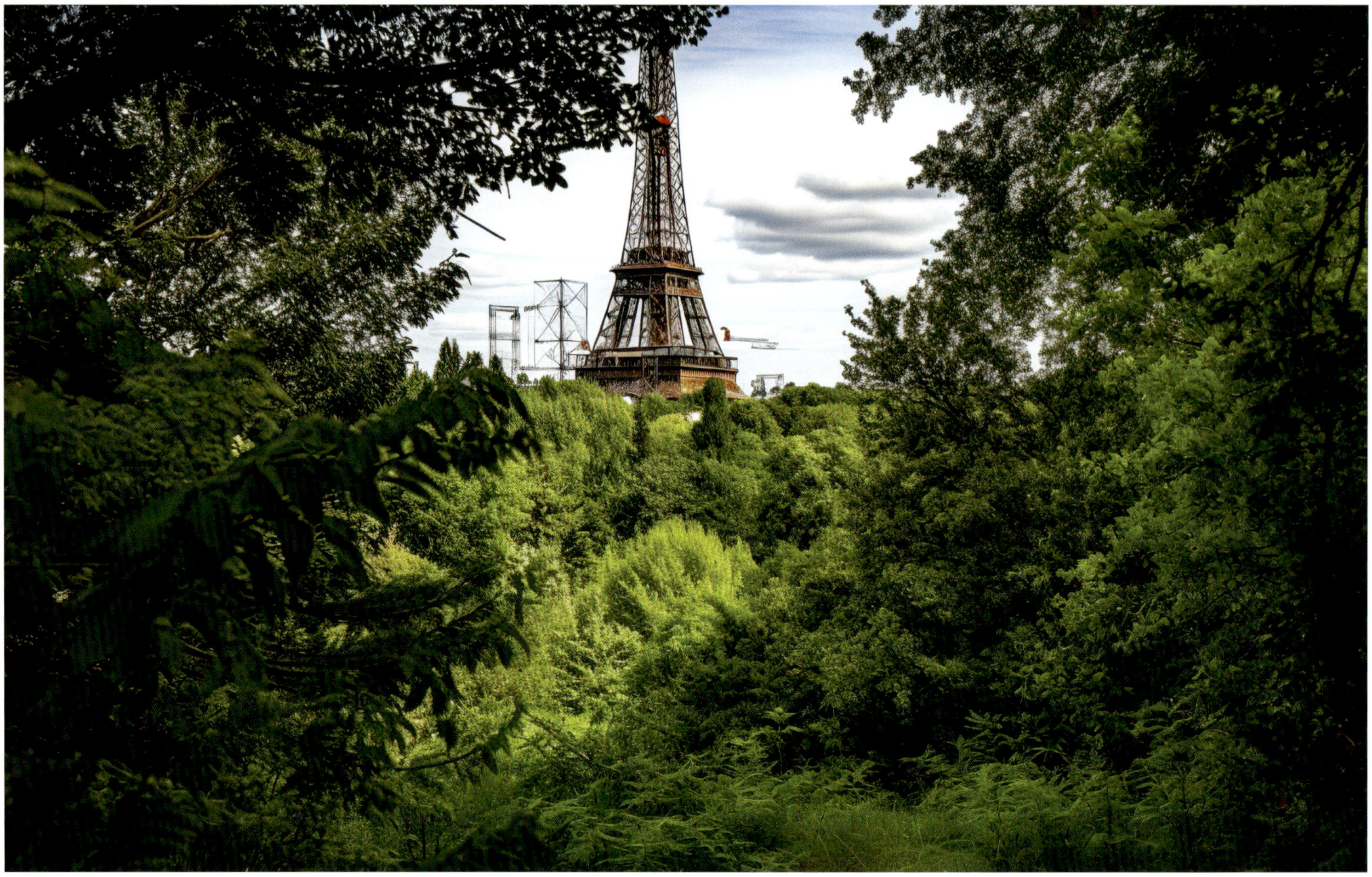

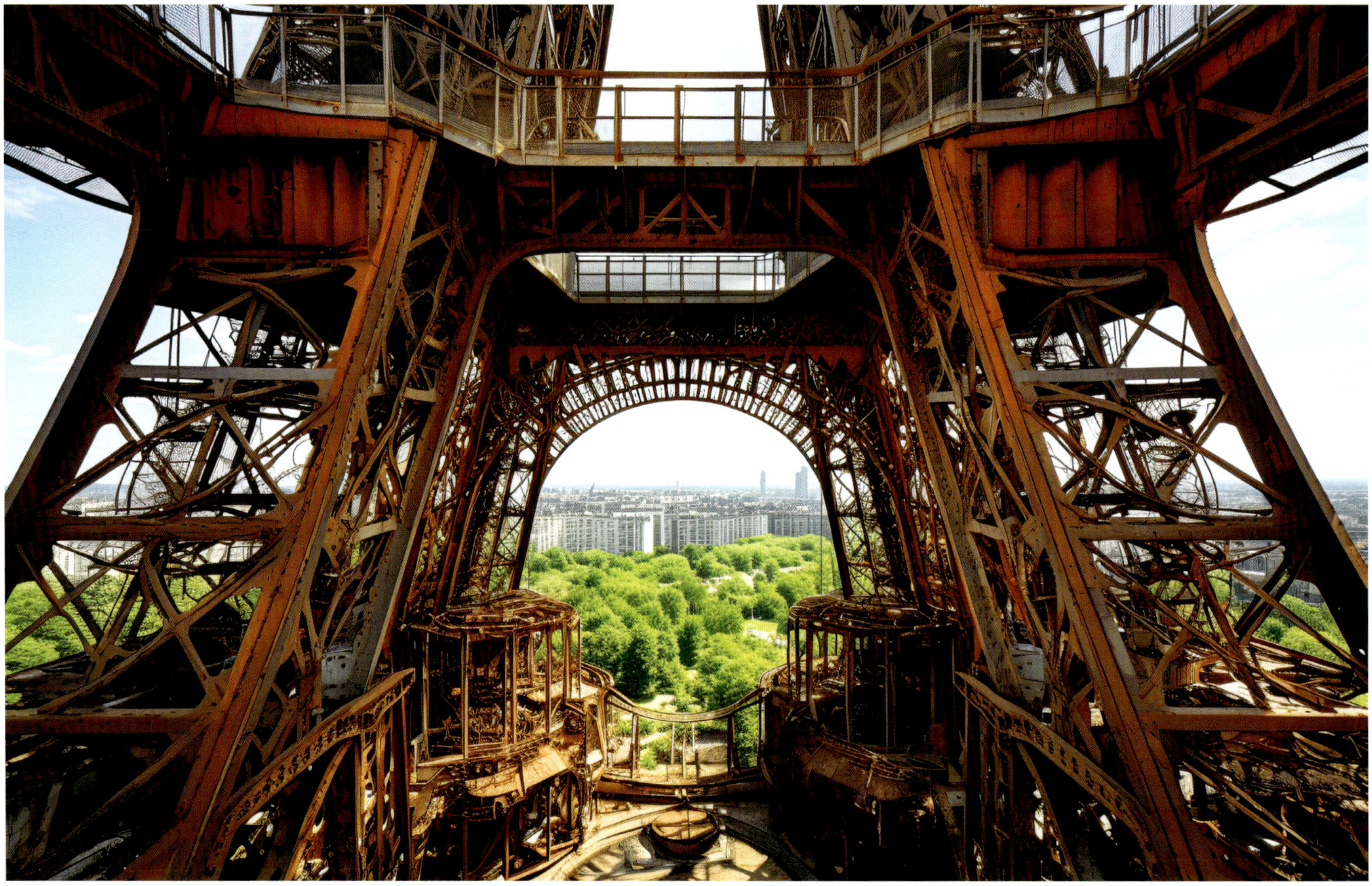

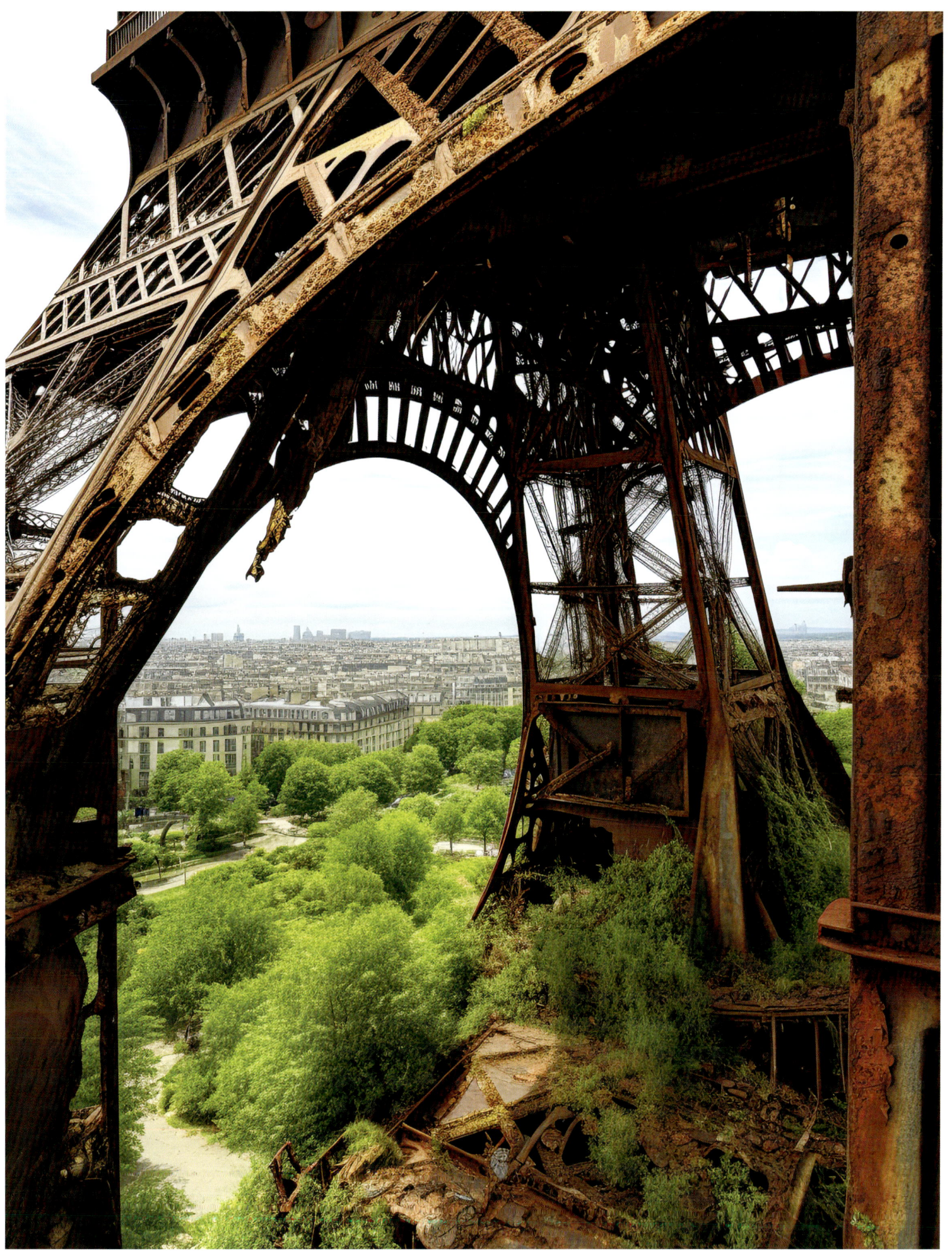

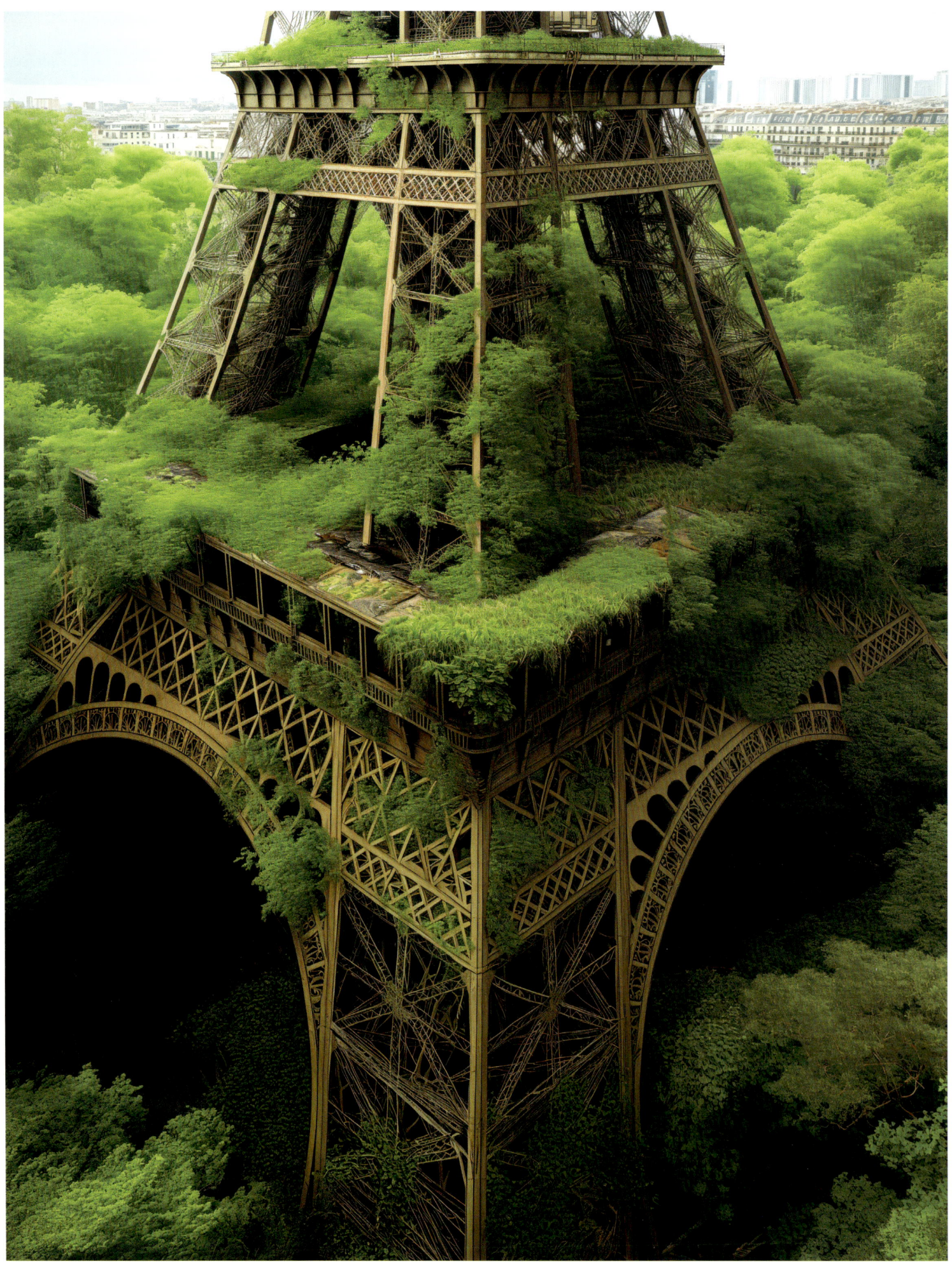

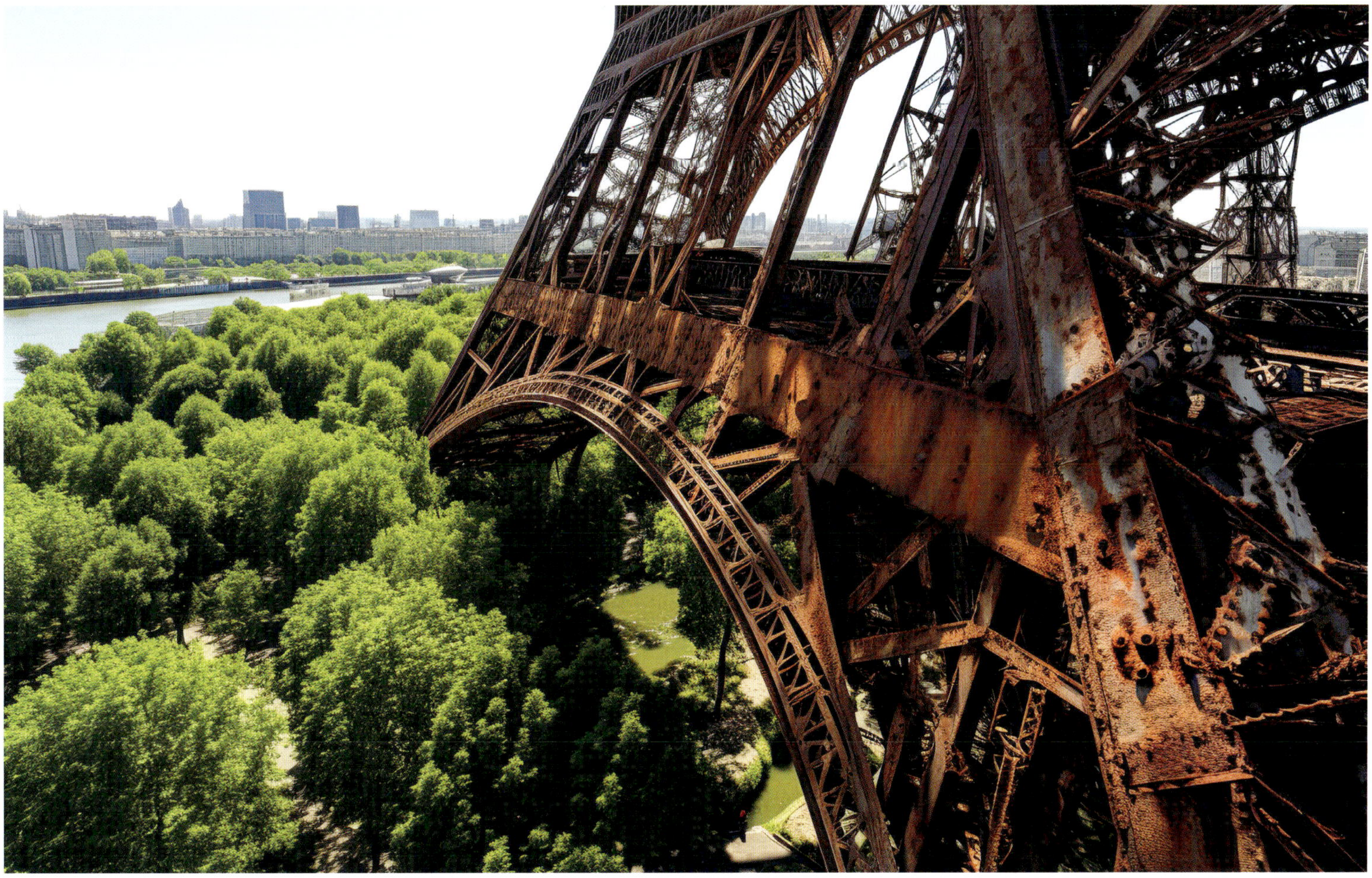

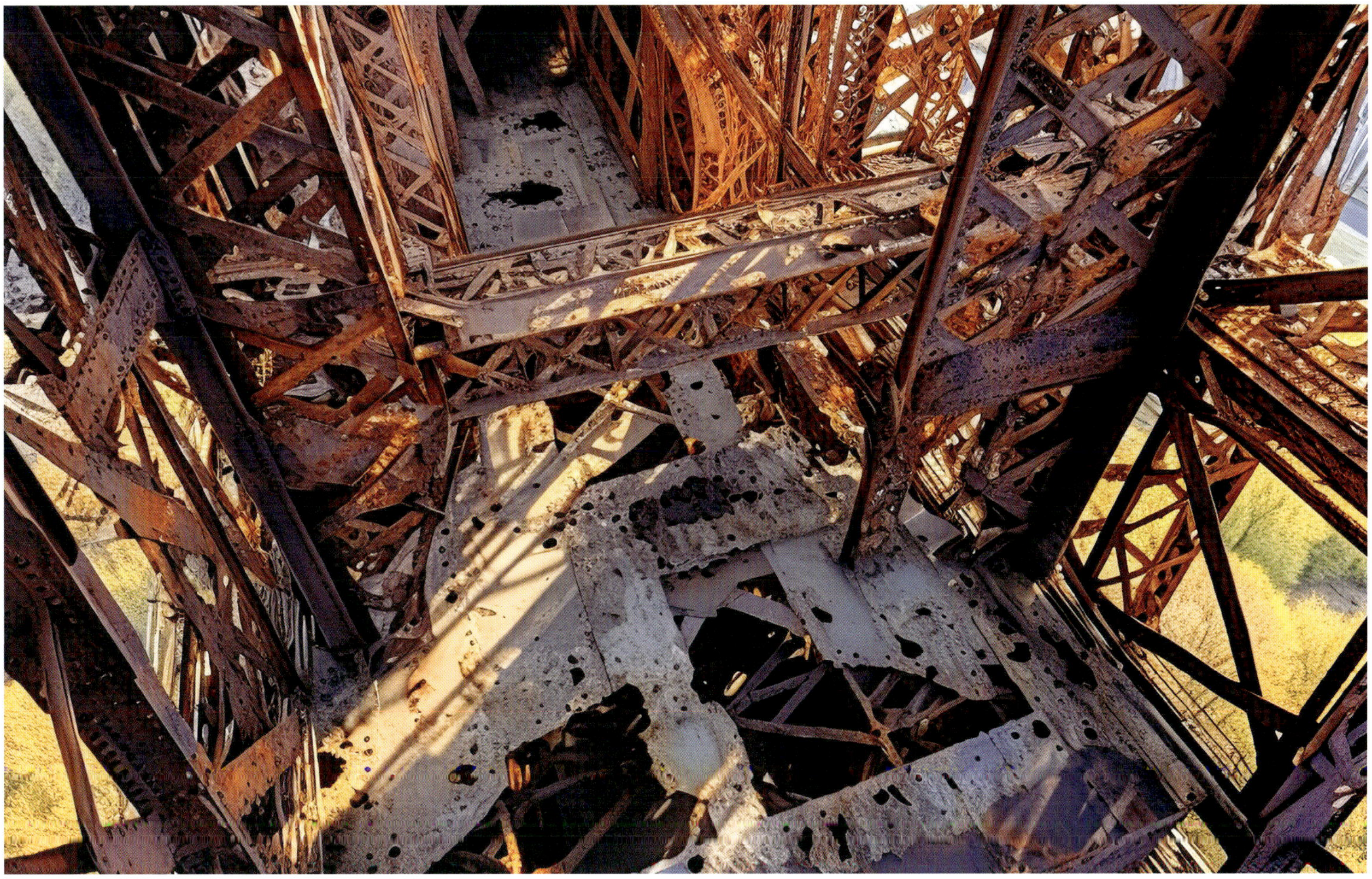

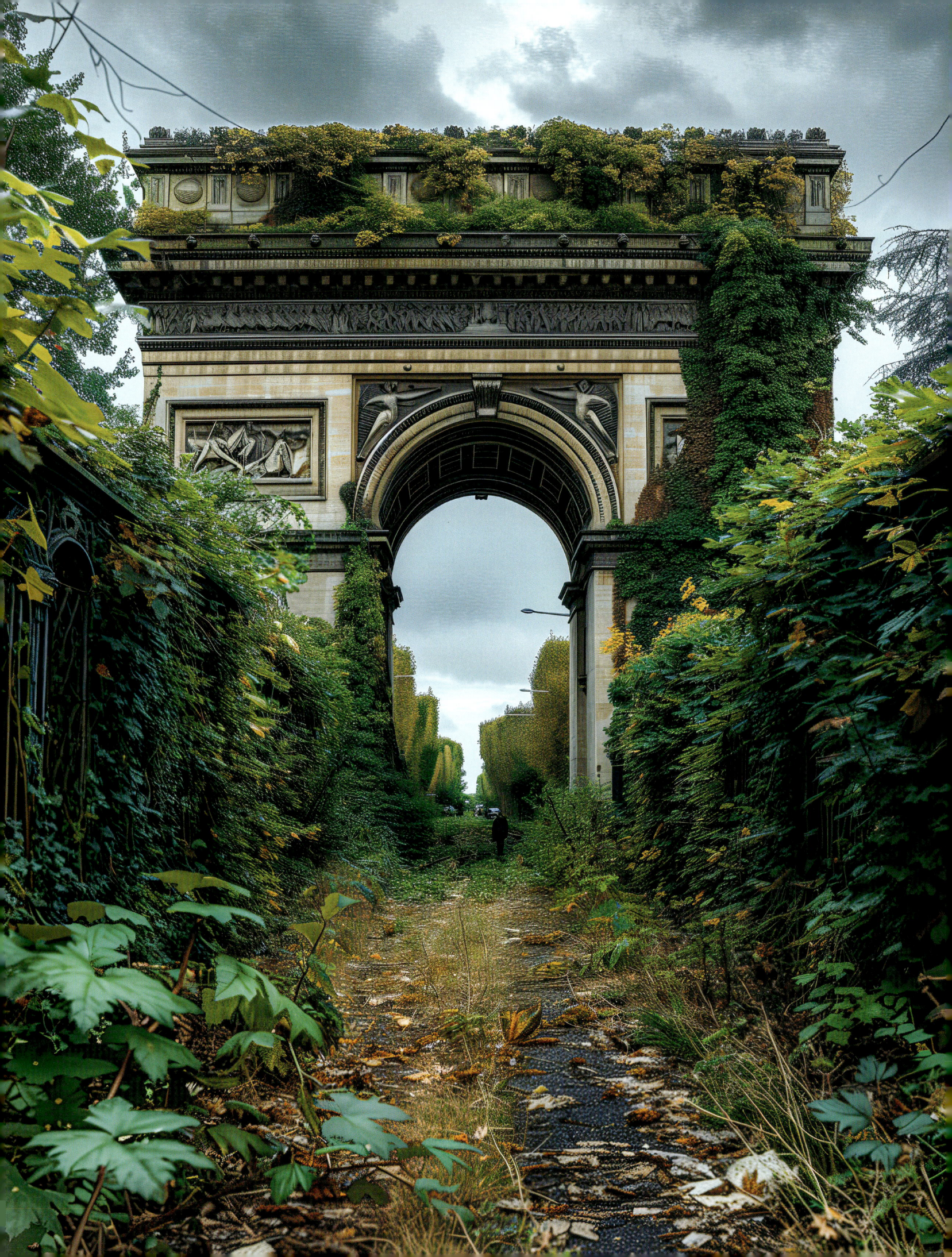

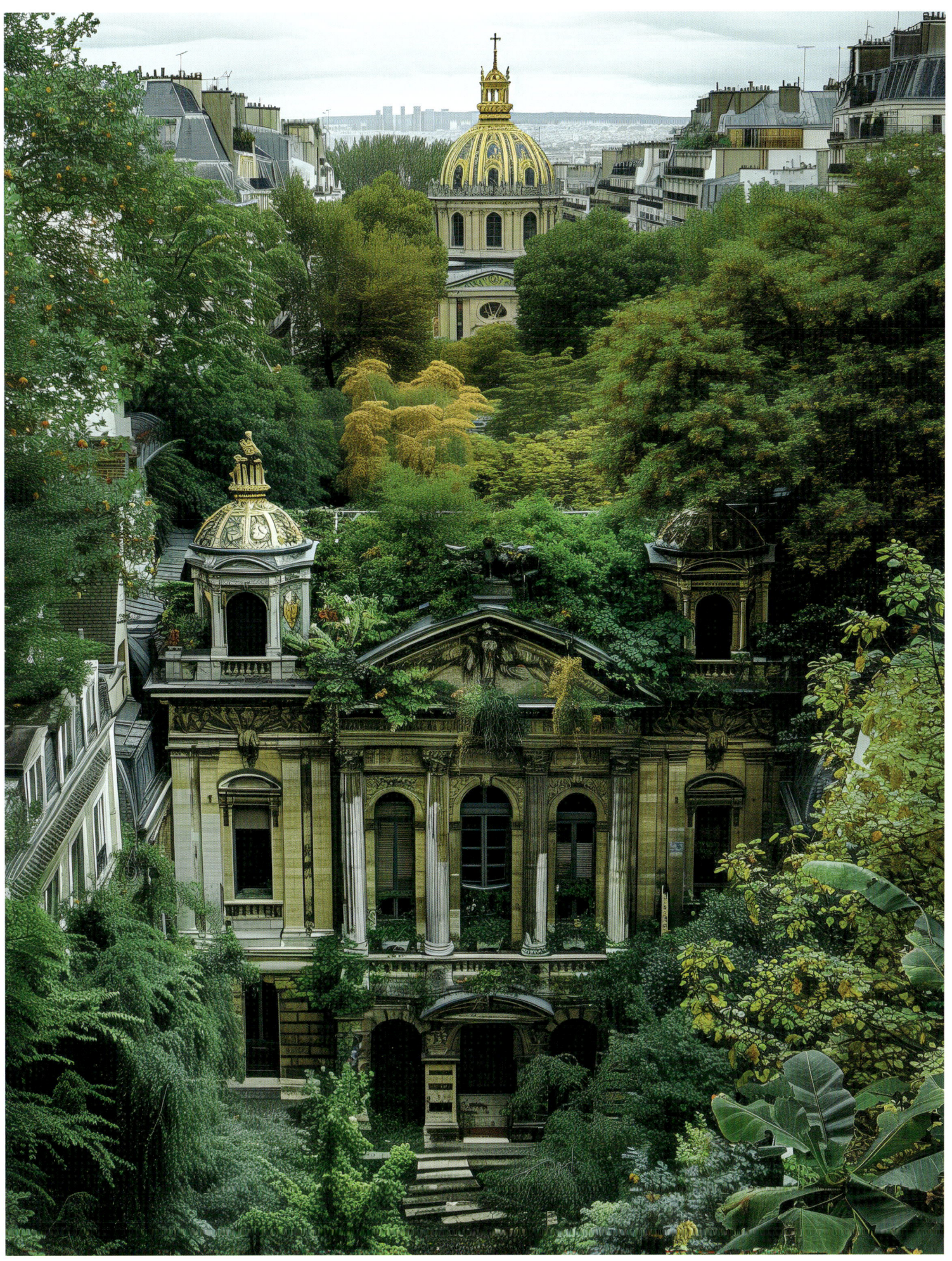

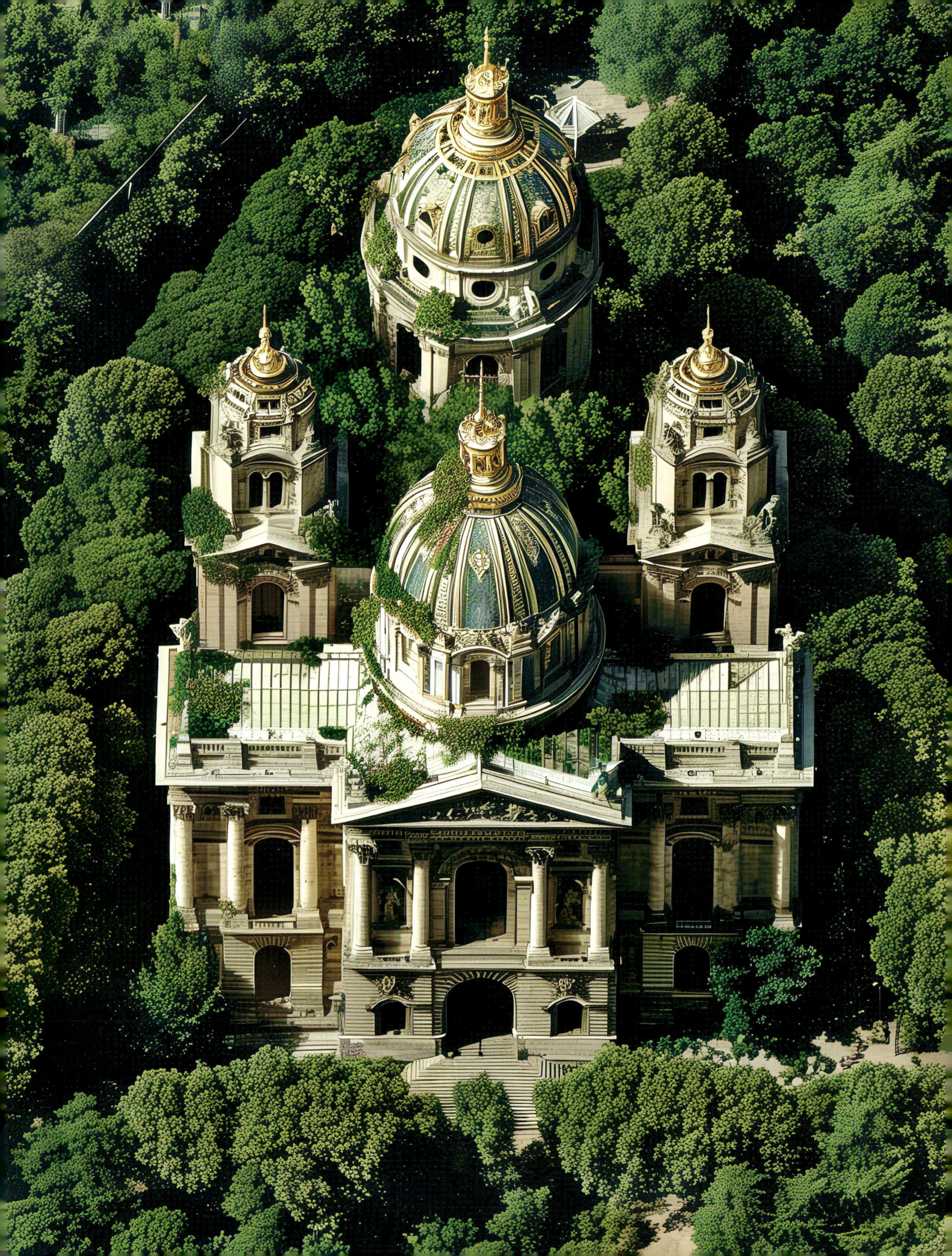

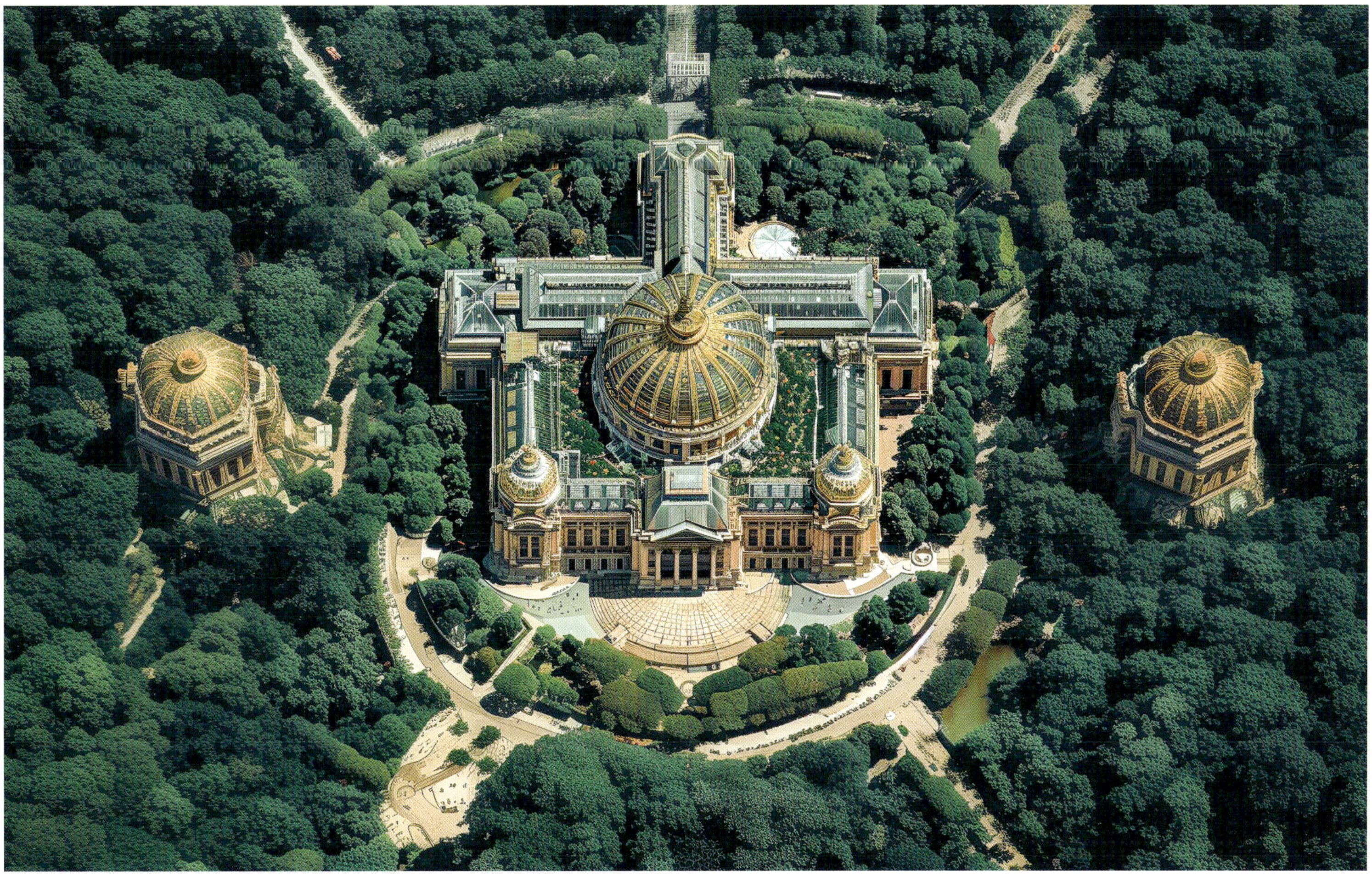

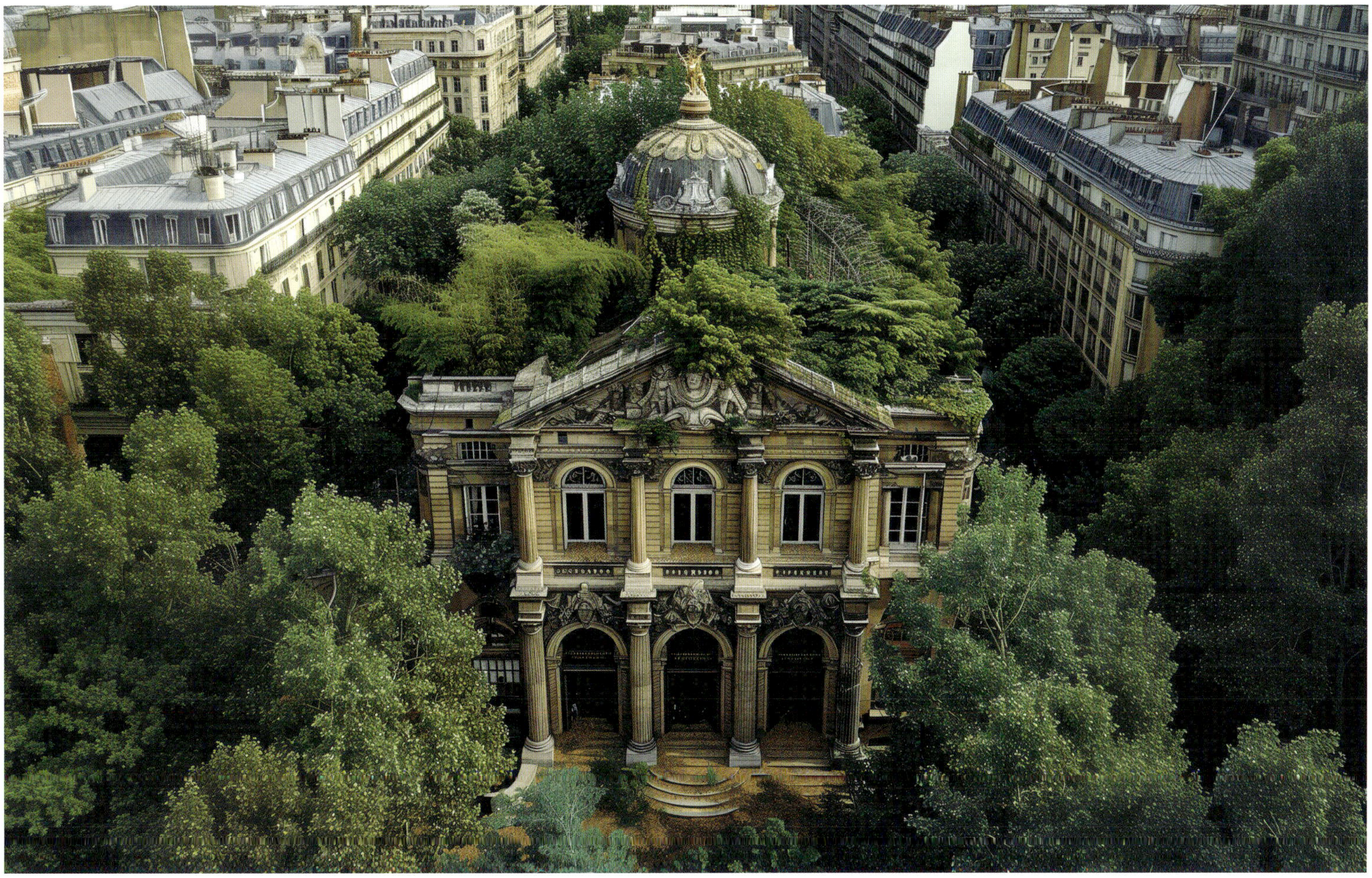

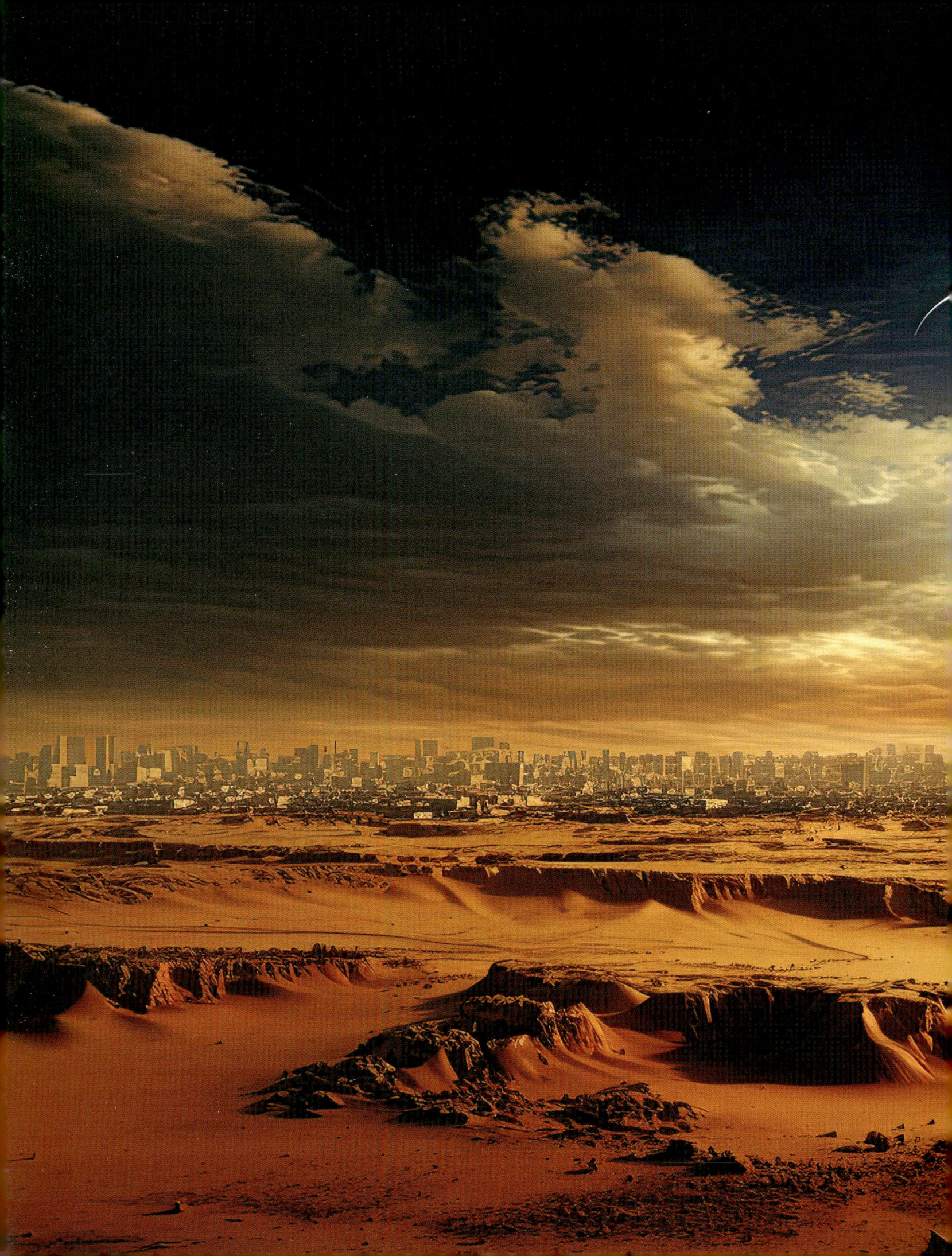

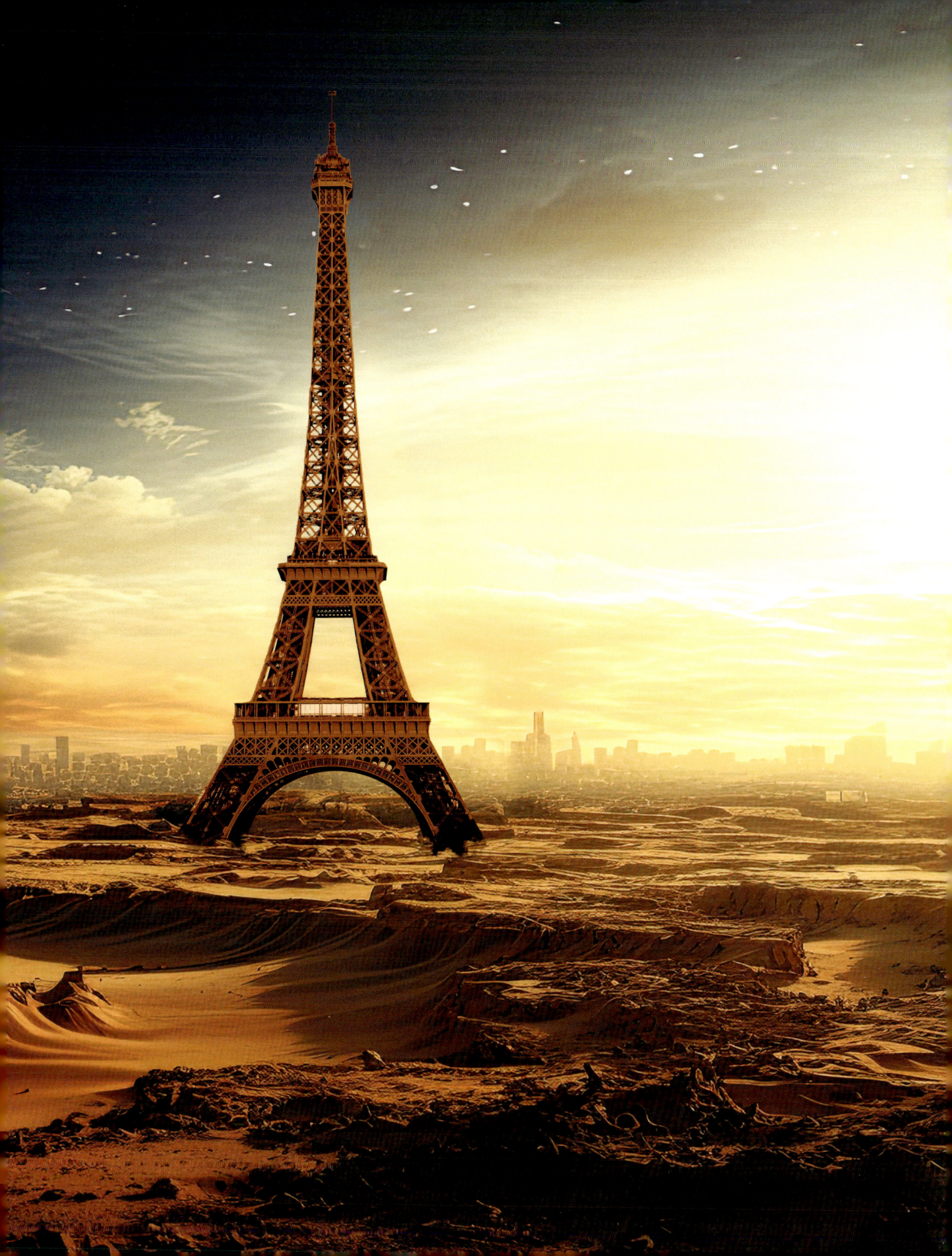

Notre-Drama

The emaciated silhouette of Notre-Dame looms as a silent witness to a time when fire devoured the sacred. The flames, insatiable, defied all attempts to save the cathedral, reducing it to a mound of ashes. Paris, already battered, bears the scars of a loss that goes far beyond stone and wood.

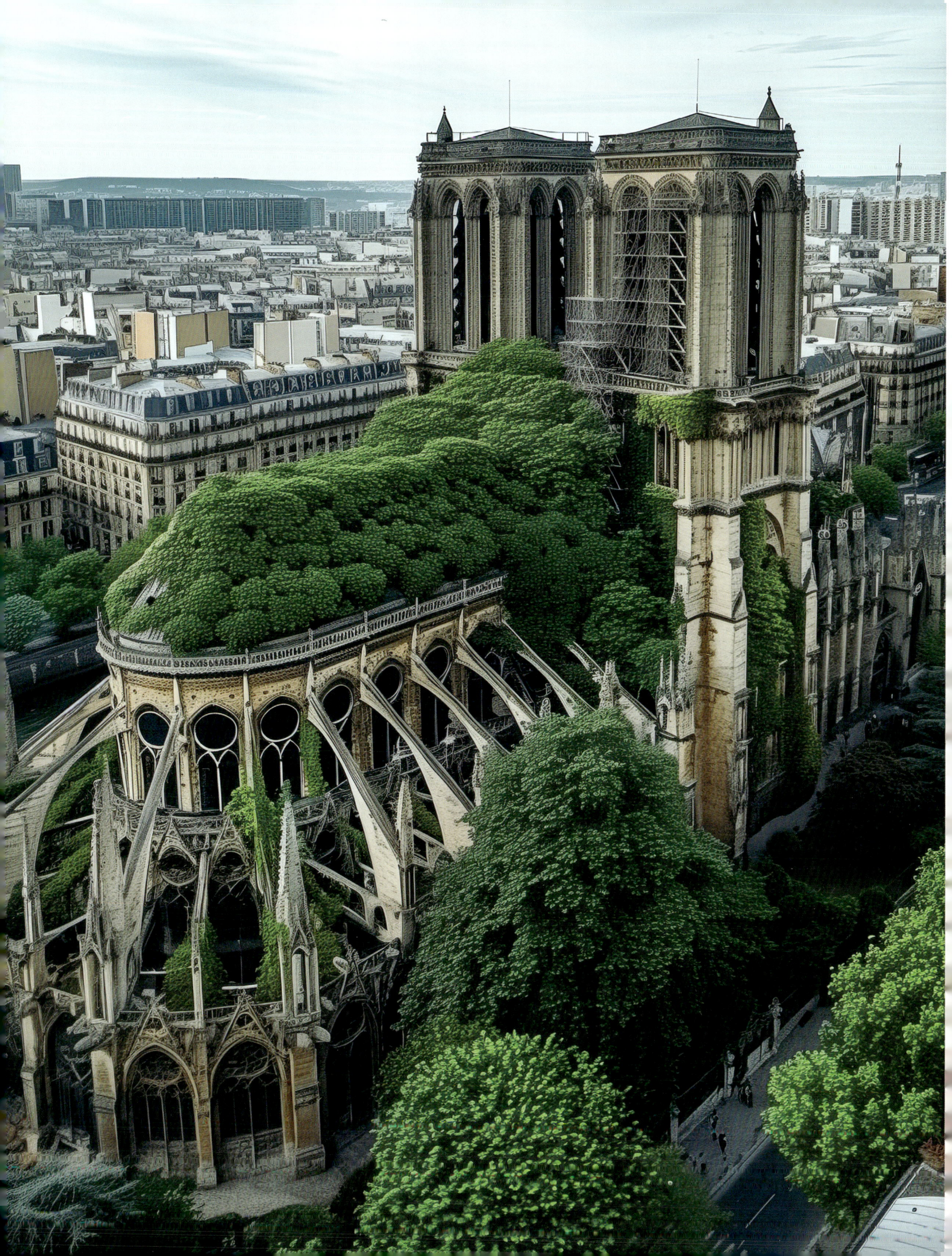

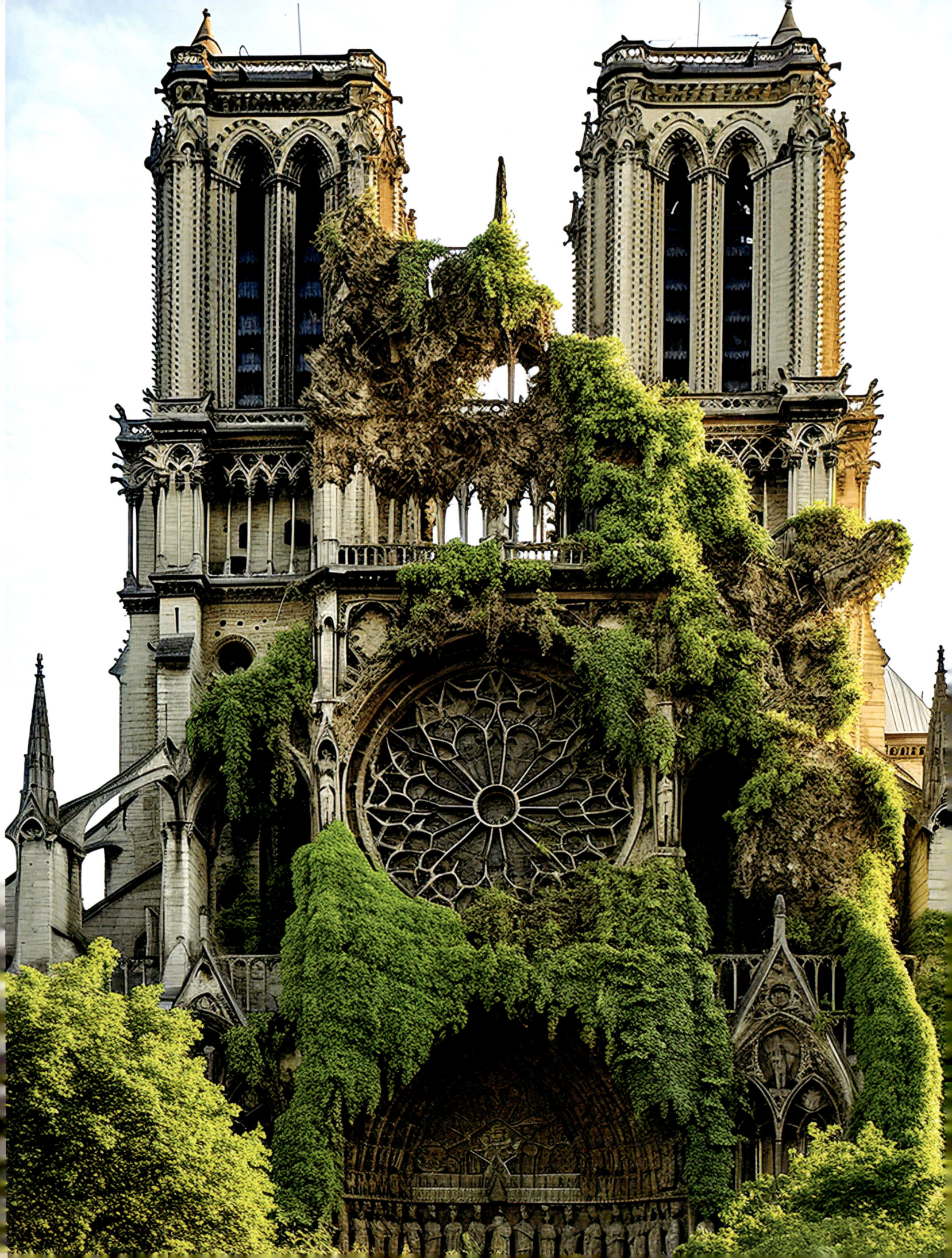

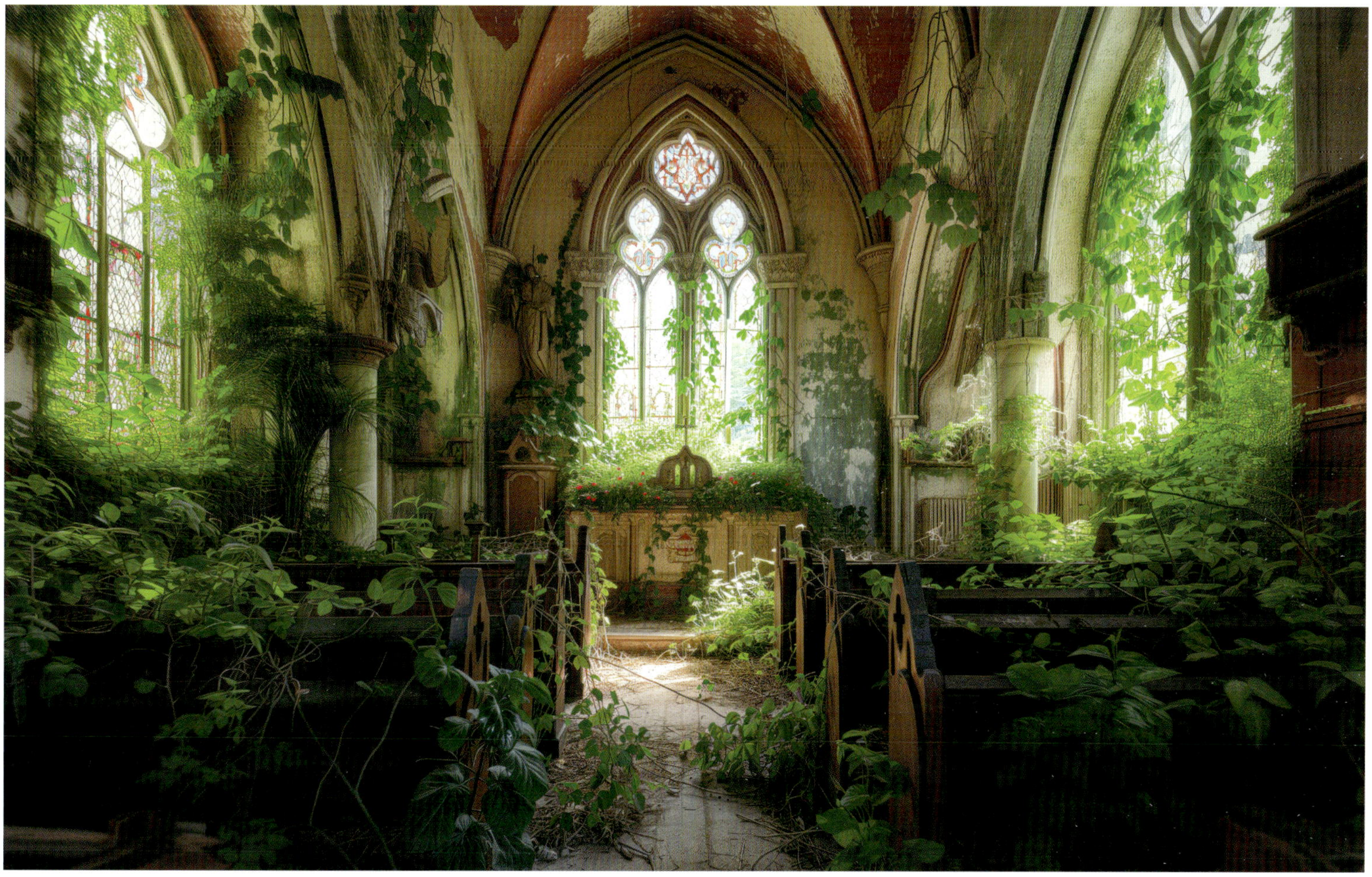

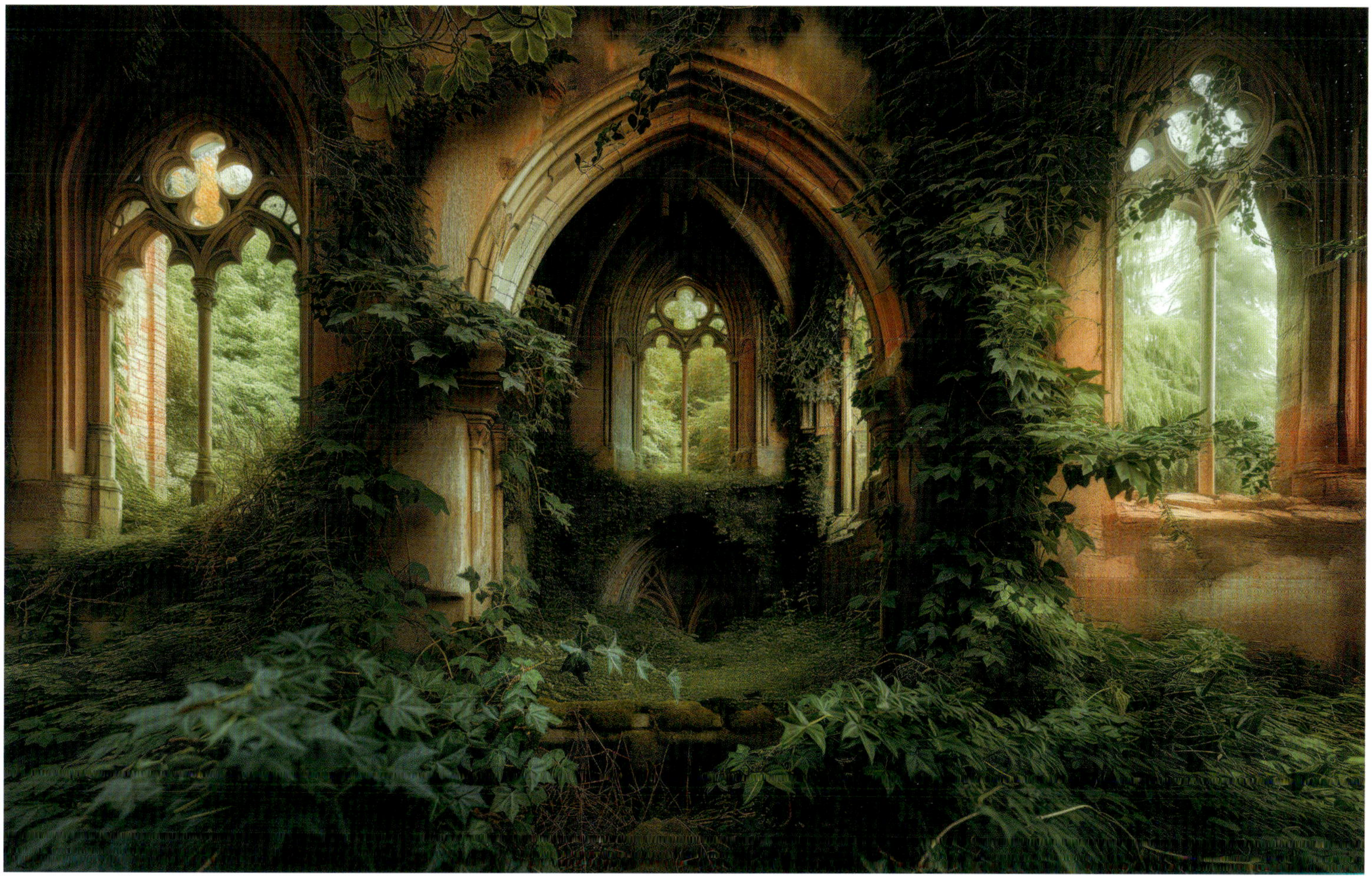

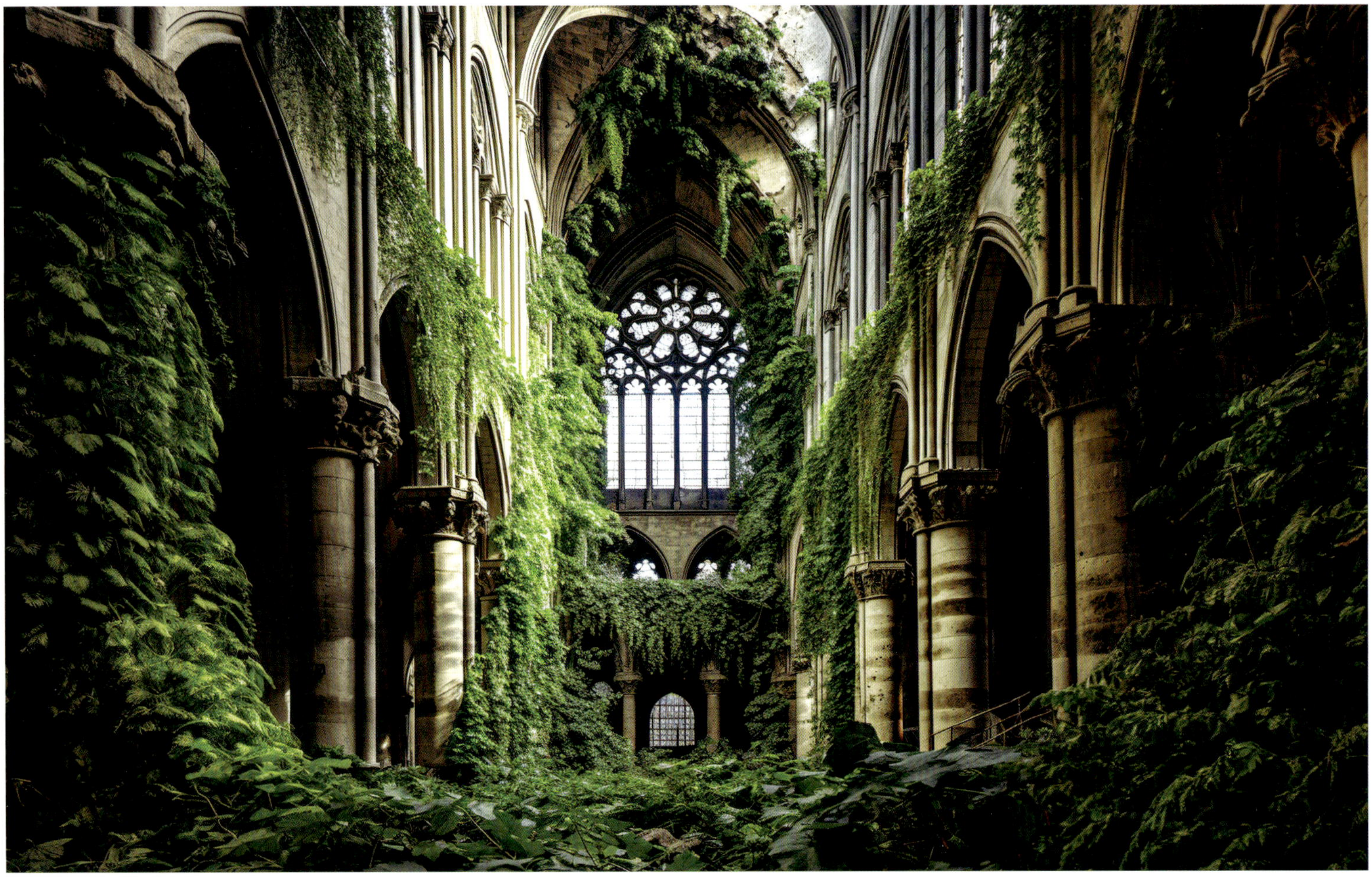

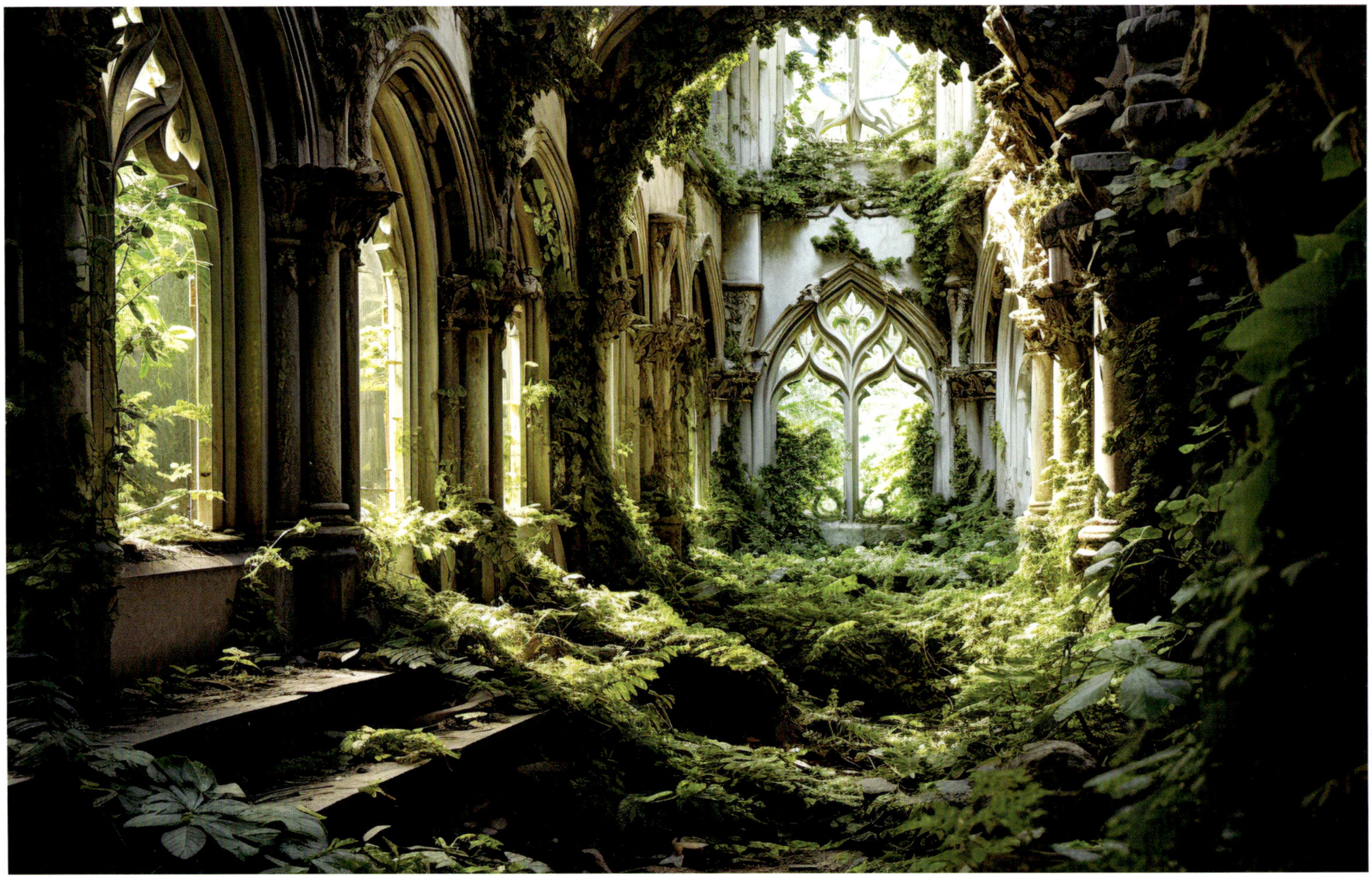

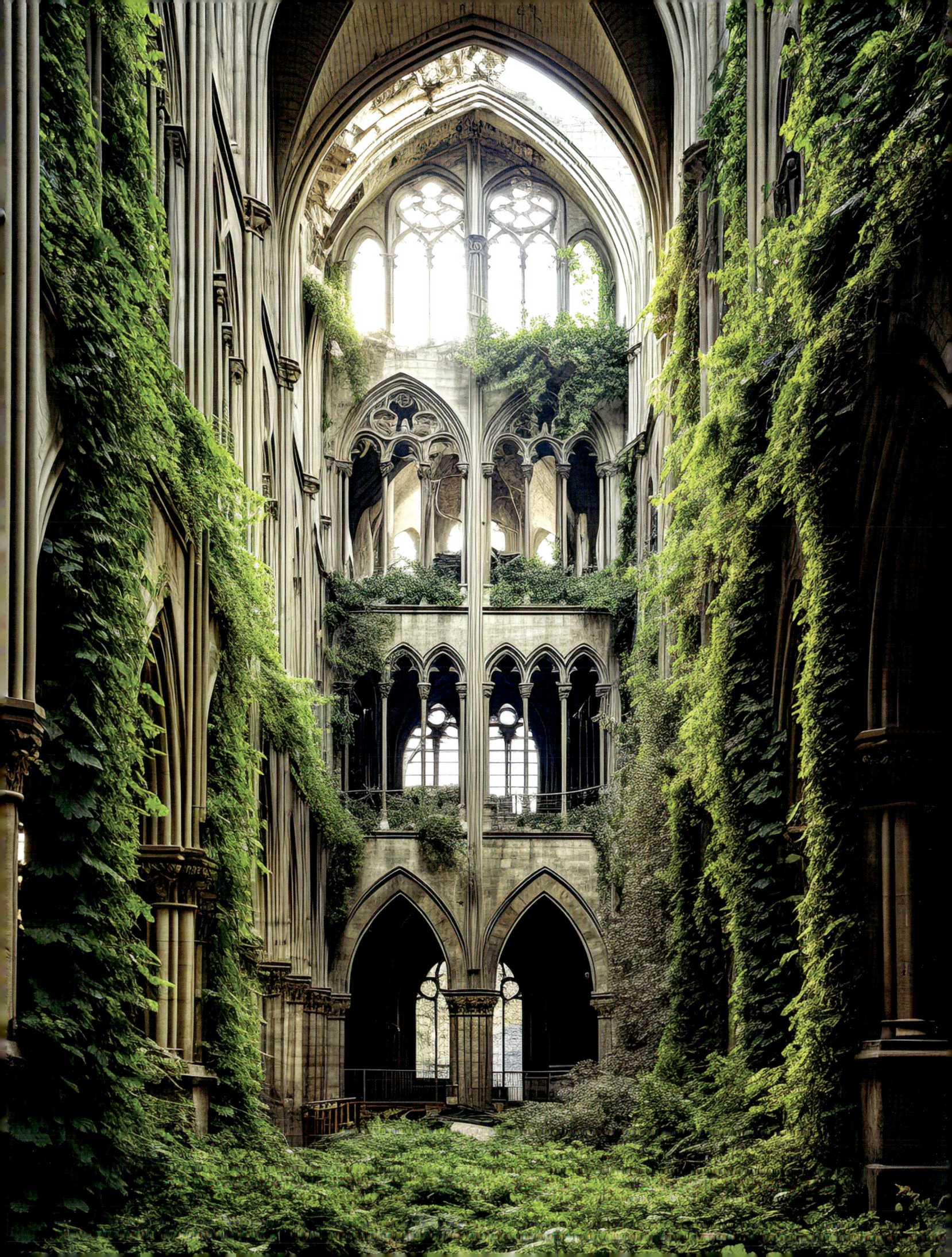

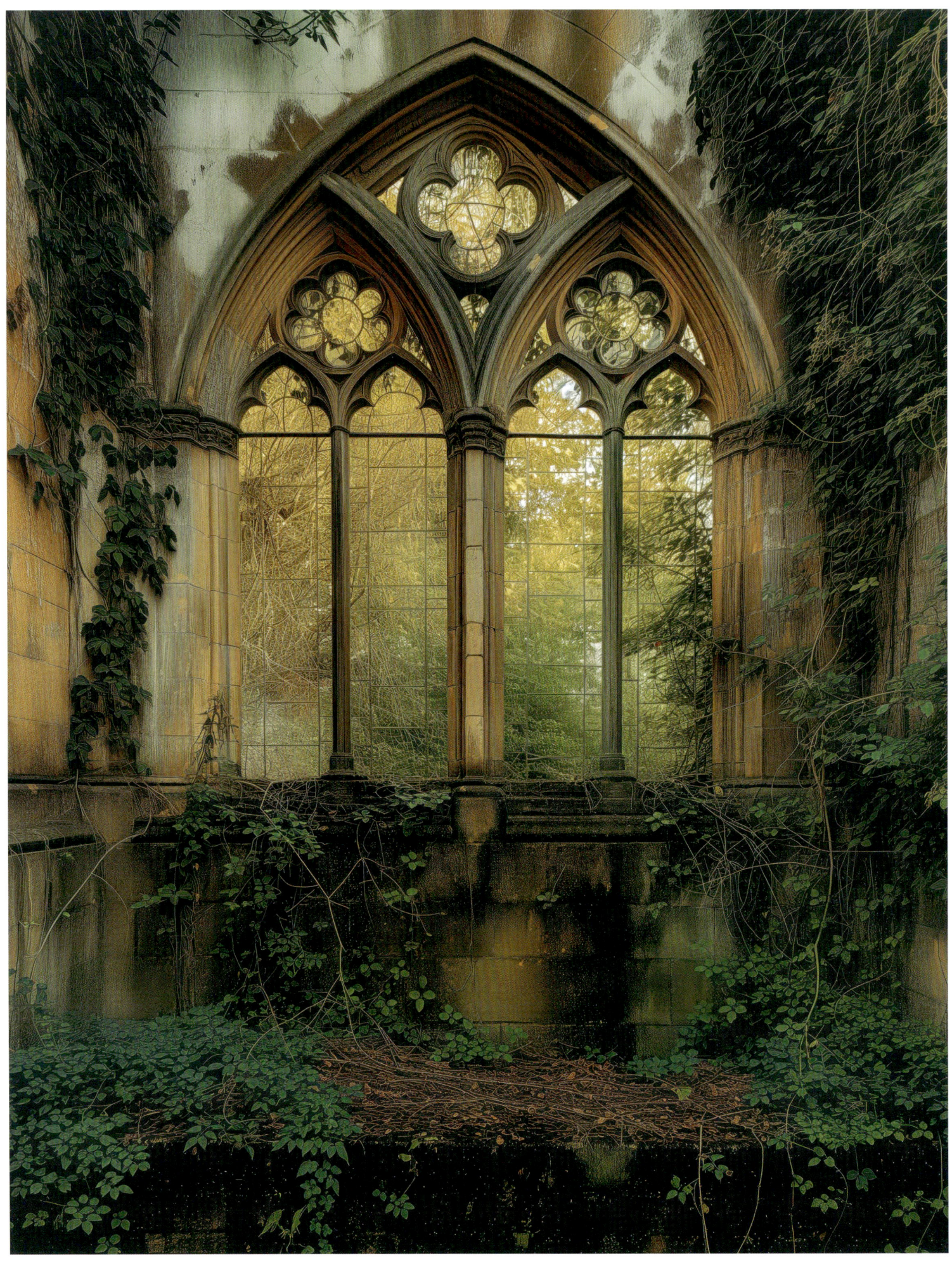

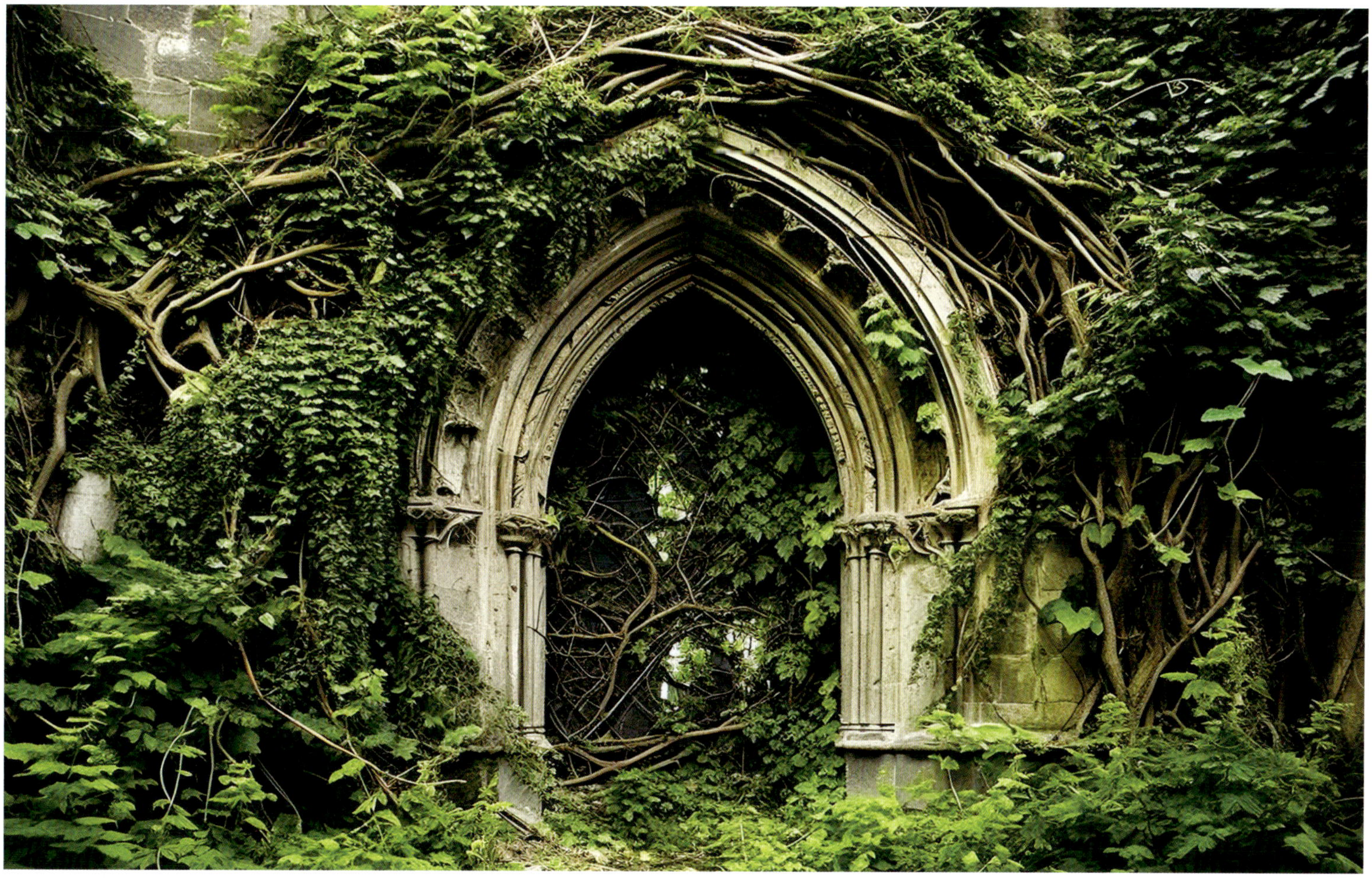

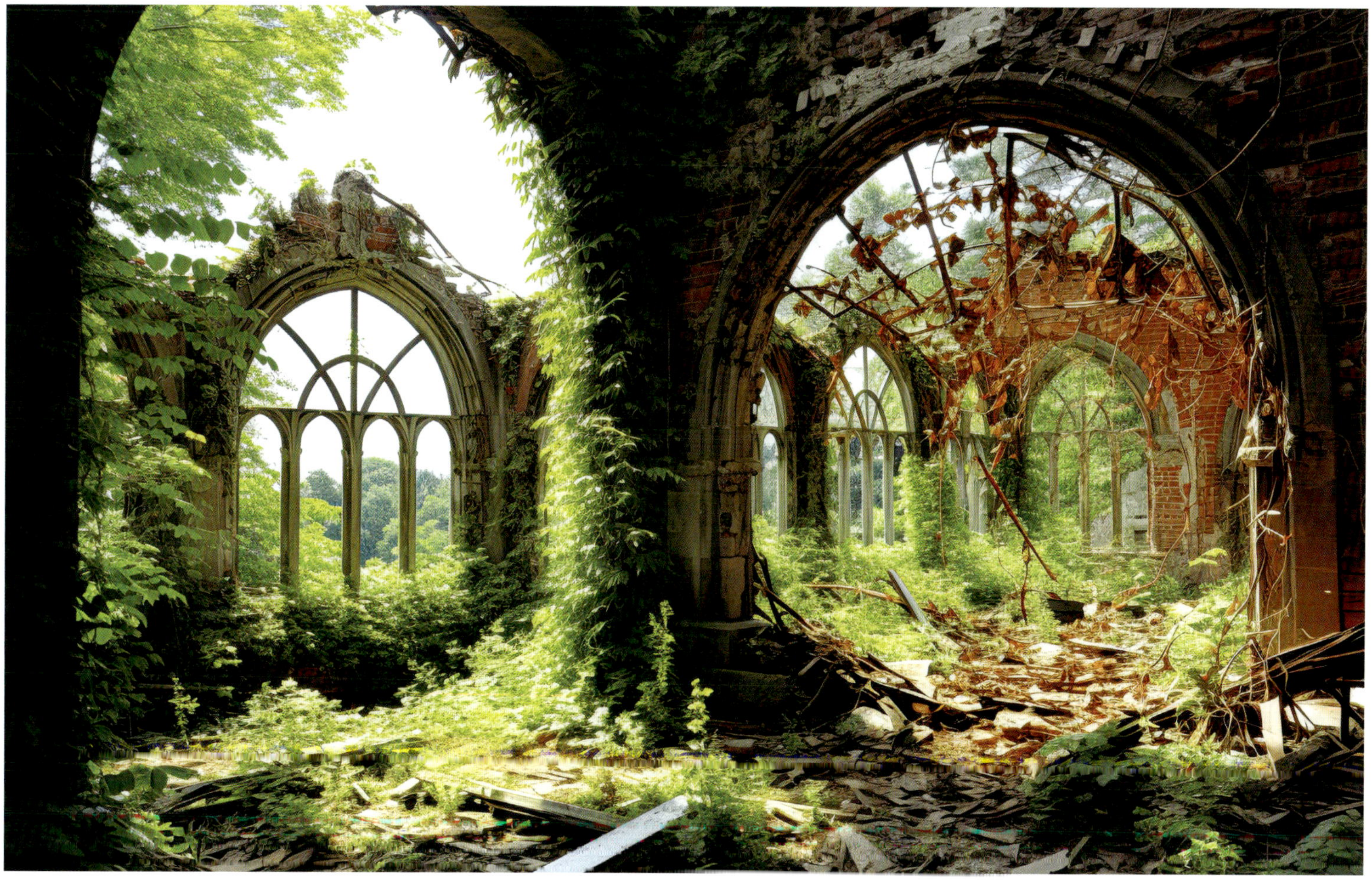

The day after

At the end of the conflict between NATO and the Eastern bloc, some European capitals were hit hard by long-range nuclear missiles fired from Russian territory. The rest of the world joined forces to quash the demonic tyrant. In an act of desperation before its defeat, the tyrant followed through on its threats. The damage and losses were considerable. Forty years on, Paris is still struggling to recover from this ordeal.

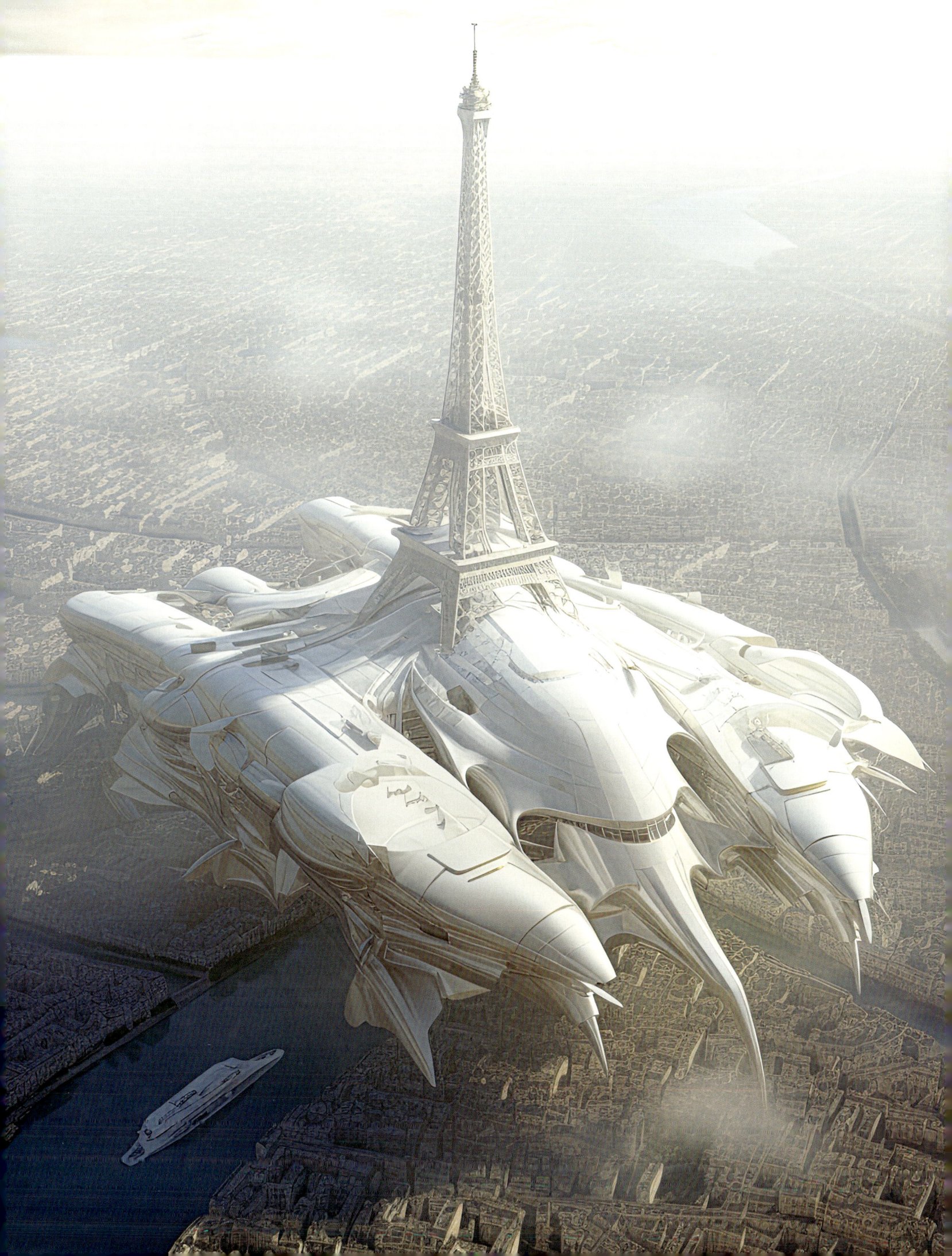

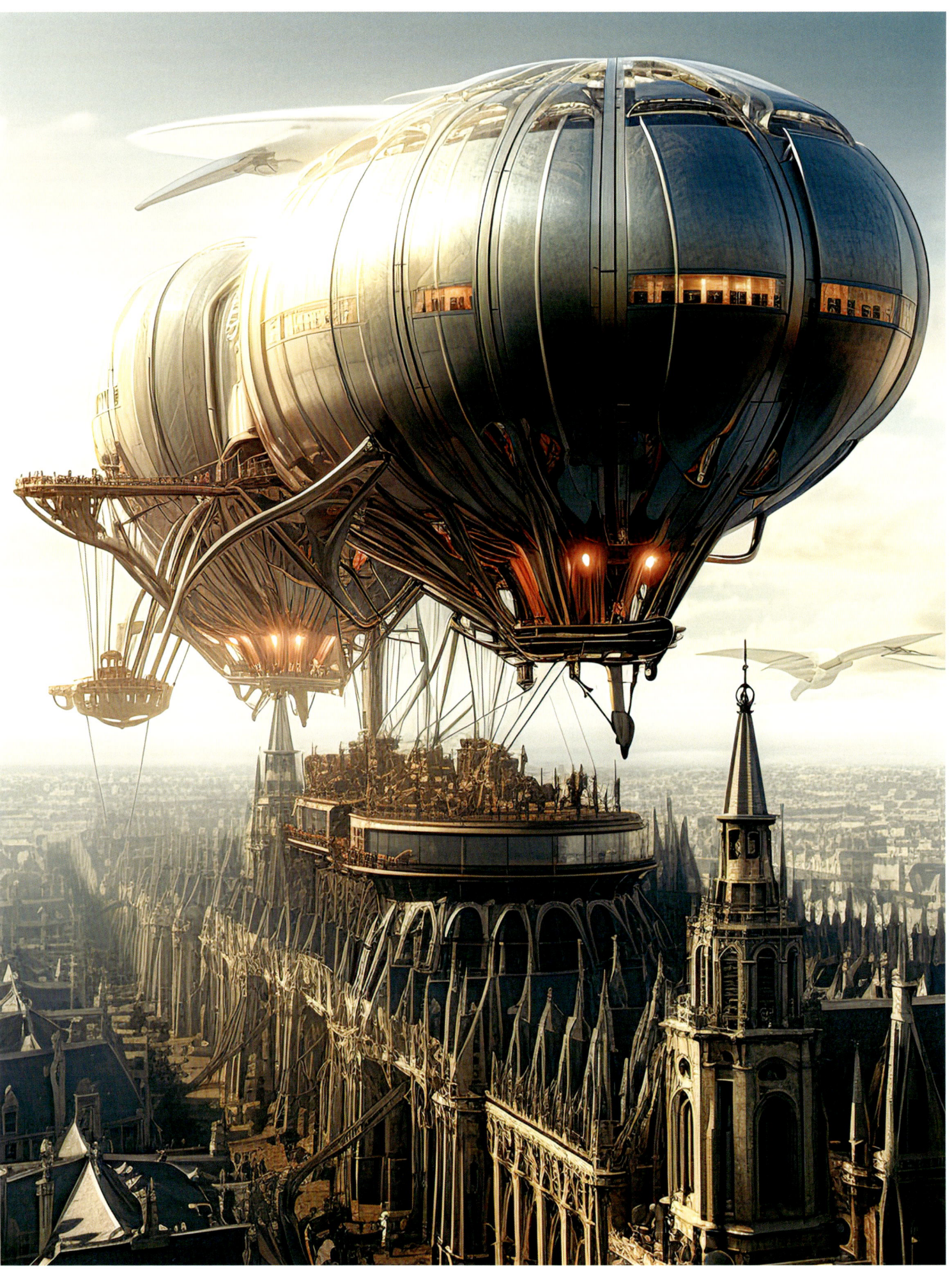

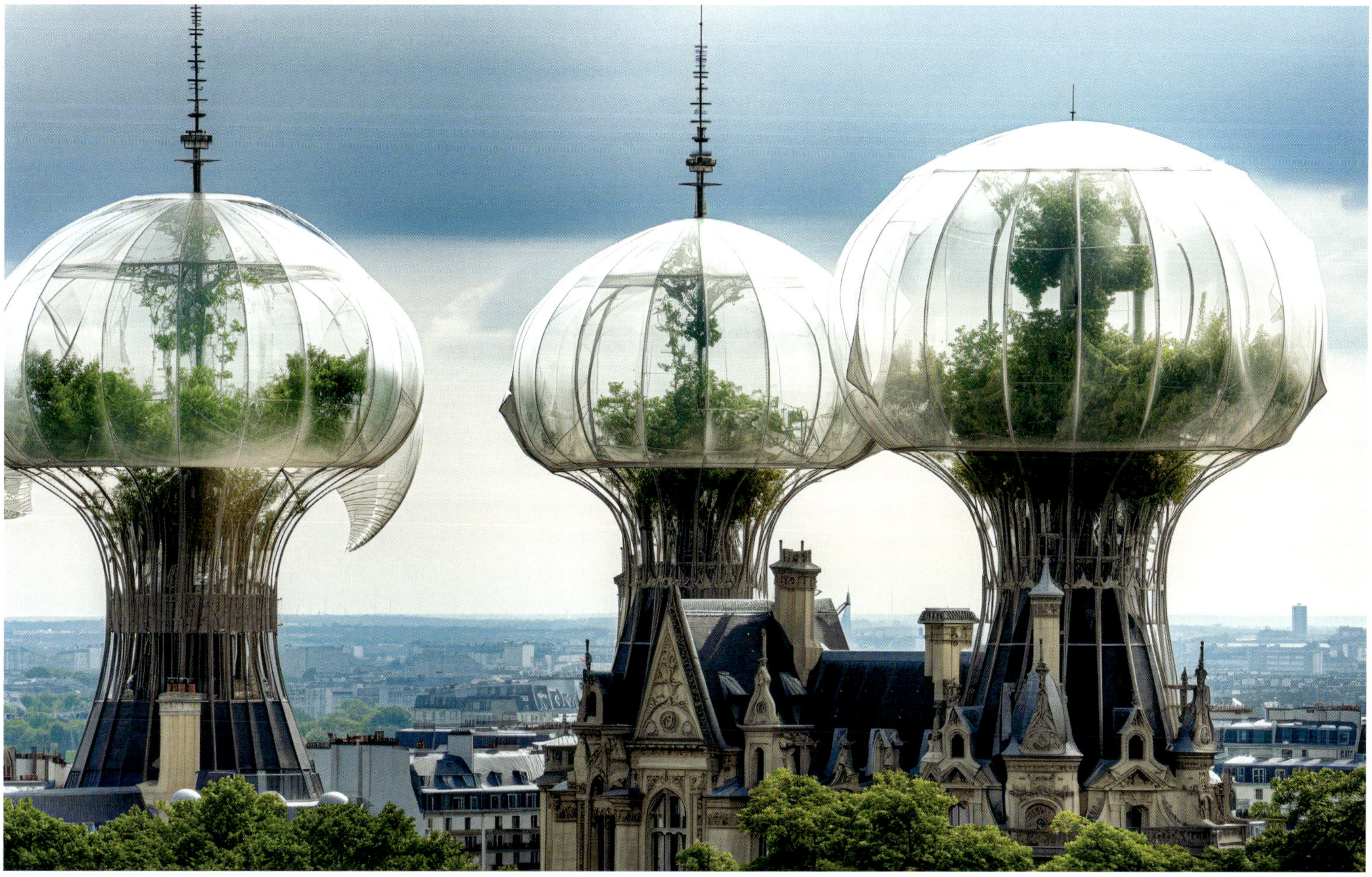

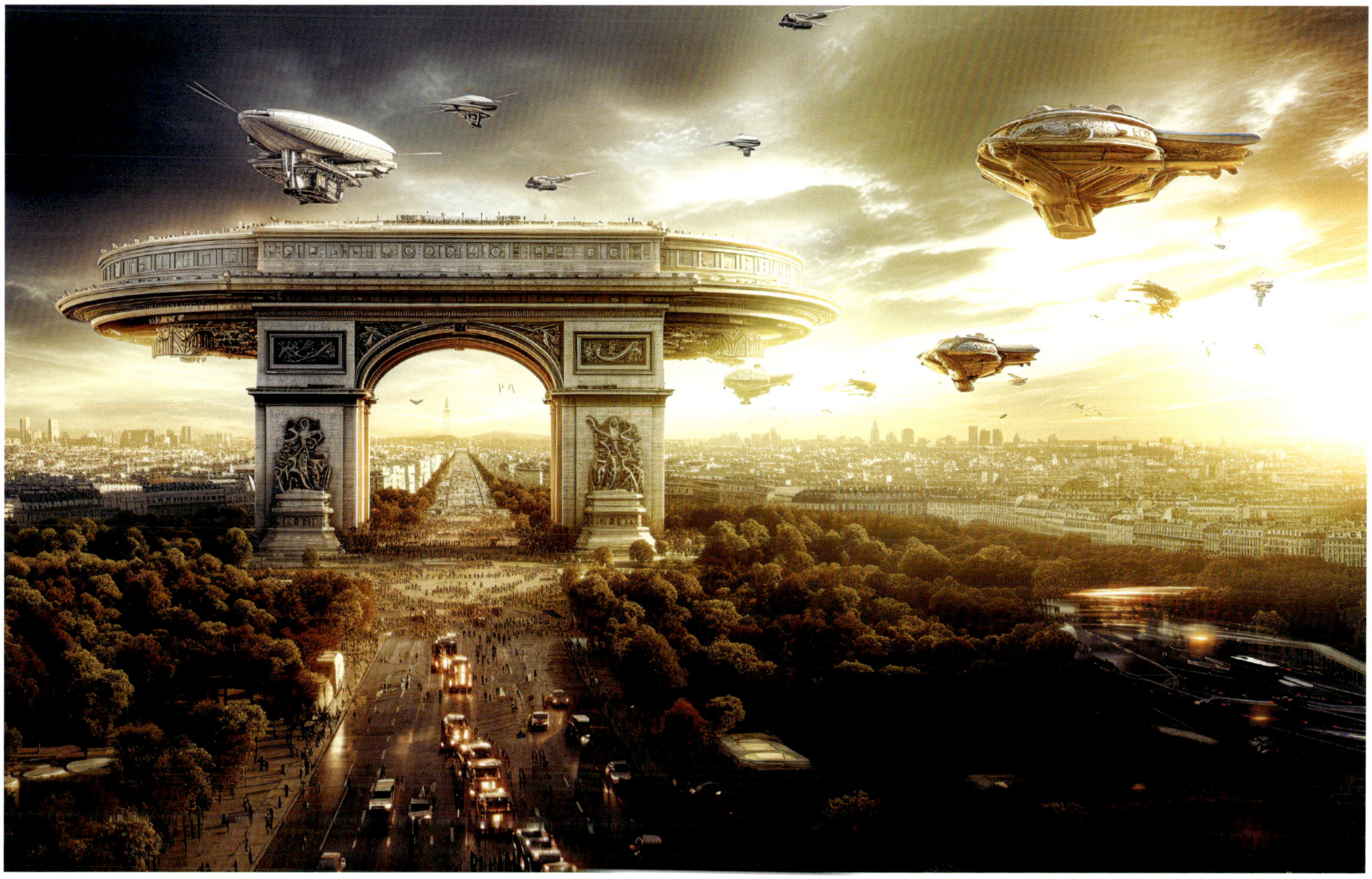

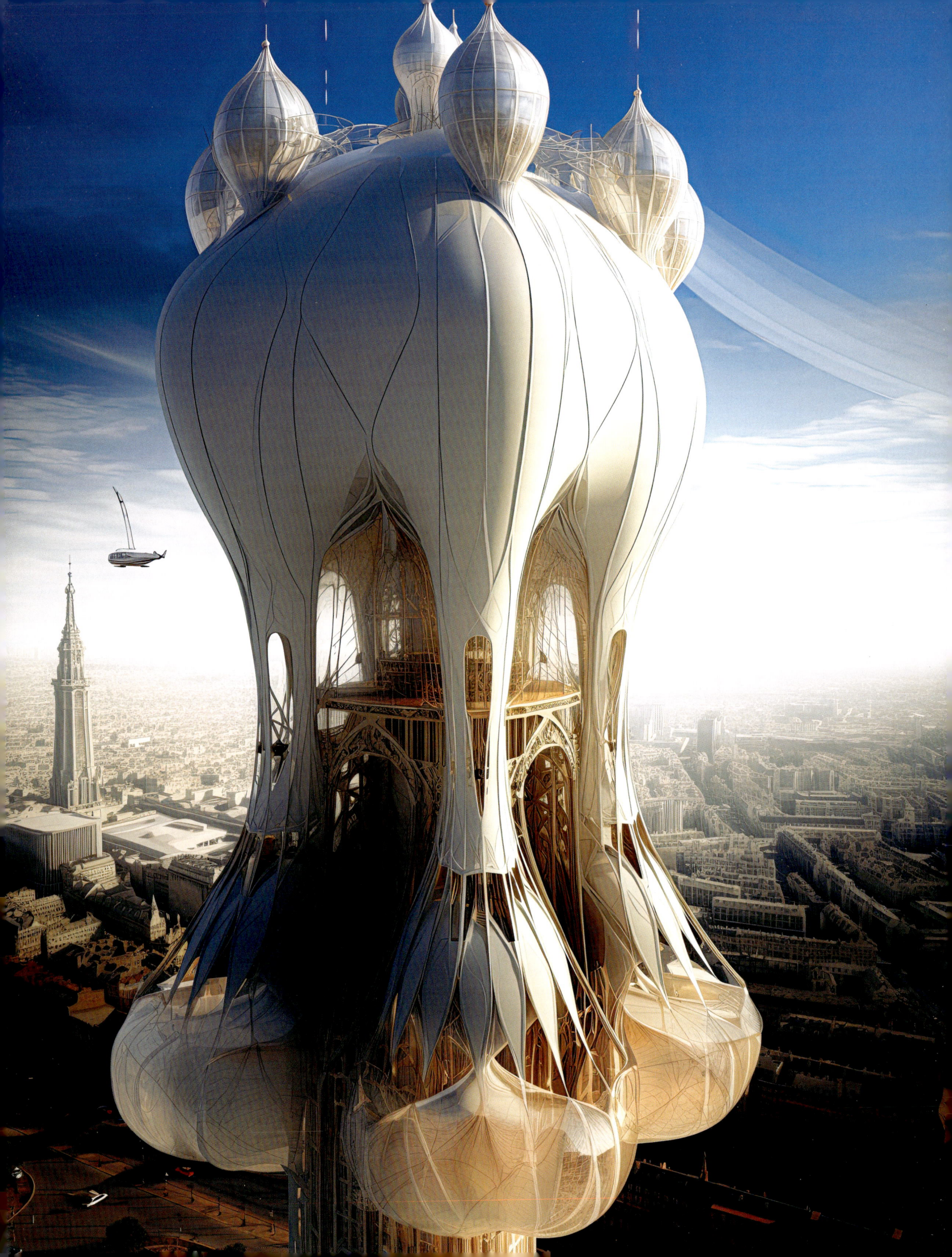

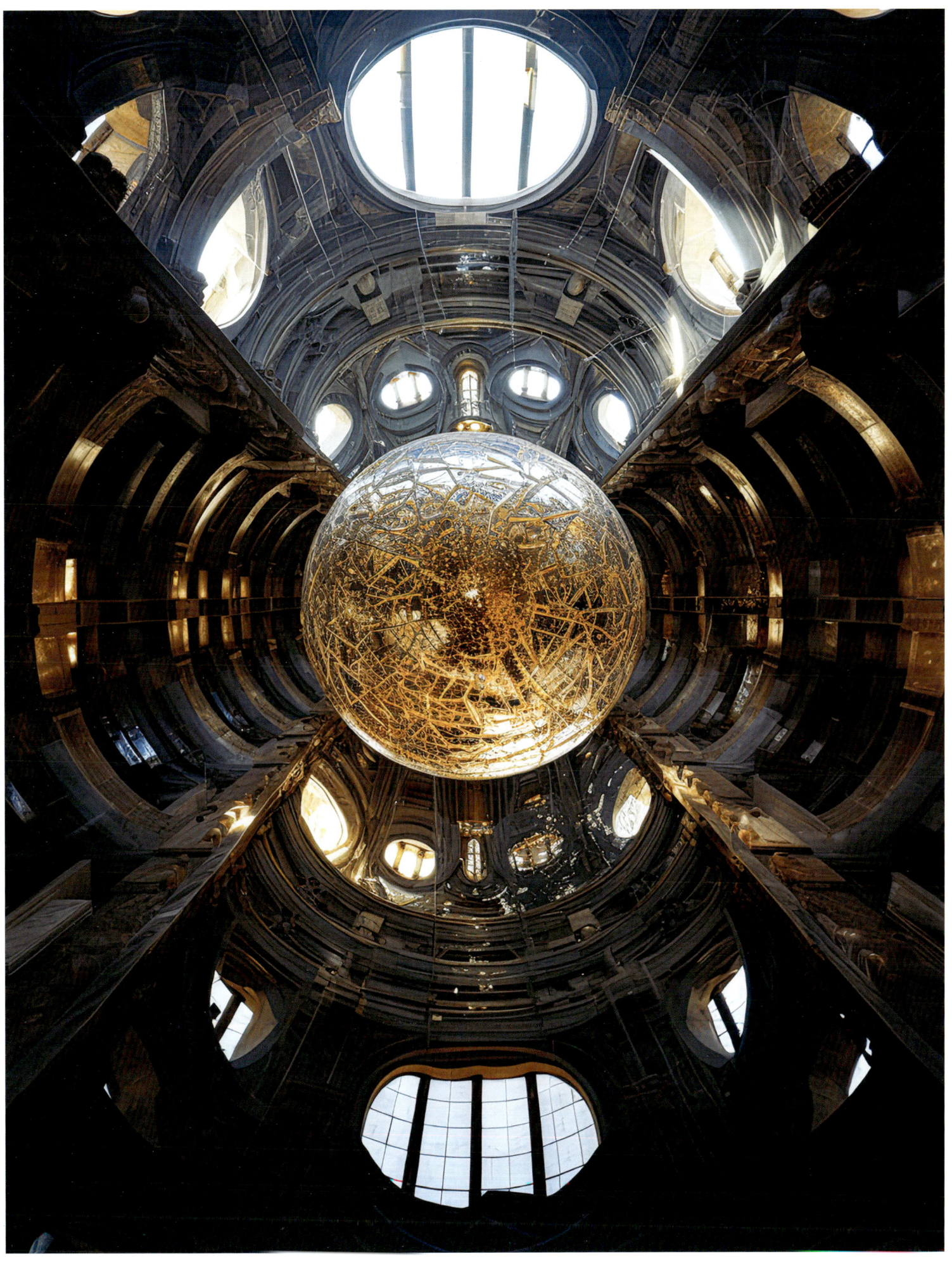

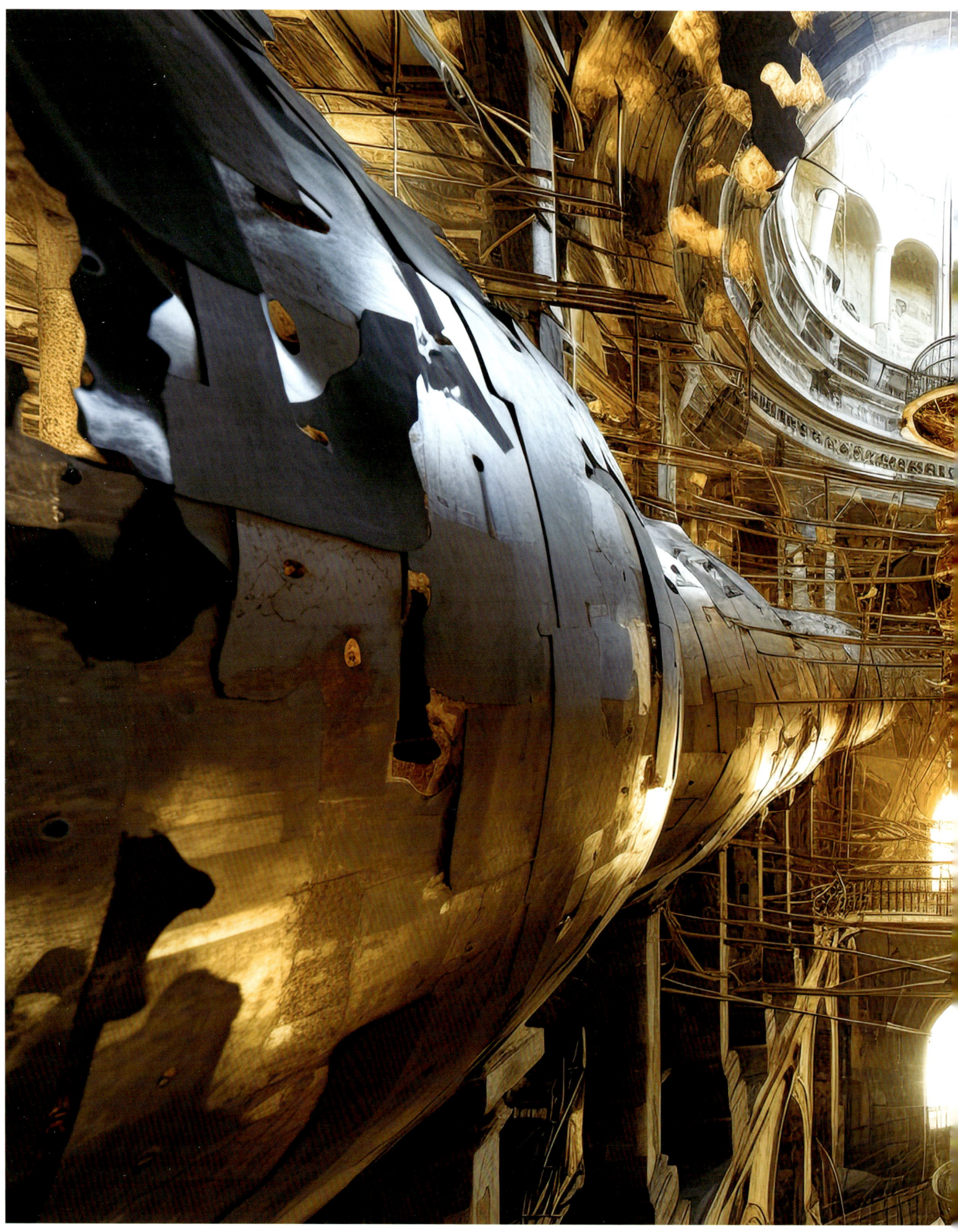

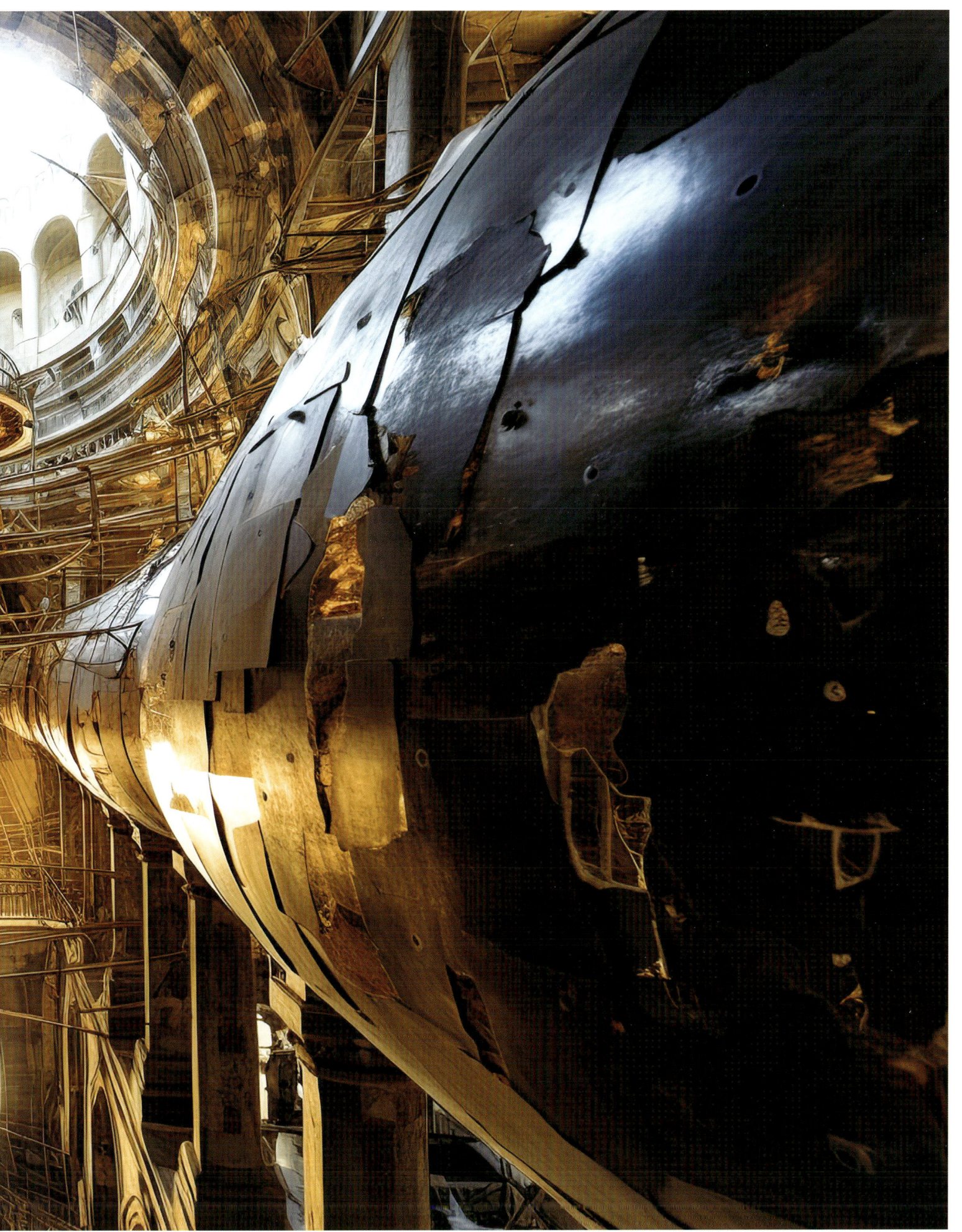

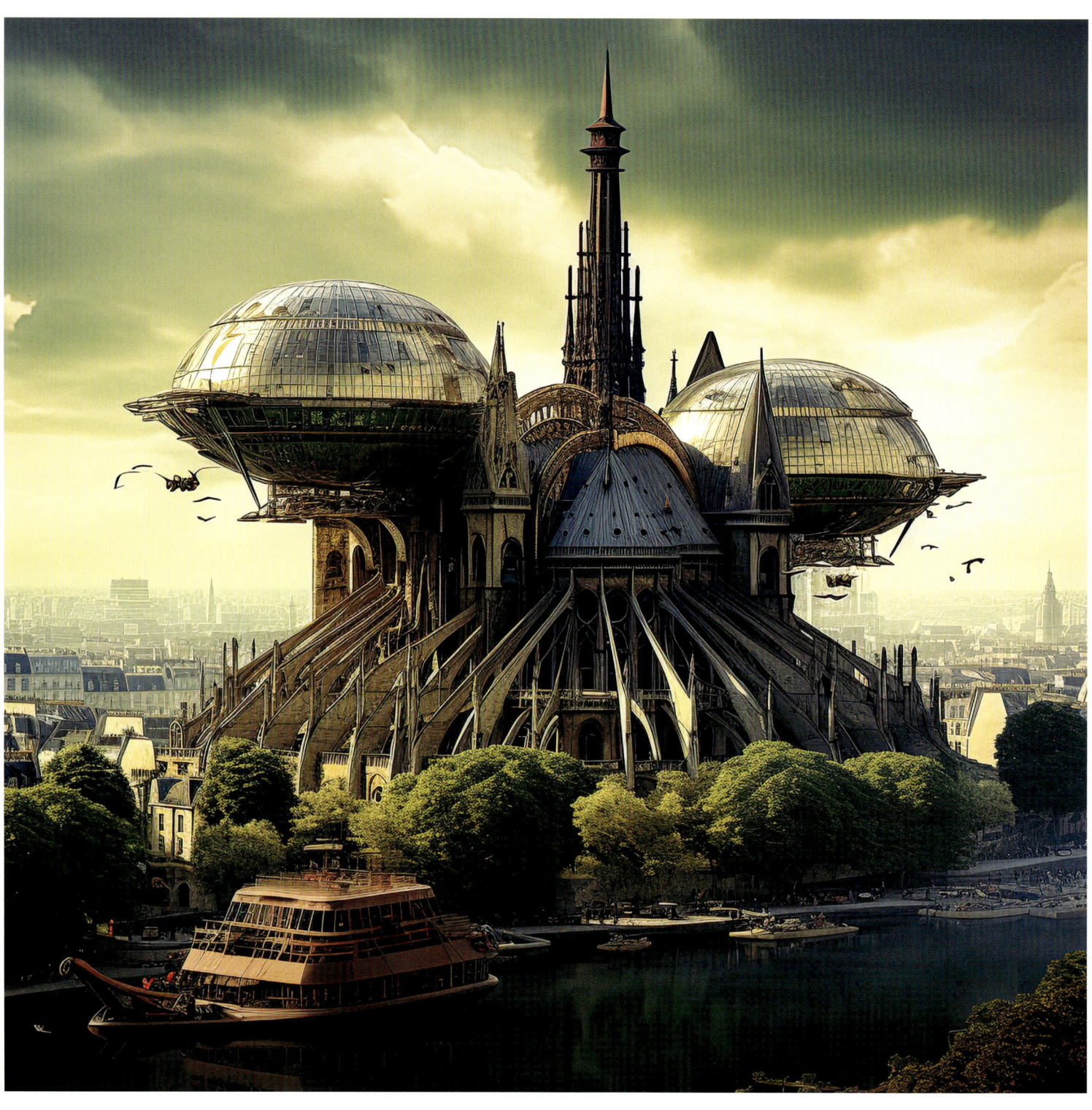

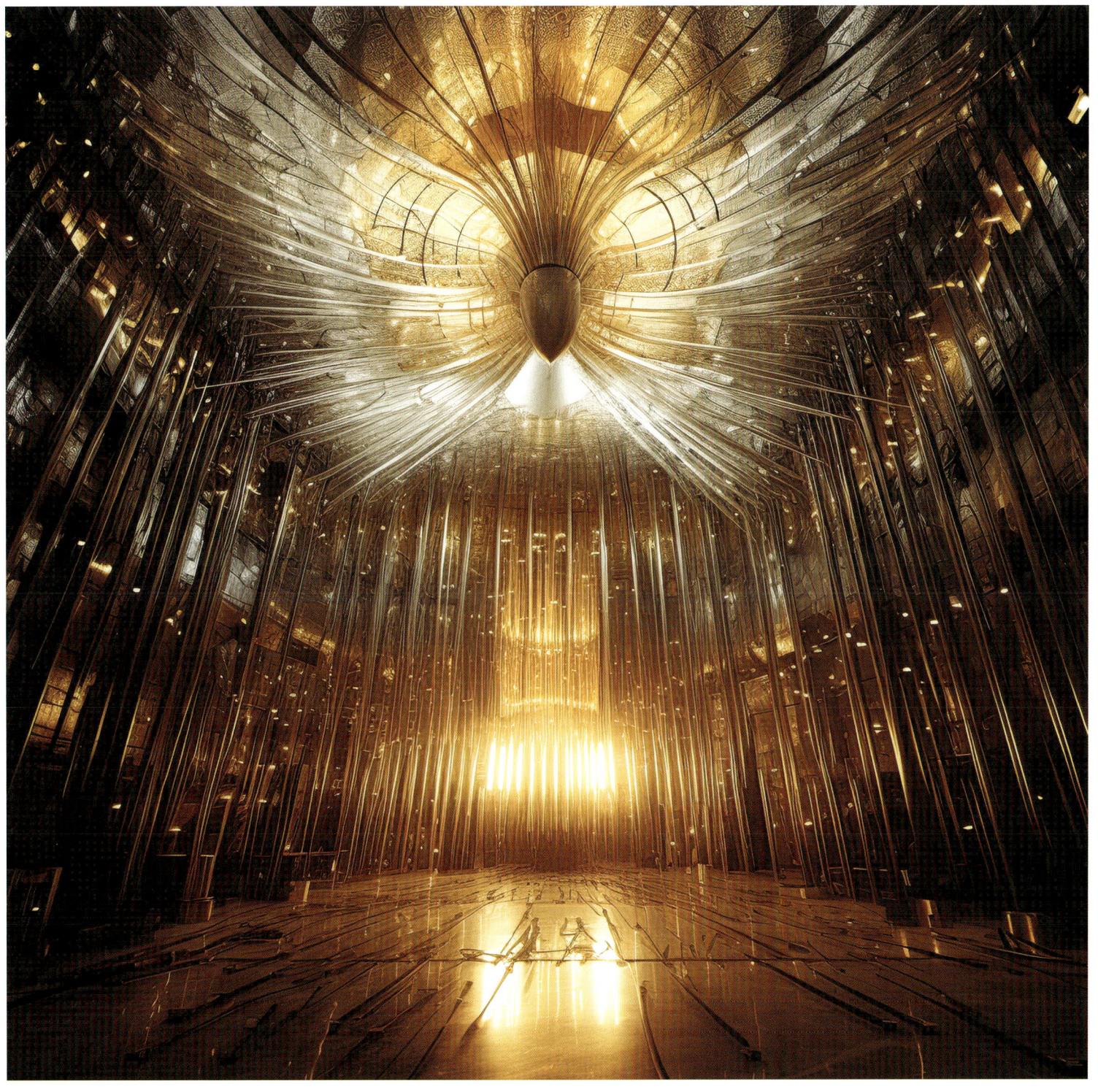

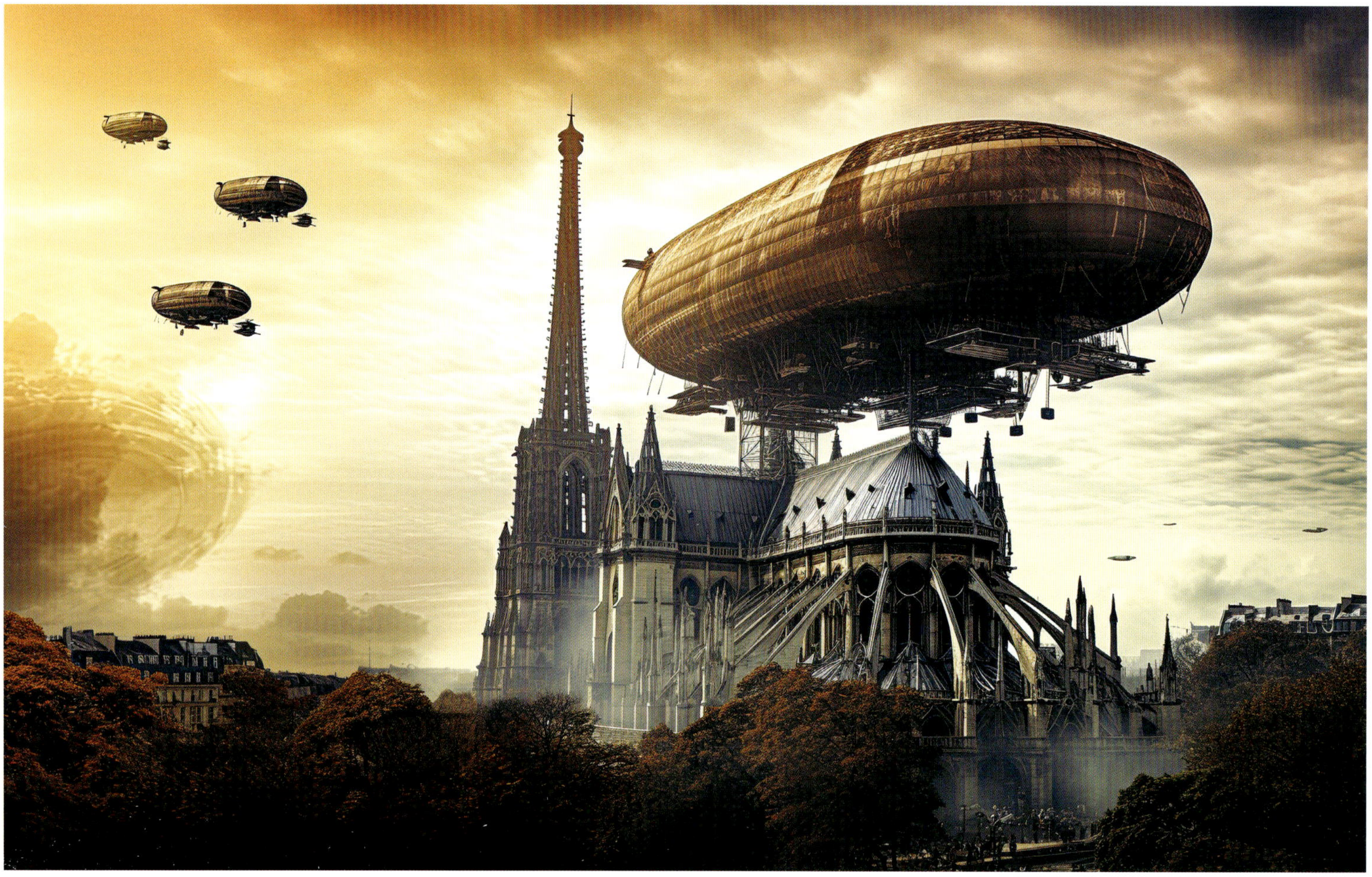

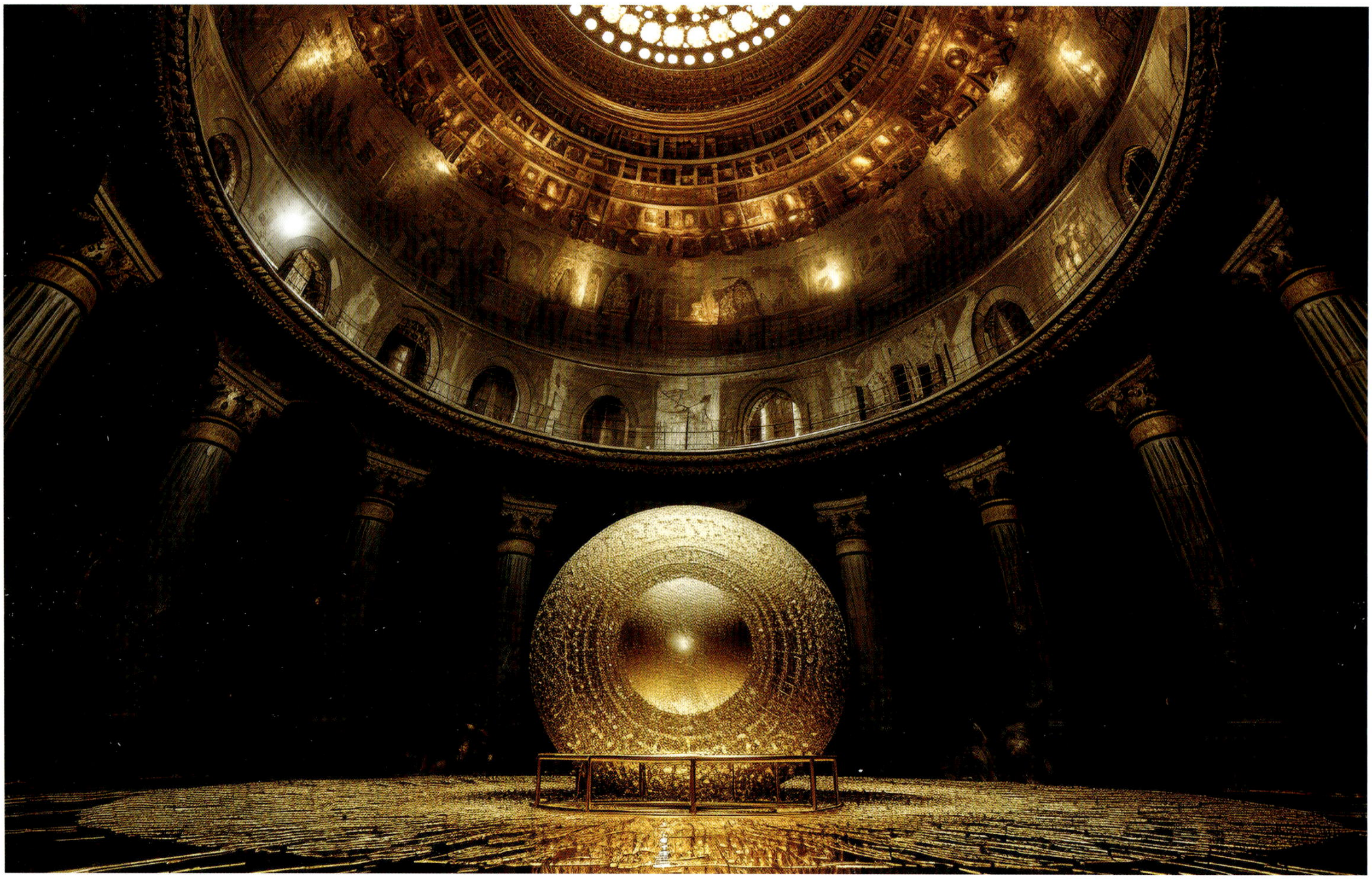

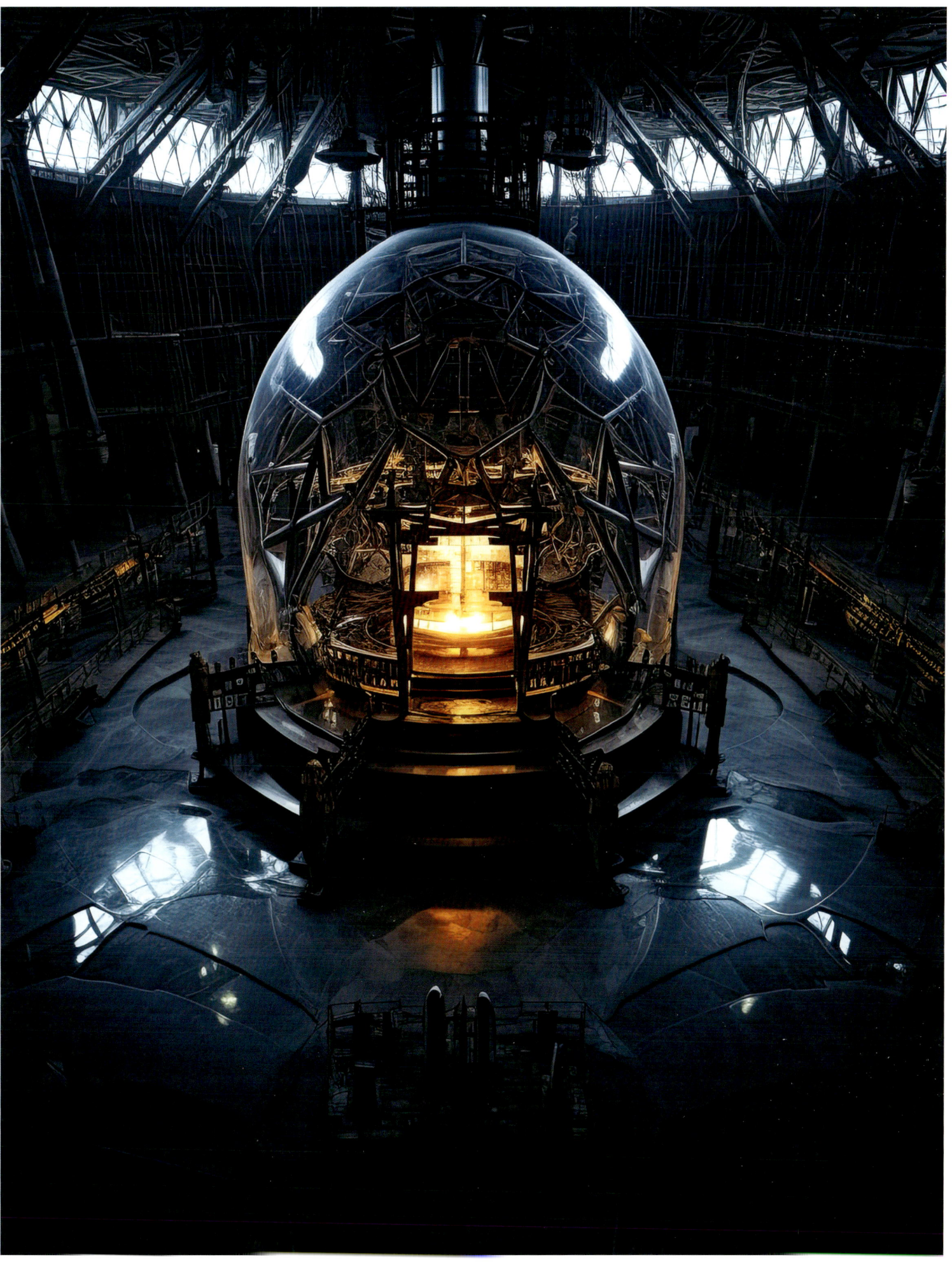

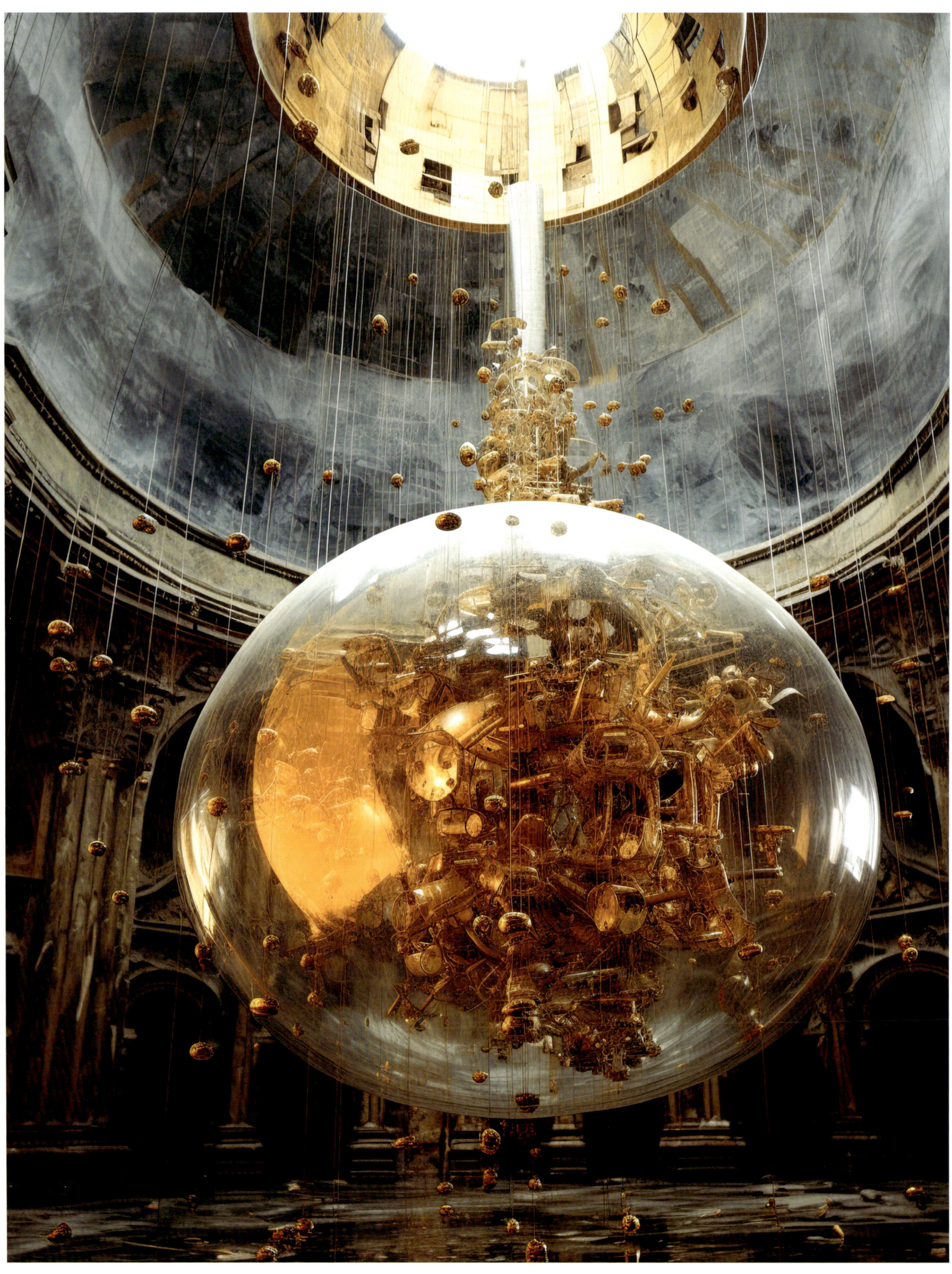

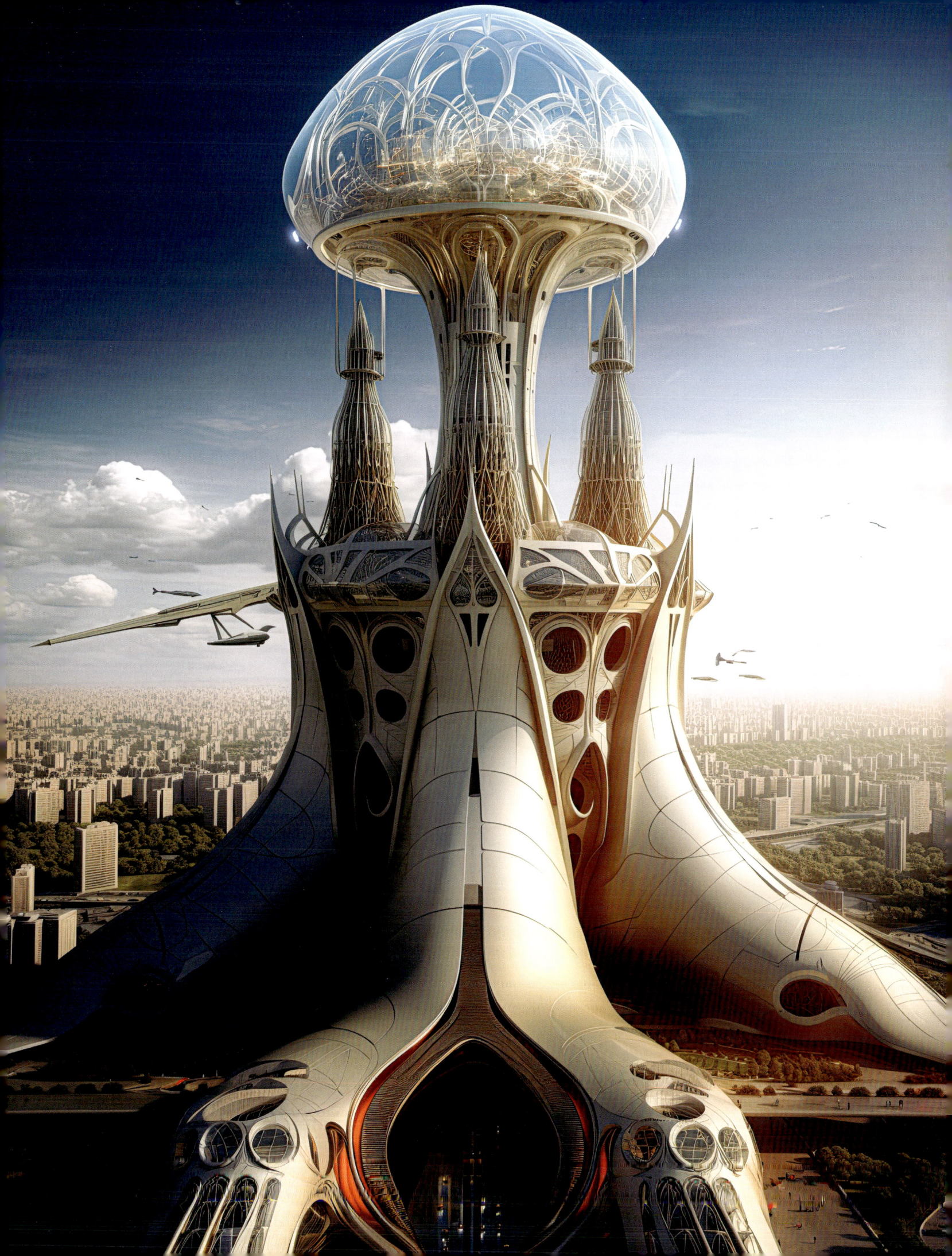

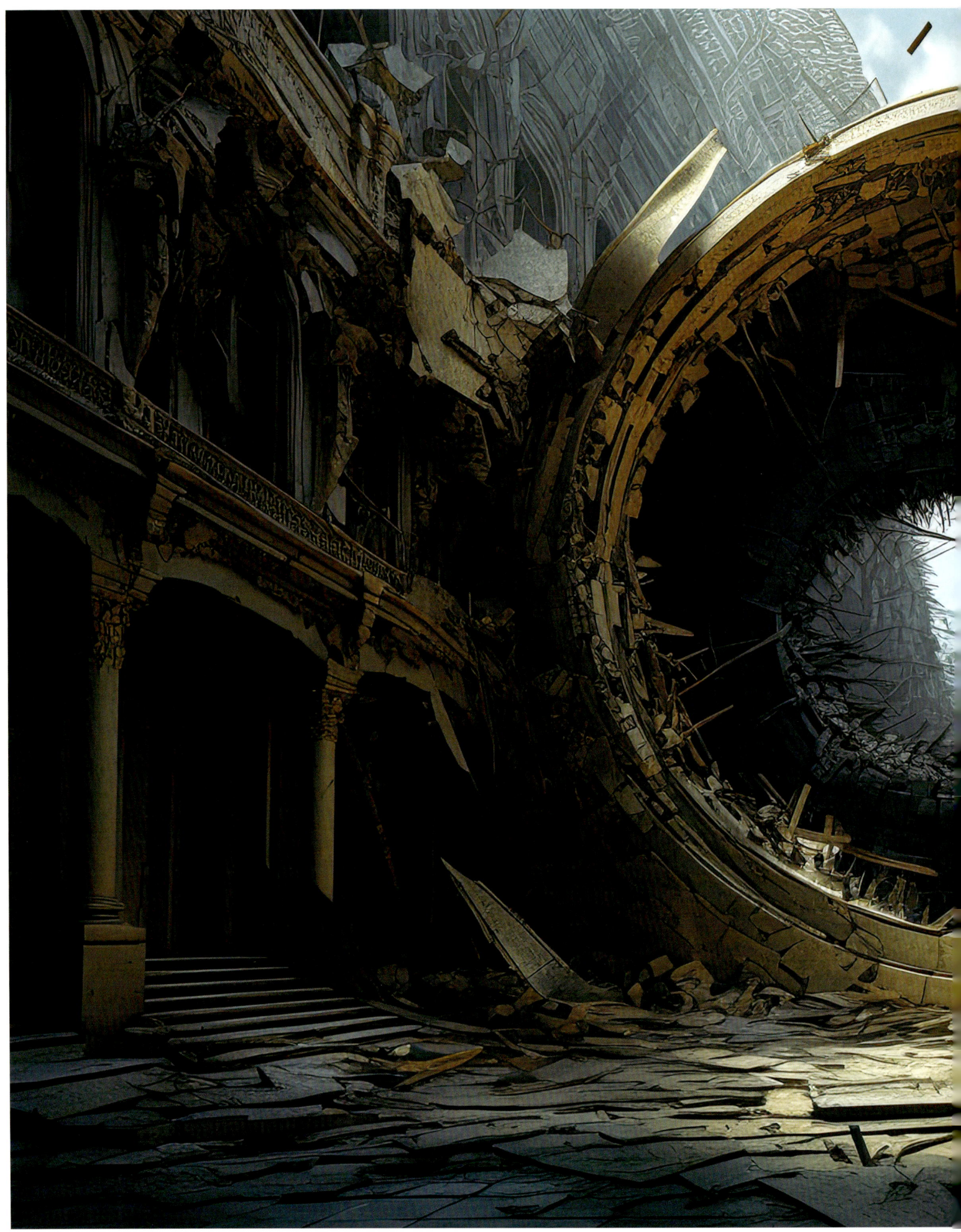

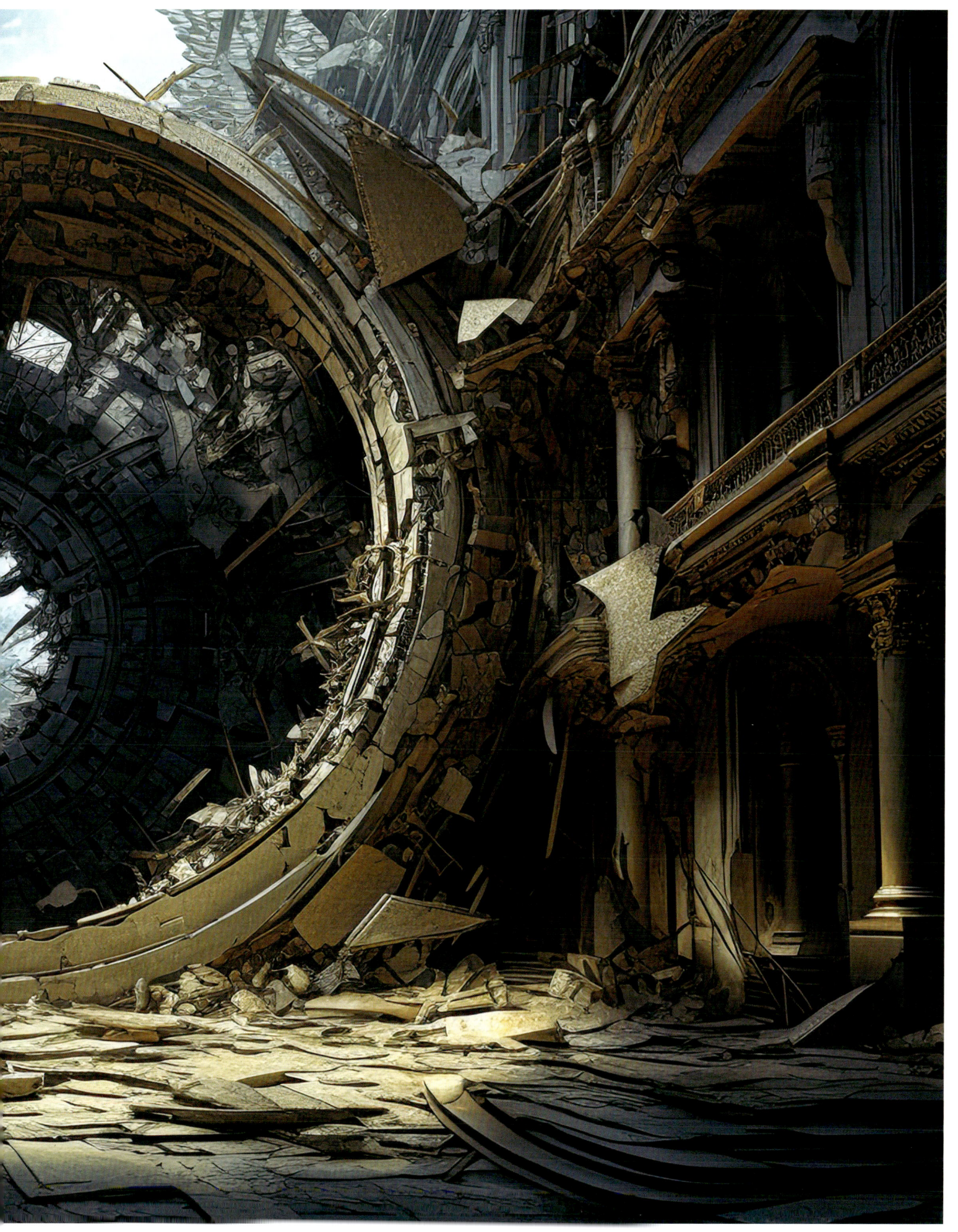

Terminal stage

In the remote areas of the former European Community, there are still no-man's-lands that it's best to avoid crossing. Like any good mushroom patch, their location has long remained secret. These areas bear witness to the merciless war waged by governments, and nature has never really been able to reclaim its rights here in a normal way, even after several decades. These zones are so toxic that only a handful of plant species have grown, drawing the sap they need to flourish from the diffuse poisons.

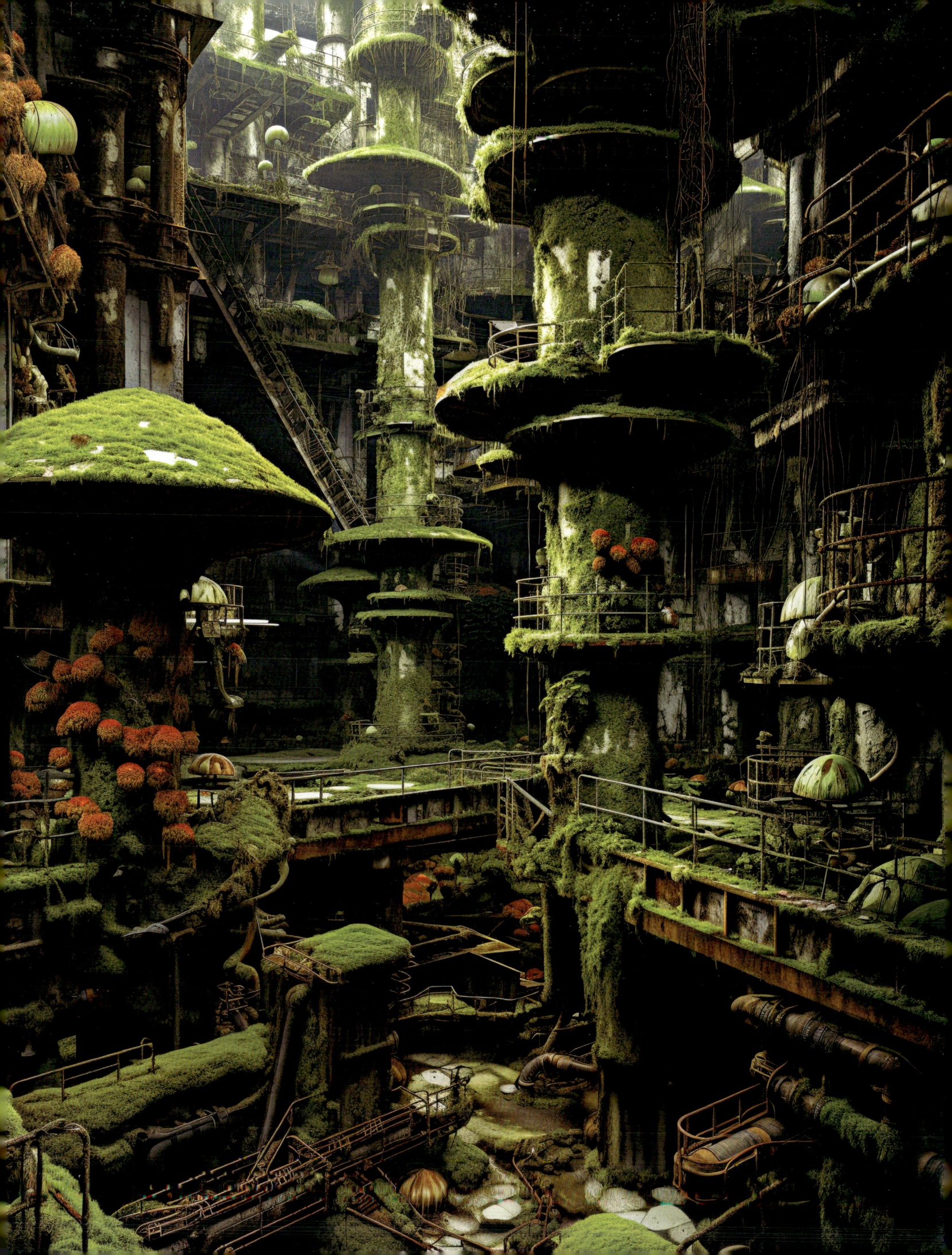

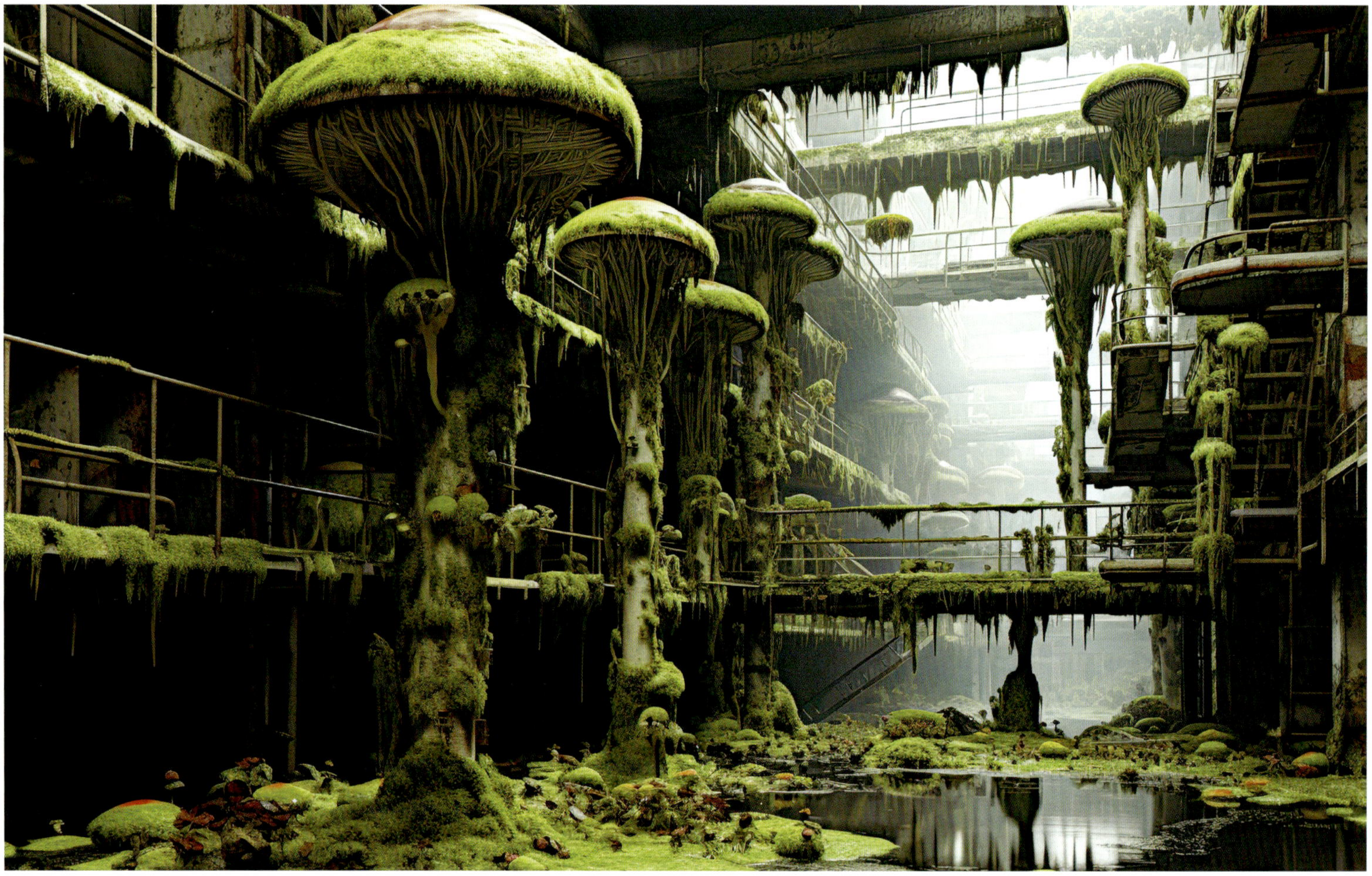

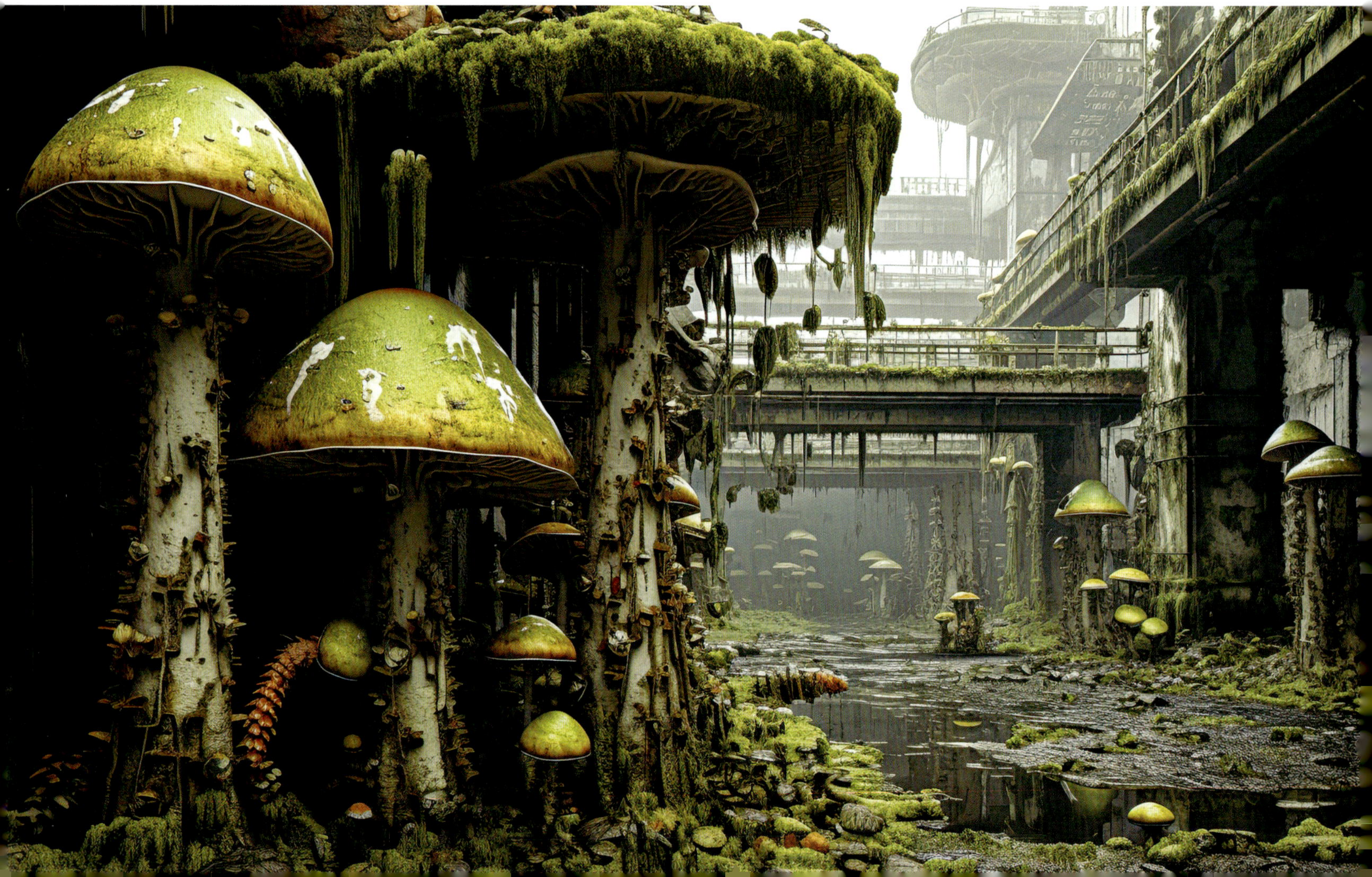

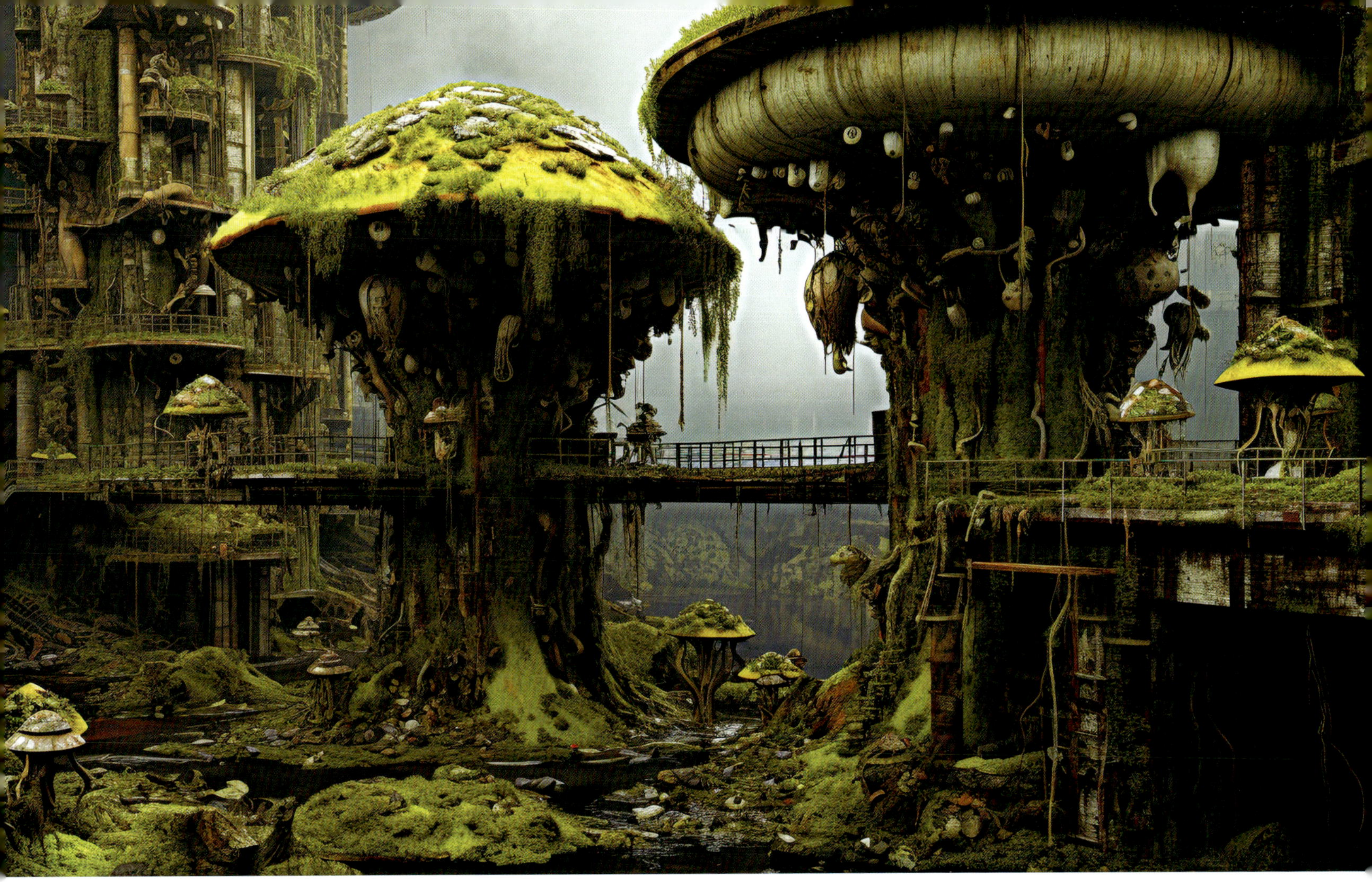

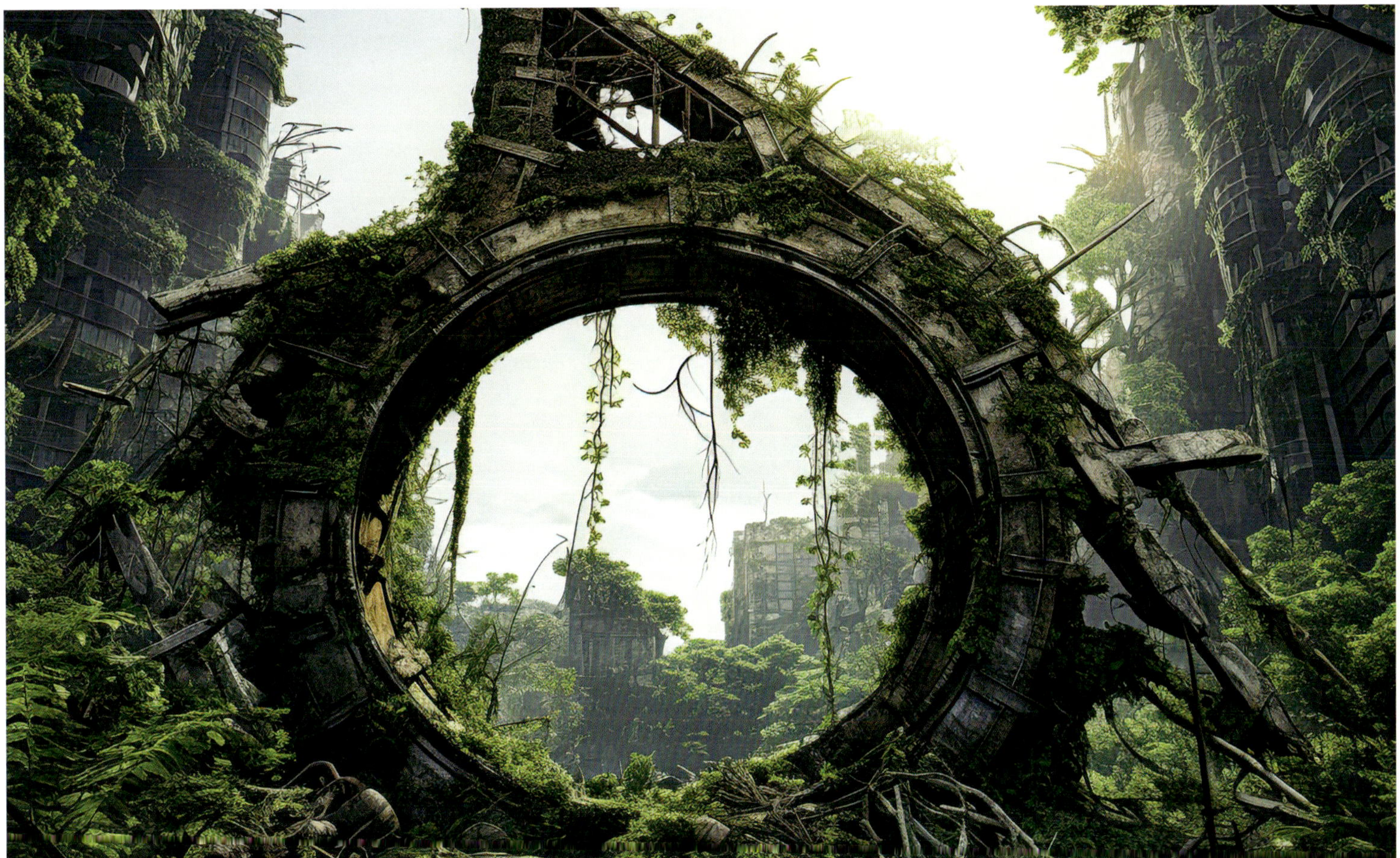

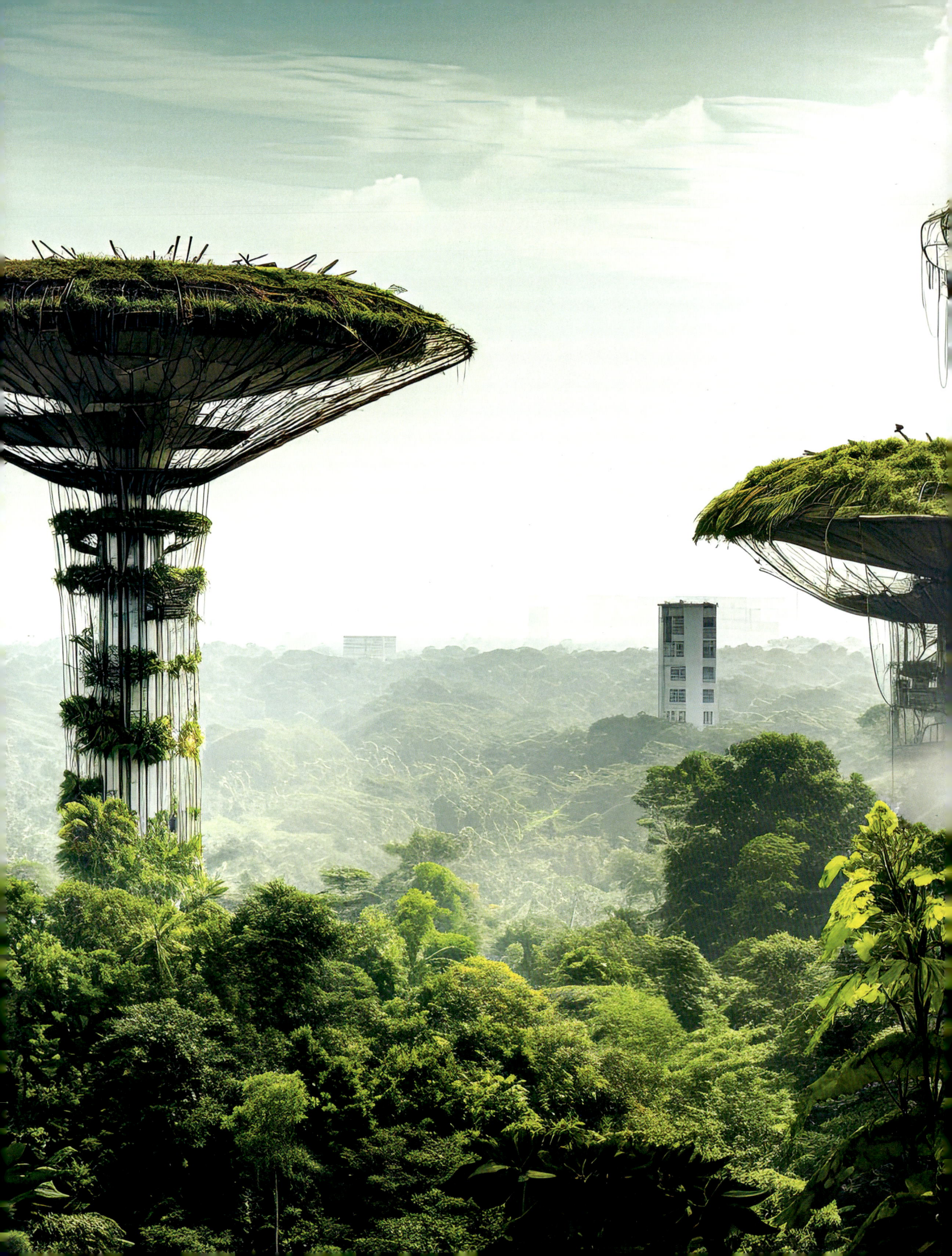

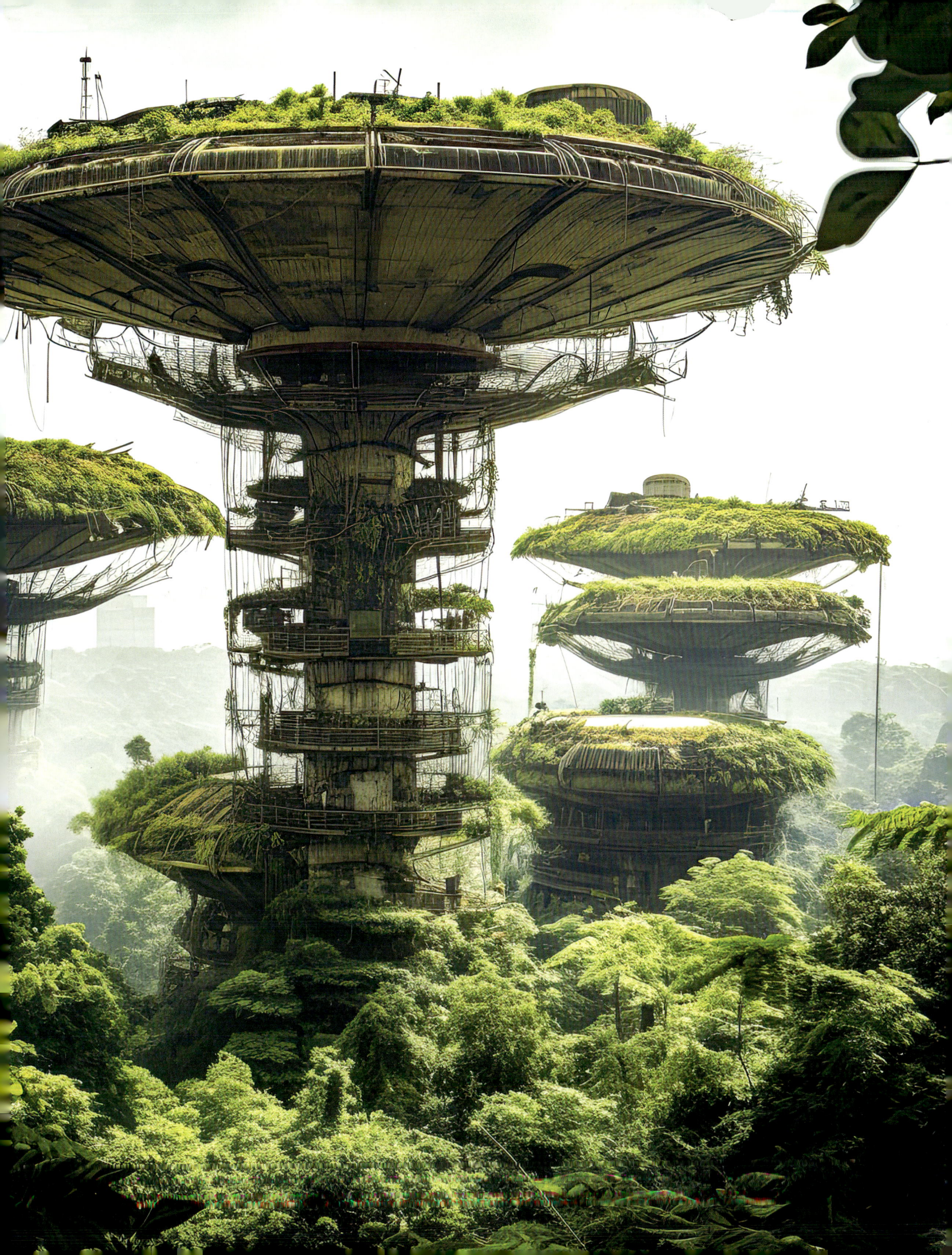

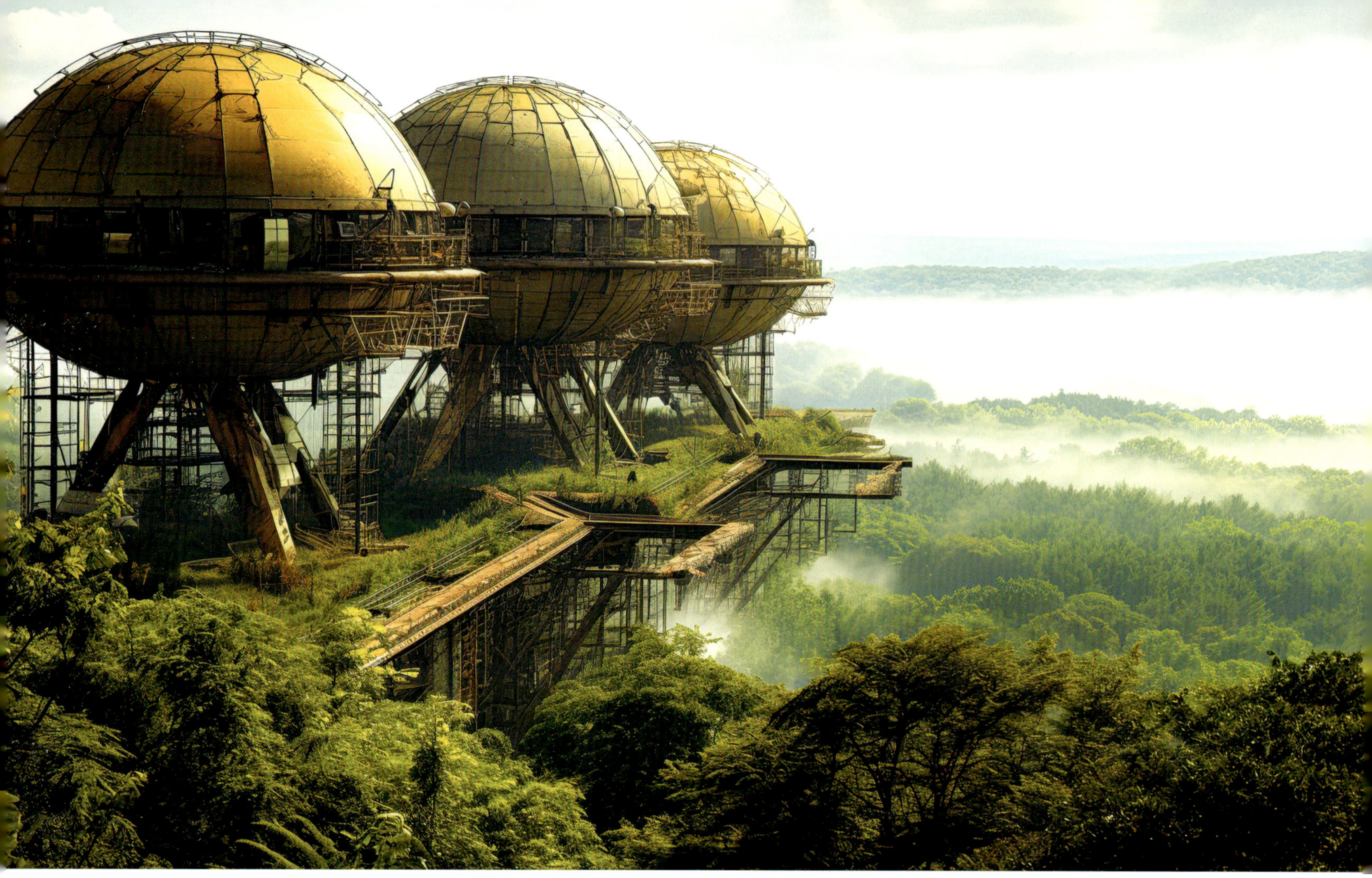

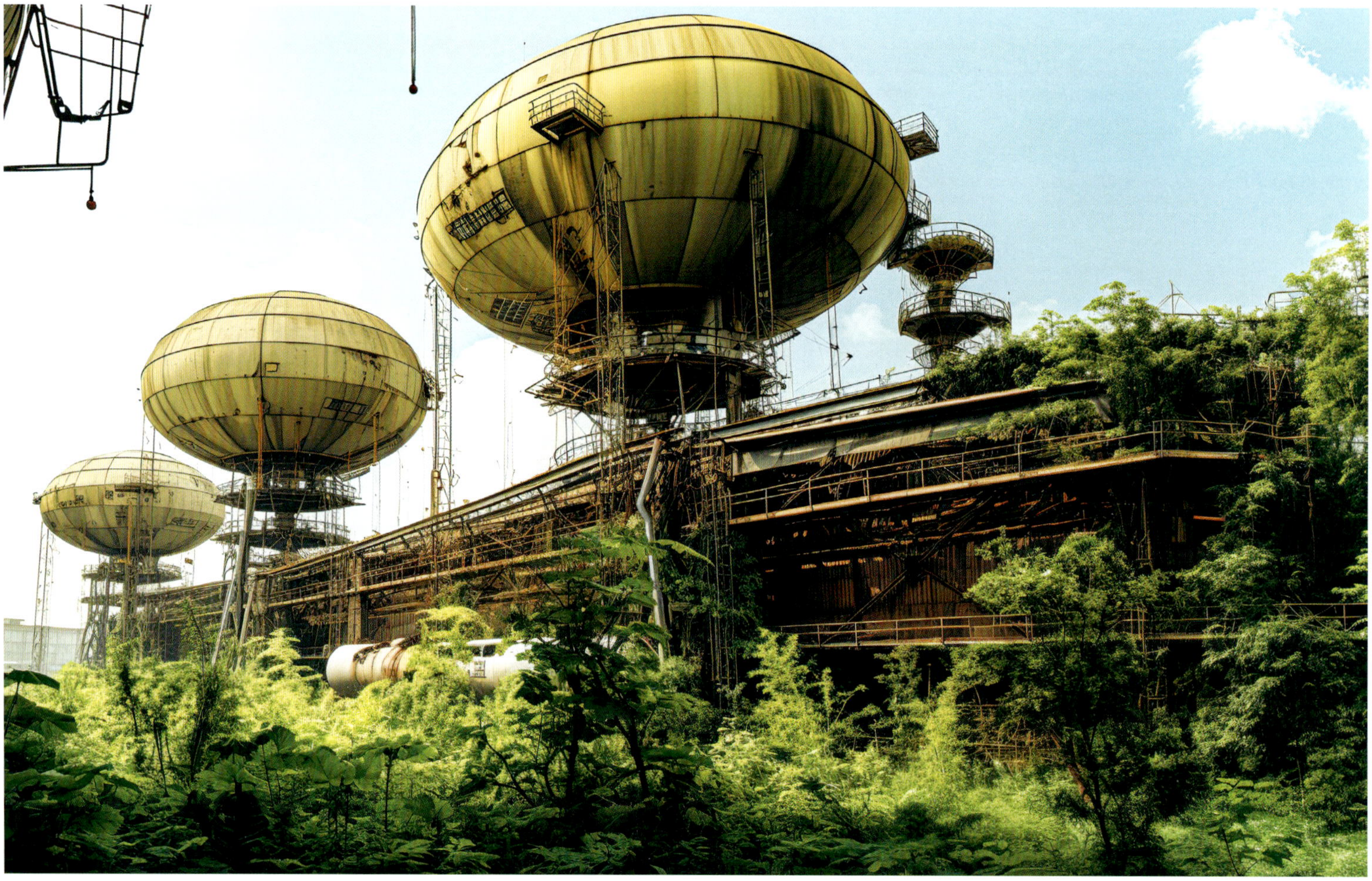

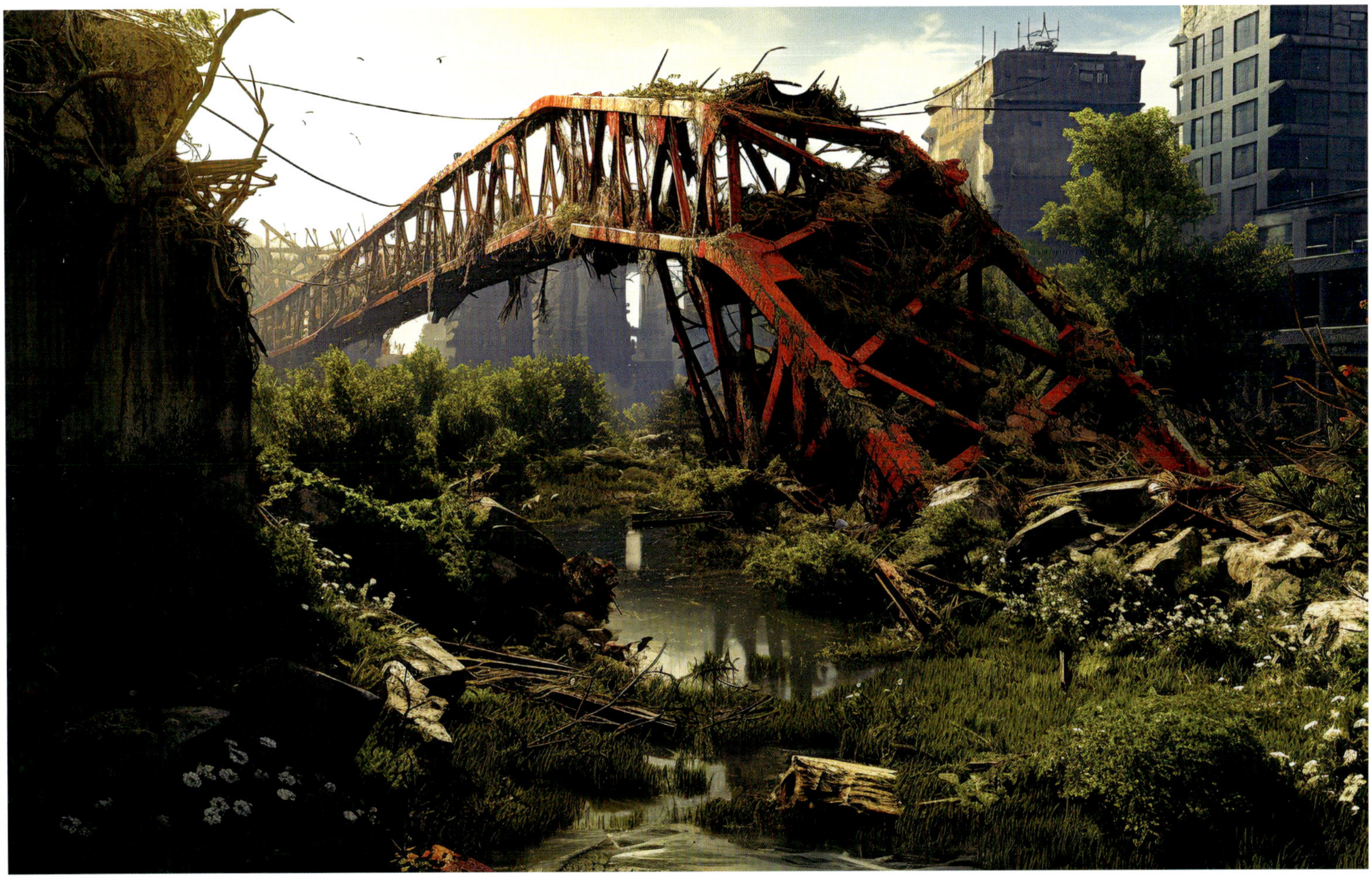

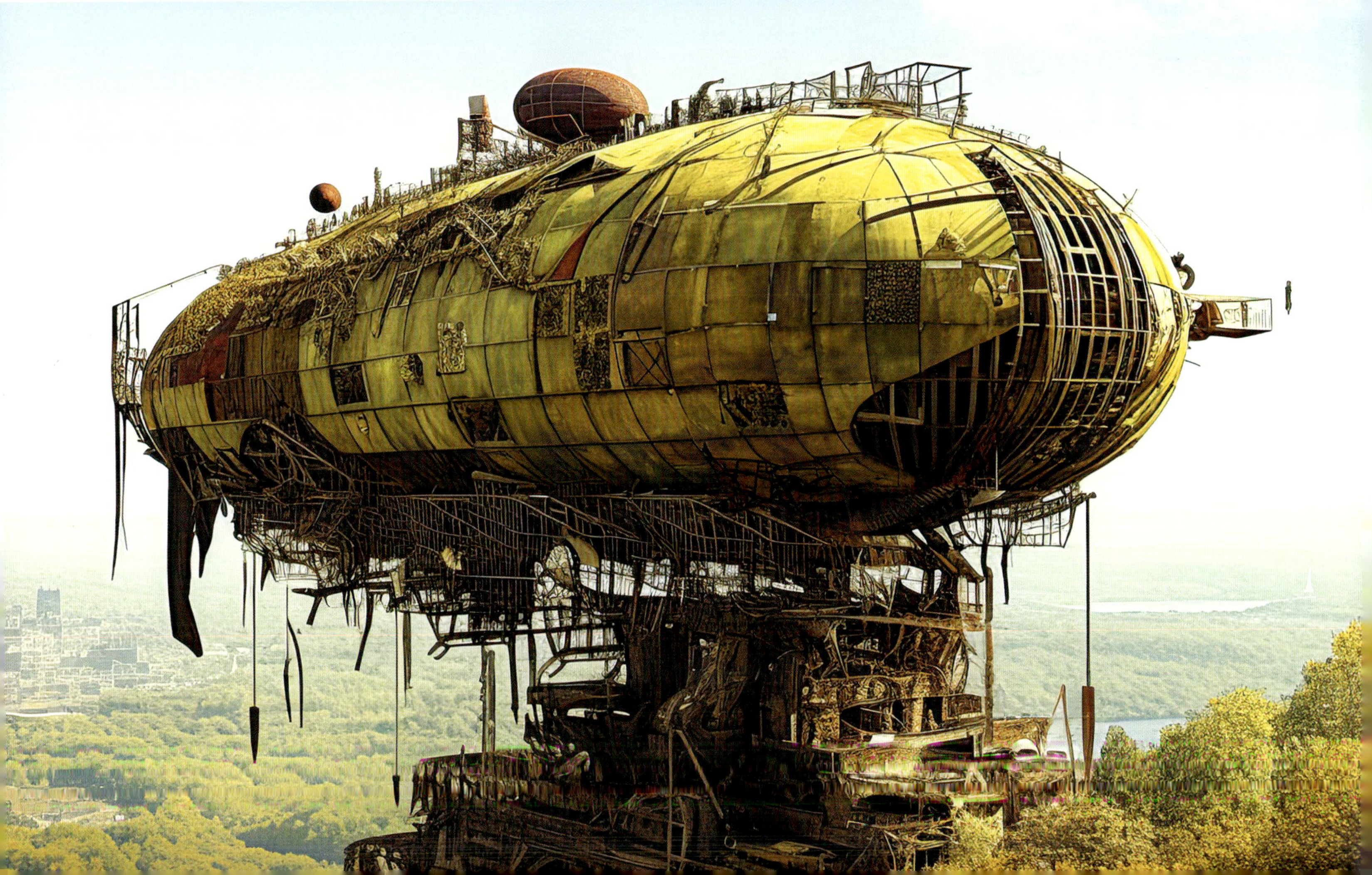

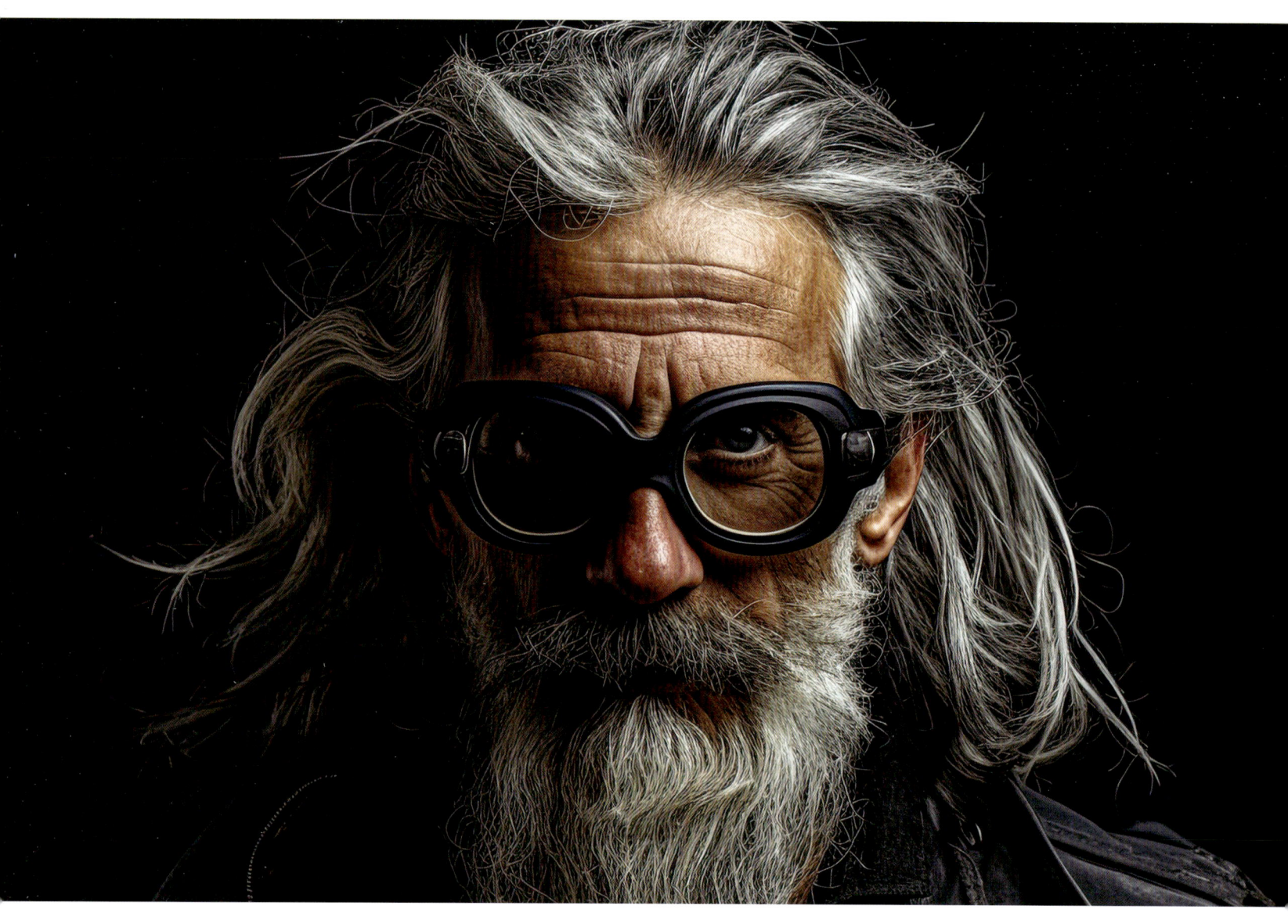

The author

Francis Meslet graduated from the National School of Art and Design of Nancy (ENSAD Nancy), where he majored in Design and Communication, in 1986. After a brief career as a designer, he turned to communications, working in advertising, first as an art director and then as a creative director.

Francis is an auteur photographer with a passion for cultural heritage, architecture and urban landscapes. In his spare time, he travels the world in search of forsaken places, sanctuaries where time has stood still since humans closed the doors. He brings back striking images, time capsules that bear witness to a silent parallel universe, conducive to escapism and questioning.

For several years now, he has been working in partnership with the Fondation du Patrimoine, helping to promote endangered sites by creating photographic portfolios.

As a further development to his work, Francis is also experimenting with artificial intelligence to conjure up imaginary worlds in a near-future hit by the advent of everything digital and by climatic and geopolitical turmoil.

www.francismeslet.com

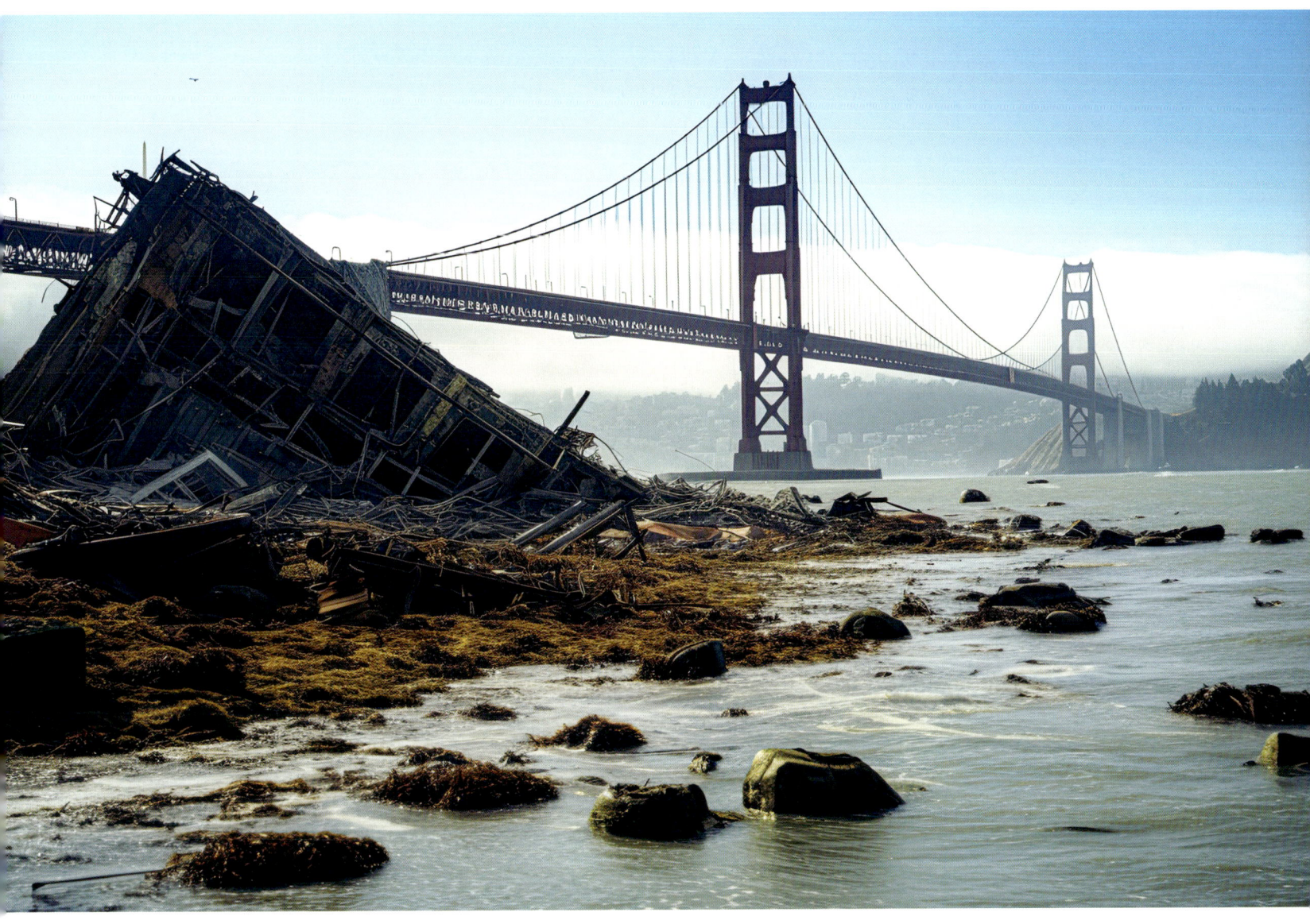

Acknowledgments

I'd like to thank all the people who have helped me pursue this passion and who have travelled a long way with me, both literally and figuratively - in particular Maxime and Quentin, with whom I've scoured many a wasteland at the expense of my trouser bottoms and a balanced diet.

Thanks also to the two confinements and two mandatory quarantines that forced me to find new ways of escaping by exploring an imaginary world with the help of AI.

Finally, thanks to my publisher Thomas Jonglez for accepting the challenge of publishing this book.

Also available from the same publisher

ATLAS

Atlas of extreme weather
Atlas of geographical curiosities
Atlas of unusual wines
Atlas of abandoned places

PHOTO BOOKS

Abandoned America
Abandoned Asylums
Abandoned Australia
Abandoned USSR
Abandoned Churches: Unclaimed places of worship
Abandoned cinemas of the world
Abandoned France
Abandoned Germany
Abandoned Italy
Abandoned Japan
Abandoned Spain
After the Final Curtain – The Fall of the American Movie Theater
After the Final Curtain – America's Abandoned Theaters
Baikonur - Vestiges of the Soviet space programme
Chernobyl's Atomic Legacy
Cinemas - A French heritage
Clickbait - A visual journey through AI-generated stories
Forbidden France
Forbidden Places – Exploring our Abandoned Heritage Vol. 1
Forbidden Places – Exploring our Abandoned Heritage Vol. 2
Forbidden Places – Exploring our Abandoned Heritage Vol. 3
Forgotten Heritage
Oblivion
Secret sacred sites
Unusual Hotels - World
Venice deserted
Venice from the skies

'SECRET' GUIDES

Secret Amsterdam
Secret Bali – An unusual guide
Secret Bangkok
Secret Barcelona
Secret Belfast
Secret Berlin
Secret Boston
Secret Brighton – An unusual guide
Secret Brooklyn
Secret Brussels
Secret Buenos Aires
Secret Campania
Secret Cape Town
Secret Copenhagen
Secret Corsica
Secret Dolomites
Secret Dublin – An unusual guide
Secret Edinburgh – An unusual guide
Secret Florence
Secret French Riviera
Secret Geneva
Secret Glasgow
Secret Granada
Secret Helsinki
Secret Istanbul
Secret Johannesburg
Secret Lisbon
Secret Liverpool – An unusual guide
Secret London – An unusual guide
Secret London – Unusual bars & restaurants
Secret Madrid
Secret Mexico City

Secret Montreal – An unusual guide
Secret Naples
Secret New Orleans
Secret New York – An unusual guide
Secret New York – Curious activities
Secret New York Hidden bars & restaurants Secret Paris
Secret Prague
Secret Provence
Secret Rio
Secret Rome
Secret Seville
Secret Singapore
Secret Stockholm
Secret Sussex – An unusual guide
Secret Tokyo
Secret Tuscany
Secret Venice
Secret Vienna
Secret Washington D.C.
Secret York – An unusual guide

'SOUL OF' GUIDES

Soul of Amsterdam - A guide to the 30 best experiences
Soul of Athens - A guide to 30 exceptional experiences
Soul of Berlin - A guide to the 30 best experiences
Soul of Kyoto - A guide to 30 exceptional experiences
Soul of Lisbon - 30 experiences
Soul of Los Angeles - A guide to 30 exceptional experiences
Soul of Marrakesh - A guide to 30 exceptional experiences
Soul of New York - A guide to 30 exceptional experiences
Soul of Rome - A guide to 30 exceptional experiences
Soul of Tokyo - A guide to 30 exceptional experiences
Soul of Venice - A guide to 30 exceptional experiences
Soul of Paris - 30 experiences
Soul of Barcelona - 30 experiences»

From the same author

Abandoned Churches - Unclaimed Places Of Worship

November 2020
ISBN: 978-2-36195-440-6
PRICE: € 35.00 — US$ 39.95 — £29.99
DIMENSIONS: 305 x 215 mm
PAGES: 224

Gold Medal at the Prix de la Photographie de Paris (PX3) in the Book and Fine Art Book categories, Silver award at the Tokyo International Foto Awards (TIFA) in the Book-Fine Art category & Honorable Mention at the International Photography Award.

Abandoned Belgium

November 2023
ISBN: 978-2-36195-683-7
PRICE: € 39.95 — US$ 39.95 — £34.99
DIMENSIONS: 230 x 297 mm
PAGES: 256

This book was created by:

Francis Meslet, texts, photographs, layout

Sophie Schlondorff, translator

Jana Gough, editing

Kimberly Bess, proofreading

Roberto Sassi, publishing manager

© JONGLEZ Publishing 2024

Registration of copyright: September 2024 – Edition: 01

ISBN: 978-2-36195-798-8